Roswell D. Hitchcock

Hymns and Songs of Praise for Public and Social Worship

Roswell D. Hitchcock

Hymns and Songs of Praise for Public and Social Worship

ISBN/EAN: 9783337286217

Printed in Europe, USA, Canada, Australia, Japan

Cover: Foto ©Lupo / pixelio.de

More available books at **www.hansebooks.com**

THE

HYMNS AND SONGS OF PRAISE,

May be had direct of the Publishers, or may be ordered of

W. G. HOLMES,
77 Madison Street, Chicago.

M. H. SARGENT,
Congregational House, Beacon Street, Boston.

HYMNS

AND

SONGS OF PRAISE

FOR

PUBLIC AND SOCIAL WORSHIP.

EDITED BY

ROSWELL D. HITCHCOCK, ZACHARY EDDY,
PHILIP SCHAFF.

NEW YORK:
ANSON D. F. RANDOLPH & COMPANY
900 BROADWAY, COR. 20th STREET.

Entered according to Act of Congress in the year 1874, by
ANSON D. F. RANDOLPH & COMPANY,
In the Office of the Librarian of Congress at Washington, D. C.

Music Electrotyper,
WARREN,
13 *Centre St, N. Y.*

Printed by
E. O. JENKINS,
20 *North William St. N. Y.*

Bindery of
ROBERT RUTTER,
82 and 84 *Beekman St., N. Y.*

PREFACE.

This Book is much larger than was at first contemplated. The Editors began their work together, now nearly four years ago, with the idea that six hundred Hymns, or, at most, eight hundred, are quite enough. Such a Selection we might have made for ourselves; and it might, perhaps, have suited some congregations. But we soon came to the conclusion that if many people are to be pleased, there must be many Hymns: a Collection, and not a Selection.

Fastidious critics may say that there are not more than two or three hundred really good Hymns in the language. And, to be sure, there are not many such Hymns as "When I survey the wondrous cross," "There is a fountain filled with blood," "Jesus, Lover of my soul," and "Rock of ages, cleft for me." But the number of Hymns that have long done good service, and will long continue to do it, is very much greater than many people suppose. And then new Hymns, which will certainly live, such as "My faith looks up to Thee," "Lead, kindly light," "Just as I am," and "Abide with me," are constantly appearing. Even the two or three hundred classic Hymns, which form the staple of our weekly use, will serve us all the better for not being made to serve alone.

Of the fourteen hundred Hymns here brought together, few, we think, could have been omitted without spiritual loss. Not all of them are designed for Public and Social Worship. Indeed, a considerable number are expressly set apart for Family Worship. And some, which need not be sung at all, are designed especially for closet use. Now and then a familiar Hymn may still be missed: omitted, perhaps, inadvertently; or because it could not be matched with appropriate music without making up an additional page; or because of its commonplace, prosaic character; or because of some doctrinal error or infelicity. But in all such cases the omitted Hymns, it is believed, will be found to have been replaced by better ones of the same general scope.

Our aim has been to make a truly catholic Book. All ages, all nations, all communions, and all types and stages of Christian experience are here represented. The older objective Hymnology, and the later subjective, are admitted to equal fellowship. Saints who had little to do with one another in their life-time, but now singing together in Heaven, are together here. Of all this goodly company, Watts still sits highest, and Charles Wesley next.

In addition to the old standard Hymns, which must go into every Book, many fine, fresh, new Hymns will be found in this Collection, some of which have been written expressly for it. We are under

PREFACE.

special obligations to Dr. RAY PALMER, the Rev. HERVEY D. GANSE, Dr. ALEXANDER R. THOMPSON, Dr. EDWARD HOPPER, the Rev. ARTHUR T. PIERSON, and Miss MARGARET E. WINSLOW.

While our Book has been carefully wrought in every part, special pains have been taken with the Hymns pertaining to Christ and the Christian life. That type of theology which makes the Person of Christ central, is here brought out in song. And while our first care has been to provide for constant and common daily and weekly wants, liberal provision has also been made for special occasions, and particularly for seasons of special religious interest.

The average length of Hymns in this Collection is somewhat greater than usual. Many chipped and fractured gems have thus been restored to their original integrity and beauty. We have seldom shortened a Hymn for merely mechanical reasons. With the quicker movement now generally practised in singing, six stanzas take no more time than used to be required for four. By making each Tune carry the first stanza of a Hymn, room has been found for many single stanzas which had better not be dropped, as well as for many additional Hymns which must otherwise have been excluded.

Immense labor, which, if foreseen, might have been thought impracticable, has been expended upon the text. In every possible instance resort has been had to original sources of information. Standard editions of Authors, instead of Hymn Books, have been employed; as, in the case of Watts, a London edition of all his Writings; and, in the case of the Wesleys, the exhaustive thirteen volume edition of their Poetical Works, recently completed. The Hymnological Library selected for the Union Theological Seminary by Mr. Daniel Sedgwick of London, has been of great service to us. Special acknowledgments are due also to the Rev. FREDERIC M. BIRD, of the Episcopal diocese of New Jersey, whose large library, and larger stores of Hymnological information, have been generously laid open to us.

With respect to the restoration of Hymns to their original forms, a middle course has been pursued. Innumerable alterations, of one sort or another, have long been current. And most of these alterations are for the worse. In all such cases restoration was felt to be simply a duty. But now and then a Hymn has been altered for the better, and the alteration has been deliberately and almost universally accepted. In such cases restoration was not to be thought of. But, of course, the alteration ought always to be acknowledged.

A word or two in explanation of the editing. The Author's name, if known, is always given in connection with the Hymn. This saves turning to an Index; and is quite as proper as naming the text of the sermon by Book, Chapter, and Verse, instead of quoting it merely as Scripture. At each opening of our Book, the dates of birth and death, if known, are given in brackets, where the Author's name occurs for the first time, or occurs but once. If it occurs again

PREFACE.

at the same opening, only the date of the Hymn is given. If the Hymn has two dates, as in the case of Montgomery's "Songs of praise the angels sang," Hymn 68 [1819, 1853], it indicates a revision of the Hymn by the Author himself. Abridgments are also indicated, as well as alterations; so that it may in every case be known whether or not we are singing a favorite Hymn entirely and exactly as the Author wrote it.

The musical editing has been done by JOHN K. PAINE, Professor of Music in Harvard University, and U. C. BURNAP, Organist of the Church on the Heights in Brooklyn, assisted by JAMES FLINT, Organist in Orange, New Jersey. The work they have done must speak for itself. As the aim has been to encourage congregational singing, most of the Tunes are familiar and easy. But some of the best Tunes in the Book are new, and must, of course, be learned and practised before they will be available for congregational use. A few pieces, like *Dies Irae*, p. 502, *Tempest*, p. 427, and some others, which musicians will easily recognize, are not meant to be sung by congregations, but by well-trained choirs on special occasions.

ROSWELL D. HITCHCOCK,
ZACHARY EDDY,
PHILIP SCHAFF.

NEW YORK, *March* 20, 1874.

Suggestions to Ministers and Directors of Church Music.

1. Do not expect any congregation to sing a new Tune at sight.
2. New Tunes demand either congregational rehearsals, or a well-trained Choir.
3. In the selection of Hymns to be sung by the congregation, be careful to select such Hymns as have familiar Tunes set to them. It is safe to assume that every American congregation is more or less familiar with the following Tunes:

L. M.—Old Hundred, Hebron, Hamburg, Ward, Windham, Wells, Duke Street, Uxbridge, Park Street (?) Retreat, Rockingham, Woodworth.

C. M.—Arlington, Avon, Balerma, Christmas, Coronation, Cowper, Dedham, Dundee, Devizes, Heber, Maitland, Mear, Marlow, Naomi, Ortonville, St. Ann's, St. Martin's, Stephens.

C. P. M.—Meribah, Ganges, Ariel (?)

S. M.—Boylston, Dennis, Laban, Olmutz, Silver Street, St. Thomas, Lebanon, Watchman.

7.—Pleyel's Hymn, Nuremberg, Hendon, Horton (?) Benevento, Martyn.

7, 6.—Amsterdam, Missionary Hymn, Webb.

8, 7, 4.—Sicily, Greenville.

8, 7.—Nettleton, Bartimeus, Stockwell, Wilmot.

L. P. M.—Dalston.

6, 4.—America, Olivet, Bethany, Italian Hymn, Portuguese Hymn, Lyons.

THE TEN COMMANDMENTS.

Exodus xx. 1-17.

God spake all these words, saying:

I am the Lord thy God, which have brought thee out of the land of Egypt, out of the house of bondage.

I. Thou shalt have no other Gods before Me.

II. Thou shalt not make unto thee any graven image, or any likeness of any thing that is in heaven above, or that is in the earth beneath, or that is in the water under the earth thou shalt not bow down thyself to them, nor serve them.

For I the Lord thy God am a jealous God, visiting the iniquity of the fathers upon the children unto the third and fourth generation of them that hate Me; and shewing mercy unto thousands of them that love Me, and keep My commandments.

III. Thou shalt not take the name of the Lord thy God in vain.

For the Lord will not hold him guiltless that taketh His name in vain.

IV. Remember the sabbath day, to keep it holy. Six days shalt thou labor, and do all thy work: but the seventh day is the sabbath of the Lord thy God: in it thou shalt not do any work, thou, nor thy son, nor thy daughter, thy man-servant, nor thy maid-servant, nor thy cattle, nor thy stranger that is within thy gates.

For in six days the Lord made heaven and earth, the sea, and all that in them is, and rested the seventh day: wherefore the Lord blessed the sabbath day, and hallowed it.

V. Honor thy father and thy mother: that thy days may be long upon the land which the Lord thy God giveth thee.

VI. Thou shalt not kill.

VII. Thou shalt not commit adultery.

VIII. Thou shalt not steal.

IX. Thou shalt not bear false witness against thy neighbor.

X. Thou shalt not covet thy neighbor's house, thou shalt not covet thy neighbor's wife, nor his man-servant, nor his maid-servant, nor his ox, nor his ass, nor any thing that is thy neighbors.

THE LORD'S PRAYER.

Matthew vi. 9-13.

Our Father who art in heaven:

Hallowed be Thy name. Thy kingdom come. Thy will be done on earth, as it is in heaven. Give us this day our daily bread. And forgive us our debts, as we forgive our debtors. And lead us not into temptation, but deliver us from evil.

For Thine is the kingdom, and the power, and the glory, forever. Amen.

THE APOSTLES' CREED.

I believe in God the Father Almighty, Maker of heaven and earth:

And in Jesus Christ His only Son our Lord; who was conceived by the Holy Ghost; born of the Virgin Mary; suffered under Pontius Pilate; was crucified, dead, and buried; He descended into hell; the third day He rose again from the dead; He ascended into heaven; and sitteth on the right hand of God the Father Almighty; from thence He shall come to judge the quick and the dead.

I believe in the Holy Ghost; the holy Catholic Church; the Communion of Saints; the Forgiveness of sins; the Resurrection of the body; and the Life everlasting. Amen.

CONTENTS.

	HYMNS.	PAGES
PREFACE		3-5
COMMANDMENTS, PRAYER, AND CREED		6
GOD	1-144	7-43
CHRIST	145-338	44-96
THE HOLY SPIRIT	339-385	97-109
THE SCRIPTURES	386-407	109-114
FREE SALVATION	408-450	114-124
THE CHRISTIAN LIFE	451-826	125-222
THE CHURCH	827-842	223-227
THE CHRISTIAN MINISTRY	843-860	227-231
BAPTISM	861-871	231-233
CONFESSION OF FAITH	872-880	234-235
THE LORD'S SUPPER	881-910	236-242
THE COMMUNION OF SAINTS	911-930	242-247
THE LORD'S DAY AND WORSHIP	931-1031	248-271
DEDICATING PLACES OF WORSHIP	1032-1037	272, 273
CHRISTIAN WORK	1038-1057	273-277
THY KINGDOM COME	1058-1141	278-297
FOR THOSE AT SEA	1142-1148	297-299
FESTIVALS AND FASTS	1149-1167	299-304
FAMILY WORSHIP	1168-1249	304-324
TIMES AND SEASONS	1250-1263	324-327
LIFE AND DEATH	1264-1336	328-346
JUDGMENT AND ETERNITY	1337-1364	347-353
HEAVEN	1365-1416	353-368
DOXOLOGIES		369, 370
CHANTS		371-381
INDEX OF SCRIPTURE TEXTS		383-384
INDEX OF SUBJECTS		385-395
INDEX OF FIRST LINES		396-410
INDEX OF FIRST LINES OF CHANTS		410
INDEX OF AUTHORS OF HYMNS		411-414

OPENING CHANT.

The Lord's Prayer
Matt. vi. 9—13.

Our Father, who | art in | heaven, || Hallowed | be — | Thy — | name.

Thy | kingdom | come. || Thy will be done on earth, | as it | is in | heaven.

Give us this day our | daily | bread. || And forgive us our debts, as | we for- | give our | debtors.

And lead us not | into temp- | tation, || But de- | liver | us from | evil:

For Thine is the kingdom, and the | power, and the | glory, || For- | ever. | A — | men.

Hymns and Songs of Praise.

GOD.

1   *"Praise Him, all ye people."*   P. M.
     Ps. cxvii. 1.   Rom. xv. 11.

1 REJOICE to-day with one accord,
    Sing out with exultation;
Rejoice and praise our mighty Lord,
    Whose arm hath brought salvation;
    His works of love proclaim
    The greatness of His name;
    For He is God alone
    Who hath His mercy shewn;
Let all His saints adore Him.

2 When in distress to Him we cried,
    He heard our sad complaining;
O trust in Him, whate'er betide,
    His love is all-sustaining;
    Triumphant songs of praise
    To Him our hearts shall raise;
    Now every voice shall say,
    "O praise our God alway;"
Let all His saints adore Him.

3 Rejoice to-day with one accord,
    Sing out with exultation:
Rejoice and praise our mighty Lord,
    Whose arm hath brought salvation;
    His works of love proclaim
    The greatness of His name;
    For He is God alone
    Who hath His mercy shewn;
Let all His saints adore Him.
    Rev. Sir Henry Williams Baker. (1821–) 1861.

2   *The Trinity invoked.*   6, 4.

1 COME, Thou Almighty King,
Help us Thy name to sing,
    Help us to praise:
Father all-glorious,
O'er all victorious,
Come, and reign over us,
    Ancient of days.

2 Jesus, our Lord, arise;
Scatter our enemies,
    And make them fall:
Let Thine almighty aid
Our sure defence be made;
Our souls on Thee be stayed;
    Lord, hear our call.

3 Come, Thou Incarnate Word,
Gird on Thy mighty sword,
    Our prayer attend:
Come, and Thy people bless,
And give Thy Word success;
Spirit of holiness,
    On us descend.

4 Come, Holy Comforter,
Thy sacred witness bear
    In this glad hour:
Thou who Almighty art,
Now rule in every heart,
And ne'er from us depart,
    Spirit of power.

5 To the great One and Three
Eternal praises be
    Hence evermore.
His sovereign majesty
May we in glory see,
And to eternity
    Love and adore.
    Rev. Charles Wesley. (1708–1788) 1757.

GOD.

3 *"Let there be light."*
Gen. i. 3. 2 Cor. iv. 6.

1 THOU, whose almighty Word
Chaos and darkness heard,
 And took their flight;
Hear us, we humbly pray,
And where the Gospel's day
Sheds not its glorious ray,
 "Let there be light."

2 Thou, who didst come to bring
On Thy redeeming wing
 Healing and sight,
Health to the sick in mind,
Sight to the inly blind,
O, now to all mankind
 "Let there be light."

3 Spirit of truth and love,
Life-giving, holy Dove,
 Speed forth Thy flight:
Move o'er the water's face,
Bearing the lamp of grace,
And in earth's darkest place
 "Let there be light."

4 Blessed and Holy Three,
Glorious Trinity,
 Wisdom, Love, Might;
Boundless as ocean's tide,
Rolling in fullest pride,
Through the world, far and wide,
 "Let there be light."
Rev. John Marriott. (1780—1825.) 1813.

4 *"God praised for His goodness and Truth."* **L. P. M.**
Ps. cxlvi.

1 I'LL praise my Maker with my breath;
And when my voice is lost in death,
 Praise shall employ my nobler powers:
My days of praise shall ne'er be past,
While life, and thought, and being last,
 Or immortality endures.

2 Happy the man whose hopes rely
On Israel's God: He made the sky,
 And earth, and seas, with all their train;
His truth forever stands secure;
He saves the opprest, He feeds the poor,
 And none shall find His promise vain.

6, 4. 3 The Lord hath eyes to give the blind;
The Lord supports the sinking mind;
 He sends the laboring conscience peace;
He helps the stranger in distress,
The widow and the fatherless,
 And grants the prisoner sweet release.

4 I'll praise Him while He lends me breath;
And when my voice is lost in death,
 Praise shall employ my nobler powers:
My days of praise shall ne'er be past,
While life and thought and being last,
 Or immortality endures.
Rev. Isaac Watts. (1674—1748.) 1719. ab.

5 *"Te Deum Laudamus."* **L. M.**

1 THEE we adore, eternal Lord,
We praise Thy name with one accord;
Thy saints, who here Thy goodness see,
Through all the world do worship Thee.

2 To Thee aloud all angels cry,
The heavens and all the powers on high,
Thee, Holy, holy, holy King,
Lord God of Hosts, they ever sing.

3 The apostles join the glorious throng;
The prophets swell the immortal song;
The martyr's noble army raise
Eternal anthems to Thy praise.

4 From day to day, O Lord, do we
Highly exalt and honor Thee;
Thy name we worship and adore,
World without end, for evermore.

5 Vouchsafe, O Lord, we humbly pray,
To keep us safe from sin this day;
Have mercy, Lord, we trust in Thee;
O let us ne'er confounded be.
Moravian Collection. 1754. ab. and alt.
Rev. Thomas Cotterill. (1779—1823.) 1810.

6 *The Trinity Adored.* **L. M.**

1 O HOLY, holy, holy Lord,
Bright in Thy deeds and in Thy name,
For ever be Thy name adored,
Thy glories let the world proclaim.

GOD.

2 O Jesus, Lamb once crucified
To take our load of sins away,
Thine be the hymn that rolls its tide
Along the realms of upper day.

3 O Holy Spirit from above,
In streams of light and glory given,
Thou source of ecstacy and love,
Thy praises ring through earth and heaven.

4 O God Triune, to Thee we owe
Our every thought, our every song;
And ever may Thy praises flow
From saint and seraph's burning tongue.
Rev. James Wallis Fastburn (1797—1819.) 1819.

7 *God with us, and in us.* L. M.

1 ETERNAL Father, when to Thee,
Beyond all worlds, by faith I soar,
Before Thy boundless majesty
I stand in silence, and adore.

2 But, Saviour, Thou art by my side:
Thy voice I hear, Thy face I see,
Thou art my friend, my daily guide;
God over all, yet *God with me*.

3 And Thou, Great Spirit, in my heart
Dost make Thy temple day by day:
The Holy Ghost of God Thou art,
Yet dwellest in this house of clay.

4 Blest Trinity, in Whom alone
All things created move or rest,
High in the heavens Thou hast Thy throne,
Thou hast Thy throne within my breast.
Rev. Hervey Doddridge Ganse. (1822—) 1872.

8 *The Trinity humbly worshipped.* L. M.

1 FATHER of heaven, whose love profound
A ransom for our souls hath found,
Before Thy throne we sinners bend:
To us Thy pardoning love extend.

2 Almighty Son, incarnate Word,
Our Prophet, Priest, Redeemer, Lord,
Before Thy throne we sinners bend:
To us Thy saving grace extend.

3 Eternal Spirit, by whose breath
The soul is raised from sin and death,
Before Thy throne we sinners bend:
To us Thy quickening power extend.

4 Jehovah,— Father, Spirit, Son,—
Mysterious Godhead, Three in One,
Before Thy throne we sinners bend:
Grace, pardon, life, to us extend.
John Cooper. 1812.

9 *Praise for Salvation.* L. M.

1 PRAISES to Him whose love has given,
In Christ, His Son, the Life of Heaven;
Who for our darkness gives us light,
And turns to day our deepest night.

2 Praises to Him, in grace who came,
To bear our woe, and sin, and shame;
Who lived to die, who died to rise,
The God-accepted sacrifice.

3 Praises to Him the chain who broke,
Opened the prison, burst the yoke,
Sent forth its captives glad and free,
Heirs of an endless liberty.

4 Praises to Him who sheds abroad
Within our hearts the love of God;
The Spirit of all truth and peace,
Fountain of joy and holiness!

5 To Father, Son, and Spirit now
The hands we lift, the knees we bow;
To Thee, Jehovah, thus we raise
The sinner's endless song of praise.
Rev. Horatius Bonar (1808—) 1861. ab. and alt.

10 *"O lucе quае tua lates."* L. M.

1 BLEST Trinity, from mortal sight
Veiled in Thine own eternal Light,
We Thee confess, in Thee believe,
To Thee with loving hearts we cleave.

2 O Father, Thou most Holy One!
O God of God, Eternal Son!
O Holy Ghost, Thou Love divine!
To join them Both is ever Thine.

3 The Father is in God the Son,
And with the Father He is One:
In Both the Spirit doth abide,
And with them Both is glorified.

4 Such as the Father, such the Son,
And such the Spirit, Three in One:
The Three one perfect Verity,
The Three one perfect Charity.

5 Eternal Father, Thee we praise;
To Thee, O Son, our hymns we raise;
O Holy Ghost, we Thee adore;
One mighty God for evermore.
Santolius Maglorianus. (1624—1684.)
Tr. by Rev. Sir Henry Williams Baker. (1821—) 1861.

11 "Te Deum laudamus." 7. D.

1 GOD eternal, Lord of all,
Lowly at Thy feet we fall.
All the earth doth worship Thee;
We amidst the throng would be.
All the holy angels cry,
Hail, thrice holy, God most High!
Lord of all the heavenly powers,
Be the same loud anthem ours.

2 Glorified apostles raise
Night and day continual praise;
Hast Thou not a mission too
For Thy children here to do?
With Thy prophets' goodly line
We in mystic bond combine;
For Thou hast to babes revealed
Things that to the wise were sealed.

3 Martyrs in a noble host,
Of Thy cross are heard to boast;
Since so bright the crown they wear,
Early we Thy cross would bear.
Offspring of a Virgin's womb;
Slain, and victor o'er the tomb;
Seated on the Judgment-throne,
Number us among Thine own.
Rev. James Elwin Millard. 1848. ab.

12 Thrice Holy. 7. D.
Is. vi. 3.

1 HOLY, holy, holy Lord
God of hosts! when heaven and earth,
Out of darkness, at Thy word,
Issued into glorious birth,
All Thy works before Thee stood,
And Thine eye beheld them good,
While They sang with sweet accord,
Holy, holy, holy Lord!

2 Holy, holy, holy! Thee,
One Jehovah evermore,
Father, Son, and Spirit, we,
Dust and ashes, would adore;
Lightly by the world esteemed,
From that world by Thee redeemed,
Sing we here, with glad accord,
Holy, holy, holy Lord!

3 Holy, holy, holy! All
Heaven's triumphant choir shall sing,
When the ransomed nations fall
At the footstool of their King;
Then shall saints and seraphim,
Hearts and voices, swell one hymn,
Round the throne with full accord,
Holy, holy, holy Lord!
James Montgomery. (1771—1854.) 1836, 1853.

13 "Glory be to God alone." 7. D.

1 FROM the vast and veiled throng,
Round the Father's heavenly throne,
Swells the everlasting song:
Glory be to God alone!
Round Immanuel's cross of pain
Mortal men, in tribes unknown,
Sing to Him who once was slain:
Glory be to God alone!

2 Blend, ye raptured songs, in one,
Men redeemed, your Father own;
Angels, worship ye the Son:
Glory be to God alone!
Spirit, 'tis within Thy light,
Streaming far from cross and throne,
Earth and heaven their songs unite:
Glory be to God alone!
Rev. Hervey Doddridge Ganse. (1822—) 1872.

14 "Singing everlastingly." 7. 6 l.

1 HOLY, holy, holy Lord,
God of Hosts, Eternal King,
By the heavens and earth adored;
Angels and Archangels sing,
Chanting everlastingly,
To the Blessed Trinity.

2 Since by Thee were all things made,
And in Thee do all things live,
Be to Thee all honor paid;
Praise to Thee let all things give,
Singing everlastingly
To the Blessed Trinity.

3 Thousands, tens of thousands, stand,
Spirits blest, before the throne,
Speeding thence at Thy command,
And, when Thy commands are done,
Singing everlastingly
To the Blessed Trinity.

4 Cherubim and Seraphim
   Veil their faces with their wings;
Eyes of angels are too dim
   To behold the King of kings,
While they sing eternally
   To the Blessed Trinity.

5 Thee apostles, prophets Thee,
   Thee the noble martyr band,
Praise with solemn jubilee,
   Thee, the Church in every land,
Singing everlastingly
   To the Blessed Trinity.

6 Hallelujah! Lord, to Thee,
   Father, Son, and Holy Ghost;
Godhead One, and Persons Three;
   Join us with the heavenly host,
Singing everlastingly
   To the Blessed Trinity.
   Bp. Christopher Wordsworth. (1807—) 1862 ab.

15   *Thrice Holy.*   8, 7.
       Is. vi. 1—3. John xii. 41.

1 ROUND the Lord in glory seated
  Cherubim and seraphim
Filled His temple, and repeated
  Each to each th' alternate hymn.

2 "Lord, Thy glory fills the heaven,
  "Earth is with its fulness stored;
  "Unto Thee be glory given,
  "Holy, holy, holy Lord!"

3 Heaven is still with glory ringing;
   Earth takes up the angel's cry,
"Holy, holy, holy," singing,
   "Lord of Hosts, the Lord most High."

4 With His seraph train before Him,
   With His holy Church below,
Thus conspire we to adore Him,
   Bid we thus our anthem flow:

5 "Lord, Thy glory fills the heaven,
   Earth is with its fulness stored:
Unto Thee be glory given,
   Holy, holy, holy Lord!"

6 Thus Thy glorious name confessing,
   We adopt the angels' cry,
Holy, holy, holy! blessing
   Thee the Lord of Hosts most High.
   Bp. Richard Mant. (1776—1848.) 1837 ab.

16   *Glory to God.*   8, 7.
          1 Tim. i. 17.

1 GLORY be to God the Father,
   Glory be to God the Son,
Glory be to God the Spirit,
   Great Jehovah, Three in One:
Glory, glory, glory, glory,
   While eternal ages run!

2 Glory be to Him who loved us,
   Washed us from each spot and stain;
Glory be to Him who bought us,
   Made us kings with Him to reign:
Glory, glory, glory, glory,
   To the Lamb that once was slain!

3 Glory to the King of angels,
   Glory to the Church's King,
Glory to the King of nations,
   Heaven and earth, your praises bring:
Glory, glory, glory, glory,
   To the King of glory bring!

4 Glory, blessing, praise eternal!
   Thus the choir of angels sings;
Honor, riches, power, dominion!
   Thus its praise creation brings:
Glory, glory, glory, glory,
   Glory to the King of kings!
   Rev. Horatius Bonar. (1808—) 1866.

17   *"Holy, holy, holy Lord."*   8, 7.

1 FATHER, Thine Elect who lovest
   With an everlasting love;
Saviour, who the bar removest
   From the holy home above;
Spirit, daily meetness bringing
   For the glory there upstored;
List to Thy glad people singing,
   "Holy, holy, holy Lord!"

2 Lord, with sin-bound souls Thou bearest,
   Struggling towards this strain divine;
Glad on mortal lips Thou hearest
   That thrice awful name of Thine.
But Thou listenest, O how sweetly!
   When from holy lips outpoured,
Rings through heaven this strain full meetly,
   "Holy, holy, holy Lord!"

3 Shall we, Lord, meet voices never
   Bring to that eternal hymn?

GOD.

Hallow us to help the endeavor
Of Thy pure-lipped Seraphim:
Hark! their own high strain we bring Thee;
Listen to the full accord!
Sweet the song we ever sing Thee,
"Holy, holy, holy Lord!"
Thomas Hornblower Gill. (1819—) 1860. ab.

18 *Prayer for Guidance.* 8, 7.
Numbers x. 33.

1 LEAD us, heavenly Father, lead us
O'er the world's tempestuous sea;
Guard us, guide us, keep us, feed us,
For we have no help but Thee;
‖: Yet possessing every blessing,
If our God our Father be. :‖

2 Saviour, breathe forgiveness o'er us;
All our weakness Thou dost know;
Thou didst tread this earth before us;
Thou didst feel its keenest woe;
‖: Lone and dreary, faint and weary,
Through the desert Thou didst go. :‖

3 Spirit of our God, descending,
Fill our hearts with heavenly joy,
Love with every passion blending,
Pleasure that can never cloy;
‖: Thus provided, pardoned, guided,
Nothing can our peace destroy. :‖
James Edmeston. (1791—1867.) 1820.

19 *"Most Hidden and Most Manifest."* L M
Ex. xxxiii. 20.

1 What secret place, what distant star
Is like, dread Lord, to Thine abode?
Why dwellest Thou from us so far?
We yearn for Thee, Thou hidden God.

2 The glory no man may abide
Doth visit us, a gracious Guest:
Thou whom "excess of light" doth hide
Here shinest sweetly manifest.

3 But sweetest, Lord, dost Thou appear
In the dear Saviour's smiling face:
The Heavenly Majesty draws near
And offers us its soft embrace.

4 To us vain searchers after God,
To us the Holy Ghost doth come;
From us Thou hidest Thine abode;
But Thou wilt make our souls Thy home.

5 O Glory that no eye may bear!
O Presence bright, our souls' sweet Guest!
O farthest off, O ever near!
Most Hidden and Most Manifest!
Thomas Hornblower Gill. 1860. ab.

20 *Praise to the Trinity.* L M

1 BLEST be the Father and His love,
To whose celestial source we owe
Rivers of endless joy above,
And rills of comfort here below.

2 Glory to Thee, great Son of God,
From whose dear wounded body rolls
A precious stream of vital blood,
Pardon and life for dying souls.

3 We give Thee, Sacred Spirit, praise,
Who, in our hearts of sin and woe,
Mak'st living springs of grace arise,
And into boundless glory flow.

4 Thus God the Father, God the Son,
And God the Spirit, we adore:
That sea of life and love unknown,
Without a bottom or a shore.
Rev. Isaac Watts. (1674—1748.) 1709.

21 *God unsearchable.* L M
Job xi. 7.

1 GOD is the name my soul adores.
Th' almighty Three, th' eternal One:
Nature and grace, with all their powers,
Confess the Infinite Unknown.

2 Thy voice produced the seas and spheres,
Bade the waves roar, and planets shine:
But nothing like Thyself appears
Through all these spacious works of Thine.

3 Still restless nature dies and grows;
From change to change the creatures run:
Thy being no succession knows,
And all Thy vast designs are one.

4 A glance of Thine runs through the globes,
Rules the bright world, and moves their frame:
Broad sheets of light compose Thy robes,
Thy guards are formed of living flame.

5 Who can behold the blazing light?
Who can approach consuming flame?
None but Thy Wisdom knows Thy might,
None but Thy Word can speak Thy name.
Rev. Isaac Watts. 1709. ab.

GOD.

22   *"Meet and right."*   7, 6.

1 MEET and right it is to sing,
    In every time and place,
Glory to our Heavenly King,
    The God of truth and grace;
Join we then with sweet accord,
    All in one thanksgiving join:
Holy, holy, holy Lord,
    Eternal praise be Thine.

2 Thee, the first-born sons of light,
    In choral symphonies,
Praise by day, day without night,
    And never, never cease.
Angels and archangels, all
    Praise the mystic Three in One
Sing, and stop, and gaze, and fall,
    O'erwhelmed before Thy throne.

3 Vying with that happy choir
    Who chant Thy praise above,
We on eagles' wings aspire,
    The wings of faith and love:
Thee they sing with glory crowned,
    We extol the slaughtered Lamb;
Lower if our voices sound
    Our theme is still the same.

4 Father, God, Thy love we praise,
    Which gave Thy Son to die;
Jesus, full of truth and grace,
    Alike we glorify;
Spirit, Comforter divine,
    Praise by all to Thee be given,
Till we in full chorus join,
    And earth is turned to heaven.
      Rev. Charles Wesley. (1708—1788.) 1749. ab. and alt.

23   *"Praise ye the Lord."*   7, 6.
    Ps. cl.

1 PRAISE the Lord, who reigns above,
    And keeps His courts below;
Praise the holy God of love,
    And all His greatness show;
Praise Him for His noble deeds,
    Praise Him for His matchless power;
Him, from whom all good proceeds,
    Let earth and heaven adore.

2 Publish, spread, to all around
    The great Jehovah's name;
Let the trumpet's martial sound
    The Lord of Hosts proclaim;
Praise Him, every tuneful string,
    All the reach of heavenly art;
All the power of music bring,
    The music of the heart.

3 Him, in whom they move and live,
    Let every creature sing;
Glory to their Maker give,
    And homage to their King:
Hallowed be His name beneath,
    As in heaven on earth adored;
Praise the Lord in every breath;
    Let all things praise the Lord.
      Rev. Charles Wesley. 1743. ab.

24   *"Te Deum laudamus."*   C. M.

1 O GOD, we praise Thee, and confess
    That Thou the only Lord
And everlasting Father art,
    By all the earth adored.

2 To Thee all angels cry aloud;
    To Thee the powers on high,
Both Cherubim and Seraphim,
    Continually do cry:

3 O holy, holy, holy Lord,
    Whom heavenly hosts obey,
The world is with the glory filled
    Of Thy majestic sway.

4 The apostles' glorious company,
    And prophets crowned with light,
With all the martyrs' noble host,
    Thy constant praise recite.

5 The holy church throughout the world,
    O Lord, confesses Thee,
That Thou eternal Father art,
    Of boundless majesty.

6 Thy honored, true, and only Son,
    And Holy Ghost, the spring
Of never ceasing joy, O Christ,
    Of glory Thou art King.
      Tate and Brady's Supplement. 1703. ab.

25   *"Gloria in excelsis."*   C. M.

1 To God be glory, peace on earth,
    To all mankind good will;
We bless, we praise, we worship Thee,
    And glorify Thee still;

2 And thanks for Thy great glory give,
    That fills our souls with light;
O Lord God, heavenly King, the God
    And Father of all might:

3 And Thou, begotten Son of God,
   Before all time begun;
   O Jesus Christ, God, Lamb of God,
   The Father's only Son:

4 Have mercy, Thou that tak'st the sins
   Of all the world away;
   Have mercy, Saviour of mankind,
   And hear us when we pray.

5 O Thou, who sitt'st at God's right hand,
   Upon the Father's throne,
   Have mercy on us, Thou, O Christ,
   Who art the Holy One!

6 Thou Lord, who with the Holy Ghost,
   Whom earth and heaven adore,
   In glory of the Father art
   Most high for evermore.
   Tate and Brady's Supplement. 1703.

26 Τριςφεγγὴς Μονὰς θεαρχική.

1 O UNITY of Threefold Light,
   Send out Thy loveliest ray,
   And scatter our transgressions' night
   And turn it into day.

2 Make us those temples pure and fair
   Thy glory loveth well,
   The spotless tabernacles where
   Thou may'st vouchsafe to dwell.

3 The glorious hosts of peerless might
   That ever see Thy Face,
   Thou mak'st the mirrors of Thy light,
   The vessels of Thy grace.

4 Thou, when their wondrous strain they weave,
   Hast pleasure in the lay;
   Deign now our praises to receive
   Albeit from lips of clay.

5 And yet Thyself they cannot know,
   Nor pierce the veil of light
   That hides Thee from the thrones below,
   As in profoundest night.

6 How then can mortal accents frame
   Due tribute to their King?
   Thou, only, while we praise Thy Name,
   Forgive us as we sing.
   Metrophanes of Smyrna. (—910).
   Tr. by Rev. John Mason Neale. (1818—1866.) 1862.

27 *"From Everlasting to Everlasting."*
Ps. xc. 2

1 Have mercy on us, God most High,
   Who lift our hearts to Thee,
   Have mercy on us worms of earth,
   Most Holy Trinity.

2 Most ancient of all mysteries,
   Before Thy Throne we lie;
   Have mercy now, most merciful,
   Most Holy Trinity.

3 When heaven and earth were yet unmade,
   When time was yet unknown,
   Thou, in Thy bliss and majesty,
   Didst live and love alone.

4 Thou wert not born; there was no fount
   From which Thy being flowed;
   There is no end which Thou can'st reach,
   But Thou art simply God.

5 How wonderful creation is,
   The work that Thou did'st bless;
   And O, what then must Thou be like,
   Eternal Loveliness?

6 Most ancient of all mysteries,
   Still at Thy Throne we lie;
   Have mercy now, most merciful,
   Most Holy Trinity.
   Rev. Frederick William Faber. (1814—1863.) 1849 ab.

28 *Praise for Creation and Redemption.*
Ps. c. 3. Rev. v. 9.

1 LET them neglect Thy glory, Lord,
   Who never knew Thy grace;
   But our loud songs shall still record
   The wonders of Thy praise.

2 We raise our shouts, O God, to Thee,
   And send them to Thy throne;
   All glory to th' united Three,
   The Undivided One.

3 'T was He, and we'll adore His name,
   That formed us by a word;
   'Tis He restores our ruined frame:
   Salvation to the Lord.

4 Hosanna, let the earth and skies
   Repeat the joyful sound:
   Rocks, hills, and vales, reflect the voice
   In one eternal round.
   Rev. Isaac Watts. (1674—1748.) 1709.

29 *A Latin Hymn to the Trinity.* 7.

1 FATHER, who didst fashion me
Image of Thyself to be,
Fill me with Thy love divine,
Let my every thought be Thine.

2 Holy Jesus, may I be
Dead and buried here with Thee;
And, by love inflamed, arise
Unto Thee a sacrifice.

3 Thou who dost all gifts impart,
Shine, sweet Spirit, in my heart;
Best of gifts, Thyself, bestow;
Make me burn Thy love to know.

4 God, the blessed Three in One,
Dwell within my heart alone;
Thou dost give Thyself to me,
May I give myself to Thee.

Le Mans Breviary.
Tr. by Rev. Sir Henry Williams Baker. (1821—) 1860.

30 *God Incarnate.* 7.

1 PRAISE to God who reigns above,
Binding earth and heaven in love;
All the armies of the sky
Worship His dread sovereignty.

2 Seraphim His praises sing,
Cherubim on fourfold wing,
Thrones, dominions, princes, powers,
Ranks of might that never cowers.

3 Angel hosts His word fulfil,
Ruling nature by His will;
Round His throne archangels pour
Songs of praise for evermore.

4 Yet on man they joy to wait,
All that bright celestial state,
For true man their Lord they see,
Christ, th' incarnate Deity.

5 On the throne our Lord, who died,
Sits in manhood glorified;
Where His people faint below,
Angels count it joy to go.

6 O the depths of joy divine,
Thrilling through those orders nine,
When the lost are found again,
When the banished come to reign.

7 Now in faith, in hope, in love,
We will join the choirs above,
Praising, with the heavenly host,
Father, Son, and Holy Ghost.

Rev. Richard Meux Benson. 1861.

31 *Prayer to the Trinity.* 7.

1 FATHER, at Thy footstool see
Those who now are one in Thee:
Draw us by Thy grace alone;
Give, O give us to Thy Son.

2 Jesus, Friend of human kind,
Let us in Thy name be joined;
Each to each unite and bless;
Keep us still in perfect peace.

3 Heavenly, all-alluring Dove,
Shed Thine overshadowing love,
Love, the sealing grace, impart,
Dwell within our single heart.

4 Father, Son, and Holy Ghost,
Be to us what Adam lost:
Let us in Thine image rise;
Give us back our Paradise.

Rev. Charles Wesley. (1708—1788.) 1749. ab. and sl. alt.

32 *The Trinity adored.* 7.

1 HOLY, holy, holy Lord,
God the Father, and the Word,
God the Comforter, receive
Blessing more than earth can give.

2 Mixed with those beyond the sky,
Chanters to the Lord Most High,
We our hearts and voices raise,
Echoing Thine eternal praise.

3 Happy they who never rest,
With Thy heavenly presence blest:
They the heights of glory see,
Sound the depths of Deity.

4 Fain with them our souls would vie;
Sink as low, and mount as high;
Fall o'erwhelmed with love, or soar;
Shout, or silently adore.

Rev. Charles Wesley. 1767. ab.

33 *All Things present to God.* 7.

1 MIGHTY God, the First, the Last,
   What are ages in Thy sight
But as yesterday when past,
   Or a watch within the night?

2 All that being ever knew,
   Down, far down, ere time had birth,
Stands as clear within Thy view
   As the present things of earth.

3 All that being e'er shall know,
   On, still on, through farthest years,
All eternity can show,
   Bright before Thee now appears.

4 In Thine all-embracing sight,
   Every change its purpose meets,
Every cloud floats into light,
   Every woe its glory greets.

5 Whatsoe'er our lot may be,
   Calmly in this thought we'll rest,—
Could we see as Thou dost see,
   We should choose it as the best.
   Mrs. Elizabeth Cleghorn Gaskell. (1810—1865.)

34 *"Round the Throne."* 7.

1 NOW with angels round the throne,
   Cherubim and Seraphim,
And the Church which still is one,
   Let us swell the solemn hymn:
Glory to the great I AM!
Glory to the Victim Lamb!

2 Blessing, honor, glory, might,
   And dominion infinite,
To the Father of our Lord,
   To the Spirit and the Word;
As it was all worlds before,
Is, and shall be evermore.
   Josiah Conder. (1789—1855.) 1824.

35 *Thanks and Praise.* 7.
  Ps. cvii.; cxvii.

1 THANK and praise Jehovah's name,
   For His mercies, firm and sure:
From eternity the same,
   To eternity endure,

2 Let the ransomed thus rejoice,
   Gathered out of every land;
As the people of His choice,
   Plucked from the destroyer's hand.

3 Praise Him, ye who know His love,
   Praise Him from the depths beneath,
Praise Him in the heights above;
   Praise your Maker, all that breathe.

4 For His truth and mercy stand,
   Past, and present, and to be,
Like the years of His right hand,
   Like His own eternity.
   James Montgomery. (1771—1854.) 1822. ab.

36 *"Take my Heart."* 7.

1 FATHER, Son, and Holy Ghost,
   One in Three, and Three in One,
As by the celestial host,
   Let Thy will on earth be done;
Praise by all to Thee be given,
Glorious Lord of earth and heaven.

2 Vilest of the fallen race,
   Lo, I answer to Thy call;
Meanest vessel of Thy grace,
   Grace divinely free for all;
Lo, I come to do Thy will,
All Thy counsel to fulfil.

3 If so poor a worm as I
   May to Thy great glory live,
All my actions sanctify,
   All my words and thoughts receive;
Claim me for Thy service, claim
All I have, and all I am.

4 Take my soul and body's powers,
   Take my memory, mind and will,
All my goods, and all my hours,
   All I know, and all I feel,
All I think, or speak, or do;
Take my heart, but make it new.
   Rev. Charles Wesley. 1745 ab.

37 Praise to the Trinity. H. M.

1 I GIVE immortal praise
    To God the Father's love,
    For all my comforts here,
    And better hopes above;
He sent His own | To die for sins
Eternal Son | That man had done.

2 To God the Son belongs
    Immortal glory too;
    Who bought us with His blood
    From everlasting woe:
And now He lives, | And sees the fruit
And now He reigns,| Of all His pains.

3 To God the Spirit's name
    Immortal worship give,
    Whose new-creating power
    Makes the dead sinner live:
His work completes | And fills the soul
The great design, | With joy divine.

4 Almighty God, to Thee
    Be endless honors done,
    The undivided Three,
    And the mysterious One:
Where reason fails, | There faith prevails,
With all her powers,| And love adores.
                    Rev. Isaac Watts. (1674—1748.) 1709.

38 Praise to the Trinity. H. M.

1 To Him that chose us first,
    Before the world began;
    To Him that bore the curse
    To save rebellious man;
To Him that formed | Is endless praise
Our hearts anew, | And glory due.

2 The Father's love shall run
    Through our immortal songs;
    We bring to God the Son
    Hosannas on our tongues:
Our lips address | With equal praise,
The Spirit's name | And zeal the same.

3 Let every saint above,
    And angels round the throne,
    Forever bless and love
    The sacred Three in One:
Thus heaven shall raise | When earth and time
His honors high, | Grow old and die.
                    Rev. Isaac Watts. 1719.

39 Praise to God from all Creatures. H. M.
Ps. cxlviii.

1 YE boundless realms of joy,
    Exalt your Maker's fame;
    His praise your songs employ
    Above the starry frame:
Your voices raise, | And seraphim,
Ye cherubim, | To sing His praise.

2 Thou moon that rul'st the night,
    And sun that guid'st the day,
    Ye glit'ring stars of light,
    To Him your homage pay:
His praise declare, | And clouds that move
Ye heavens above, | In liquid air.

3 Let them adore the Lord,
    And praise His holy name,
    By whose almighty word
    They all from nothing came:
And all shall last, | His firm decree
From changes free; | Stands ever fast.

4 United zeal be shown,
    His wondrous fame to raise,
    Whose glorious name alone
    Deserves our endless praise:
Earth's utmost ends | His glorious sway
His power obey; | The sky transcends.
                    Tate and Brady. 1696. ab.

40 Praise to God from all Creatures. H. M.
Ps. cxlviii.

1 YE tribes of Adam, join
    With heaven, and earth, and seas,
    And offer notes divine
    To your Creator's praise.
Ye holy throng | In worlds of light,
Of angels bright,| Begin the song.

2 The shining worlds above
    In glorious order stand,
    Or in swift courses move,
    By His supreme command:
He spake the word, | From nothing came,
And all their frame | To praise the Lord.

3 He moved their mighty wheels
    In unknown ages past,
    And each His word fulfils,
    While time and nature last:
In different ways | His wondrous name,
His works proclaim | And speak His praise.

GOD.

4 Let all the nations fear
The God that rules above;
He brings His people near,
And makes them taste His love:
While earth and sky | His saints shall raise
Attempt His praise, | His honors high.
Rev. Isaac Watts. (1674—1748.) 1719. ab

41 *"The Lord reigneth."* H. M.
Ps. xciii; xcvii.

1 THE Lord Jehovah reigns,
His throne is built on high;
The garments He assumes
Are light and majesty:
His glories shine | No mortal eye
With beams so bright, | Can bear the sight.

2 The thunders of His hand
Keep the wide world in awe;
His wrath and justice stand
To guard His holy law;
And where His love | His truth confirms
Resolves to bless, | And seals the grace.

3 Through all His ancient works,
Surprising wisdom shines;
Confounds the powers of hell,
And breaks their cursed designs:
Strong is His arm, | His great decrees,
And shall fulfil | His sovereign will.

4 And can this mighty King
Of glory condescend?
And will He write His name,
My Father and my Friend?
I love His name, | Join, all my powers,
I love His word; | And praise the Lord.
Rev. Isaac Watts. 1709.

42 *God's Fidelity to His Promises.* H. M.
Heb. x. 23.

1 THE promises I sing,
Which sovereign love hath spoke;
Nor will the eternal King
His words of grace revoke:
They stand secure | Not Zion's hill
And steadfast still; | Abides so sure.

2 The mountains melt away,
When once the Judge appears,
And sun and moon decay,
That measure mortal years:
But still the same, | The promise shines
In radiant lines, | Through all the flame.

3 Their harmony shall sound
Through mine attentive ears,
When thunders cleave the ground,
And dissipate the spheres:
Midst all the shock | I stand serene,
Of that dread scene, | Thy word my rock.
Rev. Philip Doddridge. (1702—1751.) 1755.

43 *God our Preserver.* H. M.
Ps. cxxi.

1 UPWARD I lift mine eyes,
From God is all my aid;
The God that built the skies,
And earth and nature made:
God is the tower | His grace is nigh
To which I fly; | In every hour.

2 My feet shall never slide,
And fall in fatal snares,
Since God, my guard and guide,
Defends me from my fears:
Those wakeful eyes, | Shall Israel keep
That never sleep, | When dangers rise.

3 No burning heats by day,
Nor blasts of evening air,
Shall take my health away,
If God be with me there:
Thou art my sun, | To guard my head
And Thou my shade, | By night or noon.

4 Hast Thou not given Thy word
To save my soul from death?
And I can trust my Lord
To keep my mortal breath:
I'll go and come, | Till from on high
Nor fear to die, | Thou call me home.
Rev. Isaac Watts. 1719.

44 *Safety in God.* H. M.
Ps. xi.

1 MY trust is in the Lord;
What foe can injure me?
Why bid me like a bird
Before the fowler flee?
The Lord is on His heavenly throne,
Omnipotent to save His own.

2 The wicked may assail,
The tempter sorely try,
All earth's foundations fail,
All nature's springs be dry;
Yet God is in His holy shrine,
And I am strong while He is mine.

3   His flock to Him is dear,
      He watches them from high;
      He sends them trials here
        To fit them for the sky;
      But safely will He tend and keep
      The humblest, feeblest, of His sheep.

4   His foes a season here
        May triumph and prevail;
      But ah, the hour is near
        When all their hopes must fail:
      While like the sun His saints shall rise,
      And shine with Him above the skies.
                    Rev. Henry Francis Lyte. (1793—1847.) 1834.

45   *The awful Majesty of God.*   S. P. M.
              Ps. xciii.

1   THE Lord Jehovah reigns,
      And royal state maintains,
    His head with awful glories crowned:
      Arrayed in robes of light,
      Begirt with sovereign might,
    And rays of majesty around.

2   Upheld by Thy commands,
      The world securely stands,
    And skies and stars obey Thy word:
      Thy throne was fixed on high
      Before the starry sky:
    Eternal is Thy kingdom, Lord.

3   In vain the noisy crowd,
      Like billows fierce and loud,
    Against Thine empire rage and roar;
      In vain with angry spite,
      The surly nations fight,
    And dash like waves against the shore.

4   Let floods and nations rage,
      And all their powers engage;
    Let swelling tides assault the sky:
      The terrors of Thy frown
      Shall beat their madness down;
    Thy throne for ever stands on high.

5   Thy promises are true,
      Thy grace is ever new;
    There fixed, Thy church shall ne'er remove:
      Thy saints with holy fear
      Shall in Thy courts appear,
    And sing Thine everlasting love.
                              Rev. Isaac Watts. 1719.

46   *All People summoned to worship.*   L. M.
              Ps. c.

1   ALL people that on earth do dwell,
      Sing to the Lord with cheerful voice:
    Him serve with fear, His praise forth tell,
      Come ye before Him, and rejoice.

2   The Lord, ye know, is God indeed,
      Without our aid He did us make:
    We are His flock, He doth us feed,
      And for His sheep He doth us take.

3   O enter then His gates with praise,
      Approach with joy His courts unto:
    Praise, laud, and bless His name always,
      For it is seemly so to do.

4   For why? the Lord our God is good,
      His mercy is forever sure:
    His truth at all times firmly stood,
      And shall from age to age endure.
                              Rev. William Kethe. 1561.

47   *Cheerful Worship.*   L. M.
              Ps. c.

1   WITH one consent, let all the earth,
      To God their cheerful voices raise;
    Glad homage pay with awful mirth,
      And sing before Him songs of praise.

2   Convinced that He is God alone,
      From whom both we and all proceed;
    We, whom He chooses for His own,
      The flock that He vouchsafes to feed.

3   O enter then His temple gate,
      Thence to His courts devoutly press,
    And still your grateful hymns repeat,
      And still His name with praises bless.

4   For He's the Lord, supremely good,
      His mercy is forever sure;
    His truth, which always firmly stood,
      To endless ages shall endure.
                              Tate and Brady. 1696

48   *Grateful Adoration.*   L. M.
              Ps. c.

1   BEFORE Jehovah's awful throne,
      Ye nations, bow with sacred joy;
    Know that the Lord is God alone;
      He can create, and He destroy.

2   His sovereign power, without our aid,
      Made us of clay, and formed us men;

And when, like wand'ring sheep, we strayed,
  He brought us to His fold again.

3 We are His people, we His care,
  Our souls and all our mortal frame:
  What lasting honors shall we rear,
  Almighty Maker, to Thy name?

4 We'll crowd Thy gates with thankful songs,
  High as the heavens our voices raise;
  And earth, with her ten thousand tongues,
  Shall fill Thy courts with sounding praise.

5 Wide as the world is Thy command,
  Vast as eternity Thy love;
  Firm as a rock Thy truth must stand,
  When rolling years shall cease to move.
    Rev. Isaac Watts (1674—1748.) 1719. ab. and alt.
    Rev. John Wesley. (1703—1791.) 1741.

49 *The Majesty and Mercy of God.* **L. M.**
Ps. lxxxii.

1 KINGDOMS and thrones to God belong;
  Crown Him, ye nations, in your song;
  His wondrous names and powers rehearse;
  His honors shall enrich your verse.

2 He shakes the heavens with loud alarms;
  How terrible is God in arms!
  In Israel are His mercies known,
  Israel is His peculiar throne.

3 Proclaim Him King, pronounce Him blest;
  He's your defence, your joy, your rest;
  When terrors rise, and nations faint,
  God is the strength of every saint.
    Rev. Isaac Watts. 1719.

50 *Praise from all Nations.* **L. M.**
Ps. cxvii.

1 FROM all that dwell below the skies,
  Let the Creator's praise arise:
  Let the Redeemer's name be sung
  Through every land, by every tongue.

2 Eternal are Thy mercies, Lord;
  Eternal truth attends Thy word;
  Thy praise shall sound from shore to shore
  Till suns shall rise and set no more.
    Rev. Isaac Watts. 1719.

51 *Universal Praise.* **L. M.**
Ps. cxlviii.

1 LOUD hallelujahs to the Lord,
  From distant worlds where creatures dwell;
  Let heaven begin the solemn word,
  And sound it dreadful down to hell.

2 High on a throne His glories dwell,
  An awful throne of shining bliss:
  Fly through the world, O sun, and tell
  How dark thy beams compared to His.

3 Let clouds, and winds, and waves agree
  To join their praise with blazing fire;
  Let the firm earth and rolling sea
  In this eternal song conspire.

4 Wide as His vast dominion lies,
  Make the Creator's name be known;
  Loud as His thunder, shout the praise,
  And sound it lofty as His throne.

5 Speak of the wonders of that love,
  Which Gabriel plays on every chord:
  From all below and all above,
  Loud hallelujahs to the Lord.
    Rev. Isaac Watts. 1719. ab.

52 *Praise for Protection, Grace, and Truth.* **L. M.**
Ps. lvii.

1 MY God, in whom are all the springs
  Of boundless love, and grace unknown.
  Hide me beneath Thy spreading wings,
  Till the dark cloud is overblown.

2 Up to the heavens I send my cry:
  The Lord will my desires perform:
  He sends His angels from the sky,
  And saves me from the threat'ning storm.

3 High o'er the earth Thy mercy reigns,
  And reaches to the utmost sky;
  His truth to endless years remains,
  When lower worlds dissolve and die.

4 Be Thou exalted, O my God,
  Above the heavens where angels dwell;
  Thy power on earth be known abroad,
  And land to land Thy wonders tell.
    Rev. Isaac Watts. 1719. ab.

53 *Praise from the whole Creation.* **8, 7.**
Ps. cxlviii.

1 PRAISE the Lord, ye heavens, adore Him,
  Praise Him, angels, in the height;
  Sun and moon, rejoice before Him;
  Praise Him, all ye stars and light.

2 Praise the Lord, for He hath spoken;
   Worlds His mighty voice obeyed;
   Laws which never shall be broken,
   For their guidance He hath made.

3 Praise the Lord, for He is glorious;
   Never shall His promise fail;
   God hath made His saints victorious;
   Sin and death shall not prevail.

4 Praise the God of our salvation;
   Hosts on high, His power proclaim;
   Heaven and earth, and all creation,
   Laud and magnify His name.
   Rev. John Kempthorne. (1775—1838.) 1809.

54 *"God is Love."* 8, 7.
1 John iv. 8.

1 GOD is love; His mercy brightens
   All the path in which we rove;
   Bliss He wakes, and woe He lightens;
   God is wisdom, God is love.

2 Chance and change are busy ever;
   Man decays, and ages move;
   But His mercy waneth never:
   God is wisdom, God is love.

3 E'en the hour that darkest seemeth
   Will His changeless goodness prove;
   From the mist His brightness streameth:
   God is wisdom, God is love.

4 He with earthly cares entwineth
   Hope and comfort from above;
   Everywhere His glory shineth:
   God is wisdom, God is love.
   Sir John Bowring. (1792—1872.) 1825.

55 *Praise on Earth and in Heaven.* 8, 7.
Rev. iv. 11.

1 PRAISE to Thee, Thou great Creator,
   Praise be Thine from every tongue;
   Join, my soul, with every creature,
   Join the universal song.

2 Father, Source of all compassion,
   Pure unbounded grace is Thine:
   Hail the God of our salvation,
   Praise Him for His love divine.

3 For ten thousand blessings given,
   For the richest gifts bestowed,
   Sound His praise through earth and heaven,
   Sound Jehovah's praise aloud.

4 Joyfully on earth adore Him,
   Till in Heaven our song we raise:
   There, enraptured fall before Him,
   Lost in wonder, love, and praise.
   Rev. John Fawcett. (1739—1817.) 1767.) alt.

56 *The Majesty and Mercy of God.* 10, 11.
Ps. civ.

1 O WORSHIP the King all glorious above;
   O gratefully sing His power and His love;
   Our Shield and Defender, the Ancient of days,
   Pavilioned in splendor, and girded with praise.

2 O tell of His might, O sing of His grace,
   Whose robe is the light, whose canopy space;
   His chariots of wrath deep thunder-clouds form,
   And dark is His path on the wings of the storm.

3 The earth, with its store of wonders untold,
   Almighty, Thy power hath founded of old,
   Hath stablished it fast by a changeless decree,
   And round it hath cast, like a mantle, the sea.

4 Thy bountiful care what tongue can recite?
   It breathes in the air, it shines in the light,
   It streams from the hills, it descends to the plain,
   And sweetly distils in the dew and the rain.

5 Frail children of dust, and feeble as frail,
   In Thee do we trust, nor find Thee to fail:
   Thy mercies how tender, how firm to the end,
   Our Maker, Defender, Redeemer, and Friend.

6 O measureless Might, ineffable Love,
   While angels delight to hymn Thee above,
   The humbler creation, though feeble their lays,
   With true adoration shall lisp to Thy praise.
   Sir Robert Grant. (1785—1838.) 1839.

57 *"Stand up, and Bless the Lord."* S. M.
Neh. ix. 5.

1 STAND up, and bless the Lord,
   Ye people of His choice;
   Stand up and bless the Lord, your God,
   With heart, and soul, and voice.

2 O for the living flame,
   From His own altar brought,
   To touch our lips, our minds inspire,
   And wing to heaven our thought.

GOD.

3 God is our strength and song,
   And His salvation ours;
   Then be His love in Christ proclaimed
   With all our ransomed powers.

4 Stand up, and bless the Lord,
   The Lord your God adore;
   Stand up, and bless His glorious name,
   Henceforth for evermore.
   James Montgomery. (1771—1854.) 1825. ab.

58 *Exhortation to Worship.* **S. M.**
Ps. xcv.

1 COME, sound His praise abroad,
   And hymns of glory sing:
   Jehovah is the sovereign God,
   The universal King.

2 He formed the deeps unknown,
   He gave the seas their bound;
   The watery worlds are all His own,
   And all the solid ground.

3 Come, worship at His throne,
   Come, bow before the Lord,
   We are His work, and not our own;
   He formed us by His word.

4 To-day attend His voice,
   Nor dare provoke His rod;
   Come, like the people of His choice,
   And own your gracious God.
   Rev. Isaac Watts. (1674—1748.) 1719. ab.

59 *Universal Praise.* **S. M.**
Ps. cxlviii.

1 LET every creature join
   To praise the eternal God,
   Ye heavenly hosts, the song begin,
   And sound His name abroad.

2 Thou sun with golden beams,
   And moon with paler rays,
   Ye starry lights, ye twinkling flames,
   Shine to your Maker's praise.

3 He built those worlds above,
   And fixed their wondrous frame;
   By His command they stand and move,
   And ever speak His name.

4 Ye vapors, when ye rise,
   Or fall in showers or snow,
   Ye thunders, murmuring round the skies,
   His power and glory show.

5 Wind, hail, and flashing fire,
   Agree to praise the Lord,
   When ye in dreadful storms conspire
   To execute His word.

6 By all His works above
   His honors be expressed;
   But saints, that taste his saving love,
   Should sing His praises best.
   Rev. Isaac Watts. 1719.

60 *The Divine Sovereignty and Goodness.* **S. M.**
Ps. viii.

1 O LORD, our heavenly King,
   Thy name is all divine;
   Thy glories round the earth are spread,
   And o'er the heavens they shine.

2 When to Thy works on high
   I raise my wondering eyes,
   And see the moon, complete in light,
   Adorn the darksome skies;

3 When I survey the stars,
   And all their shining forms,
   Lord, what is man, that worthless thing,
   Akin to dust and worms?

4 Lord, what is worthless man,
   That Thou shouldst love Him so?
   Next to Thine angels is he placed,
   And lord of all below.

5 How rich thy bounties are,
   And wondrous are Thy ways;
   Of dust and worms Thy power can frame
   A monument of praise.

6 O Lord, our heavenly King,
   Thy name is all divine;
   Thy glories round the earth are spread,
   And o'er the heavens they shine.
   Rev. Isaac Watts. 1719. ab.

61 *A holy God worshipped with Reverence.* **S. M.**
Ps. xcix.

1 EXALT the Lord our God,
   And worship at His feet;
   His nature is all holiness,
   And mercy is His seat.

2 When Israel was His church,
   When Aaron was His priest,
   When Moses cried, when Samuel prayed,
   He gave His people rest.

3 Oft He forgave their sins,
    Nor would destroy their race;
  And oft He made His vengeance known
    When they abused His grace.

4 Exalt the Lord our God,
    Whose grace is still the same;
  Still He's a God of holiness,
    And jealous for His name.
                        Rev. Isaac Watts. 1719.

62   *"The only Wise."*   S. M.
Jude 24, 25.

1 To God the only wise,
    Our Saviour and our King,
  Let all the saints below the skies
    Their humble praises bring.

2 'Tis His almighty love,
    His counsel and His care,
  Preserves us safe from sin and death,
    And every hurtful snare.

3 He will present our souls,
    Unblemished and complete,
  Before the glory of His face,
    With joys divinely great.

4 Then all the chosen seed
    Shall meet around the throne,
  Shall bless the conduct of His grace,
    And make His wonders known.

5 To our Redeemer God
    Wisdom and power belongs,
  Immortal crowns of majesty,
    And everlasting songs.
                        Rev. Isaac Watts. 1709.

63   *"The Heavens declare the Glory of God."*   L. M.
Ps. xix.

1 THE spacious firmament on high,
  With all the blue ethereal sky,
  And spangled heavens, a shining frame,
  Their great Original proclaim.

2 The unwearied sun, from day to day,
  Does his Creator's power display,
  And publishes to every land
  The work of an Almighty Hand.

3 Soon as the evening shades prevail,
  The moon takes up the wondrous tale,
  And nightly to the listening earth
  Repeats the story of her birth;

4 Whilst all the stars that round her burn,
  And all the planets in their turn,
  Confirm the tidings as they roll,
  And spread the truth from pole to pole.

5 What though in solemn silence all
  Move round the dark terrestrial ball?
  What though no real voice nor sound
  Amid their radiant orbs be found?

6 In reason's ear they all rejoice,
  And utter forth a glorious voice;
  For ever singing, as they shine,
  "The Hand that made us is divine."
                        Joseph Addison. (1672—1719.) 1712.

64   *God's Glory and Nearness to us.*   L. M.
Acts xvii. 24—28.

1 LORD of all being: throned afar,
  Thy glory flames from sun and star;
  Centre and soul of every sphere,
  Yet to each loving heart how near.

2 Sun of our life, Thy quickening ray
  Sheds on our path the glow of day;
  Star of our hope, Thy softened light
  Cheers the long watches of the night.

3 Our midnight is Thy smile withdrawn;
  Our noontide is Thy gracious dawn;
  Our rainbow arch Thy mercy's sign;
  All, save the clouds of sin, are Thine.

4 Lord of all life, below, above,
  Whose light is truth, whose warmth is love,
  Before Thy ever-blazing throne
  We ask no lustre of our own.

5 Grant us Thy truth to make us free,
  And kindling hearts that burn for Thee,
  Till all Thy living altars claim
  One holy light, one heavenly flame.
                        Oliver Wendell Holmes. (1809—) 1848.

65   *God's Love our Refuge.*   L. M.

1 O SOURCE divine, and Life of all,
  The Fount of being's wondrous sea,
  Thy depth would every heart appall,
  That saw not Love supreme in Thee.

2 We shrink before Thy vast abyss,
  Where worlds on worlds eternal brood;
  We know Thee truly but in this,
  That Thou bestowest all our good.

GOD.

3 And so, 'mid boundless time and space,
   O grant us still in Thee to dwell,
And through the ceaseless web to trace
   Thy presence working all things well.
4 Nor let Thou life's delightful play
   Thy truth's transcendent vision hide;
Nor strength and gladness lead astray
   From Thee, our nature's only guide.
5 Bestow on every joyous thrill
   Thy deeper tone of reverent awe;
Make pure Thy children's erring will,
   And teach their hearts to love Thy law.
                    Rev. John Sterling. (1806—1844.) 1839.

66   *God in Nature.*   L. M.
         Ps. lxxiv. 16, 17.

1 THOU art, O God, the life and light
   Of all this wondrous world we see;
Its glow by day, its smile by night,
   Are but reflections caught from Thee,
Where'er we turn, Thy glories shine,
And all things fair and bright are Thine.

2 When day, with farewell beam, delays
   Among the opening clouds of even,
And we can almost think we gaze
   Through golden vistas into heaven,
Those hues that mark the sun's decline,
So soft, so radiant, Lord, are Thine.

3 When night, with wings of starry gloom,
   O'ershadows all the earth and skies,
Like some dark, beauteous bird, whose plume
   Is sparkling with unnumbered eyes,
That sacred gloom, those fires divine,
So grand, so countless, Lord, are Thine.

4 When youthful spring around us breathes,
   Thy spirit warms her fragrant sigh;
And every flower the summer wreathes
   Is born beneath that kindling eye,
Where'er we turn, Thy glories shine,
And all things fair and bright are Thine.
                    Thomas Moore. (1779—1852.) 1816.

67   *"The Heavens declare the Glory of God."*   L. M.
         Ps. xix.

1 THY glory, Lord, the heavens declare,
   The firmament displays Thy skill;
The changing clouds, the viewless air,
   Tempest and calm Thy word fulfil;
Day unto day doth utter speech,
And night to night Thy knowledge teach.

2 Though voice nor sound inform the ear,
   Well known the language of their song,
When one by one the stars appear,
   Led by the silent moon along,
Till round the earth, from all the sky,
Thy beauty beams on every eye.

3 Waked by Thy touch the morning sun
   Comes like a bridegroom from his bower,
And, like a giant, glad to run
   His bright career with speed and power;
Thy flaming messenger, to dart
Life through the depth of nature's heart.

4 While these transporting visions shine
   Along the path of Providence,
Glory eternal, joy divine,
   Thy word reveals, transcending sense;
My soul Thy goodness longs to see,
Thy love to man, Thy love to me.
                    James Montgomery. (1771—1854.) 1822.

68   *"Glory to God in the highest."*   7.
         Luke ii. 13.

1 SONGS of praise the angels sang,
   Heaven with hallelujahs rang,
When Jehovah's work begun,
   When He spake, and it was done.

2 Songs of praise awoke the morn,
   When the Prince of Peace was born;
Songs of praise arose, when He
   Captive led captivity.

3 Heaven and earth must pass away,
   Songs of praise shall crown that day;
God will make new heavens, new earth,
   Songs of praise shall hail their birth.

4 And can man alone be dumb
   Till that glorious kingdom come?
No: the Church delights to raise
   Psalms, and hymns, and songs of praise.

5 Saints below, with heart and voice,
   Still in songs of praise rejoice;
Learning here, by faith and love,
   Songs of praise to sing above.

6 Borne upon their latest breath,
   Songs of praise shall conquer death;
Then, amidst eternal joy,
   Songs of praise their powers employ.
                    James Montgomery. (1771—1854.) 1819, 1853.

69
God praise{d} for His Mercies.
Ps. lxv.

1 PRAISE on Thee in Zion's gates,
Daily, O Jehovah, waits:
Unto Thee, O God, belong
Grateful words and holy song.

2 Thou the Hope and Refuge art
Of remotest lands apart;
Distant isles and tribes unknown,
'Mid the ocean waste and lone.

3 By Thy boundless might set fast,
Rise the mountains firm and vast:
Thou canst with a word assuage
Ocean's wide and deafening rage.

4 When Thy signs in heaven appear,
Earth's remotest regions fear;
And the bounties of Thy hand
Fill with gladness every land.

5 Thou dost visit earth, and rain
Blessings on the thirsty plain,
From the copious founts on high,
From the rivers of the sky.

6 Thus the clouds Thy power confess,
And Thy paths drop fruitfulness,
And the voice of song and mirth
Rises from the tribes of earth.

Josiah Conder. (1789—1855.) 1836.

70
"Hail, celestial Goodness, hail!"

1 HOLY, holy, holy Lord,
Be Thy glorious name adored:
Lord, Thy mercies never fail;
Hail, celestial Goodness, hail!

2 Though unworthy, Lord, Thine ear,
Deign our humble songs to hear;
Purer praise we hope to bring,
When around Thy throne we sing.

3 While on earth ordained to stay,
Guide our footsteps in Thy way,
Till we come to dwell with Thee,
Till we all Thy glory see.

4 Then with angel-harps again
We will wake a nobler strain;
There, in joyful songs of praise,
Our triumphant voices raise.

5 There no tongue shall silent be,
All shall join in harmony;
That through heaven's capacious round
Praise to Thee may ever sound.

6 Lord, Thy mercies never fail;
Hail, celestial Goodness, hail!
Holy, holy, holy Lord,
Be Thy glorious name adored.

Rev. Benjamin Williams. 1778.

71
"Gloria in excelsis."

1 GLORY be to God on high,
God, whose glory fills the sky;
Peace on earth to man forgiven,
Man, the well-beloved of Heaven.

2 Sovereign Father, heavenly King,
Thee we now presume to sing;
Glad, Thine attributes confess,
Glorious all, and numberless.

3 Hail, by all Thy works adored,
Hail, the everlasting Lord:
Thee, with thankful hearts we prove
God of power, and God of love.

4 Christ our Lord and God we own,
Christ, the Father's Only Son;
Lamb of God, for sinners slain,
Saviour of offending man.

5 Bow Thine ear, in mercy bow;
Hear, the world's Atonement Thou:
Jesus, in Thy name we pray,
Take, O take our sins away.

6 Hear, for Thou, O Christ, alone
Art with Thy great Father One;
One, the Holy Ghost with Thee;
One supreme, eternal Three.

Rev. Charles Wesley. (1708—1788.) 1739. ab.

72
Praise from all.
Ps. cxvii.

1 ALL ye Gentiles, praise the Lord,
All ye lands, your voices raise;
Heaven and earth, with loud accord,
Praise the Lord, forever praise.

2 For His truth and mercy stand,
Past, and present, and to be,
Like the years of His right hand,
Like His own eternity.

3 Praise Him, ye who know His love;
Praise Him, from the depths beneath;
Praise Him, in the heights above;
Praise your Maker, all that breathe.

James Montgomery. 1822.

GOD.

73 *God immutable.* C. M.
Ps. cii.

1 THROUGH endless years, Thou art the same,
  O Thou eternal God;
  Ages to come shall know Thy name,
  And tell Thy works abroad.

2 The strong foundations of the earth
  Of old by Thee were laid;
  By Thee the beauteous arch of heaven
  With matchless skill was made.

3 Soon shall this goodly frame of things,
  Formed by Thy powerful hand,
  Be, like a vesture, laid aside,
  And changed at Thy command.

4 But Thy perfections, all divine,
  Eternal as Thy days,
  Through everlasting ages shine,
  With undiminished rays.

5 Our children's children, still Thy care,
  Shall own their Father's God;
  To latest times Thy favor share,
  And spread Thy praise abroad.
  Tate and Brady. 1696 ab. and alt.

74 *Man frail, and God eternal.* C. M.
Ps. xc

1 OUR God, our help in ages past,
  Our hope for years to come;
  Our shelter from the stormy blast,
  And our eternal home:

2 Under the shadow of Thy throne
  Thy saints have dwelt secure;
  Sufficient is Thine arm alone,
  And our defence is sure.

3 Before the hills in order stood,
  Or earth received her frame,
  From everlasting Thou art God,
  To endless years the same.

4 A thousand ages, in Thy sight,
  Are like an evening gone;
  Short as the watch that ends the night,
  Before the rising sun.

5 Time, like an ever-rolling stream,
  Bears all its sons away;
  They fly, forgotten, as a dream
  Dies at the opening day.

6 Our God, our help in ages past,
  Our hope for years to come,
  Be Thou our guard while troubles last,
  And our eternal home.
  Rev. Isaac Watts. (1674—1748) 1719. ab.

75 *My Father.* C. M.

1 O GOD, Thy power is wonderful,
  Thy glory passing bright;
  Thy wisdom, with its deep on deep,
  A rapture to the sight.

2 I see Thee in the eternal years
  In glory all alone,
  Ere round Thine uncreated fires
  Created light had shone.

3 I see Thee walk in Eden's shade,
  I see Thee all through time;
  Thy patience and compassion seem
  New attributes sublime.

4 I see Thee when the doom is o'er,
  And outworn time is done,
  Still, still incomprehensible,
  O God, yet not alone.

5 Angelic spirits, countless souls,
  Of Thee have drunk their fill;
  And to eternity will drink
  Thy joy and glory still.

6 From Thee were drawn those worlds of life,
  The Saviour's heart and soul;
  And, undiminished still, Thy waves
  Of calmest glory roll.
  Rev. Frederick William Faber. (1814—1863). 1849. ab.

76 *God's eternal Dominion.* C. M.

1 GREAT God, how infinite art Thou,
  What worthless worms are we:
  Let the whole race of creatures bow,
  And pay their praise to Thee.

2 Thy throne eternal ages stood,
  Ere seas or stars were made;
  Thou art the ever-living God,
  Were all the nations dead.

3 Eternity, with all its years,
  Stands present in Thy view;
  To Thee there's nothing old appears,
  Great God, there's nothing new.

4 Our lives through various scenes are drawn,
    And vexed with trifling cares;
    While Thine eternal thought moves on
    Thine undisturbed affairs.

5 Great God, how infinite art Thou,
    What worthless worms are we;
    Let the whole race of creatures bow,
    And pay their praise to Thee.
          Rev. Isaac Watts. 1709. ab.

77   *Our Heavenly Father.*   7.

1 MY God, how wonderful Thou art,
    Thy majesty how bright,
    How beautiful Thy mercy-seat
    In depths of burning light.

2 How dread are Thine eternal years,
    O Everlasting Lord;
    By prostrate spirits day and night
    Incessantly adored.

3 How beautiful, how beautiful,
    The sight of Thee must be,
    Thine endless wisdom, boundless power,
    And awful purity.

4 O how I fear Thee, Living God,
    With deepest, tenderest fears,
    And worship Thee with trembling hope,
    And penitential tears.

5 Yet I may love Thee too, O Lord,
    Almighty as Thou art;
    For Thou hast stooped to ask of me
    The love of my poor heart.

6 No earthly father loves like Thee,
    No mother half so mild
    Bears and forbears, as Thou hast done
    With me, Thy sinful child.

7 Father of Jesus, love's reward,
    What rapture will it be,
    Prostrate before Thy throne to lie,
    And gaze, and gaze on Thee.
          Rev. Frederick William Faber. 1849. ab.

78   *The Condescension of God.*   7.
          Ps. cxiii.

1 HALLELUJAH, raise, O raise
    To our God the song of praise:
    All His servants, join to sing
    God our Saviour and our King.

2 Blesséd be for evermore
    That dread name which we adore:
    O'er all nations God alone,
    Higher than the heavens His throne.

3 Yet to view the heavens He bends;
    Yea, to earth He condescends;
    Passing by the rich and great,
    For the low and desolate.

4 He can raise the poor to stand
    With the princes of the land;
    Wealth upon the needy shower;
    Set the meanest high in power.

5 He the broken spirit cheers,
    Turns to joy the mourner's tears;
    Such the wonders of His ways:
    Praise His name, forever praise.
          Josiah Conder. (1789—1855.) 1837. ab.

79   *Praise from all God's Creatures.*   7.
          Ps. cxlviii.

1 HERALDS of creation, cry,
    Praise the Lord, the Lord most high:
    Heaven and earth, obey the call,
    Praise the Lord, the Lord of all.

2 For He spake, and forth from night,
    Sprang the universe to light;
    He commanded, Nature heard,
    And stood fast upon His word.

3 Praise Him, all ye hosts above;
    Spirits perfected in love;
    Sun and moon, your voices raise;
    Sing, ye stars, your Maker's praise.

4 Earth, from all thy depths below,
    Ocean's hallelujahs flow;
    Lightning, vapor, wind, and storm,
    Hail and snow, His will perform.

5 Birds, on wings of rapture soar,
    Warble at His temple-door;
    Joyful sounds from herds and flocks,
    Echo back, ye caves and rocks.

6 High above all height His throne,
    Excellent His name alone;
    Him let all His works confess;
    Him let every being bless.
          James Montgomery. (1771—1854.) 1822. ab.

80 *Exhortation to Praise.* 7.
Ps. cl.

1 PRAISE the Lord, His glories show,
  Saints within His courts below,
  Angels round His throne above,
  Praise Him, all that share His love.

2 Earth, to heaven exalt the strain,
  Send it, heaven, to earth again;
  Age to age, and shore to shore,
  Praise Him, praise Him, evermore.

3 Praise the Lord; His goodness trace,
  All the wonders of His grace;
  All that He hath borne and done,
  All He sends us through His Son.

4 Strings and voices, hands and hearts,
  In the concert bear your parts;
  All that breathe, your Lord adore,
  Praise Him, praise Him, evermore.
  Rev. Henry Francis Lyte. (1793—1847.) 1834, 1841.

81 *Wonders of Creation, Providence, and Grace.* 7.
Ps. cxxxvi.

1 LET us, with a gladsome mind,
  Praise the Lord, for He is kind:
    For His mercies shall endure,
    Ever faithful, ever sure.

2 He, with all-commanding might,
  Filled the new-made world with light:
    For His mercies shall endure,
    Ever faithful, ever sure.

3 He His chosen race did bless
  In the wasteful wilderness:
    For His mercies shall endure,
    Ever faithful, ever sure.

4 He hath, with a piteous eye,
  Looked upon our misery:
    For His mercies shall endure,
    Ever faithful, ever sure.

5 All things living He doth feed,
  His full hand supplies their need:
    For His mercies shall endure,
    Ever faithful ever sure.

6 Let us therefore warble forth
  His high majesty and worth:
    For His mercies shall endure,
    Ever faithful, ever sure.
  John Milton. (1608—1674.) 1674. ab. and alt.

82 *The Eternal Shepherd.* 7.
Ps. xxiii.

1 TO Thy pastures fair and large,
  Heavenly Shepherd, lead Thy charge,
  And my couch, with tenderest care,
  Mid the springing grass prepare.

2 When I faint with summer's heat
  Thou shalt guide my weary feet
  To the streams that, still and slow,
  Through the verdant meadows flow.

3 Safe the dreary vale I tread,
  By the shades of death o'erspread,
  With Thy rod and staff supplied,
  This my guard, and that my guide.

4 Constant to my latest end,
  Thou my footsteps shalt attend;
  And shalt bid Thy hallowed dome
  Yield me an eternal home.
  Rev. James Merrick. (1720—1769.) 1765. ab. and alt.

83 *"Praise the Lord."* 7.
Ps. cl.

1 PRAISE the Lord, His power confess,
  Praise Him in His holiness;
  Praise Him as the theme inspires,
  Praise Him as His fame requires.

2 Let the trumpet's lofty sound
  Spread its loudest notes around;
  Let the harp unite, in praise,
  With the sacred minstrel's lays.

3 Let the organ join to bless
  God, the Lord of righteousness;
  Tune your voice to spread the fame
  Of the great Jehovah's name.

4 All who dwell beneath His light,
  In His praise your hearts unite;
  While the stream of song is poured,
  Praise and magnify the Lord.
  William Wrangham. (—1832.) 1829.

84 *The Lord our Shepherd.* S. M.
Ps. xxiii.

1 THE Lord my Shepherd is;
    I shall be well supplied:
  Since He is mine, I am His,
    What can I want beside?

2 He leads me to the place
    Where heavenly pasture grows;

Where living waters gently pass,
  And full salvation flows.

3 If e'er I go astray,
  He doth my soul reclaim;
  And guides me, in His own right way,
  For His most holy name.

4 While He affords His aid,
  I cannot yield to fear;
  Tho' I should walk thro' death's dark shade,
  My Shepherd's with me there.

5 In spite of all my foes,
  Thou dost my table spread;
  My cup with blessings overflows,
  And joy exalts my head.

6 The bounties of Thy love
  Shall crown my following days;
  Nor from Thy house will I remove,
  Nor cease to speak Thy praise.
            Rev. Isaac Watts. (1674—1748.) 1719.

85   *The Heavenly Shepherd.*   S. M.
            Ps. xxiii.

1 WHILE my Redeemer's near,
  My shepherd and my guide,
  I bid farewell to anxious fear;
  My wants are all supplied.

2 To ever fragrant meads,
  Where rich abundance grows,
  His gracious hand indulgent leads,
  And guards my sweet repose.

3 Dear Shepherd, if I stray,
  My wandering feet restore;
  To Thy fair pastures guide my way,
  And let me rove no more.

4 Unworthy, as I am,
  Of Thy protecting care,
  Jesus, I plead Thy gracious name,
  For all my hopes are there.
            Miss Anne Steele. (1717—1778.) 1760. ab.

86   *Seeking God.*   S. M.
            Ps. lxiii.

1 My God, permit my tongue
  This joy, to call Thee mine;
  And let my early cries prevail
  To taste Thy love divine.

2 My thirsty, fainting soul
  Thy mercy doth implore;

Not travellers in desert lands
  Can pant for water more.

3 In wakeful hours at night,
  I call my God to mind;
  I think how wise Thy counsels are,
  And all Thy dealings kind.

4 Since Thou hast been my help,
  To Thee my spirit flies;
  And on Thy watchful providence
  My cheerful hope relies.

5 The shadow of Thy wings
  My soul in safety keeps;
  I follow where my Father leads,
  And He supports my steps.
            Rev. Isaac Watts. 1719. ab.

87   *Praise for temporal and spiritual Mercies.*   S. M.
            Ps. ciii. 1—7.

1 O bless the Lord, my soul,
  Let all within me join,
  And aid my tongue to bless His name,
  Whose favors are divine.

2 O bless the Lord, my soul,
  Nor let His mercies lie
  Forgotten in unthankfulness,
  And without praises die.

3 'Tis He forgives thy sins,
  'Tis He relieves thy pain,
  'Tis He that heals thy sicknesses,
  And makes thee young again.

4 He crowns thy life with love,
  When ransomed from the grave;
  He that redeemed my soul from hell,
  Hath sovereign power to save.

5 He fills the poor with good;
  He gives the sufferers rest;
  The Lord hath judgments for the proud,
  And justice for th'oppressed.

6 His wondrous works and ways
  He made by Moses known;
  But sent the world His truth and grace
  By His beloved Son.
            Rev. Isaac Watts. 1719.

88   *Abounding Compassion of God.*   S. M.
            Ps. ciii. 8—17.

1 My soul, repeat His praise
  Whose mercies are so great;

GOD.

Whose anger is so slow to rise,
  So ready to abate.

2 God will not always chide;
  And when His strokes are felt,
  His strokes are fewer than our crimes,
  And lighter than our guilt.

3 High as the heavens are raised
  Above the ground we tread,
  So far the riches of His grace
  Our highest thoughts exceed.

4 His power subdues our sins,
  And His forgiving love,
  Far as the east is from the west,
  Doth all our guilt remove.
      Rev. Isaac Watts. (1674—1748.) 1719.

89   *"He knoweth our Frame."*   **S. M.**
     Ps. ciii. 13—18.

1 THE pity of the Lord
  To those that fear His name,
  Is such as tender parents feel;
  He knows our feeble frame.

2 He knows we are but dust,
  Scattered with every breath;
  His anger, like a rising wind,
  Can send us swift to death.

3 Our days are as the grass,
  Or like the morning flower;
  If one sharp blast sweep o'er the field,
  It withers in an hour.

4 But Thy compassions, Lord,
  To endless years endure;
  And children's children ever find
  Thy words of promise sure.
      Rev. Isaac Watts. 1719.

90   *Mercies of God recounted.*   **C. M.**

1 WHEN all Thy mercies, O my God,
  My rising soul surveys,
  Transported with the view, I'm lost
  In wonder, love, and praise.

2 Unnumbered comforts to my soul
  Thy tender care bestowed,
  Before my infant heart conceived
  From whom those comforts flowed.

3 When worn with sickness, oft hast Thou
  With health renewed my face;
  And, when in sins and sorrows sunk,
  Revived my soul with grace.

4 Ten thousand thousand precious gifts
  My daily thanks employ;
  Nor is the least a cheerful heart
  That tastes those gifts with joy.

5 Through every period of my life
  Thy goodness I'll pursue;
  And after death, in distant worlds,
  The glorious theme renew.

6 Through all eternity to Thee
  A joyful song I'll raise;
  For O, eternity's too short
  To utter all Thy praise.
      Joseph Addison. (1672—1719.) 1712. ab.

91   *A merciful God.*   **C. M.**
     Deut. iv. 31.

1 FATHER of mercies, God of love,
  My Father and my God;
  I'll sing the honors of Thy name,
  And spread Thy praise abroad.

2 In every period of my life
  Thy kindest thoughts appear;
  Thy mercies gild each transient scene,
  And crown each circling year.

3 In all these mercies may my soul
  A Father's bounty see,
  Nor let the gifts Thy grace bestows
  Estrange my heart from Thee.

4 Teach me, in times of deep distress,
  To own Thy hand, my God,
  And in submissive silence learn
  The lessons of Thy rod.

5 In every varying mortal state,
  Each bright, each dreary scene,
  Give me a meek and humble mind,
  Still equal and serene.

6 Then shall I close my eyes in death,
  Without one anxious fear;
  For death itself, my God, is life,
  If Thou art with me there.
      Rev. Ottiwell Heginbothom. (1744—1768.) 1766. ab.

GOD.

92   *"Lord of all."*   C. M.

1 The Lord our God is Lord of all;
   His station who can find?
   I hear Him in the waterfall,
   I hear Him in the wind.

2 He lives, He reigns in every land,
   From winter's polar snows
   To where, across the burning sand,
   The blazing meteor goes.

3 If in the gloom of night I shroud,
   His face I cannot fly;
   I see Him in the evening cloud,
   And in the morning sky.

4 He smiles, we live, He frowns, we die;
   We hang upon His word;
   He rears His red right arm on high,
   And ruin bares the sword.

5 He bids His blasts the fields deform;
   Then when His thunders cease,
   He paints His rainbow on the storm,
   And lulls the winds to peace.
       Henry Kirke White. (1785—1806.) 1806. alt.

93   *Reverential Worship.*   C. M.
       Ps. lxxxix. 7.

1 WITH rev'rence let the saints appear,
   And bow before the Lord;
   His high commands with rev'rence hear,
   And tremble at His word.

2 How terrible Thy glories rise,
   How bright Thine armies shine:
   Where is the power with Thee that vies,
   Or truth compared with Thine?

3 The northern pole and southern rest
   On Thy supporting hand;
   Darkness and day, from east to west,
   Move round at Thy command.

4 Thy words the raging winds control,
   And rule the boisterous deep;
   Thou mak'st the sleeping billows roll,
   The rolling billows sleep.

5 Justice and judgment are Thy throne,
   Yet wondrous is Thy grace;
   While truth and mercy, joined in one,
   Invite us near Thy face.
       Rev. Isaac Watts. 1719. ab.

94   *God is everywhere.*   C. M.
       Ps. cxxxix.

1 IN all my vast concerns with Thee,
   In vain my soul would try
   To shun Thy presence, Lord, or flee
   The notice of Thine eye.

2 Thine all-surrounding sight surveys
   My rising and my rest,
   My public walks, my private ways,
   And secrets of my breast.

3 My thoughts lie open to the Lord,
   Before they're formed within;
   And ere my lips pronounce the word,
   He knows the sense I mean.

4 If winged with beams of morning light,
   I fly beyond the west,
   Thy hand, which must support my flight,
   Would soon betray my rest.

5 If o'er my sins I seek to draw
   The curtains of the night,
   Those flaming eyes that guard Thy law
   Would turn the shades to light.

6 The beams of noon, the midnight hour,
   Are both alike to Thee:
   O may I ne'er provoke that power
   From which I cannot flee.
       Rev. Isaac Watts. 1719. ab.

95   *The All-seeing God.*   L. M.
       Ps. cxxxix.

1 LORD, Thou hast searched and seen me through;
   Thine eye commands with piercing view,
   My rising and my resting hours,
   My heart and flesh with all their powers.

2 My thoughts, before they are my own,
   Are to my God distinctly known;
   He knows the words I mean to speak,
   Ere from my opening lips they break.

3 Within Thy circling power I stand;
   On every side I find Thy hand:
   Awake, asleep, at home, abroad,
   I am surrounded still with God.

4 Amazing knowledge, vast and great,
   What large extent, what lofty height:
   My soul, with all the powers I boast,
   Is in the boundless prospect lost.

GOD.

5 O may these thoughts possess my breast,
  Where'er I rove, where'er I rest,
  Nor let my weaker passions dare
  Consent to sin, for God is there.
  Rev. Isaac Watts. (1674—1748.) 1719.

96   *The Faithfulness of God.*
Ps. cxv.

1 NOT unto us, Almighty Lord,
  But to Thyself the glory be;
  Created by Thine awful word,
  We only live to honor Thee.

2 Where is their God? the heathen cry,
  And bow to senseless wood and stone;
  Our God, we tell them, fills the sky,
  And calls ten thousand worlds His own.

3 Vain gods, vain men! the Lord alone
  Is Israel's Worship, Israel's Friend;
  O fear His power, His goodness own,
  And love Him, trust Him, to the end.

4 Who lean on Him, from strength to strength,
  From light to light, shall onward move,
  Till through the grave they pass at length,
  To sing on high His saving love.
  Rev. Henry Francis Lyte. (1793—1847.) 1834.

97   *"Bless the Lord."*   L. M.
Ps. ciii.

1 BLESS, O my soul, the living God,
  Call home thy thoughts that rove abroad;
  Let all the powers within me join
  In work and worship so divine.

2 Bless, O my soul, the God of grace;
  His favors claim thy highest praise;
  Why should the wonders He hath wrought
  Be lost in silence and forgot?

3 'Tis He, my soul, that sent His Son
  To die for crimes which thou hast done;
  He owns the ransom, and forgives
  The hourly follies of our lives.

4 Let the whole earth His power confess;
  Let the whole earth adore His grace;
  The Gentile with the Jew shall join
  In work and worship so divine.
  Rev. Isaac Watts. 1719. ab.

98   *The Lord our Shepherd.*   L. M.
Ps. xxiii.

1 THE Lord my pasture shall prepare,
  And feed me with a shepherd's care;
  His presence shall my wants supply,
  And guard me with a watchful eye;
  My noonday walks He shall attend,
  And all my midnight hours defend.

2 When in the sultry glebe I faint,
  Or on the thirsty mountain pant,
  To fertile vales, and dewy meads,
  My weary, wandering steps He leads,
  Where peaceful rivers, soft and slow,
  Amid the verdant landscape flow.

3 Though in the paths of death I tread,
  With gloomy horrors overspread,
  My steadfast heart shall fear no ill,
  For Thou, O Lord, art with me still:
  Thy friendly crook shall give me aid,
  And guide me through the dreadful shade.

4 Though in a bare and rugged way,
  Through devious, lonely wilds I stray,
  Thy bounty shall my pains beguile:
  The barren wilderness shall smile,
  With sudden greens and herbage crowned,
  And streams shall murmur all around.
  Joseph Addison. (1672—1719.) 1712.

99   *Daily Duties, Dependence, and Enjoyment.*   L. M.
Rom. xiv. 8.

1 WHEN, streaming from the eastern skies,
  The morning light salutes mine eyes,
  O Sun of righteousness divine,
  On me with beams of mercy shine:
  Chase the dark clouds of guilt away,
  And turn my darkness into day.

2 And when to Heaven's all-glorious King
  My morning sacrifice I bring,
  And, mourning o'er my guilt and shame,
  Ask mercy in my Saviour's name,
  Then, Jesus, cleanse me with Thy blood,
  And be my Advocate with God.

3 When each day's scenes and labors close,
  And wearied nature seeks repose,
  With pardoning mercy richly blest,
  Guard me, my Saviour, while I rest;
  And as each morning sun shall rise,
  O lead me onward to the skies.

GOD.

4 And at my life's last setting sun,
My conflicts o'er, my labors done,
Jesus, Thy heavenly radiance shed,
To cheer and bless my dying bed;
And from death's gloom my spirit raise,
To see Thy face, and sing Thy praise.
William Shrubsole, Jr. (1759—1829.) 1813. ab. and alt.

100 *God's Care of His People.* **L. M.**
Ps. cvi.

1 O RENDER thanks to God above,
The fountain of eternal love,
Whose mercy firm through ages past
Has stood, and shall forever last.

2 Who can His mighty deeds express,
Not only vast but numberless?
What mortal eloquence can raise
His tribute of immortal praise?

3 Extend to me that favor, Lord,
Thou to Thy chosen dost afford;
When Thou return'st to set them free,
Let Thy salvation visit me.

4 O may I worthy prove to see
Thy saints in full prosperity,
That I the joyful choir may join,
And count Thy people's triumph mine.
Tate and Brady. 1696. ab.

101 *God's eternal Kingdom.* **L. M.**
Ps. xciii.

1 WITH glory clad, with strength arrayed,
The Lord that o'er all nature reigns,
The world's foundation strongly laid,
And the vast fabric still sustains.

2 How surely stablished is Thy throne,
Which shall no change or period see;
For Thou, O Lord, and Thou alone,
Art God from all eternity.

3 The floods, O Lord, lift up their voice,
And toss the troubled waves on high;
But God above can still their noise,
And make the angry sea comply.

4 Thy promise, Lord, is ever sure,
And they that in Thy house would dwell,
That happy station to secure,
Must still in holiness excel.
Tate and Brady. 1696.

102 *The Greatness of God.* **L. M.**
Ps. cxlv.

1 MY God, my King, Thy various praise
Shall fill the remnant of my days:
Thy grace employ my humble tongue
Till death and glory raise the song.

2 The wings of every hour shall bear
Some thankful tribute to Thine ear;
And every setting sun shall see
New works of duty done for Thee.

3 Thy truth and justice I'll proclaim;
Thy bounty flows an endless stream;
Thy mercy swift; thine anger slow,
But dreadful to the stubborn foe.

4 Thy works with sovereign glory shine,
And speak Thy majesty divine:
Let Zion in her courts proclaim
The sound and honor of Thy name.

5 Let distant times and nations raise
The long succession of Thy praise;
And unborn ages make my song
The joy and labor of their tongue.

6 But who can speak Thy wondrous deeds?
Thy greatness all our thoughts exceeds:
Vast and unsearchable Thy ways;
Vast and immortal be Thy praise.
Rev. Isaac Watts. 1719. ab. and alt.

103 *An Exhortation to praise God.* **L. M.**
Ps. xcv. 1–6.

1 O COME, loud anthems let us sing,
Loud thanks to our Almighty King;
For we our voices high should raise,
When our salvation's Rock we praise.

2 The depths of earth are in His hand,
Her secret wealth at His command;
The strength of hills, that threat the skies,
Subjected to His empire lies.

3 The rolling ocean's vast abyss
By the same sovereign right is His;
'T is moved by His almighty hand,
That formed and fixed the solid land.

4 O let us to His courts repair,
And bow with adoration there;
Down on our knees devoutly al
Before the Lord our Maker fall.
Tate and Brady. 1696. ab.

GOD.

104 *General Providence and special Grace.* L. M.
Ps. xxxvi. 5—9.

1 HIGH in the heavens, eternal God,
   Thy goodness in full glory shines;
   Thy truth shall break through every cloud
   That veils and darkens Thy designs.

2 Forever firm Thy justice stands,
   As mountains their foundations keep;
   Wise are the wonders of Thy hands;
   Thy judgments are a mighty deep.

3 Thy providence is kind and large;
   Both man and beast Thy bounty share:
   The whole creation is Thy charge,
   But saints are Thy peculiar care.

4 My God, how excellent Thy grace,
   Whence all our hope and comfort springs;
   The sons of Adam in distress
   Fly to the shadow of Thy wings.

5 From the provisions of Thy house
   We shall be fed with sweet repast:
   There mercy like a river flows,
   And brings salvation to our taste.

6 Life, like a fountain rich and free,
   Springs from the presence of my Lord;
   And in Thy light our souls shall see
   The glories promised in Thy word.
   Rev. Isaac Watts. (1674—1748.) 1719.

105 *Wonders of Creation and Grace.* L. M.
Ps. cxxxvi.

1 GIVE to our God immortal praise;
   Mercy and truth are all His ways:
   Wonders of grace to God belong;
   Repeat His mercies in your song.

2 He built the earth, He spread the sky,
   And fixed the starry lights on high:
   Wonders of grace to God belong;
   Repeat His mercies in your song.

3 He sent His Son with power to save,
   From guilt, and darkness, and the grave:
   Wonders of grace to God belong;
   Repeat His mercies in your song.

4 Through this vain world He guides our feet,
   And leads us to His heavenly seat:
   His mercies ever shall endure,
   When this vain world shall be no more.
   Rev. Isaac Watts. 1719. ab.

106 *The Divine Perfections.* L. M

1 JEHOVAH reigns; His throne is high,
   His robes are light and majesty;
   His glory shines with beams so bright,
   No mortal can sustain the sight.

2 His terrors keep the world in awe,
   His justice guards His holy law,
   His love reveals a smiling face,
   His truth and promise seal the grace.

3 Through all His works His wisdom shines,
   And baffles Satan's deep designs;
   His power is sovereign to fulfil
   The noblest counsels of His will.

4 And will the glorious Lord descend
   To be my Father and my Friend?
   Then let my songs with angels join;
   Heaven is secure, if God be mine.
   Rev. Isaac Watts. 1709.

107 *Joyful Worship.* L. M.
Ps. c.

1 YE nations round the earth, rejoice
   Before the Lord, your sovereign King:
   Serve Him with cheerful heart and voice,
   With all your tongues His glory sing.

2 The Lord is God; 'tis He alone
   Doth life, and breath, and being give:
   We are His work, and not our own,
   The sheep that on His pastures live.

3 Enter His gates with songs of joy,
   With praises to His courts repair;
   And make it your divine employ
   To pay your thanks and honors there.

4 The Lord is good, the Lord is kind;
   Great is His grace, His mercy sure;
   And the whole race of man shall find
   His truth from age to age endure.
   Rev. Isaac Watts. 1719.

108 *The Eternal and Sovereign God.* L. M
Ps. xciii.

1 JEHOVAH reigns; He dwells in light,
   Girded with majesty and might:
   The world, created by His hands,
   Still on its first foundation stands.

2 But ere this spacious world was made,
   Or had its first foundation laid,
   Thy throne eternal ages stood,
   Thyself the ever-living God.

GOD.

3 Like floods the angry nations rise,
   And aim their rage against the skies:
   Vain floods, that aim their rage so high!
   At Thy rebuke the billows die.

4 Forever shall Thy throne endure;
   Thy promise stands forever sure;
   And everlasting holiness
   Becomes the dwellings of Thy grace.
                    Rev. Isaac Watts. 1719.

109   *"Mightier than the mighty Sea."*   L. M.
        Ps. xciii. 3—5

1 THE floods, O Lord, lift up their voice,
   The mighty floods lift up their roar;
   The floods in tumult loud rejoice,
   And climb in foam the sounding shore.

2 But mightier than the mighty sea,
   The Lord of glory reigns on high:
   Far o'er its waves we look to Thee,
   And see their fury break and die.

3 Thy word is true, Thy promise sure,
   That ancient promise, sealed in love;
   Here be Thy temple ever pure,
   As Thy pure mansions shine above.
                    Bp. George Burgess. (1809–1866.) 1840.

110   *"The Lord reigneth."*   L. M.
        Ps. xcvii.

1 THE Lord is King: lift up thy voice,
   O earth, and all ye heavens rejoice:
   From world to world the joy shall ring,
   The Lord omnipotent is King.

2 The Lord is King: who then shall dare
   Resist His will, distrust His care,
   Or murmur at His wise decrees,
   Or doubt His royal promises?

3 The Lord is King: child of the dust,
   The Judge of all the earth is just;
   Holy and true are all His ways:
   Let every creature speak His praise.

4 O when His wisdom can mistake,
   His might decay, His love forsake,
   Then may His children cease to sing,
   The Lord Omnipotent is King.
                    Josiah Conder. (1789–1855.) 1824. ab.

111   *Praising God forever.*   L. M.
        Ps. cxlvi.

1 GOD of my life, through all its days
   My grateful powers shall sound Thy praise;
   The song shall wake with opening light,
   And warble to the silent night.

2 When anxious cares would break my rest,
   And griefs would tear my throbbing breast,
   Thy tuneful praises, raised on high,
   Shall check the murmur and the sigh.

3 When death o'er nature shall prevail,
   And all its powers of language fail,
   Joy through my swimming eyes shall break
   And mean the thanks I cannot speak.

4 But O, when that last conflict's o'er,
   And I am chained to flesh no more,
   With what glad accents shall I rise,
   To join the music of the skies!

5 Soon shall I learn the exalted strains
   Which echo o'er the heavenly plains;
   And emulate, with joy unknown,
   The glowing seraphs round Thy throne.
                  Rev. Philip Doddridge. (1702–1751.) 1755.

112   *God's unspeakable Glory.*   L. M.

1 COME, O my soul, in sacred lays
   Attempt thy great Creator's praise:
   But O, what tongue can speak His fame?
   What mortal verse can reach the theme?

2 Enthroned amid the radiant spheres,
   He glory like a garment wears;
   To form a robe of light divine,
   Ten thousand suns around Him shine.

3 In all our Maker's grand designs,
   Almighty power with wisdom shines;
   His works, through all this wondrous frame,
   Declare the glory of His name.

4 Raised on devotion's lofty wing,
   Do thou, my soul, His glories sing;
   And let His praise employ thy tongue,
   Till listening worlds shall join the song.
                  Rev. Thomas Blacklock. (1721–1791.) 1754.

113   *The Majesty of God.*   C. M.

1 THE Lord our God is full of might;
   The winds obey His will;
   He speaks, and in His heavenly height
   The rolling sun stands still.

2 Rebel, ye waves, and o'er the land
   With threatening aspect roar:
   The Lord uplifts His awful hand,
   And chains you to the shore.

3 Howl, winds of night, your force combine;
 Without His high behest,
 Ye shall not in the mountain pine
 Disturb the sparrow's nest.

4 His voice sublime is heard afar,
 In distant peals it dies;
 He yokes the whirlwind to His car,
 And sweeps the howling skies.

5 Ye nations, bend, in reverence bend;
 Ye monarchs wait His nod;
 And bid the choral song ascend,
 To celebrate our God.
   Henry Kirke White. (1785—1806.) 1806.

114   *Joy in the Lord.*   **C. M.**
   Ps. xxxiii.

1 LET all the just, to God with joy
 Their cheerful voices raise;
 For well the righteous it becomes
 To sing glad songs of praise.

2 For faithful is the word of God;
 His works with truth abound:
 He justice loves, and all the earth
 Is with His goodness crowned.

3 Whate'er the mighty Lord decrees,
 Shall stand forever sure;
 The settled purpose of His heart
 To ages shall endure.

4 Our soul on God with patience waits;
 Our help and shield is He:
 Then, Lord, let still our hearts rejoice,
 Because we trust in Thee.

5 The riches of Thy mercies, Lord
 Do Thou to us extend;
 Since we, for all we want or wish,
 On Thee alone depend.
   Tate and Brady. 1696. ab.

115   *The Divine Decrees.*   **C. M.**

1 KEEP silence, all created things,
 And wait your Maker's nod;
 My soul stands trembling while she sings
 The honors of her God.

2 Life, death, and hell, and worlds unknown,
 Hang on His firm decree;
 He sits on no precarious throne,
 Nor borrows leave to be.

3 Chained to His throne a volume lies,
 With all the fates of men;
 With every angel's form and size,
 Drawn by the eternal pen.

4 His providence unfolds the book,
 And makes His counsels shine;
 Each opening leaf, and every stroke,
 Fulfils some deep design.

5 Here He exalts neglected worms
 To sceptres and a crown;
 Anon the following page He turns,
 And treads the monarchs down.

6 Not Gabriel asks the reason why,
 Nor God the reason gives;
 Nor dares the favorite angel pry
 Between the folded leaves.

7 My God, I would not long to see
 My fate with curious eyes,
 What gloomy lines are writ for me,
 Or what bright scenes shall rise.

8 In Thy fair book of life and grace
 O may I find my name,
 Recorded in some humble place,
 Beneath my Lord, the Lamb.
   Rev. Isaac Watts. (1674—1748.) 1706. ab. and alt.

116   *The Mysteries of Providence.*   **C. M**

1 GOD moves in a mysterious way
 His wonders to perform;
 He plants His footsteps in the sea,
 And rides upon the storm.

2 Deep in unfathomable mines
 Of never-failing skill,
 He treasures up His bright designs,
 And works His sovereign will.

3 Ye fearful saints, fresh courage take;
 The clouds ye so much dread
 Are big with mercy, and shall break
 In blessings on your head.

4 Judge not the Lord by feeble sense,
 But trust Him for His grace;
 Behind a frowning providence
 He hides a smiling face.

5 His purposes will ripen fast,
 Unfolding every hour;
 The bud may have a bitter taste,
 But sweet will be the flower.

6 Blind unbelief is sure to err,
  And scan His work in vain;
  God is His own Intrepreter,
  And He will make it plain.
        William Cowper. (1731—1800.) 1779.

117 *"We know in part."* C. M.
        1 Cor. xiii. 9.

1 THY way, O God, is in the sea,
  Thy paths I cannot trace;
  Nor comprehend the mystery
  Of Thine unbounded grace.

2 'Tis but in part I know Thy will,
  I bless Thee for the sight;
  When will Thy love the rest reveal
  In glory's clearer light?

3 Here the dark veils of flesh and sense
  My captive soul surround,
  Mysterious deeps of providence
  My wondering thoughts confound.

4 When will the day of perfect light,
  The happy morn arise,
  That shall remove the shades of night
  From my beclouded eyes?

5 With rapture shall I then survey
  Thy providence and grace;
  And spend an everlasting day
  In wonder, love, and praise.
        Rev. John Fawcett. (1739—1817.) 1782. ab.

118 *Divine Protection.* L. M.
        Ps. cxxi.

1 UP to the hills I lift mine eyes,
  Th' eternal hills beyond the skies;
  Thence all her help my soul derives,
  There my Almighty Refuge lives.

2 He lives, the everlasting God,
  That built the world, that spread the flood;
  The heavens with all their hosts He made,
  And the dark regions of the dead.

3 He guides our feet, He guards our way;
  His morning smiles bless all the day;
  He spreads the evening veil, and keeps
  The silent hours while Israel sleeps.

4 Israel, a name divinely blest,
  May rise secure, securely rest;
  Thy holy Guardian's wakeful eyes
  Admit no slumber, nor surprise.

5 No sun shall smite thy head by day;
  Nor the pale moon with sickly ray
  Shall blast thy couch; no baleful star
  Dart his malignant fire so far.

6 Should earth and hell with malice burn,
  Still thou shalt go, and still return,
  Safe in the Lord; His heavenly care
  Defends thy life from every snare.

7 On thee foul spirits have no power;
  And, in thy last departing hour,
  Angels, that trace the airy road,
  Shall bear thee homeward to thy God.
        Rev. Isaac Watts. 1719.

119 *The Pillars of Cloud and Fire.* L. M.
        Ex. xiii. 21.

1 WHEN Israel, of the Lord beloved,
  Out from the land of bondage came,
  Her fathers' God before her moved,
  An awful guide, in smoke and flame.

2 By day, along th' astonished lands,
  The cloudy pillar glided slow;
  By night, Arabia's crimsoned sands
  Returned the fiery column's glow.

3 Thus present still, though now unseen,
  O Lord, when shines the prosperous day,
  Be thoughts of Thee a cloudy screen,
  To temper the deceitful ray.

4 And O, when gathers on our path,
  In shade and storm, the frequent night,
  Be Thou long-suffering, slow to wrath,
  A burning and a shining light.
        Sir Walter Scott. (1771—1832.) 1822. ab. and alt.

120 *God's Faithfulness and Mercy.* L. M.
        Ps. xxxvi.

1 MY God, what monuments I see
  In all around of Thine and Thee!
  I view Thee in the heavens above;
  More high than these is heavenly love.

2 I mark the strong eternal hill,
  Thy faithfulness is stronger still;
  I gaze on ocean deep and broad,
  More deep Thy counsels are, O God.

3 O give me 'neath Thy wings to rest,
  To lean on Thy parental breast,
  To feed on Thee, the living bread,
  And drink at mercy's fountain head.

4 The springs of life are all Thine own,
   They flow from Thy eternal throne;
   Light in Thy light alone we see,
   O save us, for we rest on Thee.
   Rev. Henry Francis Lyte. (1793—1847.) 1834.

121   *Safety and Triumph of God's People.*   L. M.
Ps. xlvi.

1 GOD is the refuge of His saints
   When storms of sharp distress invade;
   Ere we can offer our complaints,
   Behold Him present with His aid.

2 Let mountains from their seats be hurled
   Down to the deep, and buried there,
   Convulsions shake the solid world;
   Our faith shall never yield to fear.

3 Loud may the troubled ocean roar;
   In sacred peace our souls abide,
   While every nation, every shore,
   Trembles, and dreads the swelling tide.

4 There is a stream, whose gentle flow
   Supplies the city of our God,
   Life, love, and joy, still gliding through,
   And watering our divine abode.

5 That sacred stream, Thine holy word,
   Our grief allays, our fear controls;
   Sweet peace Thy promises afford,
   And give new strength to fainting souls.

6 Zion enjoys her monarch's love,
   Secure against a threatening hour;
   Nor can her firm foundations move,
   Built on His truth, and armed with power.
   Rev. Isaac Watts. (1674—1748.) 1719. alt. 2l. 5v.

122   *Trust in God.*   L. M.
Ps. xviii.

1 No change of times shall ever shock
   My firm affection, Lord, to Thee;
   For Thou hast always been my rock,
   A fortress and defence to me.

2 Thou my deliverer art, my God;
   My trust is in Thy mighty power:
   Thou art my shield from foes abroad,
   At home my safeguard and my tower.

3 To Thee I will address my prayer,
   To whom all praise we justly owe,
   So shall I, by Thy watchful care,
   Be guarded from my treacherous foe.

4 Let the eternal Lord be praised,
   The rock on whose defence I rest:
   O'er highest heavens His name be raised,
   Who me with His salvation blest.

5 To Heaven I made my mournful prayer,
   To God addressed my humble moan,
   Who graciously inclined His ear,
   And heard me from His lofty throne.
   Tate and Brady. 1696. ab.

123   *The Wisdom of God.*   L. M.

1 WAIT, O my soul, thy Maker's will,
   Tumultuous passions, all be still,
   Nor let a murmuring thought arise;
   His ways are just, His counsels wise.

2 He in the thickest darkness dwells,
   Performs His work, the cause conceals;
   And though His footsteps are unknown,
   Judgment and truth support His throne.

3 In heaven and earth, in air and seas,
   He executes His wise decrees;
   And by His saints it stands confessed,
   That what He does is ever best.

4 Then, O my soul, submissive wait,
   With reverence bow before His seat;
   And midst the terrors of His rod,
   Trust in a wise and gracious God.
   Rev. Benjamin Beddome. (1717—1795.) 1818.

124   *Habitual Devotion.*   C. M.

1 WHILE Thee I seek, protecting Power,
   Be my vain wishes stilled;
   And may this consecrated hour
   With better hopes be filled.

   Thy love the powers of thought bestowed,
   To Thee my thoughts would soar;
   Thy mercy o'er my life has flowed,
   That mercy I adore.

2 In each event of life, how clear
   Thy ruling hand I see:
   Each blessing to my soul more dear,
   Because conferred by Thee.
   In every joy that crowns my days,
   In every pain I bear,
   My heart shall find delight in praise,
   Or seek relief in prayer.

3 When gladness wings my favored hour,
   Thy love my thoughts shall fill;

GOD.

Resigned, when storms of sorrow lower,
My soul shall meet Thy will.
My lifted eye, without a tear,
The lowering storm shall see;
My steadfast heart shall know no fear,
That heart will rest on Thee.
<small>Miss Helen Maria Williams. (1762—1827.) 1786.</small>

125 *Humble Reliance.* **C. M.**

1 MY God, my Father, blissful name,
O may I call Thee mine?
May I with sweet assurance claim
A portion so divine?
This only can my fears control,
And bid my sorrows fly;
What harm can ever reach my soul
Beneath my Father's eye?

2 Whate'er Thy providence denies,
I calmly would resign,
For Thou art good and just and wise:
O bend my will to Thine.
Whate'er Thy sacred will ordains,
O give me strength to bear;
And let me know my Father reigns,
And trust His tender care.

3 Thy sovereign ways are all unknown
To my weak, erring sight;
Yet let my soul adoring own
That all Thy ways are right.
My God, my Father, be Thy name
My solace and my stay;
O wilt Thou seal my humble claim,
And drive my fears away.
<small>Miss Anne Steele. (1717—1778.) 1760. ab.</small>

126 *"Sweet Will of God."* **C. M.**

1 I WORSHIP Thee, sweet Will of God,
And all Thy ways adore;
And every day I live, I seem
To love Thee more and more.

2 I love to kiss each print where Thou
Hast set Thine unseen feet;
I cannot fear Thee, blessed Will,
Thine empire is so sweet.

3 I have no cares, O blessed Will,
For all my cares are Thine;
I live in triumph, Lord, for Thou
Hast made Thy triumphs mine.

4 He always wins who sides with God,
To him no chance is lost;
God's will is sweetest to him when
It triumphs at his cost.

5 Ill that He blesses is our good,
And unblest good is ill;
And all is right that seems most wrong,
If it be His sweet will.
<small>Rev. Frederick William Faber. (1814—1863.) 1849. ab.</small>

127 *God's Way best for us.* **7, 6.**

1 OUR yet unfinished story
Is tending all to this:
To God the greatest glory,
To us the greatest bliss.
Our plans may be disjointed,
But we may calmly rest:
What God has once appointed
Is better than our best.

2 We cannot see before us,
But our all-seeing Friend
Is always watching o'er us,
And knows the very end;
And when amid our blindness
His disappointments fall,
We trust His loving-kindness
Whose wisdom sends them all.

3 They are the purple fringes
That hide His glorious feet;
They are the fire-wrought hinges
Where truth and mercy meet;
By them the golden portal
Of Providence shall ope,
And lift to praise immortal
The songs of faith and hope.
<small>Miss Frances Ridley Havergal. 1872. ab.</small>

128 *"He bowed the Heavens."* **C. M**
<small>Ps. xviii.</small>

1 THE Lord descended from above,
And bowed the heavens most high;
And underneath His feet He cast
The darkness of the sky.

2 On cherub and on cherubim
Full royally He rode;
And on the wings of all the winds
Came flying all abroad.

3 He sat serene upon the floods,
 Their fury to restrain;
And He, as Sovereign Lord and King,
 For evermore shall reign.

4 The Lord will give His people strength
 Whereby they shall increase;
And He will bless His chosen flock
 With everlasting peace.

5 Give glory to His awful name,
 And honor Him alone;
Give worship to His majesty
 Upon His holy throne.
Thomas Sternhold. (—1549.) ab. and alt.

129 *Creating Wisdom.* C. M.

1 ETERNAL Wisdom, Thee we praise,
 Thee the creation sings;
With Thy loved name, rocks, hills and seas,
 And heaven's high palace rings.

2 Thy hand, how wide it spread the sky!
 How glorious to behold,
Tinged with a blue of heavenly dye,
 And starred with sparkling gold.

3 Thy glories blaze all nature round,
 And strike the gazing sight,
Through skies, and seas, and solid ground,
 With terror and delight.

4 Infinite strength, and equal skill,
 Shine through the worlds abroad,
Our souls with vast amazement fill,
 And speak the builder God.

5 But the sweet beauties of Thy grace
 Our softer passions move;
Pity divine in Jesus' face
 We see, adore, and love.
Rev. Isaac Watts. (1674—1748.) 1706. ab.

130 *Omnipresence and Omniscience of God.* C. M.
 Ps. cxxxix.

1 JEHOVAH, God, Thy gracious power
 On every hand we see;
O may the blessings of each hour
 Lead all our thoughts to Thee.

2 If on the wings of morn we speed
 To earth's remotest bound,
Thy hand will there our footsteps lead,
 Thy love our path surround.

3 Thy power is in the ocean deeps,
 And reaches to the skies;
Thine eye of mercy never sleeps,
 Thy goodness never dies.

4 From morn till noon, till latest eve,
 Thy hand, O God, we see;
And all the blessings we receive,
 Proceed alone from Thee.

5 In all the varying scenes of time,
 On Thee our hopes depend;
Through every age, in every clime,
 Our Father, and our Friend.
Dr. John Thomson. (—1841.)

131 *The Goodness of God.* C. M.
 Ps. cxlv.

1 SWEET is the memory of Thy grace,
 My God, my heavenly King!
Let age to age Thy righteousness
 In sounds of glory sing.

2 God reigns on high, but not confines
 His goodness to the skies;
Through the whole earth His bounty shines,
 And every want supplies.

3 With longing eyes Thy creatures wait
 On Thee for daily food;
Thy liberal hand provides their meat,
 And fills their mouths with good.

4 How kind are Thy compassions, Lord!
 How slow Thine anger moves!
But soon He sends His pardoning word
 To cheer the souls He loves.

5 Creatures, with all their endless race,
 Thy power and praise proclaim;
But saints that taste Thy richer grace
 Delight to bless Thy name.
Rev. Isaac Watts. 1719.

132 *God's Care of us.* C. M.
 Ps. xxiii.

1 THE Lord Himself, the mighty Lord,
 Vouchsafes to be my guide;
The Shepherd, by whose constant care
 My wants are all supplied.

2 In tender grass He makes me feed,
 And gently there repose;
Then leads me to cool shades, and where
 Refreshing waters flows.

CHRIST.

3 He does my wandering soul reclaim,
And, to His endless praise,
Instruct with humble zeal to walk
In His most righteous ways.

4 I pass the gloomy vale of death,
From fear and danger free;
For there His aiding rod and staff
Defend and comfort me.

5 Since God doth thus His wondrous love
Through all my life extend,
That life to Him I will devote,
And in His temple spend.
Tate and Brady. 1696.

133 *Praise for Creation and Providence.* **C. M.**
Heb. iii. 4.

1 I SING the almighty power of God,
That made the mountains rise,
That spread the flowing seas abroad,
And built the lofty skies.

2 I sing the wisdom that ordained
The sun to rule the day;
The moon shines full at His command,
And all the stars obey.

3 I sing the goodness of the Lord,
That filled the earth with food;
He formed the creatures with His word,
And then pronounced them good.

4 There's not a plant or flower below
But makes Thy glories known;
And clouds arise, and tempest blow,
By order from Thy throne.

5 Creatures that borrow life from Thee
Are subject to Thy care;
There's not a place where we can flee,
But God is present there.
Rev. Isaac Watts. 1715. ab. and alt.

134 *God exalted.* **L. M.**
Ps. lvii.

1 BE Thou, O God, exalted high;
And, as Thy glory fills the sky,
So let it be on earth displayed,
Till Thou art here, as there, obeyed.

2 O God, my heart is fixed, 't is bent,
Its thankful tribute to present;
And with my heart my voice I'll raise
To Thee, my God, in songs of praise.

3 Thy praises, Lord, I will resound
To all the listening nations round:
Thy mercy highest heaven transcends,
Thy truth beyond the clouds extends.

4 Be Thou, O God, exalted high;
And, as Thy glory fills the sky,
So let it be on earth displayed,
Till Thou art here, as there, obeyed.
Tate and Brady. 1696.

135 *God's tender Mercy to His People.* **L. M.**
Ps. ciii.

1 THE Lord, how wondrous are His ways,
How firm His truth, how large His grace:
He takes His mercy for His throne,
And thence He makes His glories known.

2 Not half so high His power hath spread
The starry heavens above our head,
As His rich love exceeds our praise,
Exceeds the highest hopes we raise.

3 Not half so far has nature placed
The rising morning from the west,
As His forgiving grace removes
The daily guilt of those He loves.

4 How slowly doth His wrath arise!
On swifter wings salvation flies:
And, if He lets His anger burn,
How soon His frowns to pity turn!

5 His everlasting love is sure
To all the saints, and shall endure;
From age to age His truth shall reign,
Nor children's children hope in vain.
Rev. Isaac Watts. 1719.

136 *Unbounded Empire.* **L. M.**
Ps. civ.

1 BLESS God, my soul; Thou, Lord, alone
Possessest empire without bounds,
With honor Thou art crowned, Thy throne
Eternal majesty surrounds.

2 With light Thou dost Thyself enrobe,
And glory for a garment take;
Heaven's curtains stretch beyond the globe,
Thy canopy of state to make.

3 God builds on liquid air, and forms
   His palace-chambers in the skies;
   The clouds His chariot are, and storms
   The swift-wing'd steeds with which He flies.

4 As bright as flame, and swift as wind,
   His ministers heaven's palace fill;
   They have their sundry tasks assigned,
   All prompt to do their Sovereign's will.

5 In praising God, while He prolongs
   My breath, I will that breath employ;
   And join devotion to my songs,
   Sincere as is in Him my joy.
   Tate and Brady. 1696. ab. and alt.

137 *God's Condescension.* L. M.
Ps. cxiii.

1 SERVANTS of God, in joyful lays,
   Sing ye the Lord Jehovah's praise:
   His glorious Name let all adore,
   From age to age, for evermore.

2 Blest be that Name, supremely blest,
   From the sun's rising to its rest;
   Above the heavens His power is known,
   Through all the earth His goodness shown.

3 Who is like God? so great, so high,
   He bows Himself to view the sky;
   And yet, with condescending grace,
   Looks down upon the human race.

4 He hears the uncomplaining moan
   Of those who sit and weep alone;
   He lifts the mourner from the dust,
   In Him the poor may safely trust.

5 Servants of God; in joyful lays,
   Sing ye the Lord Jehovah's praise;
   His glorious Name let all adore,
   From age to age, forevermore.
   James Montgomery. (1771—1854.) 1822.

138 *God in the Storm.* L. M.
Ps. xxix.

1 GIVE to the Lord, ye sons of fame,
   Give to the Lord renown and power;
   Ascribe due honors to His name,
   And His eternal might adore.

2 The Lord proclaims His power aloud,
   Over the ocean and the land;
   His voice divides the watery cloud,
   And lightnings blaze at His command.

3 The Lord sits Sovereign on the flood;
   The Thunderer reigns forever King;
   But makes His church His blest abode,
   Where we His awful glories sing.

4 In gentler language there the Lord
   The counsels of His grace imparts;
   Amid the raging storm His word
   Speaks peace and courage to our hearts.
   Rev. Isaac Watts. (1674—1748.) 1719. ab.

139 *God leading us.* L. M.
Ps. cvii.

1 GIVE thanks to God; He reigns above;
   Kind are His thoughts, His name is Love:
   His mercy ages past have known,
   And ages long to come shall own.

2 Let the redeemed of the Lord
   The wonders of His grace record;
   Israel, the nation whom He chose,
   And rescued from their mighty foes.

3 He feeds and clothes us all the way,
   He guides our footsteps lest we stray;
   He guards us with a powerful hand,
   And brings us to the heavenly land.

4 O let the saints with joy record
   The truth and goodness of the Lord:
   How great His works! how kind His ways!
   Let every tongue pronounce His praise.
   Rev. Isaac Watts. 1719. ab.

140 "*O Gott du Tiefe sonder Grund.*" L. M.

1 THINE, Lord, is wisdom, Thine alone!
   Justice and truth before Thee stand;
   Yet, nearer to Thy sacred throne,
   Mercy withholds Thy lifted hand.

2 Each evening shows Thy tender love,
   Each rising morn Thy plenteous grace;
   Thy wakened wrath doth slowly move,
   Thy willing mercy flies apace.

3 To Thy benign, indulgent care,
　Father, this light, this breath we owe;
　And all we have, and all we are,
　From Thee, great Source of being, flow.

4 Thrice Holy, Thine the kingdom is,
　The power omnipotent is Thine;
　And when created nature dies,
　Thy never-ceasing glories shine.
　　　Ernest Lange. (1650—1727.) 1711 ab.
　　Tr. by Rev. John Wesley. (1703—1791.) 1739.

141 *"Thy Mercy is in the Heavens."* **L. M.**
　　　Ps. xxxvi.

1 O LORD, Thy mercy, my sure hope,
　The highest orb of heaven transcends;
　Thy sacred truth's unmeasured scope
　Beyond the spreading sky extends.

2 Thy justice like the hills remains,
　Unfathomed depths Thy judgments are;
　Thy providence the world sustains,
　The whole creation is Thy care.

3 Since of Thy goodness all partake,
　With what assurance should the just
　Thy sheltering wings their refuge make,
　And saints to Thy protection trust.

4 Such guests shall to Thy courts be led,
　To banquet on Thy love's repast;
　And drink, as from a fountain's head,
　Of joys that shall forever last.

5 With Thee the springs of life remain,
　Thy presence is eternal day;
　O let Thy saints Thy favor gain,
　To upright hearts Thy truth display.
　　　Tate and Brady 1696. ab. and alt.

142 *Safety in God.* **C. M.**
　　　Ps. xxxiv.

1 THROUGH all the changing scenes of life,
　In trouble and in joy,
　The praises of my God shall still
　My heart and tongue employ.

2 Of His deliverance I will boast,
　Till all that are distressed
　From my example comfort take,
　And charm their griefs to rest.

3 O magnify the Lord with me,
　With me exalt His name;
　When in distress to Him I called,
　He to my rescue came.

4 The hosts of God encamp around
　The dwellings of the just;
　Deliverance He affords to all
　Who on His succor trust.

5 O make but trial of His love:
　Experience will decide
　How blest are they, and only they,
　Who in is truth confide.

6 Fear Him, ye saints, and you will then
　Have nothing else to fear;
　Make you His service your delight,
　Your wants shall be His care.
　　　Tate and Brady 1696. ab.

143 *God's Goodness in moderating Affliction.* **C. M.**
　　　Is. xxvii 8.

1 GREAT Ruler of all nature's frame,
　We own Thy power divine;
　We hear Thy breath in every storm,
　For all the winds are Thine.

2 Wide as they sweep their sounding way,
　They work Thy sovereign will;
　And, awed by Thy majestic voice,
　Confusion shall be still.

3 Thy mercy tempers every blast
　To them that seek Thy face,
　And mingles with the tempest's roar
　The whispers of Thy grace.

4 Those gentle whispers let me hear,
　Till all the tumult cease;
　And gales of Paradise shall lull
　My weary soul to peace.
　　　Rev. Philip Doddridge. (1702—1751.) 1755.

144 *"Holy and reverend."* **C. M.**
　　　Ps. cxi 9.

1 HOLY and reverend is the name
　Of our eternal King;
　"Thrice Holy Lord," the angels cry;
　"Thrice Holy," let us sing.

2 The deepest reverence of the mind
  Pay, O my soul, to God;
  Lift, with thy hands, a holy heart,
  To His sublime abode.

3 With sacred awe pronounce His name,
  Whom words nor thoughts can reach;
  A contrite heart shall please Him more
  Than noblest forms of speech.

4 Thou Holy God, preserve my soul
  From all pollution free;
  The pure in heart are Thy delight,
  And they Thy face shall see.
  Rev. John Needham. 1768.

145 *Christ's Coming.* C. M.
Ps. xcvi.

1 SING to the Lord, ye distant lands,
  Ye tribes of every tongue;
  His new discovered grace demands
  A new and nobler song.

2 Say to the nations, Jesus reigns,
  God's own almighty Son;
  His power the sinking world sustains,
  And grace surrounds His throne.

3 Let heaven proclaim the joyful day,
  Joy through the earth be seen;
  Let cities shine in bright array,
  And fields in cheerful green.

4 Let an unusual joy surprise
  The islands of the sea;
  Ye mountains sink, ye valleys rise,
  Prepare the Lord His way.

5 Behold He comes, He comes to bless
  The nations as their God;
  To show the world His righteousness,
  And send His truth abroad.
  Rev. Isaac Watts. (1674—1748.) 1719. ab.

146 *"Lo, I come."* C. M.
Ps. xl. 5—7.

1 O LORD, how infinite Thy love!
  How marvellous Thy ways!
  Let earth beneath, and Heaven above,
  Combine to sing Thy praise.

2 Man in immortal beauty shone,
  Thy noblest work below;
  Too soon by sin made heir alone
  To death and endless woe.

3 Then, "Lo, I come," the Saviour said:
  O be His name adored!
  And with His blood our ransom paid,
  And life and bliss restored.

4 O Lord, how infinite Thy love!
  How marvellous Thy ways!
  Let earth beneath, and Heaven above,
  Combine to sing Thy praise.
  Miss Harriet Auber. (1773—1862.) 1829.

147 *Praise to the Redeemer.* C. M.

1 PLUNGED in a gulf of dark despair,
  We wretched sinners lay,
  Without one cheerful beam of hope,
  Or spark of glimmering day.

2 With pitying eyes the Prince of grace
  Beheld our helpless grief;
  He saw, and (O amazing love!)
  He ran to our relief.

3 Down from the shining seats above,
  With joyful haste He fled,
  Entered the grave in mortal flesh,
  And dwelt among the dead.

4 O for this love, let rocks and hills
  Their lasting silence break;
  And all harmonious human tongues
  The Saviour's praises speak.

5 Angels, assist our mighty joys,
  Strike all your harps of gold;
  But when you raise your highest notes,
  His love can ne'er be told.
  Rev. Isaac Watts. 1709. ab.

148 *Wisdom.* 6, 7. D.
Prov. viii. 22—31.

1 ERE God had built the mountains,
  Or raised the fruitful hills;
  Before He filled the fountains
  That feed the running rills;
  In me from everlasting
  The wonderful I AM
  Found pleasures never wasting,
  And WISDOM is My name.

2 When like a tent to dwell in,
  He spread the skies abroad,
  And swathed about the swelling
  Of ocean's mighty flood;

He wrought by weight and measure,
  And I was with Him then;
Myself the Father's pleasure,
  And mine the sons of men.

3 Thus wisdom's words discover
  Thy glory and Thy grace,
Thou everlasting Lover
  Of our unworthy race:
Thy gracious eyes surveyed us
  Ere stars were seen above;
In wisdom Thou hast made us,
  And died for us in love.

4 And couldst Thou be delighted
  With creatures such as we,
Who, when we saw Thee, slighted,
  And nailed Thee to a tree?
Unfathomable wonder,
  And mystery divine:
The voice, that speaks in thunder,
  Says, "Sinner, I am thine."
         William Cowper. (1731—1800.) 1779.

149 *"Wie Soll ich dich empfangen."* 6, 7. D.

1 O HOW shall I receive Thee,
    How meet Thee on Thy way;
  Blest hope of every nation,
    My soul's delight and stay?
  O Jesus, Jesus, give me
    Now by Thine own pure light,
  To know whate'er is pleasing
    And welcome in Thy sight.

2 Thy Zion palms is strewing,
    And branches fresh and fair:
  My soul, in praise awaking,
    Her anthem shall prepare.
  Perpetual thanks and praises
    Forth from my heart shall spring;
  And to Thy Name the service
    Of all my powers I bring.

3 Ye who with guilty terror
    Are trembling, fear no more:
  With love and grace the Saviour
    Shall you to hope restore.
  He comes, who contrite sinners
    Will with the children place,
  The children of His Father,
    The heirs of life and grace.
         Rev. Paul Gerhardt. (1606—1676.) 1653.
  Tr. by Rev. Arthur Tozer Russell. (1806—) 1848. ab.

150 *The Deity and Humanity of Christ.* L. M.
           John i. 1, 3, 14.

1 ERE the blue heav'ns were stretch'd abroad,
  From everlasting was the Word;
With God He was, the Word was God,
  And must divinely be adored.

2 By His own power were all things made;
  By Him supported, all things stand:
He is the whole creation's head,
  And angels fly at His command.

3 But lo, He leaves those heavenly forms;
  The Word descends and dwells in clay.
That He may hold converse with worms,
  Dressed in such feeble flesh as they.

4 Mortals with joy beheld His face,
  Th' eternal Father's only Son;
How full of truth, how full of grace,
  When through His eyes the Godhead shone.

5 Archangels leave their high abode,
  To learn new mysteries here, and tell
The love of our descending God,
  The glories of Immanuel.
         Rev. Isaac Watts. 1709. ab.

151 *God the Son equal with the Father.* L. M

1 BRIGHT King of glory, dreadful God,
  Our spirits bow before Thy seat;
To Thee we lift an humble thought,
  And worship at Thine awful feet.

2 A thousand seraphs, strong and bright,
  Stand round the glorious Deity;
But who among the sons of light
  Pretends comparison with Thee?

3 Yet there is one, of human frame,
  Jesus, arrayed in flesh and blood,
Thinks it no robbery to claim
  A full equality with God.

4 Then let the name of Christ, our King,
  With equal honors be adored;
His praise let every angel sing,
  And all the nations own Him Lord.
         Rev. Isaac Watts. 1709.

152 *"Macht hoch die Thür."* L. M.
           Ps. xxiv.

1 LIFT up your heads, ye mighty gates,
  Behold the King of glory waits;
The King of kings is drawing near,
  The Saviour of the world is here.

2 The Lord is just, a helper tried,
   Mercy is ever at His side;
   His kingly crown is holiness,
   His sceptre, pity in distress.

3 O blest the land, the city blest
   Where Christ, the Ruler is confessed:
   O happy hearts and happy homes,
   To whom this King of triumph comes.

4 Fling wide the portals of your heart,
   Make it a temple set apart
   From earthly use for heaven's employ,
   Adorned with prayer and love and joy.

5 Redeemer, come, I open wide
   My heart to Thee; here, Lord, abide:
   Let me Thy inner presence feel,
   Thy grace and love in me reveal.

6 So come, my Sovereign, enter in;
   Let new and nobler life begin:
   Thy Holy Spirit guide us on,
   Until our glorious goal is won.
   Rev. George Weissel. (1590—1635.) Bet. 1623—1635.
   Tr. by Miss Catherine Winkworth. (1829—) 1855, ab. and alt.

153 *God's Goodness to Man.* C. M.
Ps. viii

1 O LORD, how good, how great art Thou,
   In heaven and earth the same;
   There angels at Thy footstool bow,
   Here babes Thy grace proclaim.

2 When glorious in the nightly sky
   Thy moon and stars I see,
   O, what is man, I wondering cry,
   To be so loved by Thee.

3 To him Thou hourly deign'st to give
   New mercies from on high;
   Didst quit Thy Throne with him to live,
   For him in pain to die.

4 Close to Thine own bright seraphim
   His favored path is trod;
   And all beside are serving him,
   That he may serve his God.

5 O Lord, how good, how great art Thou,
   In heaven and earth the same;
   There angels at Thy footstool bow,
   Here babes Thy grace proclaim.
   Rev. Henry Francis Lyte. (1793—1847.) 1834.

154 *The approaching Saviour.* C. M.

1 MESSIAH, at Thy glad approach
   The howling wilds are still;
   Thy praises fill the lonely waste,
   And breathe from every hill.

2 The hidden fountains, at Thy call,
   Their sacred stores unlock;
   Loud in the desert sudden streams
   Burst living from the rock.

3 The incense of the spring ascends
   Upon the morning gale;
   Red o'er the hill the roses bloom,
   The lilies in the vale.

4 Renewed, the earth a robe of light,
   A robe of beauty wears;
   And in new heavens a brighter sun
   Leads on the promised years.

5 Let Israel to the Prince of Peace
   The loud hosanna sing;
   With hallelujahs and with hymns,
   O Zion, hail thy King.
   Michael Bruce. (1746—1767.) 1781. ab.

155 *The Saviour's Errand.* C. M.
Is. lxi.

1 HARK, the glad sound, the Saviour comes,
   The Saviour promised long;
   Let every heart prepare a throne,
   And every voice a song.

2 He comes, the prisoners to release
   In Satan's bondage held;
   The gates of brass before Him burst,
   The iron fetters yield.

3 He comes, from thickest films of vice
   To clear the mental ray,
   And on the eyeballs of the blind
   To pour celestial day.

4 He comes, the broken heart to bind,
   The bleeding soul to cure,
   And with the treasures of His grace
   To enrich the humble poor.

5 Our glad hosannas, Prince of Peace,
   Thy welcome shall proclaim,
   And heaven's eternal arches ring
   With Thy beloved name.
   Rev. Philip Doddridge. (1702—1751.) 1735.

156 *"Joy to the World."* C. M.
Ps. xcviii.

1 JOY to the world, the Lord is come:
  Let earth receive her King;
  Let every heart prepare Him room,
  And heaven and nature sing.

2 Joy to the earth, the Saviour reigns:
  Let men their songs employ;
  While fields and floods, rocks, hills, and plains,
  Repeat the sounding joy.

3 No more let sins and sorrows grow,
  Nor thorns infest the ground:
  He comes to make His blessings flow
  Far as the curse is found.

4 He rules the world with truth and grace,
  And makes the nations prove
  The glories of His righteousness,
  And wonders of His love.
        Rev. Isaac Watts. (1674—1748.) 1719.

157 *The Messiah's Coming and Kingdom.* C. M.
Is. ix. 1—7.

1 THE race that long in darkness pined
  Have seen a glorious Light;
  The people dwell in Day, who dwelt
  In Death's surrounding night.

2 To hail Thy rise, Thou better Sun,
  The gathering nations come,
  Joyous as when the reapers bear
  The harvest-treasures home.

3 For Thou our burden hast removed,
  And quelled th' oppressor's sway,
  Quick as the slaughtered squadrons fell
  In Midian's evil day.

4 To us a Child of Hope is born,
  To us a Son is given;
  Him shall the tribes of earth obey,
  Him all the hosts of heaven.

5 His name shall be the Prince of Peace,
  Forevermore adored,
  The Wonderful, the Counsellor,
  The great and mighty Lord.

6 His power increasing still shall spread,
  His reign no end shall know:

  Justice shall guard His throne above,
  And Peace abound below.
        Rev. John Morrison. (1749—1798.) 1771.

158 *Christmas Carol.* C. M.

1 IT came upon the midnight clear,
  That glorious song of old,
  From angels bending near the earth,
  To touch their harps of gold:
  "Peace on the earth, good will to men
  From heaven's all gracious King."
  The world in solemn stillness lay
  To hear the angels sing.

2 Still through the cloven skies they come,
  With peaceful wings unfurled;
  And still their heavenly music floats
  O'er all the weary world:
  Above its sad and lowly plains
  They bend on hovering wing,
  And ever o'er its Babel sounds
  The blessed angels sing.

3 But with the woes of sin and strife
  The world has suffered long;
  Beneath the angel-strain have rolled
  Two thousand years of wrong;
  And man, at war with man, hears not
  The love song which they bring:
  O hush the noise, ye men of strife,
  And hear the angels sing.

4 And ye, beneath life's crushing load
  Whose forms are bending low,
  Who toil along the climbing way,
  With painful steps and slow,—
  Look now; for glad and golden hours
  Come swiftly on the wing:
  O rest beside the weary road,
  And hear the angels sing.

5 For lo, the days are hastening on
  By prophet bards foretold,
  When with the ever circling years
  Comes round the age of gold:
  When Peace shall over all the earth
  Its ancient splendors fling,
  And the whole world give back the song
  Which now the angels sing.
        Rev. Edmund Hamilton Sears. (1810—) 1850.

159   *Christmas Song.*   C. M.

1 Calm on the listening ear of night
  Come heaven's melodious strains,
Where wild Judea stretches far
  Her silver-mantled plains;
Celestial choirs from courts above
  Shed sacred glories there;
And angels, with their sparkling lyres,
  Make music on the air.

2 The answering hills of Palestine
  Send back the glad reply,
And greet from all their holy heights
  The day-spring from on high:
O'er the blue depths of Galilee
  There comes a holier calm;
And Sharon waves in solemn praise
  Her silent groves of palm.

3 Glory to God! the lofty strain
  The realm of ether fills:
How sweeps the song of solemn joy
  O'er Judah's sacred hills!
"Glory to God!" the sounding skies
  Loud with their anthems ring:
"Peace on the earth; good-will to men,
  From heaven's eternal King."

4 Light on thy hills, Jerusalem!
  The Saviour now is born:
More bright on Bethlehem's joyous plains
  Breaks the first Christmas morn;
And brighter on Moriah's brow,
  Crowned with her temple-spires,
Which first proclaim the new-born light,
  Clothed with its orient fires.

5 This day shall Christian tongues be mute,
  And Christian hearts be cold?
O catch the anthem that from heaven
  O'er Judah's mountains rolled!
When nightly burst from seraph-harps
  The high and solemn lay,—
"Glory to God; on earth be peace;
  Salvation comes to-day!"
          Rev. Edmund Hamilton Sears. 1835.

160   *Song of the Angels.*   C. M.
                Luke ii. 7—15.

1 While shepherds watched their flocks by
  All seated on the ground,   [night,
The angel of the Lord came down,
  And glory shone around.

2 "Fear not," said he, for mighty dread
  Had seized their troubled mind;
"Glad tidings of great joy I bring
  To you, and all mankind.

3 "To you, in David's town, this day,
  Is born of David's line,
The Saviour, who is Christ, the Lord;
  And this shall be the sign:

4 "The heavenly babe you there shall find
  To human view displayed,
All meanly wrapped in swathing bands,
  And in a manger laid."

5 Thus spake the seraph, and forthwith
  Appeared a shining throng
Of angels, praising God, and thus
  Addressed their joyful song:

6 "All glory be to God on high,
  And to the earth be peace;
Good-will henceforth from heaven to men
  Begin, and never cease."
          Tate and Brady's Supplement. 1703

161   *The Nativity of Christ.*   C. M.

1 Mortals, awake, with angels join,
  And chant the solemn lay;
Joy, love, and gratitude combine
  To hail the auspicious day.

2 In heaven the rapturous song began,
  And sweet seraphic fire
Through all the shining regions ran,
  And strung and tuned the lyre.

3 Swift through the vast expanse it flew,
  And loud the echo rolled;
The theme, the song, the joy, was new,
  'T was more than heaven could hold.

4 Down to the portals of the sky
  The impetuous torrent ran;
And angels rushed with eager joy,
  To bear the news to man.

5 Hark, the cherubic armies shout,
  And glory leads the song;
Good-will and peace are heard throughout
  The harmonious heavenly throng.

6 With joy the chorus we repeat,
  "Glory to God on high!
Good-will and peace are now complete;
  Jesus was born to die."
          Rev. Samuel Medley. (1738—1799.) 1800. ab.

162   *"Adeste fideles."*   11.

1 O COME, all ye faithful, triumphantly sing,
    Come, see in the manger the angels' dread King;
    To Bethlehem hasten, with joyful accord;
    O hasten, O hasten, to worship the Lord.

2 True Son of the Father, He comes from the skies;
    The womb of the Virgin He doth not despise;
    To Bethlehem hasten, with joyful accord;
    O hasten, O hasten, to worship the Lord.

3 O hark to the angels, all singing in heaven,
    "To God in the highest, all glory be given."
    To Bethlehem hasten, with joyful accord;
    O hasten, O hasten, to worship the Lord.

4 To Thee, then, O Jesus, this day of Thy birth,
    Be glory and honor through heaven and earth;
    True Godhead Incarnate, Omnipotent Word:
    O hasten, O hasten, to worship the Lord.
        Unknown Author, of uncertain date.
        Tr. by Rev. Edward Caswall. (1814—) 1849.

163   *"Christ is born."*   8,3,3,6,8,3,3,6.
        Luke ii. 11.

1 ALL my heart this night rejoices,
    As I hear,
    Far and near,
  Sweetest angel voices:
  "Christ is born," their choirs are singing,
    Till the air
    Every-where
  Now with joy is ringing.

2 Hark, a voice from yonder manger,
    Soft and sweet,
    Doth entreat,
  "Flee from woe and danger;
  Brethren, come: from all that grieves you
    You are freed;
    All you need
  I will surely give you."

3 Come then, let us hasten yonder;
    Here let all,
    Great and small,
  Kneel in awe and wonder;

  Love Him who with love is yearning;
    Hail the star
    That from far
  Bright with hope is burning.

4 Ye who pine in weary sadness,
    Weep no more,
    For the door
  Now is found of gladness:
  Cling to Him, for He will guide you
    Where no cross,
    Pain or loss,
  Can again betide you.

5 Blessèd Saviour, let me find Thee;
    Keep Thou me
    Close to Thee,
  Cast me not behind Thee:
  Life of life, my heart Thou stillest,
    Calm I rest
    On Thy breast,
  All this void Thou fillest.

6 Heedfully my Lord I'll cherish,
    Live to Thee,
    And with Thee
  Dying, shall not perish;
  But shall dwell with Thee forever,
    Far on high,
    In the joy
  That can alter never.
        Rev. Paul Gerhardt (1606—1676), 1651
        Tr. by Miss Catherine Winkworth. (1829—) 1858.

164   *Song of the Angels.*   8, 7.

1 HARK, what mean those holy voices,
    Sweetly warbling in the skies?
  Sure th' angelic host rejoices,
    Loudest hallelujahs rise.

2 Listen to the wondrous story,
    Which they chant in hymns of joy:
  "Glory in the highest, glory,
    Glory be to God most high.

3 "Peace on earth, good-will from heaven,
    Reaching far as man is found;
  Souls redeemed, and sins forgiven,
    Loud our golden harps shall sound.

4 "Christ is born, the great Anointed;
    Heaven and earth His glory sing;
  Glad receive whom God appointed
    For your Prophet, Priest, and King.

5 "Hasten, mortals, to adore Him;
  Learn His name and taste His joy:
  Till in heaven you sing before Him,
  'Glory be to God most high.'"

6 Let us learn the wondrous story
  Of our great Redeemer's birth,
  Spread the brightness of His glory,
  Till it cover all the earth.
  Rev. John Cawood. (1775—1852.) 1819.

165   *Desired of all Nations.*   8, 7.

1 Come, Thou long-expected Jesus,
  Born to set Thy people free:
  From our fears and sins release us,
  Let us find our rest in Thee.

2 Israel's Strength and Consolation,
  Hope of all the earth Thou art;
  Dear Desire of every nation,
  Joy of every longing heart.

3 Born Thy people to deliver,
  Born a Child, and yet a King,
  Born to reign in us for ever,
  Now Thy gracious kingdom bring.

4 By Thine own eternal Spirit,
  Rule in all our hearts alone;
  By Thine all-sufficient merit,
  Raise us to Thy glorious throne.
  Rev. Charles Wesley. (1708—1788.) 1744.

166   *The glad Song.*   8, 7.

1 Hark, the hosts of heaven are singing
  Praises to their new-born Lord,
  Strains of sweetest music flinging,
  Not a note or word unheard.

2 On this night, all nights excelling,
  God's high praises sounded forth,
  While the angels' songs were telling
  Of the Lord's mysterious birth.

3 Through the darkness, strangely splendid
  Flashed the light on shepherds' eyes;
  As their lowly flocks they tended,
  Came new tidings from the skies.

4 All the hosts of heaven are chanting
  Songs with power to stir and thrill,
  And the universe is panting
  Joy's deep longings to fulfil.

5 On this day then through creation
  Let the glorious hymn ring out;
  Let men hail the great salvation,
  "God with us," with song and shout.
  Rev. Edward Hayes Plumptre. (1821—)

167   *Praise for Redemption.*   C, 7.

1 Mighty God, while angels bless Thee,
  May a mortal sing Thy name?
  Lord of men, as well as angels,
  Thou art every creature's theme.

2 Lord of every land and nation,
  Ancient of eternal days,
  Sounded through the wide creation,
  Be Thy just and lawful praise.

3 For the grandeur of Thy nature,
  Grand beyond a seraph's thought;
  For the wonders of creation,
  Works with skill and kindness wrought:

4 For Thy providence, that governs
  Through Thine empire's wide domain,
  Wings an angel, guides a sparrow;
  Blessed be Thy gentle reign.

5 For Thy rich, Thy free redemption,
  Bright, though veiled in darkness long,
  Thought is poor, and poor expression;
  Who can sing that wondrous song?
  Rev. Robert Robinson. (1735—1790.) 1774. alt.

168   *Christ praised.*   C, 7.

1 Brightness of the Father's glory,
  Shall Thy praise unuttered lie?
  Fly, my tongue, such guilty silence,
  Sing the Lord who came to die.

2 Did archangels sing Thy coming?
  Did the shepherds learn their lays?
  Shame would cover me ungrateful,
  Should my tongue refuse to praise.

3 From the highest throne of glory,
  To the cross of deepest woe—
  All to ransom guilty captives:
  Flow, my praise, forever flow.

4 Go, return, immortal Saviour,
  Leave Thy footstool, take Thy throne;
  Thence return and reign forever;
  Be the Kingdom all Thine own.
  Rev. Robert Robinson. 1774. sl. alt.

CHRIST.

169   "*O sola magnarum urbium.*"   8, 7.

1 BETHLEHEM, of noblest cities
None can once with thee compare;
Thou alone the Lord from Heaven
Didst for us Incarnate bear.

2 Fairer than the sun at morning
Was the star that told His birth;
To the lands their God announcing,
Hid beneath a form of earth.

3 By its lambent beauty guided,
See, the Eastern kings appear;
See them bend, their gifts to offer,
Gifts of incense, gold, and myrrh.

4 Offerings of mystic meaning:
Incense doth the God disclose;
Gold a royal child proclaimeth;
Myrrh a future tomb foreshows.

5 Holy Jesus, in Thy brightness
To the Gentile world displayed!
With the Father, and the Spirit,
Endless praise to Thee be paid.
    Aurelius Clemens Prudentius. (348—413.)
    Tr. by Rev. Edward Caswall. (1814—) 1849.

170   "*Christ the Lord is born To-day.*"   7. D.

1 HARK the herald angels sing,
"Glory to the new born King!
Peace on earth, and mercy mild,
God and sinners reconciled!"
Joyful all ye nations, rise,
Join the triumph of the skies;
Universal nature say,
"Christ the Lord is born to-day."

2 Christ, by highest heaven adored!
Christ the everlasting Lord!
Late in time behold Him come,
Offspring of a Virgin's womb!
Veiled in flesh the Godhead see,
Hail, the incarnate Deity!
Pleased as Man with men to dwell,
Jesus, our Immanuel.

3 Hail, the heavenly Prince of Peace!
Hail, the Sun of Righteousness!
Light and life to all He brings,
Risen with healing in His wings.
Mild He lays His glory by,
Born that man no more may die,
Born to raise the sons of earth,
Born to give them second birth.

4 Come, Desire of nations, come,
Fix in us Thy humble home;
Rise, the Woman's conquering seed,
Bruise in us the serpent's head.
Now display Thy saving power,
Ruined nature now restore;
Now in mystic union join
Thine to ours, and ours to Thine.

5 Adam's likeness, Lord, efface,
Stamp Thy image in its place;
Second Adam from above,
Reinstate us in Thy love.
Let us Thee, though lost, regain,
Thee, the Life, the Inner man:
O, to all Thyself impart,
Formed in each believing heart.
    Rev. Charles Wesley. 1739 alt.

171   *The Names and Offices of Christ.*   7. D.

1 BRIGHT and joyful is the morn,
For to us a Child is born;
From the highest realms of heaven
Unto us a Son is given.
On His shoulder He shall bear
Power and majesty, and wear
On His vesture and His thigh
Names most awful, names most high.

2 Wonderful in counsel, He,
The incarnate Deity,
Sire of ages ne'er to cease,
King of kings, and Prince of Peace.
Come and worship at His feet,
Yield to Christ the homage meet;
From His manger to His throne,
Homage due to God alone.
    James Montgomery. (1771—1854.) 1853.

172   *The Coming of the Messiah*   7.
    Is. ix. 6.

1 HAIL, all hail the joyful morn!
Tell it forth from earth to heaven,
That "to us a Child is born,"
That "to us a Son is given."

2 Angels bending from the sky,
Chanted at the wondrous birth,
"Glory be to God on high,
Peace, good-will to man on earth."

CHRIST.

3 Him prophetic strains proclaim
   King of kings, the Incarnate Word;
   Great and wonderful His name,
   Prince of Peace, the Mighty God.

4 Join we then our feeble lays,
   To the chorus of the sky;
   And, in songs of grateful praise,
   Glory give to God on high.
   Miss Harriet Auber. (1773—1862.) 1829.

173 *Response to the Song of the Angels.* 7.

1 HAIL the night, all hail the morn,
   When the Prince of Peace was born:
   When, amid the watchful fold,
   Tidings good the angel told.

2 Now our solemn chant we raise
   Duly to the Saviour's praise;
   Now with carol hymns we bless
   Christ the Lord, our Righteousness.

3 While resounds the joyful cry,
   "Glory be to God on high,
   Peace on earth, good-will to men!"
   Gladly we respond, "Amen!"

4 We in perfect peace would live,
   We to God would glory give;
   Lauding, with the heavenly host,
   Father, Son, and Holy Ghost.
   From the German. The Sabbath Hymn Book. 1858. ab.

174 *"Watchman, what of the Night?"* 7.
Is. xxi. 11.

1 WATCHMAN, tell us of the night,
   What its signs of promise are;
   Traveller, o'er yon mountain's height
   See that glory-beaming star!

2 Watchman, does its beauteous ray
   Aught of joy or hope foretell?
   Traveller, yes; it brings the day,
   Promised day of Israel.

3 Watchman, tell us of the night;
   Higher yet that star ascends:
   Traveller, blessedness and light,
   Peace and truth, its course portends.

4 Watchman, will its beams alone
   Gild the spot that gave them birth?
   Traveller, ages are its own,
   See, it bursts o'er all the earth.

5 Watchman, tell us of the night,
   For the morning seems to dawn:
   Traveller, darkness takes its flight,
   Doubt and terror are withdrawn.

6 Watchman, let thy wanderings cease;
   Hie thee to thy quiet home:
   Traveller, lo, the Prince of Peace,
   Lo, the Son of God is come!
   Sir John Bowring. (1792—1872.) 1825 sl. alt.

175 *The Star of Jacob.* 7.

1 SONS of men, behold from far,
   Hail the long-expected star:
   Jacob's Star, that gilds the night,
   Guides bewildered nature right.

2 Fear not hence that ill should flow,
   Wars or pestilence below:
   Wars it bids and tumults cease,
   Ushering in the Prince of Peace.

3 Mild He shines on all beneath,
   Piercing through the shades of death,
   Scattering error's wide-spread night,
   Kindling darkness into light.

4 Nations all, far off and near,
   Haste to see your God appear;
   Haste, for Him your hearts prepare,
   Meet Him manifested there.

5 There behold the day-spring rise,
   Pouring eye-sight on your eyes;
   God in His own light survey,
   Shining to the perfect day.
   Rev. Charles Wesley. (1708—1788.) 1739.

176 *The angelic Choir.* H. M.

1 HARK, what celestial sounds,
   What music fills the air?
   Soft warbling to the morn,
   It strikes the ravished ear;
   Now all is still; | In tuneful notes,
   Now wild it floats | Loud, sweet, and shrill.

2 The angelic hosts descend
   With harmony divine;
   See how from heaven they bend,
   And in full chorus join:
   "Fear not," say they; | Jesus, your King,
   "Great joy we bring: | Is born to-day.

3 "He comes, your souls to save
   From death's eternal gloom;

CHRIST.

  To realms of bliss and light
   He lifts you from the tomb:
Your voices raise; | Your songs unite
With sons of light | Of endless praise."

4 "Glory to God on high!
  Ye mortals, spread the sound,
  And let your raptures fly
   To earth's remotest bound;
For peace on earth, | To man is given,
From God in heaven | At Jesus' birth."
    Salisbury Collection. 1778. ab. and alt.

177 *Good Will to Men.* H. M.

1 LO, God, our God, has come!
  To us a Child is born,
  To us a Son is given;
   Bless, bless the blessed morn,
O happy, lowly, lofty birth,
Now God, our God, has come to earth.

2 Rejoice, our God has come,
  In love and lowliness;
  The Son of God has come,
   The sons of men to bless:
God with us now descends to dwell,
God in our flesh, Immanuel.

3 Praise ye the Word made flesh!
  True God, true man is He:
  Praise ye the Christ of God!
   To whom all glory be:
Praise ye the Lamb that once was slain,
Praise ye the King that comes to reign.
    Rev. Horatius Bonar. (1808—) 1866.

178 "*Unto us a Child is born.*" H. M.
    Is. ix. 6.

1 THE long-expected morn
  Has dawned upon the earth;
  The Saviour Christ is born,
   And angels sing His birth:
We'll join the bright seraphic throng,
We'll share their joys, and swell their song.

2 Now sing of peace divine,
  Of grace to guilty man;
  No wisdom, Lord, but Thine
   Could form the wondrous plan:
Where peace and righteousness embrace,
And justice goes along with grace.

3 Give praise to God on high,
  With angels round His throne;
  Give praise to God with joy,
   Give praise to God alone:
'T is meet His saints their song should raise,
And give the Saviour endless praise.
    Rev. Thomas Kelly. (1769—1855.) 1806, 1836. ab.

179 "*Bear the Tidings round.*" H. M.

1 HARK, hark, the notes of joy
  Roll o'er the heavenly plains,
  And seraphs find employ
   For their sublimest strains;
Some new delight in heaven is known;
Loud ring the harps around the throne.

2 Hark, hark, the sounds draw nigh,
  The joyful hosts descend;
  Jesus forsakes the sky,
   To earth His footsteps bend;
He comes to bless our fallen race,
He comes with messages of grace.

3 Bear, bear the tidings round;
  Let every mortal know
  What love in God is found,
   What pity He can show:
Ye winds that blow, ye waves that roll,
Bear the glad news from pole to pole.

4 Strike, strike the harps again,
  To great Immanuel's name;
  Arise, ye sons of men,
   And all His grace proclaim:
Angels and men, wake every string,
'Tis God the Saviour's praise we sing.
    Rev. Andrew Reed. (1787—1862.) 1842.

180 "*The Debt we owe.*" H. M.

1 COME, every pious heart
  That loves the Saviour's name,
  Your noblest power exert
   To celebrate His fame:
Tell all above, | The debt of love
And all below, | To Him you owe.

2 He left His starry crown,
  And laid His robes aside;
  On wings of love came down,
   And wept, and bled, and died:
What He endured, | To save our souls
O who can tell, | From death and hell.

CHRIST.

3 From the dark grave He rose,
   The mansion of the dead;
   And thence His mighty foes
   In glorious triumph led:
Up through the sky | And reigns on high,
The conqueror rode, | The Saviour, God.

4 From thence He'll quickly come,
   His chariot will not stay,
   And bear our spirits home
   To realms of endless day:
There shall we see | And ever be
His lovely face, | In His embrace.

5 Jesus, we ne'er can pay
   The debt we owe Thy love;
   Yet tell us how we may
   Our gratitude approve:
Our hearts, our all, | The gift though small
To Thee we give; | Do Thou receive.
         Rev. Samuel Stennett. (1727—1795.) 1787.

181   "Good Tidings of great Joy."   8, 7.
             Luke ii. 10.

1 ANGELS, from the realms of glory,
   Wing your flight o'er all the earth,
   Ye who sang creation's story,
   Now proclaim Messiah's birth:
     Come and worship,
   Worship Christ, the new-born King.

2 Shepherds, in the field abiding,
   Watching o'er your flocks by night,
   God with man is now residing:
   Yonder shines the infant-light:
     Come and worship,
   Worship Christ, the new-born King.

3 Sages, leave your contemplations,
   Brighter visions beam afar;
   Seek the great Desire of nations:
   Ye have seen His natal star:
     Come and worship,
   Worship Christ, the new-born King.

4 Saints, before the altar bending,
   Watching long in hope and fear,
   Suddenly the Lord, descending,
   In His temple shall appear:
     Come and worship,
   Worship Christ, the new-born King.

5 Sinners, wrung with true repentance,
   Doomed for guilt to endless pains,
   Justice now revokes the sentence;
   Mercy calls you, break your chains:
     Come and worship,
   Worship Christ, the new-born King.
        James Montgomery. (1771—1854.) 1819, 1825.

182   Christ's Coming.   8, 7.

1 JESUS came, the heavens adoring,
   Came with peace from realms on high;
   Jesus came for man's redemption,
   Lowly came on earth to die;
     Hallelujah! Hallelujah!
   Came in deep humility.

2 Jesus comes again in mercy,
   When our hearts are bowed with care;
   Jesus comes again in answer
   To an earnest heartfelt prayer;
     Hallelujah! Hallelujah!
   Comes to save us from despair.

3 Jesus comes to hearts rejoicing,
   Bringing news of sins forgiven;
   Jesus comes in sounds of gladness,
   Leading souls redeemed to heaven;
     Hallelujah! Hallelujah!
   Now the gate of death is riven.

4 Jesus comes in joy and sorrow,
   Shares alike our hopes and fears;
   Jesus comes whate'er befalls us,
   Glads our hearts, and dries our tears;
     Hallelujah! Hallelujah!
   Cheering e'en our failing years.

5 Jesus comes on clouds triumphant,
   When the heavens shall pass away;
   Jesus comes again in glory;
   Let us then our homage pay,
     Hallelujah! ever singing,
   Till the dawn of endless day.
            Rev. Godfrey Thring. (1823—) 1866.

183   "Star of the East."   11, 10.

1 BRIGHTEST and best of the sons of the
     morning,
   Dawn on our darkness and lend us thine
     aid;
   Star of the East, the horizon adorning,
   Guide where our infant Redeemer is laid.

CHRIST.

2 Cold on His cradle the dew-drops are shining,
  Low lies His head with the beasts of the stall;
Angels adore Him in slumber reclining,
  Maker, and Monarch, and Saviour of all.

3 Say, shall we yield Him in costly devotion,
  Odors of Edom, and offerings divine,
Gems of the mountain, and pearls of the ocean,
  Myrrh from the forest, or gold from the mine?

4 Vainly we offer each ample oblation;
  Vainly with gifts would His favor secure:
Richer by far is the heart's adoration;
  Dearer to God are the prayers of the poor.

5 Brightest and best of the sons of the morning,
  Dawn on our darkness, and lend us Thine aid;
Star of the East, the horizon adorning,
  Guide where our infant Redeemer is laid.
        Bp. Reginald Heber. (1783—1826.) 1811.

184   *"Gelobet seist Du, Jesu Christ."*   L. M.

1 ALL praise to Thee, eternal Lord,
Clothed in the garb of flesh and blood;
Choosing a manger for Thy throne,
While world on worlds are Thine alone.

2 Once did the skies before Thee bow;
A virgin's arms contain Thee now:
Angels who did in Thee rejoice
Now listen for Thine infant voice.

3 A little child Thou art our guest,
That weary ones in Thee may rest;
Forlorn and lowly is Thy birth,
That we may rise to heaven from earth.

4 Thou comest in the darksome night
To make us children of the light,
To make us, in the realms divine,
Like Thine own angels round Thee shine.

5 All this for us Thy love hath done;
By this to Thee our love is won:
For this we tune our cheerful lays,
And shout our thanks in ceaseless praise.
        Martin Luther. (1483—1546.) 1524. ab.

185   *The Birth at Bethlehem.*   L. M.

1 WHEN Jordan hushed his waters still,
And silence slept on Zion's hill;
When Bethlehem's shepherds thro' the night
Watched o'er their flocks by starry light:

2 Hark, from the midnight hills around,
A voice of more than mortal sound
In distant hallelujahs stole,
Wild murmuring o'er the raptured soul.

3 On wheels of light, on wings of flame,
The glorious hosts of Zion came;
High heaven with songs of triumph rung,
While thus they struck their harps, and sung:

4 "O Zion, lift thy raptured eye,
The long-expected hour is nigh;
Renewed, creation smiles again,
The Prince of Salem comes to reign.

5 "He comes to cheer the trembling heart,
Bid Satan and his host depart;
Again the Daystar gilds the gloom,
Again the bowers of Eden bloom."
        Thomas Campbell. (1777—1844.) 1800. ab.

186   *"Quae stella sole pulchrior."*   L. M.

1 WHAT star is this, with beams so bright,
Which shame the sun's less radiant light?
It shines to announce a new-born King,
Glad tidings of our God to bring.

2 'Tis now fulfilled what God decreed,
"From Jacob shall a star proceed."
And lo, the Eastern sages stand,
To read in heaven the Lord's command.

3 While outward signs the star displays,
An inward light the Lord conveys,
And urges them, with force benign,
To seek the Giver of the sign.

4 True love can brook no dull delay,
Nor toil nor dangers stop their way;
Home, kindred, fatherland, and all,
They leave at once, at God's high call.

5 O Jesus, while the star of grace
Invites us now to seek Thy face,
May we no more that grace repel,
Or quench that light which shines so well.
        Prof. Charles Coffin. (1676—1749.) 1736. alt.
        Tr. by Rev. John Chandler. (1806—) 1837. ab.

CHRIST.

187 *The Star of Bethlehem.* L. M.

1 WHEN marshalled on the nightly plain,
　The glittering host bestud the sky;
　One star alone of all the train
　Can fix the sinner's wandering eye.

2 Hark! hark! to God the chorus breaks,
　From every host, from every gem;
　But one alone the Saviour speaks,
　It is the Star of Bethlehem.

3 Once on the raging seas I rode,
　The storm was loud, the night was dark,
　The ocean yawned, and rudely blowed
　The wind that tossed my foundering bark.

4 Deep horror then my vitals froze;
　Death-struck, I ceased the tide to stem;
　When suddenly a star arose,
　It was the Star of Bethlehem.

5 It was my guide, my light, my all,
　It bade my dark forebodings cease;
　And, through the storm and danger's thrall,
　It led me to the port of peace.

6 Now safely moored, my perils o'er,
　I'll sing, first in night's diadem,
　Forever and for evermore,
　The Star, the Star of Bethlehem.
　　　Henry Kirke White. (1785—1806.) 1806.

188 *"Von Himmel hoch da komm ich her."*

1 GOOD news from heaven the angels bring,
　Glad tidings to the earth they sing:
　To us this day a Child is given,
　To crown us with the joy of heaven.

2 This is the Christ, our God and Lord,
　Who in all need shall aid afford:
　He will Himself our Saviour be,
　From sin and sorrow set us free.

3 To us that blessedness He brings,
　Which from the Father's bounty springs:
　That in the heavenly realm we may
　With Him enjoy eternal day.

4 Were earth a thousand times as fair,
　Beset with gold and jewels rare,
　She yet were far too poor to be
　A narrow cradle, Lord, for Thee.

5 Ah, dearest Jesus, Holy Child,
　Make Thee a bed, soft, undefiled,
　Within my heart, that it may be
　A quiet chamber kept for Thee.
　　　Martin Luther. (1483—1546.) 1535.
　Tr. by Rev. Arthur Tozer Russell. (1806—) 1848. ab.

189 *Christ incomparable.* L. M.

1 Go, worship at Immanuel's feet;
　See in His face what wonders meet:
　Earth is too narrow to express
　His worth, His glory, or His grace.

2 The whole creation can afford
　But some faint shadows of my Lord;
　Nature, to make his beauties known,
　Must mingle colors not her own.

3 O let me climb those higher skies,
　Where storms and darkness never rise;
　There He displays His powers abroad,
　And shines, and reigns, the incarnate God.

4 Nor earth, nor seas, nor sun, nor stars,
　Nor heaven, His full resemblance bears;
　His beauties we can never trace,
　Till we behold Him face to face.
　　　Rev. Isaac Watts. (1674—1748.) 1709. ab.

190 *The guiding Star.* 7. 6l.
　Matt. ii. 10.

1 As with gladness men of old
　Did the guiding star behold;
　As with joy they hailed its light,
　Leading onward, beaming bright;
　So, most gracious Lord, may we
　Evermore be led to Thee.

2 As with joyful steps they sped
　To that lowly manger-bed,
　There to bend the knee before
　Him whom heaven and earth adore;
　So may we with willing feet
　Ever seek the mercy-seat.

3 As they offered gifts most rare
　At that manger rude and bare;
　So may we with holy joy,
　Pure, and free from sin's alloy,
　All our costliest treasures bring,
　Christ, to Thee, our heavenly King.

4 Holy Jesus, every day
　Keep us in the narrow way;

And, when earthly things are past,
Bring our ransomed souls at last
Where they need no star to guide,
Where no clouds Thy glory hide.

5 In the heavenly country bright
Need they no created light;
Thou its Light, its Joy, its Crown,
Thou its Sun, which goes not down:
There forever may we sing
Alleluias to our King.
William Chatterton Dix. (1837—) 1860.

191 *On the Birth of Christ.* 7. 6 l.

1 AMPLEST grace in Thee I find,
Friend and Saviour of mankind,
Richest merit to atone
For our sins before the throne.

2 Well might wondering angels cry,
"Glory be to God on high,
Peace on earth, good will to men,
Lost mankind is found again."

3 Join, my soul, their holy song,
Emulate the brighter throng,
Hail the everlasting Word,
Welcome thy descending Lord.

4 Grace unequalled, love unknown!
Jesus lays aside His crown,
Clothes Himself with flesh and blood,
Takes the manhood into God.
Rev. Augustus Montague Toplady. (1740—1778.) 1759. ab.

192 *The guiding Star.* C. M.

1 BRIGHT was the guiding star that led,
  With mild benignant ray,
The Gentiles to the lowly shed,
  Where the Redeemer lay.

2 But lo, a brighter, clearer light
  Now points to His abode;
It shines through sin and sorrow's night,
  To guide us to our God.

3 O haste to follow where it leads,
  The gracious call obey;
Be rugged wilds, or flowery meads,
  The Christian's destined way.

4 O gladly tread the narrow path
  While light and grace are given;

Who meekly follow Christ on earth,
  Shall reign with Him in heaven.
Miss Harriet Auber. (1773—1862.) 1829.

193 *Prayer for Guidance.* C. M.

1 O THOU, who by a star didst guide
  The wise men on their way,
Until it came and stood beside
  The place where Jesus lay:

2 Although by stars Thou dost not lead
  Thy servants now below,
Thy Holy Spirit, when they need,
  Will show them how to go.

3 As yet we know Thee but in part:
  But still we trust Thy word,
That blessèd are the pure in heart,
  For they shall see the Lord.

4 O Saviour, give us then Thy grace,
  To make us pure in heart,
That we may see Thee face to face
  Hereafter, as Thou art.
Rev. John Mason Neale. (1818—1866.) 1850.

194 *The Angels' Song at Christ's Birth.* C. M.

1 HIGH let us swell our tuneful notes,
  And join the angelic throng;
For angels no such love have known
  To wake a cheerful song.

2 Good-will to sinful men is shown,
  And peace on earth is given;
For lo, the incarnate Saviour comes
  With messages from heaven.

3 Justice and grace, with sweet accord,
  His rising beams adorn;
Let heaven and earth in concert join,
  To us a Child is born.

4 Glory to God in highest strains,
  In highest worlds be paid;
His glory by our lips proclaimed,
  And by our lives displayed.

5 When shall we reach those blissful realms
  Where Christ exalted reigns,
And learn of the celestial choir
  Their own immortal strains?
Rev. Philip Doddridge. (1702—1751.) 1755. alt.

195   *"Glory to God."*   C. M.

1 ANGELS rejoiced and sweetly sung,
    At our Redeemer's birth;
Mortals, awake; let every tongue
    Proclaim His matchless worth.

2 Glory to God, who dwells on high,
    And sent His only Son
To take a servant's form, and die
    For evils we had done.

3 Good-will to men; ye fallen race,
    Arise, and shout for joy;
He comes, with rich, abounding grace
    To save, and not destroy.

4 Lord, send the gracious tidings forth,
    And fill the world with light,
That Jew, and Gentile, through the earth,
    May know Thy saving might.
        Rev. William Hurn. (1754–1856.) 1813

196   *"The Incarnate Word."*   C. M.

1 HOSANNA, raise the pealing hymn
    To David's Son and Lord;
With Cherubim and Seraphim
    Exalt the Incarnate Word.

2 Hosanna, Sovereign, Prophet, Priest,
    How vast Thy gifts, how free;
Thy blood, our life; Thy word, our feast;
    Thy Name, our only plea.

3 Hosanna, Master, lo, we bring
    Our offerings to Thy throne;
Not gold, nor myrrh, nor mortal thing,
    But hearts to be Thine own.

4 Hosanna, once Thy gracious ear
    Approved a lisping throng;
Be gracious still, and deign to hear
    Our poor but grateful song.

5 O Saviour, if, redeemed by Thee,
    Thy temple we behold,
Hosannas through eternity
    We'll sing to harps of gold.
        Rev. William Henry Havergal. (1793–1870.) 1838. ab.

197   *"Divine crescebas puer."*   C. M.

1 IN stature grows the Heavenly Child,
    With death before His eyes;
A Lamb unblemished, meek, and mild,
    Prepared for sacrifice.

2 The Son of God His glory hides
    With parents mean and poor;
And He who made the Heaven abides
    In dwelling-place obscure.

3 Those Mighty Hands that stay the sky
    No earthly toil refuse;
And He who set the stars on high
    A humble trade pursues.

4 He whom the choirs of angels praise,
    At whose command they fly,
His earthly parents now obeys,
    And lays His glory by.
        Santolius Victorinus. (1630–1697.) ab.
        Tr. by Rev. John Chandler. (1806–) 1837. alt.

198   *"Who went about doing Good."*   C. M.
    Acts x. 38.

1 BEHOLD, where, in the Friend of man,
    Appears each grace divine;
The virtues, all in Jesus met,
    With mildest radiance shine.

2 To spread the rays of heavenly light,
    To give the mourner joy,
To preach glad tidings to the poor,
    Was His divine employ.

3 Lowly in heart, to all His friends
    A Friend and Servant found;
He washed their feet, He wiped their tears,
    And healed each bleeding wound.

4 'Midst keen reproach, and cruel scorn,
    Patient and meek He stood;
His foes, ungrateful, sought His life;
    He labored for their good.

5 To God He left His righteous cause,
    And still His task pursued;
With humble prayer, and holy faith,
    His fainting strength renewed.

6 In the last hour of deep distress,
    Before His Father's throne,
With soul resigned, He bowed, and said,
    "Thy will, not mine, be done."

7 Be Christ our pattern and our guide,
    His image may we bear;
O may we tread His holy steps,
    His joy and glory share.
        Prof. William Enfield. (1741–1797.) 1771.

199 *The Man of Sorrows.* C. M.
Is. liii. 4.

1 A PILGRIM through this lonely world,
    The blessèd Saviour passed;
  A mourner all His life was He,
    A dying Lamb at last.

2 That tender heart that felt for all,
    For all its life-blood gave;
  It found on earth no resting place,
    Save only in the grave.

3 Such was our Lord; and shall we fear
    The cross with all its scorn?
  Or love a faithless, evil world,
    That wreathed His brow with thorn?

4 No, facing all its frowns or smiles,
    Like Him, obedient still,
  We homeward press, through storm or calm,
    To Zion's blessèd hill.

5 In tents we dwell amid the waste,
    Nor turn aside to roam
  In folly's paths, nor seek our rest,
    Where Jesus had no home.

6 Dead to the world, with Him who died
    To win our hearts, our love,
  We, risen with our risen Head,
    In spirit dwell above.

7 By faith, His boundless glories there
    Our wondering eyes behold:
  Those glories which eternal years
    Shall never all unfold.
            Sir Edward Denny. (1796—) 1839. ab.

200 *The Example of Christ.* L. M.
1 Pet. ii. 21.

1 My dear Redeemer, and my Lord,
  I read my duty in Thy word;
  But in Thy life the law appears,
  Drawn out in living characters.

2 Such was Thy truth, and such Thy zeal,
  Such deference to Thy Father's will,
  Such love, and meekness so divine,
  I would transcribe and make them mine.

3 Cold mountains and the midnight air
  Witnessed the fervor of Thy prayer;
  The desert Thy temptations knew,
  Thy conflict and Thy victory too.

4 Be Thou my pattern; make me bear
  More of Thy gracious image here;

CHRIST.

Then God, the Judge, shall own my name
Amongst the followers of the Lamb.
            Rev. Isaac Watts. (1674—1748) 1709.

201 *Christ in the Desert.* L. M.

1 AWHILE in spirit, Lord, to Thee
  Into the desert would we flee;
  Awhile upon the barren steep
  Thy Fast with Thee in spirit keep;

2 Awhile from Thy temptation learn
  The daily snares of sin to spurn,
  And in our hearts to feel and own
  Man liveth not by bread alone.

3 And while at Thy command we pray,
  Give us our bread from day to day,
  May we with Thee, O Christ, be fed,
  Thou Word of God, Thou Living Bread.

4 Incarnate Lord, we come to Thee,
  Thou knowest our infirmity;
  Be Thou our Helper in the strife,
  Be Thou our true, our inward Life.
            Rev. Joseph Francis Thrupp. 1860?

202 *The Miracles of Christ.* L. M.

1 BEHOLD, the blind their sight receive;
  Behold, the dead awake and live;
  The dumb speak wonders, and the lame
  Leap like the hart, and bless His name.

2 Thus doth the eternal Spirit own
  And seal the mission of the Son;
  The Father vindicates His cause,
  While He hangs bleeding on the cross.

3 He dies, the heavens in mourning stood;
  He rises, the triumphant God;
  Behold the Lord ascending high.
  No more to bleed, no more to die.

4 Hence, and for ever, from my heart,
  I bid my doubts and fears depart;
  And to those hands my soul resign,
  Which bear credentials so divine.
            Rev. Isaac Watts. 1709.

203 *"Jordanis oras prævia vox ecce Baptistæ quatit"* L. M.

1 ON Jordan's bank the Baptist's cry
  Announces that the Lord is nigh:
  Come then and hearken, for he brings
  Glad tidings from the King of kings.

CHRIST.

2 E'en now the air, the sea, the land,
  Feel that their Maker is at hand;
  The very elements rejoice,
  And welcome Him with cheerful voice.

3 Then cleansed be every Christian breast,
  And furnished for so great a Guest;
  Yea, let us each our hearts prepare
  For Christ to come and enter there.

4 For Thou art our Salvation, Lord,
  Our Refuge, and our great Reward;
  Without Thy grace our souls must fade,
  And wither like a flower decayed.

5 Stretch forth Thy hand to heal our sore,
  And make us rise to fall no more;
  Once more upon Thy people shine,
  And fill the world with love divine.
  Prof. Charles Coffin. (1676—1749.) 1736.
  Tr. by Rev. John Chandler. (1814—) 1837. ab.

204 *Christ's Works of Mercy.* L. M.

1 WHEN, like a stranger on our sphere,
  The lowly Jesus sojourned here,
  Where'er He went, affliction fled,
  And sickness reared her drooping head.

2 The eye that rolled in irksome night
  Beheld His face, for He was light;
  The opening ear, the loosened tongue,
  His precepts heard, His praises sung.

3 Demoniac madness, dark and wild,
  With melancholy transport smiled;
  The storm of horror ceased to roll,
  And reason lightened through the soul.

4 His touch the outcast leper healed,
  His lips the sinner's pardon sealed;
  Warm tears o'er Lazarus He shed,
  Then spake the word that raised the dead.
  James Montgomery. (1771—1854.) 1797. ab.

205 *Christ's Teaching.* L. M.
       Luke iv. 22.

1 How sweetly flowed the gospel's sound
  From lips of gentleness and grace,
  When listening thousands gathered round,
  And joy and reverence filled the place.

2 From heaven He came, of heaven He spoke,
  To heaven He led His followers' way;
  Dark clouds of gloomy night He broke,
  Unveiling an immortal day.

3 "Come, wanderers, to My Father's home,
  Come, all ye weary ones, and rest:"
  Yes, sacred Teacher, we will come,
  Obey Thee, love Thee, and be blest.

4 Decay then, tenements of dust;
  Pillars of earthly pride, decay:
  A nobler mansion waits the just,
  And Jesus has prepared the way.
  Sir John Bowring. (1792—1872.) 1823.

206 *The Meekness of Christ.* L. M.

1 How beauteous were the marks divine,
  That in Thy meekness used to shine,
  That lit Thy lonely pathway, trod
  In wondrous love, O Son of God.

2 O who like Thee, so mild, so bright,
  Thou Son of Man, Thou Light of Light,
  O who like Thee did ever go
  So patient, through a world of woe?

3 O who like Thee so humbly bore
  The scorn, the scoffs of men, before?
  So meek, so lowly, yet so high,
  So glorious in humility?

4 And death, that sets the prisoner free,
  Was pang, and scoff, and scorn to Thee;
  Yet love through all Thy torture glowed,
  And mercy with Thy life-blood flowed.

5 O wondrous Lord, my soul would be
  Still more and more conformed to Thee,
  And learn of Thee, the lowly One,
  And like Thee, all my journey run.
  Bp. Arthur Cleveland Coxe. (1818—) 1840, 1869. ab.

207 *Hymn to Jesus.* C. M.

1 O LORD, when we the path retrace
  Which Thou on earth hast trod,
  To man Thy wondrous love and grace,
  Thy faithfulness to God:—

2 Thy love, by man so sorely tried,
  Proved stronger than the grave;
  The very spear that pierced Thy side
  Drew forth the blood to save.

3 Faithful amidst unfaithfulness,
  Midst darkness only light,
  Thou didst Thy Father's name confess,
  And in His will delight.

4 Unmoved by Satan's subtle wiles,
  Or suffering shame, and loss,
  Thy path, uncheered by earthly smiles,
  Led only to the cross.
5 O Lord, with sorrow and with shame,
  We meekly would confess
  How little we who bear Thy name,
  Thy mind, Thy ways, express.
6 Give us Thy meek, Thy lowly mind:
  We would obedient be;
  And all our rest and pleasure find
  In fellowship with Thee.
          James George Deck. 1838.

208   "*Grace is poured into Thy Lips.*"   C. M.
          Ps. xlv. 2
1 WHAT grace, O Lord, and beauty shone
  Around Thy steps below:
  What patient love was seen in all
  Thy life and death of woe.
2 Forever on Thy burdened heart
  A weight of sorrow hung;
  Yet no ungentle, murmuring word
  Escaped Thy silent tongue.
3 Thy foes might hate, despise, revile,
  Thy friends unfaithful prove;
  Unwearied in forgiveness still,
  Thy heart could only love.
4 O give us hearts to love like Thee,
  Like Thee, O Lord, to grieve,
  Far more for others' sins, than all
  The wrongs that we receive.
5 One with Thyself, may every eye
  In us, Thy brethren, see
  That gentleness and grace that springs
  From union, Lord, with Thee.
          Sir Edward Denny. (1796—) 1839.

209   *The Demoniac of Gadara*   C. M.
          Mark v. 1—21.
1 THE winds were howling o'er the deep,
  Each wave a watery hill;
  The Saviour wakened from His sleep,
  He spake, and all was still.
2 The madman in a tomb had made
  His mansion of despair;
  Woe to the traveller who strayed
  With heedless footsteps there.

3 The chains hung broken from his arm,
  Such strength can hell supply;
  And fiendish hate, and fierce alarm,
  Flashed from his hollow eye.
4 He met that glance so thrilling sweet,
  He heard those accents mild;
  And melting at Messiah's feet,
  Wept like a weaned child.
5 O, madder than the raving man,
  O, deafer than the sea:
  How long the time since Christ began
  To call in vain to me.
6 Yet could I hear Him once again,
  As I have heard of old,
  Methinks He should not call in vain
  His wanderer to the fold.
          Bp. Reginald Heber. (1783—1826.) 1827. ab.

210   "*O Where is He that trod the Sea.*"   C. M. D.
1 O, WHERE is He that trod the sea,
  O, where is He that spake.
  And demons from their victims flee,
  The dead their slumbers break;
  The palsied rise in freedom strong,
  The dumb men talk and sing,
  And from blind eyes, benighted long,
  Bright beams of morning spring.
2 O, where is He that trod the sea,
  O, where is He that spake,
  And dark waves, rolling heavily,
  A glassy smoothness take;
  And lepers, whose own flesh has been
  A solitary grave,
  See with amaze that they are clean,
  And cry, '*T is He can save.*
3 O, where is He that trod the sea,
  'T is only He can save;
  To thousands hungering wearily,
  A wondrous meal He gave:
  Full soon, celestially fed,
  Their mystic fare they take;
  'T was springtide when He blest the bread,
  And harvest when He brake.
4 O, where is He that trod the sea,
  My soul, the Lord is here;
  Let all thy fears be hushed in thee;
  To leap, to look, to hear,

Be thine: thy needs He'll satisfy;
Art thou diseased, or dumb?
Or dost thou in thy hunger cry?
"I come," saith Christ, "I come."
Rev. Thomas Toke Lynch. (1818—1871.) 1855. ab.

211   *"Strong to heal and save."*
            Matt. xiv. 35, 36.

1 THINE arm, O Lord, in days of old
Was strong to heal and save;
It triumphed o'er disease and death,
O'er darkness and the grave:
To Thee they went, the blind, the dumb,
The palsied and the lame,
The leper with his tainted life,
The sick with fevered frame.

2 And lo, Thy touch brought life and health,
Gave speech, and strength, and sight;
And youth renewed and frenzy calmed
Owned Thee, the Lord of Light:
And now, O Lord, be near to bless,
Almighty as of yore,
In crowded street, by restless couch,
As by Gennesareth's shore.

3 Be Thou our great Deliverer still,
Thou Lord of life and death;
Restore and quicken, soothe and bless
With Thine almighty breath.
To hands that work and eyes that see
Give wisdom's heavenly lore,
That whole and sick, and weak and strong,
May praise Thee evermore.
Rev. Edward Hayes Plumptre. (1821—) 1866.

212   *"It is good for us to be here."*
           Matt. xvii. 4   L. M. D.

1 O MASTER, it is good to be
High on the mountain here with Thee;
Where stand revealed to mortal gaze
Those glorious saints of other days:
Who once received on Horeb's height
The eternal laws of truth and right;
Or caught the still small whisper, higher
Than storm, than earthquake, or than fire.

2 O Master, it is good to be
With Thee, and with Thy faithful Three:
Here, where the apostle's heart of rock
Is nerved against temptation's shock;
Here, where the son of thunder learns
The tho't that breathes, and word that burns;
Here, where on eagle's wings we move
With Him whose last best creed is love.

3 O Master, it is good to be
Entranced, enwrapt, alone with Thee;
And watch Thy glistering raiment glow
Whiter than Hermon's whitest snow;
The human lineaments that shine
Irradiant with a light divine:
Till we too change from grace to grace,
Gazing on that transfigured Face.

4 O Master, it is good to be
Here on the holy mount with Thee:
When darkling in the depths of night,
When dazzled with excess of light,
We bow before the heavenly Voice
That bids bewildered souls rejoice,
Though love wax cold, and faith be dim,
"This is My Son, O hear ye Him."
Rev. Arthur Penrhyn Stanley. (1815—) 1872.

213   *"Cælestis formam gloriæ."*   L. M. D.

1 O WONDROUS type, O vision fair
Of glory that the Church shall share,
Which Christ upon the mountain shows,
Where brighter than the sun He glows!
From age to age the tale declare,
How with the three disciples there,
Where Moses and Elias meet,
The Lord holds converse high and sweet.

2 The law and prophets there have place,
Two chosen witnesses of grace;
The Father's voice from out the cloud
Proclaims His Only Son aloud.
With shining face and bright array,
Christ deigns to manifest to-day
What glory shall be theirs above
Who joy in God with perfect love.
Sarum Breviary. 15th cent.
Tr. by Rev. John Mason Neale. (1818—1866.) 1861. ab.

214   *"Exultet cor præcordiis."*   L. M.

1 LET every heart exulting beat
With joy at Jesus' name of bliss:
With every pure delight replete
And passing sweet its music is.

2 Jesus the comfortless consoles,
Jesus each sinful fever quells,
Jesus the power of hell controls,
Jesus each deadly foe repels.

CHRIST.

3 O speak His lofty Name abroad!
   Jesus let every tongue confess,
   Let every heart and voice accord,
   The Healer of our souls to bless.

4 Jesus, the sinner's Friend, abide
   With us, and hearken to our prayer;
   Thy frail and erring wanderers guide,
   And all our dread transgressions spare.
        Unknown Author, of ancient date.
Tr. by Rev. John David Chambers. 1857. ab. and alt.

215 *"Greater Love hath no Man than this."* **L. M.**

1 "SEE how He loved!" exclaimed the Jews,
   As tender tears from Jesus fell:
   My grateful heart the thought pursues,
   And on the theme delights to dwell.

2 See how He loved, who travelled on,
   Teaching the doctrine from the skies;
   Who bade disease and pain be gone,
   And called the sleeping dead to rise.

3 See how He loved, who, firm yet mild,
   Patient endured the scoffing tongue:
   Though oft provoked, He ne'er reviled,
   Or did His greatest foe a wrong.

4 See how He loved, who never shrank
   From toil or danger, pain or death;
   Who all the cup of sorrow drank,
   And meekly yielded up His breath.

5 Such love can we unmoved survey?
   O may our breasts with ardor glow
   To tread His steps, His laws obey,
   And thus our warm affections show.
        Mrs. Sarah Bache. (1744—1808.)

216 *What Christ did for me.* **L. M.**

1 IN love, the Father's sinless child
   Sojourned at Nazareth for me:
   With sinners dwelt the Undefiled,
   The Holy One in Galilee.

2 Jesus, whom angel hosts adore,
   Became a man of griefs for me:
   In love, though rich, becoming poor,
   That I, through Him, enriched might be.

3 Though Lord of all, above, below,
   He went to Olivet for me:
   He drank my cup of wrath and woe,
   And bled in dark Gethsemane.

4 The ever-blessed Son of God
   Went up to Calvary for me;
   There paid my debt, there bore my load
   In His own body on the tree.

5 Jesus, whose dwelling is the skies,
   Went down into the grave for me;
   There overcame my enemies,
   There won the glorious victory.

6 'Tis finished all: the veil is rent,
   The welcome sure, the access free;
   Now then, we leave our banishment,
   O Father, to return to Thee!
        Rev. Horatius Bonar. (1808—) 1857. ab.

217 *The triumphal Entry into Jerusalem.* **L. M.**
    Matt. xxi. 1—11.

1 RIDE on, ride on in majesty!
   Hark, all the tribes Hosanna cry;
   O Saviour meek, pursue Thy road
   With palms and scattered garments strowed.

2 Ride on, ride on in majesty!
   In lowly pomp, ride on to die:
   O Christ, Thy triumphs now begin
   O'er captive death and conquered sin.

3 Ride on, ride on in majesty!
   The wingéd squadrons of the sky
   Look down with sad and wondering eyes
   To see the approaching sacrifice.

4 Ride on, ride on in majesty!
   Thy last and fiercest strife is nigh:
   The Father on His sapphire Throne
   Expects His own anointed Son.

5 Ride on, ride on in majesty!
   In lowly pomp, ride on to die:
   Bow Thy meek head to mortal pain,
   Then take, O God, Thy power, and reign.
        Rev. Henry Hart Milman. (1791—1868) 1827. ab.

218 *Hosanna to the Son of David.* **L. M.**

1 To Thee be glory, honor, praise,
   Jesus, Redeemer, Saviour, King!
   Inspired with joy at Thine approach,
   Thy children loud hosannas sing.

2 Hail, Israel's King! Hail, David's Son!
   Hail, Thou that in Jehovah's name
   Didst come Thy people to redeem,
   And comest now Thy crown to claim!

3 Then, in Thy way to Salem's courts,
    They met Thee with triumphal palms;
    Now, for Thy glad return we watch
    With longing prayers, and vows and psalms.

4 Then, from the shouts of fickle joy
    Thou passedst to Thy cross, Thy grave;
    Now, from the dawn of endless day,
    We welcome Him that comes to save.

5 To Thee, Redeemer, Saviour, King,
    To Thee be glory, honor, praise!
    At Thine approach, with joy inspired,
    Thy children loud hosannas raise.
                Bp. Theodulph of Orleans. (—821.)
                Tr. by C. 1861.

219   "*Hosanna in the highest.*"   L. M.

1 WHAT are those soul-reviving strains
    Which echo thus from Salem's plains?
    What anthems loud, and louder still,
    Sweetly resound from Zion's hill?

2 Lo, 'tis an infant chorus sings
    Hosanna to the King of kings:
    The Saviour comes, and babes proclaim
    Salvation sent in Jesus' name.

3 Nor these alone their voice shall raise,
    For we will join this song of praise;
    Still Israel's children forward press,
    To hail the Lord their Righteousness.

4 Messiah's name shall joy impart
    Alike to Jew and Gentile heart:
    He bled for us, He bled for you,
    And we will sing hosanna too.

5 Proclaim hosannas, loud and clear;
    See David's Son and Lord appear:
    Glory and praise on earth be given;
    Hosanna in the highest heaven.
                James Montgomery. (1771—1854.) 1829.

220   *Christ in Gethsemane.*   L. M.

1 'T IS midnight; and on Olive's brow
    The star is dimmed that lately shone:
    'T is midnight; in the garden, now,
    The suffering Saviour prays alone.

2 'T is midnight; and from all removed,
    The Saviour wrestles lone with fears;
    E'en that disciple whom He loved
    Heeds not his Master's grief and tears.

3 'T is midnight; and for others' guilt
    The Man of Sorrows weeps in blood;
    Yet He that hath in anguish knelt
    Is not forsaken by His God.

4 'T is midnight; and from ether-plains
    Is borne the song that angels know;
    Unheard by mortals are the strains
    That sweetly soothe the Saviour's woe.
                Rev. William Bingham Tappan. (1794—1849.) 1819.

221   "*Behold the Man!*"   L. M.

1 BEHOLD the Man! How glorious He:
    Before His foes He stands unawed,
    And without wrong or blasphemy,
    He claims equality with God.

2 Behold the Man! By all condemned,
    Assaulted by a host of foes;
    His person and His claim contemned,
    A Man of sufferings and of woes.

3 Behold the Man! He stands alone,
    His foes are ready to devour;
    Not one of all His friends will own
    Their Master in this trying hour.

4 Behold the Man! Though scorned below,
    He bears the greatest name above;
    The angels at His footstool bow,
    And all His royal claims approve.

5 Behold the Man! a King He is,
    His throne is built in heaven above,
    And there the people who are His
    Shall see His face, and sing His love.
                Rev. Thomas Kelly. (1769—1855.) 1804. ab

222   *Christ's Passion.*   L. M.

1 THE morning dawns upon the place
    Where Jesus spent the night in prayer;
    Through yielding glooms behold His face,
    Nor form, nor comeliness is there.

2 Brought forth to judgment, now He stands
    Arraigned, condemned, at Pilate's bar;
    Here, spurned by fierce prætorian bands,
    There, mocked by Herod's men of war.

3 He bears their buffeting and scorn,
    Mock-homage of the lip, the knee,
    The purple robe, the crown of thorn,
    The scourge, the nail, the accursèd tree.

4 No guile within His mouth is found;
   He neither threatens, nor complains;
   Meek as a lamb, for slaughter bound,
   Dumb 'midst His murderers He remains.

5 But hark, He prays, 'tis for His foes;
   He speaks, 'tis comfort to His friends;
   Answers, and paradise bestows;
   He bows His head, the conflict ends.
          James Montgomery. 1819, 1825. ab.

223   *Christ's Agony in the Garden.*   7. 6l.

1 MANY woes had Christ endured,
   Many sore temptations met,
   Patient and to pains inured;
   But the sorest trial yet
   Was to be sustained in thee,
   Gloomy, sad Gethsemane.

2 Came at length the dreadful night;
   Vengeance, with its iron rod,
   Stood, and with collected might,
   Bruised the harmless Lamb of God:
   See, my soul, thy Saviour see
   Prostrate in Gethsemane.

3 There my God bore all my guilt;
   This, through grace, can be believed;
   But the horrors which He felt
   Are too vast to be conceived:
   None can penetrate through thee,
   Doleful, dark Gethsemane.

4 Sins against a holy God,
   Sins against His righteous laws,
   Sins against His love, His blood,
   Sins against His name and cause,
   Sins immense as is the sea —
   Hide me, O Gethsemane!

5 Here's my claim, and here alone:
   None a Saviour more can need;
   Deeds of righteousness I've none;
   No, not one good work to plead:
   Not a glimpse of hope for me,
   Only in Gethsemane.
          Rev. Joseph Hart. (1712–1768.) 1759. ab. and alt.

224   *"By Thy Night of Agony."*   7. 6l.

1 LORD, in this Thy mercy's day,
   Ere from us it pass away,
   On our knees we fall and pray;
   Holy Jesus, grant us tears,
   Fill us with heart-searching fears,
   Ere that day of doom appears.

2 By Thy night of agony,
   By Thy supplicating cry,
   By Thy willingness to die,
   By Thy tears of bitter woe
   For Jerusalem below,
   Let us not Thy love forego.

3 Lord, on us Thy Spirit pour,
   Kneeling lowly at the door,
   Ere it close for evermore.
   Judge and Saviour of our race,
   Grant us, when we see Thy face,
   With Thy ransomed ones a place.
          Rev. Isaac Williams. (1802–1865.) 1844. ab. and alt.

225   *"Vuit e orle Mediator alto."*   8, 7. 6l.

1 ZION'S Daughter, weep no more,
   Though thy troubled heart be sore:
   He of Whom the Psalmist sung,
   He Who woke the Prophet's tongue,
   Christ the Mediator blest,
   Brings thee everlasting rest.

2 In a garden, man became
   Heir of sin, and death, and shame:
   Jesus in a garden wins
   Life, and pardon for our sins;
   Through His hour of agony
   Praying in Gethsemane.

3 There for us He intercedes;
   There with God the Father pleads;
   Willing there for us to drain
   To the dregs the cup of pain,
   That in everlasting day
   He may wipe our tears away.

4 Therefore to His name be given
   Glory both in earth and heaven;
   To the Father, and the Son,
   And the Spirit, Three in One,
   Honor, praise, and glory be,
   Now and through eternity.
          Roman Breviary.
     Tr. by Rev. Sir Henry Williams Baker. (1821–) 1861.

226 *Christ our Example in Suffering.* 8, 7, 6l.

1 Go to dark Gethsemane,
    Ye that feel the tempter's power;
    Your Redeemer's conflict see,
    Watch with Him one bitter hour:
    Turn not from His griefs away,
    Learn of Jesus Christ to pray.

2 Follow to the judgment-hall,
    View the Lord of life arraigned;
    O the wormwood and the gall!
    O the pangs His soul sustained!
    Shun not suffering, shame, or loss;
    Learn of Him to bear the cross.

3 Calvary's mournful mountain climb;
    There, adoring at His feet,
    Mark that miracle of time,
    God's own sacrifice complete:
    "It is finished," hear the cry;
    Learn of Jesus Christ to die.

4 Early hasten to the tomb,
    Where they laid His breathless clay;
    All is solitude and gloom;
    Who hath taken Him away?
    Christ is risen; He meets our eyes;
    Saviour, teach us so to rise.
        James Montgomery. (1771—1854.) 1822, 1853.

227 *T was I that did it.* C. M.

1 I SEE the crowd in Pilate's hall,
    I mark their wrathful mien;
    Their shouts of "crucify" appall,
    With blasphemy between.

2 And of that shouting multitude
    I feel that I am one;
    And in that din of voices rude,
    I recognize my own.

3 I see the scourges tear His back,
    I see the piercing crown,
    And of that crowd who smite and mock
    I feel that I am one.

4 Around yon cross the throng I see,
    Mocking the sufferer's groan;
    Yet still my voice it seems to be,
    As if I mocked alone.

5 'Twas I that shed the sacred blood,
    I nailed Him to the tree,
    I crucified the Christ of God,
    I joined the mockery.

6 Yet not the less that blood avails
    To cleanse away my sin;
    And not the less that cross prevails
    To give me peace within.
        Rev. Horatius Bonar. (1808—) 1857.

228 *"His Hands and His Feet."* C. M.

1 FOR me vouchsafed the unspotted Lamb
    His Father's wrath to bear;
    I see His feet, and read my name
    Engraven deeply there.

2 Forth from the Lord His gushing blood
    In purple currents ran;
    And every wound proclaimed aloud
    His wondrous love to man.

3 For me the Saviour's blood avails,
    Almighty to atone;
    The hands He gave to piercing nails
    Shall lead me to His throne.
        Rev. Augustus Montague Toplady. (1740—1778.) 1759. ab.

229 *Calvary and the Kingdom.* C. M.

1 To Calvary, Lord, in spirit now,
    Our weary souls repair,
    To dwell upon Thy dying love,
    And taste its sweetness there.

2 Sweet resting-place of every heart
    That feels the plague of sin,
    Yet knows that deep mysterious joy,
    The peace of God within.

3 There, through Thine hour of deepest woe,
    Thy suffering spirit passed;
    Grace there its wondrous victory gained,
    And love endured its last.

4 Dear suffering Lamb, Thy bleeding wounds,
    With cords of love divine,
    Have drawn our willing hearts to Thee,
    And linked our life with Thine.

5 Thy sympathies and hopes are ours:
    Dear Lord, we wait to see
    Creation, all —below, above,
    Redeemed and blest by Thee.

6 Our longing eyes would fain behold
    That bright and blessed brow,
    Once wrung with bitterest anguish, wear
    Its crown of glory now.
        Sir Edward Denny. (1796—) 1839. ab.

230 *Godly Sorrow in View of Christ's Sufferings.* C. M.

1 ALAS, and did my Saviour bleed?
And did my Sovereign die?
Would He devote that sacred head
For such a worm as I?

2 Was it for crimes that I had done
He groaned upon the tree?
Amazing pity! grace unknown!
And love beyond degree!

3 Well might the sun in darkness hide,
And shut his glories in,
When God, the mighty Maker, died
For man the creature's sin.

4 Thus might I hide my blushing face,
While His dear cross appears:
Dissolve, my heart, in thankfulness,
And melt, mine eyes, to tears.

5 But drops of grief can ne'er repay
The debt of love I owe:
Here, Lord, I give myself away;
'Tis all that I can do.
     Rev. Isaac Watts. (1674—1748.) 1709. ab.

231 *He died for thee.* C. M.

1 BEHOLD the Saviour of mankind
Nailed to the shameful tree:
How vast the love that Him inclined
To bleed and die for thee!

2 Hark, how He groans, while nature shakes,
And earth's strong pillars bend:
The temple's veil in sunder breaks,
The solid marbles rend.

3 'Tis done, the precious ransom's paid,
"Receive my soul," He cries:
See where He bows His sacred head;
He bows His head and dies.

4 But soon He'll break death's envious chain,
And in full glory shine:
O Lamb of God, was ever pain,
Was ever love like Thine?
     Rev. Samuel Wesley. (1662—1735.) 1709.

232 *Kneeling at the Cross.* C. M.

1 O JESUS, sweet the tears I shed,
While on Thy cross I kneel,
Gaze at Thy wounded, fainting head,
And all Thy sorrows feel.

2 My heart dissolves to see Thee bleed,
This heart so hard before;
I hear Thee for the guilty plead,
And grief o'erflows the more.

3 'Twas for the sinful Thou didst die,
And I a sinner stand:
What love speaks from Thy dying eye,
And from each pierced hand.

4 I know this cleansing blood of Thine
Was shed, dear Lord, for me:
For me, for all, O grace divine!
Who look by faith on Thee.

5 O Christ of God, O spotless Lamb,
By love my soul is drawn;
Henceforth, for ever, Thine I am;
Here life and peace are born.

6 In patient hope, the cross I'll bear,
Thine arm shall be my stay;
And Thou, enthroned, my soul shalt spare,
On Thy great judgment-day.
     Rev. Ray Palmer. (1808—) 1867.

233 *"Stavo dolorosa turbha."* S. M.

1 O'ERWHELMED in depths of woe,
Upon the tree of scorn
Hangs the Redeemer of mankind,
With racking anguish torn.

2 See how the nails those hands
And feet so tender rend;
See down His face, and neck, and breast,
His sacred blood descend.

3 Hark, with what awful cry
His Spirit takes its flight,
That cry, it pierced His Mother's heart,
And whelmed her soul in night.

4 Earth hears, and to its base
Rocks wildly to and fro;
Tombs burst; seas, rivers, mountains quake;
The veil is rent in two.

5 The sun withdraws his light;
The midday heavens grow pale;
The moon, the stars, the universe
Their Maker's death bewail.

6 Shall man alone be mute?
Come, youth and hoary hairs,
Come, rich and poor, come, all mankind,
And bathe those feet in tears.

CHRIST.

7 Come, fall before His cross
   Who shed for us His blood;
   Who died the Victim of pure love,
   To make us sons of God.

8 Jesus, all praise to Thee,
   Our joy and endless rest;
   Be Thou our guide while pilgrims here,
   Our crown amid the blest.
                    Roman Breviary.
          Tr. by Rev Edward Caswall. (1814—) 1849.

234 *Faith in Christ our Sacrifice.* S. M.

1 NOT all the blood of beasts
   On Jewish altars slain,
   Could give the guilty conscience peace,
   Or wash away the stain.

2 But Christ, the heavenly Lamb,
   Takes all our sins away;
   A sacrifice of nobler name,
   And richer blood, than they.

3 My faith would lay her hand
   On that dear head of Thine,
   While like a penitent I stand,
   And there confess my sin.

4 My soul looks back to see
   The burdens Thou didst bear,
   When hanging on the cursèd tree,
   And hopes her guilt was there.

5 Believing, we rejoice
   To see the curse remove;
   We bless the Lamb with cheerful voice,
   And sing His bleeding love.
           Rev. Isaac Watts. (1674—1748.) 1709.

235 *The Humiliation and Exaltation of Christ.*
              Is. liii. 6—12.   S. M.

1 LIKE sheep we went astray,
   And broke the fold of God;
   Each wandering in a different way,
   But all the downward road.

2 How dreadful was the hour
   When God our wanderings laid,
   And did at once His vengeance pour,
   Upon the shepherd's head.

3 How glorious was the grace,
   When Christ sustained the stroke!
   His life and blood the Shepherd pays,
   A ransom for the flock.

4 His honor and His breath
   Were taken both away;
   Joined with the wicked in His death,
   And made as vile as they.

5 But God shall raise His head
   O'er all the sons of men;
   And make Him see a numerous seed,
   To recompense His pain.

6 "I'll give Him," saith the Lord,
   "A portion with the strong;
   "He shall possess a large reward,
   "And hold His honors long."
                Rev. Isaac Watts. 1709.

236 *"Jesus, the Christ of God."* S. M.

1 JESUS, the Christ of God,
   The Father's blessed Son,
   The Father's bosom Thine abode,
   The Father's love Thine own.

2 Jesus, the Lamb of God,
   Who us from hell to raise,
   Hast shed Thy reconciling blood;
   We give Thee endless praise.

3 God, and yet Man, Thou art;
   True God, true Man art Thou;
   Of man, and of man's earth a part,
   One with us Thou art now.

4 Great Sacrifice for sin,
   Giver of life for life,
   Restorer of the peace within,
   True Ender of the strife.

5 To Thee, the Christ of God,
   Thy saints exulting sing;
   The bearer of our heavy load,
   Our own anointed King.

6 Rest of the weary, Thou!
   To Thee, our Rest, we come;
   In Thee to find our dwelling now,
   Our everlasting home.
           Rev. Horatius Bonar. (1808–) 1861, an.

237 *Christ sent to save us.* S. M.

1 RAISE your triumphant songs
   To an immortal tune;
   Let the wide earth resound the deeds
   Celestial grace has done.

CHRIST.

2 Sing how Eternal Love
  Its chief beloved chose,
  And bade Him raise our wretched race
  From their abyss of woes.

3 'Twas mercy filled the throne,
  And wrath stood silent by,
  When Christ was sent with pardons down
  To rebels doomed to die.

4 Now, sinners, dry your tears,
  Let hopeless sorrow cease;
  Bow to the sceptre of His love,
  And take the offered peace.

5 Lord, we obey Thy call;
  We lay a humble claim
  To the salvation Thou hast brought,
  And love and praise Thy name.

Rev. Isaac Watts. 1709. ab.

238 "*Salve, caput cruentatum.*" 7, 6. D.

1 O SACRED Head, now wounded,
    With grief and shame weighed down,
  Now scornfully surrounded
    With thorns, Thine only crown;
  O sacred Head, what glory,
    What bliss, till now was Thine!
  Yet, though despised and gory,
    I joy to call Thee mine.

2 What Thou, my Lord, hast suffered
    Was all for sinners' gain:
  Mine, mine was the transgression,
    But Thine the deadly pain:
  Lo, here I fall, my Saviour!
    'T is I deserve Thy place;
  Look on me with Thy favor,
    Vouchsafe to me Thy grace.

3 The joy can ne'er be spoken,
    Above all joys beside,
  When in Thy body broken
    I thus with safety hide:
  My Lord of life, desiring
    Thy glory now to see,
  Beside the cross expiring,
    I'd breathe my soul to Thee.

4 What language shall I borrow
    To thank Thee, dearest Friend,
  For this Thy dying sorrow,
    Thy pity without end?

  O make me Thine forever;
    And should I fainting be,
  Lord, let me never, never,
    Outlive my love to Thee.

5 And when I am departing,
    O part not Thou from me;
  When mortal pangs are darting,
    Come, Lord, and set me free;
  And when my heart must languish
    Amidst the final throe,
  Release me from mine anguish,
    By Thine own pain and woe.

6 Be near me when I'm dying,
    O show Thy cross to me;
  And for my succor flying,
    Come, Lord, and set me free:
  These eyes, new faith receiving,
    From Jesus shall not move;
  For he who dies believing,
    Dies safely, through Thy love.

Bernard of Clairvaux (1091—1153.)
Rev. Paul Gerhardt. (1606—1676.) 1659.
Rev. James Waddell Alexander. (1804—1859.) 1849. ab.

239 *Jesus on the Cross.* 7, 6. l

1 O JESUS, we adore Thee,
    Upon the cross, our King:
  We bow our hearts before Thee;
    Thy gracious Name we sing:
  That Name hath brought salvation,
    That Name, in life our stay;
  Our peace, our consolation
    When life shall fade away.

2 Yet doth the world disdain Thee,
    Still passing by Thy cross;
  Lord, may our hearts retain Thee;
    All else we count but loss.
  The grief Thy soul endured,
    Who can that grief declare?
  Thy pains have thus assured
    That Thou Thy foes wilt spare.

3 Ah, Lord, our sins arraigned Thee,
    And nailed Thee to the tree:
  Our pride, O Lord, disdained Thee;
    Yet deign our Hope to be.
  O glorious King, we bless Thee,
    No longer pass Thee by;
  O Jesus, we confess Thee
    Our Lord enthroned on high.

4 Thy wounds, Thy grief beholding,
　With Thee, O Lord, we grieve;
　Thee in our hearts enfolding,
　Our hearts Thy wounds receive:
　Lord, grant to us remission;
　Life through Thy death restore;
　Yea, grant us the fruition
　Of life for evermore.
　　　Rev. Arthur Tozer Russell. (1806—) 1851.

240　　　*Jesu Intercessor.*　　7, 6. D.

1 O BLESSED feet of Jesus,
　Weary with seeking me,
　Stand at God's bar of judgment,
　And intercede for me.
　O knees which bent in anguish
　In dark Gethsemane,
　Kneel at the throne of glory
　And intercede for me.

2 O hands that were extended
　Upon the awful tree,
　Hold up those precious nail-prints
　Which intercede for me.
　O side from whence the spear-point
　Brought blood and water free,
　For healing and for cleansing,
　Now intercede for me.

3 O head so deeply piercéd
　With thorns which sharpest be,
　Bend low before Thy Father,
　And intercede for me.
　O sacred heart, such sorrows
　This world may never see,
　As those which are Thy warrant
　To intercede for me.

4 O body, scarred, and wounded,
　My sacrifice to be,
　Present Thy perfect offering,
　And intercede for me.
　O loving, risen Saviour,
　From death and sorrow free,
　Though throned in endless glory,
　Still intercede for me.
　　　Miss Margaret Elizabeth Winslow. (1836—) 1871.

241　　　*Jesus at the Door.*　　7, 6. D.

1 O JESUS, Thou art standing
　Outside the fast-closed door,
　In lowly patience waiting
　To pass the threshold o'er:
　Shame on us, Christian brethren,
　His Name and sign who bear,
　O shame, thrice shame upon us,
　To keep Him standing there.

2 O Jesus, Thou art knocking:
　And lo, that hand is scarred,
　And thorns Thy brow encircle,
　And tears Thy face have marred.
　O love that passeth knowledge,
　So patiently to wait!
　O sin that hath no equal,
　So fast to bar the gate!

3 O Jesus, Thou art pleading
　In accents meek and low,
　"I died for you, My children,
　And will ye treat Me so?"
　O Lord, with shame and sorrow
　We open now the door:
　Dear Saviour, enter, enter,
　And leave us never more.
　　　Rev. William Walsham How. (1823—) 1854.

242 *"The Fountain gushing from His Side."* L. M.

1 YE that pass by, behold the Man,
　The Man of Griefs condemned for you:
　The Lamb of God for sinner's slain,
　Weeping to Calvary pursue.

2 His sacred limbs they stretch, they tear;
　With nails they fasten to the wood;
　His sacred limbs, exposed and bare,
　Or only covered with His blood.

3 See there, His temples crowned with thorn,
　His bleeding hands extended wide,
　His streaming feet transfixed and torn,
　The fountain gushing from His side.

4 O Thou dear suffering Son of God,
　How doth Thy heart to sinners move:
　Sprinkle on us Thy precious blood,
　And melt us with Thy dying love.

5 The rocks could feel Thy powerful death,
　And tremble and asunder part:
　O rend with Thine expiring breath
　The harder marble of my heart.
　　　Rev. Charles Wesley. (1708—1788.) 1742. ab.

243 — Gazing upon the Cross. L. M.

1 LORD Jesus, when we stand afar
   And gaze upon Thy holy cross,
   In love of Thee and scorn of self,
   O may we count the world as loss.

2 When we behold Thy bleeding wounds,
   And the rough way that Thou hast trod,
   Make us to hate the load of sin
   That lay so heavy on our God.

3 O Holy Lord, uplifted high
   With outstretched arms, in mortal woe,
   Embracing in Thy wondrous love
   The sinful world that lies below.

4 Give us an ever-living faith
   To gaze beyond the things we see;
   And, in the mystery of Thy death,
   Draw us and all men unto Thee.
            Rev. William Walsham How. 1854.

244 — "Our Lord is crucified." L. M.

1 O COME, and mourn with me awhile;
   O come ye to the Saviour's side;
   O come, together let us mourn;
   Jesus, our Lord, is crucified.

2 Have we no tears to shed for Him,
   While soldiers scoff and Jews deride?
   Ah, look how patiently He hangs;
   Jesus, our Lord, is crucified.

3 How fast His hands and feet are nailed;
   His throat with parching thirst is dried;
   His failing eyes are dimmed with blood,
   Jesus, our Lord, is crucified.

4 Seven times He spake, seven words of love;
   And all three hours His silence cried
   For mercy on the souls of men;
   Jesus, our Lord, is crucified.

5 Come, let us stand beneath the cross;
   So may the blood from out His side
   Fall gently on us drop by drop;
   Jesus, our Lord, is crucified.

6 A broken heart, a fount of tears
   Ask, and they will not be denied;
   Lord Jesus, may we love and weep,
   Since Thou for us art crucified.
     Rev. Frederick William Faber. (1814—1863) 1849. ab. and alt

245 — Crucifixion to the World. L. M.

1 WHEN I survey the wondrous cross
   On which the Prince of Glory died,
   My richest gain I count but loss,
   And pour contempt on all my pride.

2 Forbid it, Lord, that I should boast,
   Save in the death of Christ, my God;
   All the vain things that charm me most,
   I sacrifice them to His blood.

3 See, from His head, His hands, His feet,
   Sorrow and love flow mingled down:
   Did e'er such love and sorrow meet,
   Or thorns compose so rich a crown?

4 His dying crimson, like a robe,
   Spreads o'er His body on the tree;
   Then am I dead to all the globe,
   And all the globe is dead to me.

5 Were the whole realm of nature mine,
   That were a present far too small;
   Love so amazing, so divine,
   Demands my soul, my life, my all.
          Rev. Isaac Watts. (1674—1748.) 1709.

246 — "It is finished!" John xix. 30. L. M.

1 "'Tis finished!" so the Saviour cried,
   And meekly bowed His head, and died:
   "'Tis finished!" yes, the race is run,
   The battle fought, the victory won.

2 'Tis finished! all that heaven decreed,
   And all the ancient Prophets said
   Is now fulfilled, as was designed,
   In Me, the Saviour of mankind.

3 'Tis finished! this My dying groan
   Shall sins of every kind atone;
   Millions shall be redeemed from death,
   By this My last expiring breath.

4 'Tis finished! let the joyful sound
   Be heard through all the nations round;
   'Tis finished! let the echo fly
   Thro' heaven and hell, thro' earth and sky.
      Rev. Samuel Stennett. (1727—1795.) 1778. ab.

247 — The Hiding of the Father's Face. L. M.

1 FROM Calvary a cry was heard,
   A bitter and heart-rending cry:
   My Saviour, every mournful word
   Bespeaks Thy soul's deep agony.

CHRIST.

2 A horror of great darkness fell
   On Thee, Thou spotless, holy One;
   And all the swarming hosts of hell
   Conspired to tempt God's only Son.

3 The scourge, the thorns, the deep disgrace,
   These Thou could'st bear, nor once repine;
   But when Jehovah veiled His face,
   Unutterable pangs were Thine.

4 Let the dumb world its silence break;
   Let pealing anthems rend the sky;
   Awake, my sluggish soul, awake!
   He died, that we might never die.

5 Lord, on Thy cross I fix mine eye;
   If e'er I lose its strong control,
   O let that dying, piercing cry
   Melt and reclaim my wandering soul.
   Rev. John William Cunningham. (1780—1861.) 1820.

248   "*He hath borne our Griefs.*"   7. 6l.
   Is. liii. 4, 5, 12.

1 SURELY Christ thy griefs hath borne;
   Weeping soul, no longer mourn:
   View Him bleeding on the tree:
   Pouring out His life for thee:
   There thy every sin He bore;
   Weeping soul lament no more.

2 Weary sinner, keep thine eyes
   On the atoning sacrifice:
   There the incarnate Deity
   Numbered with transgressors see;
   There His Father's absence mourns,
   Nailed and bruised, and crowned with thorns.

3 See Thy God His head bow down,
   Hear the Man of Sorrows groan;
   For thy ransom, there condemned,
   Stripped, derided, and blasphemed;
   Bleeds the guiltless for the unclean,
   Made an offering for thy sin.

4 Cast Thy guilty soul on Him,
   Find Him mighty to redeem;
   At His feet thy burden lay,
   Look thy doubts and cares away;
   Now by faith the Son embrace,
   Plead His promise, trust His grace.

5 Lord, Thine arm must be revealed,
   Ere I can by faith be healed;
   Since I scarce can look to Thee,
   Cast a gracious eye on me:

At Thy feet myself I lay;
Shine, O shine my fears away.
Rev. Augustus Montague Toplady. (1740—1778.) 1759. 1770. ab.

249   *The three Mountains.*   7.

1 WHEN on Sinai's top I see
   God descend in majesty,
   To proclaim His holy law,
   All my spirit sinks with awe.

2 When, in ecstasy sublime,
   Tabor's glorious steep I climb,
   At the too transporting light,
   Darkness rushes o'er my sight.

3 When on Calvary I rest,
   God, in flesh made manifest,
   Shines in my Redeemer's face,
   Full of beauty, truth, and grace.

4 Here I would forever stay,
   Weep and gaze my soul away:
   Thou art heaven on earth to me,
   Lovely, mournful Calvary.
   James Montgomery. (1771—1854.) 1812.

250   "*Stabat Mater dolorosa.*"   8, 8, 7.

1 NEAR the cross was Mary weeping,
   There her mournful station keeping,
      Gazing on her dying Son:
   There in speechless anguish groaning,
   Yearning, trembling, sighing, moaning,
      Through her soul the sword had gone.

2 What He for His people suffered,
   Stripes, and scoffs, and insults offered,
      His fond mother saw the whole:
   Never from the scene retiring,
   Till He bowed His head expiring,
      And to God breathed out His soul.

3 But we have no need to borrow
   Motives from the mother's sorrow,
      At our Saviour's cross to mourn.
   'T was our sins brought Him from heaven,
   These the cruel nails had driven:
      All His griefs for us were borne.

4 When no eye its pity gave us,
   When there was no arm to save us,
      He His love and power displayed:
   By His stripes He wrought our healing,
   By His death, our life revealing,
      He for us the ransom paid.

CHRIST.

5 Jesus, may Thy love constrain us,
   That from sin we may refrain us,
   In Thy griefs may deeply grieve:
   Thee our best affections giving,
   To Thy glory ever living,
   May we in Thy glory live.
   Jacoponi da Todi. (—1306.)
   Tr. by Rev. James Waddell Alexander. (1804—1859.) 1642. ab.

251. *The Lessons of the Cross.* 8, 8, 7.

1 FROM the cross the blood is falling,
   And to us a voice is calling
   Like a trumpet silver-clear.
   'T is the voice announcing pardon,
   It is finished, is its burden,
   Pardon to the far and near.

2 Peace that glorious blood is sealing,
   All our wounds forever healing,
   And removing every load;
   Words of peace that voice has spoken,
   Peace that shall no more be broken,
   Peace between the soul and God.

3 *God is Love ;*—we read the writing
   Traced so deeply in the smiting
   Of the glorious Surety there.
   God is Light ;—we see it beaming,
   Like a heavenly dayspring gleaming,
   So divinely sweet and fair.

4 Cross of shame, yet tree of glory,
   Round thee winds the one great story
   Of this ever-changing earth;
   Centre of the true and holy,
   Grave of human sin and folly,
   Womb of nature's second birth.
   Rev. Horatius Bonar. (1808—) 1866. ab.

252. *"It is finished!"* 8, 7, 4.

1 HARK, the voice of love and mercy
   Sounds aloud from Calvary;
   See, it rends the rocks asunder,
   Shakes the earth, and veils the sky:
        "It is finished!"
   Hear the dying Saviour cry.

2 "It is finished!" O what pleasure
   Do these charming words afford!
   Heavenly blessings without measure
   Flow to us from Christ, the Lord:
        "It is finished!"
   Saints, the dying words record.

3 Finished all the types and shadows
   Of the ceremonial law!
   Finished all that God had promised;
   Death and hell no more shall awe:
        "It is finished!"
   Saints, from hence your comfort draw.

4 Tune your harps anew, ye seraphs,
   Join to sing the pleasing theme;
   All on earth and all in heaven,
   Join to praise Immanuel's name:
        Hallelujah!
   Glory to the bleeding Lamb.
   Rev. Jonathan Evans. (1749—1809.) 1787. ab.

253. *A Fountain opened.* 8, 7, 6 l.

1 COME to Calvary's holy mountain,
   Sinners ruined by the fall;
   Here a pure and healing fountain
   Flows to you, to me, to all,
   In a full, perpetual tide,
   Opened when our Saviour died.

2 Come in poverty and meanness,
   Come defiled, without, within;
   From infection and uncleanness,
   From the leprosy of sin,
   Wash your robes and make them white;
   Ye shall walk with God in light.

3 Come, in sorrow and contrition,
   Wounded, impotent, and blind;
   Here the guilty, free remission,
   Here the troubled, peace may find;
   Health this fountain will restore,
   He that drinks shall thirst no more: –

4 He that drinks shall live forever;
   'T is a soul-renewing flood:
   God is faithful; God will never
   Break His covenant in blood,
   Signed when our Redeemer died,
   Sealed when He was glorified.
   James Montgomery. 1819.

254. *"Promo vocem, meus, canoram."* 8, 7, 6 l.

1 Now, my soul, thy voice upraising,
   Tell in sweet and mournful strain,
   How the Crucified, enduring
   Grief, and wounds, and dying pain,
   Freely of His love was offered,
   Sinless was for sinners slain.

2 Scourged with unrelenting fury
   For the sins which we deplore,
By His livid stripes He heals us,
   Raising us to fall no more:
All our bruises gently soothing,
   Binding up the bleeding sore.

3 See, His hands and feet are fastened;
   So He makes His people free:
Not a wound whence blood is flowing
   But a fount of grace shall be;
Yea the very nails which nail Him
   Nail us also to the tree.

4 Through His heart the spear is piercing,
   Though His foes have seen Him die;
Blood and water thence are streaming
   In a tide of mystery,
Water from our guilt to cleanse us,
   Blood to win us crowns on high.

5 Jesus, may those precious fountains
   Drink to thirsting souls afford;
Let them be our cup and healing,
   And at length our full reward;
So a ransomed world shall ever
   Praise Thee, its redeeming Lord.
Santolius Maglorianus. (1628—1684.)
Tr. by Rev. Sir Henry Williams Baker. (1821—) 1861.

255   *"Ira justa Conditoris."*   8, 7. 6l.

1 HE, who once in righteous vengeance
   Whelmed the world beneath the flood,
Once again in mercy cleansed it
   With His own most precious blood;
Coming from His throne on high,
On the painful cross to die.

2 O the wisdom of the Eternal!
   O its depth, and height divine!
O the sweetness of that mercy
   Which in Jesus Christ did shine!
We were sinners doomed to die;
Jesus paid the penalty.

3 When before the Judge we tremble,
   Conscious of His broken laws,
May the blood of His atonement
   Cry aloud, and plead our cause;
Bid our guilty terrors cease,
Be our pardon and our peace.
Roman Breviary.
Tr. by Rev. Edward Caswall. (1814—)1849. ab. and alt.

256   *Looking at the Cross.*   C. M.

1 IN evil long I took delight,
   Unawed by shame or fear,
Till a new object struck my sight,
   And stopped my wild career.

2 I saw One hanging on a tree,
   In agonies and blood;
Who fixed His languid eyes on me,
   As near His cross I stood.

3 Sure, never till my latest breath,
   Can I forget that look;
It seemed to charge me with His death,
   Though not a word He spoke.

4 My conscience felt and owned the guilt,
   And plunged me in despair;
I saw my sins His blood had spilt,
   And helped to nail Him there.

5 Alas, I knew not what I did,
   But all my tears were vain;
Where could my trembling soul be hid,
   For I the Lord had slain.

6 A second look He gave, that said,
   "I freely all forgive;
This blood is for thy ransom paid,
   I die that thou mayest live."

7 Thus, while His death my sin displays
   In all its blackest hue,
Such is the mystery of grace,
   It seals my pardon too.

8 With pleasing grief, and mournful joy,
   My spirit now is filled,
That I should such a life destroy,
   Yet live by Him I killed.
Rev. John Newton. (1725—1807.) 1772.

257   *The Tomb of Jesus.*   C. M.

1 COME, see the place where Jesus lies:
   The last sad rite is done;
With aching hearts, and weeping eyes,
   The faithful few are gone.

2 They washed with tears each bloody trace
   On those dear limbs that lay;
Then spread the napkin o'er His face,
   And turned and went their way.

3 By the sealed stones with grounded spears
  The guards their vigils keep:
  They wist not other eyes than theirs
  Watch o'er the Saviour's sleep.

4 All Heaven above, all Hell beneath,
  Bright hope and blank dismay,
  Look on to see if grisly Death
  Can hold his mighty prey.

5 Now, grisly Death, thy powers combine!
  Now gird thee to the strife!
  Yet needs there stronger arm than thine
  To keep the Lord of life.

6 'T is done! O Death, thy Victor-guest
  Hath smoothed thy visage grim;
  O Grave, thou place of blessed rest
  To all who sleep in Him!

Rev. Thomas Edwards Hankinson. (1805—1843.) 1843.

258   *Christ in the Tomb.*   7. 6l.

1 RESTING from His work to-day,
  In the tomb the Saviour lay;
  Still He slept, from head to feet
  Shrouded in the winding sheet,
  Lying in the rock alone,
  Hidden by the sealed stone.

2 Late at even there was seen
  Watching long the Magdalene
  Early, ere the break of day,
  Sorrowful she took her way
  To the holy garden glade,
  Where her buried Lord was laid.

3 So with Thee, till life shall end,
  I would solemn vigil spend;
  Let me hew Thee, Lord, a shrine
  In this rocky heart of mine,
  Where in pure embalmed cell
  None but Thee may ever dwell.

4 Myrrh and spices will I bring,
  True affection's offering;
  Close the door from sight and sound
  Of the busy world around;
  And in patient watch remain
  Till my Lord appear again.

Rev. Thomas Whytehead. (1815—1843.) 1842. ab. and alt.

259   *"All is o'er."*   7. 6l.

1 ALL is o'er, the pain, the sorrow,
  Human taunts and fiendish spite;
  Death shall be despoiled to-morrow
  Of the prey he grasps to-night;
  Yet once more to seal his doom,
  Christ must sleep within the tomb.

2 Close and still the cell that holds Him,
  While in brief repose He lies;
  Deep the slumber that enfolds Him,
  Veiled awhile from mortal eyes;
  Slumber such as needs must be
  After hard-won victory.

3 Fierce and deadly was the anguish,
  Which on yonder cross He bore;
  How did soul and body languish,
  Till the toil of death was o'er;
  But that toil, so fierce and dread,
  Bruised and crushed the serpent's head.

4 Now to-night, with plaintive voicing,
  Chant His requiem soft and low;
  Loftier strain of loud rejoicing
  From to-morrow's harps shall flow;
  "Death and hell at length are slain,
  Christ hath triumphed, Christ doth reign."

Rev. John Moultrie. (1804—) 1836. ab. and sl. alt.

260   *"He is risen."*   7.
  Mark. xvi. 6.

1 "CHRIST, the Lord, is risen to-day,"
  Sons of men and angels say.
  Raise your joys and triumphs high;
  Sing, ye heavens; and earth, reply.

2 Love's redeeming work is done,
  Fought the fight, the battle won.
  Lo, our Sun's eclipse is o'er;
  Lo, He sets in blood no more.

3 Vain the stone, the watch, the seal;
  Christ has burst the gates of hell;
  Death in vain forbids His rise;
  Christ has opened paradise.

4 Lives again our glorious King:
  Where, O Death, is now thy sting?
  Once He died our souls to save:
  Where thy victory, O grave?

5 Soar we now where Christ has led,
  Following our exalted Head;
  Made like Him, like Him we rise;
  Ours the Cross, the grave, the skies.

Rev. Charles Wesley. (1708—1788.) 1739. ab. and alt.

261   *"Surrexit Christus hodie."*   7.

1 JESUS Christ is risen to-day,
Our triumphant holy-day;
Who did once upon the cross
Suffer to redeem our loss.

2 Hymns of praise then let us sing
Unto Christ our heavenly King,
Who endured the cross and grave,
Sinners to redeem and save.

3 But the pains which He endured,
Our salvation have procured:
Now above the sky He's king,
Where the angels ever sing.

4 Sing we to our God above
Praise eternal as His love;
Praise Him, all ye heavenly host,
Father, Son, and Holy Ghost.

           Unknown Author of the 15th cent.
First three verses in Tate and Brady's Supplement. 1703.

262   *The Women at the Sepulchre.*   7.
        Luke xxiv. 1—10.

1 HAIL to Thee, our risen King,
Joyfully Thy praise we sing;
For, the mighty conflict o'er,
Now Thou livest evermore.

2 Thou within the tomb hast slept,
Angel-guards Thy vigil kept:
'Twas their word to Mary brought
Tidings of the Lord she sought:—

3 "Seek Him not among the dead,
He is risen, as He said:"
Gladdened by the angelic word,
Turning, she beheld her Lord.

4 Fain like Mary, Lord, would we
In Thy glorious presence be;
Hear Thy voice, behold Thy face,
Praise Thee for Thy wondrous grace.

5 Resurrection-life hast Thou
Given to Thy people now;
Haste the time when, raised to Thee,
We shall manifested be.

           S. A. 1863. ab.

263   *Resurrection of Christ.*

1 ANGELS, roll the rock away,
Death, yield up thy mighty prey:
See, He rises from the tomb,
Glowing with immortal bloom.

2 'Tis the Saviour, angels raise
Fame's eternal trump of praise;
Let the earth's remotest bound
Hear the joy-inspiring sound.

3 Now, ye saints, lift up your eyes,
Now to glory see Him rise
In full triumph up the sky,
Up to waiting worlds on high.

4 Heaven displays her portals wide,
Glorious Hero, through them ride;
King of Glory, mount Thy throne,
Thy great Father's and Thine own.

5 Praise Him, all ye heavenly choirs,
Strike and sweep your golden lyres:
Shout, O earth, in rapturous song,
Let the strains be sweet and strong.

6 Every note with wonder swell,
Sin o'erthrown and captived hell;
Where is hell's once dreaded King?
Where, O death, thy mortal sting?

           Rev. Thomas Scott. (—1776.) 1709. ab.

264   *"The Lord is risen."*   7.

1 CHRIST, the Lord, is risen to-day,
Our triumphant holy-day:
He endured the cross and grave,
Sinners to redeem and save.

2 Lo, He rises, mighty King:
Where, O death, is now thy sting?
Lo, He claims His native sky:
Grave, where is thy victory?

3 Sinners, see your ransom paid,
Peace with God forever made:
With your risen Saviour rise;
Claim with Him the purchased skies.

4 Christ, the Lord, is risen to-day,
Our triumphant holy-day;
Loud the song of victory raise:
Shout the great Redeemer's praise.

       Rev. Josiah Pratt's (1768—1844.) Collection. 1829.

265   *"Christus ist erstanden."*   7.

1 CHRIST, the Lord, is risen again,
Christ hath broken every chain:
Hark, the angels shout for joy,
Singing evermore on high.

2 He who bore all pain and loss
Comfortless upon the cross,

CHRIST.

    Lives in glory now on high,
    Pleads for us, and hears our cry.
3 He who slumbered in the grave,
    Is exalted now to save;
    Now through Christendom it rings,
    That the Lamb is King of kings.
4 Now He bids us tell abroad,
    How the lost may be restored,
    How the penitent forgiven,
    How we, too, may enter heaven.
5 Thou our Paschal Lamb indeed,
    Christ, to-day Thy people feed;
    Take our sins and guilt away;
    Let us sing by night and day.
Rev. Michael Weisse. (—1540.) 1531.
Tr. by Miss Catherine Winkworth. (1829—) 1858. ab.

266   *The Resurrection of Christ.*   H. M.
              Luke xxiv. 34.
1 YES, the Redeemer rose;
    The Saviour left the dead;
    And o'er our hellish foes
      High raised His conquering head;
    In wild dismay, the guards around
    Fell to the ground, and sunk away.
2 Lo, the angelic bands
    In full assembly meet,
    To wait His high commands,
      And worship at His feet:
    Joyful they come, and wing their way,
    From realms of day, to such a tomb.
3 Then back to heaven they fly,
    And the glad tidings bear;
    Hark, as they soar on high,
      What music fills the air:
    Their anthems say, 'Jesus, who bled,
    Hath left the dead; He rose to-day.'
4 Ye mortals, catch the sound,
    Redeemed by Him from hell;
    And send the echo round
      The globe on which you dwell:
    Transported cry, 'Jesus, who bled,
    Hath left the dead, no more to die.'
5 All hail, triumphant Lord,
    Who savest us with Thy blood!
    Wide be Thy name adored,
      Thou rising, reigning God.
    With Thee we rise, with Thee we reign,
    And empires gain beyond the skies.
Rev. Philip Doddridge. (1702—1751.) 1755.

267   *Captivity led captive.*   H. M.
           Ps. lxviii. 18. Eph. iv. 8.
1 THE happy morn is come;
    The Saviour leaves the grave;
    His glorious work is done,
      Almighty now to save:
    Captivity is captive led,
    Since Jesus liveth that was dead.
2 Who to our charge shall lay
      Iniquity and guilt?
    All sin is done away,
      Since His rich blood was spilt:
    Captivity is captive led,
    Since Jesus liveth that was dead.
3 Christ hath the ransom paid;
      The glorious work is done;
    On Him our help is laid,
      The victory is won:
    Captivity is captive led,
    Since Jesus liveth that was dead.
4 Hail the triumphant Lord!
      The resurrection Thou!
    We bless Thy sacred word,
      Before Thy throne we bow:
    Captivity is captive led,
    Since Jesus liveth that was dead.
Rev. Thomas Haweis. (1732—1820.) 1792. ab.

268   *Christ our High Priest.*   H. M.
             Heb. x. 21.
1 THE atoning work is done,
    The victim's blood is shed,
    And Jesus now is gone
      His people's cause to plead:
    He stands in heaven their great High Priest,
    And bears their names upon His breast.
2 He sprinkles with His blood
      The mercy-seat above;
    For justice had withstood
      The purposes of love:
    But justice now objects no more,
    And mercy yields her boundless store.
3 No temple made with hands
      His place of service is;
    In heaven itself He stands,
      A heavenly priesthood His:
    In Him the shadows of the law
    Are all fulfilled, and now withdraw.

4 And though awhile He be
    Hid from the eyes of men,
  His people look to see
    Their great High Priest again:
  In brightest glory He will come,
  And take His waiting people home.
              Rev. Thomas Kelly. (1769—1855.) 1804.

269   *The Work that saves.*   H. M.

1 DONE is the work that saves,
    Once and forever done;
  Finished the righteousness
    That clothes the unrighteous one:
  The love that blesses us below
  Is flowing freely to us now.

2 The sacrifice is o'er,
    The veil is rent in twain,
  The mercy seat is red
    With blood of victim slain:
  Why stand we then without, in fear?
  The blood divine invites us near.

3 The gate is open wide,
    The new and living way
  Is clear, and free, and bright,
    With love, and peace, and day:
  Into the holiest now we come,
  Our present and our endless home.

4 Upon the mercy-seat
    The High Priest sits within;
  The blood is in His hand
    Which makes and keeps us clean:
  With boldness let us now draw near;
  That blood has banished every fear.
              Rev. Horatius Bonar. (1808—) 1866. ab.

270   *Weeping Mary.*   7. D.
           John xx 11—16.

1 MARY to her Saviour's tomb
    Hasted at the early dawn;
  Spice she brought and sweet perfume;
    But the Lord she loved was gone.
  For awhile she weeping stood,
  Struck with sorrow and surprise,
  Shedding tears, a plenteous flood,
    For her heart supplied her eyes.

2 Jesus, who is always near,
    Though too often unperceived,
  Came, His drooping child to cheer,
    Kindly asking why she grieved.
  Though at first she knew Him not,
    When He called her by her name,
  Then her griefs were all forgot,
    For she found He was the same.

3 Grief and sighing quickly fled
    When she heard His welcome voice;
  Just before, she thought Him dead,
    Now, He bids her heart rejoice.
  What a change His word can make,
    Turning darkness into day!
  You who weep for Jesus' sake,
    He will wipe your tears away.

4 He who came to comfort her,
    When she thought her all was lost,
  Will for your relief appear,
    Though you now are tempest-tost.
  On His word your burden cast,
    On His love your thoughts employ;
  Weeping for a while may last,
    But the morning brings the joy.
              Rev. John Newton. (1725—1807.) 1779.

271   *The Shout of Triumph.*   7. D.

1 SONS of Zion, raise your songs,
  Praise to Zion's King belongs;
  His the victor's crown and fame,
  Glory to the Saviour's name.
  Sore the strife, but rich the prize,
  Precious in the Victor's eyes;
  Glorious is the work achieved,
  Satan vanquished, man relieved.

2 Sing we then the Victor's praise,
  Go ye forth and strew the ways;
  Bid Him welcome to His throne,
  He is worthy, He alone.
  Place the crown upon His brow;
  Every knee to Him shall bow;
  Him the brightest seraph sings,
  Heaven proclaims Him "King of kings."
              Rev. Thomas Kelly. 1839.

272 *The Sepulchre on Sabbath Morning.* C. L. M.

1 How calm and beautiful the morn,
    That gilds the sacred tomb,
  Where Christ the crucified was borne,
    And veiled in midnight gloom!
  O weep no more the Saviour slain,
  The Lord is risen, He lives again.

2 Ye mourning saints, dry every tear
　For your departed Lord;
"Behold the place, He is not here,"
　The tomb is all unbarred:
The gates of death were closed in vain,
The Lord is risen—He lives again.

3 Now cheerful to the house of prayer
　Your early footsteps bend;
The Saviour will Himself be there,
　Your Advocate and Friend:
Once by the law your hopes were slain,
But now in Christ ye live again.

4 How tranquil now the rising day!
　'Tis Jesus still appears,
A risen Lord, to chase away
　Your unbelieving fears:
O weep no more your comforts slain,
The Lord is risen, He lives again.

5 And when the shades of evening fall,
　When life's last hour draws nigh,
If Jesus shines upon the soul,
　How blissful then to die!
Since He has risen that once was slain,
Ye die in Christ to live again.
　　　　　　Thomas Hastings. (1792—1872.) 1832.

273　　"*Aurora Cœlum purpurat.*"　　C. M.

1 THE morning purples all the sky,
　The air with praises rings;
Defeated hell stands sullen by,
　The world exulting sings:
Glory to God! our glad lips cry;
All glory be to God Most High!

2 While He, the King all strong to save,
　Rends the dark doors away,
And through the breaches of the grave
　Strides forth into the day,
Glory to God! our glad lips cry;
All glory be to God Most High!

3 Death's captive, in his gloomy prison
　Fast fettered He has lain;
But He has mastered death, is risen,
　And death wears now the chain.
Glory to God! our glad lips cry;
All glory be to God Most High!

4 The shining angels cry, "Away
　With grief; no spices bring;
Not tears, but songs, this joyful day,
　Should greet the rising king!"
Glory to God! our glad lips cry;
All glory be to God Most High!

5 That Thou our Paschal Lamb mayst be,
　And endless joy begin,
Jesus, Deliverer, set us free
　From the dread death of sin.
Glory to God! our glad lips cry;
All glory be to God Most High!
　　　　　　Ambrose of Milan. (340—397.
Tr. by Rev. Alexander Ramsay Thompson. (1822—) 1869.
　　　　　　　　　　　　　　　　1873.

274　　"*Ich sage Jedem dass Er lebt.*"　　C. M.

1 I SAY to all men, far and near,
　That He is risen again;
That He is with us now and here,
　And ever shall remain.

2 And what I say, let each this morn
　Go tell it to his friend,
That soon in every place shall dawn
　His Kingdom without end.

3 Now first to souls who thus awake
　Seems earth a Fatherland:
A new and endless life they take
　With rapture from His hand.

4 The fears of death and of the grave
　Are whelmed beneath the sea,
And every heart, now light and brave,
　May face the things to be.

5 The way of darkness that He trod
　To heaven at last shall come,
And he who hearkens to His word
　Shall reach His Father's home.
　　　　　Frederich von Hardenburg (1772—1801.) 1799.
　　　　　Tr. by Miss Catharine Winkworth. 1856. ab.

275　　*Christ's Triumph over death.*　　C. M.

1 YE choirs of new Jerusalem,
　Your sweetest notes employ,
The Paschal victory to hymn
　In strains of holy joy.

2 For Judah's Lion bursts His chains,
　Crushing the serpent's head;
And cries aloud through death's domains,
　To wake the imprisoned dead.

CHRIST.

4 Triumphant in His glory now,
   To him all power is given;
   To Him in one communion bow
   All saints in earth and heaven.

5 While we, His soldiers, praise our King,
   His mercy we implore,
   Within His palace bright to bring
   And keep us evermore.
      Fulbert of Chartres. (— c. 1029.)
     Tr. by Robert Campbell. (—1868.) 1850. ab.

276 *Trust in Christ.* C. M.

1 O JESUS, when I think of Thee,
   Thy manger, cross, and throne,
   My spirit trusts exultingly
   In Thee, and Thee alone.

2 I see Thee in Thy weakness first;
   Then, glorious from Thy shame,
   I see Thee death's strong fetters burst,
   And reach heaven's mightiest name.

3 In each, a brother's love I trace
   By power divine exprest,
   One in Thy Father God's embrace,
   As on Thy mother's breast.

4 For me Thou didst become a man,
   For me didst weep and die;
   For me achieve Thy wondrous plan,
   For me ascend on high.

5 O let me share Thy holy birth,
   Thy faith, Thy death to sin!
   And, strong amidst the toils of earth,
   My heavenly life begin.

6 Then shall I know what means the strain
   Triumphant of Saint Paul:
   "To live is Christ, to die is gain;"
   "Christ is my all in all."
    Rev. George Washington Bethune. (1805—1862.) 1847.

277 *"The Lord is risen indeed."* S. M.
   Luke xxiv. 34.

1 "THE Lord is risen indeed,"
   Then is His work performed;
   The captive surety now is freed,
   And death, our foe, disarmed.

2 "The Lord is risen indeed,"
   Then hell has lost his prey;
   With Him is risen the ransomed seed,
   To reign in endless day.

3 "The Lord is risen indeed,"
   He lives, to die no more;
   He lives, the sinner's cause to plead,
   Whose curse and shame He bore.

4 "The Lord is risen indeed,"
   Attending angels, hear;
   Up to the courts of heaven, with speed,
   The joyful tidings bear.

5 Then take your golden lyres,
   And strike each cheerful chord;
   Join all the bright celestial choirs,
   To sing our risen Lord.
     Rev. Thomas Kelly. (1769—1855.) 1812. ab.

278 *Gone into Heaven.* S. M.

1 THOU art gone up on high
   To mansions in the skies;
   And round Thy throne unceasingly
   The songs of praise arise.

2 But we are lingering here
   With sin and care oppressed:
   Lord, send Thy promised Comforter,
   And lead us to Thy rest.

3 Thou art gone up on high:
   But Thou didst first come down,
   Through earth's most bitter agony
   To pass unto Thy crown.

4 And girt with griefs and fears
   Our onward course must be;
   But only let that path of tears
   Lead us at last to Thee.

5 Thou art gone up on high:
   But thou shalt come again,
   With all the bright ones of the sky
   Attendant in Thy train.

6 O by Thy saving power
   So make us live and die,
   That we may stand, in that dread hour,
   At Thy right hand on high.
      Mrs. Emma Toke. (1812—) 1851.

279 *"The Conqueror reigns."* S. M.

1 JESUS, the Conqueror, reigns,
   In glorious strength arrayed;
   His kingdom over all maintains,
   And bids the earth be glad.

2 Ye sons of men, rejoice
   In Jesus' mighty love;
  Lift up your heart, lift up your voice,
   To Him who rules above.

3 Extol His kingly power;
   Kiss the exalted Son,
  Who died, and lives to die no more,
   High on His Father's throne.

4 Our Advocate with God,
   He undertakes our cause,
  And spreads through all the earth abroad
   The victory of His cross.
       Rev. Charles Wesley. (1708—1788.) 1749. ab.

280   *"Our Lord is risen."*   S. M.
          Ps. xxiv.

1 OUR Lord is risen from the dead,
   Our Jesus is gone up on high;
  The powers of hell are captive led,
   Dragged to the portals of the sky.

2 There His triumphal chariot waits,
   And angels chant the solemn lay:—
  "Lift up your heads, ye heavenly gates,
   Ye everlasting doors, give way.

3 "Loose all your bars of massy light,
   And wide unfold the ethereal scene;
  He claims these mansions as His right;
   Receive the King of glory in."

4 "Who is this King of glory, who?"
  "The Lord that all His foes o'ercame;
   The world, sin, death, and hell o'erthrew;
   And Jesus is the conqueror's name."

5 Lo, His triumphal chariot waits,
   And angels chant the solemn lay:—
  "Lift up your heads, ye heavenly gates,
   Ye everlasting doors, give way."

6 "Who is this King of glory, who?"
  "The Lord of glorious power possessed,
   The King of saints and angels, too;
   God over all, forever blessed."
       Rev. Charles Wesley. 1743. ab.

281   *"The Ascended Saviour."*   7.
          Ps. lxviii.

1 LORD, Thy Church hath seen Thee rise
  To Thy temple in the skies:
  God my Saviour, God my King;
  While Thy ransomed round Thee sing.

2 When in glories all divine,
  Through the earth Thy Church shall shine,
  Kings in prayer and praise shall wait,
  Bending at Thy temple's gate.
       Rev. William Goode. (1762—1816.) 1811. ab.

282   *"My Redeemer Lives."*   L. M.

1 "I KNOW that my Redeemer lives:"
  What comfort this sweet sentence gives,
  He lives, He lives, who once was dead,
  He lives, my ever-living head.

2 He lives to bless me with His love,
  He lives to plead for me above,
  He lives my hungry soul to feed,
  He lives to help in time of need.

3 He lives to grant me rich supply,
  He lives to guide me with His eye,
  He lives to comfort me when faint,
  He lives to hear my souls complaint.

4 He lives to silence all my fears,
  He lives to stoop and wipe my tears,
  He lives to calm my troubled heart,
  He lives all blessings to impart.

5 He lives, my kind, my faithful Friend,
  He lives and loves me to the end,
  He lives, and while he lives I'll sing,
  He lives, my Prophet, Priest, and King.

6 He lives, and grants me daily breath,
  He lives, and I shall conquer death,
  He lives my mansion to prepare,
  He lives to bring me safely there.

7 He lives, all glory to His Name;
  He lives, my Jesus, still the same:
  O the sweet joy this sentence gives,
  "I know that my Redeemer lives."
       Rev. Samuel Medley. (1738—1799.) 1789. ab.

283   *Christ dying, rising, and reigning.*   L. M.

1 HE dies, the Friend of sinners dies;
  Lo, Salem's daughters weep around;
  A solemn darkness veils the skies;
  A sudden trembling shakes the ground.

2 Here's love and grief beyond degree;
  The Lord of glory dies for men;
  But lo, what sudden joys I see,
  Jesus, the dead, revives again.

3 The rising God forsakes the tomb,
   Up to His Father's court He flies;
   Cherubic legions guard Him home,
   And shout Him welcome to the skies.

4 Break off your tears, ye saints, and tell
   How high our great Deliverer reigns;
   Sing how He spoiled the hosts of hell,
   And led the monster death in chains.

5 Say, "Live forever, wondrous King,
   Born to redeem, and strong to save!"
   Then ask the monster, "Where's thy sting?"
   "And where's thy victory, boasting grave?"
   Rev. Isaac Watts. (1674—1748.) 1706, ab.
   Alt. by Rev. John Wesley. (1703—1791.)

284 *Christ interceding.* L. M.
Heb. vii. 25.

1 He lives, the Great Redeemer lives,
   What joy the blest assurance gives;
   And now, before His Father, God,
   Pleads the full merits of His blood.

2 Repeated crimes awake our fears,
   And justice armed with frowns appears;
   But in the Saviour's lovely face
   Sweet mercy smiles, and all is peace.

3 Hence, then, ye black, despairing thoughts;
   Above our fears, above our faults,
   His powerful intercessions rise,
   And guilt recedes, and terror dies.

4 In every dark, distressful hour,
   When sin and Satan join their power,
   Let this dear hope repel the dart,
   That Jesus bears us on His heart.

5 Great Advocate, Almighty Friend,
   On Him our humble hopes depend;
   Our cause can never, never fail,
   For Jesus pleads, and must prevail.
   Miss Anne Steele. (1716—1778.) 1760.

285 "*Aeterne Rex altissime.*" L. M.

1 O LORD most High, Eternal King,
   By Thee redeemed Thy praise we sing;
   The bonds of death are burst by Thee,
   And grace has won the victory.

2 Ascending to the Father's throne
   Thou claim'st the kingdom as Thine own;
   Thy days of mortal weakness o'er,
   All power is Thine for evermore.

3 To Thee the whole creation now
   Shall, in its threefold order, bow,
   Of things on earth, and things on high,
   And things that underneath us lie.

4 Be Thou our joy, O mighty Lord,
   As Thou wilt be our great reward;
   Let all our glory be in Thee
   Both now and through eternity.

5 All praise from every heart and tongue
   To Thee, ascended Lord, be sung;
   All praise to God the Father be,
   And Holy Ghost, eternally.
   Ambrose of Milan. (340—397.)
   Tr. by Rev. John Mason Neale. (1818—1866.) 1861, ab. and alt.

286 *Christ ascending.*

1 HAIL the day that sees Him rise,
   Ravished from our wishful eyes;
   Christ, awhile to mortals given,
   Re-ascends His native heaven.
   There the glorious triumph waits,
   Lift your heads, eternal gates;
   Wide unfold the radiant scene,
   Take the King of Glory in.

2 Him though highest heaven receives,
   Still He loves the earth He leaves:
   Though returning to His throne,
   Still He calls mankind His own.
   See, He lifts His hands above;
   See, He shows the prints of love;
   Hark, His gracious lips bestow
   Blessings on His Church below.

3 Still for us His death He pleads;
   Prevalent, He intercedes;
   Near Himself prepares our place,
   Harbinger of human race.
   Lord, though parted from our sight,
   High above yon azure height,
   Grant our hearts may thither rise,
   Following Thee beyond the skies.
   Rev. Charles Wesley. (1708—1788.) 1739. ab.

287 "*He is gone.*"

1 HE is gone! and we remain
   In this world of sin and pain:
   In the void which He has left,

On this earth of Him bereft,
We have still His work to do,
We can still His path pursue;
Seek Him both in friend and foe,
In ourselves His image show.

2 He is gone! we heard Him say,
"Good that I should go away;"
Gone is that dear form and face,
But not gone His present grace:
Though Himself no more we see,
Comfortless we cannot be;
No, His Spirit still is ours,
Quickening, freshening all our powers.

3 He is gone! unto their goal
World and Church must on ward roll;
Far behind we leave the past;
Forward all our glances cast:
Still His words before us range
Through the ages, as they change;
Wheresoe'er the truth shall lead,
He will give whate'er we need.

4 He is gone! but we once more
Shall behold Him as before,
In the heaven of heavens the same
As on earth he went and came:
In the many mansions there,
Place for us he will prepare:
In that world, unseen, unknown,
He and we shall yet be one.
Rev. Arthur Penrhyn Stanley. (1815—) 1859. ab. and sl alt.

288 *"And yet have believed."* L. M. 6l.
John xx. 29.

1 We did not see Thee lifted high,
Amid that wild and savage crew,
Nor heard Thy meek, imploring cry:
"Forgive, they know not what they do!"
Yet we believe the deed was done
Which shook the earth, and veiled the sun.

2 We stood not by the empty tomb
Where late Thy sacred body lay,
Nor sat within that upper room,
Nor met Thee in the open way:
But we believe that angels said
"Why seek the living with the dead?"

3 We did not mark the chosen few,
When Thou didst thro' the clouds ascend,
First lift to heaven their wondering view,
Then to the earth all prostrate bend:
Yet we believe that mortal eyes
Beheld that journey to the skies.

4 And now that Thou dost reign on high,
And thence Thy waiting people bless;
No ray of glory from the sky
Doth shine upon our wilderness:
But we believe Thy faithful word,
And trust in our redeeming Lord.
Rev. John Hampden Gurney. (1802—1862.) 1238, 1851. alt.

289 *"Ich habe nun den Grund gefunden."* L. M. 6l.

1 Now I have found the ground wherein
Sure my soul's anchor may remain:
The wounds of Jesus, for my sin
Before the world's foundation slain;
Whose mercy shall unshaken stay
When heaven and earth are fled away.

2 O Love, Thou bottomless abyss!
My sins are swallowed up in Thee:
Covered is my unrighteousness,
Nor spot of guilt remains in me:
While Jesus' blood through earth and skies,
Mercy, free, boundless mercy, cries!

3 With faith I plunge me in this sea;
Here is my hope, my joy, my rest;
Hither, when hell assails, I flee,
I look into my Saviour's breast.
Away, sad doubt and anxious fear!
Mercy is all that's written there.

4 Though waves and storms go o'er my head;
Though strength, and health, and friends be gone,
Though joys be withered all and dead;
Though every comfort be withdrawn:
On this my steadfast souls relies:
Father, Thy mercy never dies.
Rev. John Andrew Rothe. (1688—1758.) 1728.
Tr. by Rev. John Wesley. (1703—1791.) 1740. ab.

290 *Ascension.* 6,4.

1 Rise, glorious Conqueror, rise
Into Thy native skies;
Assume Thy right;
And where in many a fold
The clouds are backward rolled,
Pass through those gates of gold,
And reign in light.

CHRIST.

2 Victor o'er death and hell,
  Cherubic legions swell
    The radiant train:
  Praises all heaven inspire;
  Each angel sweeps his lyre,
  And claps his wings of fire,
    Thou Lamb once slain.

3 Enter, Incarnate God!
  No feet but Thine have trod
    The serpent down:
  Blow the full trumpets, blow,
  Wider yon portals throw,
  Saviour, triumphant, go,
    And take Thy crown.

4 Lion of Judah, Hail!
  And let Thy name prevail
    From age to age:
  Lord of the rolling years,
  Claim for Thine own the spheres,
  For Thou hast bought with tears
    Thy heritage.
            Matthew Bridges. 1848. ab.

291   "*King of Saints.*"   6, 4.
            Rev xv 3.

1 LET us awake our joys,
  Strike up with cheerful voice,
    Each creature sing:
  Angels, begin the song,
  Mortals, the strain prolong,
  In accents sweet and strong,
    "Jesus is King."

2 Proclaim abroad His name,
  Tell of His matchless fame;
    What wonders done:
  Shout through hell's dark profound;
  Let all the earth resound,
  'Till the high heavens rebound,
    "The victory's won."

3 He vanquished sin and hell,
  And the last foe will quell;
    Mourners, rejoice!
  His dying love adore,
  Praise Him, now raised in power,
  And triumph evermore,
    With a glad voice.

4 All hail the glorious day,
  When through the heavenly way
    Lo, He shall come!

While they who pierced Him wail,
His promise shall not fail;
Saints, see your King prevail·
  Come, dear Lord, come!
        Rev. William Kingsbury. (1744—1818.) 1806.

292   "*Worthy the Lamb!*"   6, 4.

1 GLORY to God on high,
  Let praises fill the sky!
    Praise ye His name.
  Angels His name adore,
  Who all our sorrows bore,
  And saints cry evermore,
    "Worthy the Lamb!"

2 All they around the throne
  Cheerfully join in one,
    Praising His name.
  We who have felt His blood
  Sealing our peace with God,
  Spread His dear fame abroad:
    "Worthy the Lamb!"

3 To Him our hearts we raise;
  None else shall have our praise;
    Praise ye His name!
  Him, our exalted Lord,
  By us below adored,
  We praise with one accord,
    "Worthy the Lamb!"

4 Join all the human race,
  Our Lord and God to bless;
    Praise ye His name!
  In Him we will rejoice,
  Making a cheerful noise,
  And say with heart and voice,
    "Worthy the Lamb!"

5 Though we must change our place,
  Our souls shall never cease
    Praising His name;
  To Him we'll tribute bring,
  Laud Him our gracious King,
  And without ceasing sing,
    "Worthy the Lamb!"
        Rev. James Allen. (1734—1804.) 1761. ab.

293   *Praise to Jesus*   6, 4.

1 COME, all ye saints of God,
  Wide through the earth abroad
    Spread Jesus' fame;

CHRIST.

    Tell what His love has done;
    Trust in His name alone;
    Shout to His lofty throne,
      "Worthy the Lamb!"

2 Hence, gloomy doubts and fears;
    Dry up your mournful tears;
    Join our glad theme;
    Beauty for ashes bring;
    Strike each melodious string;
    Join heart and voice to sing,
      "Worthy the Lamb!"

3 Hark how the choirs above,
    Filled with the Saviour's love,
    Dwell on His name;
    There too may we be found,
    With light and glory crowned,
    While all the heavens resound,
      "Worthy the Lamb!"
        Rev. James Boden. (1757—1841.) 1801. sl. alt.

294   "*Willkommen Held im Streit.*"   C. M.

1 WELCOME, Thou victor in the strife,
    Now welcome from the cave!
    To-day we triumph in Thy life
    Around Thine empty grave.

2 Our enemy is put to shame,
    His short-lived triumph o'er;
    Our God is with us, we exclaim,
    We fear our foe no more.

3 O share with us the spoils, we pray,
    Thou diedst to achieve;
    We meet within Thy house to-day
    Our portion to receive.

4 And let Thy conquering banner wave
    O'er hearts Thou makest free,
    And point the path that from the grave
    Leads heavenward up to Thee.

5 We bury all our sin and crime
    Deep in our Saviour's tomb,
    And seek the treasure there, that time
    Nor change can e'er consume.

6 We die with Thee: O let us live
    Henceforth to Thee aright;
    The blessings Thou hast died to give
    Be daily in our sight.

7 Fearless we lay us in the tomb,
    And sleep the night away,

    If Thou art there to break the gloom,
    And call us back to day.
        Rev. Benjamin Schmolck. (1672—1737.) 1712.
        Tr. by Miss Catherine Winkworth. (1829—) 1855. ab.

295   *Jesus seen of Angels.*   C. M.
        1 Tim. iii. 16.

1 BEYOND the glittering starry skies,
    Far as the eternal hills,
    There, in the boundless worlds of light,
    Our dear Redeemer dwells.

2 Immortal angels, bright and fair,
    In countless armies shine;
    At His right hand, with golden harps,
    They offer songs divine.

3 In all His toils, and dangerous paths,
    They did His steps attend;
    Oft paused, and wondered how at last
    This scene of love would end.

4 And when the powers of hell combined
    To fill His cup of woe,
    Their pitying eyes beheld His tears
    In bloody anguish flow.

5 As on the torturing tree He hung,
    And darkness veiled the sky,
    They saw, aghast, that awful sight,
    The Lord of glory die.

6 Anon He bursts the gates of death,
    And quells the tyrant's power;
    They saw the illustrious Conqueror rise,
    And hailed the blessed hour.

7 They thronged His chariot up the sky,
    And bore Him to His throne;
    Then swept their golden harps and cried,
    "The glorious work is done!"

8 My soul the joyful triumph feels,
    And thinks the moments long,
    Ere she her Saviour's glory sees,
    And joins the rapturous song.
        Rev. James Fanch. 1776.
    Rev. Daniel Turner. (1710—1798.) 1791. ab. and alt.

296   "*On His Head were many Crowns.*"   S. M.
        Rev. xix. 12.

1 CROWN Him with many crowns,
    The Lamb upon His throne!
    Hark, how the heavenly anthem drowns
    All music but its own.

2 Crown Him the Lord of love!
  Behold His hands and side,—
  Rich wounds, yet visible above,
  In beauty glorified.

3 Crown Him the Lord of peace!
  Whose power a sceptre sways,
  From pole to pole, that wars may cease,
  Absorbed in prayer and praise.

4 Crown Him the Lord of years,
  The Potentate of time,
  Creator of the rolling spheres,
  Ineffably sublime!

5 Crown Him the Lord of Heaven!
  One with the Father known,—
  And the blest Spirit, through Him given
  From yonder triune throne!

6 All hail! Redeemer, hail!
  For Thou hast died for me:
  Thy praise shall never, never fail
  Throughout eternity.
  Matthew Bridges. (1800—) 1847. ab.

297 *Jesus enthroned in Glory.* S. M.

1 Throned high is Jesus now,
  Upon His heavenly seat;
  The kingly crown is on His brow,
  The saints are at His feet.

2 In shining white they stand,
  A great and countless throng;
  A palmy sceptre in each hand,
  On every lip a song.

3 They sing the Lamb of God,
  Once slain on earth for them;
  The Lamb, through whose atoning blood
  Each wears his diadem.

4 Thy grace, O Holy Ghost,
  Thy blessed help supply,
  That we may join the radiant host,
  Who circle Christ on high.
  Rev. Thomas James Judkin. (1788—1871.) 1831.

298 *"Ascendens in altum Dominus.* S. M.

1 The Lord on high ascends,
  Once more to take His seat;
  Celestial powers rejoicing fly,
  His glad return to greet.

2 The mighty battle gained,
  The world's great Prince undone,
  Before His Father He presents
  The mortal palm He won.

3 Upborne above the clouds,
  Sweet hope He sheds on all;
  He flings the gates of Eden back,
  Shut fast by Adam's fall.

4 To our Redeemer's name
  All thanks and praise be given,
  That He hath borne our mortal shape,
  To tread the courts of heaven.

5 May we, while waiting Christ,
  To heavenly works arise,
  And ever live such saintly lives,
  That we may reach the skies.
  Ambrose of Milan. (340—397.)
Tr. by Robert Corbet Singleton. 1870. ab.

299 *Christ ascending and reigning.* C. M.
Ps. xlvii.

1 O for a shout of sacred joy
  To God, the sovereign King!
  Let every land their tongues employ,
  And hymns of triumph sing.

2 Jesus, our God, ascends on high;
  His heavenly guards around
  Attend Him rising through the sky,
  With trumpet's joyful sound.

3 While angels shout, and praise their King,
  Let mortals learn their strains;
  Let all the earth His honor sing;
  O'er all the earth He reigns.

4 Rehearse His praise with awe profound,
  Let knowledge lead the song;
  Nor mock Him with a solemn sound
  Upon a thoughtless tongue.

5 In Israel stood His ancient throne;
  He loved that chosen race:
  But now He calls the world His own,
  And heathens taste His grace.
  Rev. Isaac Watts. (1674—1748.) 1719. ab.

300 *"The King of Glory."* C. M.
S. xxiv. 7—10.

1 Lift up your heads, eternal gates,
  Unfold to entertain
  The King of glory; see, He comes
  With His celestial train.

CHRIST.

2 Who is this King of glory—who?
   The Lord, for strength renowned;
   In battle mighty; o'er His foes
   Eternal Victor crowned.

3 Lift up your heads, ye gates, unfold
   In state to entertain
   The King of glory; see, He comes
   With all His shining train.

4 Who is the King of glory—who?
   The Lord of hosts renowned:
   Of glory He alone is King,
   Who is with glory crowned.
                    Tate and Brady. 1696. sl. alt.

301   *"Gone in before us."*   C. M.

1 THE eternal gates lift up their heads,
   The doors are opened wide;
   The King of glory is gone up
   Unto His Father's side.

2 Thou art gone in before us, Lord,
   Thou hast prepared a place,
   That we may be where now Thou art,
   And look upon Thy face.

3 And ever on Thine earthly path
   A gleam of glory lies;
   A light still breaks behind the cloud
   That veils Thee from our eyes.

4 Lift up our thoughts, lift up our songs,
   And let Thy grace be given,
   That while we linger yet below,
   Our hearts may be in heaven;

5 That where Thou art at God's right hand,
   Our hope, our love may be:
   Dwell in us now, that we may dwell
   For evermore in Thee.
                    Mrs Cecil Frances Alexander. 1858.

302   *"Perfect through Sufferings."*   C. M.
                    Heb. ii. 10

THE head that once was crowned with thorns
   Is crowned with glory now;
   A royal diadem adorns
   The mighty Victor's brow.

2 The highest place that heaven affords
   Is His, is His by right,
   "The King of kings, and Lord of lords,"
   And heaven's eternal light.

3 The joy of all who dwell above,
   The joy of all below
   To whom He manifests His love,
   And grants His name to know:

4 To them the cross, with all its shame,
   With all its grace, is given;
   Their name, an everlasting name,
   Their joy, the joy of heaven.

5 They suffer with their Lord below,
   They reign with Him above;
   Their profit and their joy to know
   The mystery of His love.

6 The cross He bore is life and health,
   Though shame and death to Him;
   His people's hope, His people's wealth,
   Their everlasting theme.
                    Rev. Thomas Kelly. (1769—1855.) 1820

303   *"The Desire of all Nations."*   C. M.
                    Hag. ii. 7

1 INFINITE excellence is Thine,
   Thou glorious Prince of Grace!
   Thy uncreated beauties shine
   With never-fading rays.

2 Sinners, from earth's remotest end,
   Come bending at Thy feet;
   To Thee their prayers and songs ascend,
   In Thee their wishes meet.

3 Millions of happy spirits live
   On Thy exhaustless store;
   From Thee they all their bliss receive,
   And still Thou givest more.

4 Thou art their triumph, and their joy;
   They find their all in Thee;
   Thy glories will their tongues employ
   Through all eternity.
                    Rev. John Fawcett. (1739—1817.) 1782 ab.

304   *"The Way, the Truth, the Life."*   C. M.
                    John xiv. 6

1 THOU art the Way: to Thee alone
   From sin and death we flee;
   And he who would the Father seek,
   Must seek Him, Lord, by Thee.

2 Thou art the Truth: Thy word alone
   True wisdom can impart;
   Thou only canst inform the mind,
   And purify the heart.

3 Thou art the Life: the rending tomb
   Proclaims Thy conquering arm,
   And those who put their trust in Thee
   Nor death, nor hell shall harm.

4 Thou art the Way, the Truth, the Life;
   Grant us that Way to know,
   That Truth to keep, that Life to win,
   Whose joys eternal flow.
         Bp. George Washington Doane. (1799—1859.) 1824.

305 "*And He shall reign forever and ever.*" 8, 7, 4.
        Rev. xi. 15.

1 LOOK, ye saints, the sight is glorious,
     See "the Man of Sorrows" now;
   From the fight returned victorious,
     Every knee to Him shall bow:
       Crown Him, crown Him;
   Crowns become the Victor's brow.

2 Crown the Saviour, angels, crown Him:
     Rich the trophies Jesus brings:
   In the seat of power enthrone Him,
     While the vault of heaven rings:
       Crown Him, crown Him;
   Crown the Saviour "King of kings."

3 Sinners in derision crowned Him,
     Mocking thus the Saviour's claim;
   Saints and angels crowd around Him,
     Own His title, praise His name:
       Crown Him, crown Him;
   Spread abroad the Victor's fame.

4 Hark, those bursts of acclamation!
     Hark, those loud triumphant chords!
   Jesus takes the highest station:
     O what joy the sight affords!
       Crown Him, crown Him;
   "King of kings, and Lord of lords."
         Rev. Thomas Kelly. (1769—1855.) 1809.

306   "*Thou art worthy, O Lord.*"   8, 7, 4.
              Rev. iv. 11.

1 GLORY, glory everlasting
     Be to Him who bore the cross!
   Who redeemed our souls, by tasting
     Death, the death deserved by us;
       Spread His glory,
   Who redeemed His people thus.

2 His is love, 'tis love unbounded,
     Without measure, without end;
   Human thought is here confounded,
     'T is too vast to comprehend:
       Praise the Saviour!
   Magnify the sinner's Friend.

3 While we hear the wondrous story
     Of the Saviour's cross and shame,
   Sing we "Everlasting glory
     Be to God, and to the Lamb:"
       Saints and angels,
   Give ye glory to His name.
         Rev. Thomas Kelly. 1809.

307   *Worshipped of Angels.*   8, 7, 6 l.
              Heb. i. 6.

1 HARK, ten thousand harps and voices
   Sound the note of praise above!
   Jesus reigns, and heaven rejoices;
   Jesus reigns, the God of love;
   See He sits on yonder throne;
   Jesus rules the world alone.

2 King of glory, reign forever!
   Thine an everlasting crown;
   Nothing from Thy love shall sever
   Those whom Thou hast made Thine own;
   Happy objects of Thy grace,
   Destined to behold Thy face.

3 Saviour, hasten Thine appearing;
   Bring, O bring the glorious day,
   When the awful summons hearing,
   Heaven and earth shall pass away:
   Then, with golden harps, we'll sing,
   "Glory, glory to our King!"
         Rev. Thomas Kelly. 1804. ab.

308 *A Hymn of Praise to the Redeemer.* 8, 7. 6 l.

1 COME, ye faithful, raise the anthem,
   Cleave the skies with shouts of praise;
   Sing to Him Who found the ransom,
   Ancient of eternal days:
   God Eternal, Word Incarnate,
   Whom the Heaven of heavens obeys.

2 Ere He raised the lofty mountains,
   Formed the sea, or built the sky,
   Love eternal, free, and boundless,
   Forced the Lord of Life to die:
   Lifted up the Prince of princes
   On the throne of Calvary.

3 Now on those eternal mountains
   Stands the sapphire throne, all bright,
 Where unceasing hallelujahs
   They upraise, the sons of light:
 Zion's people tell His praises,
   Victor after hard-won fight.

4 Bring your harps and bring your incense,
   Sweep the string and pour the lay;
 Let the earth proclaim His wonders,
   King of that celestial day.
 He, the Lamb once slain, is worthy,
   Who was dead and lives for aye.
        Rev. Joh Hupton. (1762—1849.) 1808. ab.
   Alt. by Rev. John Mason Neale. (1818—1866.) 1851

309 Ἰησοῦς ὁ Ζωοδότης. 8, 7. 6 l.

1 JESUS, Lord of Life eternal,
   Taking those He loved the best,
 Stood upon the Mount of Olives,
   And His own the last time blest:
 Then, though He had never left it,
   Sought again His Father's breast.

2 Knit is now our flesh to Godhead,
   Knit in everlasting bands:
 Call the world to highest festal:
   Floods and oceans, clap your hands:
 Angels, raise the song of triumph:
   Make response, ye distant lands.

3 Loosing death with all its terrors
   Thou ascendedst up on high;
 And to mortals, now immortal,
   Gavest immortality,
 As Thine own disciples saw Thee
   Mounting Victor to the sky.
        Joseph of the Studium, (d—833.)
   Tr. by Rev. John Mason Neale. 1862. ab. 2nd alt

310 "Enthroned in Glory." 8, 7. D.

1 HAIL, Thou once despised Jesus,
   Hail, thou Galilean king!
 Thou didst suffer to release us,
   Thou didst free salvation bring:
 Hail, Thou agonizing Saviour,
   Bearer of our sin and shame;
 By Thy merits we find favor;
   Life is given through Thy Name.

2 Paschal Lamb, by God appointed,
   All our sins on Thee were laid;
 By Almighty Love anointed,
   Thou hast full atonement made:

All Thy people are forgiven
   Through the virtue of Thy blood;
 Opened is the gate of heaven;
   Peace is made 'twixt man and God.

3 Jesus, hail, enthroned in glory,
   There forever to abide;
 All the heavenly hosts adore Thee,
   Seated at Thy Father's side.
 There for sinners Thou art pleading;
   There Thou dost our place prepare;
 Ever for us interceding
   Till in glory we appear.

4 Worship, honor, power, and blessing,
   Thou art worthy to receive;
 Loudest praises, without ceasing,
   Meet it is for us to give.
 Help, ye bright angelic spirits,
   Bring your sweetest, noblest lays;
 Help to sing our Saviour's merits,
   Help to chant Immanuel's praise.

5 Soon we shall, with those in glory,
   His transcendent grace relate;
 Gladly sing the amazing story
   Of His dying love so great:
 In that blessed contemplation
   We for evermore shall dwell,
 Crowned with bliss and consolation,
   Such as none below can tell.
        Rev. John Bakewell. (1721—1819.) 1760. alt
   Rev. Augustus Montague Toplady. (1740—1778.) 1776.

311 "Christ the First-fruits." 8, 7. D.
        1 Cor. xv. 20—23.

1 Hallelujah! hallelujah!
   Hearts to heaven and voices raise;
 Sing to God a hymn of gladness,
   Sing to God a hymn of praise;
 He, who on the cross a Victim
   For the world's salvation bled,
 Jesus Christ, the King of glory,
   Now is risen from the dead.

2 Christ is risen, Christ the First-fruits
   Of the holy harvest field,
 Which will all its full abundance
   At His second coming yield;
 Then the golden ears of harvest
   Will their heads before Him wave,
 Ripened by His glorious sunshine
   From the furrows of the grave.

CHRIST.

3 Christ is risen, we are risen;
　Shed upon us heavenly grace,
　Rain, and dew, and gleams of glory
　　From the brightness of Thy face;
　That we, with our hearts in heaven,
　　Here on earth may fruitful be,
　And by angel-hands be gathered,
　　And be ever, Lord, with Thee.
　　　Bp. Christopher Wordsworth. (1807—) 1862. ab.

312　　*Mounting in Triumph.*　　8, 7. D.

1 SEE the Conqueror mounts in triumph,
　　See the King in royal state,
　Riding on the clouds His chariot
　　To His heavenly palace-gate;
　Hark, the choirs of angel voices
　　Joyful hallelujahs sing,
　And the portals high are lifted,
　　To receive their Heavenly King.

2 Who is this that comes in glory,
　　With the trump of jubilee?
　Lord of battles, God of armies,
　　He has gained the victory;
　He who on the cross did suffer,
　　He who from the grave arose,
　He has vanquished sin and Satan,
　　He by death has spoiled His foes.

3 Thou hast raised our human nature
　　On the clouds to God's right hand,
　There we sit in heavenly places,
　　There with Thee in glory stand;
　Jesus reigns adored by angels,
　　Man with God is on the throne;
　Mighty Lord, in Thine ascension
　　We by faith behold our own.

4 Lift us up from earth to heaven,
　　Give us wings of faith and love,
　Gales of holy aspiration
　　Wafting us to realms above;
　That, with hearts and minds uplifted,
　　We with Christ our Lord may dwell,
　Where He sits enthroned in glory
　　In the heavenly citadel.

5 So at last, when He appeareth,
　　We from out our graves may spring,
　With our youth renewed like eagles',
　　Flocking round our heavenly King,

　Caught up on the clouds of heaven,
　　And may meet Him in the air,
　Rise to realms where He is reigning,
　　And may reign forever there.
　　　Bp. Christopher Wordsworth. 1862. ab.

313　　*The Glory of Christ.*　　L. M
　　　　　　Ps. xlv.

1 Now be my heart inspired to sing
　The glories of my Saviour King:
　Jesus, the Lord, how heavenly fair
　His form! how bright His beauties are!

2 O'er all the sons of human race
　He shines with a superior grace;
　Love from His lips divinely flows,
　And blessings all His state compose.

3 Thy throne, O God, forever stands;
　Grace is the sceptre in Thy hands;
　Thy laws and works are just and right;
　Justice and grace are Thy delight.

4 God, Thine own God, has richly shed
　His oil of gladness on Thy head;
　And with His sacred Spirit blest
　His first-born Son above the rest.
　　　Rev. Isaac Watts. (1674—1748.) 1719. ab.

314　　*"Rex Christe, factor omnium."*　　L. M.

1 O CHRIST, our King, Creator, Lord,
　Saviour of all who trust Thy word,
　To them who seek Thee ever near,
　Now to our praises bend Thine ear.

2 In Thy dear cross a grace is found,
　It flows from every streaming wound,
　Whose power our inbred sin controls,
　Breaks the firm bond, and frees our souls.

3 Thou didst create the stars of night,
　Yet Thou hast veiled in flesh Thy light;
　Hast deigned a mortal form to wear,
　A mortal's painful lot to bear.

4 When Thou didst hang upon the tree,
　The quaking earth acknowledged Thee;
　When Thou didst there yield up Thy breath,
　The world grew dark as shades of death.

5 Now in the Father's glory high,
　Great Conqueror, never more to die,
　Us by Thy mighty power defend,
　And reign through ages without end.
　　　Gregory the Great (540—604.)
　　　Tr. by Rev. Ray Palmer. (1808—) 1858

CHRIST.

315 *Christ's Humiliation and Exaltation.* L. M.
Rev. v. 12.

1 WHAT equal honors shall we bring,
To Thee, O Lord our God, the Lamb,
When all the notes that angels sing,
Are far inferior to Thy name?

2 Worthy is He that once was slain,
The Prince of peace that groaned and died,
Worthy to rise, and live, and reign
At His Almighty Father's side.

3 All riches are His native right,
Yet He sustained amazing loss;
To Him ascribe eternal might,
Who left His weakness on the cross.

4 Honor immortal must be paid,
Instead of scandal and of scorn;
While glory shines around His head,
And a bright crown without a thorn.

5 Blessings forever on the Lamb,
Who bore the curse for wretched men;
Let angels sound His sacred name,
And every creature say, Amen.
Rev. Isaac Watts. 1709. ab.

2 He who for men in mercy stood,
And poured on earth His precious blood,
Pursues in heaven His plan of grace,
The Guardian God of human race.

3 Though now ascended up on high,
He bends on earth a brother's eye;
Partaker of the human name,
He knows the frailty of our frame.

4 Our fellow-sufferer yet retains
A fellow-feeling of our pains;
And still remembers in the skies
His tears, and agonies, and cries.

5 In every pang that rends the heart,
The Man of sorrows had a part;
He sympathizes in our grief,
And to the sufferer sends relief.

6 With boldness, therefore, at the throne,
Let us make all our sorrows known,
And ask the aids of heavenly power,
To help us in the evil hour.
Michael Bruce. (1746—1767.) 1781.

316 *"Optatus votis omnium."* L. M.

1 O MIGHTY joy to all our race!
The Virgin-born, who bore for us
The stripes, the spitting, and the cross,
Takes on the Father's throne His place.

2 To Thee let ceaseless praises rise,
Champion of our salvation Thou,
Bearing Thy Human Body now
In the high palace of the skies.

3 One common joy this day shall fill
The hearts of angels and of men;
To them that Thou art come again,
To us that Thou art with us still.

4 Now, following in the steps He trod,
'Tis ours to look for Christ from heaven,
And so to live that it be given
To rise with Him at last to God.
Ambrose of Milan. (340—397.)
Tr. by Mrs. Elizabeth Charles. 1865. ab.

317 *The enthroned High Priest.* L. M.

1 WHERE high the heavenly temple stands,
The house of God not made with hands,
A great High Priest our nature wears,
The Patron of mankind appears.

318 *"King of kings, and Lord of lords."* L. M.
Rev. xix. 16.

1 O CHRIST, the Lord of heaven, to Thee,
Clothed with all majesty divine,
Eternal power and glory be,
Eternal praise of right is Thine.

2 Reign, Prince of life, that once Thy brow
Didst yield to wear the wounding thorn;
Reign, throned beside Thy Father now,
Adored the Son of God first-born!

3 From angel hosts that round Thee stand,
With forms more pure than spotless snow,
From the bright burning seraph band,
Let praise in loftiest numbers flow!

4 To Thee, the Lamb, our mortal songs,
Born of deep fervent love, shall rise;
All honor to Thy name belongs,
Our lips would sound it through the skies.

5 "Jesus!"—all earth shall speak the word;
"Jesus!"—all heaven resound it still;
Immanuel, Saviour, Conqueror, Lord,
Thy praise the universe shall fill.
Rev. Ray Palmer.

CHRIST.

319 *Rejoicing in Hope.* C. M.
Rom. xii. 12.

1 I KNOW that my Redeemer lives,
    And ever prays for me;
  A token of His love He gives,
    A pledge of liberty.

2 I find Him lifting up my head,
    He brings salvation near;
  His presence makes me free indeed,
    And He will soon appear.

3 Far spent is the Egyptian night
    Of fear, and pain, and grief;
  And lo, I see the morning light
    That brings assured relief.

4 Jesus, I hang upon Thy word;
    I steadfastly believe
  Thou wilt return, and claim me, Lord,
    And to Thyself receive.

5 When God is mine, and I am His,
    Of paradise possessed,
  I taste unutterable bliss,
    And everlasting rest.
        Rev. Charles Wesley. (1708—1788.) 1742 ab.

320 *Christ's Compassion to the Weak and Tempted.* C. M.
Heb. iv. 16, v. 7. Matt. xii. 20.

1 WITH joy we meditate the grace
    Of our High Priest above;
  His heart is made of tenderness,
    His bosom glows with love.

2 Touched with a sympathy within,
    He knows our feeble frame;
  He knows what sore temptations mean,
    For He hath felt the same.

3 He, in the days of feeble flesh,
    Poured out His cries and tears;
  And, in His measure, feels afresh
    What every member bears.

4 He'll never quench the smoking flax,
    But raise it to a flame;
  The bruiséd reed He never breaks,
    Nor scorns the meanest name.

5 Then let our humble faith address
    His mercy and His power;
  We shall obtain delivering grace
    In the distressing hour.
        Rev. Isaac Watts. (1674—1748.) 1709. alt.

321 *"The Incarnate Mystery."* C. M.
1 Cor. i. 22—23.

1 DEAREST of all the names above,
    My Jesus and my God,
  Who can resist Thy heavenly love,
    Or trifle with Thy blood?

2 'Tis by the merits of Thy death
    Thy Father smiles again;
  'Tis by Thine interceding breath
    The Spirit dwells with men.

3 Till God in human flesh I see,
    My thoughts no comfort find:
  The holy, just, and sacred Three
    Are terrors to my mind.

4 But if Immanuel's face appear,
    My hope, my joy, begins:
  His name forbids my slavish fear,
    His grace removes my sins.

5 While Jews on their own law rely,
    And Greeks of wisdom boast,
  I love the incarnate Mystery,
    And there I fix my trust.
        Rev. Isaac Watts. (1674—1748.) 1709.

322 *The Gates opened.* C. M.

1 COME, let us lift our joyful eyes
    Up to the courts above,
  And smile to see our Father there,
    Upon a throne of love.

2 Now we may bow before His feet,
    And venture near the Lord:
  No fiery cherub guards His seat,
    Nor double flaming sword.

3 The peaceful gates of heavenly bliss
    Are opened by the Son;
  High let us raise our notes of praise,
    And reach the almighty throne.

4 To Thee ten thousand thanks we bring,
    Great Advocate on high;
  And glory to the eternal King,
    That lays His fury by.
        Rev. Isaac Watts. 1709 ab.

323 *Seated on the Throne.* C. M.

1 HE who on earth as man was known,
    And bore our sins and pains,
  Now, seated on the eternal throne,
    The God of glory reigns.

CHRIST.

2 His hands the wheels of nature guide
   With an unerring skill,
   And countless worlds, extended wide,
   Obey His sovereign will.

3 While harps unnumbered sound His praise
   In yonder world above,
   His saints on earth admire His ways,
   And glory in His love.

4 When troubles, like a burning sun,
   Beat heavy on their head,
   To this almighty Rock they run,
   And find a pleasing shade.

5 How glorious He, how happy they
   In such a glorious Friend!
   Whose love secures them all the way,
   And crowns them at the end.
   Rev. John Newton. (1725—1807.) 1779. ab.

324 *"Clothed with our Nature still."* C. M.

1 COME, let us join in songs of praise
   To our ascended Priest;
   He entered heaven, with all our names
   Engraven on His breast.

2 Below He washed our guilt away,
   By His atoning blood;
   Now He appears before the throne,
   And pleads our cause with God.

3 Clothed with our nature still, He knows
   The weakness of our frame,
   And how to shield us from the foes
   Which He Himself o'ercame.

4 Nor time, nor distance, e'er shall quench
   The fervors of His love;
   For us He died in kindness here,
   Nor is less kind above.

5 O may we ne'er forget His grace,
   Nor blush to wear His name;
   Still may our hearts hold fast His faith,
   Our mouths His praise proclaim.
   Rev. Alexander Pirie. (—1804.) 1786.

325 *Our double Kindred to Emmanuel.* C. M.
       1 Cor. xv. 47, 49.

1 O MEAN may seem this house of clay,
   Yet 't was the Lord's abode;
   Our feet may mourn this thorny way,
   Yet here Emmanuel trod.

2 This fleshly robe the Lord did wear;
   This watch the Lord did keep;
   These burdens sore the Lord did bear;
   These tears the Lord did weep.

3 O vale of tears no longer sad,
   Wherein the Lord did dwell!
   O happy robe of flesh that clad
   Our own Emmanuel!

4 But not this fleshly robe alone
   Shall link us, Lord, to Thee;
   Not only in the tear and groan
   Shall the dear kindred be.

5 We shall be reckoned for Thine own,
   Because Thy heaven we share,
   Because we sing around Thy throne,
   And Thy bright raiment wear.

6 O mighty grace, our life to live,
   To make our earth divine!
   O mighty grace, Thy heaven to give
   And lift our life to Thine!
   Thomas Hornblower Gill. (1819—) 1860. ab.

326 *To the Lamb that was slain.* C. M.
       Rev. v. 6—12.

1 BEHOLD the glories of the Lamb,
   Amidst His Father's throne:
   Prepare new honors for His name,
   And songs before unknown.

2 Let elders worship at His feet,
   The church adore around,
   With vials full of odors sweet,
   And harps of sweeter sound.

3 Those are the prayers of all the saints,
   And these the hymns they raise:
   Jesus is kind to our complaints,
   He loves to hear our praise.

4 Now to the Lamb that once was slain,
   Be endless blessings paid;
   Salvation, glory, joy remain
   Forever on Thy head.

5 Thou hast redeemed our souls with blood,
   Hast set the prisoners free,
   Hast made us kings and priests to God,
   And we shall reign with Thee.
   Rev. Isaac Watts. 1709. ab.

CHRIST.

327 *Jesu, nostra redemptio.* C. M.

1 O CHRIST, our hope, our heart's desire,
 Redemption's only spring,
 Creator of the world art Thou,
 Its Saviour and its King.

2 How vast the mercy and the love,
 Which laid our sins on Thee,
 And led Thee to a cruel death,
 To set Thy people free!

3 But now the bonds of death are burst,
 The ransom has been paid;
 And Thou art on Thy Father's throne
 In glorious robes arrayed.

4 O may Thy mighty love prevail
 Our sinful souls to spare;
 O may we come before Thy throne,
 And find acceptance there!

Ambrosian. Tr. by Rev. John Chandler. (1806—) 1837. ab.

328 *"Our great High Priest above."* C. M.

1 Now let our cheerful eyes survey
 Our great High Priest above,
 And celebrate His constant care,
 And sympathetic love.

2 Though raised to a superior throne,
 Where angels bow around,
 And high o'er all the shining train
 With matchless honors crowned;

3 The names of all His saints He bears,
 Deep graven on His heart:
 Nor shall the meanest Christian say
 That he hath lost his part.

4 Those characters shall fair abide,
 Our everlasting trust,
 When gems, and monuments, and crowns,
 Are mouldered down to dust.

5 So, gracious Saviour, on my breast
 May Thy dear name be worn,
 A sacred ornament and guard,
 To endless ages borne.

Rev. Philip Doddridge. (1702—1751.) 1755.

329 *"Lord of all."* Acts x. 36. C. M.

1 ALL hail the power of Jesus' name!
 Let angels prostrate fall,
 Bring forth the royal diadem,
 And crown Him Lord of all.

2 Crown Him, ye morning stars of light,
 Who fixed this floating ball;
 Now hail the strength of Israel's might,
 And crown Him Lord of all.

3 Crown Him, ye martyrs of your God,
 Who from His altar call;
 Extol the stem of Jesse's rod,
 And crown Him Lord of all.

4 Ye seed of Israel's chosen race,
 Ye ransomed of the fall,
 Hail Him, who saves you by His grace,
 And crown Him Lord of all.

5 Sinners, whose love can ne'er forget
 The wormwood and the gall,
 Go, spread your trophies at His feet,
 And crown Him Lord of all.

6 Let every kindred, every tribe,
 On this terrestrial ball,
 To Him all majesty ascribe,
 And crown Him Lord of all.

Rev. Edward Perronet. (—1792.) 1780. ab. and alt.

330 *The Lamb worshipped by all Creatures.* C. M.
 Rev. v. 11—13.

1 COME, let us join our cheerful songs
 With angels round the throne;
 Ten thousand thousand are their tongues,
 But all their joys are one.

2 "Worthy the Lamb that died," they cry,
 "To be exalted thus;"
 "Worthy the Lamb," our lips reply,
 "For He was slain for us."

3 Jesus is worthy to receive
 Honor and power divine;
 And blessings, more than we can give,
 Be, Lord, for ever Thine.

4 Let all that dwell above the sky,
 And air, and earth, and seas,
 Conspire to lift Thy glories high,
 And speak Thine endless praise.

5 The whole creation join in one,
 To bless the sacred name
 Of Him that sits upon the throne,
 And to adore the Lamb.

Rev. Isaac Watts. (1674—1748.) 1709.

CHRIST.

331 *"Hosanna to our conquering King."* C. M.

1 HOSANNA to our conquering King,
All hail, incarnate Love!
Ten thousand songs and glories wait
To crown Thy head above.

2 Thy victories, and Thy deathless fame,
Through the wide world shall run,
And everlasting ages sing
The triumphs Thou hast won.
Rev. Isaac Watts. 1709. ab.

332 *The Word made Flesh.* 7.

1 HALLELUJAH! Praise to God
For the love He sheds abroad,
Lightening o'er a world of sin,
Glowing in the heart within:
Hallelujah!

2 For the pristine promise made
E'en in Eden's darkened shade,
For the light of sacrifice
Till the Morning Star should rise:
Hallelujah!

3 For the harp of prophecy,
Singing of Redemption nigh,
For the Branch of Jesse's stem,
For the birth at Bethlehem:
Hallelujah!

4 For the sacred standard spread,
For the life our Pattern led,
For His precepts pure and true,
For His doctrine, like the dew:
Hallelujah!

5 For the crown of thorns He wore,
For the painful cross He bore,
For the dying word He said,
Sealed with blood of sprinkling shed:
Hallelujah!

6 For the radiant rising dawn,
For the sting of death withdrawn,
For the victory gained so well
O'er the grave and over hell:
Hallelujah!

7 For His glorious reign on high,
When He rose from Bethany,
For the heavenly peace He leaves,
For the Comforter He gives:
Hallelujah!

8 For the pledge that we shall rise,
In His likeness, to the skies;
For the merciful decree
That our Friend our Judge shall be:
Hallelujah!
William Ball. 1864. ab. and alt.

333 *"The Man Christ Jesus."* 7.
1 Tim. ii. 5.

1 CHRIST to heaven is gone before
In the body here He wore;
He that as our Brother died,
Is our Brother glorified.

2 All the angels wondering own
'Tis our nature on the throne;
"How He loved them, behold!"
Trembles on the harps of gold.

3 Fear not, ye of little faith,
For He hath abolished death;
Death, no longer now we die,
We but follow Christ on high.

4 And before each fainting one,
Dreading the dark way alone,
Now appear His footsteps bright,
Far diffusing holiest light.

5 As our Shepherd He is there,
With the comfort of His care;
Fear no evil, doubt no more,
Christ to heaven is gone before.
George Rawson. (1807—) 1857.

334 *He rules over all.* 10, 11.

1 YE servants of God, your Master proclaim,
And publish abroad His wonderful Name;
The Name all-victorious of Jesus extol;
His kingdom is glorious, and rules over all.

2 God ruleth on high, almighty to save;
And still He is nigh, His presence we have;
The great congregation His triumph shall sing,
Ascribing salvation to Jesus our King.

3 "Salvation to God who sits on the throne,"
Let all cry aloud, and honor the Son;
The praises of Jesus the angels proclaim,
Fall down on their faces, and worship the Lamb.

CHRIST. THE HOLY SPIRIT.

4 Then let us adore, and give Him His right.
All glory and power, and wisdom and might;
All honor and blessing, with angels above,
And thanks never ceasing, and infinite love.
  Rev. Charles Wesley. (1708—1788.) 1744. ab.

335   *Praise for Salvation.*   10, 11.

1 OUR Saviour alone, the Lord let us bless,
Who reigns on His throne, the Prince of
 our peace ;
Who evermore saves us by shedding His
 blood :
All hail, holy Jesus, our Lord and our God !

2 We thankfully sing Thy glory and praise,
Thou merciful Spring of pity and grace.
Thy kindness forever to men will we tell :
And say our dear Saviour redeemed us
 from hell.

3 Preserve us in love while here we abide :
O never remove Thy presence, nor hide
Thy glorious salvation, till each of us see,
With joy, the blest vision completed in
 Thee !
  Rev. John Cennick. (1717—1755.) 1743. alt.

336   *"He is not here."*   C. P. M.
    Matt. xxviii. 6.

1 COME, see the place where Jesus lay,
And hear angelic watchers say
"He lives, who once was slain :
Why seek the living 'midst the dead?
Remember how the Saviour said
That He would rise again."

2 O joyful sound ! O glorious hour,
When by His own almighty power
He rose, and left the grave !
Now let our songs His triumph tell,
Who burst the bands of death and hell,
And ever lives to save.

3 The First-begotten of the dead,
For us He rose, our glorious Head,
Immortal life to bring ;
What though the saints like Him shall die,
They share their Leader's victory,
And triumph with their King.

4 No more they tremble at the grave,
For Jesus will their spirits save,
And raise their slumbering dust :
O risen Lord, in Thee we live,

To Thee our ransomed souls we give,
To Thee our bodies trust.
  Rev. Thomas Kelly. (1769—1855.) 1806. ab. and alt.

337   *Looking unto Jesus.*   C. P. M.
    John xiv. 1.

1 CHILDREN of light, arise and shine !
Your birth, your hopes, are all divine,
 Your home is in the skies.
O then, for heavenly glory born,
Look down on all with holy scorn
 That earthly spirits prize.

2 With Christ, with glory full in view,
O what is all the world to you?
 What is it all but loss?
Come on, then, cleave no more to earth,
Nor wrong your high celestial birth,
 Ye pilgrims of the cross.

3 The cross is ours, we bear it now ;
But did He not beneath it bow,
 And suffer there at last ?
All that we feel can Jesus tell ;
His gracious soul remembers well
 The sorrows of the past.

4 O blessèd Lord, we yet shall reign,
Redeemed from sorrow, sin, and pain,
 And walk with Thee in white.
We suffer now, but O, at last
We'll bless Thee, Lord, for all the past,
 And own our cross was light.
  Sir Edward Denny. (1796—) 1839.

338   *"The Lord is King."*   H. M.

1 REJOICE, the Lord is King,
 Your Lord and King adore ;
Mortals, give thanks and sing,
 And triumph evermore ;
Lift up your heart, lift up your voice,
Rejoice, again I say, rejoice.

2 Jesus the Saviour reigns,
 The God of truth and love ;
When He had purged our stains,
 He took His seat above ;
Lift up your heart, lift up your voice,
Rejoice, again I say, rejoice.

3 His kingdom cannot fail,
 He rules o'er earth and heaven ;
The keys of death and hell
 Are to our Jesus given ;

Lift up your heart, lift up your voice,
Rejoice, again I say, rejoice.

4 He sits at God's right hand
    Till all His foes submit,
    And bow to His command,
    And fall beneath His feet:
Lift up your heart, lift up your voice,
Rejoice, again I say, rejoice.

5 He all His foes shall quell,
    Shall all our sins destroy,
    And every bosom swell
    With pure seraphic joy:
Lift up your heart, lift up your voice,
Rejoice, again I say, rejoice.

6 Rejoice in glorious hope;
    Jesus, the Judge, shall come,
    And take His servants up
    To their eternal home:
We soon shall hear the archangel's voice,
The trump of God shall sound. Rejoice.
Rev. Charles Wesley. 1748

339   *"I will send Him unto you."*   H. M.
John xvi. 7.

1 SINNERS, lift up your hearts,
    The promise to receive:
Jesus Himself imparts,
    He comes in man to live;
The Holy Ghost to man is given;
Rejoice in God sent down from heaven.

2 Jesus is glorified,
    And gives the Comforter.
His Spirit, to reside
    In all His members here:
The Holy Ghost to man is given;
Rejoice in God sent down from heaven.

3 To make an end of sin,
    And Satan's works destroy,
He brings His kingdom in,
    Peace, righteousness, and joy:
The Holy Ghost to man is given;
Rejoice in God sent down from heaven.

4 Sent down to make us meet
    To see His glorious Face,
And grant us each a seat
    In that thrice happy place,
The Holy Ghost to man is given;
Rejoice in God sent down from heaven.

5 From heaven He shall once more
    Triumphantly descend,
And all His saints restore
    To joys that never end:
Then, then, when all our joys are given,
Rejoice in God, rejoice in heaven.
Rev. John Wesley. (1703—1791.) 1746. ab.

340   *The Comforter comes.*   8, 6, 8, 4.
John xvi. 7.

1 OUR blest Redeemer, ere He breathed
    His tender last farewell,
A Guide, a Comforter, bequeathed
    With us to dwell.

2 He came in semblance of a dove
    With sheltering wings outspread,
The holy balm of peace and love
    On earth to shed.

3 He came sweet influence to impart,
    A gracious, willing guest,
While He can find one humble heart
    Wherein to rest.

4 And His that gentle voice we hear
    Soft as the breath of even,
That checks each tho't, that calms each fear,
    And speaks of heaven.

5 And every virtue we possess,
    And every victory won,
And every thought of holiness
    Are His alone.

6 Spirit of purity and grace,
    Our weakness, pitying, see:
O make our hearts Thy dwelling-place,
    And meet for Thee.
Miss Harriet Auber. (1773—1862.) 1829. ab.

341   *Pentecost.*   C. M.
Acts ii. 1—4.

1 No track is on the sunny sky,
    No footprints on the air;
Jesus hath gone; the face of earth
    Is desolate and bare.

2 That Upper Room is heaven on earth:
    Within its precincts lie
All that earth has of faith, or hope,
    Or heaven-born charity.

3 He comes! He comes! that mighty Breath
    From heaven's eternal shores;
His uncreated freshness fills
    His Bride, as she adores.

4 Earth quakes before that rushing blast,
 Heaven echoes back the sound,
 And mightily the tempest wheels
 That Upper Room around.

5 One moment—and the Spirit hung
 O'er all with dread desire;
 Then broke upon the heads of all
 In cloven tongues of fire.

6 The Spirit came into the Church
 With His unfailing power;
 He is the living Heart that beats
 Within her at this hour.

7 Most tender Spirit, mighty God,
 Sweet must Thy presence be,
 If loss of Jesus can be gain,
 So long as we have Thee!
 *Rev. Frederick William Faber. (1814—1863.) 1849.
 ab. and sl. alt.*

342   *Pentecost.*   C. M.

1 WHEN God of old came down from heaven,
 In power and wrath He came;
 Before His feet the clouds were riven,
 Half darkness and half flame.

2 But when He came the second time,
 He came in power and love;
 Softer than gale at morning prime,
 Hovered His holy Dove.

3 The fires, that rushed on Sinai down
 In sudden torrents dread,
 Now gently light, a glorious crown,
 On every sainted head.

4 And, as on Israel's awe-struck ear
 The voice exceeding loud,
 The tramp that angels quake to hear,
 Thrilled from the deep dark cloud;

5 So, when the Spirit of our God
 Came down His flock to find,
 A voice from heaven was heard abroad,
 A rushing mighty wind.

6 It fills the Church of God, it fills
 The sinful world around;
 Only in stubborn hearts and wills
 No place for it is found.

7 Come, Lord, come Wisdom, Love, and Power
 Open our ears to hear;
 Let us not miss the accepted hour;
 Save, Lord, by love or fear.
 Rev. John Keble. (1792—1866.) 1827. ab.

343   *Prayer to the Spirit.*   C. M.

1 SPIRIT Divine, attend our prayers,
 And make this house Thy home;
 Descend with all Thy gracious powers,
 O come, Great Spirit, come!

2 Come as the light; to us reveal
 Our sinfulness and woe;
 And lead us in those paths of life
 Where all the righteous go.

3 Come as the fire, and purge our hearts,
 Like sacrificial flame;
 Let our whole soul an offering be
 To our Redeemer's name.

4 Come as the dew, and sweetly bless
 This consecrated hour;
 May barrenness rejoice to own
 Thy fertilizing power.

5 Come as the wind, with rushing sound,
 With Pentecostal grace;
 And make the great salvation known,
 Wide as the human race.

6 Spirit Divine, attend our prayers,
 Make a lost world Thy home;
 Descend with all Thy gracious powers,
 O come, Great Spirit, come!
 Rev. Andrew Reed. (1787—1862.) 1843. ab.

344   *The Promise fulfilled.*   C. M.

1 LET songs of praises fill the sky;
 Christ, our ascended Lord,
 Sends down His Spirit from on high,
 According to His word.

2 The Spirit, by His heavenly breath,
 New life creates within;
 He quickens sinners from the death
 Of trespasses and sin.

3 The things of Christ the Spirit takes,
 And shows them unto men;
 The fallen soul His temple makes,
 God's image stamps again.

4 Come, Holy Spirit, from above,
 With Thy celestial fire;
 Come, and with flames of zeal and love,
 Our hearts and tongues inspire.
 Rev. Thomas Cotterill. (1779—1823.) 1819. ab.

345 *The Spirit entreated to come* 8, 7. D.

1 COME, Thou everlasting Spirit,
    Bring to every thankful mind
  All the Saviour's dying merit,
    All His sufferings for mankind:
  True recorder of His passion,
    Now the living faith impart;
  Now reveal His great salvation,
    Preach His gospel to our heart.

2 Come, Thou Witness of His dying,
    Come, Remembrancer divine;
  Let us feel Thy power applying
    Christ to every soul, and mine;
  Let us groan Thine inward groaning,
    Look on Him we pierced, and grieve,
  All receive the grace atoning,
    All the sprinkled blood receive.
            Rev. Charles Wesley. (1708—1788.) 1745.

346 *Prayer for Light.* 8, 7. D.

1 LIGHT of those whose dreary dwelling
    Borders on the shades of death,
  Come, and by Thy love's revealing
    Dissipate the clouds beneath:
  The new heaven and earth's Creator,
    In our deepest darkness rise,
  Scattering all the night of nature,
    Pouring eye-sight on our eyes.

2 Still we wait for Thine appearing;
    Life and joy Thy beams impart,
  Chasing all our fears, and cheering
    Every poor benighted heart:
  Come, and manifest the favor
    God hath for our ransomed race;
  Come, Thou glorious God and Saviour,
    Come, and bring the gospel-grace.

3 Save us in Thy great compassion,
    O thou mild, pacific Prince,
  Give the knowledge of salvation,
    Give the pardon of our sins;
  By Thine all-restoring merit,
    Every burdened soul release,
  Every weary, wandering spirit
    Guide into Thy perfect peace.
                Rev. Charles Wesley. 1745.

347 *"Love Divine."* 8, 7. D.

1 LOVE Divine, all love excelling,
    Joy of heaven, to earth come down;
  Fix in us Thy humble dwelling,
    All Thy faithful mercies crown:
  Jesus, Thou art all compassion,
    Pure, unbounded love Thou art;
  Visit us with Thy salvation,
    Enter every trembling heart.

2 Breathe, O breathe, Thy loving Spirit
    Into every troubled breast;
  Let us all in Thee inherit,
    Let us find that second rest;
  Take away our power of sinning,
    Alpha and Omega be,
  End of faith, as its beginning,
    Set our hearts at liberty.

3 Come, almighty to deliver,
    Let us all Thy life receive;
  Suddenly return, and never,
    Never more Thy temples leave.
  Thee we would be always blessing,
    Serve Thee as Thy hosts above,
  Pray, and praise Thee without ceasing,
    Glory in Thy perfect love.

4 Finish then Thy new creation,
    Pure, and spotless let us be;
  Let us see Thy great salvation
    Perfectly restored in Thee:
  Changed from glory into glory,
    Till in heaven we take our place,
  Till we cast our crowns before Thee,
    Lost in wonder, love, and praise.
            Rev. Charles Wesley. 1747. sl. alt.

348 *The Spirit still given.* 8, 7. D.

1 DAY divine, when sudden streaming
    To the Lord's first lovers came
  Glory new and treasures teeming,
    Mighty gifts and tongues of flame!
  Day to happy souls commended,
    When the Holy Ghost was given,
  When the Comforter descended,
    And brought down the joy of heaven!

2 Hath the Holy Ghost been holden
    By those ancient saints alone?
  Only may the ages olden
    Call the Comforter their own?
  Wonders we may not inherit,
    Signs and tongues we may not crave;
  Yet we still receive the Spirit,
    Still the Comforter we have.

THE HOLY SPIRIT.

3 Sure the Holy Ghost is dwelling
   With the souls that holier grow;
   Signs most glorious, all excelling,
   Witness brightest we may show:
   Hope that makes ashamèd never,
   Perfect peace that passeth thought,
   Mighty joy that stayeth ever,
   Love Divine that changeth not.
   Thomas Hornblower Gill. (1819—) 1860. ab.

349 *The Descent of the Spirit.* S. M.

1 LORD God, the Holy Ghost,
   In this accepted hour,
   As on the day of Pentecost,
   Descend in all Thy power.

2 We meet with one accord
   In our appointed place,
   And wait the promise of our Lord,
   The Spirit of all grace.

3 Like mighty rushing wind
   Upon the waves beneath,
   Move with one impulse every mind,
   One soul, one feeling breathe.

4 The young, the old inspire
   With wisdom from above:
   And give us hearts and tongues of fire
   To pray, and praise, and love.

5 Spirit of light, explore,
   And chase our gloom away,
   With lustre shining more and more
   Unto the perfect day.

6 Spirit of truth, be Thou,
   In life and death, our guide;
   O Spirit of adoption, *now*
   May we be sanctified.
   James Montgomery. (1771—1854) 1819, 1825.

350 *Invocation.* S. M.

1 COME, Holy Spirit, come,
   With energy divine,
   And on this poor benighted soul,
   With beams of mercy shine.

2 From the celestial hills,
   Light, life, and joy dispense;
   And may I daily, hourly feel
   Thy quickening influence.

3 O melt this frozen heart,
   This stubborn will subdue;
   Each evil passion overcome,
   And form me all anew.

4 The profit will be mine,
   But Thine shall be the praise;
   Cheerful to Thee will I devote
   The remnant of my days.
   Rev. Benjamin Beddome. (1717—1795.) 1818.

351 *Prayer for the Spirit.* S. M.

1 O FOR the happy hour
   When God will hear our cry,
   And send, with a reviving power,
   His Spirit from on high.

2 We meet, we sing, we pray,
   We listen to the word,
   In vain:—we see no cheering ray,
   No cheering voice is heard.

3 While many crowd Thy house,
   How few, around Thy board,
   Meet to record their solemn vows,
   And bless Thee as their Lord.

4 Thou, Thou alone canst give
   Thy gospel sure success,
   And bid the dying sinner live
   Anew in holiness.

5 Come, with Thy power divine,
   Spirit of life and love;
   Then shall our people all be Thine,
   Our church like that above.
   Rev. George Washington Bethune. (1805—1862)
   1843, 1848. ab.

352 *To the Holy Ghost.* S. M.

1 COME, Holy Spirit, come,
   Let Thy bright beams arise,
   Dispel the darkness from our minds,
   And open all our eyes.

2 Revive our drooping faith,
   Our doubts and fears remove,
   And kindle in our breasts the flame
   Of never-dying love.

3 Convince us of our sin,
   Then lead to Jesus' blood,
   And to our wondering view reveal
   The secret love of God.

4 Show us that loving Man
   That rules the courts of bliss,
  The Lord of Hosts, the Mighty God,
   The Eternal Prince of Peace.

5 'T is Thine to cleanse the heart,
   To sanctify the soul,
  To pour fresh life in every part,
   And new-create the whole.

6 Dwell therefore in our hearts,
   Our minds from bondage free;
  Then we shall know, and praise, and love
   The Father, Son, and Thee.
            Rev. Joseph Hart. (1712—1768.) 1759. ab.

353   *Leadings of the Spirit.*   S. M.

1 THAT we might walk with God,
   He forms our hearts anew;
  Takes us, like Ephraim, by the hand,
   And teaches us to go.

2 He by His Spirit leads
   In paths before unknown;
  The work to be performed is ours,
   The strength is all His own.

3 Assisted by His grace,
   We still pursue our way;
  And hope at last to reach the prize,
   Secure in endless day.

4 'T is He that works to will,
   'T is He that works to do;
  His is the power by which we act,
   His be the glory too.
            Rev. Benjamin Beddome. 1818.

354   *Invocation to the Holy Spirit.*   S. M.

1 BLEST Comforter Divine,
   Whose rays of heavenly love
  Amid our gloom and darkness shine,
   And point our souls above;

2 Thou, who with "still small voice,"
   Dost stop the sinner's way,
  And bid the mourning saint rejoice,
   Though earthly joys decay;

3 Thou, whose inspiring breath
   Can make the cloud of care,
  And e'en the gloomy vale of death,
   A smile of glory wear;

4 Thou, who dost fill the heart
   With love to all our race;
  Blest Comforter, to us impart
   The blessings of Thy grace.
       Mrs. Lydia Howard Huntley Sigourney. (1791—1865.) 1824.

355   *The witnessing and sealing Spirit.*   C. M.
             Rom. viii. 14, 16. Eph. i. 13, 14.

1 WHY should the children of a King
   Go mourning all their days?
  Great Comforter, descend and bring
   Some tokens of Thy grace.

2 Dost Thou not dwell in all the saints,
   And seal the heirs of heaven?
  When wilt Thou banish my complaints,
   And show my sins forgiven?

3 Assure my conscience of her part
   In the Redeemer's blood;
  And bear Thy witness with my heart,
   That I am born of God.

4 Thou art the earnest of His love,
   The pledge of joys to come;
  And Thy soft wings, celestial Dove,
   Will safe convey me home.
            Rev. Isaac Watts. (1674—1748.) 1709.

356   *The Spirit's Influences desired.*   C. M.
                   Acts x. 44.

1 GREAT Father of each perfect gift,
   Behold Thy servants wait;
  With longing eyes and lifted hands,
   We flock around Thy gate.

2 O shed abroad that royal gift,
   Thy Spirit from above,
  To bless our eyes with sacred light,
   And fire our hearts with love.

3 Blest earnest of eternal joy,
   Declare our sins forgiven;
  And bear, with energy divine,
   Our raptured thoughts to heaven.

4 Diffuse, O God, those copious showers,
   That earth its fruit may yield,
  And change the barren wilderness
   To Carmel's flowery field.
       Rev. Philip Doddridge. (1702—1751.) 1755. ab.

THE HOLY SPIRIT.

357 *"O fons amoris, Spiritus."* C. M.

1 O HOLY Spirit, Fount of love,
   Blest source of gifts divine,
Kindle, we pray Thee, from above
   The inmost souls of Thine.

2 Shed in each faithful heart abroad
   Love that doth all excel;
That God in us, and we in God,
   For evermore may dwell.
Prof. Charles Coffin (1676—1740.) 1736. ab.
Tr. by Miss Jane E. Leeson. 1864.

358 *"The Comforter is come."* C. M.

1 MY God, my reconciled God,
   Creator of my peace:
Thee will I love, and praise, and sing,
   Till life and breath shall cease.

2 My soul doth magnify the Lord,
   My spirit doth rejoice
In God my Saviour, and my God;
   I hear His joyful voice.

3 I need not go abroad for joy,
   Who have a feast at home;
My sighs are turned into songs,
   The Comforter is come.

4 Down from above the blessed Dove
   Is come into my breast,
To witness God's eternal love:
   This is my heavenly feast.

5 My God, my reconciled God,
   Creator of my peace:
Thee will I love, and praise, and sing,
   Till life and breath shall cease.
Rev. John Mason. (—1694.) 1683. ab.

Breathing after the Holy Spirit. C. M.

1 COME, Holy Spirit, heavenly Dove,
   With all Thy quickening powers,
Kindle a flame of sacred love
   In these cold hearts of ours.

2 Look how we grovel here below,
   Fond of these trifling toys:
Our souls can neither fly nor go
   To reach eternal joys.

3 In vain we tune our formal songs,
   In vain we strive to rise;
Hosannas languish on our tongues,
   And our devotion dies.

4 Dear Lord, and shall we ever live
   At this poor dying rate,
Our love so faint, so cold to Thee,
   And Thine to us so great?

5 Come, Holy Spirit, heavenly Dove,
   With all Thy quickening powers,
Come, shed abroad a Saviour's love,
   And that shall kindle ours.
Rev. Isaac Watts. (1674—1748.) 1709.

360 *"Thy Spirit in our Heart."* C. M.

1 ENTHRONED on high, Almighty Lord,
   Thy Holy Ghost send down;
Fulfil in us Thy faithful word,
   And all Thy mercies crown.

2 Though on our heads no tongues of fire
   Their wondrous powers impart,
Grant, Saviour, what we more desire,
   Thy Spirit in our heart.

3 Spirit of life, and light, and love,
   Thy heavenly influence give;
Quicken our souls, born from above,
   In Christ that we may live.

4 To our benighted minds reveal
   The glories of His grace,
And bring us where no clouds conceal
   The brightness of His face.

5 His love within us shed abroad,
   Life's ever-springing well;
Till God in us, and we in God,
   In love eternal dwell.
Rev. Thomas Haweis. (1732—1820.) 1792.

361 *For a well-grounded Hope of Salvation.* C. M.

1 ETERNAL Spirit, Source of truth,
   Our contrite hearts inspire;
Kindle the flame of heavenly love,
   And feed the pure desire.

2 'T is Thine to soothe the sorrowing mind,
   With Satan's yoke oppressed;
'T is Thine to bid the dying live,
   And give the weary rest.

3 Subdue the power of every sin,
   Whate'er that sin may be;
That we, in singleness of heart,
   May worship only Thee.

4 Then with our spirits witness bear
  That we're the sons of God,
  Redeemed from sin, and death, and hell,
  Through Christ's atoning blood.
      Rev. Joseph Hart. (1712—1768.) 1759. much alt.
      Rev. Thomas Cotterill. (1779—1823.) 1810. ab.

362   "*Veni Creator Spiritus.*"   L. M.

1 COME, O Creator-Spirit blest,
  And in our souls take up Thy rest;
  Come, with Thy grace and heavenly aid,
  To fill the hearts which Thou hast made.

2 Great Comforter, to Thee we cry;
  O highest gift of God most high,
  O Fount of life, O Fire of love,
  And sweet anointing from above!

3 Kindle our senses from above,
  And make our hearts o'erflow with love;
  With patience firm, and virtue high,
  The weakness of our flesh supply.

4 Far from us drive the foe we dread,
  And grant us Thy true peace instead;
  So shall we not, with Thee for guide,
  Turn from the path of life aside.
      Unknown Author of the 7th or 8th Century.
      Tr. by Rev. Edward Caswall. (1814—) 1849. ab. and alt.

363   *The Operations of the Spirit.*   L. M.

1 ETERNAL Spirit, we confess
  And sing the wonders of Thy grace;
  Thy power conveys our blessings down
  From God the Father and the Son.

2 Enlightened by Thy heavenly ray,
  Our shades and darkness turn to day;
  Thine inward teachings make us know
  Our danger and our refuge too.

3 Thy power and glory work within,
  And break the chains of reigning sin:
  Do our imperious lusts subdue,
  And form our wretched hearts anew.

4 The troubled conscience knows Thy voice;
  Thy cheering words awake our joys;
  Thy words allay the stormy wind,
  And calm the surges of the mind.
      Rev. Isaac Watts. 1709.

364   *Teachings of the Spirit.*   L. M.

1 COME, blessèd Spirit, Source of light,
  Whose power and grace are unconfined.

Dispel the gloomy shades of night,
The thicker darkness of the mind.

2 To mine illumined eyes display
  The glorious truths Thy word reveals;
  Cause me to run the heavenly way;
  The book unfold, and loose the seals.

3 Thine inward teachings make me know
  The mysteries of redeeming love,
  The vanity of things below,
  And excellence of things above.

4 While through this dubious maze I stray,
  Spread, like the sun, Thy beams abroad,
  To show the dangers of the way,
  And guide my feeble steps to God.
      Rev. Benjamin Beddome. (1717—1795.) 1818.

365   *Prayer for Rest in God.*   L. M.

1 COME, Holy Spirit, calm my mind,
  And fit me to approach my God;
  Remove each vain, each worldly thought,
  And lead me to Thy blest abode.

2 Hast Thou imparted to my soul
  A living spark of heavenly fire?
  O kindle now the sacred flame;
  Teach it to burn with pure desire.

3 A brighter faith and hope impart,
  And let me now the Saviour see:
  O soothe and cheer my burdened heart,
  And bid my Spirit rest in Thee.
      Rev. Henry Forster Burder's Coll. 1826.

366   *Prayer for Light and Guidance.*   L. M.

1 COME, Holy Spirit, heavenly Dove,
  My sinful maladies remove:
  Be Thou my Light, be Thou my Guide,
  O'er every thought and step preside.

2 The light of truth to me display,
  That I may know and choose my way;
  Plant holy fear within my heart,
  That I from God may ne'er depart.

3 Conduct me safe, conduct me far
  From every sin and hurtful snare;
  Lead me to God, my final Rest,
  In His enjoyment to be blest.

4 Lead me to Christ, the Living Way,
  Nor let me from His pastures stray;
  Lead me to Heaven, the seat of bliss,
  Where pleasure in perfection is.

5 Lead me to holiness, the road
  That I must take to dwell with God;
  Lead to Thy Word, that rules must give,
  And sure directions how to live.
      Rev. Simon Browne. (1680—1732.) 1720. ab.

367 *The Spirit dwelling in us.* L. M.
       John xiv. 16, 17.

1 SURE the blest Comforter is nigh;
  'Tis He sustains my fainting heart:
  Else would my hope for ever die,
  And every cheering ray depart.

2 When some kind promise glads my soul,
  Do I not find His healing voice
  The tempest of my fears control,
  And bid my drooping powers rejoice?

3 Whene'er to call the Saviour mine,
  With ardent wish my heart aspires,
  Can it be less than power divine,
  That animates these strong desires?

4 And when my cheerful hope can say,
  I love my God, and taste His grace,
  Lord, is it not Thy blissful ray
  Which brings this dawn of sacred peace?

5 Let Thy kind Spirit in my heart
  For ever dwell, O God of love,
  And light and heavenly peace impart,
  Sweet earnest of the joys above.
      Miss Anne Steele. (1717—1778.) 1760. ab.

368 *"Spirit of Mercy, Truth, and Love."* L. M.

1 SPIRIT of mercy, truth, and love,
  O shed Thine influence from above;
  And still through endless time convey
  The wonders of this sacred day.

2 In every clime, by every tongue,
  Be God's surpassing glory sung;
  Let all the listening earth be taught
  The wonders by our Saviour wrought.

3 Unfailing Comfort, Heavenly Guide,
  Still in our longing hearts abide;
  Still let mankind Thy blessings prove,
  Spirit of mercy, truth, and love.
      Rev. R. W. Kyle. 1775.

369 *Prayer for Peace and Rest.* 7.

1 GRACIOUS Spirit, Dove Divine,
  Let Thy light within me shine;
  All my guilty fears remove,
  Fill me full of heaven and love.

2 Speak Thy pardoning grace to me,
  Set the burdened sinner free,
  Lead me to the Lamb of God,
  Wash me in His precious blood.

3 Life and peace to me impart,
  Seal salvation on my heart,
  Breathe Thyself into my breast,
  Earnest of immortal rest.

4 Let me never from Thee stray,
  Keep me in the narrow way,
  Fill my soul with joy divine,
  Keep me, Lord, forever Thine.
      John Stocker. 1776. ab.

370 *With Light, with Power, with Joy.* 7.

1 HOLY GHOST, with light divine,
  Shine upon this heart of mine;
  Chase the shades of night away,
  Turn the darkness into day.

2 Holy Ghost, with power divine,
  Cleanse this guilty heart of mine;
  Long has sin, without control,
  Held dominion o'er my soul.

3 Holy Ghost, with joy divine,
  Cheer this saddened heart of mine;
  Bid my many woes depart,
  Heal my wounded, bleeding heart.

4 Holy Spirit, all Divine,
  Dwell within this heart of mine,
  Cast down every idol-throne;
  Reign supreme, and reign alone.
      Rev. Andrew Reed. (1787—1862.) 1843. ab.

371 *"Hail the joyful Day's Return."* 7.

1 HAIL the joyful day's return,
  Hail the Pentecostal morn,
  Morn when our ascended Head
  On His Church His Spirit shed.
  Like to cloven tongues of flame
  On the twelve the Spirit came;
  Tongues, that earth may hear the call;
  Fire, that love may burn in all.

2 Hear the speech before unknown;
  Trembling crowds the wonder own:
  What though hardened some abide,
  And the holy work deride?

THE HOLY SPIRIT.

Lord, to Thee Thy people bend,
Unto us Thy Spirit send:
Blessings of this sacred day
Grant us, dearest Lord, we pray.

3 Thou who didst our fathers guide,
With their children still abide;
Grant us pardon, grant us peace,
Till our earthly wanderings cease.
To the Father praises sing,
Praise to Christ, our risen King,
Praise to Thee, the Lord of love,
Blessed Spirit, Holy Dove.
Robert Campbell. (—1868.) 1850.

372 *"Granted is the Saviour's Prayer."*
1 GRANTED is the Saviour's prayer,
Sent the gracious Comforter,
Promise of our parting Lord,
Jesus, to His heaven restored.

2 Christ, who now gone up on high,
Captive leads captivity,
While His foes from Him receive
Grace, that God with man may live.

3 God, the everlasting God,
Makes with mortals His abode;
Whom the heavens cannot contain,
He vouchsafes to dwell in man.

4 Never will He thence depart,
Inmate of a humble heart;
Carrying on His work within,
Striving till He cast out sin.

5 There He helps our feeble moans,
Deepens our imperfect groans;
Intercedes in silence there,
Sighs the unutterable prayer.

6 Come, divine and peaceful Guest,
Enter our devoted breast;
Holy Ghost, our hearts inspire,
Kindle there the gospel fire.

7 Crown the agonizing strife,
Principle and Lord of life:
Life divine in us renew,
Thou the Gift and Giver too!
Rev. Charles Wesley. (1708—1788.) 1739. ab.

373 *"Dwell with me."*
1 GRACIOUS Spirit, dwell with me;
I myself would gracious be,
And with words that help and heal
Would Thy life in mine reveal,
And with actions bold and meek
Would for Christ my Saviour speak.

2 Truthful Spirit, dwell with me;
I myself would truthful be,
And with wisdom kind and clear
Let Thy life in mine appear,
And with actions brotherly
Speak my Lord's sincerity.

3 Tender Spirit, dwell with me;
I myself would tender be,
Shut my heart up like a flower
At temptation's darksome hour,
Open it when shines the sun,
And His love by fragrance own.

4 Silent Spirit, dwell with me;
I myself would quiet be,
Quiet as the growing blade
Which through earth its way has made;
Silently, like morning light,
Putting mists and chills to flight.

5 Mighty Spirit, dwell with me;
I myself would mighty be,
Mighty so as to prevail
Where unaided man must fail,
Ever by a mighty hope
Pressing on and bearing up.

6 Holy Spirit, dwell with me;
I myself would holy be;
Separate from sin, I would
Choose and cherish all things good,
And what ever I can be
Give to Him, who gave me Thee!
Rev. Thomas Toke Lynch. (1818—1871.) 1850.

374 *"Veni Sancte Spiritus."* 6, 4.
1 COME, Holy Ghost, in love,
   Shed on us from above
      Thine own bright ray!
   Divinely good Thou art;
   Thy sacred gifts impart
   To gladden each sad heart:
      O come to-day!

2 Come, tenderest Friend, and best,
Our most delightful guest,
  With soothing power;
Rest, which the weary know,
Shade, 'mid the noontide glow,
Peace, when deep griefs o'erflow,
  Cheer us, this hour!

3 Come, Light serene, and still
Our inmost bosoms fill;
  Dwell in each breast;
We know no dawn but Thine,
Send forth Thy beams divine,
On our dark souls to shine,
  And make us blest!

4 Exalt our low desires;
Extinguish passion's fires;
  Heal every wound;
Our stubborn spirits bend;
Our icy coldness end;
Our devious steps attend,
  While heavenward bound.

5 Come, all the faithful bless;
Let all who Christ confess,
  His praise employ;
Give virtue's rich reward;
Victorious death accord,
And, with our glorious Lord,
  Eternal joy!
    Robert II, King of France. (972—1031.)
    Tr. by Rev. Ray Palmer. (1808—) 1858.

375   *"Come, O promised Comforter."*   7. 6 l.

1 COME, O promised Comforter;
Light upon our darkness pour.
Father of the poor Thou art;
Then to us Thy gifts impart.
Light of everlasting Day!
Lord, direct us on our way.

2 Consolation all divine,
Blessed Comforter, is Thine;
Be our strength in weariness;
Thou the weeping heart dost bless;
Sweet repose in every toil,
Thou dost all our griefs beguile.

3 Lord, Thy perfect gifts bestow
On the fold of Christ below;
Crown our days with heavenly grace,
Help us when we close our race;

Help us when we look to Thee;
Grant us endless joy to see.
    Rev. Arthur Tozer Russell. (1806—) 1848, 1851.

376   *"Holy Ghost, the Infinite."*   7. 5.

1 HOLY GHOST, the infinite,
Shine upon our nature's night
With Thy blessed inward light,
  Comforter Divine!

2 We are sinful, cleanse us, Lord;
We are faint, Thy strength afford;
Lost, until by Thee restored,
  Comforter Divine!

3 Like the dew, Thy peace distil;
Guide, subdue our wayward will,
Things of Christ unfolding still,
  Comforter Divine!

4 In us, for us, intercede,
And with voiceless groaning plead
Our unutterable need,
  Comforter Divine!

5 In us "Abba, Father," cry,
Earnest of our bliss on high,
Seal of immortality,
  Comforter Divine!

6 Search for us the depths of God;
Bear us up the starry road,
To the height of Thine abode,
  Comforter Divine!
    George Rawson. (1807—) 1853. alt.

377   *"Holy, heavenly Love."*   7. 5.

1 GRACIOUS Spirit, Holy Ghost,
Taught by Thee, we covet most,
Of Thy gifts at Pentecost,
  Holy, heavenly Love.

2 Love is kind, and suffers long,
Love is meek, and thinks no wrong,
Love than death itself more strong:
  Give us heavenly Love.

3 Prophecy will fade away,
Melting in the light of day;
Love will ever with us stay:
  Give us heavenly Love.

4 Faith will vanish into sight,
Hope be emptied in delight;

Love in heaven will shine more bright:
Give us heavenly Love.

5 Faith and Hope and Love we see
Joining hand in hand agree;
But the greatest of the three,
And the best, is Love.
Bp. Christopher Wordsworth. (1807—) 1862. ab. and alt.

378   *A Prayer to the Holy Ghost.*

1 THOU who like the wind dost come,
Come to me; but ne'er depart:
Blessed Spirit, make Thy home
In my thankful heart.

2 Answer not with tongues of light;
Brood not o'er me like a dove;
Fall upon me in Thy might;
Fill me with Thy love.

3 Sin has ruled me; set me free.
Sin has scourged me; bring me rest.
Help my fainting soul to flee
To my Saviour's breast.

4 Tell me much of cleansing blood;
Show me sin, but sin forgiven:
Step by step, where Christ has trod,
Help me home to heaven.
Rev. Hervey Doddridge Ganse. (1822—) 1873.

379   *"Come, Holy Ghost."*   L. M. 6l.

1 COME, Holy Ghost, all quickening fire,
Come, and in me delight to rest;
Drawn by the lure of strong desire,
O come and consecrate my breast;
The temple of my soul prepare,
And fix Thy sacred presence there.

2 My peace, my life, my comfort now,
My treasure, and my all Thou art;
True Witness of my sonship Thou,
Engraving pardon on my heart:
Seal of my sins in Christ forgiven,
Earnest of love, and pledge of heaven.

3 Come, then, my God, mark out Thine heir,
Of heaven a larger earnest give,
With clearer light Thy witness bear;
More sensibly within me live:
Let all my powers Thy entrance feel,
And deeper stamp Thyself the Seal.
Rev. Charles Wesley. (1708—1788) 1739. ab.

380   *"Veni Creator Spiritus."*   L. M. 6l.

1 COME, Holy Ghost, our souls inspire,
And lighten with celestial fire;
Thou the anointing Spirit art,
Who dost Thy seven-fold gifts impart:
Thy blessed unction from above
Is comfort, life, and fire of love.

2 Enable with perpetual light
The dullness of our blinded sight;
Anoint and cheer our soiled face
With the abundance of Thy grace;
Keep far our foes, give peace at home;
Where Thou art guide, no ill can come.

3 Teach us to know the Father, Son,
And Thee, of both, to be but one;
That through the ages all along,
This still may be our endless song:
All praise, with all the heavenly host,
To Father, Son, and Holy Ghost!
Unknown Author of the 7th or 8th century.
Tr. by Bp. John Cosin. (1594—1672.) 1627. alt.

381   *"Come, condescending Spirit, come."*   L. M. 6l.

1 ETERNAL Spirit, Source of light,
Enlivening, consecrating Fire,
Descend, and with celestial heat
Our dull, our frozen hearts inspire;
Our souls refine, our dross consume:
Come, condescending Spirit, come.

2 In our cold breast, O strike a spark
Of the pure flame which seraphs feel;
Nor let us wander in the dark,
Or lie benumbed and stupid still:
Come, vivifying Spirit, come,
And make our hearts Thy constant home.

3 Whatever guilt and madness dare,
We would not quench the heavenly fire;
Our hearts as fuel we prepare,
Though in the flame we should expire;
Our breasts expand to make Thee room:
Come, purifying Spirit, come.

4 Let pure devotion's fervors rise;
Let every pious passion glow;
O let the raptures of the skies
Kindle in our cold hearts below:
Come, condescending Spirit, come,
And make our souls Thy constant home.
Rev. Samuel Davies (1724-1761.) 1769.

382   "*Veni Sancte Spiritus.*"   7. 3 l.

1 HOLY Spirit, Lord of light,
From Thy clear celestial height,
   Thy pure beaming radiance give.

2 Come, Thou Father of the poor,
Come, with treasures which endure,
   Come, Thou Light of all that live.

3 Thou, of all consolers best,
Visiting the troubled breast,
   Dost refreshing peace bestow.

4 Thou in toil art comfort sweet,
Pleasant coolness in the heat,
   Solace in the midst of woe.

5 Light immortal, Light divine,
Visit Thou these hearts of Thine,
   And our inmost being fill.

6 If Thou take Thy grace away,
Nothing pure in man will stay;
   All his good is turned to ill.

7 Heal our wounds, our strength renew,
On our dryness pour Thy dew;
   Wash the stains of guilt away.

8 Bend the stubborn heart and will,
Melt the frozen, warm the chill;
   Guide the steps that go astray.

9 Thou, on those who evermore
Thee confess and Thee adore,
   In Thy sevenfold gifts descend.

10 Give them comfort when they die,
Give them life with Thee on high;
   Give them joys which never end.
       Robert II. King of France. (972—1031.)
       Tr. by Rev. Edward Caswall. (1814—) 1849.

383   "*The Promise of the Father.*"   7. 3 l.
       Acts i. 4.

1 HOLY Ghost that, promised, came
With the Pentecostal flame,
   Comforter, we hail Thy name.

2 For Thy mighty help we call;
On our waiting spirits fall;
   Fill us, cheer us, rule us all.

3 'Neath Thy breath our graces bloom;
Flee our wintry shades and gloom;
   Come! our hearts prepare Thee room.

4 If but Thou within us move,
We shall mount on wings of love,
   Joyous as the hosts above.

5 O what raptures may we feel,
If but Thou our eyes unseal,
   And the things of Christ reveal.

6 Blessed Helper, by Thee led,
On, our willing feet shall tread,
   Till we see our glorious Head.

7 Then, immortal years begun,
While the eternal circuits run,
   Praise, all Heaven, the Three in One!
       Rev. Ray Palmer, (1808—) 1873.

384   "*Veni Creator Spiritus.*"   L. M. 6 l.

1 CREATOR Spirit, by whose aid
The world's foundations first were laid,
Come, visit every pious mind,
Come, pour Thy joys on human kind;
From sin and sorrow set us free,
And make Thy temples worthy Thee.

2 O Source of uncreated light,
The Father's promised Paraclete;
Thrice holy Fount, thrice holy Fire,
Our hearts with heavenly love inspire;
Come, and Thy sacred unction bring,
To sanctify us while we sing.

3 Plenteous of grace, descend from high,
Rich in Thy sevenfold energy;
Thou Strength of His almighty hand,
Whose power doth heaven and earth command,
Proceeding Spirit, our Defence,
Who dost the gift of tongues dispense.

4 Refine and purge our earthly parts;
But, O inflame and fire our hearts;
Make us eternal truths receive,
And practise all that we believe;
Give us Thyself, that we may see
The Father and the Son, by Thee.

5 Immortal honors, endless fame,
Attend the almighty Father's name!
The Saviour Son be glorified,
Who for lost man's redemption died!
And equal adoration be,
Eternal Paraclete, to Thee!
       Unknown Author of the 7th or 8th century.
       Tr. by John Dryden. (1631—1700.) 1699. ab.

385 *Groaning for the Spirit of Adoption.* L. M. 1.

1 WHEN shall I hear the inward voice,
   Which only faithful souls can hear?
   Pardon, and peace, and heavenly joys
   Attend the promised Comforter:
   He comes! and righteousness divine,
   And Christ, and all with Christ, is mine.

2 O that the Comforter would come,
   Nor visit as a transient guest;
   But fix in me His constant home,
   And keep possession of my breast,
   And make my soul His loved abode,
   The temple of indwelling God.

3 Come, Holy Ghost, my heart inspire;
   Attest that I am born again;
   Come, and baptize me now with fire,
   Or all Thy former gifts are vain.
   I cannot rest in sins forgiven;
   Where is the earnest of my heaven?

4 Where the indubitable seal,
   That ascertains the kingdom mine?
   The powerful stamp I long to feel,
   The signature of love divine:
   O shed it in my heart abroad,
   Fulness of love, of heaven, of God!
          Rev. Charles Wesley (1708—1788) 1740 ab.

386 *The Uses of Scripture* L. P. M.
          Ps. xix.

1 I LOVE the volumes of Thy word:
   What light and joy those leaves afford
   To souls benighted and distressed:
   Thy precepts guide my doubtful way,
   Thy fear forbids my feet to stray,
   Thy promise leads my heart to rest.

2 From the discoveries of Thy law
   The perfect rules of life I draw:
   These are my study and delight;
   Not honey so invites the taste,
   Nor gold that hath the furnace past
   Appears so pleasing to the sight.

3 Thy threatenings wake my slumbering eyes,
   And warn me where my danger lies;
   But 'tis Thy blessed gospel, Lord,
   That makes my guilty conscience clean,
   Converts my soul, subdues my sin,
   And gives a free, but large reward.

4 Who knows the errors of his thoughts?
   My God, forgive my secret faults,
   And from presumptuous sins restrain;
   Accept my poor attempts of praise,
   That I have read Thy book of grace,
   And book of nature, not in vain.
          Rev. Isaac Watts (1674—1748) 1719.

387 *God praised for His Word.* L. P. M.
          Ps. lxi.

1 JOIN, all ye servants of the Lord,
   To praise Him for His sacred word,
   That word, like manna, sent from heaven,
   To all who seek it freely given;
   Its promises our fears remove,
   And fill our hearts with joy and love.

2 It tells us, though oppressed with cares,
   The God of mercy hears our prayers;
   Though steep and rough the appointed way,
   His mighty arm shall be our stay;
   Though deadly foes assail our peace,
   His power shall bid their malice cease.

3 It tells who first inspired our breath,
   Whose blood redeemed our souls from death:
   It tells of grace, grace freely given,
   And shows the path to God and heaven:
   O bless we, then, our gracious Lord
   For all the treasures of His word.
          Miss Harriet Auber (1773—1862) 1829.

388 *To understand God's Word.* L. P. M.

1 SPIRIT of Truth, essential God,
   Who didst Thine ancient saints inspire,
   Shed in their hearts Thy love abroad,
   And touch their hallowed lips with fire,
   Our God from all eternity,
   World without end we worship Thee.

2 Still we believe, Almighty Lord,
   Whose presence fills both earth and heaven,
   The meaning of the written word
   Is still by inspiration given;
   Thou only dost Thyself explain
   The secret mind of God to man.
          Rev Charles Wesley. 1767. ab.

389 *"Holy Bible, Book divine."* 7.

1 HOLY Bible, book Divine,
   Precious treasure, thou art mine;
   Mine to tell me whence I came,
   Mine to teach me what I am.

THE SCRIPTURES.

2 Mine to chide me when I rove,
   Mine to show a Saviour's love;
   Mine art thou to guide my feet,
   Mine to judge, condemn, acquit.

3 Mine to comfort in distress,
   If the Holy Spirit bless;
   Mine to show by living faith
   Man can triumph over death.

4 Mine to tell of joys to come,
   Light and life beyond the tomb;
   Holy Bible, book divine,
   Precious treasure, thou art mine.
                    John Burton (1773—1846.) 1805.

390   *"Immer muss ich wieder lesen."*   7.

1 EVER would I fain be reading,
   In the ancient holy Book,
   Of my Saviour's gentle pleading,
   Truth in every word and look.

2 How when children came He blessed them,
   Suffered no man to reprove;
   Took them in His arms and pressed them
   To His heart with words of love.

3 How He healed the sick and dying,
   Heard the contrite sinner's moan,
   Sought the poor, and stilled their crying,
   Called them brothers and His own.

4 Still I read the ancient story,
   And my joy is ever new;
   How for us He left His glory,
   How He still is kind and true.

5 Let me kneel, my Lord, before Thee,
   Let my heart in tears o'erflow,
   Melted by Thy love adore Thee,
   Blest in Thee mid joy or woe.
              Miss Luise Hensel. (1798—) 1829.
   Tr. by Miss Catherine Winkworth. (1829—) 1858, ab. and alt.

391   *"Walte, walte nah und fern."*   7.

1 SPREAD, O spread, thou mighty word,
   Spread the kingdom of the Lord,
   Wheresoe'er His breath has given
   Life to beings meant for heaven.

2 Tell them how the Father's will
   Made the world, and keeps it still;
   How He sent His Son to save
   All who help and comfort crave.

3 Tell of our Redeemer's love,
   Who for ever doth remove,
   By His holy sacrifice,
   All the guilt that on us lies.

4 Tell them of the Spirit given
   Now, to guide us up to heaven,
   Strong and holy, just and true
   Working both to will and do.

5 Word of life, most pure and strong,
   Lo, for Thee the nations long;
   Spread, till from its dreary night
   All the world awakes to light.

6 Lord of harvest, let there be
   Joy and strength to work for Thee;
   Let the nations, far and near,
   See Thy light, and learn Thy fear.
        Rev. Jonathan Frederic Bahnmaier. (1774—1841.) 1823.
           Tr. by Miss Catherine Winkworth. 1858, ab.

392   *The Scriptures our only Help and Guide.*   C. M.

1 LADEN with guilt, and full of fears,
   I fly to Thee, my Lord,
   And not a glimpse of hope appears,
   But in Thy written word.

2 The volume of my Father's grace,
   Does all my grief assuage;
   Here I behold my Saviour's face
   Almost in every page.

3 Here consecrated water flows,
   To quench my thirst of sin;
   Here the fair tree of knowledge grows,
   Nor danger dwells therein.

4 This is the field where hidden lies
   The pearl of price unknown;
   That merchant is divinely wise,
   Who makes the pearl his own.

5 This is the judge that ends the strife,
   Where wit and reason fail;
   My guide to everlasting life,
   Through all this gloomy vale.

6 O may Thy counsels, mighty God,
   My roving feet command;
   Nor I forsake the happy road,
   That leads to Thy right hand.
              Rev. Isaac Watts. (1674—1748.) 1709.

THE SCRIPTURES.

393 *The Excellency and Variety of Scripture.* C. M.
Ps. cxix. 111.

1 LORD, I have made Thy word my choice,
My lasting heritage:
There shall my noblest powers rejoice,
My warmest thoughts engage.

2 I'll read the histories of Thy love,
And keep Thy laws in sight;
While through the promises I rove
With ever fresh delight.

3 'T is a broad land of wealth unknown,
Where springs of life arise,
Seeds of immortal bliss are sown,
And hidden glory lies.

4 The best relief that mourners have;
It makes our sorrows blest;
Our fairest hope beyond the grave,
And our eternal rest.
Rev. Isaac Watts. 1719.

394 *Instruction from Scripture.* C. M.
Ps. cxix. 9, 30, 105, 113, 160.

1 How shall the young secure their hearts,
And guard their lives from sin?
Thy word the choicest rules imparts,
To keep the conscience clean.

2 When once it enters to the mind,
It spreads such light abroad,
The meanest souls instruction find,
And raise their thoughts to God.

3 'T is like the sun, a heavenly light,
That guides us all the day;
And, through the dangers of the night,
A lamp to lead our way.

4 Thy precepts make me truly wise:
I hate the sinner's road;
I hate my own vain thoughts that rise,
But love Thy law, my God.

5 Thy word is everlasting truth;
How pure is every page!
That holy book shall guide our youth,
And well support our age.
Rev. Isaac Watts. 1719 ab.

395 *The Light and Glory of the Word.* C. M.
Ps. cxix. 130. 2 Cor. iv. 4.

1 THE Spirit breathes upon the word,
And brings the truth to sight;
Precepts and promises afford
A sanctifying light.

2 A glory gilds the sacred page,
Majestic, like the sun;
It gives a light to every age,
It gives, but borrows none.

3 The hand, that gave it, still supplies
The gracious light and heat;
Its truths upon the nations rise,
They rise, but never set.

4 Let everlasting thanks be Thine,
For such a bright display
As makes a world of darkness shine
With beams of heavenly day.

5 My soul rejoices to pursue
The steps of Him I love,
Till glory breaks upon my view,
In brighter worlds above.
William Cowper (1731–1800.) 1779.

396 *The Riches of God's Word.* C. M.
Ps. cxix.

1 FATHER of mercies, in Thy word
What endless glory shines!
Forever be Thy name adored
For these celestial lines.

2 Here may the wretched sons of want
Exhaustless riches find;
Riches above what earth can grant,
And lasting as the mind.

3 Here the Redeemer's welcome voice
Spreads heavenly peace around;
And life and everlasting joys
Attend the blissful sound.

4 O may these heavenly pages be
My ever dear delight;
And still new beauties may I see,
And still increasing light.

5 Divine Instructor, gracious Lord,
Be Thou forever near;
Teach me to love Thy sacred word,
And view my Saviour there.
Miss Anne Steele. (1717–1778.) 1760. ab.

397 *A Lamp, and a Light.* C. M.
Ps. cxix. 105. 2 Tim. iii. 16.

1 How precious is the book divine,
By inspiration given:
Bright as a lamp its doctrines shine,
To guide our souls to heaven.

THE SCRIPTURES.

2 Its light, descending from above,
　Our gloomy world to cheer,
　Displays a Saviour's boundless love,
　And brings His glories near.

3 It shows to man his wandering ways,
　And where his feet have trod ;
　And brings to view the matchless grace
　Of a forgiving God.

4 It sweetly cheers our drooping hearts,
　In this dark vale of tears;
　Life, light, and joy it still imparts,
　And quells our rising fears.

5 This lamp, through all the tedious night
　Of life, shall guide our way,
　Till we behold the clearer light
　Of an eternal day.
　　　　Rev. John Fawcett. (1733—1817.) 1772. ab.

398　　　*God's Word in His Works*　　C. M.
　　　　　　Rom. i. 20

1 THERE is a book, who runs may read,
　Which heavenly truth imparts,
　And all the lore its scholars need,
　Pure eyes and Christian hearts.

2 The works of God, above, below,
　Within us and around,
　Are pages in that book to show
　How God Himself is found.

3 The glorious sky, embracing all,
　Is like the Maker's love,
　Wherewith encompassed, great and small
　In peace and order move.

4 The Saviour lends the light and heat
　That crowns His holy hill ;
　The saints, like stars, around His seat
　Perform their courses still.

5 Thou, who hast given me eyes to see
　And love this sight so fair,
　Give me a heart to find out Thee,
　And read Thee everywhere.
　　　　Rev. John Keble. (1792—1866.) 1827. ab.

399　　　*Delight in Scripture*　　C. M.
　　　　　　Ps. cxix. 97, 148, 54, 175.

1 O HOW I love Thy holy law,
　'T is daily my delight ;
　And thence my meditations draw
　Divine advice by night.

2 My waking eyes prevent the day
　To meditate Thy word ;
　My soul with longing melts away
　To hear Thy gospel, Lord.

3 How doth Thy word my heart engage,
　How well employ my tongue ;
　And in my tiresome pilgrimage
　Yields me a heavenly song.

4 When nature sinks, and spirits droop,
　Thy promises of grace
　Are pillars to support my hope,
　And there I write Thy praise.
　　　　Rev. Isaac Watts. (1674—1748.) 1719. ab.

400　　　*Perfection of Scripture.*　　C. M.
　　　　　　Ps. cxix. 96.

1 LET all the heathen writers join
　To form one perfect book ;
　Great God, if once compared with Thine,
　How mean their writings look !

2 Not the most perfect rules they gave
　Could show one sin forgiven,
　Nor lead a step beyond the grave ;
　But Thine conduct to heaven.

3 Yet men would fain be just with God,
　By works their hands have wrought ;
　But Thy commands, exceeding broad,
　Extend to every thought.

4 Our faith, and love, and every grace,
　Fall far below Thy word ;
　But perfect truth and righteousness
　Dwell only with the Lord.
　　　　Rev. Isaac Watts. 1719. ab.

401　　　*"Lamp of our Feet."*　　C. M.

1 LAMP of our feet, whereby we trace
　Our path when wont to stray ;
　Stream from the Fount of heavenly grace,
　Brook by the traveller's way ;

2 Bread of our souls, whereon we feed,
　True manna from on high ;
　Our guide and chart, wherein we read
　Of realms beyond the sky ;

3 Pillar of fire through watches dark,
　And radiant cloud by day ;
　When waves would whelm our tossing bark
　Our anchor and our stay ;

THE SCRIPTURES.

4 Word of the Everlasting God,
   Will of His glorious Son;
   Without thee how could earth be trod,
   Or heaven itself be won?

5 Lord, grant us all aright to learn
   The wisdom it imparts;
   And to its heavenly teaching turn,
   With simple, child-like hearts.
   Bernard Barton. (1784–1849.) 1827. ab.

402   *"Hail, sacred Truth."*   C. M.

1 HAIL, sacred truth, whose piercing rays
   Dispel the shades of night;
   Diffusing, o'er the mental world,
   The healing beams of light.

2 Jesus, Thy word, with friendly aid,
   Restores our wandering feet;
   Converts the sorrows of the mind
   To joys divinely sweet.

3 O send Thy light and truth abroad,
   In all their radiant blaze;
   And bid the admiring world adore
   The glories of Thy grace.
   John Burtress. 1820.

403   *The two Revelations.*   L. M.
               Ps. xix.

1 THE heavens declare Thy glory, Lord;
   In every star Thy wisdom shines;
   But when our eyes behold Thy word,
   We read Thy name in fairer lines.

2 The rolling sun, the changing light,
   And nights and days, Thy power confess;
   But the blest volume Thou hast writ,
   Reveals Thy justice and Thy grace.

3 Sun, moon, and stars, convey Thy praise
   Round the whole earth, and never stand:
   So when Thy truth began its race,
   It touched and glanced on every land.

4 Nor shall Thy spreading gospel rest,
   Till through the world Thy truth has run;
   Till Christ has all the nations blessed
   That see the light, or feel the sun.

5 Great Sun of Righteousness, arise,
   Bless the dark world with heavenly light;
   Thy gospel makes the simple wise,
   Thy laws are pure, Thy judgments right.
   Rev. Isaac Watts. 1719 ab.

404   *Prophecy and Inspiration.*   L. M.
               2 Tim. iii. 16.

1 'T WAS by an order from the Lord,
   The ancient prophets spoke His word:
   His spirit did their tongues inspire,
   And warmed their hearts with heavenly fire.

2 The works and wonders which they wrought
   Confirmed the messages they brought;
   The prophet's pen succeeds his breath,
   To save the holy words from death.

3 Great God, mine eyes with pleasure look
   On the dear volume of Thy book;
   There my Redeemer's face I see,
   And read His name who died for me.

4 Let the false raptures of the mind
   Be lost, and vanish in the wind;
   Here I can fix my hope secure;
   This is Thy word, and must endure.
   Rev. Isaac Watts. 1709.

405   *God's Word our Guide.*   L. M.

1 GOD, in the gospel of His Son,
   Makes His eternal counsels known:
   Where love in all its glory shines,
   And truth is drawn in fairest lines.

2 Here sinners, of an humble frame,
   May taste His grace, and learn His name;
   May read, in characters of blood,
   The wisdom, power, and grace of God.

3 The prisoner here may break his chains;
   The weary rest from all his pains;
   The captive feel his bondage cease;
   The mourner find the way of peace.

4 Here faith reveals to mortal eyes
   A brighter world beyond the skies;
   Here shines the light which guides our way
   From earth to realms of endless day.

5 O grant us grace, Almighty Lord,
   To read and mark Thy holy word;
   Its truth with meekness to receive,
   And by its holy precepts live.
   Rev. Benjamin Beddome (1717–1795.) 1787. ab. and alt.
   Rev. Thomas Cotterill. (1779–1823.) 1819.

406   *"The starry Firmament."*
               Ps. xix.

1 THE starry firmament on high,
   And all the glories of the sky,
   Yet shine not to Thy praise, O Lord,
   So brightly as Thy written word.

2 The hopes that holy word supplies,
    Its truths divine, and precepts wise,
    In each a heavenly beam I see,
    And every beam conducts to Thee.

3 When, taught by painful proof to know
    That all is vanity below,
    The sinner roams from comfort far,
    And looks in vain for sun or star;

4 Soft gleaming then those lights divine
    Through all the cheerless darkness shine,
    And sweetly to the ravished eye
    Disclose the Day-spring from on high.

5 Almighty Lord, the sun shall fail,
    The moon forget her nightly tale,
    And deepest silence hush on high
    The radiant chorus of the sky;

6 But, fixed for everlasting years,
    Unmoved amid the wreck of spheres,
    Thy word shall shine in cloudless day,
    When heaven and earth have passed away.
    Sir Robert Grant. (1785—1838.) 1815.

407 *"O Word of God incarnate."* 7. 6 l.

1 O WORD of God Incarnate,
    O Wisdom from on high,
    O Truth unchanged, unchanging,
    O Light of our dark sky;
    We praise Thee for the radiance
    That from the hallowed page,
    A lantern to our footsteps,
    Shines on from age to age.

2 The Church from Thee, her Master,
    Received the gift divine;
    And still that light she lifteth
    O'er all the earth to shine.
    It is the golden casket
    Where gems of truth are stored;
    It is the heaven-drawn picture
    Of Thee, the living Word.

3 It floateth like a banner
    Before God's host unfurled;
    It shineth like a beacon
    Above the darkling world;
    It is the chart and compass,
    That o'er life's surging sea,
    Mid mists, and rocks, and quicksands,
    Still guide, O Christ, to Thee.

4 O make Thy Church, dear Saviour,
    A lamp of burnished gold,
    To bear before the nations
    Thy true light, as of old.
    O teach Thy wandering pilgrims
    By this their path to trace,
    Till, clouds and darkness ended,
    They see Thee face to face.
    Rev. William Walsham How. (1823—) 1867.

408 *"Let him come unto Me."* 7. 6 l.
        John. vii. 37.

1 FROM the cross uplifted high,
    Where the Saviour deigns to die,
    What melodious sounds I hear,
    Bursting on my ravished ear:
    "Love's redeeming work is done,
    Come and welcome, sinner, come.

2 "Sprinkled now with blood the throne;
    Why beneath thy burdens groan?
    On My pierced body laid,
    Justice owns the ransom paid:
    Bow the knee, and kiss the Son,
    Come and welcome, sinner, come.

3 "Spread for thee, the festal board
    See with richest dainties stored;
    To thy Father's bosom prest,
    Yet again a child confest,
    Never from His house to roam:
    Come and welcome, sinner, come.

4 "Soon the days of life shall end;
    Lo I come, your Saviour, Friend,
    Safe your spirits to convey
    To the realms of endless day,
    Up to My eternal home:
    Come and welcome, sinner, come.
    Rev. Thomas Haweis. (1732—1820.) 1792.

409 *"Take the Peace the Gospel brings."* 7. 6 l.
        Ps. lxxxv. 2

1 YE that in His courts are found,
    Listening to the joyful sound,
    Lost and helpless as ye are,
    Sons of sorrow, sin, and care:
    Glorify the King of kings,
    Take the peace the gospel brings.

2 Turn to Christ your longing eyes,
    View His bloody sacrifice;
    See, in Him, your sins forgiven,

Pardon, holiness, and heaven:
Glorify the King of kings,
Take the peace the gospel brings.
    Rev. Rowland Hill (1744—1833.) 1774.

410 *The Heart breaking before the Cross.*

1 HEART of stone, relent, relent;
Break, by Jesus' cross subdued!
See His body mangled, rent,
Covered with a gore of blood;
Sinful soul, what hast thou done?
Crucified the Incarnate Son.

2 Yes, thy sins have done the deed,
Driven the nails that fixed Him there,
Crowned with thorns His sacred head,
Pierced Him with the cruel spear,
Made His soul a sacrifice,
While for sinful man He dies.

3 Wilt thou let Him bleed in vain?
Still to death thy Lord pursue?
Open all His wounds again,
And the shameful cross renew?
No; with all my sins I'll part;
Break, O break, my bleeding heart!
    Rev. Charles Wesley. (1708—1783.) 1745. alt.

411 *"The Voice of free Grace."* 12, 11.

1 THE voice of free grace cries, Escape to the mountain;
For Adam's lost race, Christ hath opened a fountain;
For sin, and uncleanness, and every transgression,
His blood flows most freely, in streams of salvation.
Hallelujah to the Lamb, who hath purchased our pardon,
We'll praise Him again, when we pass over Jordan.

2 Ye souls that are wounded, O flee to the Saviour;
He calls you in mercy, 'tis infinite favor;
Your sins are increased as high as a mountain,
His blood can remove them, it flows from the fountain.
    Hallelujah, etc.

3 Now Jesus, our King, reigns triumphantly glorious;
O'er sin, death, and hell, He is more than victorious;
With shouting proclaim it, O trust in His passion,
He saves us most freely, O glorious salvation!
    Hallelujah, etc.

4 With joy shall we stand, when escaped to the shore;
With harps in our hands, we will praise Him the more;
We'll range the sweet plains on the banks of the river,
And sing of salvation for ever and ever.
Hallelujah to the Lamb, who hath purchased our pardon,
We'll praise Him again, when we pass over Jordan.
    Rev. Richard Burdsall. (1735—1824.) 1796. ab. and alt.

412 *"O come to the merciful Saviour."* 12, 11.

1 O COME to the merciful Saviour that calls you,
O come to the Lord who forgives and forgets;
Though dark be the fortune on earth that befalls you,
There's a bright home above, where the sun never sets.

2 O come then to Jesus, whose arms are extended
To fold His dear children in closest embrace.
O come, for your exile will shortly be ended,
And Jesus will show you His beautiful face.

3 Then come to the Saviour, whose mercy grows brighter
The longer you look at the depths of His love;
And fear not, 'tis Jesus, and life's cares grow lighter
As you think of the home and the glory above.
    Rev. Frederick William Faber. (1814—1863) 1849. ab.

413 *"O turn ye, O turn ye."* 11.

1 O TURN ye, O turn ye, for why will ye die,
When God in great mercy is coming so nigh?
Now Jesus invites you, the Spirit says, "Come!"
And angels are waiting to welcome you home.

FREE SALVATION.

2 How vain the delusion, that, while you delay,
Your hearts may grow better by staying away!
Come wretched, come starving, come just as
 you be,
While streams of salvation are flowing so free.

3 And now Christ is ready your souls to re-
 ceive;
O how can you question, if you will believe?
If sin is your burden, why will you not come?
'T is you He bids welcome; He bids you come
 home.

4 In riches, in pleasures, what can you obtain,
To soothe your affliction, or banish your pain?
To bear up your spirit when summoned to die,
Or waft you to mansions of glory on high?

5 Why will you be starving, and feeding on air?
There's mercy in Jesus, enough and to spare;
If still you are doubting, make trial and see,
And prove that His mercy is boundless and
 free.
Rev. Josiah Hopkins. 1830.

414   "To-Day."   6, 4.

1 TO-DAY the Saviour calls:
 Ye wanderers come;
 O ye benighted souls,
 Why longer roam?

2 To-day the Saviour calls:
 O hear Him now;
 Within these sacred walls
 To Jesus bow.

3 To-day the Saviour calls:
 For refuge fly;
 The storm of justice falls,
 And death is nigh.

4 The Spirit calls to-day:
 Yield to His power;
 O grieve Him not away:
 'T is mercy's hour.

415   The gracious Call. Matt. xi. 28–30.   7.

1 COME, said Jesus' sacred voice,
 Come, and make My path your choice;
 I will guide you to your home,
 Weary pilgrim, hither come.

2 Thou who, houseless, sole, forlorn,
 Long hast borne the proud world's scorn,
 Long hast roamed the barren waste,
 Weary pilgrim, hither haste.

3 Ye who, tossed on beds of pain,
 Seek for ease, but seek in vain;
 Ye, by fiercer anguish torn,
 In remorse for guilt who mourn;

4 Hither come, for here is found
 Balm that flows for every wound,
 Peace that ever shall endure,
 Rest eternal, sacred, sure.
Mrs. Anna Lætitia Barbauld. (1743–1825.) 1825. ab. and alt.

416   "Why will ye die?" Ezek. xviii. 31.   7.

1 SINNERS, turn, why will ye die?
 God, your Maker, asks you why;
 God, who did your being give,
 Made you with himself to live;
 He the fatal cause demands,
 Asks the work of His own hands,
 Why, ye thankless creatures, why
 Will ye cross His love, and die?

2 Sinners, turn, why will ye die?
 God, your Saviour, asks you why;
 God who did your souls retrieve,
 Died Himself that ye might live:
 Will you let Him die in vain?
 Crucify your Lord again?
 Why, ye ransomed sinners, why
 Will you slight His grace, and die?

3 Sinners, turn, why will ye die?
 God, the Spirit, asks you why;
 He, who all your lives hath strove,
 Wooed you to embrace His love:
 Will you not His grace receive?
 Will you still refuse to live?
 Why, ye long-sought sinners, why
 Will ye grieve your God, and die?
Rev. Charles Wesley. (1708–1788.) 1745. ab.

417   "The Year of Jubilee is come."   H. M.

1 BLOW ye the trumpet, blow
 The gladly solemn sound;
 Let all the nations know,
 To earth's remotest bound,
 The year of jubilee is come;
 Return, ye ransomed sinners, home.

2 Jesus, our great High-Priest,
  Hath full atonement made;
  Ye weary Spirits, rest,
  Ye mournful souls, be glad,
  The year of jubilee is come:
  Return, ye ransomed sinners, home.

3 Extol the Lamb of God,
  The all-atoning Lamb;
  Redemption in His blood
  Throughout the world proclaim;
  The year of jubilee is come:
  Return, ye ransomed sinners, home.

4 Ye slaves of sin and hell,
  Your liberty receive,
  And safe in Jesus dwell,
  And blest in Jesus live;
  The year of jubilee is come:
  Return, ye ransomed sinners, home.

5 Ye, who have sold for naught
  Your heritage above,
  Shall have it back unbought,
  The gift of Jesus' love;
  The year of jubilee is come:
  Return, ye ransomed sinners, home.

6 The gospel trumpet hear,
  The news of heavenly grace;
  And, saved from earth, appear
  Before your Saviour's face;
  The year of jubilee is come:
  Return, ye ransomed sinners, home.
      Rev Charles Wesley (1708—1788) 1750

418   *"It is the Year of Jubilee"*   H. M.

1 FAIR shines the morning star;
  The silver trumpets sound,
  Their notes re-echoing far,
  While dawns the day around;
  Joy to the slave; the slave is free:
  It is the year of jubilee.

2 Prisoners of hope, in gloom
  And silence left to die,
  With Christ's unfolding tomb,
  Your portals open fly;
  Rise with your Lord; He sets you free:
  It is the year of jubilee.

3 Ye, who have sold for naught
  The land your fathers won,
  Behold, how God hath wrought

  Redemption through His Son;
  Your heritage again is free;
  It is the year of Jubilee.

4 Ye, who yourselves have sold
  For debts to justice due,
  Ransomed, but not with gold,
  He gave Himself for you;
  The blood of Christ hath made you free:
  It is the year of jubilee.

5 Captives of sin and shame,
  O'er earth and ocean, hear
  An angel's voice proclaim
  The Lord's accepted year;
  Let Jacob rise, be Israel free;
  It is the year of jubilee.
      James Montgomery. (1777—1854) 1825.

419   *"Come, and welcome"*   8, 7, 4.

1 COME, ye sinners poor and wretched,
    Weak and wounded, sick and sore;
  Jesus ready stands to save you,
    Full of pity, joined with power;
      He is able,
  He is willing; doubt no more.

2 Ho, ye needy, come and welcome;
    God's free bounty glorify;
  True belief, and true repentance,
    Every grace that brings us nigh,
      Without money,
  Come to Jesus Christ and buy.

3 Let not conscience make you linger,
    Nor of fitness fondly dream;
  All the fitness He requireth
    Is to feel your need of Him:
      This He gives you;
  'Tis the Spirit's rising beam.

4 Come, ye weary, heavy-laden,
    Bruised and mangled by the fall;
  If you tarry till you're better,
    You will never come at all.
      Not the righteous,
  Sinners, Jesus came to call.

5 Lo, the Incarnate God. ascended,
    Pleads the merit of His blood;
  Venture on Him, venture wholly,
    Let no other trust intrude;
      None but Jesus
  Can do helpless sinners good.
      Rev. Joseph Hart (1712—1768) 1759. ab.

FREE SALVATION.

420   "*Hear, and live.*"   8, 7, 4.

1 SINNERS, will you scorn the message
    Sent in mercy from above?
Every sentence, O how tender!
    Every line is full of love:
      Listen to it;
    Every line is full of love.

2 Hear the heralds of the gospel
    News from Zion's King proclaim:
"Pardon to each rebel sinner,
    Free forgiveness in His name:"
      How important!
    "Free forgiveness in His name."

3 Tempted souls, they bring you succor;
    Fearful hearts, they quell your fears,
And, with news of consolation,
    Chase away the falling tears:
      Tender heralds!
    Chase away the falling tears.

4 O ye angels, hovering round us,
    Waiting spirits, speed your way;
Haste ye to the court of heaven,
    Tidings bear without delay,
      Rebel sinners
    Glad the message will obey.

        Rev. Jonathan Allen. 1801. ab.

421   *This our only Probation.*   Eccl. ix. 10.   L. M.

1 LIFE is the time to serve the Lord,
The time to insure the great reward
And while the lamp holds out to burn,
The vilest sinner may return.

2 Life is the hour that God has given
T' escape from hell and fly to heaven;
The day of grace, and mortals may
Secure the blessings of the day.

3 Then what my thoughts design to do,
My hands, with all your might pursue,
Since no device, nor work is found,
Nor faith, nor hope, beneath the ground.

4 There are no acts of pardon passed
In the cold grave to which we haste;
But darkness, death, and long despair
Reign in eternal silence there.

        Rev. Isaac Watts (1674—1748.) 1709. ab.

422   "*The one Thing needful.*"   Luke x. 42.   L. M.

1 WHY will ye waste on trifling cares
That life which God's compassion spares,
While, in the various range of thought,
The one thing needful is forgot?

2 Shall God invite you from above?
Shall Jesus urge His dying love?
Shall troubled conscience give you pain?
And all these pleas unite in vain?

3 Not so your eyes will always view
Those objects which you now pursue:
Not so will heaven and hell appear,
When death's decisive hour is near.

4 Almighty God, Thy grace impart;
Fix deep conviction on each heart;
Nor let us waste on trifling cares
That life which Thy compassion spares.

        Rev. Philip Doddridge. (1702—1751.) 1755. ab. and alt.

423   *No Hope after Death.*   L. M.

1 WHILE life prolongs its precious light,
Mercy is found and peace is given;
But soon, ah, soon approaching night
Shall blot out every hope of heaven.

2 While God invites, how blest the day!
How sweet the gospel's charming sound!
Come, sinners, haste, O haste away,
While yet a pardoning God He's found.

3 Soon, borne on time's most rapid wing,
Shall death command you to the grave,
Before His bar your spirits bring,
And none be found to hear or save.

4 In that lone land of deep despair
No Sabbath's heavenly light shall rise;
No God regard your bitter prayer,
Nor Saviour call you to the skies.

5 Now God invites, how blest the day!
How sweet the gospel's charming sound!
Come, sinners, haste, O haste away,
While yet a pardoning God is found.

        Rev. Timothy Dwight. (1752—1817.) 1800.

424   "*Haste, Traveler, haste!*"   L. M.

1 HASTE, traveller, haste! the night comes on,
And many a shining hour is gone;
The storm is gathering in the west,
And thou art far from home and rest.

FREE SALVATION. 119

2 O far from home thy footsteps stray;
Christ is the Life, and Christ the Way;
And Christ the Light, thy setting Sun,
Sinks ere thy morning is begun.

3 The rising tempest sweeps the sky;
The rains descend, the winds are high;
The waters swell, and death and fear
Beset thy path, nor refuge near.

4 Then linger not in all the plain,
Flee for thy life, the mountain gain;
Look not behind, make no delay,
O speed thee, speed thee on thy way.
  Rev. William Bengo Collyer. (1782–1854.) 1829. ab.

425   *"Grieve not the Spirit"*   L. M.

1 SAY, sinner, hath a voice within
Oft whispered to thy secret soul,
Urged thee to leave the ways of sin,
And yield thy heart to God's control?

2 Sinner, it was a heavenly voice,
It was the Spirit's gracious call;
It bade thee make the better choice,
And haste to seek in Christ thine all.

3 Spurn not the call to life and light;
Regard in time the warning kind;
That call thou may'st not always slight,
And yet the gate of mercy find.

4 God's Spirit will not always strive
With hardened, self-destroying man;
Ye, who persist His love to grieve,
May never hear His voice again.

5 Sinner, perhaps this very day
Thy last accepted time may be;
O should'st thou grieve Him now away,
Then hope may never beam on thee.
  Mrs. Ann Beadley Hyde. (–1872.) 1824. ab.

426   *"The Gospel Feast"*
    Luke xiv. 16–24.   L. M.

1 COME, sinners, to the gospel feast,
Let every soul be Jesus' guest;
You need not one be left behind,
For God has bidden all mankind.

2 Sent by my Lord, on you I call,
The invitation is to all:
Come all the world; come, sinner, thou;
All things in Christ are ready now.

3 Come, then, ye souls by sins opprest,
Ye restless wanderers after rest;
Ye poor, and maimed, and halt, and blind,
In Christ a hearty welcome find.
  Rev. Charles Wesley. (1708–1788.) 1747. ab.

427   *"All Things are now ready."*
    Luke xiv. 17.   L. M.

1 SINNERS, obey the gospel word;
Haste to the supper of my Lord;
Be wise to know your gracious day;
All things are ready, come away.

2 Ready the Father is to own,
And kiss His late-returning son;
Ready your loving Saviour stands,
And spreads for you His bleeding hands.

3 Ready the Spirit of His love,
Just now the stony to remove,
T' apply and witness with the blood,
And wash and seal the sons of God.

4 Ready for you the angels wait,
To triumph in your blest estate;
Tuning their harps, they long to praise
The wonders of redeeming grace.

5 The Father, Son, and Holy Ghost,
Are ready, with Their shining host:
All heaven is ready to resound,
"The dead's alive, the lost is found!"
  Rev. Charles Wesley. 1749. ab.

428   *Christ knocking at the Door.*
    Cant. v. 2. Rev. iii. 20.   L. M.

1 BEHOLD, a stranger's at the door;
He gently knocks, has knocked before;
Has waited long, is waiting still;
You treat no other friend so ill.

2 But will He prove a friend indeed?
He will, the very friend you need;
The Man of Nazareth, 'tis He,
With garments dyed at Calvary.

3 O lovely attitude! He stands
With melting heart, and laden hands;
O matchless kindness! and He shows
This matchless kindness to His foes.

4 Rise, touched with gratitude divine;
Turn out His enemy and thine,
That soul-destroying monster, Sin;
And let the Heavenly Stranger in.

FREE SALVATION.

5 Admit Him, for the human breast
Ne'er entertained so kind a Guest.
Admit Him, for you can't expel;
Where'er He comes, He comes to dwell.

6 Admit Him, ere His anger burn;
His feet, departed, ne'er return!
Admit Him, or the hour 's at hand
When at His door denied you'll stand.
Rev. Joseph Grigg. (—1768.) 1765. ab. and alt.

429 *Christ's Invitation to Sinners.* L. M.
Matt. xi. 28—30.

1 "Come hither, all ye weary souls,
Ye heavy-laden sinners, come;
I'll give you rest from all your toils,
And raise you to My heavenly home.

2 "They shall find rest that learn of Me;
I'm of a meek and lowly mind;
But passion rages like the sea,
And pride is restless as the wind.

3 "Blest is the man, whose shoulders take
My yoke, and bear it with delight;
My yoke is easy to his neck.
My grace shall make the burden light."

4 Jesus, we come at Thy command;
With faith, and hope, and humble zeal,
Resign our spirits to Thy hand,
To mould and guide us at Thy will.
Rev. Isaac Watts (1674—1748.) 1709.

430 *"Jesu auctor clementia."* L. M.

1 Of Him who did salvation bring,
I could forever think and sing;
Arise, ye needy, He'll relieve;
Arise, ye guilty, He'll forgive.

2 Ask but His grace, and lo, 'tis given;
Ask, and He turns your hell to heaven:
Though sin and sorrow wound my soul,
Jesus, Thy balm will make it whole.

3 To shame our sins, He blushed in blood;
He closed His eyes to show us God:
Let all the world fall down and know,
That none but God such love can show.

4 'Tis Thee I love, for Thee alone
I shed my tears and make my moan;
Where'er I am, where'er I move,
I meet the object of my love.

5 Insatiate, to this spring I fly;
I drink, and yet am ever dry:
Ah, who against Thy charms is proof?
Ah, who that loves can love enough?
Bernard of Clairvaux (1091—1153.) 1140.
Tr. Rev. Anthony Wilhelm Boehm. (1673—1722.) 1712. alt.

431 *"Return, O Wanderer, return."* L. M.
Jer. xxxi. 18—20.

1 Return, O wanderer, return,
And seek an injured Father's face;
Those warm desires that in thee burn,
Were kindled by reclaiming grace.

2 Return, O wanderer, return,
And seek a Father's melting heart;
Whose pitying eyes thy grief discern,
Whose hand can heal thine inward smart.

3 Return, O wanderer, return,
He heard thy deep repentant sigh,
He saw thy softened spirit mourn,
When no intruding ear was nigh.

4 Return, O wanderer, return,
Thy Saviour bids thy spirit live;
Go to His bleeding feet, and learn
How freely Jesus can forgive.

5 Return, O wanderer, return,
And wipe away the falling tear;
'T is God who says, "No longer mourn,"
'T is mercy's voice invites thee near.
Rev. William Bengo Collyer (1782—1854.) 1812. ab.

432 *"Come, weary Souls."* L. M.
Matt. xi. 28.

1 Come, weary souls, with sin distrest,
The Saviour offers heavenly rest;
The kind, the gracious call obey,
And cast your gloomy fears away.

2 Oppressed with guilt, a painful load,
O come and spread your woes abroad;
Divine compassion, mighty love,
Will all the painful load remove.

3 Here mercy's boundless ocean flows,
To cleanse your guilt and heal your woes;
Pardon, and life, and endless peace,
How rich the gift, how free the grace!

4 Lord, we accept with thankful heart
The hope Thy gracious words impart;
We come with trembling, yet rejoice,
And bless the kind inviting voice.

FREE SALVATION.

5 Dear Saviour, let Thy powerful love
Confirm our faith, our fears remove;
O sweetly reign in every breast,
And guide us to eternal rest.
  Miss Anne Steele. (1717—1778.) 1760. sl. alt.

433   "*All Things are now ready.*"   L. M.
          Luke xiv. 17.

1 O COME, ye sinners, to your Lord,
In Christ to paradise restored;
His proffered benefits embrace,
The plentitude of gospel grace:

2 A pardon written with His blood,
The favor and the peace of God,
The seeing eye, the feeling sense,
The mystic joys of penitence:

3 The godly grief, the pleasing smart,
The meltings of a broken heart,
The tears that tell your sins forgiven,
The sighs that waft your souls to heaven:

4 The guiltless shame, the sweet distress,
The unutterable tenderness,
The genuine, meek humility,
The wonder, "Why such love to me!"—

5 The o'erwhelming power of saving grace,
The sight that veils the seraph's face,
The speechless awe that dares not move,
And all the silent heaven of love.
  Rev. Charles Wesley. (1708—1788.) 1749. ab. and sl. alt.

434   "*Come, ye disconsolate.*"   11, 10.

1 COME, ye disconsolate, where'er ye languish,
Come to the mercy-seat, fervently kneel;
Here bring your wounded hearts, here tell your anguish,
Earth has no sorrows that heaven cannot heal.

2 Joy of the desolate, Light of the straying,
Hope of the penitent, fadeless and pure,
Here speaks the Comforter, tenderly saying,
Earth has no sorrows that heaven cannot cure.

3 Here see the Bread of Life; see waters flowing
Forth from the throne of God, pure from above;
Come to the feast prepared, come, ever knowing
Earth has no sorrows but heaven can remove.
  Thomas Moore. (1779—1852.) 1816. v. 1, 2. alt.
                Thomas Hastings. (1784—1872.) v. 3.

435   "*Peace, troubled Soul.*"   L. M. 6l.

1 PEACE, troubled soul, whose plaintive moan
Hath taught each scene the note of woe;
Cease thy complaint, suppress thy groan,
And let thy tears forget to flow:
Behold, the precious balm is found,
Which lulls thy pain, which heals thy wound.

2 Come, freely come, by sin opprest;
Unburden here thy weighty load;
Here find thy refuge and thy rest,
Safe in the mercy of thy God:
Thy God's thy Saviour, glorious word!
O hear, believe, and bless the Lord.
  Hon. and Rev. Walter Shirley. (1725—1786.) 1774. ab.

436   Κόπον τε καὶ κάματον.   8, 5, 8, 3.

1 ART thou weary, art thou languid,
  Art thou sore distrest?
"Come to me," saith One, "and coming
  Be at rest!"

2 Hath He marks to lead me to Him,
  If He be my Guide?
"In His feet and hands are wound-prints,
  And His side."

3 Is there diadem, as Monarch,
  That His brow adorns?
"Yea, a crown in very surety,
  But of thorns!"

4 If I still hold closely to Him,
  What hath He at last?
"Sorrow vanquished, labor ended,
  Jordan past!"

5 If I ask Him to receive me,
  Will He say me nay?
"Not till earth, and not till heaven
  Pass away!"
  Stephen of St. Sabas. (725—794.)
  Tr. by Rev. John Mason Neale. (1818—1866.) 1862. ab.

437   *Christ giving Rest.*   11, 10.

1 COME unto me, when shadows darkly gather,
When the sad heart is weary and distrest,
Seeking for comfort from your Heavenly Father,
Come unto me, and I will give you rest.

FREE SALVATION.

2 Large are the mansions in thy Father's dwelling,
Glad are the homes that sorrows never dim;
Sweet are the harps in holy music swelling,
Soft are the tones which raise the heavenly hymn.

3 There, like an Eden blossoming in gladness,
Bloom the fair flowers the earth too rudely pressed;
Come unto me all ye who droop in sadness,
Come unto me, and I will give you rest?
Unknown Author 1854. ab.

438 *The Gospel Trumpet.* S. M.

1 YE trembling captives, hear;
The gospel-trumpet sounds;
No music more can charm the ear,
Or heal your heart-felt wounds.

2 'T is not the trump of war,
Nor Sinai's awful roar;
Salvation's news is spread afar,
And vengeance is no more.

3 Forgiveness, love, and peace,
Glad heaven aloud proclaims;
And earth, the jubilee's release
With eager rapture claims.

4 Far, far to distant lands
The saving news shall spread,
And Jesus all His willing bands
In glorious triumph lead.
Samuel Boyce. 1801. sl. alt.

439 *"Now is the accepted Time"* S. M.
2 Cor. vi. 2.

1 NOW is the accepted time,
Now is the day of grace;
Now, sinners, come without delay,
And seek the Saviour's face.

2 Now is the accepted time,
The Saviour calls to-day;
Pardon and peace He freely gives;
Then why should you delay?

3 Now is the accepted time,
The gospel bids you come;
And every promise in His word
Declares there yet is room.

4 Lord, draw reluctant souls,
And feast them with Thy love:

Then will the angels clap their wings,
And bear the news above.
John Dobell. (1757–1840.) 1806. ab.

440 *"Come, take His Offers now."* C. M.

1 COME, take His offers now,
From every sin depart,
Perform thy oft-repeated vow,
And render Him thy heart.

2 Repent, return, receive
The grace through Jesus given;
Sure, if with God on earth we live,
We live with God in heaven.
Rev. Charles Wesley. (1708–1788.) ab. and alt.
Rev. Nehemiah Adams. (1806–) 1864.

441 *"All Things are ready."* S. M.
Matt. xxii. 4.

1 "All things are ready," Come,
Come to the supper spread;
Come, rich and poor, come, old and young,
Come, and be richly fed.

2 "All things are ready," Come,
The invitation's given,
Through Him who now in glory sits
At God's right hand in heaven.

3 "All things are ready," Come,
The door is open wide;
O feast upon the love of God,
For Christ, His Son, has died.

4 "All things are ready," Come,
All hindrance is removed;
And God, in Christ, His precious love
To fallen man has proved.

5 "All things are ready," Come,
To-morrow may not be;
O sinner, come, the Saviour waits
This hour to welcome thee.
Albert Midlane. (1825–) 1862.

442 *And the Spirit and the Bride say, Come* S. M.
Rev. xxii. 17.

1 THE Spirit, in our hearts,
Is whispering, "Sinner, come;"
The bride, the Church of Christ, proclaims
To all His children, "Come."

2 Let him that heareth, say
To all about him, "Come;"
Let him that thirsts for righteousness,
To Christ, the Fountain, come.

3 Yes, whosoever will,
  O let him freely come,
And freely drink the stream of life;
  'Tis Jesus bids him come.

4 Lo, Jesus, who invites,
  Declares, "I quickly come;"
Lord, even so; I wait Thine hour;
  Jesus, my Saviour, come.

Bp. Henry Ustick Onderdonk. (1789—1858.) 1826.

443 *"The Land of Peace."* S. M.

1 COME to the land of peace;
  From shadows come away;
Where all the sounds of weeping cease,
  And storms no more have sway.

2 Fear hath no dwelling here;
  But pure repose and love
Breathe through the bright, celestial air
  The spirit of the dove.

3 Come to the bright and blest,
  Gathered from every land;
For here thy soul shall find its rest
  Amid the shining band.

4 In this divine abode
  Change leaves no saddening trace;
Come, trusting spirit, to thy God,
  Thy holy resting-place.

5 "Come to our peaceful home,"
  The saints and angels say,
"Forsake the world, no longer roam;
  O wanderer, come away!"

Briggs' Collection.

444 *"Behold the Ark of God."* S. M.

1 LIKE Noah's weary dove,
  That soared the earth around,
But not a resting-place above
  The cheerless waters found;

O cease, my wandering soul,
  On restless wing to roam;
All the wide world, to either pole,
  Has not for thee a home.

3 Behold the Ark of God,
  Behold the open door;
Hasten to gain that dear abode,
  And rove, my soul, no more.

4 There, safe thou shalt abide,
  There, sweet shall be thy rest,
And every longing satisfied,
  With full salvation blest.

5 And when the waves of ire
  Again the earth shall fill,
The Ark shall ride the sea of fire;
  Then rest on Zion's hill.

Rev. William Augustus Muhlenberg. (1796—) 1826.

445 *Salvation.* C. M.

1 SALVATION! O the joyful sound!
  'Tis pleasure to our ears;
A sovereign balm for every wound,
  A cordial for our fears.

2 Buried in sorrow and in sin,
  At hell's dark door we lay;
But we arise, by grace divine,
  To see a heavenly day.

3 Salvation! Let the echo fly
  The spacious earth around,
While all the armies of the sky
  Conspire to raise the sound.

Rev. Isaac Watts. (1674—1748.) 1709.

446 *"Without Money and without Price."* Is. lv. 1, 2. C. M.

1 LET every mortal ear attend,
  And every heart rejoice;
The trumpet of the gospel sounds,
  With an inviting voice.

2 Ho, all ye hungry, starving souls,
  That feed upon the wind,
And vainly strive, with earthly toys,
  To fill an empty mind;

3 Eternal wisdom has prepared
  A soul-reviving feast,
And bids your longing appetites
  The rich provision taste.

4 Ho, ye that pant for living streams,
  And pine away and die,
Here you may quench your raging thirst
  With springs that never dry.

5 Rivers of love and mercy here
  In a rich ocean join;
Salvation in abundance flows,
  Like floods of milk and wine.

FREE SALVATION.

6 The happy gates of gospel grace
　Stand open night and day;
　Lord, we are come to seek supplies,
　And drive our wants away.
　　　　Rev. Isaac Watts. (1674—1748.) 1709.

447　　"*The Saviour calls.*"　　C. M.
　　　　　John vii. 37.

1 THE Saviour calls, let every ear
　Attend the heavenly sound;
　Ye doubting souls, dismiss your fear,
　Hope smiles reviving round.

2 For every thirsty, longing heart,
　Here streams of bounty flow,
　And life, and health, and bliss impart,
　To banish mortal woe.

3 Ye sinners, come, 't is mercy's voice,
　The gracious call obey;
　Mercy invites to heavenly joys,
　And can you yet delay?

4 Dear Saviour, draw reluctant hearts,
　To Thee let sinners fly,
　And take the bliss Thy love imparts,
　And drink and never die.
　　　　Miss Anne Steele (1717—1778.) 1760. ab.

448　　*Invited to the Feast.*　　C. M.
　　　　　Luke xiv. 22.

1 YE wretched, hungry, starving poor,
　Behold a royal feast;
　Where mercy spreads her bounteous store,
　For every humble guest.

2 See, Jesus stands with open arms;
　He calls, He bids you come:
　Guilt holds you back, and fear alarms;
　But see, there yet is room.

3 Room in the Saviour's bleeding heart:
　There love and pity meet;
　Nor will He bid the soul depart
　That trembles at His feet.

4 In Him the Father, reconciled,
　Invites your souls to come;
　The rebel shall be called a child,
　And kindly welcomed home.

5 There, with united heart and voice,
　Before the eternal throne,
　Ten thousand thousand souls rejoice
　In ecstacies unknown.

6 And yet ten thousand thousand more
　Are welcome still to come:
　Ye longing souls, the grace adore;
　Approach, there yet is room.
　　　　Miss Anne Steele. 1760. ab.

449　　*Christ's Commission.*　　C. M.
　　　　　John iii. 16, 17.

1 COME, happy souls, approach your God
　With new, melodious songs;
　Come, render to almighty grace
　The tribute of your tongues.

2 So strange, so boundless, was the love
　That pitied dying men,
　The Father sent His equal Son
　To give them life again.

3 Thy hands, dear Jesus, were not armed
　With a revenging rod,
　No hard commission to perform
　The vengeance of a God.

4 But all was mercy, all was mild,
　And wrath forsook the throne,
　When Christ on the kind errand came,
　And brought salvation down.

5 Here, sinners, you may heal your wounds,
　And wipe your sorrows dry;
　Trust in the mighty Saviour's name,
　And you shall never die.

6 See, dearest Lord, our willing souls
　Accept Thine offered grace;
　We bless the great Redeemer's love,
　And give the Father praise.
　　　　Rev. Isaac Watts. 1709.

450　　"*Child of Sin and Sorrow.*"　　P. M.

1 CHILD of sin and sorrow,
　Filled with dismay,
　Wait not for to-morrow,
　Yield thee to-day;
　Heaven bids thee come,
　While yet there's room.
　Child of sin and sorrow,
　Hear and obey.

2 Child of sin and sorrow,
　Why wilt thou die?
　Come while thou canst borrow
　Help from on high;

PENITENCE.

Grieve not that love
Which from above,
Child of sin and sorrow,
Would bring thee nigh.

3 Child of sin and sorrow,
Thy moments glide,
Like the flitting arrow,
Or the rushing tide;
Ere time is o'er,
Heaven's grace implore;
Child of sin and sorrow,
In Christ confide.

Thomas Hastings. (1784—1872.) 1832.

451   *At Christ's Feet.*   C. M.

1 PROSTRATE, dear Jesus, at Thy feet,
A guilty rebel lies;
And upwards to Thy mercy-seat
Presumes to lift his eyes.

2 O let not justice frown me hence;
Stay, stay the vengeful storm:
Forbid it, that Omnipotence
Should crush a feeble worm.

3 If tears of sorrow would suffice
To pay the debt I owe,
Tears should from both my weeping eyes
In ceaseless torrents flow.

4 But no such sacrifice I plead
To expiate my guilt;
No tears but those which Thou hast shed,
No blood but Thou hast spilt.

5 Think of Thy sorrows, dearest Lord,
And all my sins forgive;
Justice will well approve the word,
That bids the sinner live.

Rev. Samuel Stennett. (1727 - 1795.) 1787.

452   *Sueing for Mercy.*   C. M.

1 LORD, at Thy feet a sinner lies,
And knocks at mercy's door,
With heavy heart and downcast eyes,
Thy favor to implore.

2 On me the vast extent display
Of Thy forgiving love;
Take all my heinous guilt away,
This heavy load remove.

3 'T is mercy, mercy I implore;
I would Thy pity move;
Thy grace is an exhaustless store,
And Thou Thyself art Love.

4 O for Thine own, for Jesus' sake,
My many sins forgive;
This grace my rocky heart will break,
My breaking heart relieve.

5 Thus melt me down, thus make me bend,
And Thy dominion own,
Nor let a rival more pretend
To repossess Thy throne.

Rev. Simon Browne. (1680—1732.) 1720. ab. and sl. alt.

453   *"One only Hand."*   C M.

1 WHEN wounded sore the stricken soul
Lies bleeding and unbound,
One only hand, a pierced hand,
Can salve the sinner's wound.

2 When sorrow swells the laden breast,
And tears of anguish flow,
One only heart, a broken heart,
Can feel the sinner's woe.

3 When penitence has wept in vain
Over some foul dark spot,
One only stream, a stream of blood,
Can wash away the blot.

4 'T is Jesus' blood that washes white,
His hand that brings relief,
His heart that's touched with all our joys,
And feeleth for our grief.

5 Lift up Thy bleeding hand, O Lord;
Unseal that cleansing tide;
We have no shelter from our sin
But in Thy wounded side.

Mrs. Cecil Frances Alexander. 1858.

454   *A Cry for Mercy.*   C. M.

1 O LORD, turn not Thy face from me,
Who lie in woeful state,
Lamenting all my sinful life,
Before Thy mercy-gate:

2 A gate that opens wide to those
That do lament their sin;
Shut not that gate against me, Lord,
But let me enter in.

PENITENCE.

3 And call me not to strict account
   How I have sojourned here;
   For then my guilty conscience knows
   How vile I shall appear.

4 Mercy, good Lord, mercy I ask;
   This is my humble prayer;
   For mercy, Lord, is all my suit,
   O let Thy mercy spare.

5 To Father, Son, and Holy Ghost,
   The God whom we adore,
   Be glory, as it was, is now,
   And shall be evermore.
                    John Mardley, 1562. ab. and alt.

455 *Coming to Christ.* C. M.

1 APPROACH, my soul, the mercy-seat,
   Where Jesus answers prayer;
   There humbly fall before His feet,
   For none can perish there.

2 Thy promise is my only plea,
   With this I venture nigh;
   Thou callest burdened souls to Thee,
   And such, O Lord, am I.

3 Bowed down beneath a load of sin,
   By Satan sorely prest,
   By war without, and fears within,
   I come to Thee for rest.

4 Be Thou my shield and hiding-place,
   That, sheltered near Thy side,
   I may my fierce accuser face,
   And tell him, Thou hast died.

5 O wondrous love, to bleed and die,
   To bear the cross and shame,
   That guilty sinners, such as I,
   Might plead Thy gracious Name.
                    Rev. John Newton. (1725—1807.) 1779. ab.

456 *Returning to God.* C. M.

1 O THOU, whose tender mercy hears
   Contrition's humble sigh,
   Whose hand indulgent wipes the tears
   From sorrow's weeping eye;

2 See, low before Thy throne of grace,
   A wretched wanderer mourn;
   Hast Thou not bid me seek Thy face?
   Hast Thou not said, return?

3 And shall my guilty fears prevail,
   To drive me from Thy feet!
   O let not this dear refuge fail,
   This only safe retreat!

4 O shine on this benighted heart,
   With beams of mercy shine!
   And let Thy healing voice impart
   A taste of joys divine.

5 Thy presence only can bestow
   Delights which never cloy:
   Be this my solace here below,
   And my eternal joy!
                    Miss Anne Steele (1717—1778.) 1760 a.

457 *"Remember me."* C. M.

1 JESUS, Thou art the sinner's Friend;
   As such I look to Thee;
   Now, in the fullness of Thy love,
   O Lord, remember me.

2 Remember Thy pure word of grace,
   Remember Calvary;
   Remember all Thy dying groans,
   And then remember me.

3 Thou wondrous Advocate with God,
   I yield myself to Thee;
   While Thou art sitting on Thy throne,
   Dear Lord, remember me.

4 Lord, I am guilty, I am vile,
   But Thy salvation's free;
   Then in Thine all-abounding grace,
   Dear Lord, remember me.

5 And when I close my eyes in death,
   When creature-helps all flee,
   Then, O my dear Redeemer God,
   I pray, remember me.
                    Rev. Richard Burnham (1749—1810.) 1783. ab.

458 *"Have Mercy upon me, O God."* S. M.
         Ps. li.

1 HAVE mercy, Lord, on me,
   As Thou wert ever kind;
   Let me oppressed with loads of guilt,
   Thy wonted mercy find.

2 Wash off my foul offence,
   And cleanse me from my sin;
   For I confess my crime, and see
   How great my guilt has been.

PENITENCE.

3 Against Thee, Lord, alone,
  And only in Thy sight,
Have I transgressed; and, tho' condemned,
  Must own Thy judgment right.

4 Blot out my crying sins,
  Nor me in anger view:
Create in me a heart that's clean,
  An upright mind renew.

5 Withdraw not Thou Thy help,
  Nor cast me from Thy sight;
Nor let Thy Holy Spirit take
  His everlasting flight.

  Tate and Brady. 1696. ab.

459 *Tears of Penitence.* S. M.

1 DID Christ o'er sinners weep,
  And shall our cheeks be dry?
Let floods of penitential grief
  Burst forth from every eye.

2 The Son of God in tears
  Angels with wonder see:
Be thou astonished, O my soul,
  He shed those tears for thee.

3 He wept that we might weep;
  Each sin demands a tear;
In heaven alone no sin is found,
  And there's no weeping there.

  Rev. Benjamin Beddome. (1717—1795.) 1787.

460 *God's Goodness leading to Repentance.* S. M.
       Rom. ii. 4

1 Is this the kind return,
  And these the thanks we owe,
Thus to abuse eternal love,
  Whence all our blessings flow?

2 To what a stubborn frame
  Hath sin reduced our mind!
What strange, rebellious wretches we,
  And God as strangely kind!

3 Turn, turn us, mighty God,
  And mould our souls afresh;
Break, sovereign grace, these hearts of stone,
  And give us hearts of flesh.

4 Let old ingratitude
  Provoke our weeping eyes;
And hourly, as new mercies fall,
  Let hourly thanks arise.

  Rev. Isaac Watts. (1674—1748.) 1709. ab.

461 *Mercy implored.* S. M.

1 THOU Lord of all above,
  And all below the sky,
Prostrate before Thy feet I fall,
  And for Thy mercy cry.

2 Forgive my follies past,
  The crimes which I have done;
Bid a repenting sinner live,
  Through Thine incarnate Son.

3 Guilt, like a heavy load,
  Upon my conscience lies;
To Thee I make my sorrows known,
  And lift my weeping eyes.

4 The burden which I feel,
  Thou canst alone remove;
Do Thou display Thy pardoning grace,
  And Thine unbounded love.

5 One gracious look of Thine
  Will ease my troubled breast;
O let me know my sins forgiven,
  And I shall then be blest.

  Rev. Benjamin Beddome. 1818.

462 *The Issues of Life and Death.* S. M.

1 O WHERE shall rest be found,
  Rest for the weary soul?
'T were vain the ocean-depths to sound,
  Or pierce to either pole.

2 The world can never give
  The bliss for which we sigh;
'T is not the *whole* of life to live,
  Nor *all* of death to die.

3 Beyond this vale of tears
  There is a life above,
Unmeasured by the flight of years;
  And all that life is love.

4 There is a death, whose pang
  Outlasts the fleeting breath:
O what eternal horrors hang
  Around the second death!

5 Lord God of truth and grace,
  Teach us that death to shun,
Lest we be banished from Thy face,
  And evermore undone.

  James Montgomery. (1771—1854.) 1819, 1853. ab.

PENITENCE.

463 *"Out of the Depths."* S. M.
Ps. cxxx

1 OUT of the deep I call
  To Thee, O Lord, to Thee;
Before Thy throne of grace I fall,
  Be merciful to me.

2 Out of the deep I cry,
  The woful deep of sin,
Of evil done in days gone by,
  Of evil now within.

3 Out of the deep of fear,
  And dread of coming shame,
From morning watch till night is near
  I plead the Precious Name.

Rev. Sir Henry Williams Baker. (1821—) 1868. ab.

464 *The shining Light.* S. M.

1 MY former hopes are fled,
  My terror now begins;
I feel, alas, that I am dead
  In trespasses and sins.

2 Ah, whither shall I fly?
  I hear the thunder roar;
The law proclaims destruction nigh,
  And vengeance at the door.

3 When I review my ways,
  I dread impending doom;
But sure a friendly whisper says,
  "Flee from the wrath to come."

4 I see, or think I see,
  A glimmering from afar;
A beam of day, that shines for me,
  To save me from despair.

5 Forerunner of the sun,
  It marks the pilgrim's way;
I'll gaze upon it while I run,
  And watch the rising day.

William Cowper. (1731—1800.) 1779.

465 *Pleading for Pardon.* L. M.
Ps. li.

1 SHOW pity, Lord, O Lord, forgive:
Let a repenting rebel live:
Are not Thy mercies large and free?
May not a sinner trust in Thee?

2 My crimes are great, but don't surpass
The power and glory of Thy grace;
Great God, Thy nature hath no bound,
So let Thy pardoning love be found.

3 O wash my soul from every sin,
And make my guilty conscience clean;
Here on my heart the burden lies,
And past offences pain mine eyes.

4 My lips with shame my sins confess,
Against Thy law, against Thy grace;
Lord, should Thy judgments grow severe,
I am condemned, but Thou art clear.

5 Should sudden vengeance seize my breath,
I must pronounce Thee just in death;
And if my soul were sent to hell,
Thy righteous law approves it well.

6 Yet save a trembling sinner, Lord,
Whose hope, still hovering round Thy word,
Would light on some sweet promise there,
Some sure support against despair.

Rev. Isaac Watts. (1674–1748.) 1719.

466 *Prayer for renewing and helping Grace.* L. M.
Ps. li.

1 O THOU that hearest when sinners cry,
Though all my crimes before Thee lie,
Behold me not with angry look,
But blot their memory from Thy book.

2 Create my nature pure within,
And form my soul averse to sin;
Let Thy good Spirit ne'er depart,
Nor hide Thy presence from my heart.

3 I cannot live without Thy light,
Cast out and banished from Thy sight;
Thy holy joys, my God, restore,
And guard me, that I fall no more.

4 Though I have grieved Thy Spirit, Lord,
His help and comfort still afford:
And let a wretch come near Thy throne,
To plead the merits of Thy Son.

Rev. Isaac Watts. 1719.

467 *Sin confessed.* L. M.
Ps. li.

1 LORD, I am vile, conceived in sin,
And born unholy and unclean;
Sprung from the man whose guilty fall
Corrupts the race, and taints us all.

2 Soon as we draw our infant breath,
The seeds of sin grow up for death;
Thy law demands a perfect heart;
But we're defiled in every part.

PENITENCE.

3 Behold, I fall before Thy face;
  My only refuge is Thy grace;
  No outward forms can make me clean;
  The leprosy lies deep within.

4 No bleeding bird, nor bleeding beast,
  Nor hyssop branch, nor sprinkling priest,
  Nor running brook, nor flood, nor sea,
  Can wash the dismal stain away.

5 Jesus, my God, Thy blood alone
  Hath power sufficient to atone;
  Thy blood can make me white as snow;
  No Jewish types could cleanse me so.

  Rev. Isaac Watts. 1719. ab.

468. *Seeking Rest in Christ.* L. M.
Matt. xi. 28

1 O THAT my load of sin were gone!
  O that I could at last submit
  At Jesus' feet to lay it down
  To lay my soul at Jesus' feet!

2 Rest for my soul I long to find;
  Saviour of all, if mine Thou art,
  Give me Thy meek and lowly mind,
  And stamp Thine image on my heart.

3 Break off the yoke of inbred sin,
  And fully set my spirit free;
  I cannot rest till pure within,
  Till I am wholly lost in Thee.

4 Fain would I learn of Thee, my God,
  Thy light and easy burden prove,
  The cross all stained with hallowed blood,
  The labor of Thy dying love.

5 I would, but Thou must give the power;
  My heart from every sin release;
  Bring near, bring near the joyful hour,
  And fill me with Thy perfect peace.

  Rev. Charles Wesley (1708-1788) 1742. ab.

469 *Help only in Christ.* L. M.
Gal. iii. 22.

1 JESUS, the sinner's Friend, to Thee,
  Lost and undone, for aid I flee,
  Weary of earth, myself, and sin:
  Open Thine arms and take me in.

2 Pity and heal my sin-sick soul;
  'Tis Thou alone canst make me whole;
  Fallen, till in me Thine image shine,
  And lost I am, till Thou art mine.

3 The mansion for Thyself prepare;
  Dispose my heart by entering there:
  'T is this alone can make me clean,
  'T is this alone can cast out sin.

4 Long have I vainly hoped and strove
  To force my hardness into love,
  To give Thee all Thy laws require,
  And labored in the purging fire.

5 At last I own it cannot be
  That I should fit myself for Thee:
  Here, then, to Thee I all resign;
  Thine is the work, and only Thine.

  Rev. Charles Wesley. 1739. ab.

470 *The Spirit entreated to stay.* L. M.

1 STAY, Thou insulted Spirit, stay,
  Though I have done Thee such despite,
  Nor cast the sinner quite away,
  Nor take Thine everlasting flight.

2 Though I have steeled my stubborn heart,
  And shaken off my guilty fears;
  And vexed, and urged Thee to depart,
  For many long rebellious years;

3 Though I have most unfaithful been
  Of all who e'er Thy grace received;
  Ten thousand times Thy goodness seen,
  Ten thousand times Thy goodness grieved;

4 Yet, O the chief of sinners spare,
  In honor of my great High Priest;
  Nor in Thy righteous anger swear
  To exclude me from Thy people's rest.

5 Now, Lord, my weary soul release,
  Upraise me with Thy gracious hand,
  And guide into Thy perfect peace,
  And bring me to the promised land.

  Rev. Charles Wesley 1749. ab.

471 *After a Relapse into Sin.* 7.
Heb. x. 29

1 DEPTH of mercy, can there be
  Mercy still reserved for me?
  Can my God His wrath forbear?
  Me, the chief of sinners, spare?

2 I have long withstood His grace,
  Long provoked Him to His face;
  Would not hearken to His calls;
  Grieved Him by a thousand falls.

PENITENCE.

3 Kindled His relentings are;
  Me He now delights to spare;
  Cries, "How shall I give thee up?"
  Lets the lifted thunder drop.

4 There for me the Saviour stands,
  Shows His wounds, and spreads His hands;
  God is love: I know, I feel;
  Jesus weeps, but loves me still.
            Rev. Charles Wesley. (1708—1788.) 1740. ab.

472   *Rest in Christ.*   7.

1 COME, ye weary sinners, come,
    All who groan beneath your load;
  Jesus calls His wanderers home:
    Hasten to your pardoning God.

2 Come, ye guilty souls opprest,
    Answer to the Saviour's call:
  "Come, and I will give you rest;
    Come, and I will save you all."

3 Jesus, full of truth and love,
    We Thy kindest word obey:
  Faithful let Thy mercies prove,
    Take our load of guilt away.

4 Weary of this war within,
    Weary of this endless strife,
  Weary of ourselves and sin,
    Weary of a wretched life;

5 Fain we would on Thee rely,
    Cast on Thee our every care,
  To Thine arms of mercy fly,
    Find our lasting quiet there.

6 Burdened with a world of grief,
    Burdened with our sinful load,
  Burdened with this unbelief,
    Burdened with the wrath of God;

7 Lo, we come to Thee for ease,
    True and gracious as Thou art;
  Now our groaning soul release,
    Write forgiveness on our heart.
            Rev. Charles Wesley. 1747. ab. and alt.
            Rev. John Wesley. (1703—1791.) 1779.

473   *The Penitent pardoned.*   7.

1 SOVEREIGN Ruler, Lord of all,
  Prostrate at Thy feet I fall;
  Hear, O hear my ardent cry,
  Frown not, lest I faint and die.

2 Vilest of the sons of men,
  Worst of rebels I have been;
  Oft abused Thee to Thy face,
  Trampled on Thy richest grace.

3 Justly might Thy vengeful dart
  Pierce this bleeding, broken heart;
  Justly might Thy kindled ire
  Blast me in eternal fire.

4 But with Thee there's mercy found,
  Balm to heal my every wound:
  Thou canst soothe the troubled breast,
  Give the weary wanderer rest.
            Rev. Thomas Raffles. (1788—1863.) 1812. ab.

474   *Looking to Jesus.*   7.

1 THOU, who didst on Calvary bleed,
  Thou, who dost for sinners plead,
  Help me in my time of need,
  Jesus, Saviour, hear my cry.

2 In my darkness and my grief,
  With my heart of unbelief,
  I, who am of sinners chief,
  Jesus, lift to Thee mine eye.

3 Foes without and fears within,
  With no plea Thy grace to win,
  But that Thou canst save from sin,
  Jesus, to Thy cross I fly.

4 There on Thee I cast my care,
  There to Thee I raise my prayer,
  Jesus, save me from despair,
  Save me, save me, or I die.

5 When the storms of trial lower,
  When I feel temptation's power,
  In the last and darkest hour,
  Jesus, Saviour, be Thou nigh.
            Rev. James Drummond Burns. (1823—1864.) 1858.

475   *Christ our only Hope.*   7.

1 HOLY Spirit, from on high
  Bend on us a pitying eye;
  Animate the drooping heart,
  Bid the power of sin depart.

2 Light up every dark recess
  Of our heart's ungodliness;
  Show us every devious way
  Where our steps have gone astray.

PENITENCE.

3 Teach us, with repentant grief,
   Humbly to implore relief;
   Then the Saviour's blood reveal,
   All our deep disease to heal.

4 Other groundwork should we lay,
   Sweep those empty hopes away;
   Make us feel that Christ alone
   Can for human guilt atone.
   Rev. William Hiley Bathurst. (1796—) 1831 ab.

476   *Rest for the weary.*   **7.**
           Gen. viii.

1 DOES the Gospel word proclaim
   Rest for those that weary be?
   Then, my soul, put in thy claim,
   Sure that promise speaks to thee.

2 Marks of grace I cannot show,
   All polluted is my best;
   But I weary am, I know,
   And the weary long for rest.

3 Burdened with a load of sin,
   Harrassed with tormenting doubt,
   Hourly conflicts from within,
   Hourly crosses from without;

4 All my little strength is gone,
   Sink I must without supply;
   Sure upon the earth is none
   Can more weary be than I.

5 In the ark the weary dove
   Found a welcome resting-place;
   Thus my spirit longs to prove
   Rest in Christ, the Ark of grace.

6 Tempest-tossed I long have been,
   And the flood increases fast;
   Open, Lord, and take me in,
   Till the storm be overpast.
   Rev. John Newton. (1725—1807) 1779. ab.

477   *"Gott ruft noch."*   **L. M.**

1 GOD calling yet! shall I not hear?
   Earth's pleasures shall I still hold dear?
   Shall life's swift passing years all fly,
   And still my soul in slumber lie?

2 God calling yet! shall I not rise?
   Can I His loving voice despise,
   And basely His kind care repay?
   He calls me still; can I delay?

3 God calling yet! and shall He knock,
   And I my heart the closer lock?
   He still is waiting to receive,
   And shall I dare His Spirit grieve?

4 God calling yet! and shall I give
   No heed, but still in bondage live?
   I wait, but He does not forsake;
   He calls me still; my heart, awake!

5 God calling yet! I cannot stay;
   My heart I yield without delay:
   Vain world, farewell, from thee I part;
   The voice of God hath reached my heart.
   Gerhard Tersteegen. (1697—1769) 1730.
   Tr. by Miss Jane Borthwick. 1854 ab and alt.

478   *Communing with our Hearts.*   **L. M.**
           Ps. iv. 4.

1 RETURN, my roving heart, return,
   And chase these shadowy forms no more;
   Seek out some solitude to mourn,
   And thy forsaken God implore.

2 And Thou my God, whose piercing eye
   Distinct surveys each deep recess,
   In these abstracted hours draw nigh,
   And with Thy presence fill the place.

3 Through all the mazes of my heart,
   My search let heavenly wisdom guide;
   And still its radiant beams impart,
   Till all be searched and purified.

4 Then, with the visits of Thy love,
   Vouchsafe my inmost soul to cheer,
   Till every grace shall join to prove,
   That God has fixed His dwelling there.
   Rev. Philip Doddridge. (1702—1751) 1755. ab.

479   *The Dawn of Grace.*   **L. M.**

1 HEART-BROKEN, friendless, poor, cast down
   Where shall the chief of sinners fly,
   Almighty Vengeance, from Thy frown?
   Eternal Justice, from Thine eye?

2 Lo, through the gloom of guilty fears,
   My faith discerns a dawn of grace;
   The sun of Righteousness appears
   In Jesus' reconciling face.
   James Montgomery. (1771—1854) 1819 ab.

480   *A contrite Heart.*   **L. M.**
           Ps. li.

1 A BROKEN heart, my God, my King,
   Is all the sacrifice I bring;
   The God of grace will ne'er despise
   A broken heart for sacrifice.

PENITENCE.

2 My soul lies humbled in the dust,
And owns Thy dreadful sentence just;
Look down, O Lord, with pitying eye,
And save the soul condemned to die.

3 Then will I teach the world Thy ways:
Sinners shall learn Thy sovereign grace;
I'll lead them to my Saviour's blood,
And they shall praise a pardoning God.

4 O may Thy love inspire my tongue!
Salvation shall be all my song;
And all my powers shall join to bless
The Lord, my strength and righteousness.
Rev. Isaac Watts. (1674—1748.) 1719. sl. alt.

481 *The Prayer of the Publican.* L. M.
Luke xviii. 13.

1 WITH broken heart and contrite sigh,
A trembling sinner, Lord I cry:
Thy pardoning grace is rich and free;
O God, be merciful to me.

2 I smite upon my troubled breast,
With deep and conscious guilt opprest,
Christ and His cross my only plea;
O God, be merciful to me.

3 Far off I stand with tearful eyes,
Nor dare uplift them to the skies;
But Thou dost all my anguish see;
O God, be merciful to me.

4 Nor alms, nor deeds that I have done,
Can for a single sin atone;
To Calvary alone I flee;
O God, be merciful to me.

5 And when, redeemed from sin and hell,
With all the ransomed throng I dwell,
My raptured song shall ever be,
God has been merciful to me.
Rev. Cornelius Elven. (1797—) 1852.

482 *"God be merciful to me a Sinner."* L. M.
Luke xviii. 13.

1 HEAR, gracious God, a sinner's cry,
For I have nowhere else to fly;
My hope, my only hope's in Thee;
O God, be merciful to me.

2 To Thee I come, a sinner poor,
And wait for mercy at Thy door;
Indeed, I've nowhere else to flee;
O God, be merciful to me.

3 To Thee I come, a sinner weak,
And scarce know how to pray or speak;
From fear and weakness set me free;
O God, be merciful to me.

4 To Thee I come, a sinner great,
And well Thou knowest all my state;
Yet full forgiveness is with Thee;
O God, be merciful to me.

5 To Thee I come, a sinner lost,
Nor have I aught wherein to trust;
But where Thou art, Lord, I would be;
O God, be merciful to me.
Rev. Samuel Medley. (1738—1799.) 1789 ab.

483 *The stony Heart.* L. M.

1 O FOR a glance of heavenly day,
To take this stubborn stone away,
And thaw, with beams of love divine,
This heart, this frozen heart of mine.

2 The rocks can rend; the earth can quake;
The seas can roar; the mountains shake;
Of feeling all things show some sign,
But this unfeeling heart of mine.

3 To hear the sorrows Thou hast felt,
Dear Lord, an adamant would melt;
But I can read each moving line,
And nothing move this heart of mine.

4 Thy judgment, too, which devils fear,
Amazing thought!—unmoved I hear;
Goodness and wrath in vain combine
To stir this stupid heart of mine.

5 But power divine can do the deed;
And, Lord, that power I greatly need:
Thy Spirit can from dross refine,
And melt and change this heart of mine.
Rev. Joseph Hart. (1712—1768.) 1762. alt.

484 *"I'll go to Jesus."* C. M.

1 COME, humble sinner, in whose breast,
A thousand thoughts revolve;
Come, with your guilt and fear oppressed,
And make this last resolve:

2 "I'll go to Jesus; though my sin
Hath like a mountain rose:
I know His courts, I'll enter in,
Whatever may oppose.

3 "Prostrate I'll lie before His throne,
  And there my guilt confess;
  I'll tell Him I'm a wretch undone,
  Without His sovereign grace.

4 "I'll to the gracious King approach,
  Whose sceptre pardon gives;
  Perhaps He may command my touch,
  And then the suppliant lives.

5 "Perhaps He will admit my plea,
  Perhaps will hear my prayer;
  But, if I perish, I will pray,
  And perish only there.

6 "I can but perish if I go,
  I am resolved to try;
  For if I stay away, I know
  I must forever die."

  Rev. Edmund Jones. (1732—1765.) c. 1760.

485   Christ our Righteousness.   C. M.
1 Cor. i. 30

1 JESUS, Thou art my Righteousness,
  For all my sins were Thine;
  Thy death hath bought of God my peace,
  Thy life hath made Him mine.

2 Spotless and just in Thee I am,
  I feel my sins forgiven;
  I taste salvation in Thy name,
  And antedate my heaven.

3 Forever here my rest shall be,
  Close to Thy bleeding side;
  This all my hope, and all my plea,
  For *me* the Saviour died.

4 My dying Saviour, and my God,
  Fountain for guilt and sin,
  Sprinkle me ever with Thy blood,
  And cleanse, and keep me clean.

5 Wash me, and make me thus Thine own;
  Wash me, and mine Thou art;
  Wash me, but not my feet alone,
  My hands, my head, my heart.

6 The atonement of Thy blood apply,
  Till faith to sight improve;
  Till hope shall in fruition die,
  And all my soul be love.

  Rev. Charles Wesley. (1708—1788.) 1740.

486   Giving up all for Christ.   C. M.
Phil. iii. 8.

1 AND must I part with all I have,
  My dearest Lord, for Thee?
  It is but right, since Thou hast done
  Much more than this for me.

2 Yes, let it go!—one look from Thee
  Will more than make amends
  For all the losses I sustain
  Of credit, riches, friends.

3 Ten thousand worlds, ten thousand lives,
  How worthless they appear,
  Compared with Thee, supremely good,
  Divinely bright and fair.

4 Saviour of souls, could I from Thee
  A single smile obtain,
  The loss of all things I could bear,
  And glory in my gain.

  Rev. Benjamin Beddome. (1717—1795.) 1787.

487   "Bless me, even me also."   8, 7.
Gen. xxvii. 34.

1 LORD, I hear of showers of blessing
  Thou art scattering full and free;
  Showers, the thirsty land refreshing;
    Let some droppings fall on me,
      Even me.

2 Pass me not, O gracious Father,
  Sinful though my heart may be;
  Thou might'st curse me, but the rather
    Let Thy mercy light on me,
      Even me.

3 Pass me not, O tender Saviour,
  Let me love and cling to Thee;
  I am longing for Thy favor;
    When Thou comest, call for me,
      Even me.

4 Pass me not, O mighty Spirit,
  Thou canst make the blind to see;
  Witnesser of Jesus' merit,
    Speak the word of power to me,
      Even me.

5 Love of God, so pure and changeless,
  Blood of God, so rich and free,
  Grace of God, so strong and boundless,
    Magnify them all in me,
      Even me.

  Mrs. Elizabeth Codner. 1860. ab.

PENITENCE.

488 "*Pass me not.*" 8, 5.

1 PASS me not, O gentle Saviour,
  Hear my humble cry;
While on others Thou art smiling,
  Do not pass me by!

2 Let me at a throne of mercy
  Find a sweet relief,
Kneeling there in deep contrition,
  Help my unbelief!

3 Trusting only in Thy merits,
  Would I seek Thy face,
Heal my wounded, broken spirit,
  Save me by Thy grace!

4 Thou the Spring of all my comfort,
  More than life to me,
Whom on earth have I besides Thee,
  Whom in heaven but Thee!
  Mrs. Fanny Jane Crosby Van Alstyne. (1821—) 1869.

489 "*Wretched, helpless, and distrest.*"
  Rev. iii. 17. 7, 6, 7, 7, 6.

1 WRETCHED, helpless, and distrest,
  Ah, whither shall I fly?
Ever panting after rest,
  I cannot find it nigh:
Naked, sick, and poor, and blind,
Bound in sin and misery,
Friend of sinners, let me find
  My help, my all in Thee.

2 In the wilderness I stray,
  My foolish heart is blind;
Nothing do I know; the way
  Of peace I cannot find:
Jesus, Lord, restore my sight,
Take, O take the veil away;
Turn my darkness into light,
  My midnight into day.

3 Naked of Thine image, Lord,
  Forsaken, and alone,
Unrenewed, and unrestored,
  I have not Thee put on:
Over me Thy mantle spread,
Send Thy likeness from above;
Let Thy goodness be displayed,
  And wrap me in Thy love.

4 Clothe me with Thy holiness,
  Thy meek humility;

Put on me Thy glorious dress,
  Endue my soul with Thee;
Let Thine image be restored,
  Let me now Thy nature prove;
With Thy fulness fill me, Lord,
  And perfect me in love.
  Rev. Charles Wesley. (1708—1788.) 1742. ab. and sl. alt.

490 *Waiting for Christ the Prophet.* 7, 6, 7, 7, 6.

1 OPEN, Lord, my inward ear,
  And bid my heart rejoice;
Bid my quiet spirit hear
  Thy comfortable voice;
Never in the whirlwind found,
Or where earthquakes rock the place;
Still and silent is the sound,
  The whisper of Thy grace.

2 From the world of sin, and noise,
  And hurry, I withdraw;
For the small and inward voice
  I wait with humble awe:
Silent am I now and still,
Dare not in Thy presence move;
To my waiting soul reveal
  The secret of Thy love.

3 Thou didst undertake for me,
  For me to death wast sold;
Wisdom in a mystery
  Of bleeding love unfold;
Teach the lesson of Thy cross,
Let me die, with Thee to reign;
All things let me count but loss,
  So I may Thee regain.
  Rev. Charles Wesley. 1742. ab.

491 Ἰησοῦ γλυκύτατε. 7, 6, 8, 7.

1 JESUS, Name all names above,
  Jesus, best and dearest,
Jesus, Fount of perfect love,
  Holiest, tenderest, nearest;
Jesus, Source of grace completest,
Jesus purest, Jesus sweetest,
Jesus, Well of power divine,
Make me, keep me, seal me Thine.

2 Jesus, open me the gate
  Which the sinner entered,
Who, in his last dying state,
  Wholly on Thee ventured;

PENITENCE.

Thou, whose wounds are ever pleading,
And Thy passion interceding,
From my misery let me rise
To a home in Paradise.

3 Thou didst call the prodigal;
Thou didst pardon Mary;
Thou, whose words can never fall,
Love can never vary;
Lord, to heal my lost condition
Give, for Thou canst give, contrition;
Thou canst pardon all my ill,
If Thou wilt: O say, "I will!"

4 Woe, that I have turned aside
After fleshly pleasure!
Woe, that I have never tried
For the heavenly treasure!
Treasure, safe in homes supernal,
Incorruptible, eternal:
Treasure no less price hath won
Than the passion of the Son.

5 Jesus, crowned with thorns for me,
Scourged for my transgression,
Witnessing, through agony,
That Thy good confession;
Jesus, clad in purple raiment,
For my evil making payment;
Let not all Thy woe and pain,
Let not Calvary, be in vain.

6 When I cross death's bitter sea,
And its waves roll higher,
Help the more forsaking me
As the storm draws nigher;
Jesus, leave me not to languish,
Helpless, hopeless, full of anguish,
Tell me, "Verily, I say,
"Thou shalt be with Me to-day."

Theoctistus of the Studium (?—890.)
Tr. by Rev. John Mason Neale (1818–1866.) 1862.

492 *"Have Mercy."*
Mark x. 47.   8, 7.

1 JESUS, full of all compassion,
Hear Thy humble suppliant's cry;
Let me know Thy great salvation;
See, I languish, faint, and die.

2 Guilty, but with heart relenting,
Overwhelmed with helpless grief,
Prostrate at Thy feet repenting,
Send, O send me quick relief.

3 Whither should a wretch be flying,
But to Him who comfort gives?
Whither, from the dread of dying,
But to Him who ever lives?

4 While I view Thee, wounded, grieving,
Breathless, on the cursèd tree,
Fain I'd feel my heart believing
Thou didst suffer thus for me.

5 Hear, then, blessed Saviour, hear me!
My soul cleaveth to the dust;
Send the Comforter to cheer me;
Lo, in Thee I put my trust.

6 On the word Thy blood hath sealed
Hangs my everlasting all;
Let Thy arm be now revealed;
Stay, O stay me, lest I fall.

7 In the world of endless ruin,
Let it never, Lord, be said,
"Here's a soul that perished suing
For the boasted Saviour's aid."

8 *Saved!*—the deed shall spread new glory
Through the shining realms above;
Angels sing the pleasing story,
All enraptured with Thy love.

Rev. Daniel Turner (1710–1798.) 1787 ab.

493 *"Take me."*   8, 7.

1 TAKE me, O my Father, take me,
Take me, save me, through Thy Son;
That, which Thou would'st have me, make me,
Let Thy will in me be done. [me,

2 Long from Thee my footsteps straying,
Thorny proved the way I trod;
Weary come I now, and praying,
Take me to Thy love, my God.

3 Fruitless years with grief recalling,
Humbly I confess my sin;
At Thy feet, O Father, falling,
To Thy household take me in.

4 Freely now to Thee I proffer
This relenting heart of mine:
Freely, life and soul I offer,
Gift unworthy love like Thine.

5 Once the world's Redeemer dying,
Bore our sins upon the tree;
On that sacrifice relying,
Now I look in hope to Thee;

CHOICE OF CHRIST. FAITH.

6 Father, take me; all forgiving,
   Fold me to Thy loving breast;
   In Thy love for ever living,
   I must be for ever blest.
                    Rev. Ray Palmer. (1808—) 1865.

494 *"Make my Heart Thy lasting home."* H. M.

1 COME, my Redeemer, come,
   And deign to dwell with me,
   Come, make my heart Thy home,
   And bid Thy rivals flee:
   Come, my Redeemer, quickly come,
   And make my heart Thy lasting home.

2 Why should the world presume
   To occupy Thy throne?
   Come, all Thy right assume,
   I would be Thine alone:
   Come, my Redeemer, quickly come,
   And make my heart Thy lasting home.

3 Exert Thy mighty power,
   And banish all my sin,
   In this auspicious hour,
   Bring all Thy graces in:
   Come, my Redeemer, quickly come,
   And make my heart Thy lasting home.

4 Rule Thou in every thought
   And passion of my soul,
   Till all my powers are brought
   Beneath Thy full control:
   Come, my Redeemer, quickly come,
   And make my heart Thy lasting home.

5 Then shall my days be Thine,
   And all my heart be love;
   And joy and peace be mine,
   Such as are known above:
   Come, my Redeemer, quickly come,
   And make my heart Thy lasting home.
                    Rev. Andrew Reed (1787—1862) 1842.

495 *"O for a Trumpet Voice."* H. M.

1 JESUS, transporting sound!
   The joy of earth and heaven!
   No other help is found,
   No other name is given,
   By which we can salvation have
   But Jesus came the world to save.

2 His name the sinner hears,
   And is from sin set free;
   'T is music in his ears,
   'T is life and victory;
   New songs do now his lips employ,
   And dances his glad heart for joy.

3 O unexampled love!
   O all-redeeming grace!
   How swiftly didst Thou move
   To save a fallen race!
   What shall I do to make it known,
   What Thou for all mankind hast done?

4 O for a trumpet voice,
   On all the world to call,
   To bid their hearts rejoice
   In Him who died for all:
   For all my Lord was crucified;
   For all, for all, my Saviour died.
                    Rev. Charles Wesley. (1708—1788.) 1741. ab.

496 *"Just as I am."* L. M.
John vi. 37.

1 JUST as I am, without one plea
   But that Thy blood was shed for me,
   And that Thou bidd'st me come to Thee,
   O Lamb of God, I come.

2 Just as I am, and waiting not
   To rid my soul of one dark blot,
   To Thee, whose blood can cleanse each spot,
   O Lamb of God, I come.

3 Just as I am, though tossed about
   With many a conflict, many a doubt,
   With fears within, and foes without,
   O Lamb of God, I come.

4 Just as I am, poor, wretched, blind;
   Sight, riches, healing of the mind,
   Yea, all I need, in Thee to find,
   O Lamb of God, I come.

5 Just as I am, Thou wilt receive,
   Wilt welcome, pardon, cleanse, relieve:
   Because Thy promise I believe,
   O Lamb of God, I come.

6 Just as I am, Thy love unknown
   Has broken every barrier down:
   Now, to be Thine, yea, *Thine alone*,
   O Lamb of God, I come.
                    Miss Charlotte Elliott. (1789—1871.) 1836.

FAITH.

497 *"Just as thou art."*

1 JUST as thou art, without one trace
Of love, or joy, or inward grace,
Or meetness for the heavenly place,
O guilty sinner, come, O come.

2 Thy sins I bore on Calvary's tree;
The stripes, thy due, were laid on Me,
That peace and pardon might be free;
O wretched sinner, come, O come.

3 Come, leave thy burden at the cross,
Count all thy gains but empty dross:
My grace repays all earthly loss;
O needy sinner, come, O come.
Rev. Russell Sturgis Cook. (1814—1864.) 1850. ab.

498 *The Prodigal's Welcome.* L. M.

1 THE wanderer no more will roam,
The lost one to the fold hath come,
The prodigal is welcomed home,
O Lamb of God, in Thee.

2 Though clothed with shame, by sin defiled,
The Father hath embraced His child,
And I am pardoned, reconciled,
O Lamb of God, in Thee.

3 It is the Father's joy to bless;
His love provides for me a dress,
A robe of spotless righteousness,
O Lamb of God, in Thee.

4 Now shall my famished soul be fed,
A feast of love for me is spread,
I feed upon the children's bread,
O Lamb of God, in Thee.

5 Yea, in the fulness of His grace,
He puts me in the children's place,
Where I may gaze upon His face,
O Lamb of God, in Thee.

6 I cannot half His love express;
Yet, Lord, with joy my lips confess,
This blessèd portion I possess,
O Lamb of God, in Thee.
Mrs. Mary Jane Walker. 1847. ab.

499 *"Rock of Ages."* 7.

1 ROCK of ages, cleft for me,
Let me hide myself in Thee;
Let the water and the blood,
From Thy riven side which flowed,
Be of sin the double cure,
Cleanse me from its guilt and power.

2 Not the labors of my hands
Can fulfil Thy law's demands;
Could my zeal no respite know,
Could my tears for ever flow,
All for sin could not atone;
Thou must save, and Thou alone.

3 Nothing in my hand I bring;
Simply to Thy cross I cling;
Naked, come to Thee for dress;
Helpless, look to Thee for grace;
Foul, I to the fountain fly;
Wash me, Saviour, or I die.

4 While I draw this fleeting breath,
When my eye-lids close in death,
When I soar to worlds unknown,
See Thee on Thy judgment throne,
Rock of ages, cleft for me,
Let me hide myself in Thee.
Rev. Augustus Montague Toplady. (1740—1778.) 1776. sl. alt.

500 *"Son of God, to Thee I cry."* 7.

1 SON of God, to Thee I cry:
By the holy mystery
Of Thy dwelling here on earth;
By Thy pure and holy birth,
Lord, Thy presence let me see,
Manifest Thyself to me.

2 Lamb of God, to Thee I cry:
By Thy bitter agony,
By Thy pangs to us unknown,
By Thy Spirit's parting groan,
Lord, Thy presence let me see,
Manifest Thyself to me.

3 Prince of Life, to Thee I cry:
By Thy glorious majesty,
By Thy triumph o'er the grave,
Meek to suffer, strong to save,
Lord, Thy presence let me see,
Manifest Thyself to me.

4 Lord of glory, God most High,
Man exalted to the sky,
With Thy love my bosom fill,
Prompt me to perform Thy will;
Then Thy glory I shall see,
Thou wilt bring me home to Thee.
Bp. Richard Mant. (1776—1848.) 1828.

FAITH.

501   *"A Fountain opened."*   C. M.
     Zech. xiii. 1.

1 THERE is a fountain filled with blood
     Drawn from Emmanuel's veins;
   And sinners, plunged beneath that flood,
     Lose all their guilty stains.

2 The dying thief rejoiced to see
     That fountain in his day;
   And there have I, as vile as he,
     Washed all my sins away.

3 Dear dying Lamb, Thy precious Blood
     Shall never lose its power,
   Till all the ransomed Church of God
     Be saved, to sin no more.

4 E'er since, by faith, I saw the stream
     Thy flowing wounds supply,
   Redeeming love has been my theme,
     And shall be till I die.

5 Then in a nobler, sweeter song,
     I'll sing Thy power to save,
   When this poor lisping, stammering tongue
     Lies silent in the grave.

6 Lord, I believe Thou hast prepared,
     Unworthy though I be,
   For me a blood-bought free reward,
     A golden harp for me.

7 'T is strung, and tuned for endless years,
     And formed by power divine,
   To sound in God the Father's ears
     No other name but Thine.
         William Cowper. (1731—1800.) 1779.

502   *"Vexilla Regis prodeunt."*   C. M.

1 THE royal banner is unfurled,
     The cross is reared on high,
   On which the Saviour of the world
     Is stretched in agony.

2 See through His holy hands and feet
     The cruel nails they drive:
   Our ransom thus is made complete,
     Our souls are saved alive.

3 And see, the spear hath pierced His side,
     And shed that sacred flood,
   That holy reconciling tide,
     The water and the blood.

4 Hail, holy cross, from thee we learn
     The only way to heaven;
   And O, to thee may sinners turn,
     And look, and be forgiven!

5 Jehovah, we Thy name adore,
     In Thee we will rejoice,
   And sing, till time shall be no more,
     The triumphs of the cross.
     Venantius Fortunatus. (530—609.) 580. ab.
     Tr. by Rev. John Chandler. (1806—) 1837.

503   *Fear disarmed.*   C. M.

1 THE Saviour! O what endless charms
     Dwell in the blissful sound!
   Its influence every fear disarms,
     And spreads sweet comfort round.

2 Wrapt in the gloom of dark despair,
     We helpless, hopeless lay;
   But sovereign mercy reached us there,
     And smiled despair away.

3 The almighty Former of the skies
     Stooped to our vile abode;
   While angels viewed with wondering eyes,
     And hailed the incarnate God.

4 O the rich depths of love divine,
     Of bliss a boundless store!
   Dear Saviour, let me call Thee mine;
     I cannot wish for more.

5 On Thee alone my hope relies,
     Beneath Thy cross I fall,
   My Lord, my Life, my Sacrifice,
     My Saviour, and my All.
     Miss Anne Steele. (1717—1778.) 1763. ab.

504   *The sweet Name.*   C. M.

1 How sweet the Name of Jesus sounds
     In a believer's ear;
   It soothes his sorrows, heals his wounds,
     And drives away his fear.

2 It makes the wounded spirit whole,
     And calms the troubled breast;
   'T is manna to the hungry soul,
     And to the weary rest.

3 Dear Name! the rock on which I build,
     My shield and hiding-place,
   My never-failing treasury, filled
     With boundless stores of grace.

4 By Thee my prayers acceptance gain,
   Although with sin defiled;
   Satan accuses me in vain,
   And I am owned a child.

5 Jesus, my Shepherd, Husband, Friend,
   My Prophet, Priest, and King;
   My Lord, my Life, my Way, my End,
   Accept the praise I bring.

6 Weak is the effort of my heart,
   And cold my warmest thought;
   But when I see Thee as Thou art,
   I'll praise Thee as I ought.

7 Till then I would Thy love proclaim
   With every fleeting breath;
   And may the music of Thy Name
   Refresh my soul in death.
   Rev. John Newton. (1725—1807.) 1779.

505   *"The Name high over all."*   C. M.

1 JESUS, the name high over all,
   In hell, or earth, or sky;
   Angels and men before it fall,
   And devils fear and fly.

2 Jesus, the name to sinners dear,
   The name to sinners given;
   It scatters all their guilty fear,
   And turns their hell to heaven.

3 Jesus the prisoner's fetters breaks,
   And bruises Satan's head;
   Power into strengthless souls He speaks,
   And life into the dead.

4 O that the world might taste and see
   The riches of His grace;
   The arms of love that compass me,
   Would all mankind embrace.

5 His only righteousness I show,
   His saving truth proclaim:
   'T is all my business here below,
   To cry, Behold the Lamb!

6 Happy, if with my latest breath
   I may but gasp His name;
   Preach Him to all, and cry in death,
   Behold, behold the Lamb!
   Rev. Charles Wesley (1708—1788.) 1749 ab.

506   *"I bless the Christ of God."*   S. M.

1 I BLESS the Christ of God;
   I rest on love divine;
   And with unfaltering lip and heart,
   I call this Saviour mine.

2 His cross dispels each doubt;
   I bury in His tomb
   Each thought of unbelief and fear,
   Each lingering shade of gloom.

3 I praise the God of grace;
   I trust His truth and might;
   He calls me His, I call Him mine,
   My God, my joy, my light.

4 In Him is only good,
   In me is only ill;
   My ill but draws His goodness forth,
   And me He loveth still.

5 'T is He who saveth me,
   And freely pardon gives;
   I love because He loveth me,
   I live because He lives.

6 My life with Him is hid,
   My death has passed away,
   My clouds have melted into light,
   My midnight into day.
   Rev. Horatius Bonar. (1808—) 1863.

507   *"To love Thee for Thyself."*   S. M.

1 BLEST be Thy love, dear Lord,
   That taught us this sweet way,
   Only to love Thee for Thyself
   And for that love obey.

2 O Thou, our souls' chief hope,
   We to Thy mercy fly;
   Where'er we are, Thou canst protect,
   Whate'er we need, supply.

3 Whether we sleep or wake,
   To Thee we both resign;
   By night we see, as well as day,
   If Thy light on us shine.

4 Whether we live or die,
   Both we submit to Thee;
   In death we live, as well as life,
   If Thine in death we be.
   John Austin (1613—1669.) 1668 ab.

FAITH.

508 *Other Lords rejected.* S. M.
Is. xxvi. 13.

1 O LORD, Thou art my Lord,
My portion and delight;
All other lords I now reject,
And cast them from my sight.

2 Thy sovereign right I own,
Thy glorious power confess;
Thy law shall ever rule my heart,
While I adore Thy grace.

3 Too long my feet have strayed
In sin's forbidden way;
But since Thou hast my soul reclaimed,
To Thee my vows I'll pay.

4 My soul, to Jesus joined
By faith and hope and love,
Now seeks to dwell among Thy saints,
And rest with them above.

5 Accept, O Lord, my heart;
To Thee myself I give;
Nor suffer me from hence to stray,
Or cause Thy saints to grieve.
Rev. Benjamin Beddome. (1717—1795.) 1818.

509 *The Surrender.* S. M.

1 AH, what avails my strife,
My wandering to and fro?
Thou hast the words of endless life;
Ah, whither should I go?

2 Thy condescending grace
To me did freely move;
It calls me still to seek Thy face,
And stoops to ask my love.

3 Lord, at Thy feet I fall,
I groan to be set free;
I fain would now obey the call,
And give up all for Thee.
Rev. Charles Wesley. (1708—1788.) 1740. ab.

510 *"And can I yet delay?"* S. M.

1 AND can I yet delay
My little all to give?
To tear my soul from earth away,
For Jesus to receive?

2 Nay, but I yield, I yield,
I can hold out no more;
I sink, by dying love compelled,
And own Thee Conqueror.

3 Though late, I all forsake,
My friends, my all resign;
Gracious Redeemer, take, O take,
And seal me ever Thine.

4 Come, and possess me whole,
Nor hence again remove;
Settle and fix my wavering soul
With all Thy weight of love.

5 My one desire be this,
Thine only love to know;
To seek and taste no other bliss,
No other good below.

6 My Life, my Portion thou,
Thou all-sufficient art;
My Hope, my heavenly Treasure, now
Enter, and keep my heart.
Rev. Charles Wesley. 1740. ab.

511 *The Blessedness of the Pardoned.* S. M.
Ps. xxxii.

1 O BLESSED souls are they,
Whose sins are covered o'er;
Divinely blest, to whom the Lord
Imputes their guilt no more.

2 They mourn their follies past,
And keep their hearts with care;
Their lips and lives without deceit
Shall prove their faith sincere.

3 While I concealed my guilt,
I felt the festering wound;
Till I confessed my sins to Thee,
And ready pardon found.

4 Let sinners learn to pray,
Let saints keep near the throne;
Our help in times of deep distress
Is found in God alone.
Rev. Isaac Watts. (1674—1748.) 1719.

512 *Sweet Subjection.* S. M.

1 DEAR Lord and Master mine,
Thy happy servant see:
My Conqueror, with what joy divine
Thy captive clings to Thee.

2 I love Thy yoke to wear,
To feel Thy gracious bands,
Sweetly restrained by Thy care,
And happy in Thy hands.

3 No bar would I remove;
    No bond would I unbind;
    Within the limits of Thy love
    Full liberty I find.
4 I would not walk alone,
    But still with Thee, my God;
    At every step my blindness own,
    And ask of Thee the road.
5 The weakness I enjoy
    That casts me on Thy breast;
    The conflicts that Thy strength employ
    Make me divinely blest.
6 Dear Lord and Master mine,
    Still keep Thy servant true;
    My Guardian and my Guide divine,
    Bring, bring Thy pilgrim through.
7 My Conqueror and my King,
    Still keep me in Thy train;
    And with Thee Thy glad captive bring,
    When Thou return'st to reign.
        Thomas Hornblower Gill. (1819—) 1859.

513 *"Behold the Man."* H. M.
1 ARISE, my soul, arise,
    Shake off thy guilty fears;
    The bleeding Sacrifice
    In my behalf appears;
    Before the throne my Surety stands,
    My name is written on His hands.
2 He ever lives above,
    For me to intercede,
    His all-redeeming love,
    His precious blood, to plead;
    His blood atoned for all our race,
    And sprinkles now the throne of grace.
3 The Father hears Him pray,
    His dear anointed One:
    He cannot turn away
    The presence of His Son;
    His Spirit answers to the blood,
    And tells me I am born of God.
4 My God is reconciled,
    His pardoning voice I hear,
    He owns me for His child;
    I can no longer fear,
    With confidence I now draw nigh,
    And Father, Abba, Father, cry.
        Rev. Charles Wesley. 1742. ab.

514 *Prophet, Priest, and King.* H. M.
1 JOIN all the glorious names
    Of wisdom, love, and power
    That ever mortals knew,
    That angels ever bore:
    All are too mean to speak His worth,
    Too mean to set my Saviour forth.
2 Great Prophet of my God,
    My tongue would bless Thy name;
    By Thee the joyful news
    Of our salvation came:
    The joyful news of sins forgiven,
    Of hell subdued, and peace with heaven.
3 Jesus, my great High Priest,
    Offered His blood and died;
    My guilty conscience seeks
    No sacrifice beside:
    His powerful blood did once atone,
    And now it pleads before the throne.
4 My dear Almighty Lord,
    My Conqueror and my King,
    Thy sceptre and Thy sword,
    Thy reigning grace I sing:
    Thine is the power; behold, I sit,
    In willing bonds, beneath Thy feet.
5 Now let my soul arise,
    And tread the tempter down;
    My Captain leads me forth
    To conquest and a crown;
    A feeble saint shall win the day,
    Though death and hell obstruct the way.
        Rev. Isaac Watts. 1709. ab.

515 *The Fountain of Life.* H. M.
    Zech. xiii. 1.
1 HAIL, everlasting Spring,
    Celestial Fountain, hail,
    Thy streams salvation bring,
    The waters never fail;
    Still they endure, and still they flow
    For all our woe a sovereign cure.
2 Blest be His wounded side,
    And blest His bleeding heart,
    Who all in anguish died,
    Such favors to impart:
    His sacred blood shall make us clean
    From every sin, and fit for God.

3 To that dear source of love
   Our souls this day would come;
   And thither from above,
   Lord, call the nations home:
 That Jew and Greek, with rapturous songs,
   On all their tongues, Thy praise may speak.
   Rev. Philip Doddridge. (1702–1751.) 1755

516 *"Wounded for our Transgressions."* H. M.
Is. liii. 5

1 THY works, not mine, O Christ,
   Speak gladness to this heart;
   They tell me all is done;
   They bid my fear depart:
 To whom save Thee, who canst alone
   For sin atone, Lord, shall I flee?

2 Thy tears, not mine, O Christ,
   Have wept my guilt away,
   And turned this night of mine
   Into a blessèd day:
 To whom, save Thee, who canst alone
   For sin atone, Lord, shall I flee?

3 Thy wounds, not mine, O Christ,
   Can heal my bruisèd soul;
   Thy stripes, not mine, contain
   The balm that makes me whole:
 To whom save Thee, who canst alone
   For sin atone, Lord, shall I flee?

4 Thy cross, not mine, O Christ,
   Has borne the awful load
   Of sins that none in heaven
   Or earth could bear but God:
 To whom save Thee, who canst alone
   For sin atone, Lord, shall I flee?

5 Thy death, not mine, O Christ,
   Has paid the ransom due;
   Ten thousand deaths like mine
   Would have been all too few:
 To whom save Thee, who canst alone
   For sin atone, Lord, shall I flee?
   Rev. Horatius Bonar. (1808–) 1857. ab

517 *Blind Bartimeus* 8. 7.
Mark x 47, 48

1 "MERCY, O Thou Son of David,"
   Thus blind Bartimeus prayed;
 "Others by Thy word are saved,
   Now to me afford Thine aid."

2 Many for his crying chid him,
   But he called the louder still;
 Till the gracious Saviour bid him
   Come, and ask Me what you will.

3 Money was not what he wanted,
   Though by begging used to live;
 But he asked, and Jesus granted,
   Alms which none but He could give.

4 "Lord, remove this grievous blindness,
   Let mine eyes behold the day!"
 Straight he saw and, won by kindness,
   Followed Jesus in the way.

5 O methinks I hear him praising,
   Publishing to all around,
 "Friends, is not my case amazing?
   What a Saviour I have found!

6 "O that all the blind but knew Him,
   And would be advised by me,
 Surely they would hasten to Him,
   He would cause them all to see."
   Rev. John Newton. (1725–1807.) 1779.

518 *"He received his Sight."* 8. 7.
Mark x. 51, 52.

1 LORD, I know Thy grace is nigh me,
   Though Thyself I cannot see;
 Jesus, Master, pass not by me;
   Son of David, pity me.

2 While I sit in weary blindness,
   Longing for the blessèd light,
 Many taste Thy loving-kindness;
   "Lord, I would receive my sight."

3 I would see Thee and adore Thee,
   And Thy word the power can give;
 Hear the sightless soul implore Thee:
   Let me see Thy face and live.

4 Ah, what touch is this that thrills me?
   What this burst of strange delight?
 Lo, the rapturous vision fills me!
   This is Jesus! this is sight!

5 Room, ye saints that throng behind Him!
   Let me follow in the way;
 I will teach the blind to find Him
   Who can turn their night to day.
   Rev Hervey Doddridge Ganse (1822–) 1869.

FAITH.

519   *"Open, Lord, and let me in."*   8. 7.

1 AT the door of mercy sighing
    With the burden of my sin,
Day and night my soul is crying,
    "Open, Lord, and let me in."

2 Waiting 'mid the darkness dreary,
    Stretching out my hands to Thee,
In the refuge for the weary
    Is there not a place for me?

3 Hark, what sounds my ear receiveth,
    Sweet as songs of seraphim!
He that in the Lord believeth
    Life eternal hath in Him.

4 At the outer door why staying?
    Nothing, soul, hast thou to pay:
Christ in love to thee is saying,
    "Weary child, come in to-day."
        Thomas MacKellar. (1812—) 1872.

520   *Free Mercy.*   P. M.

1 BY faith I view my Saviour dying
    On the tree, on the tree;
To every nation He is crying,
    Look to me, look to me,
He bids the guilty now draw near,
Repent, believe, dismiss their fear;
Hark, hark, what precious words I hear:
    Mercy's free, mercy's free.

2 Jesus, the Lord of life, hath spoken
    Peace to me, peace to me;
Now all my chains of sin are broken,
    I am free, I am free,
Soon as I in His name believed,
His pardoning grace my soul received
And was from sin and death retrieved
    Mercy's free, mercy's free.

3 This precious truth, ye sinners hear it,
    Mercy's free, mercy's free;
Ye ministers of God declare it,
    Mercy's free, mercy's free.
Visit the heathen's dark abode,
Proclaim to all the love of God,
And spread the glorious news abroad,
    Mercy's free, mercy's free.

4 Long as I live I'll still be crying,
    Mercy's free, mercy's free.

And this shall be my theme when dying,
    Mercy's free, mercy's free.
And when the vale of death I've passed,
When lodged above the stormy blast,
I'll sing, while endless ages last,
    Mercy's free, mercy's free.
        R. Jukes. 1842.

521   *"How happy are they."*   11, 9.

1 O HOW happy are they
    Who the Saviour obey,
And have laid up their treasures above;
    Tongue can never express
    The sweet comfort and peace
Of a soul in its earliest love.

2 That sweet comfort was mine,
    When the favor divine
I first found in the blood of the Lamb;
    When my heart it believed,
    What a joy it received,
What a heaven in Jesus's name!

3 'T was a heaven below
    My Redeemer to know,
And the angels could do nothing more
    Than to fall at His feet,
    And the story repeat,
And the Lover of sinners adore.

4 O the rapturous height
    Of that holy delight,
Which I felt in the life-giving blood!
    Of my Saviour possessed,
    I was perfectly blest,
As if filled with the fulness of God.
    Rev. Charles Wesley. (1708—1788) 1749. ab. and sl. alt.

522   *The Surrender.*   C. P. M.
        Acts ix. 6.

1 LORD, Thou hast won, at length I yield;
  My heart, by mighty grace compelled,
    Surrenders all to Thee;
Against Thy terrors long I strove,
But who can stand against Thy love?
    Love conquers even me.

2 If Thou hadst bid Thy thunders roll,
And lightnings flash to blast my soul,
    I still had stubborn been;
But mercy has my heart subdued,
A bleeding Saviour I have viewed,
    And now I hate my sin.

FAITH.

3 Now, Lord, I would be Thine alone,
  Come, take possession of Thine own,
  For Thou hast set me free;
  Released from Satan's hard command,
  See all my powers in waiting stand,
  To be employed by Thee.
        Rev. John Newton. (1725—1807.) 1779. ab.

523   *Sinai, and the Saviour.*   C. P. M.

1 AWAKED by Sinai's awful sound,
  My soul in bonds of guilt I found,
  And knew not where to go;
  Eternal truth did loud proclaim,
  "The sinner must be born again,
  Or sink to endless woe."

2 When to the law I trembling fled,
  It poured its curses on my head,
  I no relief could find;
  This fearful truth increased my pain,
  "The sinner must be born again,"
  And whelmed my tortured mind.

3 The saints I heard with rapture tell
  How Jesus conquered death and hell,
  And broke the fowler's snare;
  Yet, when I found this truth remain,
  "The sinner must be born again,"
  I sunk in deep despair.

4 But while I thus in anguish lay,
  The gracious Saviour passed this way,
  And felt His pity move;
  The sinner, by His justice slain,
  Now by His grace is born again,
  And sings redeeming love.
        Rev. Sampson Occum. (1723—1792.) 1760. alt.
        Rev. Asahel Nettleton. (1783—1844.) 1824. ab.

524   *The true Convert.*   C. P. M.

1 WHEN with a mind devoutly pressed,
  Dear Saviour, my revolving breast
  Would past offences trace;
  Trembling I make the black review,
  Yet pleased behold, admiring too,
  The power of changing grace.

2 This tongue with blasphemies defiled,
  These feet to erring paths beguiled,
  In heavenly league agree;
  Who would believe such lips could praise,
  Or think my dark and winding ways
  Should ever lead to Thee?

3 These eyes that once abused the light
  Now lift to Thee their watery sight,
  And weep a silent flood;
  These hands ascend in ceaseless prayer;
  O wash away the stains they wear,
  In pure, redeeming blood.

4 Thus art Thou served in every part;
  O wouldst Thou but transform my heart,
  That drossy thing refine;
  That grace might nature's powers control,
  And a new creature, body, soul,
  Be all, be ever Thine.
        Rev. Moses Browne. (1703—1787.) 1739. ab.

525   *The Prayer of Faith.*   C. P. M.

1 O THOU that hear'st the prayer of faith,
  Wilt Thou not save a soul from death,
  That casts itself on Thee?
  I have no refuge of my own,
  But fly to what my Lord hath done,
  And suffered once for me.

2 Slain in the guilty sinner's stead,
  His spotless righteousness I plead,
  And His availing blood:
  Thy merit, Lord, my robe shall be,
  Thy merit shall atone for me,
  And bring me near to God.

3 Then snatch me from eternal death,
  The Spirit of adoption breathe,
  His consolations send;
  By Him some word of life impart,
  And sweetly whisper to my heart,
  "Thy Maker is thy Friend."

4 The king of terrors *then* would be
  A welcome messenger to me,
  That bids me come away:
  Unclogged by earth, or earthly things,
  I'd mount upon his sable wings
  To everlasting day.
        Rev. Augustus Montague Toplady. (1740—1778.) 1759.

526   *"Jesus paid it all."*   7, 6.

1 NOTHING, either great or small,
  Remains for me to do;
  Jesus died and paid it all,
  Yes all the debt I owe.

2 When He from His lofty throne,
  Stooped down to die and die,

Every thing was fully done;
"'T is finished!" was His cry.

3 Weary, working, plodding one,
O wherefore toil you so?
Cease your doing; all was done,
Yes, ages long ago.

4 Till to Jesus' work you cling,
Alone by simple faith,
"Doing" is a deadly thing,
Your "doing" ends in death.

5 Cast your deadly "doing" down,
Down all at Jesus' feet;
Stand in Him, in Him alone,
All glorious and complete.

Rev. James Procter. 1858. ab. and alt.

527   *Singing for Joy.*   C. M.

1 I'VE found the pearl of greatest price,
My heart doth sing for joy;
And sing I must; for Christ is mine,
Christ shall my song employ.

2 Christ is my Prophet, Priest, and King;
A Prophet full of light,
My great High-Priest before the throne,
My King of heavenly might.

3 For He indeed is Lord of lords,
And He the King of kings;
He is the Sun of righteousness,
With healing in His wings.

4 Christ is my Peace; he died for me,
For me He gave his blood;
And as my wondrous Sacrifice,
Offered Himself to God.

5 Christ Jesus is my All in all,
My Comfort and my Love,
My Life below, and He shall be
My Joy and Crown above.

Rev. John Mason. (—1694.) 1683. ab. and alt.

528   *Converting Grace commemorated.*   C. M.

1 O FOR a thousand tongues to sing
My dear Redeemer's praise;
The glories of my God and King,
The triumphs of His grace.

2 My gracious Master and my God,
Assist me to proclaim,

To spread through all the earth abroad,
The honors of Thy name.

3 Jesus, the name that charms our fears,
That bids our sorrows cease;
'T is music in the sinner's ears,
'T is life, and health, and peace.

4 He breaks the power of cancelled sin,
He sets the prisoners free;
His blood can make the foulest clean,
His blood availed for *me*.

5 He speaks, and, listening to His voice,
New life the dead receive;
The mournful, broken hearts rejoice;
The humble poor believe.

Rev. Charles Wesley. (1708—1788.) 1740. ab.

529   *"Old Things are passed away."*   C. M.
2 Cor. v. 17.

1 LET worldly minds the world pursue,
It has no charms for me;
Once I admired its trifles too,
But grace has set me free.

2 Its pleasures now no longer please,
No more content afford;
Far from my heart be joys like these,
Now I have seen the Lord.

3 As by the light of opening day
The stars are all concealed,
So earthly pleasures fade away,
When Jesus is revealed.

4 Creatures no more divide my choice,
I bid them all depart;
His name, and love, and gracious voice,
Have fixed my roving heart.

5 Now, Lord, I would be Thine alone,
And wholly live to Thee;
For if Thou hadst not loved me first,
I had refused still Thee.

Rev. John Newton. 1779. ab.

530   *Unseen, but loved.*   C. M.
1 Pet. i. 8.

1 JESUS, these eyes have never seen
That radiant form of Thine;
The veil of sense hangs dark between
Thy blessèd face and mine.

2 I see Thee not, I hear Thee not,
   Yet art Thou oft with me;
   And earth hath ne'er so dear a spot,
   As where I meet with Thee.

3 Like some bright dream that comes unsought
   When slumbers o'er me roll,
   Thine image ever fills my thought,
   And charms my ravished soul.

4 Yet though I have not seen, and still
   Must rest in faith alone,
   I love Thee, dearest Lord,—and will,
   Unseen, but not Unknown.

5 When death these mortal eyes shall seal,
   And still this throbbing heart,
   The rending veil shall Thee reveal,
   All-glorious as Thou art.
        Rev. Ray Palmer. (1808—) 1858.

531   *Jesus, my God and my All.*   C. M.

1 O JESUS, Jesus, dearest Lord,
   Forgive me, if I say,
   For very love, Thy sacred name
   A thousand times a day.

2 I love Thee so, I know not how
   My transports to control;
   Thy love is like a burning fire
   Within my very soul.

3 O wonderful! that Thou shouldst let
   So vile a heart as mine
   Love Thee with such a love as this,
   And make so free with Thine.

4 O Light in darkness, Joy in grief,
   O Heaven begun on earth!
   Jesus, my Love, my Treasure, who
   Can tell what Thou art worth?

5 O Jesus, Jesus, sweetest Lord,
   What art Thou not to me?
   Each hour brings joys before unknown,
   Each day new liberty.
        Rev. Frederick William Faber. (1814—1863.) 1849. ab.

532   *Jesu Rex admirabilis*   C. M.

1 O JESUS, King most wonderful,
   Thou Conqueror renowned,
   Thou sweetness most ineffable,
   In whom all joys are found:

2 When once Thou visitest the heart,
   Then truth begins to shine,
   Then earthly vanities depart,
   Then kindles love divine.

3 O Jesus, Light of all below,
   Thou Fount of life and fire,
   Surpassing all the joys we know,
   All that we can desire:

4 May every heart confess Thy name,
   And ever Thee adore;
   And seeking Thee, itself inflame
   To seek Thee more and more.

5 Thee may our tongues forever bless;
   Thee may we love alone;
   And ever in our lives express
   The image of Thine own.
        Bernard of Clairvaux. (1091—1153.) 1140.
        Tr. by Rev. Edward Caswall. (1814—) 1849.

533   *"I'm a Miracle of Grace."*   8, 7. D.

1 HAIL, my ever blessed Jesus!
   Only Thee I wish to sing;
   To my soul Thy name is precious,
   Thou my Prophet, Priest and King.
   O what mercy flows from Heaven,
   O what joy and happiness!
   Love I much, I've much forgiven;
   I'm a miracle of grace.

2 Once with Adam's race in ruin,
   Unconcerned in sin I lay,
   Swift destruction still pursuing,
   Till my Saviour passed that way.
   Witness, all ye host of heaven,
   My Redeemer's tenderness.
   Love I much, I've much forgiven;
   I'm a miracle of grace.

3 Shout, ye bright, angelic choir,
   Praise the Lamb enthroned above,
   While, astonished, I admire
   God's free grace and boundless love.
   That blest moment I received Him
   Filled my soul with joy and peace.
   Love I much, I've much forgiven;
   I'm a miracle of grace.
        John Wingrove. 1806.

534   *Bought with a Price*   8, 7. D.

1 WHEN I view my Saviour bleeding,
   For my sins, upon the tree;

LOVE—JOY—TRUST. GRATITUDE.

O how wondrous, how exceeding
    Great His love appears to me!
Floods of deep distress and anguish,
    To impede His labors, came;
Yet they all could not extinguish
    Love's eternal, burning flame.

2 Now redemption is completed,
    Full salvation is procured;
Death and Satan are defeated,
    By the sufferings He endured.
Now the gracious Mediator,
    Risen to the courts of bliss,
Claims for me, a sinful creature,
    Pardon, righteousness, and peace.

3 Sure, such infinite affection
    Lays the highest claims to mine;
All my powers, without exception,
    Should in fervent praises join.
Jesus, fit me for Thy service;
    Form me for Thyself alone;
I am Thy most costly purchase,
    Take possession of Thine own.
                     Richard Lee. 1794.

535   *Praise for pardoning Grace*   **8, 7. D.**

1 LORD, with glowing heart I'd praise Thee,
    For the bliss Thy love bestows,
For the pardoning grace that saves me,
    And the peace that from it flows.
Help, O God, my weak endeavor,
    This dull soul to rapture raise;
Thou must light the flame, or never
    Can my love be warmed to praise.

2 Praise, my soul, the God that sought thee,
    Wretched wanderer, far astray;
Found thee lost, and kindly brought thee
    From the paths of death away.
Praise, with love's devoutest feeling,
    Him who saw thy guilt-born fear,
And, the light of hope revealing,
    Bade the blood-stained cross appear.

3 Lord, this bosom's ardent feeling
    Vainly would my lips express;
Low before Thy footstool kneeling,
    Deign Thy suppliant's prayer to bless.
Let Thy grace, my soul's chief treasure,
    Love's pure flame within me raise;
And since words can never measure,
    Let my life show forth Thy praise.
              Francis Scott Key (1799—1843.) 1857.

536   *Grateful Recollection.*   **8, 7. D.**

1 COME, thou Fount of every blessing,
    Tune my heart to sing Thy grace;
Streams of mercy never ceasing,
    Call for songs of loudest praise:
Teach me some melodious sonnet,
    Sung by flaming tongues above;
Praise the mount, I'm fixed upon it,
    Mount of God's unchanging love.

2 Here I raise my Ebenezer,
    Hither by Thy help I'm come;
And I hope, by Thy good pleasure,
    Safely to arrive at home:
Jesus sought me, when a stranger,
    Wandering from the fold of God;
He, to rescue me from danger,
    Interposed His precious blood.

3 O to grace how great a debtor,
    Daily I'm constrained to be:
Let that grace now, like a fetter,
    Bind my wandering heart to Thee:
Prone to wander, Lord, I feel it,
    Prone to leave the God I love;
Here's my heart, O take and seal it,
    Seal it from Thy courts above.
       Rev. Robert Robinson. (1735—1790.) 1758.

537   *"Bless the Lord, O my Soul."*   **8, 7. D.**
        Ps. ciii.

1 PRAISE, my soul, the King of Heaven;
    To His feet thy tribute bring;
Ransomed, healed, restored, forgiven,
    Evermore His praises sing:
        Alleluia! Alleluia!
    Praise the everlasting King.

2 Praise Him for His grace and favor
    To our fathers in distress;
Praise Him still the same as ever,
    Slow to chide, and swift to bless:
        Alleluia! Alleluia!
    Glorious in His faithfulness.

3 Father-like, He tends and spares us,
    Well our feeble frame He knows;
In His hands He gently bears us,
    Rescues us from all our foes:
        Alleluia! Alleluia!
    Praise with us the God of grace.
   Rev. Henry Francis Lyte. (1793—1847.) 1834. ab. and alt.
   Rev. Sir Henry Williams Baker. (1821—) 1861.

GRATITUDE.

538 *A full Surrender.* 8. 7.

1 WELCOME, welcome, dear Redeemer,
  Welcome to this heart of mine:
Lord, I make a full surrender,
  Every power and thought be Thine,
    Thine entirely,
  Through eternal ages Thine.

2 Known to all to be Thy mansion,
  Earth and hell will disappear;
Or in vain attempt possession,
  When they find the Lord is near;
    Shout, O Zion,
  Shout, ye saints, the Lord is here.
      Rev. William Mason. (1725—1797.) 1704.

539 *Lost but found.* S. M.

1 I WAS a wandering sheep,
    I did not love the fold;
  I did not love my Shepherd's voice,
    I would not be controlled:
  I was a wayward child,
    I did not love my home,
  I did not love my Father's voice,
    I loved afar to roam.

2 The Shepherd sought His sheep,
    The Father sought His child,
  They followed me o'er vale and hill,
    O'er deserts waste and wild:
  They found me nigh to death,
    Famished, and faint, and lone;
  They bound me with the bands of love;
    They saved the wandering one.

3 Jesus my Shepherd is,
    'Twas He that loved my soul,
  'Twas He that washed me in His blood,
    'Twas He that made me whole;
  'Twas He that sought the lost,
    That found the wandering sheep,
  'Twas He that brought me to the fold,
    'Tis He that still doth keep.

4 I was a wandering sheep,
    I would not be controlled:
  But now I love my Shepherd's voice,
    I love, I love the fold:
  I was a wayward child;
    I once preferred to roam;
  But now I love my Father's voice,
    I love, I love His home.
      Rev. Horatius Bonar. (1808—) 1844. ab.

540 *"Who can forbear to sing?"* S. M.

1 WHO can forbear to sing,
    Who can refuse to praise,
  When Zion's high, celestial King
    His saving power displays?
  When sinners at His feet,
    By mercy conquered, fall?
  When grace, and truth, and justice meet,
    And peace unites them all?

2 When heaven's opening gates
    Invite the pilgrims' feet;
  And Jesus, at their entrance waits,
    To place them on His seat
  Who can forbear to praise
    Our high, celestial King,
  When sovereign, rich, redeeming grace
    Invites our tongues to sing?
      Rev. Joseph Swain. (1761—1796.) 1792.

541 *"Is this the Son of God?"* S. M.

1 Is this the Son of God
    That dies in agony?
  And did He choose this cross of shame,
    This bitter death, *for me?*
  Is this the Holy Ghost
    That moves within my breast,
  And shows me all my wretchedness,
    And makes me long for rest?

2 Is this the Father's voice
    That speaks above my fears,
  And with its sweetness melts my soul
    To penitence and tears?
  To me, O God, *to me*
    Is this great pity shown?
  Take me, I yield: and from this hour,
    Dear Lord, I am Thine own.
      Rev. Hervey Doddridge Ganse. (1822—) 1872.

542 *"Du ach bestes Gotteskind."* S. M.

1 ONCE blind with sin and self,
    Along the treacherous way,
  That ends in ruin at the last,
    I hastened far astray;
  Then God sent down His Son;
    For with a love most deep,
  Most underserved, His heart still yearned
    O'er me, poor wandering sheep.

2 God with His life of love
    To me was far and strange,

GRATITUDE.

My heart clung only to the world
Of sight and sense and change;
In Thee, Immanuel,
Are God and man made one;
In Thee my heart hath peace with God,
And union in the Son.

3 O ponder this, my soul,
Our God hath loved us thus,
That even His only dearest Son
He freely giveth us.
Thou precious gift of God,
The pledge and bond of love,
With thankful heart I kneel to take
This treasure from above.
Gerhard Tersteegen. (1679—1769.) 1731.
Tr. by Miss Catherine Winkworth. (1829—) 1858. ab.

543   *"Ist Gott für mich so trete."*   S. M. D.

1 HERE I can firmly rest,
I dare to boast of this,
That God, the Highest and the Best,
My Friend and Father is.
From dangerous snares He saves;
Where'er He bids me go
He checks the storms and calms the waves,
That naught can work me woe.

2 He whispers in my breast
Sweet words of holy cheer,
How he who seeks in God his rest
Shall ever find Him near;
How God hath built above
A city fair and new,
Where eye and heart shall see and prove
What faith has counted true.

3 My heart for gladness springs,
It cannot more be sad,
For very joy it laughs and sings,
Sees naught but sunshine glad.
The sun that glads mine eyes
Is Christ the Lord I love;
I sing for joy of that which lies
Stored up for us above.
Rev. Paul Gerhardt. (1606—1676.) 1650.
Tr. by Miss Catherine Winkworth. 1855. ab.

544   *"Closer than a Brother."*   8,7,8,7,7,7.
Prov. xviii. 24.

1 ONE there is above all others,
Well deserves the name of Friend;
His is love beyond a brother's,
Costly, free, and knows no end:
They who once His kindness prove,
Find it everlasting love.

2 Which of all our friends, to save us,
Could or would have shed his blood?
But our Jesus died to have us
Reconciled in Him to God:
This was boundless love indeed;
Jesus is a Friend in need.

3 When He lived on earth abased,
Friend of sinners was His name;
Now, above all glory raised,
He rejoices in the same;
Still He calls them brethren, friends,
And to all their wants attends.

4 Could we bear from one another
What He daily bears from us?
Yet this glorious Friend and Brother
Loves us, though we treat Him thus:
Though for good we render ill,
He accounts us brethren still.

5 O for grace our hearts to soften;
Teach us, Lord, at length to love;
We, alas, forget too often
What a Friend we have above:
But when home our souls are brought,
We will love Thee as we ought.
Rev. John Newton. (1725—1807.) 1779. ab.

545   *"Ich will Dich lieben."*   8,7,8,7,7,7.
1 Pet. i. 8.

1 I WILL love Thee, all my treasure;
I will love Thee, all my strength;
I will love Thee without measure,
And will love Thee right at length:
I will love Thee, Light Divine,
Till I die and find Thee mine.

2 I will praise Thee, Sun of Glory,
For Thy beams have gladness brought;
I will praise Thee, will adore Thee,
For the light I vainly sought;
Praise Thee that Thy words so blest
Spake my sin-sick soul to rest.

3 Be my heart more warmly glowing,
Sweet and calm the tears I shed;
And its love, its ardor, showing,
Let my spirit onward tread:
Near to Thee, and nearer still,
Draw this heart, this mind, this will.

GRATITUDE.

4 I will love in joy or sorrow,
Crowning joy! will love Thee well;
I will love to-day, to-morrow,
While I in this body dwell:
I will love Thee, Light Divine,
Till I die, and find Thee mine.
Johann Angelus. (1624—1677.) 1657.
Tr. by Miss Jane Borthwick. 1854. ab.

546 *Gloriosi Salvatoris.* 8, 7, 7.

1 JESUS is the Name we treasure;
Name beyond what words can tell;
Name of gladness, Name of pleasure,
Ear and heart delighting well;
Name of sweetness, passing measure,
Saving us from sin and hell.

2 'Tis the Name for adoration,
Name for songs of victory,
Name for holy meditation
In this vale of misery,
Name for joyful veneration
By the citizens on high.

3 Jesus is the Name exalted
Over every other name;
In this Name, whene'er assaulted,
We can put our foes to shame;
Strength to them who else had halted,
Eyes to blind, and feet to lame.

4 Therefore we in love adoring,
This most blessèd Name revere;
Holy Jesus, Thee imploring
So to write it in us here,
That hereafter heavenward soaring,
We may sing with angels there.
Unknown Author of the 14th or 15th Century.
Tr by Rev John Mason Neale. (1818—1866.) 1851. ab. and alt.

547 *"I would love Thee."* 8, 7, 7.

1 I WOULD love Thee, God and Father,
My Redeemer and my King:
I would love Thee; for, without Thee,
Life is but a bitter thing.
I would love Thee; look upon me,
Ever guide me with Thine eye:
I would love Thee; if not nourished
By Thy love, my soul would die.

2 I would love Thee; may Thy brightness
Dazzle my rejoicing eyes;

I would love Thee; may Thy goodness
Watch from heaven o'er all I prize.
I would love Thee, I have vowed it;
On Thy love my heart is set;
While I love Thee, I will never
My Redeemer's blood forget.
Madame Jeanne M. B. de la M. Guyon. (1648—1717.) 1710.

548 *"I love Thee best."* 8, 7, 7.

1 SOMETHING every heart is loving;
If not Jesus, none can rest;
Lord, my heart to Thee is given,
Take it, for it loves Thee best.
Thus I cast the world behind me;
Jesus most beloved shall be;
Beauteous more than all things beauteous,
He alone is joy to me.

2 Bright with all eternal radiance,
Is the glory of Thy face;
Thou art loving, sweet and tender,
Full of pity, full of grace.
Keep my heart still faithful to Thee,
That my earthly life may be
But a shadow to that glory
Of my hidden life in Thee.
Gerhard Tersteegen. (1697—1769.) 1730.

549 *"To live is Christ, and to die is Gain."* Phil i. 21 7.

1 CHRIST, of all my hopes the Ground,
Christ, the Spring of all my joy,
Still in Thee may I be found,
Still for Thee my powers employ.
Fountain of o'erflowing grace,
Freely from Thy fulness give;
Till I close my earthly race,
May I prove it, "Christ to live."

2 When I touch the blessèd shore,
Back the closing waves shall roll;
Death's dark stream shall never more
Part from Thee my ravished soul.
Thus, O thus, an entrance give
To the land of cloudless sky;
Having known it, "Christ to live,"
Let me know it, "Gain to die."

3 Gain, to part from all my grief;
Gain, to bid my sins farewell;
Gain, of all my gains the chief,
Ever with the Lord to dwell:

GRATITUDE.

This Thy people's portion, Lord,
  Peace on earth, and bliss on high ;
This their ever-sure reward,
  "Christ to live, and Gain to die."
        Rev. Ralph Wardlaw. (1779—1853.) 1817.

550   *"Blessèd Fountain."*
              Zech. xiii. 1.   7.

1 BLESSÈD Fountain, full of grace,
    Grace for sinners, grace for me,
  To this source alone I trace
    What I am, and hope to be:
  What I am, as one redeemed,
    Saved and rescued by the Lord ;
  Hating what I once esteemed,
    Loving what I once abhorred :

2 What I hope to be, ere long,
    When I take my place above,
  When I join the heavenly throng,
    When I see the God of love ;
  Then I hope like Him to be,
    Who redeemed His saints from sin,
  Whom I now obscurely see,
    Through a cloud that stands between.

3 When I see Him as He is,
    No corruption can remain :
  Such their portion who are His,
    Such the happy state they gain.
  Blessèd Fountain, full of grace,
    Grace for sinners, grace for me,
  To this source alone I trace
    What I am, and hope to be.
        Rev. Thomas Kelly. (1769—1855.) 1809, 1853.

551   *Parting Hymn to Christ.*

1 BLESSÈD Jesus, ere we part,
  Speak Thy blessing to each heart :
  Blessèd Jesus, Son of God,
  Wash us in Thy precious blood :
  Blessèd Jesus, Light divine,
  Let Thy presence round us shine :
  Blessèd Jesus, Saviour bright,
  Guide us safe to realms of light.
        Rev. Christian Henry Bateman. (1813—) 1848. ab.

552   *"Sing unto the Lord."*
             Ps. xxxi. 2.   8, 5.

1 SING of Jesus, sing for ever,
    Of the love that changes never.
  Who or what from Him can sever
    Those He makes His own?

2 With His blood the Lord has bought them ;
  When they knew Him not, He sought them,
  And from all their wand'rings brought them ;
    His the praise alone.

3 Through the desert Jesus leads them,
  With the bread of heaven He feeds them,
  And through all the way He speeds them
    To their home above.

4 There they see the Lord who bought them,
  Him who came from heaven, and sought
    them,
  Him who by His Spirit taught them,
    Him they serve and love.

5 Let His people sing with gladness,
  Other mirth than this is madness,
  Mirth it is that ends in sadness,
    Be it far away.

6 'Tis the saints have solid treasure,
  They can sing with holy pleasure,
  And their joy will know no measure,
    In the final day.
        Rev. Thomas Kelly. 1815.

553 *Our Song on Earth and in Heaven.*   8, 5.

1 SAINTS in glory, we together
  Know the song that ceases never ;
  Song of songs Thou art, O Saviour,
    All that endless day.

2 Theme of Adam, when forgiven,
  Theme of Abraham, David, Stephen ;
  Souls, ye chant it entering heaven,
    Now, henceforth, alway.

3 O the God-man ! O Immanuel !
  Cloud by day ! Jehovah-Angel !
  Fire by night ! He led His Israel,
    So He leads us home.

4 Come, ye angels, round us gather,
  While to Jesus we draw nearer ;
  In His throne He 'll seat forever
    Those for whom He died.

5 Underneath His throne a river,
  Clear as crystal, flows forever,
  Like His fulness, failing never :
    Hail, enthronèd Lamb !

6 O the unsearchable Redeemer !
  Shoreless Ocean, sounded never !
  Yesterday, to-day, forever,
    Jesus Christ, the same.
        S. E. Mahmied. ab.

GRATITUDE.

554 *"Behold the Way to God!"* L. M.

1 JESUS, my All, to heaven is gone,
He that I placed my hopes upon;
His track I see, and I'll pursue
The narrow way till Him I view.

2 The way the holy Prophets went,
The way that leads from banishment,
The King's highway of holiness,
I'll go; for all the paths are peace.

3 This is the way I long have sought,
And mourned because I found it not;
My grief, my burden, long have been
Because I could not cease from sin.

4 The more I strove against its power
I sinned and stumbled but the more;
Till late I heard my Saviour say,
"Come hither, soul, for I'm the Way."

5 Lo, glad I come; and Thou, dear Lamb,
Shalt take me to Thee, as I am:
Nothing but sin I Thee can give;
Yet help me, and Thy praise I'll live.

6 I'll tell to all poor sinners round
What a dear Saviour I have found;
I'll point to Thy redeeming blood,
And say, "Behold the way to God!"
    Rev. John Cennick. (1717—1755.) 1743.

555 *The Hiding place.* L. M.
Is. xxxii. 2.

1 HAIL, sovereign Love, that first began
The scheme to rescue fallen man;
Hail, matchless, free, eternal grace,
That gave my soul a Hiding-place.

2 Against the God that rules the sky
I fought with hand uplifted high;
Despised His rich, abounding grace,
Too proud to seek a Hiding-place.

3 Indignant justice stood in view;
To Sinai's fiery mount I flew:
But Justice cried, with frowning face,
"This mountain is no Hiding-place."

4 Vain every hope, until I heard
The voice of mercy in Thy word,
Proclaiming free redeeming grace,
And Jesus, as my Hiding-place.

5 A few more rolling waves, at most,
Will land me safe on Canaan's coast;
Where I shall see Him face to face.
Jesus, my glorious Hiding-place.
    Rev. Jehoida Brewer. (1752—1817.) 1776. ab.

556 *Christ, our Light and Life.* L. M.

1 LORD, I was blind! I could not see
In Thy marred visage any grace;
But now the beauty of Thy face
In radiant vision dawns on me.

2 Lord, I was deaf! I could not hear
The thrilling music of Thy voice;
But now I hear Thee and rejoice,
And all Thy uttered words are dear.

3 Lord, I was dumb! I could not speak
The grace and glory of Thy name;
But now, as touched with living flame,
My lips Thine eager praises wake.

4 Lord, I was dead! I could not stir
My lifeless soul to come to Thee;
But now, since Thou hast quickened me,
I rise from sin's dark sepulchre.

5 For Thou hast made the blind to see,
The deaf to hear, the dumb to speak,
The dead to live, and lo, I break
The chains of my captivity.
    Rev. William Tidd Matson. 1866.

557 *The new Joy.* L. M.

1 TREMBLING before Thine awful Throne,
O Lord, in dust my sins I own;
Justice and mercy for my life
Contend; O smile, and heal the strife.

2 The Saviour smiles: upon my soul
New tides of hope tumultuous roll;
His voice proclaims my pardon found,
Seraphic transport wings the sound.

3 Earth has a joy unknown to heaven,
The new-born peace of sins forgiven;
Tears of such pure and deep delight,
Ye angels, never dimmed your sight.

4 Ye saw of old, on chaos rise
The beauteous pillars of the skies;
Ye know where morn exulting springs,
And evening folds her drooping wings.

PRAISE TO CHRIST.

5 Bright heralds of the Eternal Will,
　Abroad His errands ye fulfil;
　Or, throned in floods of beamy day,
　Symphonious in His presence play.

6 Loud is the song, the heavenly plain
　Is shaken with the choral strain;
　And dying echoes, floating far,
　Draw music from each chiming star.

7 But I amid your choirs shall shine,
　And all your knowledge shall be mine;
　Ye on your harps must lean to hear
　A secret chord that mine will bear.
　　　　Abraham Lucas Hillhouse. (1792—1859.) 1822.

558　　*Parting with carnal Joys.*　　L. M.

1 I SEND the joys of earth away;
　Away, ye tempters of the mind,
　False as the smooth, deceitful sea,
　And empty as the whistling wind.

2 Your streams were floating me along
　Down to the gulf of dark despair;
　And while I listened to your song, [there.
　Your streams had e'en conveyed me

3 Lord, I adore Thy matchless grace,
　That warned me of that dark abyss,
　That drew me from those treacherous seas,
　And bade me seek superior bliss.

4 Now to the shining realms above
　I stretch my hands and glance my eyes;
　O for the pinions of a dove,
　To bear me to the upper skies!

5 There, from the bosom of my God,
　Oceans of endless pleasure roll;
　There would I fix my last abode,
　And drown the sorrows of my soul.
　　　　Rev. Isaac Watts. (1674—1748.) 1709.

559　*Longing for Communion with Christ.*　L. M.

1 O that I could for ever dwell
　With Mary at my Saviour's feet,
　And view the form I love so well,
　And all His tender words repeat.

2 The world shut out from all my soul,
　And heaven brought in with all its bliss,
　O, is there aught, from pole to pole,
　One moment to compare with this?

3 This is the hidden life I prize,
　A life of penitential love,
　When most my follies I despise,
　And raise the highest thoughts above.

4 Thus would I live till nature fail,
　And all my former sins forsake;
　Then rise to God within the vail,
　And of eternal joys partake.
　　　　Rev. Andrew Reed. (1787—1862.) 1842. ab.

560　　*Jesus the Best Beloved.*　　L. M.

1 JESUS, this heart within me burns,
　To tell Thee all its conscious love;
　And from earth's low delights it turns,
　To taste a joy like that above.

2 When Thou to meet me dost descend,
　In love divine, Thou Blessed One,
　The moments that with Thee I spend,
　Seem e'en as heaven itself begun.

3 Though oft these lips my love have told,
　They still the story would repeat;
　To me the rapture ne'er grows old
　That thrills me bending at Thy feet.

4 I breathe my words into Thine ear;
　I seem to fix mine eyes on Thine;
　And sure that Thou dost wait to hear,
　I dare in faith to call Thee mine.

5 Reign Thou sole Sovereign of my heart,
　My all I yield to Thy control;
　O let me never from Thee part,
　Thou Best Belovéd of my soul.
　　　　Rev. Ray Palmer. (1808—) 1869.

561　　*"Majestic Sweetness."*　　C. M.

1 MAJESTIC sweetness sits enthroned
　Upon the Saviour's brow;
　His head with radiant glories crowned,
　His lips with grace o'erflow.

2 No mortal can with Him compare
　Among the sons of men;
　Fairer is He than all the fair
　That fill the heavenly train.

3 He saw me plunged in deep distress,
　He flew to my relief;
　For me He bore the shameful cross,
　And carried all my grief.

PRAISE TO CHRIST.

4 To Him I owe my life and breath,
    And all the joys I have;
  He makes me triumph over death,
    He saves me from the grave.

5 To heaven, the place of His abode,
    He brings my weary feet,
  Shows me the glories of my God,
    And makes my joy complete.

6 Since from His bounty I receive
    Such proofs of love divine,
  Had I a thousand hearts to give,
    Lord, they should all be Thine.
        Rev. Samuel Stennett. (1727—1795.) 1787.

562 "*A Priest for ever.*" C. M.
        Ps. cx. 4 Heb. v. 6.

1 THOU dear Redeemer, dying Lamb,
    I love to hear of Thee;
  No music's like Thy charming name,
    Nor half so sweet can be.

2 O let me ever hear Thy voice
    In mercy to me speak;
  In Thee, my Priest, will I rejoice,
    And Thy salvation seek.

3 My Jesus shall be still my theme,
    While in this world I stay;
  I'll sing my Jesus' lovely name
    When all things else decay.

4 When I appear in yonder cloud,
    With all Thy favored throng,
  Then will I sing more sweet, more loud,
    And Christ shall be my song.
        Rev. John Cennick. (1717—1755.) 1745. alt.

563 *Christ precious.* C. M.
        1 Pet. ii. 7.

1 JESUS, I love Thy charming name,
    'T is music to mine ear:
  Fain would I sound it out so loud
    That earth and heaven should hear.

2 Yes, Thou art precious to my soul,
    My Transport and my Trust;
  Jewels to Thee are gaudy toys,
    And gold is sordid dust.

3 All my capacious powers can wish
    In Thee doth richly meet;
  Not to mine eyes is light so dear,
    Nor friendship half so sweet.

4 Thy grace still dwells upon my heart,
    And sheds its fragrance there;
  The noblest balm of all its wounds,
    The cordial of its care.

5 I'll speak the honors of Thy name
    With my last laboring breath;
  Then, speechless, clasp Thee in mine arms,
    The antidote of death.
        Rev. Philip Doddridge. (1702—1751.) 1755.

564 "*Jesu dulcis memoria.*" C. M.

1 JESUS, the very thought of Thee
    With sweetness fills my breast;
  But sweeter far Thy face to see,
    And in Thy presence rest.

2 Nor voice can sing, nor heart can frame,
    Nor can the memory find
  A sweeter sound than Thy blest name,
    O Saviour of mankind!

3 O Hope of every contrite heart,
    O Joy of all the meek,
  To those who fall, how kind Thou art!
    How good to those who seek!

4 But what to those who find? Ah, this
    Nor tongue nor pen can show:
  The love of Jesus, what it is,
    None but His loved ones know.

5 Jesus, our only Joy be Thou,
    As Thou our Prize wilt be;
  Jesus, be Thou our Glory now,
    And through eternity.
        Bernard of Clairvaux. (1091—1153.) 1140.
        Tr. by Rev. Edward Caswall. (1814—) 1849.

565 "*Lead on, dear Shepherd.*" C. M.

1 TO Thee, my Shepherd and my Lord,
    A grateful song I'll raise;
  O let the feeblest of Thy flock
    Attempt to speak Thy praise.

2 My life, my joy, my hope, I owe
    To Thine amazing love;
  Ten thousand thousand comforts here,
    And nobler bliss above.

3 To Thee my trembling spirit flies,
    With sin and grief oppressed;
  Thy gentle voice dispels my fears,
    And lulls my cares to rest.

4 Nay, should I walk thro' death's dark vale
    With double horrors spread,
  Thy rod would guide my doubtful steps,
    And guard my drooping head.

5 Lead on, dear Shepherd; led by Thee,
    No evil shall I fear;
  Soon shall I reach Thy fold above,
    And praise Thee better there.
      Rev. Ottiwell Heginbotham. (1744—1768.) 1765.

566   *To be one with Christ.*   C. M.

1 COMPARED with Christ, in all beside
    No comeliness I see;
  The one thing needful, dearest Lord,
    Is to be one with Thee.

2 The sense of Thy redeeming love
    Into my soul convey;
  Thyself bestow; for Thee alone,
    My All in all, I pray.

3 Less than Thyself will not suffice
    My comfort to restore:
  More than Thyself I cannot have;
    And Thou canst give no more.

4 Loved of my God, for Him again
    With love intense I burn;
  Chosen of Thee ere time began,
    I choose Thee in return.

5 Whate'er consists not with Thy love,
    O teach me to resign;
  I'm rich to all the intents of bliss,
    If Thou, O God, art mine.
      Rev. Augustus Montague Toplady. (1740—1778.) 1772.
      ab. and alt.

567   *"O Jesu Christu, wachs in mir."*   C. M.

1 O JESUS Christ, grow Thou in me,
    And all things else recede;
  My heart be daily nearer Thee,
    From sin be daily freed.

2 Each day, let Thy supporting might
    My weakness still embrace;
  My darkness vanish in Thy light,
    Thy life my death efface.

3 In Thy bright beams, which on me fall,
    Fade every evil thought;
  That I am nothing, Thou art all,
    I would be daily taught.

4 Make this poor self grow less and less,
    Be Thou my life and aim,
  O, make me daily, through Thy grace,
    More worthy of Thy name;

5 Let faith in Thee and in Thy might
    My every motive move;
  Be Thou alone my soul's delight,
    My passion and my love.
      Rev. Johann Caspar Lavater. (1741—1801.) 1780.
      Tr. by Mrs. Elizabeth Lee Smith. (1817—) 1869. ab.

568   *"O make me love Thee more and more."*   L. M. 6 l.

1 JESUS, my Lord, my God, my all,
  Hear me, blest Saviour, when I call;
  Hear me, and from Thy dwelling place
  Pour down the riches of Thy grace;
  Jesus, my Lord, I Thee adore,
  O make me love Thee more and more.

2 Jesus, too late I Thee have sought,
  How can I love Thee as I ought;
  And how extol Thy matchless fame,
  The glorious beauty of Thy Name?
  Jesus, my Lord, I Thee adore,
  O make me love Thee more and more.

3 Jesus, what didst Thou find in me,
  That Thou hast dealt so lovingly?
  How great the joy that Thou hast brought,
  So far exceeding hope or thought!
  Jesus, my Lord, I Thee adore,
  O make me love Thee more and more.

4 Jesus, of Thee shall be my song,
  To Thee my heart and soul belong;
  All that I have or am is Thine,
  And Thou, blest Saviour, Thou art mine:
  Jesus, my Lord, I Thee adore,
  O make me love Thee more and more.
      Rev. Henry Collins. 1852.

569   *"My All in all."*   L. M. 6 l.

1 THOU hidden Source of calm repose,
  Thou all-sufficient Love divine,
  My help and refuge from my foes,
  Secure I am while Thou art mine;
  And lo, from sin, and grief, and shame,
  I hide me, Jesus, in Thy name.

2 Thy mighty name salvation is,
  And keeps my happy soul above;
  Comfort it brings, and power, and peace,

And joy, and everlasting love;
To me, with Thy dear name, are given
Pardon, and holiness, and heaven.

3 Jesus, my All in all Thou art;
My rest in toil, my ease in pain;
The medicine of my broken heart;
In war, my peace; in loss, my gain;
My smile beneath the tyrant's frown;
In shame, my glory and my crown;

4 In want, my plentiful supply;
In weakness, my almighty power;
In bonds, my perfect liberty;
My light, in Satan's darkest hour;
In grief, my joy unspeakable;
My life in death, my All in all.

Rev. Charles Wesley. (1708—1788.) 1749. sl. alt.

570 *"Ich will Dich lieben, meine Stärke."* L.M.6l.

1 THEE will I love, my Strength, my Tower,
Thee will I love, my Joy, my Crown;
Thee will I love with all my power,
In all Thy works, and Thee alone:
Thee will I love, till sacred fire
Fills my whole soul with pure desire.

2 I thank Thee, uncreated Sun,
That Thy bright beams on me have shined;
I thank Thee, who hast overthrown
My foes, and healed my wounded mind;
I thank Thee, whose enlivening voice
Bids my freed heart in Thee rejoice.

3 Uphold me in the doubtful race,
Nor suffer me again to stray;
Strengthen my feet, with steady pace
Still to press forward in Thy way;
That all my powers, with all their might,
In Thy sole glory may unite.

4 Thee will I love, my Joy, my Crown;
Thee will I love, my Lord, my God;
Thee will I love, beneath Thy frown
Or smile, Thy sceptre or Thy rod;
What though my flesh and heart decay,
Thee shall I love in endless day.

Johann Angelus Silesius. (1624—1677.) 1657.
Tr. by Rev. John Wesley. (1703—1791.) 1739. ab.

571 *"O Jesu Christ, mein schönstes Licht."* L.M.6l.

1 JESUS, Thy boundless love to me
No thought can reach, no tongue declare;
O knit my thankful heart to Thee,
And reign without a rival there:
Thine wholly, Thine alone, I am;
Be thou alone my constant flame.

2 O grant, that nothing in my soul
May dwell but Thy pure love alone:
O may Thy love possess me whole,
My joy, my treasure, and my crown;
Strange fires far from my soul remove;
My every act, word, thought, be love.

3 Unwearied may I this pursue,
Dauntless to the high prize aspire;
Hourly within my breast renew
This holy flame, this heavenly fire;
And day and night, be all my care
To guard this sacred treasure there.

4 In suffering be Thy love my peace,
In weakness be Thy love my power;
And when the storms of life shall cease,
Jesus in that important hour,
In death as life be Thou my guide,
And save me, who for me hast died.

Rev. Paul Gerhardt (1606—1676.) 1653.
Tr. by Rev. John Wesley. 1739. ab.

572 *"Jesu dulcis memoria."* L. M.

1 JESUS, how sweet Thy memory is!
Thinking of Thee is truest bliss;
Beyond all honeyed sweets below
Thy presence is it here to know.

2 Tongue cannot speak a lovelier word,
Naught more melodious can be heard,
Naught sweeter can be thought upon,
Than Jesus Christ, God's only Son.

3 Jesus, Thou Hope of those who turn,
Gentle to those who pray and mourn,
Ever to those who seek Thee, kind,
What must Thou be to those who find?

4 Jesus, Thou dost true pleasures bring,
Light of the heart, and living Spring;
Higher than highest pleasures roll,
Or warmest wishes of the soul.

5 Lord, in our bosoms ever dwell,
And of our souls the night dispel,
Pour on our inmost mind the ray,
And fill our earth with blissful day.

Bernard of Clairvaux. (1091—1153.) 1140.
Tr. Rev. James Waddell Alexander (1804—1859.) 1859. ab.

573   *"The Song of Songs."*   L. M.

1 COME, let us sing the song of songs,
   The saints in heaven began the strain,
The homage which to Christ belongs:
   "Worthy the Lamb, for He was slain!"

2 Slain to redeem us by His blood,
   To cleanse from every sinful stain,
And make us kings and priests to God:
   "Worthy the Lamb, for He was slain!"

3 To Him who suffered on the tree,
   Our souls at His soul's price to gain,
Blessing, and praise, and glory be:
   "Worthy the Lamb, for He was slain!"

4 To Him, enthroned by filial right,
   All power in heaven and earth proclaim,
Honor, and majesty, and might:
   "Worthy the Lamb, for He was slain!"

5 Long as we live, and when we die,
   And while in heaven with Him we reign,
This song our song of songs shall be:
   "Worthy the Lamb, for He was slain!"

James Montgomery. (1771—1854.) 1853. ab. and alt.

574   *All in all.*   Col. iii. 11.   L. M.

1 IN Christ I've all my soul's desire;
His spirit does my heart inspire
With boundless wishes large and high;
And Christ will all my wants supply.

2 Christ is my Hope, my Strength, and Guide;
For me He bled, and groaned, and died;
He is my Sun, to give me light,
He is my soul's supreme Delight.

3 Christ is the Source of all my bliss;
My wisdom and my righteousness;
My Saviour, Brother, and my Friend;
On Him alone I now depend.

4 Christ is my King, to rule and bless,
And all my troubles to redress;
He's my Salvation and my All,
Whate'er on earth shall me befall.

5 Christ is my Strength and Portion too;
My soul in Him can all things do;
Through Him I'll triumph o'er the grave,
And death and hell my soul outbrave.

*W. G. In The Christian Magazine, 1790. alt.
John Dobell's (1757—1840) Collection. 1806.*

575   *"The Loving Kindness of the Lord."*   Is. lxiii. 7.   L. M.

1 AWAKE, my soul, in joyful lays,
And sing thy great Redeemer's praise:
He justly claims a song from me,
His loving-kindness is so free.

2 He saw me ruined in the fall,
Yet loved me notwithstanding all,
And saved me from my lost estate,
His loving-kindness is so great.

3 Through mighty hosts of cruel foes,
Where earth and hell my way oppose,
He safely leads my soul along,
His loving-kindness is so strong.

4 So when I pass death's gloomy vale,
And life and mortal powers shall fail,
O may my last expiring breath
His loving-kindness sing in death.

5 Then shall I mount, and soar away
To the bright world of endless day;
There shall I sing, with sweet surprise,
His loving-kindness in the skies.

Rev. Samuel Medley. (1738—1799.) 1787. ab.

576   *"Thy Loving-Kindness."*   L. M.

1 THY loving-kindness, Lord, I sing,
Of grace and life the sacred spring;
The spring o'erflowing, rich, and free,
In precious blood, once shed for me.

2 I to Thy mercy-seat repair,
And find Thy loving-kindness there;
And when to Thy sweet word I go,
Thy loving-kindness there I know.

3 Lord, from the moment of my birth,
I've nothing known but love on earth;
By day, by night, where'er I be,
Thy loving-kindness follows me.

4 From daily sin and daily woe
Thy loving-kindness saves me now;
And I will praise, for sins forgiven,
Thy loving-kindness all, in heaven.

Rev. George Barrell Cheever. (1807—) 1845. ab.

577   *"O Deus, ego amo Te."*   L. M.

1 JESUS, I love Thee evermore,
For Thou hast loved me, Lord, before;

PRAISE TO CHRIST.

I have no freedom but to be
A willing servant, Lord, to Thee.

2 Let memory then no thought retain
Except the glory of Thy reign;
Nor let my mind desire below
Aught but the love of Christ to know.

3 I cannot have a wish or thought,
Except to love Thee as I ought;
What, by Thy gracious gift, is mine,
With joy I freely make it Thine.

4 From Thee I have, to Thee I give,
In Thy commands, O let me live!
My wants will then be all supplied,
For all are only dreams beside.

Of unknown authorship and date.
Tr. by Erastus Cornelius Benedict. (1800—) 1868, 1873.

578 *"Jesus Christ, the Crucified."* 7.

1 ASK ye what great thing I know
That delights and stirs me so?
What the high reward I win?
Whose the name I glory in?
Jesus Christ, the Crucified.

2 What is faith's foundation strong?
What awakes my lips to song?
He who bore my sinful load,
Purchased for me peace with God,
Jesus Christ, the Crucified.

3 Who defeats my fiercest foes?
Who consoles my saddest woes?
Who revives my fainting heart,
Healing all its hidden smart?
Jesus Christ, the Crucified.

4 Who is Life in life to me?
Who the Death of death will be?
Who will place me on His right
With the countless hosts of light?
Jesus Christ, the Crucified.

5 This is that great thing I know;
This delights and stirs me so:
Faith in Him who died to save,
Him who triumphed o'er the grave,
Jesus Christ, the Crucified.

Rev. John Samuel Bewley Monsell (1811–) 1863

579 *"Now Thine Anger's turned away."* 7.
Is. xii. 1.

1 I WILL praise Thee every day
Now Thine anger's turned away;

Comfortable thoughts arise
From the bleeding Sacrifice.

2 Jesus is become at length
My Salvation and my Strength;
And His praises shall prolong,
While I live, my pleasant song.

3 Praise ye, then, His glorious Name,
Publish His exalted fame!
Still His worth your praise exceeds,
Excellent are all His deeds.

4 Raise again the joyful sound,
Let the nations roll it round!
Zion, shout! for this is He;
God the Saviour dwells in Thee!

William Cowper (1731–1800) 1779. ab.

580 *"Keine Schönheit hat die Welt."* 7.

1 EARTH has nothing sweet or fair,
Lovely forms or beauties rare,
But before my eyes they bring
Christ, of beauty Source and Spring.

2 When the morning paints the skies,
When the golden sunbeams rise,
Then my Saviour's form I find
Brightly imaged on my mind.

3 When, as moonlight softly steals,
Heaven its thousand eyes reveals,
Then I think: Who made their light
Is a thousand times more bright.

4 When I see, in spring-tide gay,
Fields their varied tints display,
Wakes the awful thought in me,
What must their Creator be!

5 Lord of all that's fair to see,
Come, reveal Thyself to me;
Let me, 'mid Thy radiant light,
See Thine unveiled glories bright.

Johann Angelus Silesius (1624–1677) 1657. ab.
Tr. by Miss Frances Elizabeth Cox 1841. ab.

581 *None but Jesus.* 8. D.
Ps. lxxiii. 25.

1 How tedious and tasteless the hours
    When Jesus no longer I see!
Sweet prospects, sweet birds, and sweet
    flowers

Have all lost their sweetness with me.
The mid-summer sun shines but dim,
The fields strive in vain to look gay;
But when I am happy in Him,
December's as pleasant as May.

2 His name yields the richest perfume,
And sweeter than music His voice;
His presence disperses my gloom,
And makes all within me rejoice.
I should, were He always thus nigh,
Have nothing to wish or to fear;
No mortal so happy as I,
My summer would last all the year.

3 Content with beholding His face,
My all to His pleasure resigned,
No changes of season or place
Would make any change in my mind.
While blest with a sense of His love,
A palace a toy would appear;
And prisons would palaces prove,
If Jesus would dwell with me there.
  Rev. John Newton. (1725—1807.) 1779. ab.

582   "Schönster Herr Jesu"   5, 5, 10.

1 FAIREST Lord Jesus,
  Ruler of all nature,
O Thou of God and man the Son!
  Thee will I cherish,
  Thee will I honor;
Thou, my soul's glory, joy and crown.

2   Fair are the meadows,
    Fairer still the woodlands,
Robed in the blooming garb of spring:
    Jesus is fairer,
    Jesus is purer,
Who makes the woeful heart to sing.

3   Fair is the sunshine,
    Fairer still the moonlight,
And the twinkling starry host:
    Jesus shines brighter,
    Jesus shines purer
Than all the angels heaven can boast.
  Unknown Author of the 12th century.

583   Only Jesus, and Him crucified.
         1 Cor. ii. 2   7, 6. D.

1 VAIN, delusive world, adieu,
    With all of creature good;
  Only Jesus I pursue,
    Who bought me with His blood;
  All thy pleasures I forego:
    All thy pomps, thy wealth and pride:
  Only Jesus will I know,
    And Jesus crucified.

2 Other knowledge I disdain,
    'T is all but vanity;
  Christ, the Lamb of God, was slain,
    He tasted death for me;
  Me to save from endless woe,
    Christ, th' atoning Victim died:
  Only Jesus will I know,
    And Jesus crucified.

3 Him to know is life and peace
    And pleasure without end;
  This is all my happiness,
    On Jesus to depend;
  Daily in His grace to grow,
    Ever in His faith abide:
  Only Jesus will I know,
    And Jesus crucified.

4 Him in all my works I seek,
    Who hung upon the tree;
  Only of His love I speak,
    Who freely died for me;
  While I sojourn here below,
    Nothing will I seek beside:
  Only Jesus will I know,
    And Jesus crucified.
      Rev. Charles Wesley. 1742. ab. and alt.

584   The Sinner's Plea.
         1 Tim. i. 15   7, 6. D.

1 LET the world their virtue boast,
    Their works of righteousness;
  I, a wretch undone and lost,
    Am freely saved by grace;
  Other title I disclaim,
    This, only this, is all my plea:
  I the chief of sinners am,
    But Jesus died for me.

2 Happy they whose joys abound
    Like Jordan's swelling stream,
  Who their heaven in Christ have found;
    And give the praise to Him;
  Meanest follower of the Lamb,
    His steps I at a distance see:
  I the chief of sinners am,
    But Jesus died for me.

3 Jesus, Thou for me hast died,
　And Thou in me wilt live;
　I shall feel Thy death applied;
　I shall Thy life receive;
　Yet, when melted in the flame
　　Of love, this shall be all my plea:
　I the chief of sinners am,
　　But Jesus died for me.
　　　Rev. Charles Wesley. (1708—1788.) 1742. ab.

585　　*Rejoicing on our Way.*　　7.

1 CHILDREN of the Heavenly King,
　As ye journey, sweetly sing;
　Sing your Saviour's worthy praise,
　Glorious in His works and ways.

2 We are traveling home to God,
　In the way the fathers trod:
　They are happy now, and we
　Soon their happiness shall see.

3 Shout, ye little flock, and blest,
　You on Jesus' throne shall rest;
　There your seat is now prepared,
　There your kingdom and reward.

4 Fear not, brethren, joyful stand
　On the borders of your land;
　Jesus Christ, your Father's Son,
　Bids you undismayed go on.

5 Lord, obediently we go,
　Gladly leaving all below;
　Only Thou our Leader be,
　And we still will follow Thee.
　　Rev. John Cennick. (1717—1755.) 1742. ab.

586　　*Onward, and still onward.*　　7.

1 MUCH in sorrow, oft in woe,
　Onward, Christians, onward go;
　Fight the fight, and, worn with strife,
　Steep with tears the Bread of Life.

2 Onward, Christians, onward go;
　Join the war, and face the foe;
　Faint not; much doth yet remain;
　Dreary is the long campaign.

3 Shrink not, Christians, will ye yield?
　Will ye quit the painful field?
　Will ye flee in danger's hour?
　Know ye not your Captain's power?

4 Let your drooping hearts be glad;
　March, in heavenly armor clad;
　Fight, nor think the battle long;
　Victory soon shall tune your song.

5 Onward then to battle move;
　More than conquerors ye shall prove;
　Though opposed by many a foe,
　Christian soldiers, onward go.
　　Henry Kirke White. (1785—1806.) First 10 lines.
　　Miss Fanny Fuller Maitland. 1827. ab.

587　　*Redeeming Love.*　　7.

1 Now begin the heavenly theme,
　Sing aloud in Jesus' name;
　Ye who Jesus' kindness prove,
　Triumph in redeeming love.

2 Ye who see the Father's grace
　Beaming in the Saviour's face,
　As to Canaan on ye move,
　Praise and bless redeeming love.

3 Mourning souls, dry up your tears;
　Banish all your guilty fears;
　See your guilt and curse remove,
　Cancelled by redeeming love.

4 Welcome, all by sin opprest,
　Welcome to His sacred rest;
　Nothing brought Him from above,
　Nothing but redeeming love.

5 Hither, then, your music bring,
　Strike aloud each joyful string;
　Mortals, join the host above,
　Join to praise redeeming love.
　　Rev. Martin Madan? (1726—1790.) 1763. ab.

588　　*"Make His Praise glorious."*
　　　Ps. lxvi. 2.　　C. P. M.

1 O COULD I speak the matchless worth,
　O could I sound the glories forth,
　　Which in my Saviour shine,
　I'd soar and touch the heavenly strings,
　And vie with Gabriel while he sings
　　In notes almost divine.

2 I'd sing the precious blood He spilt,
　My ransom from the dreadful guilt
　　Of sin, and wrath divine;
　I'd sing His glorious righteousness,
　In which all-perfect, heavenly dress
　　My soul shall ever shine.

3 I'd sing the characters He bears,
   And all the forms of love He wears,
      Exalted on His throne;
   In loftiest songs of sweetest praise,
   I would to everlasting days
      Make all His glories known.

4 Well, the delightful day will come
   When my dear Lord will bring me home,
      And I shall see His face;
   Then with my Saviour, Brother, Friend,
   A blest eternity I'll spend,
      Triumphant in His grace.
         Rev. Samuel Medley. (1738—1799.) 1789 ab

589   *Desiring to love.*   C. P. M.

1 O LOVE divine, how sweet thou art!
   When shall I find my willing heart
      All taken up by Thee?
   I thirst, and faint, and die to prove
   The greatness of redeeming love,
      The love of Christ to me.

2 Stronger His love than death or hell;
   Its riches are unsearchable;
      The first-born sons of light
   In vain desire its depths to see;
   They cannot reach the mystery,
      The length, and breadth, and height.

3 God only knows the love of God;
   O that it now were shed abroad
      In this poor, stony heart!
   For love I sigh, for love I pine:
   This only portion, Lord, be mine,
      Be mine this better part.

4 O that I could forever sit
   With Mary at the Master's feet
      Be this my happy choice,
   My only care, delight, and bliss,
   My joy, my heaven on earth, be this,
      To hear the Bridegroom's voice.

5 O that I could, with favored John,
   Recline my weary head upon
      The dear Redeemer's breast!
   From care and sin and sorrow free,
   Give me, O Lord, to find in Thee
      My everlasting rest.
         Rev. Charles Wesley. 1749. ab.

590   *"Only Thee."*   7.

1 BLESSÉD Saviour, Thee I love,
   All my other joys above;
   All my hopes in Thee abide,
   Thou my Hope, and naught beside;
   Ever let my glory be,
   Only, only, only Thee.

2 Once again beside the cross,
   All my gain I count but loss;
   Earthly pleasures fade away;
   Clouds they are that hide my day;
   Hence, vain shadows, let me see
   Jesus, crucified for me.

3 From beneath that thorny crown
   Trickle drops of cleansing down;
   Pardon from Thy piercéd hand
   Now I take, while here I stand;
   Only then I live to Thee,
   When Thy wounded side I see.

4 Blesséd Saviour, Thine am I,
   Thine to live, and Thine to die;
   Height or depth, or earthly power,
   Ne'er shall hide my Saviour more:
   Ever shall my glory be,
   Only, only, only Thee.
      Rev. George Duffield, Jr. (1818—) 1859.

591   *Happy Trust.*   7.

1 SAVIOUR, happy would I be,
   If I could but trust in Thee;
   Trust Thy wisdom me to guide;
   Trust Thy goodness to provide;
   Trust Thy saving love and power;
   Trust Thee every day and hour:

2 Trust Thee as the only light
   In the darkest hour of night;
   Trust in sickness, trust in health;
   Trust in poverty and wealth;
   Trust in joy, and trust in grief;
   Trust Thy promise for relief:

3 Trust Thy blood to cleanse my soul;
   Trust Thy grace to make me whole;
   Trust Thee living, dying, too;
   Trust Thee all my journey through;
   Trust Thee till my feet shall be
   Planted on the crystal sea.
      Rev. Edwin H. Nevin. (1814—) 1858.

592 "Whose I am." 7.

1 JESUS, Master, whose I am,
  Purchased Thine alone to be,
 By Thy blood, O spotless Lamb,
  Shed so willingly for me;
 Let my heart be all Thine own,
 Let me live to Thee alone.

2 Other lords have long held sway;
  Now Thy name alone to bear,
 Thy dear voice alone obey,
  Is my daily, hourly prayer.
 Whom have I in heaven but Thee?
 Nothing else my joy can be.

3 Jesus, Master, I am Thine;
  Keep me faithful, keep me near:
 Let Thy presence in me shine
  All my homeward way to cheer.
 Jesus, at Thy feet I fall,
 O be Thou my All in all.
                Miss Frances Ridley Havergal. 1872.

593 "Thou knowest that I love Thee." C. M.
             John xxi. 15.

1 Do not I love Thee, O my Lord?
  Behold my heart and see;
 And turned each cursed idol out,
  That dares to rival Thee.

2 Do not I love Thee from my soul?
  Then let me nothing love;
 Dead be my heart to every joy,
  When Jesus cannot move.

3 Is not Thy Name melodious still
  To mine attentive ear?
 Doth not each pulse with pleasure bound
  My Saviour's voice to hear?

4 Hast Thou a lamb in all Thy flock
  I would disdain to feed?
 Hast Thou a foe before whose face
  I fear Thy cause to plead?

5 Would not my heart pour forth its blood
  In honor of Thy Name,
 And challenge the cold hand of death
  To damp the immortal flame?

6 Thou know'st I love Thee, dearest Lord,
  But O, I long to soar
 Far from the sphere of mortal joys,
  And learn to love Thee more.
              Rev. Philip Doddridge. (1702—1751.) 1755. ab.

594 True Love. C. M.

1 THINK well how Jesus trusts Himself
  Unto our childish love,
 As though by His free ways with us
  Our earnestness to prove.

2 His sacred Name a common word
  On earth He loves to hear;
 There is no majesty in Him
  Which love may not come near.

3 The light of love is round His feet,
  His paths are never dim;
 And He comes nigh to us when we
  Dare not come nigh to Him.

4 Let us be simple with Him, then,
  Not backward, stiff, or cold,
 As though our Bethlehem could be
  What Sinai was of old.
        Rev. Frederick William Faber. (1814—1863.) 1849. ab.

595 "The great Love." C. M.
             John xv. 13

1 MY blessed Saviour, is Thy love
  So great, so full, so free?
 Behold, I give my love, my heart,
  My life, my all, to Thee.

2 I love Thee for the glorious worth
  In Thy great Self I see;
 I love Thee for that shameful cross
  Thou hast endured for me.

3 No man of greater love can boast
  Than for his friend to die;
 But for Thy foes, Lord, Thou wast slain;
  What love with Thine can vie!

4 Though in the very form of God,
  With heavenly glory crowned,
 Thou wouldst partake of human flesh
  Beset with troubles round.

5 O Lord, I'll treasure in my soul
  The memory of Thy love;
 And Thy dear name shall still to me
  A grateful odor prove.
        Rev. Joseph Stennett. (1663—1713.) 1697. ab.

596 "O Deus, ego amo Te." C. M.

1 MY God, I love Thee: not because
  I hope for heaven thereby,
 Nor yet because who love Thee not
  Must die eternally.

LOVE TO CHRIST. CHRIST'S GRACE EXTOLLED.

2 Thou, O my Jesus, Thou didst me
   Upon the cross embrace:
For me didst bear the nails, and spear,
   And manifold disgrace;

3 And griefs, and torments numberless,
   And sweat of agony;
Yea, death itself; and all for me
   Who was Thine enemy.

4 Then why, O blessèd Jesus Christ,
   Should I not love Thee well?
Not for the hope of winning heaven,
   Nor of escaping hell.

5 Not with the hope of gaining aught,
   Not seeking a reward;
But as Thyself hast lovèd me,
   O ever-loving Lord.

6 So would I love Thee, dearest Lord,
   And in Thy praise will sing;
Solely because Thou art my God,
   And my Eternal King.

        Francis Xavier (1506—1552.) 1552.
Tr. by Rev. Edward Caswall (1814—) 1849. sl. alt.

597   "*Oneness with Christ.*"   C. M.

1 LORD Jesus, are we one with Thee?
   O height, O depth of love!
With Thee we died upon the tree;
   In Thee we live above.

2 Such was Thy grace, that for our sake
   Thou didst from heaven come down.
Thou didst of flesh and blood partake,
   In all our sorrows one.

3 Our sins, our guilt, in love divine,
   Confessed and borne by Thee;
The gall, the curse, the wrath were Thine
   To set Thy members free.

4 Ascended now in glory bright,
   Still one with us Thou art;
Nor life, nor death, nor depth, nor height,
   Thy saints and Thee can part.

5 Soon, soon shall come that glorious day,
   When, seated on Thy throne,
Thou shalt to wondering worlds display
   That Thou with us art one!

        James George Deck. 1837.

598   "*Jesu decus angelicum.*"   C. M.

1 O JESUS, Thou the beauty art
   Of angel-worlds above;
Thy Name is music to the heart,
   Enchanting it with love.

2 O Jesus, Saviour, hear the sighs
   Which unto Thee I send;
To Thee my inmost spirit cries,
   My being's hope and end.

3 Stay with us, Lord, and with Thy light
   Illume the soul's abyss;
Scatter the darkness of our night,
   And fill the world with bliss.

4 O Jesus, King of earth and heaven,
   Our Life and Joy! to Thee
Be honor, thanks, and blessing given
   Through all eternity!

        Bernard of Clairvaux (1091—1153.) 1140.
Tr. by Rev. Edward Caswall. 1849. ab. and alt.

599   *The Voice from Galilee.*   C. M. D.
        John i. 16.

1 I HEARD the voice of Jesus say,
   "Come unto Me and rest;
Lay down, thou weary one, lay down
   Thy head upon my breast."
I came to Jesus as I was,
   Weary, and worn, and sad;
I found in Him a resting place,
   And He has made me glad.

2 I heard the voice of Jesus say,
   "Behold, I freely give
The living water; thirsty one,
   Stoop down, and drink, and live."
I came to Jesus, and I drank
   Of that life-giving stream;
My thirst was quenched, my soul revived,
   And now I live in Him.

3 I heard the voice of Jesus say,
   "I am this dark world's Light;
Look unto Me, thy morn shall rise,
   And all thy day be bright."
I looked to Jesus, and I found
   In Him my Star, my Sun;
And in that Light of life I'll walk
   Till all my journey's done.

        Rev. Horatius Bonar. (1808—) 1857. sl. alt.

CHRIST'S GRACE EXTOLLED.

600 *"Amazing Grace."* C. M. D.

1 AMAZING grace, how sweet the sound
  That saved a wretch like me!
  I once was lost, but now am found,
  Was blind, but now I see.
  'T was grace that taught my heart to fear,
  And grace my fears relieved;
  How precious did that grace appear
  The hour I first believed!

2 Through many dangers, toils, and snares,
  I have already come;
  'T is grace has brought me safe thus far,
  And grace will lead me home.
  The Lord has promised good to me,
  His word my hope secures;
  He will my Shield and Portion be,
  As long as life endures.

3 Yes, when this flesh and heart shall fail,
  And mortal life shall cease,
  I shall possess, within the veil,
  A life of joy and peace.
  The earth shall soon dissolve like snow,
  The sun forbear to shine;
  But God, who called me here below,
  Will be forever mine.
  Rev. John Newton. (1725—1807.) 1779.

601 *Mine and Thine.* C. M.

1 ALL that I was, my sin and guilt,
  My death was all my own;
  All that I am, I owe to Thee,
  My gracious God, alone.

2 The evil of my former state
  Was mine, and only mine;
  The good in which I now rejoice,
  Is Thine, and only Thine.

3 The darkness of my former state,
  The bondage, all was mine;
  The light of life in which I walk,
  The liberty, is Thine.

4 Thy grace first made me feel my sin,
  It taught me to believe;
  Then, in believing, peace I found;
  And now I live, I live.
  All that I am, e'en here on earth,
  All that I hope to be,
  When Jesus comes, and glory dawns,
  I owe it, Lord, to Thee.
  Rev. Horatius Bonar. 1857.

602 *Great Things done for us.* C. M.
Ps. cxxvi.

1 WHEN God revealed His gracious name,
  And changed my mournful state,
  My rapture seemed a pleasing dream
  The grace appeared so great.

2 The world beheld the glorious change,
  And did Thy hand confess:
  My tongue broke out in unknown strains,
  And sung surprising grace.

3 "Great is the work," my neighbors cried,
  And owned the power divine;
  "Great is the work," my heart replied,
  "And be the glory Thine."

4 The Lord can clear the darkest skies,
  Can give us day for night;
  Make drops of sacred sorrow rise
  To rivers of delight.

5 Let those who sow in sadness, wait
  Till the fair harvest come;
  They shall confess their sheaves are great,
  And shout the blessings home.
  Rev. Isaac Watts. (1674—1748.) 1719. ab.

603 *Converting Grace.* C. M.

1 O GIFT of gifts! O grace of faith!
  My God, how can it be
  That Thou, who hast discerning love,
  Shouldst give that gift to me?

2 How many hearts Thou mightst have had
  More innocent than mine,
  How many souls more worthy far
  Of that sweet touch of Thine!

3 Ah, grace, into unlikehest hearts
  It is thy boast to come,
  The glory of thy light to find
  In darkest spots a home.

4 The crowd of cares, the weightiest cross,
  Seem trifles less than light;
  Earth looks so little and so low
  When faith shines full and bright.

5 O happy, happy that I am!
  If Thou canst be, O faith,
  The treasure that thou art in life,
  What wilt thou be in death?
  Rev. Frederick William Faber. (1814—1863.) 1848. ab.

604 *Saving Grace.* S. M.
Eph. ii. 5.

1 GRACE, 't is a charming sound,
   Harmonious to mine ear;
   Heaven with the echo shall resound,
   And all the earth shall hear.

2 Grace first contrived a way
   To save rebellious man,
   And all the steps that grace display,
   Which drew the wondrous plan.

3 Grace taught my wandering feet
   To tread the heavenly road;
   And new supplies each hour I meet,
   While pressing on to God.

4 Grace all the work shall crown,
   Through everlasting days;
   It lays in heaven the topmost stone,
   And well deserves the praise.
   Rev. Philip Doddridge (1702—1751) 1755.

605 *Christ our Righteousness.*
1 Cor. i. 30.

1 How heavy is the night
   That hangs upon our eyes,
   Till Christ, with His reviving light,
   Over our souls arise!

2 Our guilty spirits dread
   To meet the wrath of heaven;
   But, in His righteousness arrayed,
   We see our sins forgiven.

3 Unholy and impure
   Are all our thoughts and ways;
   His hands infected nature cure,
   With sanctifying grace.

4 The powers of hell agree
   To hold our souls in vain;
   He sets the sons of bondage free,
   And breaks the cursèd chain.

5 Lord, we adore Thy ways
   To bring us near to God;
   Thy sovereign power, Thy healing grace,
   And Thine atoning blood.
   Rev. Isaac Watts, 1709.

606 *"The Song of Moses and the Lamb."* S. M.
Rev. xv. 3.

1 AWAKE, and sing the song
   Of Moses and the Lamb;
   Wake every heart and every tongue,
   To praise the Saviour's name.

2 Sing of His dying love;
   Sing of His rising power;
   Sing how He intercedes above
   For those whose sins He bore.

3 Sing till we feel our hearts
   Ascending with our tongues;
   Sing till the love of sin departs,
   And grace inspires our songs.

4 Sing on your heavenly way,
   Ye ransomed sinners, sing;
   Sing on, rejoicing every day
   In Christ the eternal King.

5 Soon shall ye hear Him say,
   "Ye blessed children, come;"
   Soon will He call you hence away,
   And take His wanderers home.

6 There shall our raptured tongue
   His endless praise proclaim,
   And sweeter voices swell the song
   Of Moses and the Lamb.
   Rev. William Hammond (—1733) 1745, alt. and alt.
   Rev. Martin Madan (1726—1790) 1760. Last 5 vs.

607 *Heavenly Joy on Earth.* S. M.

1 COME, we that love the Lord,
   And let our joys be known;
   Join in a song of sweet accord,
   And thus surround the throne.

2 Let those refuse to sing
   That never knew our God;
   But favorites of the heavenly King
   May speak their joys abroad.

3 The men of grace have found
   Glory begun below;
   Celestial fruits on earthly ground
   From faith and hope may grow.

4 The hill of Zion yields
   A thousand sacred sweets
   Before we reach the heavenly fields,
   Or walk the golden streets.

5 Then let our songs abound,
   And every tear be dry;
   We're marching thro' Immanuel's ground
   To fairer worlds on high.
   Rev. Isaac Watts, 1709, ab.

608   "Summi Parentis Filio."   S. M.

1 To Christ, the Prince of peace,
    And Son of God most high,
The Father of the world to come,
    Sing we with holy joy.

2 Deep in His heart for us
    The wound of love He bore,
That love, which still He kindles in
    The hearts that Him adore.

3 O Jesus, Victim blest,
    What else, but love divine,
Could Thee constrain to open thus
    That sacred heart of Thine?

4 O Fount of endless life,
    O Spring of waters clear,
O Flame celestial, cleansing all
    Who unto Thee draw near:

5 Hide me in Thy dear heart,
    For thither do I fly;
There seek Thy grace through life, in death
    Thine immortality.
Roman Breviary.
Tr. by Rev. Edward Caswall. (1814—) 1849.

609   Singing in the Ways of God   S. M.
Ps. cxxxviii. 5.

1 Now let our voices join
    To form a sacred song;
Ye pilgrims in Jehovah's ways,
    With music pass along.

2 How straight the path appears,
    How open, and how fair!
No lurking gins t' entrap our feet;
    No fierce destroyer there.

3 But flowers of paradise
    In rich profusion spring;
The Sun of glory gilds the path,
    And dear companions sing.

4 See Salem's golden spires
    In beauteous prospect rise;
And brighter crowns than mortals wear,
    Which sparkle through the skies.

5 All honor to His name,
    Who marks the shining way;
To Him, who leads the wanderer on
    To realms of endless day.
Rev. Philip Doddridge. (1702—1751.) 1755. ab. and alt.

610   "We have left all."   8, 7. D.
Mark x. 28

1 Jesus, I my cross have taken,
    All to leave, and follow Thee;
Destitute, despised, forsaken,
    Thou, from hence, my all shalt be:
Perish, every fond ambition,
    All I've sought, and hoped, and known,
Yet how rich is my condition,
    God and heaven are still my own!

2 Let the world despise and leave me,
    They have left my Saviour, too;
Human hearts and looks deceive me;
    Thou art not, like man, untrue;
And while Thou shalt smile upon me,
    God of wisdom, love, and might,
Foes may hate, and friends may shun me,
    Show Thy face and all is bright.

3 Go then, earthly fame and treasure!
    Come disaster, scorn, and pain!
In Thy service, pain is pleasure;
    With Thy favor, loss is gain.
I have called Thee, Abba, Father;
    I have stayed my heart on Thee:
Storms may howl, and clouds may gather,
    All must work for good to me.

4 Man may trouble and distress me,
    'T will but drive me to Thy breast;
Life with trials hard may press me,
    Heaven will bring me sweeter rest.
O 't is not in grief to harm me,
    While Thy love is left to me;
O 't were not in joy to charm me,
    Were that joy unmixed with Thee.
Rev. Henry Francis Lyte. (1793—1847.) 1825.

611   The End of Trials.   8, 7. D.
(Second part of preceding hymn.)

1 Take, my soul, thy full salvation,
    Rise o'er sin, and fear, and care;
Joy to find in every station
    Something still to do or bear.
Think what Spirit dwells within thee;
    What a Father's smile is thine;
What a Saviour died to win thee:
    Child of heaven, shouldst thou repine?

2 Haste thee on from grace to glory,
    Armed by faith, and winged by prayer

Heaven's eternal day's before thee,
God's own hand shall guide thee there.
Soon shall close thy earthly mission,
Swift shall pass thy pilgrim days,
Hope soon change to glad fruition,
Faith to sight, and prayer to praise.
Rev. Henry Francis Lyte. 1825.

612 *"In the Cross of Christ I glory."* 8, 7.
Gal. vi. 14.

1 IN the cross of Christ I glory,
　Towering o'er the wrecks of time;
　All the light of sacred story
　Gathers round its head sublime.

2 When the woes of life o'ertake me,
　Hopes deceive, and fears annoy,
　Never shall the cross forsake me;
　Lo, it glows with peace and joy.

3 When the sun of bliss is beaming
　Light and love upon my way,
　From the cross the radiance streaming
　Adds more lustre to the day.

4 Bane and blessing, pain and pleasure,
　By the cross are sanctified;
　Peace is there, that knows no measure,
　Joys that through all time abide.

5 In the cross of Christ I glory,
　Towering o'er the wrecks of time;
　All the light of sacred story
　Gathers round its head sublime.
Sir John Bowring. (1792—1872.) 1825.

613 *"Kreuz wir grüssen dich von Herzen."* 8, 7.

1 CROSS, reproach, and tribulation,
　Ye to me are welcome guests,
　When I have this consolation,
　That my soul in Jesus rests.

2 The reproach of Christ is glorious;
　Those who here His burden bear
　In the end shall prove victorious,
　And eternal gladness share.

3 Bear, then, the reproach of Jesus,
　Ye who live a life of faith;
　Lift triumphant songs and praises,
　E'en in martyrdom and death.

4 Bonds, and stripes, and evil story,
　Are our honorable crowns;

Pain is peace, and shame is glory,
Gloomy dungeons are as thrones.
Ludwig Andreas Gotter. (1660—1735.) 1735.
Moravian Collection. 1754.

614 *The watchful Servant.* 8, 7.
Matt. xxv. 7.

1 EARTHLY joys no longer please us,
　Here would we renounce them all,
　Seek our only rest in Jesus,
　Him our Lord and Master call.

2 Faith, our languid spirits cheering,
　Points to brighter worlds above,
　Bids us look for His appearing,
　Bids us triumph in His love.

3 May our lights be always burning,
　And our loins be girded round,
　Waiting for our Lord's returning,
　Longing for the welcome sound.

4 Thus the Christian life adorning,
　Never will we be afraid,
　Should He come at night or morning,
　Early dawn or evening shade.
Charles Lawrence Ford. — ab.

615 *Be not weary.* 8, 7.

1 YES, He knows the way is dreary,
　Knows the weakness of our frame,
　Knows that hand and heart are weary;
　He in all points felt the same.

2 Look to Him, and faith shall brighten,
　Hope shall soar, and faith shall burn;
　Peace once more thy heart shall brighten,
　Rise, He calleth thee, return.
Miss Frances Ridley Havergal. 1872. ab.

616 *Not ashamed of Jesus.* L. M.
Rom. i. 16. Heb. ii. 11.

1 JESUS, and shall it ever be,
　A mortal man ashamed of Thee?
　Ashamed of Thee, whom angels praise,
　Whose glories shine through endless days?

2 Ashamed of Jesus! sooner far
　Let evening blush to own a star;
　He sheds the beams of light divine
　O'er this benighted soul of mine.

3 Ashamed of Jesus! just as soon
　Let midnight be ashamed of noon;
　'Tis midnight with my soul, till He,
　Bright Morning Star, bid darkness flee.

4 Ashamed of Jesus, that dear Friend
  On whom my hopes of heaven depend!
  No, when I blush, be this my shame,
  That I no more revere His name.

5 Ashamed of Jesus! yes, I may,
  When I've no guilt to wash away,
  No tear to wipe, no good to crave,
  No fear to quell, no soul to save.

6 Till then, nor is my boasting vain,
  Till then I boast a Saviour slain;
  And O, may this my glory be,
  That Christ is not ashamed of me.
     Rev. Joseph Grigg. (—1768) 1765. alt.
     Rev. Benjamin Francis (1734—1799) 1787.

617 *Bearing the Cross for Christ.* **L. M.**

1 My precious Lord, for Thy dear Name
  I bear the cross, despise the shame;
  Nor do I faint, while Thou art near;
  I lean on Thee; how can I fear?

2 No other name but Thine is given
  To cheer my soul, in earth or heaven;
  No other wealth will I require;
  No other friend can I desire.

3 Yea, into nothing would I fall
  For Thee alone, my All in all;
  To feel Thy love, my only joy,
  To tell Thy love, my sole employ.
     Moravian Collection. 1754. ab.

618 *Glorying in the Cross of Christ.* **L. M.**
  Gal. vi. 14.

1 We sing the praise of Him who died,
  Of Him who died upon the cross;
  The sinner's hope let men deride,
  For this we count the world but loss.

2 Inscribed upon the cross we see,
  In shining letters, "God is Love;"
  He bears our sins upon the tree,
  He brings us mercy from above.

3 The cross! it takes our guilt away;
  It holds the fainting spirit up;
  It cheers with hope the gloomy day,
  And sweetens every bitter cup.

4 It makes the coward spirit brave,
  And nerves the feeble arm for fight;
  It takes its terror from the grave,
  And gilds the bed of death with light.

5 The balm of life, the cure of woe,
  The measure and the pledge of love,
  The sinner's refuge here below,
  The angels' theme in heaven above.
     Rev. Thomas Kelly. (1769—1855.) 1820.

619 *Christ's Service the Fruit of our Labors.* **L. M.**
  Phil. i. 22.

1 My gracious Lord, I own Thy right
  To every service I can pay,
  And call it my supreme delight
  To hear Thy dictates and obey.

2 What is my being but for Thee,
  Its sure support, its noblest end,
  Thine ever-smiling face to see,
  And serve the cause of such a Friend!

3 I would not breathe for worldly joy,
  Or to increase my worldly good;
  Nor future days nor powers employ
  To spread a sounding name abroad.

4 'Tis to my Saviour I would live,
  To Him who for my ransom died;
  Nor could the bowers of Eden give
  Such bliss as blossoms at His side.

5 His work my hoary age shall bless,
  When youthful vigor is no more;
  And my last hour of life confess
  His dying love, His saving power.
     Rev. Philip Doddridge. (1702—1751.) 1755. alt.

620 *For Grace to surrender all.* **L. M.**

1 Jesus, our best beloved Friend,
  Draw out our souls in pure desire;
  Jesus, in love to us descend,
  Baptize us with Thy Spirit's fire.

2 On Thy redeeming Name we call,
  Poor and unworthy though we be;
  Pardon and sanctify us all;
  Let each Thy full salvation see.

3 Our souls and bodies we resign,
  To fear and follow Thy commands;
  O take our hearts, our hearts are Thine,
  Accept the service of our hands.

4 Firm, faithful, watching unto prayer,
  May we Thy blessèd will obey;
  Toil in Thy vineyard here, and bear
  The heat and burden of the day.

5 Yet, Lord, for us a resting-place,
   In heaven, at Thy right hand prepare;
   And till we see Thee face to face,
   Be all our conversation there.
       James Montgomery (1771—1854.) 1825.

621   *Holiness and Grace.*
           Titus ii. 10-13.

1 So let our lips and lives express
   The holy gospel we profess;
   So let our works and virtues shine,
   To prove the doctrine all divine.

2 Thus shall we best proclaim abroad
   The honors of our Saviour God;
   When His salvation reigns within,
   And grace subdues the power of sin.

3 Our flesh and sense must be denied,
   Passion and envy, lust and pride;
   While justice, temperance, truth, and love,
   Our inward piety approve.

4 Religion bears our spirits up,
   While we expect that blessed hope,
   The bright appearance of the Lord,
   And faith stands leaning on His word.
       Rev. Isaac Watts (1674—1748.) 1709. sl. alt.

622   *No Cross, no Crown.*   C. M.

1 Must Jesus bear the cross alone,
   And all the world go free?
   No there's a cross for every one,
   And there's a cross for me.

2 How happy are the saints above,
   Who once went sorrowing here!
   But now they taste unmingled love,
   And joy without a tear.

3 The consecrated cross I'll bear,
   Till death shall set me free;
   And then go home my crown to wear,
   For there's a crown for me.

4 Upon the crystal pavement, down
   At Jesus' piercèd feet,
   Joyful I'll cast my golden crown,
   And His dear Name repeat.

5 And palms shall wave, and harps shall ring,
   Beneath heaven's arches high;
   The Lord that lives, the ransomed sing,
   That lives, no more to die.

6 O precious cross! O glorious crown!
   O resurrection day!
   Ye angels, from the stars come down,
   And bear my soul away.
       G. N. Allen. vs. 1-3. 1F49. alt.

623   *"I am not ashamed."*   C. M.
           2 Tim. i. 12.

1 I'm not ashamed to own my Lord,
   Or to defend His cause,
   Maintain the honor of His word,
   The glory of His cross.

2 Jesus, my God! I know His Name,
   His Name is all my trust;
   Nor will He put my soul to shame,
   Nor let my hope be lost.

3 Firm as His throne His promise stands,
   And He can well secure
   What I've committed to His hands,
   Till the decisive hour.

4 Then will He own my worthless name
   Before His Father's face,
   And in the New Jerusalem
   Appoint my soul a place.
       Rev. Isaac Watts. 1709.

624   *Christ our Example.*   C. M.
           John xv. 13.

1 Lord, as to Thy dear cross we flee,
   And plead to be forgiven,
   So let Thy life our pattern be,
   And form our souls for heaven.

2 Help us, through good report and ill,
   Our daily cross to bear;
   Like Thee, to do our Father's will,
   Our brethren's griefs to share.

3 If joy shall at Thy bidding fly,
   And grief's dark day come on,
   We in our turn would meekly cry,
   Father, Thy will be done.

4 Should friends misjudge, or foes defame,
   Or brethren faithless prove,
   Then, like Thine own, be all our aim
   To conquer them by love.

5 Kept peaceful in the midst of strife,
   Forgiving and forgiven,
   O may we lead the pilgrim's life,
   And follow Thee to heaven.
       Rev. John Hampden Gurney. (1802—1862.) 1838. ab.

WARFARE.

625 *"Quit you like Men."* C. M.
1 Cor. xvi. 13.

1 AM I a soldier of the cross,
  A follower of the Lamb?
And shall I fear to own His cause,
  Or blush to speak His name?

2 Must I be carried to the skies
  On flowery beds of ease,
While others fought to win the prize,
  And sailed through bloody seas?

3 Are there no foes for me to face?
  Must I not stem the flood?
Is this vile world a friend to grace,
  To help me on to God?

4 Sure I must fight, if I would reign;
  Increase my courage, Lord;
I'll bear the toil, endure the pain,
  Supported by Thy word.

5 Thy saints, in all this glorious war,
  Shall conquer though they die;
They view the triumph from afar,
  And seize it with their eye.

6 When that illustrious day shall rise,
  And all Thine armies shine
In robes of victory through the skies,
  The glory shall be Thine.
  Rev. Isaac Watts. (1674—1748.) 1720.

626 *"Hinder me not."* C. M.
Gen. xxiv. 56.

1 IN all my Lord's appointed ways,
  My journey I'll pursue;
Hinder me not, ye much-loved saints,
  For I must go with you.

2 Through floods and flames, if Jesus lead,
  I'll follow where He goes;
Hinder me not! shall be my cry,
  Though earth and hell oppose.

3 Through duty, and through trials too,
  I'll go at His command;
Hinder me not, for I am bound
  To my Immanuel's land.

4 And when my Saviour calls me home,
  Still this my cry shall be,
Hinder me not! come, welcome death!
  I'll gladly go with thee.
  Rev. John Ryland. (1753—1825.) 1773. ab.

627 *The Highway to Zion.* C. M.
Is. xxxv. 1-10.

1 SING, ye redeemed of the Lord,
  Your great Deliverer sing;
Pilgrims for Zion's city bound,
  Be joyful in your King.

2 A hand divine shall lead you on
  Through all the blissful road,
Till to the sacred mount you rise,
  And see your smiling God.

3 There garlands of immortal joy
  Shall bloom on every head;
While sorrow, sighing, and distress,
  Like shadows all are fled.

4 March on in your Redeemer's strength;
  Pursue His footsteps still;
And let the prospect cheer your eye,
  While laboring up the hill.
  Rev. Philip Doddridge. (1702—1751.) 1755.

628 *"The whole Armor."* S. M.
Eph. vi. 11—18.

1 SOLDIERS of Christ, arise,
  And put your armor on,
Strong in the strength which God supplies
  Through His eternal Son.

2 Strong in the Lord of hosts,
  And in His mighty power,
Who in the strength of Jesus trusts,
  Is more than conqueror.

3 Stand, then, in His great might,
  With all His strength endued,
And take, to arm you for the fight,
  The panoply of God;

4 That, having all things done,
  And all your conflicts past,
Ye may o'ercome through Christ alone,
  And stand entire at last.

5 Leave no unguarded place,
  No weakness of the soul;
Take every virtue, every grace,
  And fortify the whole.

6 To keep your armor bright,
  Attend with constant care,
Still walking in your Captain's sight,
  And watching unto prayer.
  Rev. Charles Wesley. (1708—1788.) 1749. ab.

WARFARE.

629   *"Lead on."*   S. M.

1 LEAD on, almighty Lord,
   Lead on to victory!
Encouraged by the bright reward
   With joy to follow Thee.

2 We'll follow Thee, our Guide,
   Our Saviour and our King;
We'll follow Thee, through grace supplied
   From heaven's eternal spring.

3 We hope to see the day
   When all our toils shall cease;
When we shall cast our arms away,
   And dwell in endless peace.

4 This hope supports us here,
   It makes our burdens light;
'T will serve our drooping hearts to cheer,
   Till faith shall end in sight;

5 Till, of the prize possessed,
   We hear of war no more;
And O, sweet thought! forever rest
   On yonder peaceful shore.
          Rev. Thomas Kelly. (1769—1855.) 1809.

630   *"Be on thy Guard."*   S. M.

1 MY soul, be on thy guard;
   Ten thousand foes arise,
And hosts of sins are pressing hard
   To draw Thee from the skies.

2 O watch, and fight, and pray,
   The battle ne'er give o'er;
Renew it boldly every day,
   And help divine implore.

3 Ne'er think the victory won,
   Nor once at ease sit down;
Thine arduous work will not be done
   Till Thou receive thy crown.

4 Fight on, my soul, till death
   Shall bring thee to thy God;
He'll take thee at thy parting breath,
   To His divine abode.
          George Heath. 1781.

631   *"Keep the Charge of the Lord."*   S. M.
        Lev. viii. 35.

1 A CHARGE to keep I have,
   A God to glorify,
A never-dying soul to save,
   And fit it for the sky;

2 To serve the present age,
   My calling to fulfil;
O may it all my powers engage
   To do my Master's will.

3 Arm me with jealous care,
   As in Thy sight to live,
And O Thy servant, Lord, prepare
   A strict account to give.

4 Help me to watch and pray,
   And on Thyself rely,
Assured, if I my trust betray,
   I shall for ever die.
          Rev. Charles Wesley. 1762.

632   *"Watch and pray."*   S. M.
        Eph. v. 14.

1 GRACIOUS Redeemer, shake
   This slumber from my soul;
Say to me now, "Awake, awake!
   And Christ shall make thee whole."

2 Give me on Thee to call,
   Always to watch and pray,
Lest I into temptation fall,
   And cast my shield away.

3 For each assault prepared
   And ready may I be;
For ever standing on my guard,
   And looking up to Thee.

4 Thou seest my feebleness;
   Jesus, be Thou my power,
My help and refuge in distress,
   My fortress and my tower.

5 Cause me to trust in Thee,
   Be Thou my sure abode;
My horn, and rock, and buckler be,
   My Saviour, and my God.

6 Myself I cannot save,
   Myself I cannot keep;
But strength in Thee I surely have,
   Whose eyelids never sleep.

7 My soul to Thee alone
   Now, therefore, I commend;
Thou Jesus, having loved Thine own,
   Shalt love me to the end.
          Rev. Charles Wesley. 1749. ab.

WARFARE.

633   "Weigh not thy Life."   S. M.

1 My soul, weigh not thy life
   Against thy heavenly crown;
   Nor suffer Satan's deadliest strife
   To beat thy courage down.

2 With prayer and crying strong,
   Hold on the fearful fight,
   And let the breaking day prolong
   The wrestling of the night.

3 The battle soon will yield,
   If thou thy part fulfil;
   For strong as is the hostile shield,
   Thy sword is stronger still.

4 Thine armor is divine,
   Thy feet with victory shod;
   And on thy head shall quickly shine
   The diadem of God.
           Unknown Author.

634   "Verzage nicht, du Häuflein klein."   C. P. M.

1 Fear not, O little flock, the foe
   Who madly seeks your overthrow,
     Dread not his rage and power:
   What tho' your courage sometimes faints,
   His seeming triumph o'er God's saints
     Lasts but a little hour.

2 Be of good cheer; your cause belongs
   To Him who can avenge your wrongs;
     Leave it to Him, our Lord.
   Though hidden yet from mortal eyes,
   Salvation shall for you arise:
     He girdeth on His sword!

3 As true as God's own word is true,
   Not earth nor hell with all their crew
     Against us shall prevail.
   A jest and byword are they grown:
   God is with us; we are His own;
     Our victory cannot fail.

4 Amen. Lord Jesus, grant our prayer!
   Great Captain, now Thine arm make bare;
     Fight for us once again!
   So shall Thy saints and martyrs raise
   A mighty chorus to Thy praise,
     World without end. Amen.
       Gustavus Adolphus (1594–1632) 1631. in prose.
       Rev. Jacob Fabricius. (1593–1654) 1631. in verse.
       Tr. by Miss Catherine Winkworth. (1829—) 1855. alt.

635   Casting our Care on God.   C. P. M.
           1 Pet. v. 7.

1 O Lord, how happy should we be
   If we could cast our care on Thee,
     If we from self could rest;
   And feel at heart that One above
   In perfect wisdom, perfect love,
     Is working for the best.

2 How far from this our daily life,
   How oft disturbed by anxious strife,
     By sudden wild alarms;
   O could we but relinquish all
   Our earthly props, and simply fall
     On Thine almighty arms!

3 Could we but kneel and cast our load,
   E'en while we pray, upon our God,
     Then rise with lightened cheer;
   Sure that the Father who is nigh
   To still the famished raven's cry,
     Will hear in that we fear.

4 We cannot trust Him as we should;
   So chafes weak nature's restless mood
     To cast its peace away;
   But birds and flowerets round us preach,
   All, all the present evil teach
     Sufficient for the day.

5 Lord, make these faithless hearts of ours
   Such lessons learn from birds and flowers;
     Make them from self to cease,
   Leave all things to a Father's will,
   And taste, before Him lying still,
     E'en in affliction, peace.
       Prof. Joseph Anstice. (1808–1836) 1836.

636   In Affliction.   C. P. M.

1 "Father, Thy will, not mine, be done!"
   So prayed on earth Thy suffering Son,
     So in His Name I pray:
   The spirit fails, the flesh is weak;
   Thy help in agony I seek;
     O take the cup away.

2 If such be not Thy sovereign will,
   Thy wiser purpose then fulfil;
     My wishes I resign;
   Into Thy hands my soul commend,
   On Thee for life or death depend;
     Thy will be done, not mine.
       James Montgomery. (1771–1854.) 1853.

637   *The Tempest.*   8, 6.

1 OFT when the waves of passion rise,
   And storms of life conceal the skies,
     And o'er the ocean sweep,
   Tossed in the long tempestuous night,
   We feel no ray of heavenly light
     To cheer the lonely deep.

2 But lo, in our extremity,
   The Saviour walking on the sea!
     E'en now He passes by!
   He silences our clamorous fear,
   And mildly says, "Be of good cheer,
     Be not afraid, 'tis I."

3 Ah, Lord, if it be Thou indeed,
   So near us in our time of need,
     So good, so strong to save,
   Speak the kind word of power to me,
   Bid me believe, and come to Thee,
     Swift walking on the wave.

4 He bids me come! His voice I know,
   And boldly on the waters go,
     O'er rude temptations now I bound,
   The billows yield a solid ground,
     The wave is firm as rock.

5 Come in, come in, Thou Prince of Peace,
   And all the storms of sin shall cease,
     And fall, no more to rise;
   O, if Thy Spirit still remain,
   Our rest on distant shores we gain,
     Our haven in the skies.
       Rev. Charles Wesley. (1708—1788.) 1749. ab. and alt.

638   *"Come on."*   8, 6.

1 COME on, my partners in distress,
   My comrades through the wilderness,
     Who still your bodies feel:
   Awhile forget your griefs and fears,
   And look beyond the vale of tears,
     To that celestial hill.

2 Beyond the bounds of time and space,
   Look forward to that happy place,
     The saints' secure abode;
   On faith's strong eagle pinions rise,
   And force your passage to the skies,
     And scale the mount of God.

   Who suffer for our Master here,
   We shall before His face appear,
     And by His side sit down;
   To patient faith the prize is sure;
   And all that to the end endure
     The cross, shall wear the crown.

4 Thrice blessed, bliss-inspiring hope!
   It lifts the fainting spirits up,
     It brings to life the dead:
   Our conflicts here shall soon be past,
   And you and I ascend at last,
     Triumphant with our Head.

5 That great mysterious Deity
   We soon with open face shall see:
     The beatific sight
   Shall fill the heavenly courts with praise,
   And wide diffuse the golden blaze
     Of everlasting light.
       Rev. Charles Wesley. 1749. ab.

639   *"Forward into Light!"*   6, 5.
       Ex. xiv. 15.

1 FORWARD! be our watchword,
     Steps and voices joined;
   Seek the things before us,
     Not a look behind:
   Burns the fiery pillar
     At our army's head;
   Who shall dream of shrinking,
     By our Captain led?
   Forward through the desert,
     Through the toil and fight:
   Jordan flows before us,
     Zion beams with light!

2 Forward, flock of Jesus,
     Salt of all the earth;
   Till each yearning purpose
     Spring to glorious birth:
   Sick, they ask for healing,
     Blind, they grope for day;
   Pour upon the nations
     Wisdom's loving ray.
   Forward, out of error,
     Leave behind the night;
   Forward through the darkness,
     Forward into Light!

3 Glories upon glories
     Hath our God prepared,

By the souls that love Him
One day to be shared:
Eye hath not beheld them,
Ear hath never heard;
Nor of these hath uttered
Thought or speech a word:
Forward, marching eastward
Where the heaven is bright,
Till the veil be lifted,
Till our faith be sight!

4 Far o'er yon horizon
Rise the city towers,
Where our God abideth;
That fair home is ours:
Flash the streets with jasper,
Shine the gates with gold;
Flows the gladdening river
Shedding joys untold;
Thither, onward thither,
In the Spirit's might:
Pilgrims to your country,
Forward into Light!
Rev. Henry Alford. (1810—1871.) 1865. ab.

640 *"Onward, Christian Soldiers."* 6, 5.

1 ONWARD, Christian soldiers,
Marching as to war,
With the cross of Jesus
Going on before.
Christ the royal Master
Leads against the foe;
Forward into battle,
See, his banner go.
  Onward, Christian soldiers,
  Marching as to war,
  With the cross of Jesus
  Going on before.

2 At the sign of triumph
Satan's host doth flee;
On then, Christian soldiers,
On to victory.
Hell's foundations quiver
At the shout of praise;
Brothers, lift your voices,
Loud your anthems raise.
  Onward, &c.

3 Like a mighty army
Moves the Church of God;

Brothers, we are treading
Where the saints have trod;
We are not divided,
All one body we,
One in hope and doctrine,
One in charity.
  Onward, &c.

4 Crowns and thrones may perish,
Kingdoms rise and wane,
But the Church of Jesus
Constant will remain;
Gates of hell can never
'Gainst that Church prevail;
We have Christ's own promise,
And that cannot fail.
  Onward, &c.

5 Onward, then, ye people,
Join our happy throng,
Blend with ours your voices
In the triumph-song;
Glory, laud, and honor
Unto Christ the King;
This through countless ages,
Men and angels sing.
  Onward, &c.
Rev. Sabine Baring Gould. (1834—) 1865. ab.

641 *God is our Leader.* 7, 6.
Ps. lxxvii.

1 IN time of tribulation,
Hear, Lord, my feeble cries;
With humble supplication
To Thee my spirit flies:
My heart with grief is breaking;
Scarce can my heart complain:
Mine eyes with tears kept waking,
Still watch and weep in vain.

2 Hath God cast off forever?
Can time His truth impair?
His tender mercy, never
Shall I presume to share?
Hath He His loving-kindness
Shut up in endless wrath?
No; this is mine own blindness,
That cannot see His path.

3 I call to recollection
The years of His right hand;
And, strong in His protection,
Again through faith I stand:

Thy deeds, O Lord, are wonder.
Holy are all Thy ways;
The secret place of thunder,
Shall utter forth Thy praise.

4 Thee, with the tribes assembled,
O God, the billows saw;
They saw Thee and they trembled,
Turned, and stood still with awe;
Through the wild sea Thou leddest
Thy chosen flock of yore:
Still on the waves Thou treadest,
And Thy redeemed pass o'er.

James Montgomery. (1771—1854.) 1822. ab.

642 *Christ keeps us.* 7, 6.

1 O LAMB of God, still keep me
Near to Thy wounded side;
'Tis only there in safety
And peace I can abide.
What foes and snares surround me,
What doubts and fears within!
The grace that sought and found me,
Alone can keep me clean.

2 'Tis only in Thee hiding,
I know my life secure;
Only in Thee abiding,
The conflict can endure:
Thine arm the victory gaineth
O'er every hateful foe;
Thy love my heart sustaineth,
In all its care and woe.

3 Soon shall my eyes behold Thee
With rapture face to face;
One half hath not been told me
Of all Thy power and grace;
Thy beauty, Lord, and glory,
The wonders of Thy love,
Shall be the endless story
Of all Thy saints above.

James George Deck. 1857.

643 *"Stand up, stand up for Jesus!"* 7, 6.

1 STAND up, stand up for Jesus,
Ye soldiers of the cross;
Lift high His royal banner,
It must not suffer loss:
From victory unto victory
His army shall He lead,
Till every foe is vanquished,
And Christ is Lord indeed.

2 Stand up, stand up for Jesus,
The trumpet call obey;
Forth to the mighty conflict,
In this His glorious day:
"Ye that are men, now serve Him"
Against unnumbered foes;
Let courage rise with danger,
And strength to strength oppose.

3 Stand up, stand up for Jesus,
Stand in His strength alone;
The arm of flesh will fail you,
Ye dare not trust your own:
Put on the gospel armor,
Each piece put on with prayer;
Where duty calls, or danger,
Be never wanting there.

4 Stand up, stand up for Jesus,
The strife will not be long;
This day the noise of battle,
The next the victor's song:
To him that overcometh,
A crown of life shall be;
He with the King of Glory
Shall reign eternally.

Rev. George Duffield, Jr. (1818—) 1858. ab.

644 *"Go forward, Christian Soldier."* 7, 6.

1 Go forward, Christian soldier,
Beneath His banner true:
The Lord Himself, thy Leader,
Shall all thy foes subdue.
His love foretells thy trials,
He knows thine hourly need;
He can, with bread of heaven,
Thy fainting spirit feed.

2 Go forward, Christian soldier,
Fear not the secret foe;
Far more are o'er thee watching
Than human eyes can know.
Trust only Christ, thy Captain,
Cease not to watch and pray;
Heed not the treach'rous voices,
That lure thy soul astray.

3 Go forward, Christian soldier,
Nor dream of peaceful rest,
Till Satan's host is vanquished,
And heaven is all possest;

Till Christ Himself shall call thee
    To lay thine armor by,
And wear, in endless glory,
    The crown of victory.

4 Go forward, Christian soldier,
    Fear not the gathering night;
The Lord has been thy shelter,
    The Lord will be thy light;
When morn His face revealeth,
    Thy dangers all are past;
O pray that faith and virtue
    May keep thee to the last.
        Rev. Laurence Tuttiett. (1825—) 1854.

645   *"Faint not, Christian."*   7.

1 FAINT not, Christian, though the road,
Leading to thy blest abode,
Darksome be, and dangerous too;
Christ thy Guide will bring thee through.

2 Faint not Christian, though in rage
Satan would thy soul engage;
Gird on faith's anointed shield,
Bear it to the battle-field.

3 Faint not, Christian, though the world
Has its hostile flag unfurled;
Hold the cross of Jesus fast,
Thou shalt overcome at last.

4 Faint not, Christian, though within
There's a heart so prone to sin;
Christ, the Lord, is over all,
He'll not suffer thee to fall.

5 Faint not, Christian, Jesus near
Soon in glory will appear;
And His love will then bestow
Power to conquer every foe.

6 Faint not, Christian, look on high;
See the harpers in the sky:
Patient, wait, and thou wilt join
Chant with them of love divine.
        Rev. James Harrington Evans. (1785—1840.) 1833.

646   *The Conflict soon over.*   7.

1 BRETHREN, while we sojourn here,
Fight we must, but should not fear;
Foes we have, but we've a Friend,
One that loves us to the end:
Forward, then, with courage go;
Long we shall not dwell below;

Soon the joyful news will come,
"Child, your Father calls, come home!"

2 In the way a thousand snares
Lie, to take us unawares;
Satan, with malicious art,
Watches each unguarded part:
But, from Satan's malice free,
Saints shall soon victorious be;
Soon the joyful news will come,
"Child, your Father calls, come home!"

3 But of all the foes we meet,
None so oft mislead our feet,
None betray us into sin
Like the foes that dwell within;
Yet let nothing spoil our peace,
Christ shall also conquer these;
Soon the joyful news will come,
"Child, your Father calls, come home!"
        Rev. Joseph Swain. (1761—1796.) 1792.

647   *Welcome Cross.*   7.

1 'TIS my happiness below,
Not to live without the cross,
But the Saviour's power to know,
Sanctifying every loss.

2 Trials must and will befall;
But with humble faith to see
Love inscribed upon them all,
This is happiness to me.

3 Trials make the promise sweet;
Trials give new life to prayer;
Trials bring me to His feet,
Lay me low, and keep me there.
        William Cowper. (1731—1800.) 1779. ab.

648   *Pressing on.*   C. M.
        Phil. iii. 12—14.

1 AWAKE, my soul, stretch every nerve,
    And press with vigor on:
A heavenly race demands thy zeal,
    And an immortal crown.

2 A cloud of witnesses around
    Hold thee in full survey:
Forget the steps already trod,
    And onward urge thy way.

3 'Tis God's all-animating voice
    That calls thee from on high;
'Tis His own hand presents the prize
    To thine aspiring eye:—

4 That prize with peerless glories bright,
    Which shall new lustre boast,
  When victors' wreaths and monarchs' gems
    Shall blend in common dust.

5 Blest Saviour, introduced by Thee,
    Have I my race begun;
  And crowned with victory, at Thy feet
    I'll lay my honors down.
    Rev. Philip Doddridge. (1702—1751.) 1755.

649   *The Martyr-Spirit.*   C. M.

1 THE Son of God goes forth to war,
    A kingly crown to gain;
  His blood-red banner streams afar:
    Who follows in His train?

2 Who best can drink His cup of woe,
    Triumphant over pain,
  Who patient bears His cross below,
    He follows in His train.

3 The martyr first, whose eagle eye
    Could pierce beyond the grave,
  Who saw his Master in the sky,
    And called on Him to save:

4 Like Him, with pardon on his tongue,
    In midst of mortal pain,
  He prayed for them that did the wrong:
    Who follows in his train?

5 A glorious band, the chosen few
    On whom the Spirit came,
  Twelve valiant saints, their hope they knew,
    And mocked the cross and flame;

6 They climbed the steep ascent of heaven
    Through peril, toil, and pain:
  O God, to us may grace be given
    To follow in their train.
    Bp Reginald Heber. (1783—1826.) 1827. ab.

650   *The hard Way.*   C. M.

1 OUR journey is a thorny maze,
    But we march upward still,
  Forget these troubles of the ways,
    And reach at Zion's hill.

  See the kind angels, at the gates,
    Inviting us to come !
  There Jesus, the Forerunner, waits
    To welcome travellers home.

3 There, on a green and flowery mount,
    Our weary souls shall sit,
  And, with transporting joys, recount
    The labors of our feet.

4 Eternal glories to the King,
    Who brought us safely through,
  Our tongues shall never cease to sing,
    And endless praise renew.
    Rev. Isaac Watts. (1674—1748.) 1709. ab.

651   *The Christian Warfare.*   L. M.

1 STAND up, my soul, shake off thy fears,
  And gird the gospel armor on;
  March to the gates of endless joy,
  Where Jesus our great Captain's gone.

2 Hell and thy sins resist thy course,
  But hell and sin are vanquished foes;
  Thy Jesus nailed them to the cross,
  And sung the triumph when He rose.

3 Then let my soul march boldly on,
  Press forward to the heavenly gate;
  There peace and joy eternal reign,
  And glittering robes for conquerors wait.

4 There shall I wear a starry crown,
  And triumph in almighty grace;
  While all the armies of the skies
  Join in my glorious Leader's praise.
    Rev. Isaac Watts. 1709. ab. and alt.

652   *"The good Fight."*   L. M.
    1 Tim. vi. 12.

1 FIGHT the good fight with all thy might,
  Christ is thy strength, and Christ thy right;
  Lay hold on life, and it shall be
  Thy joy and crown eternally.

2 Run the straight race through God's good
  Lift up thine eyes, and seek His face; [grace,
  Life with its way before us lies,
  Christ is the path, and Christ the prize.

3 Cast care aside, upon thy Guide
  Lean, and His mercy will provide;
  Lean, and the trusting soul shall prove
  Christ is its life, and Christ its love.

4 Faint not nor fear, His arms are near,
  He changeth not, and thou art dear;
  Only believe, and thou shalt see
  That Christ is All in all to thee.
    Rev. John Samuel Bewley Monsell. (1811—) 1863.

653   The Call to Vigilance.   L. M.

1 Awake, my soul, lift up thine eyes:
See where thy foes against thee rise,
In long array, a numerous host:
Awake, my soul, or thou art lost.

2 See where rebellious passions rage,
And fierce desires and lusts engage;
The meanest foe of all the train
Has thousands and ten thousands slain.

3 Thou tread'st upon enchanted ground,
Perils and snares beset thee round;
Beware of all, guard every part,
But most, the traitor in thy heart.

4 Come, then, my soul, now learn to wield
The weight of thine immortal shield;
Put on the armor from above
Of heavenly truth, and heavenly love.

5 The terror and the charm repel,
The powers of earth, and powers of hell;
The Man of Calvary triumphed here:
Why should His faithful followers fear?
Mrs. Anna Laetitia Barbauld. (1743—1825) 1773. ab.

654   "Uphold me, Lord."   L. M.
Ps. ix.

1 Uphold me, Lord, too prone to stray,
Uphold me in Thy narrow way;
From sin and folly bid me flee,
And turn from all who turn from Thee.

2 The cloud and pillar of Thy word,
Be this my guide, my comfort, Lord,
By day, by night, at hand to bless,
And lead me through the wilderness.
Rev. Henry Francis Lyte. (1793—1847) 1834. ab.

655   The Christian Race.   L. M.
Is. xl. 28–31.

1 Awake, our souls, away our fears,
Let every trembling thought be gone;
Awake, and run the heavenly race,
And put a cheerful courage on.

2 True, 'tis a strait and thorny road,
And mortal spirits tire and faint;
But they forget the mighty God,
Who feeds the strength of every saint:

3 The mighty God, whose matchless power
Is ever new, and ever young,
And firm endures, while endless years
Their everlasting circles run.

4 From Thee, the overflowing spring,
Our souls shall drink a full supply;
While such as trust their native strength,
Shall melt away, and droop, and die.

5 Swift as an eagle cuts the air,
We'll mount aloft to Thine abode;
On wings of love our souls shall fly,
Nor tire amidst the heavenly road.
Rev. Isaac Watts. (1674—1748.) 1707.

656   Walking by Faith.   L. M.

1 'Tis by the faith of joys to come,
We walk through deserts dark as night;
Till we arrive at heaven, our home,
Faith is our guide, and faith our light.

2 The want of sight she well supplies;
She makes the pearly gates appear;
Far into distant worlds she pries,
And brings eternal glories near.

3 Cheerful we tread the desert through,
While faith inspires a heavenly ray;
Though lions roar and tempests blow,
And rocks and dangers fill the way.

4 So Abr'am, by divine command,
Left his own house to walk with God;
His faith beheld the promised land,
And fired his zeal along the road.
Rev. Isaac Watts. 1709.

657   Our City yet to come.   L. M.
Heb. xiii. 14.

1 "We've no abiding city here:"
Sad truth, were this to be our home;
But let the thought our spirits cheer,
"We seek a city yet to come."

2 "We've no abiding city here,"
We seek a city out of sight;
Zion its name, the Lord is there,
It shines with everlasting light.

3 Zion! Jehovah is her strength!
Secure she smiles at all her foes;
And weary travellers at length
Within her sacred walls repose.

4 O sweet abode of peace and love,
Where pilgrims freed from toil are blest;
Had I the pinions of the dove,
I'd fly to thee, and be at rest.

5 But hush, my soul, nor dare repine!
   The time my God appoints is best:
   While here, to do His will be *mine*,
   And *His* to fix my time of rest.
     Rev. Thomas Kelly. (1769—1855.) 1812, 1853. ab.

658   *Seeking a Country.*   6,6,8,6,4,7.
     Heb. xi. 14

1 FROM Egypt lately come,
   Where death and darkness reign,
   We seek our new, our better home,
   Where we our rest shall gain.
    Hallelujah!
    We are on our way to God.

2 To Canaan's sacred bound
   We haste with songs of joy,
   Where peace and liberty are found,
   And sweets that never cloy.
    Hallelujah!
    We are on our way to God.

3 Our toils and conflicts cease
   On Canaan's happy shore;
   We there shall dwell in endless peace,
   And never hunger more.
    Hallelujah!
    We are on our way to God.

4 There, in celestial strains,
   Enraptured myriads sing;
   There love in every bosom reigns,
   For God Himself is King.
    Hallelujah!
    We are on our way to God.

5 We soon shall join the throng,
   Their pleasures we shall share;
   And sing the everlasting song
   With all the ransomed there.
    Hallelujah!
    We are on our way to God.

6 How sweet the prospect is!
   It cheers the pilgrim's breast;
   We're journeying thro' the wilderness,
   But soon shall gain our rest.
    Hallelujah!
    We are on our way to God.
     Rev. Thomas Kelly. 1812, 1853. ab.

659   *Pressing on.*   6,6,8,6,4,7.

1 THIS is the day of toil
   Beneath earth's sultry noon;
   This is the day of service true,
   But the rest cometh soon.
    Hallelujah!
    There remains a rest for us.

2 Serve we our God in faith,
   No work for Him is vain;
   Blessèd and holy is the toil,
   And infinite the gain.
    Hallelujah!
    There remains a rest for us.

3 Spend and be spent would we,
   While lasteth time's brief day;
   No turning back in coward fear,
   No lingering by the way.
    Hallelujah!
    There remains a rest for us.

4 Onward we press in haste,
   Upward our journey still;
   Ours is the path the Master trod,
   Through good report and ill.
    Hallelujah!
    There remains a rest for us.

5 We have forsaken all,
   Jesus, to follow Thee;
   We counted well the cost, O Lord,
   We pay it cheerfully.
    Hallelujah!
    There remains a rest for us.

6 The way may rougher grow,
   The weariness increase;
   We gird our loins, and hasten on;
   The end, the end is peace.
    Hallelujah!
    There remains a rest for us.
     Rev. Horatius Bonar. (1808—) 1856. ab.

660   *"He leadeth me."*   L. M.

1 HE leadeth me: O blessed thought,
   O words with heavenly comfort fraught!
   Whate'er I do, where'er I be,
   Still 'tis God's hand that leadeth me.
CHO. He leadeth me, He leadeth me,
   By His own hand He leadeth me;
   His faithful follower I would be,
   For by His hand He leadeth me.

2 Sometimes 'mid scenes of deepest gloom
   Sometimes where Eden's bowers bloom

PILGRIMAGE.

By waters still, o'er troubled sea,
Still 't is His hand that leadeth me. *Cho.*

3 Lord, I would clasp Thy hand in mine,
Nor ever murmur nor repine;
Content, whatever lot I see,
Since 't is my God that leadeth me. *Cho.*

4 And when my task on earth is done,
When, by Thy grace, the victory's won,
E'en death's cold wave I will not flee,
Since God through Jordan leadeth me.
Cho. Rev. J. H. Gilmore. 1859.

661 *The Lord our Shepherd.* L. M.
Ps. xxiii.

1 THE Lord Himself doth condescend
To be my Shepherd and my Friend;
I on His faithfulness rely,
His care shall all my wants supply.

2 In pastures green He doth me lead,
And there in safety makes me feed;
Refreshing streams are ever nigh,
My thirsty soul to satisfy.

3 When strayed, or languid, I complain,
His grace revives my soul again;
For His Name's sake in ways upright
He makes me walk with great delight.

4 Yea, when death's gloomy vale I tread,
With joy, e'en there, I'll lift my head:
From fear and dread He'll keep me free;
His rod and staff shall comfort me.

5 Thou spread'st a table, Lord, for me,
While foes with spite Thy goodness see;
Thou dost my head with oil anoint,
And a full cup for me appoint.

6 Goodness and mercy shall to me,
Through all my life extended be;
And when my pilgrimage is o'er,
I'll dwell with Thee for evermore.
New York Dutch Reformed Collection of Psalms. 1767.

662 *Prayer for Guidance.* 8, 7, 4.

1 GUIDE me, O Thou great Jehovah,
Pilgrim through this barren land;
I am weak, but Thou art mighty,
Hold me with Thy powerful hand:
Bread of heaven, Bread of heaven,
Feed me till I want no more.

2 Open now the crystal fountain,
Whence the healing stream doth flow;
Let the fire and cloudy pillar
Lead me all my journey through:
Strong Deliverer, strong Deliverer,
Be Thou still my strength and shield.

3 When I tread the verge of Jordan,
Bid my anxious fears subside;
Death of deaths, and hell's destruction,
Land me safe on Canaan's side:
Songs of praises, songs of praises,
I will ever give to Thee.
Rev. Peter Williams. (1719—1796.) 1771. v. 1.
Rev. William Williams. (1717—1791.) 1773. ab.

663 *"And He led them on safely."* 8, 7, 4.
Ps. lxxviii.

1 SAVIOUR, through the desert lead us,
Without Thee we cannot go;
Thou from cruel chains hast freed us,
Thou hast laid the tyrant low:
Let Thy presence
Cheer us all our journey through.

2 When we halt, no track discovering,
Fearful lest we go astray,
O'er our path the pillar hovering,
Fire by night, and cloud by day,
Shall direct us:
Thus we shall not miss our way.

3 When we hunger, Thou wilt feed us,
Manna shall our camp surround;
Faint and thirsty, Thou wilt feed us;
Streams shall from the rock abound:
Happy Israel,
What a Saviour thou hast found!

4 When our foes in arms assemble,
Ready to obstruct our way,
Suddenly their hearts shall tremble,
Thou wilt strike them with dismay;
And Thy people,
Led by Thee, shall win the day.
Rev. Thomas Kelly. (1769—1855.) 1812. ab.

664 *The better Country.* 8, 7, 4.

1 SHEPHERD of Thine Israel, lead us,
Pilgrim through this desert land;
Thou who hast from bondage freed us,
Guard us by Thy mighty hand:
Daily feed us,
Till we reach the heavenly strand.

2 As Thou didst in wondrous manner
   Guide Thy chosen flock aright,
Let Thy presence be our banner,
   Cloud by day, and fire by night:
Thy protection
Be our shield, Thy word our light.

3 When we come to Death's dark river,
   Should we dread the swelling tide,
Death of death, life's Source and Giver,
   Bid the narrow stream divide:
Joyful praises
We will sing on Canaan's side.
            Josiah Conder. (1769—1855.) 1856.

665   *In Sorrow.*   8, 7.

1 GENTLY, Lord, O gently lead us,
   Pilgrims in this vale of tears,
Through the trials yet decreed us,
   Till our last great change appears.
When temptation's darts assail us,
   When in devious paths we stray,
Let Thy goodness never fail us,
   Lead us in Thy perfect way.

2 In the hour of pain and anguish,
   In the hour when death draws near,
Suffer not our hearts to languish,
   Suffer not our souls to fear;
And, when mortal life is ended,
   Bid us in Thine arms to rest,
Till, by angel bands attended,
   We awake among the b'est.
            Thomas Hastings. (1784—1872.), 1830, 1850, 1859.

666   *The elder Brother.*   8, 7.

1 YES, for me, for me He careth
   With a brother's tender care;
Yes, with me, with me He shareth
   Every burden, every fear.
Yes, o'er me, o'er me He watcheth,
   Ceaseless watcheth, night and day;
Yes, e'en me, e'en me He snatcheth
   From the perils of the way.

2 Yes for me He standeth pleading
   At the mercy-seat above;
Ever for me interceding,
   Constant in untiring love.
Yes, in me abroad He sheddeth
   Joys unearthly, love and light;
And to cover me He spreadeth
   His paternal wing of might.

3 Yes, in me, in me He dwelleth;
   I in Him, and He in me!
And my empty soul He filleth,
   Here and through eternity.
Thus I wait for His returning,
   Singing all the way to heaven;
Such the joyful song of morning,
   Such the tranquil song of even.
            Rev. Horatius Bonar. (1808—) 1857.

667   *"Always with us."*   8, 7.

1 ALWAYS with us, always with us—
   Words of cheer and words of love;
Thus the risen Saviour whispers,
   From His dwelling place above.
With us when we toil in sadness,
   Sowing much, and reaping none;
Telling us that in the future
   Golden harvests shall be won.

2 With us when the storm is sweeping
   O'er our pathway dark and drear;
Waking hope within our bosoms,
   Stilling every anxious fear.
With us in the lonely valley,
   When we cross the chilling stream;
Lighting up the steps to glory
   With salvation's radiant beam.
            Rev. Edwin H. Nevin. (1814—) 1858.

668   *"Lead Thou me on."*   10, 4, 10.

1 LEAD, kindly Light, amid the encircling
   Lead Thou me on;   [gloom,
The night is dark, and I am far from home;
   Lead Thou me on;
Keep Thou my feet; I do not ask to see
The distant scene; one step enough for me.

2 I was not ever thus, nor prayed that Thou
   Shouldst lead me on;
I love to choose and see my path; but now
   Lead Thou me on!
I love the garish day, and, spite of fears,
Pride ruled my will. Remember not past
   years!

3 So long Thy Power has blest me, sure it still
   Will lead me on
O'er moor and fen, o'er crag and torrent, till
   The night is gone,
And with the morn those angels faces smile
Which I have loved long since, and lost
   awhile!
            Rev. John Henry Newman. (1801—) 1833.

669   *"Jesu, geh voran."*   5, 8.

1 JESUS, still lead on,
Till our rest be won;
And although the way be cheerless,
We will follow, calm and fearless:
Guide us by Thy hand
To our Fatherland.

2 If the way be drear,
If the foe be near,
Let not faithless fears o'ertake us,
Let not faith and hope forsake us;
For through many a foe,
To our home we go.

3 When we seek relief
From a long-felt grief,
When temptations come alluring,
Make us patient and enduring;
Show us that bright shore
Where we weep no more.

4 Jesus, still lead on,
Till our rest be won;
Heavenly Leader, still direct us,
Still support, console, protect us,
Till we safely stand
In our Fatherland.

Nicolaus Ludwig Zinzendorf. (1700—1760.) 1721.
Tr. by Miss Jane Borthwick. 1855. sl. alt.

670   *"Wer ist wohl wie Du?"*   5, 8.

1 JESUS, who can be
Once compared with Thee!
Source of rest and consolation,
Life and light, and full salvation;
Son of God, with Thee
None compared can be!

2 Thou hast died for me,
From all misery
And distress me to deliver,
And from death to save forever;
I am by Thy blood
Reconciled to God.

3 Grant me steadiness,
Lord, to run my race,
Following Thee with love most tender,
So that Satan may not hinder
Me by craft or force;
Further Thou my course.

4 When I hence depart,
Strengthen Thou my heart;
Where Thou art, O Lord, convey me
In Thy righteousness array me,
That at Thy right hand
Joyful I may stand.

Rev. Johann Anastasius Freylinghausen. (1670—1739.) 1713.
Tr. by Bp. John Gambold. (1710—1771.) 1754. ab. and alt.

671   *"Lay Hold on eternal Life.*   10, 11, 12.
1 Tim. vi. 12.

1 BREAST the wave, Christian, when it is strongest;
Watch for day, Christian, when night is longest;
Onward and onward still be thine endeavor;
The rest that remaineth, endureth forever.

2 Fight the fight, Christian, Jesus is o'er thee;
Run the race, Christian, heaven is before thee;
He who hath promised faltereth never;
O trust in the love that endureth forever.

3 Lift the eye, Christian, just as it closeth;
Raise the heart, Christian, ere it reposeth;
Nothing thy soul from the Saviour shall sever;
Soon shalt thou mount upward to praise Him forever.

Joseph Stammers. (1801—) 1830. alt.

672   *"All is well."*   8, 4.

1 THROUGH the love of God our Saviour,
All will be well;
Free and changless is His favor;
All, all is well.
Precious is the blood that healed us,
Perfect is the grace that sealed us;
Strong the hand stretched out to shield us;
All must be well.

2 Though we pass through tribulation
All will be well;
Ours is such a full salvation
All, all is well.
Happy, still in God confiding,
Fruitful, if in Christ abiding,
Holy, through the Spirit's guiding,
All must be well.

3 We expect a bright to-morrow;
All will be well;
Faith can sing through days of sorrow,
All, all is well.

On our Father's love relying,
  Jesus every need supplying,
  Or in living, or in dying,
    All must be well.
      Mrs. Mary Bowly Peters. (—1856.) 1847.

673   Ζοφερᾶς τρικυμίας.   6, 4. D.

1 FIERCE was the wild billow,
  Dark was the night,
Oars labored heavily,
  Foam glimmered white,
Trembled the mariners,
  Peril was high;
Then said the God of God,
  "Peace? It is I!"

2 Ridge of the mountain-wave
  Lower thy crest!
Wail of Euroclydon,
  Be thou at rest!
Sorrow can never be,
  Darkness must fly,
Where saith the Light of Light,
  "Peace! It is I!"

3 Jesus, Deliverer,
  Come Thou to me:
Soothe Thou my voyaging
  Over life's sea;
Thou, when the storm of death
  Roars, sweeping by,
Whisper, Thou Truth of Truth,
  "Peace! It is I!"
      Anatolius of Constantinople. (—458.)
  Tr. by Rev. John Mason Neale. (1818—1866.) 1862. alt.

674   Cling to Him.   6, 4. D.

1 CLING to the Mighty One,
  Cling in thy grief;
Cling to the Holy One,
  He gives relief;
Cling to the Gracious One,
  Cling in thy pain;
Cling to the Faithful One,
  He will sustain.

2 Cling to the Living One,
  Cling in Thy woe;
Cling to the Loving One,
  Through all below;

Cling to the Pardoning One,
  He speaketh peace;
Cling to the Healing One,
  Anguish shall cease.

3 Cling to the Piercéd One,
  Cling to His side;
Cling to the Risen One,
  In Him abide;
Cling to the Coming One,
  Hope shall arise;
Cling to the Reigning One,
  Joy lights thine eyes.
      Henry Bennett. (1813—1868.) 1852.

675   "Hear our solemn Litany."   7. D.

1 SAVIOUR, when in dust to Thee
Low we bend the adoring knee;
When repentant, to the skies
Scarce we lift our weeping eyes;
O, by all the pains and woe
Suffered once for man below,
Bending from Thy throne on high,
Hear our solemn Litany!

2 By Thy helpless infant years;
By Thy life of want and tears
By Thy days of sore distress
In the savage wilderness;
By the dread mysterious hour
Of the insulting tempter's power;
Turn, O turn a favoring eye,
Hear our solemn Litany!

3 By the sacred griefs that wept
O'er the grave where Lazarus slept;
By the boding tears that flowed
Over Salem's loved abode;
By the anguished sigh that told
Treachery lurked within Thy fold;
From Thy seat above the sky,
Hear our solemn Litany!

4 By Thine hour of dire despair;
By Thine agony of prayer;
By the cross, the nail, the thorn,
Piercing spear, and torturing scorn;
By the gloom that veiled the skies
O'er the dreadful sacrifice;
Listen to our humble cry,
Hear our solemn Litany!

5 By Thy deep expiring groan;
  By the sad sepulchral stone;
  By the vault, whose dark abode
  Held in vain the rising God;
  O, from earth to heaven restored,
  Mighty reascended Lord,
  Listen, listen to the cry
  Of our solemn Litany!
      Sir Robert Grant. (1785—1838.) 1815. sl. alt.

676   *"Jesus, Lover of my Soul."*   7. D.

1 JESUS, Lover of my soul,
    Let me to Thy bosom fly,
  While the nearer waters roll,
    While the tempest still is high;
  Hide me, O my Saviour, hide,
    Till the storm of life is past;
  Safe into the haven guide;
    O receive my soul at last.

2 Other refuge have I none;
    Hangs my helpless soul on Thee;
  Leave, ah leave me not alone,
    Still support and comfort me.
  All my trust on Thee is stayed,
    All my help from Thee I bring;
  Cover my defenceless head
    With the shadow of Thy wing.

3 Wilt Thou not regard my call?
    Wilt Thou not accept my prayer?
  Lo, I sink, I faint, I fall!
    Lo, on Thee I cast my care.
  Reach me out Thy gracious hand!
    While I of Thy strength receive,
  Hoping against hope I stand,
    Dying, and behold I live!
        Rev. Charles Wesley. (1708—1788.) 1740.

677   *"All I want."*   7. D.

1 THOU, O Christ, art all I want;
    More than all in Thee I find:
  Raise the fallen, cheer the faint,
    Heal the sick, and lead the blind.
  Just and holy is Thy Name;
    I am all unrighteousness;
  False and full of sin I am,
    Thou art full of truth and grace.

2 Plenteous grace with Thee is found,
    Grace to cover all my sin:
  Let the healing streams abound,
    Make and keep me pure within.
  Thou of Life the Fountain art;
    Freely let me take of Thee;
  Spring Thou up within my heart,
    Rise to all eternity.
        Rev. Charles Wesley. 1740.

678   *Declension deplored.*   7. 6l.
         Job. xxix 2.

1 ONCE I thought my mountain strong,
    Firmly fixed no more to move;
  Then Thy grace was all my song,
    Then my soul was filled with love:
  Those were happy, golden days,
  Sweetly spent in prayer and praise.

2 Little then myself I knew,
    Little thought of Satan's power;
  Now I feel my sins anew,
    Now I feel the stormy hour;
  Sin has put my joys to flight,
  Sin has changed my day to night.

3 Saviour, shine and cheer my soul;
    Bid my dying hopes revive;
  Make my wounded spirit whole;
    Far away the tempter drive;
  Speak the word, and set me free,
  Let me live alone to Thee.
      Rev. John Newton (1725—1807.) 1779. ab. and alt.

679   *"Was von aussen und von innen."*   7.

1 LORD, thou art my Rock of strength,
    And my home is in Thine arms;
  Thou wilt send me help at length,
    And I feel no wild alarms.
  Sin nor death can pierce the shield
    Thy defence has o'er me thrown;
  Up to Thee myself I yield,
    And my sorrows are Thine own.

2 When my trials tarry long,
    Unto Thee I look and wait,
  Knowing none, though keen and strong,
    Can my trust in Thee abate.
  And this faith I long have nursed
    Comes alone, O God, from Thee;
  Thou my heart didst open first,
    Thou didst set this hope in me.

3 Let Thy mercy's wings be spread
　O'er me, keep me close to Thee;
　In the peace Thy love doth shed,
　Let me dwell eternally.
　Be my all; in all I do,
　Let me only seek Thy will.
　Where the heart to Thee is true,
　All is peaceful, calm and still.
　　Rev. August Hermann Franke. (1663—1727.) 1711.
　　Tr. by Miss Catherine Winkworth. (1829—) 1855. ab.

680　　Daily Strength.　　7.

1 "As thy day, thy strength shall be!"
　This should be enough for thee;
　He who knows thy frame will spare
　Burdens more than thou canst bear.

2 When thy days are veiled in night,
　Christ shall give thee heavenly light;
　Seem they wearisome and long,
　Yet in Him thou shalt be strong.

3 Cold and wintry though they prove,
　Thine the sunshine of His love;
　Or with fervid heat opprest,
　In His shadow thou shalt rest.

4 When thy days on earth are past,
　Christ shall call thee home at last,
　His redeeming love to praise,
　Who hath strengthened all thy days.
　　Miss Frances Ridley Havergal. 1872.

681　　The forgiven Debt.　　7. 6l.
　　　　Matt. xviii. 32.

1 When this passing world is done,
　When has sunk yon glaring sun,
　When we stand with Christ in glory,
　Looking o'er life's finished story;
　Then, Lord, shall I fully know,
　Not till then, how much I owe.

2 When I stand before the throne,
　Dressed in beauty not my own;
　When I see Thee as Thou art,
　Love Thee with unsinning heart;
　Then, Lord, shall I fully know,
　Not till then, how much I owe.

3 When the praise of heaven I hear,
　Loud as thunders to the ear,
　Loud as many waters' noise,
　Sweet as harp's melodious voice;
　Then, Lord, shall I fully know,
　Not till then, how much I owe.
　　Rev. Robert Murray McCheyne. (1813—1843.) 1837. ab.

682　　Debtor to all Men.　　7. 6l.
　　　　Rom. i. 14.

1 Chosen not for good in me,
　Wakened up from wrath to flee,
　Hidden in the Saviour's side,
　By the Spirit sanctified,
　Teach me, Lord, on earth to show,
　By my love, how much I owe.

2 Oft I walk beneath the cloud,
　Dark as midnight's gloomy shroud;
　But, when fear is at the height,
　Jesus comes, and all is light:
　Blessèd Jesus, bid me show
　Doubting saints how much I owe.

3 When in flowery paths I tread,
　Oft by sin I'm captive led;
　Oft I fall, but still arise,
　Jesus comes, the tempter flies:
　Blessèd Saviour, bid me show
　Weary sinners all I owe.

4 Oft the nights of sorrow reign,
　Weeping, sickness, sighing, pain;
　But a night Thine anger burns,
　Morning comes, and joy returns:
　God of comforts, bid me show
　To Thy poor how much I owe.
　　Rev. Robert Murray McCheyne. 1837. ab. and st. alt.

683　　"Haste to help me."　　7.
　　　　Ps. lxx.

1 Hasten, Lord, to my release,
　Haste to help me, O my God!
　Foes, like armèd bands, increase;
　Turn them back the way they trod.

2 Dark temptations round me press,
　Evil thoughts my soul assail;
　Doubts and fears, in my distress,
　Rise till flesh and spirit fail.

3 Those that seek Thee shall rejoice;
　I am bowed with misery;
　Yet I make Thy law my choice;
　Turn, my God, and look on me.

4 Thou mine only Helper art,
　My Redeemer from the grave;
　Strength of my desiring heart,
　Do not tarry, haste to save.
　　James Montgomery (1771—1854.) 1821.

RENEWED CONSECRATION.

684
"A closer Walk."
Gen. v. 24.   1 John ii. 6.
C. M.

1 O FOR a closer walk with God,
   A calm and heavenly frame,
   A light to shine upon the road
   That leads me to the Lamb!

2 Where is the blessedness I knew
   When first I saw the Lord?
   Where is the soul-refreshing view
   Of Jesus and His word?

3 What peaceful hours I once enjoyed,
   How sweet their memory still!
   But they have left an aching void
   The world can never fill.

4 Return, O Holy Dove, return,
   Sweet messenger of rest:
   I hate the sins that made Thee mourn,
   And drove Thee from my breast.

5 The dearest idol I have known,
   Whate'er that idol be;
   Help me to tear it from Thy throne,
   And worship only Thee.

6 So shall my walk be close with God,
   Calm and serene my frame;
   So purer light shall mark the road
   That leads me to the Lamb.
   William Cowper. (1731—1800.) 1779.

685
"Let us return."
Hos. vi. 1-4.
C. M.

1 COME, let us to the Lord our God
   With contrite hearts return;
   Our God is gracious, nor will leave
   The desolate to mourn.

2 His voice commands the tempest forth,
   And stills the stormy wave;
   And though His arm be strong to smite,
   'T is also strong to save.

3 Long hath the night of sorrow reigned;
   The dawn shall bring us light:
   God shall appear, and we shall rise
   With gladness in His sight.

4 Our hearts, if God we seek to know,
   Shall know Him and rejoice;
   His coming like the morn shall be,
   Like morning songs His voice.

5 As dew upon the tender herb,
   Diffusing fragrance round;
   As showers that usher in the spring,
   And cheer the thirsty ground:

6 So shall His presence bless our souls,
   And shed a joyful light;
   That hallowed morn shall chase away
   The sorrows of the night.
   Rev. John Morrison. (1749—1798.) 1781.

686
"O that I were as in Months past!"
Job xxix. 2.
C. M.

1 SWEET was the time when first I felt
   The Saviour's pardoning blood
   Applied to cleanse my soul from guilt,
   And bring me home to God.

2 Soon as the morn the light revealed,
   His praises tuned my tongue;
   And when the evening shades prevailed,
   His love was all my song.

3 In prayer my soul drew near the Lord,
   And saw His glory shine;
   And when I read His holy word,
   I called each promise mine.

4 But now, when evening shade prevails,
   My soul in darkness mourns;
   And when the morn the light reveals,
   No light to me returns.

5 Rise, Saviour, help me to prevail,
   And make my soul Thy care;
   I know Thy mercy cannot fail:
   Let me that mercy share.
   Rev. John Newton. (1725—1807.) 1779. ab. and alt.

687
Panting for God.
Ps. xlii.
C. M.

1 As pants the hart for cooling streams,
   When heated in the chase,
   So pants my soul, O Lord, for Thee,
   And Thy refreshing grace.

2 For Thee, the Lord, the living Lord,
   My thirsty soul doth pine:
   O when shall I behold Thy face,
   Thou Majesty Divine?

3 I sigh to think of happier days,
   When Thou, O Lord, wert nigh;
   When every heart was tuned to praise,
   And none so blest as I.

4 Why restless, why cast down, my soul?
  Trust God, and thou shalt sing
  His praise again, and find Him still
  Thy health's eternal spring.
  Tate and Brady. 1696 alt
Rev. Henry Francis Lyte. (1793—1847.) 1834

688   *Lamenting Inconstancy.*   C. M.

1 WHY is my heart so far from Thee,
  My God, my chief Delight?
  Why are my thoughts no more by day
  With Thee, no more by night?

2 Why should my foolish passions rove?
  Where can such sweetness be,
  As I have tasted in Thy love,
  As I have found in Thee?

3 When my forgetful soul renews
  The savor of Thy grace,
  My heart presumes, I cannot lose
  The relish all my days.

4 But ere one fleeting hour is passed,
  The flattering world employs
  Some sensual bait to seize my taste,
  And to pollute my joys.

5 Wretch that I am, to wander thus,
  In chase of false delight!
  Let me be fastened to Thy cross,
  Rather than lose Thy sight.

6 Make haste, my days, to reach the goal,
  And bring my heart to rest
  On the dear centre of my soul,
  My God, my Saviour's breast.
  Rev. Isaac Watts. (1674—1748.) 1709. ab.

689   *Longing for Christ.*   C. M.

1 O COULD I find, from day to day,
  A nearness to my God;
  Then should my hours glide sweet away,
  And live upon Thy Word.

2 Lord, I desire with Thee to live,
  Anew from day to day,
  In joys the world can never give,
  Nor ever take away.

3 O Jesus, come and rule my heart,
  And I'll be wholly Thine;
  And never, never more depart,
  For Thou art wholly mine.

4 Thus, till my last expiring breath,
  Thy goodness I'll adore;
  And when my flesh dissolves in death,
  My soul shall love Thee more.
  Benjamin Cleveland. 1790. ib.

690   *Pardoning Love.*   C. M.
Jer. iii. 22. Hos. xiv. 4.

1 How oft, alas, this wretched heart
  Has wandered from the Lord!
  How oft my roving thoughts depart,
  Forgetful of His word!

2 Yet sovereign mercy calls, "Return!"
  Dear Lord, and may I come?
  My vile ingratitude I mourn;
  O take the wanderer home.

3 And canst Thou, wilt Thou yet forgive,
  And bid my crimes remove?
  And shall a pardoned rebel live,
  To speak Thy wondrous love?

4 Thy pardoning love, so free, so sweet,
  Dear Saviour, I adore;
  O keep me at Thy sacred feet,
  And let me rove no more.
  Miss Anne Steele. (1717—1778.) 1760. ab.

691   *Weak Believers encouraged.*   S. M.

1 YOUR harps, ye trembling saints,
  Down from the willows take;
  Loud to the praise of love divine
  Bid every string awake.

2 Though in a foreign land,
  We are not far from home;
  And nearer to our house above
  We every moment come.

3 His grace will to the end
  Stronger and brighter shine;
  Nor present things, nor things to come,
  Shall quench the spark divine.

4 When we in darkness walk,
  Nor feel the heavenly flame,
  Then is the time to trust our God,
  And rest upon His name.

5 Soon shall our doubts and fears
  Subside at His control;
  His loving-kindness shall break through
  The midnight of the soul.

6 Blest is the man, O God,
   That stays himself on Thee;
Who wait for Thy salvation, Lord,
   Shall Thy salvation see.
   Augustus Montague Toplady (1740—1778) 1772. ab.

692   *The Anchor of Hope.*   S. M.
          Heb. vi. 19.

1 FASTENED within the vail,
   Hope be your anchor strong;
His loving Spirit the sweet gale
   That wafts you smooth along.

2 Or, should the surges rise,
   And peace delay to come,
Blest is the sorrow, kind the storm,
   That drives us nearer home.
   Rev. Augustus Montague Toplady. 1772. ab.

693   *Waiting upon Christ.*   S. M.

1 THE people of His choice
   Christ will not cast away;
Yet do not always here expect
   On Tabor's mount to stay.

2 No wonder, when His love
   Pervades your kindling breast,
You wish forever to retain
   The heart-transporting Guest.

3 Yet learn, in every state,
   To make His will your own;
And, when the joys of sense depart,
   To walk by faith alone.

4 Still on His plighted love
   At all events rely;
The very hidings of His face
   Shall train thee up to joy.

5 Wait, till the shadows flee;
   Wait thy appointed hour;
Wait, till the Bridegroom of thy soul
   Reveal His love with power.

6 The time of love will come,
   When thou shalt clearly see,
Not only that He shed His blood,
   But that it flowed for thee.
   Rev. Augustus Montague Toplady. 1772. ab. and sl. alt.

694   *Through the Sea.*   S. M.
          Ps. cvii. 23.

1 WE'RE bound for yonder land,
   Where Jesus reigns supreme;
We leave the shore at His command,
   Forsaking all for Him.

2 The perils of the sea,
   The rocks, the waves, the wind,
Are small, whatever they may be,
   To those we leave behind.

3 Nor have we cause to fear;
   The God who rules the sea
In every danger will be near,
   And our protector be.

4 The Lord Himself will keep
   His people safe from harm;
Will hold the helm, and guide the ship,
   With His Almighty arm.

5 Then let the tempests roar,
   The billows heave and swell;
We trust to reach the peaceful shore,
   Where all the ransomed dwell.

6 And when we gain the land,
   How happy shall we be!
How shall we bless the mighty Hand
   That led us through the sea!
   Rev. Thomas Kelly. (1769–1855.) 1809. ab.

695   *"Out of the Depths."*   S. M.
          Ps. cxxx.

1 OUT of the depths of woe,
   To Thee, O Lord, I cry;
Darkness surrounds me, but I know
   That Thou art ever nigh.

2 I cast my hope on Thee;
   Thou canst, Thou wilt forgive;
Wert Thou to mark iniquity,
   Who in Thy sight could live?

3 Humbly I wait on Thee,
   Confessing all my sin;
Lord, I am knocking at Thy gate;
   Open, and take me in.

4 Glory to God above!
   The waters soon will cease;
For lo, the swift-returning Dove
   Brings home the sign of peace.

5 Though storms His face obscure,
   And dangers threaten load,
Jehovah's covenant is sure,
   His bow is in the cloud.
   James Montgomery (1771–1854.) 1822. ab.

696   *Prayer for perfect Peace.*   S. M.

1 JESUS, my Lord, attend
    Thy fallen creature's cry,
And show Thyself the sinner's Friend,
    And set me up on high.

2 From hell's oppressive power,
    From earth and sin release,
And to Thy Father's grace restore,
    And to Thy perfect peace.

3 Thy blood and righteousness
    I make my only plea;
My present and eternal peace
    Are both derived from Thee.

4 O then, impute, impart,
    To me Thy righteousness;
And let me taste how good Thou art,
    How full of truth and grace.

5 That Thou canst here forgive,
    Grant me to testify;
And justified by faith to live,
    And in that faith to die.
      Rev. Charles Wesley (1708–1758) 1747. ab.

697   *Daily Trust.*   S. M.

1 JESUS, one word from Thee
    Fills my sad soul with peace.
My griefs are like a tossing sea;
    They hear Thy voice and cease.

2 Soon as Thy pitying face
    Shone through my stormy fears,
The storm swept by, nor left a trace,
    Save the sweet dew of tears.

3 And when Thou call'st me, Lord,
    Where thickest dangers be,
Even the waves a path afford;
    I walk the waves with Thee.

4 With Thee within my bark
    I'll dare death's threatening tide;
Nor count the passage strange or dark
    With Jesus by my side.

5 Dear Lord, Thy faithful grace
    I know and I adore:
What shall it be to see Thy face
    In heaven, forevermore!
      Rev. Hervey Doddridge Ganse (1822–) 1872.

698   "*Ye shall live also.*"   L. M.
      John xiv. 19

1 WHEN sins and fears prevailing rise,
And fainting hope almost expires,
Jesus, to Thee I lift mine eyes;
To Thee I breathe my soul's desires.

2 Art Thou not mine, my Living Lord?
And can my hope, my comfort die?
Fixed on Thine everlasting word,
That word which built the earth and sky?

3 If my Immortal Saviour lives,
Then my immortal life is sure;
His word a firm foundation gives;
Here let me build, and rest secure.

4 Here let my faith unshaken dwell;
Immovable the promise stands;
Not all the powers of earth or hell
Can e'er dissolve the sacred bands.

5 Here, O my soul, thy trust repose;
If Jesus is forever mine,
Not death itself, that last of foes,
Shall break a union so divine.
      Miss Anne Steele. (1717–1778) 1760

699   *Restoring and preserving Grace*   L. M.
      Ps. cxxxviii

1 To God I cried when troubles rose;
He heard me, and subdued my foes;
He did my rising fears control,
And strength diffused through all my soul.

2 The God of heaven maintains His state,
Frowns on the proud, and scorns the great;
But from His throne descends to see
The sons of humble poverty.

3 Amid a thousand snares, I stand
Upheld and guarded by Thy hand;
Thy words my fainting soul revive,
And keep my dying faith alive.

4 Grace will complete what grace begins,
To save from sorrows and from sins;
The work that wisdom undertakes,
Eternal mercy ne'er forsakes.
      Rev. Isaac Watts (1674–1748) 1719. ab.

700   *Gift of God.*   L. M.

1 JESUS, my Lord, my chief Delight,
For Thee I long, for Thee I pray,
Amid the shadows of the night,
Amid the business of the day.

2 When shall I see Thy smiling face,
  That face which often I have seen?
  Arise, Thou Sun of righteousness,
  Scatter the clouds that intervene.

3 Thou art the glorious gift of God
  To sinners weary and distrest;
  The first of all His gifts bestowed,
  And certain pledge of all the rest.

4 Could I but say this gift is mine,
  The world should lie beneath my feet;
  Though poor, no more would I repine,
  Or look with envy on the great.

5 The precious jewel I would keep,
  And lodge it deep within my heart,
  At home, abroad, awake, asleep,
  It never should from thence depart.
     Rev. Benjamin Beddome. (1717—1795.) 1818.

701   *The Triumph of Faith.*   L. M.
           Rom. viii. 33.

1 WHO shall the Lord's elect condemn?
  'Tis God that justifies their souls,
  And mercy, like a mighty stream,
  O'er all their sins divinely rolls.

2 Who shall adjudge the saints to hell?
  'Tis Christ that suffered in their stead;
  And the salvation to fulfil,
  Behold Him rising from the dead!

3 He lives! He lives! and sits above,
  Forever interceding there:
  Who shall divide us from His love,
  Or what shall tempt us to despair?

4 Shall persecution, or distress,
  Famine, or sword, or nakedness?
  He that hath loved us bears us through,
  And makes us more than conquerors too.

5 Not all that men on earth can do,
  Nor powers on high, nor powers below,
  Shall cause His mercy to remove,
  Or wean our hearts from Christ, our Love.
     Rev. Isaac Watts. (1674—1748.) 1709. ab.

702   *Christ all sufficient.*   L. M.

1 FOUNTAIN of grace, rich, full, and free,
  What need I, that is not in Thee?
  Full pardon, strength to meet the day,
  And peace which none can take away.

2 Doth sickness fill my heart with fear?
  'T is sweet to know that Thou art near;
  Am I with dread of justice tried?
  'T is sweet to know that Christ hath died.

3 In life, Thy promises of aid
  Forbid my heart to be afraid;
  In death, peace gently veils the eyes;
  Christ rose, and I shall surely rise.

4 O all-sufficient Saviour, be
  This all-sufficiency to me;
  Nor pain, nor sin, nor death, can harm
  The weakest shielded by Thine arm.
     James Edmeston. (1791—1867.) 1844.

703   *Thirsting for God.*   L. M.

1 I THIRST, but not as once I did,
  The vain delights of earth to share;
  Thy wounds, Immanuel, all forbid
  That I should seek my pleasures there.

2 It was the sight of Thy dear cross
  First weaned my soul from earthly things,
  And taught me to esteem as dross
  The mirth of fools and pomp of kings.

3 I want that grace that springs from Thee,
  That quickens all things where it flows,
  And makes a wretched thorn like me
  Bloom as the myrtle, or the rose.

4 For sure, of all the plants that share
  The notice of Thy Father's eye,
  None proves less grateful to His care,
  Or yields Him meaner fruit than I.
     William Cowper. (1731—1800.) 1779. ab.

704   *"Seelenbräutigam O du Gottes-Lamm."*   L. M.

1 O THOU, to whose all-searching sight
  The darkness shineth as the light,
  Search, prove my heart, it pants for Thee;
  O burst these bonds, and set it free.

2 Wash out its stains, refine its dross;
  Nail my affections to the cross;
  Hallow each thought; let all within
  Be clean, as Thou, my Lord, art clean.

3 If in this darksome wild I stray,
  Be Thou my light, be Thou my way;
  No foes, no violence I fear,
  No fraud, while Thou, my God, art near.

ASSURANCE OF FAITH.

4 When rising floods my soul o'erflow,
  When sinks my heart in waves of woe,
  Jesus, Thy timely aid impart,
  And raise my head, and cheer my heart.

5 Saviour, where'er Thy steps I see,
  Dauntless, untired, I follow Thee;
  O let Thy hand support me still,
  And lead me to Thy holy hill.

  Gerhard Tersteegen. (1697—1769.)
  Tr. by Rev. John Wesley (1703—1791) 1738. ab.

705 *"Geht hin, ihr gläubigen Gedanken."* L. M.
  1 John iii. 2.

1 ERE earth's foundations yet were laid,
  Or heaven's fair roof was spread abroad;
  Ere man a living soul was made,
  Love stirred within the heart of God.

2 Thy loving counsel gave to me
  True life in Christ, Thy only Son,
  Whom Thou hast made my way to Thee,
  From whom all grace flows ever down.

3 O Love, that long ere time began,
  That precious name of child bestowed;
  That opened Heaven on earth to man,
  And called us sinners "sons of God!"

4 I am not worthy, Lord, that Thou
  Shouldst such compassion on me show:
  That He who made the world should bow
  To cheer with love a wretch so low.

5 Could I but honor Thee aright,
  Noble and sweet my song should be;
  That earth and heaven should learn Thy
      might,
  And what my God hath done for me.

  Rev. Johann Gottfried Hermann. (1707—1791.) 1742.
  Tr. by Miss Catherine Winkworth. (1829—) 1855. ab. and alt.

706 *Looking upwards in a Storm.* L. M.

1 GOD of my life, to Thee I call,
  Afflicted, at Thy feet I fall;
  When the great water-floods prevail,
  Leave not my trembling heart to fail.

2 Friend of the friendless and the faint,
  Where should I lodge my deep complaint?
  Where, but with Thee, whose open door
  Invites the helpless and the poor?

3 Did ever mourner plead with Thee,
  And Thou refuse that mourner's plea?
  Does not the word still fixed remain,
  That none shall seek Thy face in vain?

4 That were a grief I could not bear,
  Didst Thou not hear and answer prayer;
  But a prayer-hearing, answering God
  Supports me under every load.

5 Poor though I am, despised, forgot,
  Yet God, my God, forgets me not;
  And he is safe, and must succeed,
  For whom the Lord vouchsafes to plead.

  William Cowper. 1779. ab.

707 *"Come to Me!"* L. M.

1 WITH tearful eyes I look around;
  Life seems a dark and stormy sea;
  Yet 'midst the gloom I hear a sound,
  A heavenly whisper, "Come to Me!"

2 It tells me of a place of rest,
  It tells me where my soul may flee:
  O, to the weary, faint, opprest,
  How sweet the bidding, "Come to Me!"

3 When the poor heart with anguish learns
  That earthly props resigned must be,
  And from each broken cistern turns,
  It hears the accents, "Come to Me!"

4 When against sin I strive in vain,
  And cannot from its yoke get free,
  Sinking beneath the heavy chain,
  The words arrest me, "Come to Me!"

5 When nature shudders, loath to part
  From all I love, enjoy, and see;
  When a faint chill steals o'er my heart,
  A sweet voice utters, "Come to Me!"

6 "Come, for all else must fail and die;
  Earth is no resting-place for thee;
  Heavenward direct thy weeping eye;
  I am thy portion; Come to Me!"

7 O voice of mercy, voice of love,
  In conflict, grief, and agony,
  Support me, cheer me from above,
  And gently whisper, "Come to Me!"

  Miss Charlotte Elliott. (1789—1871.) 1841.

708 *"T is I; be not afraid."* L. M.
  Matt. xiv. 27.

1 TOSSED with rough winds, and faint with
  Above the tempest, soft and clear, [fear,
  What still small accents greet mine ear?
  'T is I, 't is I; be not afraid.

ASSURANCE OF FAITH.

2 'T is I who washed thy spirit white;
'T is I who gave thy blind eyes sight;
'T is I thy Lord, thy Life, thy Light:
'T is I, 'tis I; be not afraid.

3 These raging winds, this surging sea,
Have spent their deadly force on Me;
They bear no breath of wrath to thee:
'T is I, 'tis I; be not afraid.

4 This bitter cup, I drank it first;
To thee it is no draught accurst;
The hand that gives it thee is pierced:
'T is I, 'tis I; be not afraid.

5 Mine eyes are watching by thy bed,
Mine arms are underneath thy head,
My blessing is around thee shed:
'T is I, 'tis I; be not afraid.

6 When on the other side thy feet
Shall rest, 'mid thousand welcomes sweet,
One well-known voice thy heart shall greet:
'T is I, 'tis I; be not afraid.
Mrs. Elizabeth Charles. 1862, 1870. ab. and sl. alt.

709 *"Exceeding great and precious Promises." 11.*
2 Pet. i. 4.

1 How firm a foundation, ye saints of the Lord,
Is laid for your faith in His excellent word!
What more can He say than to you He hath said,
You who unto Jesus for refuge have fled?

2 "Fear not, I am with thee, O be not dismayed,
For I am thy God, and will still give thee aid;
I'll strengthen thee, help thee, and cause thee to stand,
Upheld by My righteous, omnipotent hand.

3 "When through the deep waters I call thee to go,
The rivers of woe shall not thee overflow;
For I will be with thee thy trouble to bless,
And sanctify to thee thy deepest distress.

4 "When through fiery trials thy pathway shall lie,
My grace all-sufficient shall be thy supply;
The flame shall not hurt thee: I only design
Thy dross to consume, and thy gold to refine.

5 "E'en down to old age, all My people shall prove,
My sovereign, eternal, unchangeable love;
And when hoary hairs shall their temples adorn,
Like lambs they shall still in My bosom be borne.

6 "The soul that on Jesus hath leaned for repose
I will not, I will not desert to his foes;
That soul, though all hell should endeavor to shake,
I'll never, no never, no never forsake."
George Keith. 1787. ab.

710 *"I will fear no Evil." 11.*
Ps. xxiii. 4.

1 THE Lord is my Shepherd no want shall I know;
I feed in green pastures, safe-folded I rest;
He leadeth my soul where the still waters flow,
Restores me when wandering, redeems when opprest.

2 Through the valley and shadow of death though I stray,
Since Thou art my Guardian, no evil I fear;
Thy rod shall defend me, Thy staff be my stay;
No harm can befall, with my Comforter near.

3 In the midst of affliction my table is spread;
With blessings unmeasured my cup runneth o'er;
With perfume and oil Thou anointest my head;
O what shall I ask of Thy providence more?

4 Let goodness and mercy, my bountiful God,
Still follow my steps till I meet Thee above;
I seek, by the path which my forefathers trod
Through the land of their sojourn, Thy kingdom of love.
James Montgomery. (1771–1854.) 1822.

711 *"The Lord our Righteousness." 11.*

1 I ONCE was a stranger to grace and to God,
I knew not my danger, and felt not my load;
Though friends spoke in rapture of Christ on the tree,
Jehovah, my Saviour, seemed nothing to me.

JOYFUL TRUST.

2 When free grace awoke me by light from on high,
Then legal fears shook me, I trembled to die:
No refuge, no safety, in self could I see;
Jehovah, Thou only my Saviour must be.

3 My terrors all vanished before His sweet name;
My guilty fears banished, with boldness I came
To drink at the fountain, so copious and free:
Jehovah, my Saviour, is all things to me.

4 Jehovah, the Lord, is my treasure and boast;
Jehovah, my Saviour, I ne'er can be lost;
In Thee I shall conquer, by flood and by field,
Jehovah my anchor, Jehovah my shield!

5 E'en treading the valley, the shadow of death,
This watchword shall rally my faltering breath;
For while from life's fever my God sets me free,
Jehovah, my Saviour, my death-song shall be.

Rev. Robert Murray McCheyne (1813–1843) 1834 ab. and alt.

712 *Joy and Peace* 7, 6. D.

1 SOMETIMES a light surprises
   The Christian while he sings
It is the Lord who rises
   With healing in His wings:
When comforts are declining,
   He grants the soul again
A season of clear shining,
   To cheer it after rain.

2 In holy contemplation,
   We sweetly then pursue
The theme of God's salvation,
   And find it ever new:
Set free from present sorrow,
   We cheerfully can say,
Let the unknown to-morrow
   Bring with it what it may.

3 It can bring with it nothing
   But He will bear us through;
Who gives the lilies clothing
   Will clothe His people too;
Beneath the spreading heavens,
   No creature but is fed;
And He who feeds the ravens
   Will give His children bread.

4 Though vine nor fig-tree neither,
   Their wonted fruit shall bear,
Though all the field should wither,
   Nor flocks nor herds be there;
Yet God the same abiding,
   His praise shall tune my voice,
For, while in Him confiding,
   I cannot but rejoice.

William Cowper (1731–1800) 1779

713 *The Pilgrims of Jesus.* 7, 6. D.

1 O HAPPY band of pilgrims,
   If onward ye will tread,
With Jesus as your Fellow,
   To Jesus as your Head.
O happy, if ye labor
   As Jesus did for men:
O happy, if ye hunger
   As Jesus hungered then.

2 The cross that Jesus carried
   He carried as your due:
The crown that Jesus weareth
   He weareth it for you.
The faith by which ye see Him,
   The hope in which ye yearn,
The love that through all trouble
   To Him alone will turn:

3 What are they but forerunners
   To lead you to His sight?
What are they save the effluence
   Of uncreated Light?
The trials that beset you,
   The sorrows ye endure,
The manifold temptations
   That death alone can cure:

4 What are they, but His jewels
   Of right celestial worth?
What are they but the ladder,
   Set up to heaven on earth?
O happy band of pilgrims,
   Look upward to the skies;
Where such a light affliction
   Shall win you such a prize.

Joseph of the Studium, (—883)
Rev. John Mason Neale (1818–1866) 1862 sl. alt.

714 "*Shew forth His Salvation.*" Ps. xcvi. 2. 7, 6. D.

1 To Thee, my God and Saviour,
   My heart exulting sings,

Rejoicing in Thy favor,
 Almighty, King of kings:
I'll celebrate Thy glory,
 With all thy saints above,
And tell the joyful story,
 Of Thy redeeming love.

2 Soon as the morn with roses
 Bedecks the dewy east,
And when the sun reposes
 Upon the ocean's breast,
My voice in supplication,
 Well pleased, Thou shalt hear:
O grant me Thy salvation,
 And to my soul draw near.

3 By Thee through life supported,
 I pass the dangerous road,
With heavenly hosts escorted
 Up to their bright abode;
There cast my crown before Thee;
 Now all my conflicts o'er,
And day and night adore Thee:
 What can an angel more?
  Rev. Thomas Haweis (1732–1820) 1792.

715 *"O when shall I see Jesus?"* 7, 6. D.

1 O WHEN shall I see Jesus,
 And reign with Him above;
And from that flowing fountain
 Drink everlasting love?
When shall I be delivered
 From this vain world of sin,
And with my blessèd Jesus,
 Drink endless pleasures in?

2 But now I am a soldier,
 My Captain's gone before,
He's given me my orders,
 And bid me not give o'er;
And since He has proved faithful,
 A righteous crown He'll give,
And all His valiant soldiers
 Eternal life shall have.

3 Through grace I am determined
 To conquer, though I die;
And then away to Jesus
 On wings of love I'll fly.
Farewell to sin and sorrow,
 I bid you all adieu;

Then, O my friends, prove faithful,
 And on your way pursue.
  Rev. John Leland. (1754–1741.) 1799. ab.

716 *Rejoicing in God our Saviour.* 7, 6. D.
  Luke i. 47.

1 To Thee, O dear, dear Saviour,
 My spirit turns for rest,
My peace is in Thy favor,
 My pillow on Thy breast.
Though all the world deceive me,
 I know that I am Thine;
And Thou wilt never leave me,
 O blessèd Saviour mine.

2 O Thou, whose mercy found me,
 From bondage set me free;
And then for ever bound me
 With threefold cords to Thee;
O for a heart to love Thee
 More truly as I ought,
And nothing place above Thee
 In deed, or word, or thought.
  Rev. John Samuel Bewley Monsell (1811–) 1863. ab.

717 *"In Glory, at Home."* 11.

1 'MID scenes of confusion and creature complaints,
How sweet to the soul is communion with saints:
To find at the banquet of mercy there's room,
And feel in the presence of Jesus at home.
Prepare me, dear Saviour, for glory, my home.
Home, home, sweet, sweet home.

2 Sweet bonds that unite all the children of peace!
And thrice precious Jesus, whose love cannot cease!
Though oft from Thy presence in sadness I roam,
I long to behold Thee in glory, at home.

3 I sigh from this body of sin to be free,
Which hinders my joy and communion with Thee;
Though now my temptation like billows may foam,
All, all will be peace, when I'm with Thee at home.

4 While here in the valley of conflict I stay,
  O give me submission, and strength as my
      day;
  In all my afflictions to Thee would I come,
  Rejoicing in hope of my glorious home.
5 Whate'er Thou deniest, O give me Thy
      grace,
  The Spirit's sure witness, and smiles of
      Thy face;
  Endue me with patience to wait at Thy
      throne,
  And find, even now, a sweet foretaste of
      home.
6 I long, dearest Lord, in Thy beauties to
      shine;
  No more as an exile in sorrow to pine;
  And in Thy dear image arise from the tomb,
  With glorified millions to praise Thee at
      home.
      Rev. David Denham. 1837.

718 *"My heavenly Home is bright and fair."* L. M.

1 MY heavenly home is bright and fair;
  Nor pain, nor death can enter there;
  Its glittering towers the sun outshine;
  That heavenly mansion shall be mine.
    I'm going home, I'm going home,
    I'm going home to die no more,
    To die no more, to die no more,
    I'm going home to die no more.

2 My Father's house is built on high,
  Far, far above the starry sky;
  When from this earthly prison free,
  That heavenly mansion mine shall be.
      I'm going home, &c.

3 While here, a stranger far from home,
  Affliction's waves may round me foam;
  And, though like Lazarus, sick and poor,
  My heavenly mansion is secure.
      I'm going home, &c.

4 Let others seek a home below,
  Which flames devour, or waves o'erflow,
  Be mine the happier lot to own
  A heavenly mansion near the throne.
      I'm going home, &c.

5 Then fail the earth, let stars decline,
  And sun and moon refuse to shine,
  All nature sink and cease to be,
  That heavenly mansion stands for me.
      I'm going home, &c.
      Rev. William Hunter. (1811—) 1842.

719   *Home in View.*   L. M.

1 AS when the weary traveller gains
    The height of some o'erlooking hill,
  His heart revives, if 'cross the plains
  He eyes his home, though distant still.
      I'm going home, &c.

2 So when the Christian pilgrim views,
    By faith, his mansion in the skies,
  The sight his fainting strength renews,
  And wings his speed to reach the prize.
      I'm going home, &c.

3 The thought of home his spirit cheers;
    No more he grieves for troubles past,
  Nor any future trial fears,
  So he may safe arrive at last.
      I'm going home, &c.

4 'Tis there, he says, I am to dwell
    With Jesus, in the realms of day;
  Then I shall bid my cares farewell,
  And He will wipe my tears away.
      I'm going home, &c.
      Rev. John Newton. (1725—1807) 1779. ab and alt

720   *One with Christ.*   S. M.
          1 Cor. vi. 17.

1 DEAR Saviour, I am Thine,
    By everlasting bands;
  My name, my heart, I would resign;
    My soul is in Thy hands.

2 To Thee I still would cleave
    With ever growing zeal;
  Let millions tempt me Christ to leave,
    They never shall prevail.

3 His Spirit shall unite
    My soul to Him, my Head;
  Shall form me to His image bright,
    And teach His paths to tread.

4 Death may my soul divide
    From this abode of clay;
  But love shall keep me near His side,
    Through all the gloomy way.

5 Since Christ and we are one,
　What should remain to fear?
　If He in heaven has fixed His throne,
　He'll fix His members there.
　Rev. Philip Doddridge. (1702—1751.) 1755. sl. alt.

721 *"We are the Lord's."* S. M.
Rom. xiv. 8.

1 JESUS, I live to Thee,
　The loveliest and best;
　My life in Thee, Thy life in me,
　In Thy blest love I rest.

2 Jesus, I die to Thee,
　Whenever death shall come;
　To die in Thee is life to me,
　In my eternal home.

3 Whether to live or die,
　I know not which is best;
　To live in Thee is bliss to me,
　To die is endless rest.

4 Living or dying, Lord,
　I ask but to be Thine;
　My life in Thee, Thy life in me,
　Makes heaven forever mine.
　Rev. Henry Harbaugh. (1818—1867.) 1850.

722 *Communion with God and Christ* S. M.
1 John i. 3.

1 OUR Heavenly Father calls,
　And Christ invites us near;
　With both our friendship shall be sweet,
　And our communion dear.

2 God pities all my griefs;
　He pardons every day;
　Almighty to protect my soul,
　And wise to guide my way.

3 How large His bounties are!
　What various stores of good,
　Diffused from my Redeemer's hand,
　And purchased with His blood!

4 Jesus, my living Head,
　We bless Thy faithful care;
　Mine Advocate before the throne,
　And my Forerunner there.

5 Here fix, my roving heart,
　Here wait, my warmest love,
　Till the communion be complete,
　In nobler scenes above.
　Rev. Philip Doddridge. 1755.

723 *Adoption.* S. M.
1 John iii. 1.　Gal. vi. 6.

1 BEHOLD what wondrous grace
　The Father hath bestowed
　On sinners of a mortal race,
　To call them sons of God.

2 Nor doth it yet appear
　How great we must be made;
　But when we see our Saviour here,
　We shall be like our Head.

3 A hope so much divine
　May trials well endure,
　May purge our souls from sense and sin,
　As Christ the Lord is pure.

4 If in my Father's love
　I share a filial part,
　Send down Thy Spirit, like a dove,
　To rest upon my heart.

5 We would no longer lie
　Like slaves beneath the throne;
　Our faith shall Abba, Father! cry,
　And Thou the kindred own.
　Rev. Isaac Watts. (1674—1748.) 1709. ab.

724 *"Our Captain leads us on."* S. M.

1 OUR Captain leads us on;
　He beckons from the skies;
　He reaches out a starry crown,
　And bids us take the prize.

2 "Be faithful unto death,
　Partake My victory,
　And thou shalt wear this glorious wreath,
　And thou shalt reign with Me."

3 'T is thus the righteous Lord
　To every soldier saith,
　Eternal life is the reward
　Of all-victorious faith.

4 Who conquer in His might
　The victor's meed receive;
　They claim a kingdom in His right,
　Which God will freely give.
　Rev. Charles Wesley. (1708—1788.) 1749. ab. and sl. alt.

725 *Far from Home.* S. M.
Ps. cxxxvii.

1 FAR from my heavenly home,
　Far from my Father's breast,
　Fainting I cry, "Blest Spirit, come
　And speed me to my rest."

2 Upon the willows long
  My harp has silent hung:
  How should I sing a cheerful song
  Till Thou inspire my tongue?

3 My spirit homeward turns,
  And fain would thither flee;
  My heart, O Zion, droops and yearns,
  When I remember thee.

4 To thee, to thee I press,
  A dark and toilsome road:
  When shall I pass the wilderness,
  And reach the saints' abode?

5 God of my life, be near:
  On Thee my hopes I cast;
  O guide me through the desert here,
  And bring me home at last.
    Rev. Henry Francis Lyte. (1793–1847.) 1834.

726 *The Pilgrim's Song.* 7, 6.

1 RISE my soul, and stretch thy wings,
  Thy better portion trace;
  Rise from transitory things
  Towards heaven, thy native place:
  Sun and moon and stars decay;
  Time shall soon this earth remove;
  Rise my soul, and haste away
  To seats prepared above.

2 Rivers to the ocean run,
  Nor stay in all their course;
  Fire, ascending, seeks the sun;
  Both speed them to their source:
  So a soul, that's born of God,
  Pants to view His glorious face,
  Upward tends to His abode,
  To rest in His embrace.

3 Fly me, riches, fly me, cares,
  Whilst I that coast explore;
  Flattering world, with all thy snares
  Solicit me no more!
  Pilgrims fix not here their home;
  Strangers tarry but a night;
  When the last dear morn is come,
  They'll rise to joyful light.

4 Cease, ye pilgrims, cease to mourn,
  Press onward to the prize;
  Soon our Saviour will return
  Triumphant in the skies:

  Yet a season, and you know
  Happy entrance will be given,
  All our sorrows left below,
  And earth exchanged for heaven.
    Rev. Robert Seagrave. (1693–) 1742. ab.

727 *"Time is winging us away."* 7, 6.

1 TIME is winging us away
  To our eternal home;
  Life is but a winter's day,
  A journey to the tomb;
  Youth and vigor soon will flee,
  Blooming beauty lose its charms;
  All that's mortal soon shall be
  Enclosed in death's cold arms.

2 Time is winging us away
  To our eternal home;
  Life is but a winter's day,
  A journey to the tomb;
  But the Christian shall enjoy
  Health and beauty soon, above,
  Far beyond the world's annoy,
  Secure in Jesus' love.
    John Burton. (1773–1822.) 1815.

728 *"My Faith looks up to Thee."* 6, 4.

1 MY faith looks up to Thee,
  Thou Lamb of Calvary,
  Saviour Divine:
  Now hear me while I pray,
  Take all my guilt away,
  O let me from this day
  Be wholly Thine.

2 May Thy rich grace impart
  Strength to my fainting heart,
  My zeal inspire;
  As Thou hast died for me,
  O may my love to Thee,
  Pure, warm, and changeless be,
  A living fire.

3 While life's dark maze I tread,
  And griefs around me spread,
  Be Thou my Guide;
  Bid darkness turn to day,
  Wipe sorrow's tears away,
  Nor let me ever stray
  From Thee aside.

4 When ends life's transient dream,
  When death's cold, sullen stream

Shall o'er me roll;
Blest Saviour, then, in love,
Fear and distrust remove;
O, bear me safe above,
A ransomed soul.
Rev. Ray Palmer. (1808—) 1830.

729   *"Saviour, I look to Thee."*   6, 4.

1 SAVIOUR, I look to Thee,
Be not Thou far from me,
'Mid storms that lower:
On me Thy care bestow,
Thy loving kindness show,
Thine arms around me throw,
This trying hour.

2 Saviour, I look to Thee,
Feeble as infancy,
Gird up my heart:
Author of life and light,
Thou hast an arm of might,
Thine is the sovereign right,
Thy strength impart.

3 Saviour, I look to Thee,
Let me Thy fulness see,
Save me from fear:
While at Thy cross I kneel,
All my backslidings heal,
And a free pardon seal,
My soul to cheer.

4 Saviour, I look to Thee,
Thine shall the glory be,
Hearer of prayer:
Thou art my only aid,
On Thee my soul is stayed,
Naught can my heart invade,
While Thou art near.
Thomas Hastings. (1784—1872) 1858.

730   *Panting for Heaven.*   8. D.

1 YE angels, who stand around the throne,
And view my Immanuel's face,
In rapturous songs make Him known,
Tune, tune your soft harps to His praise;
He formed you the spirit you are,
So happy, so noble, so good;
When others sunk down in despair,
Confirmed by His power, ye stood.

2 Ye saints, who stand nearer than they,
And cast your bright crowns at His feet,
His grace and His glory display,
And all His rich mercy repeat:
He snatched you from hell and the grave,
He ransomed from death and despair;
For you He was mighty to save,
Almighty to bring you safe there.

3 O when will the period appear,
When I shall unite in your song?
I'm weary of lingering here,
And I to your Saviour belong:
I'm fettered, and chained up in clay;
I struggle, and pant to be free;
I long to be soaring away,
My God and my Saviour to see.

4 I want to put on my attire,
Washed white in the blood of the Lamb;
I want to be one of your choir,
And tune my sweet harp to His name;
I want, O I want to be there,
Where sorrow and sin bid adieu,
Your joy and your friendship to share,
To wonder, and worship with you.
Miss Maria De Fleury. 1791.

731   *"What must it be to be there!"*   8. D.

1 WE speak of the realms of the blest,
That country so bright and so fair,
And oft are its glories confessed;
But what must it be to be there!
We speak of its pathways of gold,
Its walls decked with jewels most rare;
Its wonders and pleasures untold;
But what must it be to be there!

2 We speak of its freedom from sin,
From sorrow, temptation, and care;
From trials without and within;
But what must it be to be there!
We speak of its service of love,
The robes which the glorified wear;
The Church of the First-born above;
But what must it be to be there!
Mrs. Elizabeth Mills. (1805—1829) 1829. ab.

732   *Longing to be with Christ.*   8. D.

1 To Jesus, the Crown of my hope,
My soul is in haste to be gone,
O bear me, ye cherubim, up,
And waft me away to His throne.

My Saviour whom absent I love,
  Whom, not having seen, I adore,
  Whose name is exalted above
  All glory, dominion, and power;

2 Dissolve Thou these bands that detain
  My soul from her portion in Thee;
  Ah, strike off this adamant chain,
  And make me eternally free.
  When that happy era begins,
  When arrayed in Thy glories I shine,
  Nor grieve any more, by my sins,
  The bosom on which I recline;

3 O then shall the veil be removed,
  And round me Thy brightness be poured,
  I shall meet Him whom absent I loved,
  Shall see whom unseen I adored.
  And then, nevermore shall the fears,
  The trials, temptations, and woes,
  Which darken this valley of tears,
  Intrude on my blissful repose.

4 Or if yet remembered above,
  Remembrance no sadness shall raise,
  They will be but new signs of Thy love,
  New themes for my wonder and praise.
  Thus the strokes which from sin and from pain
  Shall set me eternally free,
  Will but strengthen and rivet the chain
  Which binds me, my Saviour, to Thee.
        William Cowper (1731—1800.) 1802.

733   "*The King in His Beauty.*"   8. D.
    Is. xxxiii. 17, 24.

1 I LONG to behold Him arrayed
  With glory and light from above,
  The King in His beauty displayed,
  His beauty of holiest love:
  I languish and die to be there,
  Where Jesus hath fixed His abode;
  O when shall we meet in the air,
  And fly to the mountain of God!

2 With Him I on Zion shall stand,
  For Jesus hath spoken the word;
  The breadth of Immanuel's land
  Survey by the light of my Lord.
  But when, on Thy bosom reclined,
  Thy face I am strengthened to see,
  My fulness of rapture I find,
  My heaven of heavens in Thee.

3 How happy the people that dwell
  Secure in the city above!
  No pain the inhabitants feel,
  No sickness or sorrow shall prove.
  Physician of souls, unto me
  Forgiveness and holiness give;
  And when from the body set free,
  O then to the city receive.
        Rev. Charles Wesley. (1708—1788.) 1762. ab.

734   "*Nearer, my God, to Thee.*"   6, 4.
    Gen. xxviii. 10—12.

1 NEARER, my God, to Thee,
  Nearer to Thee:
  E'en though it be a cross
  That raiseth me;
  Still all my song shall be,
  Nearer, my God, to Thee,
  Nearer to Thee.

2 Though like the wanderer,
  The sun gone down,
  Darkness be over me,
  My rest a stone;
  Yet in my dreams I'd be
  Nearer, my God, to Thee,
  Nearer to Thee.

3 There let the way appear
  Steps unto heaven;
  All that Thou send'st to me,
  In mercy given;
  Angels to beckon me
  Nearer, my God, to Thee,
  Nearer to Thee.

4 Then with my waking thoughts
  Bright with Thy praise,
  Out of my stony griefs
  Bethel I'll raise;
  So by my woes to be
  Nearer, my God, to Thee,
  Nearer to Thee.

5 Or if on joyful wing
  Cleaving the sky,
  Sun, moon, and stars forgot,
  Upwards I fly,
  Still all my song shall be,
  Nearer, my God, to Thee,
  Nearer to Thee.
        Mrs. Sarah Flower Adams. (1805—1848.) 1840.

735   "*Jesus is mine.*"   6, 4.

1 FADE, fade, each earthly joy;
   Jesus is mine.
Break, every tender tie;
   Jesus is mine.
Dark is the wilderness,
Earth has no resting-place,
Jesus alone can bless;
   Jesus is mine.

2 Tempt not my soul away;
   Jesus is mine.
Here would I ever stay;
   Jesus is mine.
Perishing things of clay,
Born but for one brief day,
Pass from my heart away;
   Jesus is mine.

3 Farewell, ye dreams of night;
   Jesus is mine.
Lost in this dawning bright,
   Jesus is mine.
All that my soul has tried,
Left but a dismal void;
Jesus has satisfied;
   Jesus is mine.

4 Farewell, mortality;
   Jesus is mine.
Welcome, eternity:
   Jesus is mine.
Welcome, O loved and blest,
Welcome, sweet scenes of rest,
Welcome, my Saviour's breast;
   Jesus is mine.
        Mrs. Horatius Bonar. (1808—) 1845.

736   "*More Love to Thee.*"   6, 4.
       John xxi. 17

1 MORE love to Thee, O Christ,
   More love to Thee!
Hear Thou the prayer I make,
   On bended knee;
This is my earnest plea,
More love, O Christ, to Thee,
   More love to Thee.

2 Once earthly joy I craved,
   Sought peace and rest;
Now Thee alone I seek,
   Give what is best:

This all my prayer shall be,
More love, O Christ, to Thee,
   More love to Thee!

3 Let sorrow do its work,
   Send grief and pain;
Sweet are Thy messengers,
   Sweet their refrain,
When they can sing with me,
More love, O Christ, to Thee,
   More love to Thee!

4 Then shall my latest breath
   Whisper Thy praise;
This be the parting cry
   My heart shall raise,
This still its prayer shall be,
More love, O Christ, to Thee,
   More love to Thee!
    Mrs. Elizabeth Payson Prentiss. (1819—) 1869.

737   "*Jesus is mine.*"   6, 4, 6, 6, 6, 4.

1 Now I have found a Friend,
   Jesus is mine;
His love shall never end,
   Jesus is mine:
Though earthly joys decrease,
Though earthly friendships cease,
Now I have lasting peace;
   Jesus is mine.

2 Though I grow poor and old,
   Jesus is mine;
Though I grow faint and cold,
   Jesus is mine:
He shall my wants supply;
His precious blood is nigh,
Naught can my hope destroy;
   Jesus is mine.

3 When earth shall pass away,
   Jesus is mine;
In the great judgment day,
   Jesus is mine:
O what a glorious thing,
Then to behold my King,
On tuneful harp to sing,
   Jesus is mine.
    Henry Joy McCracken Hope. (1805—1872.) 1852. ab

738   *Light in Darkness.*   C. M.

1 MY God, the Spring of all my joys,
   The Life of my delights,

The Glory of my brightest days,
And Comfort of my nights?

2 In darkest shades if He appear,
My dawning is begun;
He is my soul's sweet Morning Star,
And He my Rising Sun.

3 The opening heavens around me shine
With beams of sacred bliss,
While Jesus shows His heart is mine,
And whispers, *I am His.*

4 My soul would leave this heavy clay,
At that transporting word;
Run up with joy the shining way,
T' embrace my dearest Lord.

5 Fearless of hell and ghastly death,
I'd break through every foe;
The wings of love, and arms of faith,
Should bear me conqueror through.
Rev. Isaac Watts. (1674–1748.) 1709.

739 *Delighting in God.* C. M.

1 O LORD, I would delight in Thee,
And on Thy care depend;
To Thee in every trouble flee,
My best, my only Friend.

2 When all created streams are dried,
Thy fulness is the same;
May I with this be satisfied,
And glory in Thy name.

3 No good in creatures can be found,
But may be found in Thee;
I must have all things, and abound,
While God is God to me.

4 O Lord, I cast my care on Thee;
I triumph and adore;
Henceforth my great concern shall be
To love and please Thee more.
Rev. John Ryland. (1735–1825.) 1777. ab.

740 *Happiness only in God.* C. M.
Ps. lxxiii. 25.

1 My God, my Portion, and my Love,
My everlasting All,
I've none but Thee in heaven above,
Or on this earthly ball.

2 In vain the bright, the burning sun
Scatters his feeble light;

'T is Thy sweet beams create my noon;
If Thou withdraw, 't is night.

3 To Thee we owe our wealth and friends,
And health and safe abode;
Thanks to Thy name for meaner things,
But they are not my God.

4 Were I possessor of the earth,
And called the stars my own,
Without Thy graces and Thyself,
I were a wretch undone.

5 Let others stretch their arms like seas,
And grasp in all the shore,
Grant me the visits of Thy face,
And I desire no more.
Rev. Isaac Watts. 1707 ab.

741 *"Make me a clean Heart."* C. M.
Ps. li. 10.

1 O FOR a heart to praise my God,
A heart from sin set free;
A heart that always feels Thy blood
So freely spilt for me!

2 A heart resigned, submissive, meek,
My dear Redeemer's throne;
Where only Christ is heard to speak,
Where Jesus reigns alone.

3 A humble, lowly, contrite heart,
Believing, true, and clean;
Which neither life nor death can part
From Him that dwells within.

4 A heart in every thought renewed,
And full of love divine;
Perfect, and right, and pure, and good,
A copy, Lord, of Thine.

5 Thy nature, dearest Lord, impart;
Come quickly from above;
Write Thy new Name upon my heart,
Thy new, best Name of Love.
Rev. Charles Wesley. (1708–1788.) 1742. ab.

742 *"Impart Thyself to me."* C. M.

1 O LORD, impart Thyself to me,
No other good I need;
When Thou, the Son, shalt make me free,
I shall be free indeed.

2 I cannot rest till in Thy blood
   I full redemption have;
   But Thou, through whom I come to God,
   Canst to the utmost save.

3 From sin, the guilt, the power, the pain,
   Thou wilt redeem my soul:
   Lord, I believe, and not in vain;
   My faith shall make me whole.

4 I too with Thee shall walk in white;
   With all Thy saints shall prove
   The length, and depth, and breadth, and
   Of everlasting love.   [height
   Rev. Charles Wesley. (1708—1788.) 1740. ab. and alt.

743   *"Talk with me, Lord."*   C. M.
           Luke xxiv. 30.

1 TALK with me, Lord: Thyself reveal,
   While here o'er earth I rove;
   Speak to my heart, and let it feel
   The kindling of Thy love.

2 With Thee conversing, I forget
   All time, and toil, and care;
   Labor is rest, and pain is sweet,
   If Thou, my God, art here.

3 Here then, my God, vouchsafe to stay,
   And make my heart rejoice;
   My bounding heart shall own Thy sway,
   And echo to Thy voice.

4 Thou callest me to seek Thy face;
   'T is all I wish to seek;
   To attend the whispers of Thy grace,
   And hear Thee inly speak.

5 Let this my every hour employ,
   Till I Thy glory see,
   Enter into my Master's joy,
   And find my heaven in Thee.
   Rev. Charles Wesley. 1740. ab.

744   *The hidden Life.*   C. M.

1 O HAPPY soul, that lives on high,
   While men lie groveling here!
   His hopes are fixed above the sky,
   And faith forbids his fear.

2 His conscience knows no secret stings,
   While grace and joy combine
   To form a life, whose holy springs
   Are hidden and divine.

3 He waits in secret on his God,
   His God in secret sees;
   Let earth be all in arms abroad,
   He dwells in heavenly peace.

4 His pleasures rise from things unseen,
   Beyond this world and time,
   Where neither eyes nor ears have been,
   Nor thoughts of mortals climb.

5 He wants no pomp nor royal throne
   To raise his honor here,
   Content and pleased to live unknown,
   Till Christ his life appear.

6 He looks to heaven's eternal hills,
   To meet that glorious day;
   Dear Lord, how slow Thy chariot wheels.
   How long is Thy delay!
   Rev. Isaac Watts. (1674—1748.) 1720

745   *Breathing after Holiness.*   C. M.
           Ps. cxix. 5, 133, 176, 35.

1 O THAT the Lord would guide my ways,
   To keep His statutes still;
   O that my God would grant me grace,
   To know and do His will!

2 Order my footsteps by Thy word,
   And make my heart sincere;
   Let sin have no dominion, Lord,
   But keep my conscience clear.

3 My soul hath gone too far astray,
   My feet too often slip;
   Yet since I've not forgot Thy way,
   Restore Thy wandering sheep.

4 Make me to walk in Thy commands,
   'T is a delightful road;
   Nor let my head, or heart, or hands,
   Offend against my God.
   Rev. Isaac Watts. 1719. ab.

746   *For a tender Conscience.*   C. M.

1 I WANT a principle within
   Of jealous, godly fear;
   A sensibility of sin,
   A pain to feel it near.

2 From Thee that I no more may part,
   No more Thy goodness grieve,
   The filial awe, the fleshly heart,
   The tender conscience give.

3 Quick as the apple of an eye.
   O God, my conscience make;
   Awake my soul when sin is nigh,
   And keep it still awake.

4 If to the right or left I stray,
   That moment, Lord, reprove;
   And let me weep my life away
   For having grieved Thy love.

5 O may the least omission pain
   My well-instructed soul,
   And drive me to the blood again,
   Which makes the wounded whole.
   Rev. Charles Wesley. 1749. ab.

747   *Mercies and Thanks.*   C. M.

1 How can I sink with such a prop
   As my eternal God,
   Who bears the earth's huge pillars up,
   And spreads the heavens abroad?

2 How can I die while Jesus lives,
   Who rose and left the dead?
   Pardon and grace my soul receives
   From my exalted Head.

3 All that I am, and all I have,
   Shall be forever Thine;
   Whate'er my duty bids me give,
   My cheerful hands resign.

4 Yet if I might make some reserve,
   And duty did not call,
   I love my God with zeal so great.
   That I should give Him all.
   Rev. Isaac Watts. 1709.

748   *God our Portion here and hereafter.*   C. M.
   Ps. lxxiii. 23-28.

1 God, my supporter and my hope,
   My help forever near,
   Thine arm of mercy held me up
   When sinking in despair.

2 Thy counsels, Lord, shall guide my feet
   Through this dark wilderness;
   Thy hand conduct me near Thy seat,
   To dwell before Thy face.

3 Were I in heaven without my God,
   'Twould be no joy to me;
   And while this earth is my abode,
   I long for none but Thee.

4 What if the springs of life were broke,
   And flesh and heart should faint?
   God is my soul's eternal rock,
   The strength of every saint.

5 But to draw near to Thee, my God,
   Shall be my sweet employ:
   My tongue shall sound Thy works abroad,
   And tell the world my joy.
   Rev. Isaac Watts. 1719. ab.

749   *Sonship.*   C. M.

1 Grace, like an uncorrupted seed,
   Abides and reigns within;
   Immortal principles forbid
   The sons of God to sin.

2 Not by the terrors of a slave
   Do they perform His will,
   But with the noblest powers they have
   His sweet commands fulfil.

3 They find access, at every hour,
   To God within the veil;
   Hence they derive a quickening power,
   And joys that never fail.

4 O happy souls! O glorious state
   Of overflowing grace!
   To dwell so near their Father's seat,
   And see His lovely face.

5 Lord, I address Thy heavenly throne;
   Call me a child of Thine;
   Send down the Spirit of Thy Son,
   To form my heart divine.

6 There shed Thy choicest love abroad.
   And make my comforts strong;
   Then shall I say, "My Father God."
   With an unwavering tongue.
   Rev. Isaac Watts. 1709. ab.

750   *Christ our Strength and Righteousness.*   C. M.
   Ps. lxxi.

1 My Saviour, my Almighty Friend,
   When I begin Thy praise,
   Where will the growing numbers end,
   The numbers of Thy grace?

2 Thou art my everlasting trust,
   Thy goodness I adore;
   And since I knew Thy graces first,
   I speak Thy glories more.

3 My feet shall travel all the length
  Of the celestial road,
  And march with courage in Thy strength
  To see my Father, God.

4 When I am filled with sore distress
  For some surprising sin,
  I'll plead Thy perfect righteousness,
  And mention none but Thine.

5 How will my lips rejoice to tell
  The victories of my King!
  My soul, redeemed from sin and hell,
  Shall Thy salvation sing.

6 Awake, awake, my tuneful powers!
  With this delightful song
  I'll entertain the darkest hours,
  Nor think the season long.
           Rev. Isaac Watts. (1674—1748.) 1719. ab.

751   *Watching and Praying.*   S. M.
           Luke xviii. 1. Phil. iv. 13.

1 JESUS, my Strength, my Hope,
  On Thee I cast my care,
  With humble confidence look up,
  And know Thou hear'st my prayer.

2 Give me on Thee to wait,
  Till I can all things do;
  On Thee, Almighty to create,
  Almighty to renew.

3 I want a sober mind,
  A self-renouncing will,
  That tramples down, and casts behind
  The baits of pleasing ill;

4 A soul inured to pain,
  To hardship, grief, and loss,
  Bold to take up, firm to sustain
  The consecrated cross.

5 I want a godly fear,
  A quick-discerning eye,
  That looks to Thee when sin is near,
  And sees the Tempter fly;

6 A spirit still prepared,
  And armed with jealous care,
  Forever standing on its guard,
  And watching unto prayer.
           Rev. Charles Wesley. (1708—1788.) 1742. ab.

752   *Christ the Way.*   S. M.
           John xiv. 6. 1 Pet. v. 10.

1 JESUS, my Truth, my Way,
  My sure, unerring Light,
  On Thee my feeble steps I stay,
  Which Thou wilt lead aright.

2 My Wisdom and my Guide,
  My Counsellor Thou art;
  O never let me leave Thy side,
  Or from Thy paths depart.

3 I lift mine eyes to Thee,
  My lovely bleeding Lamb,
  That I may still enlightened be,
  And never put to shame.

4 I never will remove
  Out of Thy hands my cause;
  But rest in Thy redeeming love,
  And hang upon Thy cross.
           Rev. Charles Wesley. 1749. ab.

753   *God in All.*   S. M.

1 TEACH me, my God and King,
  In all things Thee to see,
  And what I do in anything,
  To do it as for Thee;

2 To scorn the senses' sway,
  While still to Thee I tend;
  In all I do be Thou the Way,
  In all be Thou the End.

3 All may of Thee partake;
  Nothing so small can be
  But draws, when acted for Thy sake,
  Greatness and worth from Thee.

4 If done to obey Thy laws,
  E'en servile labors shine;
  Hallowed is toil, if this the cause,
  The meanest work, divine.
           Rev. George Herbert. (1593—1632.) 1633. ab.

754   *"All in all."*   S. M.
           Ps. lxxiii. 25.

1 MY God, my Life, my Love,
  To Thee, to Thee I call;
  I cannot live if Thou remove,
  For Thou art All in all.

2 To Thee, and Thee alone,
  The angels owe their bliss;

They sit around Thy gracious throne,
And dwell where Jesus is.

3 Not all the harps above
Can make a heavenly place,
If God His residence remove,
Or but conceal His face.

4 Nor earth, nor all the sky,
Can one delight afford;
No, not a drop of real joy,
Without Thy presence, Lord.

5 Thou art the sea of love,
Where all my pleasures roll;
The circle where my passions move,
And centre of my soul.

Rev. Isaac Watts. 1709. ab.

755 *Jesus in the midst of us.* S. M.
Matt. xviii. 20.

1 JESUS, we look to Thee,
Thy promised presence claim;
Thou in the midst of us shalt be,
Assembled in Thy name.

2 Thy name salvation is,
Which here we come to prove;
Thy name is life, and health, and peace,
And everlasting love.

3 Not in the name of pride
Or selfishness we meet;
From nature's paths we turn aside,
And worldly thoughts forget.

4 We meet, the grace to take
Which Thou hast freely given;
We meet on earth for Thy dear sake,
That we may meet in heaven.

5 Present we know Thou art,
But O, Thyself reveal;
Now, Lord, let every bounding heart
The mighty comfort feel.

6 O might Thy quickening voice
The death of sin remove;
And bid our inmost souls rejoice,
In hope of perfect love.

Rev. Charles Wesley. 1749. ab.

756 *Pure in Heart.* S. M.
Matt. v. 8.

1 BLEST are the pure in heart,
For they shall see our God;
The secret of the Lord is theirs,
Their soul is Christ's abode.

2 Still to the lowly soul
He doth Himself impart;
And for His cradle and His throne
Chooseth the pure in heart.

3 Lord, we Thy presence seek,
May ours this blessing be;
O give the pure and lowly heart,
A temple meet for Thee.

Rev. John Keble. (1792–1866) 1819. ab. and alt

757 *"He is precious."* 7, 6, D.
1 Pet. ii. 7.

1 I NEED Thee, precious Jesus,
For I am full of sin;
My soul is dark and guilty,
My heart is dead within;
I need the cleansing fountain
Where I can always flee,
The blood of Christ most precious,
The sinner's perfect plea.

2 I need Thee, precious Jesus,
For I am very poor;
A stranger and a pilgrim,
I have no earthly store;
I need the love of Jesus
To cheer me on my way,
To guide my doubting footsteps,
To be my strength and stay.

3 I need Thee, precious Jesus,
I need a friend like Thee,
A friend to soothe and pity,
A friend to care for me.
I need the heart of Jesus
To feel each anxious care,
To tell my every trouble,
And all my sorrows share.

4 I need Thee, precious Jesus,
And hope to see Thee soon,
Encircled with the rainbow,
And seated on Thy throne:
There, with Thy blood-bought children,
My joy shall ever be,
To sing Thy praises, Jesus,
To gaze, my Lord, on Thee.

Rev. Frederick Whitfield. (1829—) 1859. ab. and cl. alt

758 "Thee, Thee only." 7, 6. D.

1 LORD Jesus, by Thy passion,
   To Thee I make my prayer;
Thou who in mercy smitest,
   Have mercy, Lord, and spare:
O wash me in the fountain
   That floweth from Thy Side;
O clothe me in the raiment
   Thy blood hath purified.

2 O hold Thou up my goings,
   And lead from strength to strength,
That unto Thee in Zion
   I may appear at length
O make my spirit worthy
   To join the ransomed throng;
O teach my lips to utter
   That everlasting song.

3 O give that last, best blessing
   That even saints can know,
To follow in Thy footsteps
   Wherever Thou dost go.
Not wisdom, might, or glory,
   I ask to win above;
I ask for Thee, Thee only,
   O Thou Eternal Love!
          Unknown Author.

759 "I will fear no Evil." Ps xxiii 4. 7, 6. D.

1 IN heavenly love abiding,
   No change my heart shall fear;
And safe is such confiding,
   For nothing changes here.
The storm may roar without me,
   My heart may low be laid,
But God is round about me,
   And can I be dismayed?

2 Wherever He may guide me,
   No want shall turn me back;
My Shepherd is beside me,
   And nothing can I lack.
His wisdom ever waketh,
   His sight is never dim,
He knows the way He taketh,
   And I will walk with Him.

3 Green pastures are before me,
   Which yet I have not seen;
Bright skies will soon be o'er me,
   Where darkest clouds have been.

My hope I cannot measure,
   My path to life is free,
My Saviour has my treasure,
   And He will walk with me.
      Miss Anna Laetitia Waring. 1850. sl. alt.

760 "O Jesu, meine Sonne." 7, 6. D.

1 I KNOW no life divided,
   O Lord of life, from Thee;
In Thee is life provided
   For all mankind and me:
I know no death, O Jesus,
   Because I live in Thee;
Thy death it is which frees us
   From death eternally.

2 I fear no tribulation,
   Since, whatsoe'er it be,
It makes no separation
   Between my Lord and me.
If Thou, my God and Teacher,
   Vouchsafe to be my own,
Though poor, I shall be richer
   Than monarch on his throne.

3 If, while on earth I wander,
   My heart is light and blest,
Ah, what shall I be yonder
   In perfect peace and rest?
O blessed thought in dying,
   We go to meet the Lord,
Where there shall be no sighing,
   A kingdom our reward.
   Rev. Carl Johann Philipp Spitta (1801–1859.) 1833.
                    Tr. by Richard Massie. 1860. ab.

761 "A calm, a thankful Heart." C. M.

1 FATHER, whate'er of earthly bliss
   Thy sovereign will denies,
Accepted at Thy throne of grace,
   Let this petition rise:

2 Give me a calm, a thankful heart,
   From every murmur free;
The blessings of Thy grace impart,
   And make me live to Thee.

3 Let the sweet hope that Thou art mine
   My life and death attend;
Thy presence through my journey shine,
   And crown my journey's end.
      Miss Anne Steele (1717–1778.) 1760. ab.

RESIGNATION AND PEACE. SEEKING CONSOLATION.

762   *"Remember me, O my God."*   C. M.
                  Neh. xiii. 31.

1 O THOU from whom all goodness flows,
    I lift my heart to Thee;
  In all my sorrows, conflicts, woes,
    Dear Lord, remember me.

2 When groaning on my burdened heart
    My sins lie heavily,
  Thy pardon speak, new peace impart,
    In love remember me.

3 Temptations sore obstruct my way,
    And ills I cannot flee;
  O give me strength, Lord, as my day;
    For good remember me.

4 Distrest with pain, disease, and grief,
    This feeble body see;
  Grant patience, rest, and kind relief;
    Hear and remember me.

5 If on my face for Thy dear name,
    Shame and reproaches be,
  All hail reproach, and welcome shame,
    If Thou remember me.

6 The hour is near; consigned to death,
    I own the just decree:
  Saviour with my last parting breath,
    I'll cry, Remember me.
            Rev. Thomas Haweis. (1732—1820.) 1792.

763   *The inner Calm.*   C. M.

1 CALM me, my God, and keep me calm,
    Soft resting on Thy breast;
  Soothe me with holy hymn and psalm,
    And bid my spirit rest.

2 Calm me, my God, and keep me calm;
    Let Thine outstretchéd wing
  Be like the shade of Elim's palm,
    Beside her desert spring.

3 Yes, keep me calm, though loud and rude
    The sounds my ear that greet;
  Calm in the closet's solitude,
    Calm in the bustling street;

4 Calm in the hour of buoyant health,
    Calm in my hour of pain;
  Calm in my poverty or wealth,
    Calm in my loss or gain;

5 Calm in the sufferance of wrong,
    Like Him who bore my shame,
  Calm 'mid the threatening, taunting throng
    Who hate Thy holy Name.
          Rev. Horatius Bonar. (1808—) 1857. ab.

764   *Our Refuge.*   C. M.

1 DEAR Refuge of my weary soul,
    On Thee, when sorrows rise,
  On Thee, when waves of trouble roll,
    My fainting hope relies.

2 To Thee I tell each rising grief,
    For Thou alone canst heal;
  Thy word can bring a sweet relief
    For every pain I feel.

3 But O, when gloomy doubts prevail,
    I fear to call Thee mine;
  The springs of comfort seem to fail,
    And all my hopes decline.

4 Yet, gracious God, where shall I flee?
    Thou art my only trust;
  And still my soul would cleave to Thee,
    Though prostrate in the dust.

5 Thy mercy-seat is open still;
    Here let my soul retreat,
  With humble hope attend Thy will,
    And wait beneath Thy feet.
        Miss Anne Steele. (1717—1778.) 1760. ab.

765   *"The secret Place."*   C. M.
             Ps. xci.

1 THERE is a safe and secret place
    Beneath the wings divine,
  Reserved for all the heirs of grace:
    O be that refuge mine!

2 The least and feeblest there may bide
    Uninjured and unawed;
  While thousands fall on every side,
    He rests secure in God.

3 The angels watch him on his way,
    And aid with friendly arm;
  And Satan, roaring for his prey,
    May hate, but cannot harm.

4 He feeds in pastures large and fair
    Of love and truth divine;
  O child of God, O glory's heir,
    How rich a lot is thine!

SEEKING CONSOLATION. SUBMISSION.

5 A hand almighty to defend,
   An ear for every call,
   An honored life, a peaceful end,
   And heaven to crown it all!
        Rev. Henry Francis Lyte. (1793–1847.) 1834.

766   *Prayer and Hope.*   C. M.
          Ps. xxvii. 8, 9, 13, 14.

1 SOON as I heard my Father say,
   "Ye children, seek My grace;"
   My heart replied without delay,
   "I'll seek my Father's face."

2 Let not Thy face be hid from me,
   Nor frown my soul away:
   God of my life, I fly to Thee
   In a distressing day.

3 Should friends and kindred near and dear
   Leave me to want, or die;
   My God would make my life His care,
   And all my need supply.

4 My fainting flesh had died with grief,
   Had not my soul believed
   To see Thy grace provide relief;
   Nor was my heart deceived.

5 Wait on the Lord, ye trembling saints,
   And keep your courage up:
   He'll raise your spirit when it faints,
   And far exceed your hope.
        Rev. Isaac Watts. (1674–1748.) 1719.

767   *"Mein Jesu, wie Du willst."*   6. D.

1 My Jesus, as Thou wilt:
   O may Thy will be mine
   Into Thy hand of love
   I would my all resign.
   Through sorrow or through joy,
   Conduct me as Thine own,
   And help me still to say,
   My Lord, Thy will be done.

2 My Jesus, as Thou wilt:
   If needy here and poor,
   Give me Thy people's bread,
   Their portion rich and sure.
   The manna of Thy word
   Let my soul feed upon;
   And if all else should fail,
   My Lord, Thy will be done.

3 My Jesus, as Thou wilt:
   Though seen through many a tear,
   Let not my star of hope
   Grow dim or disappear.
   Since Thou on earth hast wept
   And sorrowed oft alone,
   If I must weep with Thee,
   My Lord, Thy will be done.

4 My Jesus, as Thou wilt:
   All shall be well for me;
   Each changing future scene
   I gladly trust with Thee.
   Straight to my home above,
   I travel calmly on,
   And sing in life or death,
   My Lord, Thy will be done.
        Rev. Benjamin Schmolke. (1672–1737.) 1716.
        Tr. by Miss Jane Borthwick. 1853. ab.

768   *"The Rod."*   6. D.
          Micah vi. 9.

1 I DID Thee wrong, my God;
   I wronged Thy truth and love;
   I fretted at the rod,
   Against Thy power I strove.
   Come nearer, nearer still;
   Let not Thy light depart;
   Bend, break this stubborn will,
   Dissolve this iron heart.

2 Less wayward let me be,
   More pliable and mild;
   In glad simplicity
   More like a trustful child.
   Less, less of self each day,
   And more, my God, of Thee;
   O keep me in the way,
   However rough it be.

3 Less of the flesh each day,
   Less of the world and sin;
   More of Thy Son, I pray,
   More of Thyself within.
   More moulded to Thy will,
   Lord, let Thy servant be;
   Higher and higher still,
   Liker and liker Thee.
        Rev. Horatius Bonar. (1808–.) 1857. ab.

SUBMISSION.

769 *The Rest that remaineth.* 6. D.

1 THERE is a blessèd home
  Beyond this land of woe,
 Where trials never come,
  Nor tears of sorrow flow;
 Where faith is lost in sight,
  And patient hope is crowned,
 And everlasting light
  Its glory throws around.

2 There is a land of peace,
  Good angels know it well;
 Glad songs that never cease
  Within its portals swell;
 Around its glorious throne
  Ten thousand saints adore
 Christ, with the Father One
  And Spirit, evermore.

3 O joy all joys beyond,
  To see the Lamb who died,
 And count each sacred wound
  In hands, and feet, and side;
 To give to Him the praise
  Of every triumph won,
 And sing through endless days
  The great things He hath done.

4 Look up, ye saints of God,
  Nor fear to tread below
 The path your Saviour trod
  Of daily toil and woe;
 Wait but a little while
  In uncomplaining love,
 His own most gracious smile
  Shall welcome you above.
   Rev. Sir Henry Williams Baker. (1821–) 1861.

770 *"Thy Way, not mine."* 6. D.

1 THY way, not mine, O Lord,
  However dark it be!
 Lead me by Thine own hand;
  Choose out the path for me.
 I dare not choose my lot;
  I would not, if I might;
 Choose Thou for me, my God,
  So shall I walk aright.

2 The kingdom that I seek
  Is Thine: so let the way
 That leads to it be Thine,
  Else I must surely stray.

Take thou my cup, and it
 With joy or sorrow fill,
As best to Thee may seem;
 Choose Thou my good and ill.

3 Choose Thou for me my friends,
  My sickness or my health,
 Choose Thou my cares for me,
  My poverty or wealth.
 Not mine, not mine the choice,
  In things or great or small;
 Be Thou my Guide, my Strength,
  My Wisdom, and my All.
   Rev. Horatius Bonar. 1857. ab.

771 *Longing for Christ.* 6. D.

1 MY spirit longs for Thee
  Within my troubled breast,
 Unworthy though I be
  Of so Divine a Guest.
 Of so Divine a Guest
  Unworthy though I be,
 Yet has my heart no rest
  Unless it come from Thee.

2 Unless it come from Thee,
  In vain I look around;
 In all that I can see
  No rest is to be found.
 No rest is to be found
  But in Thy blessèd love:
 O let my wish be crowned,
  And send it from above.
   John Byrom. (1691–1763.) 1773.

772 *Christ's Answer.* 6. D.

1 CHEER up, desponding soul,
  Thy longing pleased I see:
 'T is part of that great whole
  Wherewith I longed for thee;
 Wherewith I longed for thee,
  And left My Father's throne,
 From death to set thee free,
  And claim thee for My own.

2 To claim thee for My own,
  I suffered on the cross:
 O were My love but known,
  All else would be as dross;
 All else would be as dross,
  And souls, through grace divine,
 Would count their gain but loss,
  To live for ever Mine.
   John Byrom. 1773.

CONSOLATION IN GOD.

773 *God's Care a Remedy for ours.* S. M.
1 Pet. v. 7

1 How gentle God's command!
   How kind His precepts are!
   "Come, cast your burdens on the Lord,
   And trust His constant care."

2 While Providence supports,
   Let saints securely dwell;
   That hand, which bears all nature up,
   Shall guide His children well.

3 Why should this anxious load
   Press down your weary mind?
   Haste to your heavenly Father's throne,
   And sweet refreshment find.

4 His goodness stands approved,
   Down to the present day;
   I'll drop my burden at His feet,
   And bear a song away.
   Rev. Philip Doddridge (1702—1751.) 1755.

774 *Affliction Blessed.* S. M.
Ps. lxxi. 71, 75

1 How tender is Thy hand,
   O Thou belovèd Lord:
   Afflictions come at Thy command,
   And leave us at Thy word.

2 How gentle was the rod
   That chastened us for sin:
   How soon we found a smiling God,
   Where deep distress had been.

3 A Father's hand we felt,
   A Father's heart we knew;
   With tears of penitence we knelt,
   And found His word was true.

4 We told Him all our grief,
   We thought of Jesus' love;
   A sense of pardon brought relief,
   And bade our pains remove.

5 Now we will bless the Lord,
   And in His strength confide;
   Forever be His name adored,
   For there is none beside.
   Thomas Hastings. (1784—1872.) 1822, 1850.

775 *Trust in Providence.* S. M.
Matt. vi. 25; 1 Pet. v. 7.

1 Commit thou all thy griefs
   And ways into His hands,

To His sure truth and tender care,
Who earth and heaven commands.

2 Who points the clouds their course,
   Whom wind and seas obey,
   He shall direct thy wandering feet,
   He shall prepare thy way.

3 Thou on the Lord rely,
   So safe shalt thou go on;
   Fix on His work thy steadfast eye,
   So shall thy work be done.

4 No profit canst thou gain
   By self-consuming care;
   To Him commend thy cause; His ear
   Attends the softest prayer.

5 And whatsoe'er Thou will'st
   Thou dost, O King of kings;
   What Thy unerring wisdom chose,
   Thy power to being brings.
   Rev. Paul Gerhardt (1606—1676.) 1659
   Tr. by Rev. John Wesley (1703—1791.) 1739. ab.

776 *"Thy Will be mine!"* S. M.

1 It is Thy hand, my God,
   My sorrow comes from Thee;
   I bow beneath Thy chastening rod,
   'T is love that bruises me.

2 I would not murmur, Lord,
   Before Thee I am dumb;
   Lest I should breathe one murmuring word,
   To Thee for help I come.

3 My God, Thy name is Love;
   A Father's hand is Thine;
   With tearful eyes I look above,
   And cry, "Thy will be mine!"

4 I know Thy will is right,
   Though it may seem severe;
   Thy path is still unsullied light,
   Though dark it may appear.

5 Jesus for me hath died;
   Thy Son Thou didst not spare;
   His piercèd hands, His bleeding side,
   Thy love for me declare.

6 Here my poor heart can rest;
   My God, it cleaves to Thee:
   Thy will is love, Thine end is best;
   All work for good to me.
   James George Deck. 1843

777   *Safety in God.*   S. M.
Ps. xxxi.

1 My spirit, on Thy care,
   Blest Saviour, I recline;
Thou wilt not leave me to despair,
   For Thou art Love divine.

2 In Thee I place my trust,
   On Thee I calmly rest;
I know Thee good, I know Thee just,
   And count Thy choice the best.

3 Whate'er events betide,
   Thy will they all perform;
Safe in Thy breast my head I hide,
   Nor fear the coming storm.

4 Let good or ill befall,
   It must be good for me;
Secure of having Thee in all,
   Of having all in Thee.
Rev. Henry Francis Lyte (1793–1847.) 1834.

778   "*Sweet is Thy Mercy.*"   S. M.
Ps. cix. 20.

1 Sweet is Thy mercy, Lord;
   Before Thy mercy-seat
My soul, adoring, pleads Thy word,
   And owns Thy mercy sweet.

2 My need, and Thy desires,
   Are all in Christ complete;
Thou hast the justice truth requires,
   And I Thy mercy sweet.

3 Where'er Thy name is blest,
   Where'er Thy people meet,
There I delight in Thee to rest,
   And find Thy mercy sweet.

4 Light Thou my weary way,
   Place Thou my weary feet,
That while I stray on earth I may
   Still find Thy mercy sweet.

5 Thus shall the heavenly host
   Hear all my songs repeat
To Father, Son, and Holy Ghost,
   My joy, Thy mercy sweet.
Rev. John Samuel Bewley Monsell. (1811–) 1862.

779   *Constant Trust in God.*   C. M. D.

1 Father of Love, our Guide and Friend,
   O lead us gently on,
Until life's trial-time shall end,
   And heavenly peace be won.
We know not what the path may be
   As yet by us untrod;
But we can trust our all to Thee,
   Our Father and our God.

2 If called, like Abraham's child, to climb
   The hill of sacrifice,
Some angel may be there in time;
   Deliverance shall arise:
Or, if some darker lot be good,
   O teach us to endure
The sorrow, pain, or solitude,
   That make the spirit pure.

3 Christ by no flowery pathway came;
   And we, His followers here,
Must do Thy will and praise Thy Name,
   In hope, and love, and fear.
And, till in Heaven we sinless bow,
   And faultless anthems raise,
O Father, Son, and Spirit, now
   Accept our feeble praise.
Rev. William Josiah Irons. (1812–) 1853.

780   *Christ cheering the Cheerless.*   C. M.

1 O Thou, whose filmed and failing eye,
   Ere yet it closed in death,
Beheld Thy mother's agony,
   The shameful cross beneath:

2 Remember them, like her, through whom
   The sword of grief is driven,
And O, to cheer their cheerless gloom,
   Be Thy dear mercy given.

3 Let Thine own word of tenderness
   Drop on them from above;
Its music shall the lone heart bless,
   Its touch shall heal with love.

4 O Son of Mary, Son of God,
   The way of mortal ill,
By Thy blest feet in triumph trod,
   Our feet are treading still.

5 But not with strength like Thine, we go
   This dark and dreadful way;
As Thou wert strengthened in Thy woe,
   So strengthen us, we pray.
Rev. Alexander Ramsay Thompson. (1822–) 1869.

781   "The Peace of God."   C. M.

1 THE world can neither give nor take,
    Nor can they comprehend
The peace of God, which Christ has bought,
    The peace which knows no end.

2 The burning bush was not consumed
    Whilst God remained there;
The Three, when Jesus made the Fourth,
    Found fire as soft as air.

3 God's furnace doth in Zion stand;
    But Zion's God sits by,
As the refiner views his gold
    With an observant eye.

4 His thoughts are high, His love is wise,
    His wounds a cure intend;
And, though He does not always smile,
    He loves unto the end.
        Rev. John Mason. (—1694) 1683. alt.
    Selina, Countess of Huntingdon. (1707—1791) 1780.

782   Steadfast Trust.   C. M.
    Ps. lxxi.

1 IN Thee I put my steadfast trust,
    Defend me, Lord, from shame;
Incline Thine ear, and save my soul,
    For righteous is Thy name.

2 Be Thou my strong abiding-place,
    To which I may resort;
Thy promise, Lord, is my defence,
    Thou art my rock and fort.

3 My steadfast and unchanging hope
    Shall on Thy power depend;
And I in grateful songs of praise
    My time to come will spend.
        Tate and Brady. 1696. ab. and alt.

783   Prayer for Pity   C. M.

1 To Thee, my God, whose presence fills
    The earth, and seas, and skies,
To Thee, whose name, whose heart is Love,
    With all my powers I rise.

2 Troubles in long succession roll;
    Wave rushes upon wave;
Pity, O pity my distress;
    Thy child, Thy suppliant save.

3 O bid the roaring tempest cease;
    Or give me strength to bear
Whate'er Thy holy will appoints,
    And save me from despair.

4 To Thee, my God, alone I look,
    On Thee alone confide;
Thou never hast deceived the soul
    That on Thy grace relied.

5 Though oft Thy ways are wrapt in clouds
    Mysterious and unknown,
Truth, Righteousness, and Mercy stand
    The pillars of Thy throne.
        Rev. Thomas Gibbons. (1720—1785) 1784.

784   The right Faith   C. M.

1 O FOR a faith that will not shrink
    Though pressed by every foe;
That will not tremble on the brink
    Of any earthly woe;

2 That will not murmur nor complain
    Beneath the chastening rod,
But, in the hour of grief or pain,
    Will lean upon its God;

3 A faith that shines more bright and clear
    When tempests rage without;
That when in danger knows no fear,
    In darkness feels no doubt;

4 A faith that keeps the narrow way
    Till life's last hour is fled,
And with a pure and heavenly ray
    Lights up a dying bed.

5 Lord, give us such a faith as this,
    And then, whate'er may come,
We'll taste, e'en here, the hallowed bliss
    Of an eternal home.
        Rev. William Hiley Bathurst. (1796—) 1831. alt.

785   Vows made in Trouble.   C. M.
    Ps. cxvi. 12.

1 WHAT shall I render to my God
    For all His kindness shown?
My feet shall visit Thine abode,
    My songs address Thy throne.

2 Among the saints that fill Thy house,
    My offering shall be paid;
There shall my zeal perform the vows
    My soul in anguish made.

3 How much is mercy Thy delight,
    Thou ever blessed God!
How dear Thy servants in Thy sight!
    How precious is their blood!

TRUST IN PROVIDENCE.

4 How happy all Thy servants are!
  How great Thy grace to me!
  My life, which Thou hast made Thy care,
  Lord, I devote to Thee.

5 Now I am Thine, forever Thine;
  Nor shall my purpose move:
  Thy hand hath loosed my bonds of pain,
  And bound me with Thy love.

6 Here in Thy courts I leave my vow,
  And Thy rich grace record;
  Witness, ye saints, who hear me now,
  If I forsake the Lord.
  Rev. Isaac Watts (1674—1748) 1719.

786 *Preservation by Day and Night.* C. M.
Ps. cxxi.

1 To heaven I lift my waiting eyes,
  There all my hopes are laid;
  The Lord, that built the earth and skies,
  Is my perpetual aid.

2 Their feet shall never slide nor fall,
  Whom He designs to keep;
  His ear attends the softest call,
  His eyes can never sleep.

3 Israel, rejoice and rest secure,
  Thy keeper is the Lord:
  His wakeful eyes employ His power
  For thine eternal guard.

4 Nor scorching sun, nor sickly moon,
  Shall have His leave to smite;
  He shields thy head from burning noon,
  From blasting damps at night.

5 He guards thy soul, He keeps thy breath,
  Where thickest dangers come;
  Go and return, secure from death,
  Till God commands thee home.
  Rev. Isaac Watts. 1719. ab.

787 *Support in God's Covenant.* C. M.
2 Sam. xxiii 5

1 My God, the covenant of Thy love
  Abides forever sure;
  And in its matchless grace I feel
  My happiness secure.

2 Since Thou, the everlasting God,
  My Father art become,
  Jesus my Guardian and my Friend,
  And heaven my final home;

3 I welcome all Thy sovereign will,
  For all that will is love;
  And when I know not what Thou dost,
  I wait the light above.

4 Thy covenant in the darkest gloom
  Shall heavenly rays impart,
  And when my eyelids close in death
  Sustain my fainting heart.
  Rev. Philip Doddridge. (1702—1751.) 1755. ab. and alt.

788 *Submission.* C. M.

1 O Lord, my best desire fulfil,
  And help me to resign
  Life, health, and comfort to Thy will,
  And make Thy pleasure mine.

2 Why should I shrink at Thy command,
  Whose love forbids my fears?
  Or tremble at the gracious Hand
  That wipes away my tears?

3 No, let me rather freely yield
  What most I prize to Thee,
  Who never hast a good withheld,
  Or wilt withhold from me.

4 Thy favor, all my journey through,
  Thou art engaged to grant;
  What else I want, or think I do,
  'T is better still to want.

5 Wisdom and mercy guide my way;
  Shall I resist them both?
  A poor blind creature of a day,
  And crushed before the moth!

6 But, ah, my inmost spirit cries,
  Still bind me to Thy sway;
  Else the next cloud that veils the skies,
  Drives all these thoughts away.
  William Cowper (1731—1800) 1779.

789 *God's Way in the Deep.* C. M.

1 Thy way is in the deep, O Lord:
  E'en there we'll go with Thee;
  We'll meet the tempest at Thy word,
  And walk upon the sea.

2 Poor tremblers at His rougher wind,
  Why do we doubt Him so?
  Who gives the storm a path, will find
  The way our feet shall go.

3 A moment may His hand be lost,
    Drear moment of delay!
  We cry, "Lord help the tempest-tost,"
    And safe we're borne away.
4 The Lord yields nothing to our tears
    And flies from selfish care;
  But comes Himself, where'er He hears
    The voice of loving prayer.
                        Unknown Author.

790   "Help us!"   C. M.

1 O HELP us, Lord, each hour of need
    Thy heavenly succor give;
  Help us in thought, and word, and deed,
    Each hour on earth we live.

2 O help us when our spirits bleed,
    With contrite anguish sore;
  And when our hearts are cold and dead,
    O help us, Lord, the more.

3 If strangers to Thy fold we call,
    Imploring at Thy feet
  The crumbs that from Thy table fall,
    'Tis all we dare entreat.

4 O help us, Jesus, from on high:
    We know no help but Thee;
  O help us so to live and die,
    As Thine in heaven to be.
  Rev. Henry Hart Milman. (1791–1868.) 1827. ab.

791   "He hath borne our Griefs."   7.
                    Isaiah 4.

1 WHEN our heads are bowed with woe,
  When our bitter tears o'erflow,
  When we mourn the lost, the dear,
  Jesus, Son of Mary, hear.

2 Thou our throbbing flesh hast worn,
  Thou our mortal griefs hast borne,
  Thou hast shed the human tear;
  Jesus, Son of Mary, hear.

3 When the solemn death-bell tolls
  For our own departing souls,
  When our final doom is near,
  Jesus, Son of Mary, hear.

4 Thou hast bowed the dying head,
  Thou the blood of life hast shed,
  Thou hast filled a mortal bier;
  Jesus, Son of Mary, hear.

5 When the heart is sad within
  With the thought of all its sin,

When the spirit shrinks with fear,
Jesus, Son of Mary, hear.

6 Thou, the shame, the grief hast known;
  Though the sins were not Thine own,
  Thou hast deigned their load to bear;
  Jesus, Son of Mary, hear.
        Rev. Henry Hart Milman. 1827. ab.

792   Prayer for Comfort.   7.

1 IN the dark and cloudy day,
  When earth's riches flee away,
  And the last hope will not stay,
  Saviour, Saviour, comfort me.

2 When the hoard of many years
  Like a fleet cloud disappears,
  And the future's full of fears,
  Saviour, Saviour, comfort me.

3 When the secret idol's gone
  That my poor heart yearned upon,
  Desolate, bereft, alone,
  Saviour, Saviour, comfort me.

4 Thou, who wast so sorely tried,
  In the darkness crucified,
  Bid me in Thy love confide;
  Saviour, Saviour, comfort me.

5 In these hours of sad distress,
  Let me know He loves no less,
  Bids me trust His faithfulness;
  Saviour, Saviour, comfort me.

6 Not unduly let me grieve,
  Meekly the kind stripes receive,
  Let me humbly still believe;
  Saviour, Saviour, comfort me.
  Rev. Robert Herrick (1591–1674.) 1647. ab. and alt.

793   "Hear and save."   7.

1 LORD of mercy and of might,
  Of mankind the Life and Light,
  Maker, Teacher Infinite,
  Jesus, Jesus, hear and save.

2 Who, when sin's primeval doom
  Gave creation to the tomb,
  Didst not scorn a Virgin's womb,
  Jesus, Jesus, hear and save.

3 Strong Creator, Saviour mild,
  Humbled to a mortal child,
  Captive, beaten, bound, reviled,
  Jesus, Jesus, hear and save.

COMMITTING THE FUTURE TO GOD.

4 Throned above celestial things,
Borne aloft on angels' wings,
Lord of lords, and King of kings,
Jesus, Jesus, hear and save.

5 Soon to come to earth again,
Judge of angels and of men,
Hear us now, and hear us then,
Jesus, Jesus, hear and save.
Bp Reginald Heber (1783—1826) 1811. alt.

794   "*Cast thy Burden upon the Lord.*"   7.
Ps. lv. 22.

1 CAST thy burden on the Lord,
Only lean upon His word;
Thou shalt soon have cause to bless,
His eternal faithfulness.

2 Ever in the raging storm
Thou shalt see His cheering form,
Hear His pledge of coming aid:
"It is I, be not afraid."

3 Cast thy burden at His feet;
Linger at His mercy-seat:
He will lead thee by the hand
Gently to the better land.

4 He will gird thee by His power,
In thy weary, fainting hour;
Lean then, loving, on His word;
Cast thy burden on the Lord.
Rev. Rowland Hill. (1744—1833.) 1783. v. 1
George Rawson. (1807—) 1857. ab. and much alt.

795   *Prayer for Guidance.*

1 HEAVENLY Father, to whose eye
Future things unfolded lie,
Through the desert where I stray,
Let Thy counsels guide my way.

2 Lord, uphold me day by day,
Shed a light upon my way,
Guide me through perplexing snares,
Care for me in all my cares.

3 All I ask for is, enough;
Only, when the way is rough,
Let Thy rod and staff impart
Strength and courage to my heart.

4 Should Thy wisdom, Lord, decree
Trials long and sharp for me,
Pain or sorrow, care or shame,
Father, glorify Thy name!

5 Let me neither faint nor fear,
Feeling still that Thou art near;

In the course my Saviour trod,
Tending still to Thee, my God.
Josiah Conder. (1789—1855.) 1837. ab.

796   *Childlike Simplicity.*   7.

1 JESUS, cast a look on me:
Give me true simplicity;
Make me poor, and keep me low,
Seeking only Thee to know.

2 All that feeds my busy pride,
Cast it evermore aside;
Bid my will to Thine submit,
Lay me humbly at Thy feet.

3 Make me like a little child,
Simple, teachable, and mild;
Seeing only in Thy light,
Walking only in Thy might;

4 Leaning on Thy loving breast,
Where a weary soul may rest;
Feeling well the peace of God
Flowing from Thy precious blood.
Rev. Charles Wesley. (1708—1788.) 1762. much alt.
Rev. John Berridge. (1716—1793.) 1785. ab.

797   "*My Times are in Thy Hand.*"   7.
Ps. xxxi. 15.

1 SOVEREIGN Ruler of the skies,
Ever gracious, ever wise,
All my times are in Thy hand,
All events at Thy command.

2 Times of sickness, times of health,
Times of penury and wealth;
Times of trial and of grief,
Times of triumph and relief;

3 Times the Tempter's power to prove,
Times to taste a Saviour's love;
All must come, and last, and end,
As shall please my heavenly Friend.

4 Plagues and deaths around me fly;
Till He bids, I cannot die:
Not a single shaft can hit
Till the God of love sees fit.

5 O Thou Gracious, Wise, and Just,
In Thy hands my life I trust:
Have I something dearer still?
I resign it to Thy will.

6 Thee at all times will I bless;
Having Thee I all possess;
How can I bereaved be,
Since I cannot part with Thee?
Rev. John Ryland. (1753—1825.) 1777 ab.

798 "Blessed are they that mourn." L. M.
Matt. v. 4.

1 O DEEM not they are blest alone,
  Whose lives a peaceful tenor keep;
  The Power, who pities man, has shown
  A blessing for the eyes that weep.

2 The light of smiles shall fill again
  The lids that overflow with tears;
  And weary hours of woe and pain
  Are promises of happier years.

3 There is a day of sunny rest
  For every dark and troubled night;
  And grief may bide an evening guest,
  But joy shall come with early light.

4 And thou, who o'er thy friend's low bier
  Sheddest the bitter drops like rain,
  Hope that a brighter, happier sphere
  Will give him to thy arms again.

5 Nor let the good man's trust depart,
  Though life its common gifts deny;
  Though, with a pierced and broken heart,
  And spurned of men, he goes to die.

6 For God has marked each sorrowing day,
  And numbered every secret tear,
  And heaven's long age of bliss shall pay
  For all His children suffer here.

William Cullen Bryant. (1794—) 1824.

799 Trials meant for Good. L. M.

1 WHY should I murmur or repine,
  O Lamb of God, who bled for me?
  What are my griefs compared with Thine,
  Thy tears, Thy groans, Thine agony!

2 If Thou the furnace dost employ,
  Thou sittest as refiner near
  To purge away the base alloy,
  Till Thine own image bright appear.

3 Though oft Thy way is in the sea,
  Thy footsteps in the winged storm;
  Though crested billows threaten me,
  Love slumbers in their frowning form.

4 Submissive would I kiss the rod,
  Needful each stroke, I humbly own;
  Help me to trust Thee, O my God,
  If now Thy wisdom be unknown.

Unknown Author.

800 Temptation. L. M.

1 THE billows swell, the winds are high,
  Clouds overcast my wintry sky;
  Out of the depths to Thee I call,
  My fears are great, my strength is small.

2 O Lord, the pilot's part perform,
  And guard and guide me through the storm;
  Defend me from each threatening ill,
  Control the waves, say, "Peace, be still!"

3 Amidst the roaring of the sea
  My soul still hangs her hope on Thee;
  Thy constant love, Thy faithful care,
  Is all that saves me from despair.

4 Dangers of every shape and name
  Attend the followers of the Lamb,
  Who leave the world's deceitful shore,
  And leave it to return no more.

5 Though tempest-tost and half a wreck,
  My Saviour through the floods I seek:
  Let neither winds nor stormy main
  Force back my shattered bark again.

William Cowper. (1731—1800.) 1779.

801 Christ able to succor the tempted. L. M. 6l.
Heb. ii. 18.

1 WHEN gathering clouds around I view,
  And days are dark, and friends are few,
  On Him I lean who not in vain
  Experienced every human pain;
  He sees my wants, allays my fears,
  And counts and treasures up my tears.

2 If aught should tempt my soul to stray
  From heavenly wisdom's narrow way;
  To fly the good I would pursue,
  Or do the sin I would not do;
  Still He who felt temptation's power,
  Shall guard me in that dangerous hour.

3 When sorrowing o'er some stone I bend
  Which covers what was once a friend,
  And from his voice, his hand, his smile,
  Divides me for a little while;
  Thou, Saviour, mark'st the tears I shed,
  For Thou didst weep o'er Lazarus dead.

4 And O, when I have safely past
  Through every conflict but the last,
  Still, still unchanging, watch beside

CHRIST OUR CONSOLER. CONFIDENCE IN GOD.

My painful bed, for Thou hast died;
Then point to realms of cloudless day,
And wipe the latest tear away.
Sir Robert Grant. (1785—1838.) 1806, 1812. ab.

802   *"Continually with Thee."*   L. M.
Ps. lxxiii. 23—26.

1 WHEN, in the hour of lonely woe,
   I give my sorrows leave to flow,
   And anxious fear and dark distrust
   Weigh down my spirit to the dust;

2 When not e'en friendship's gentle aid
   Can heal the wounds the world has made,
   O, this shall check each rising sigh,
   My Saviour is forever nigh!

3 His counsels and upholding care
   My safety and my comfort are;
   And He shall guide me all my days,
   Till glory crown the work of grace.

4 Jesus, in whom but Thee above
   Can I repose my trust, my love?
   And shall an earthly object be
   Loved in comparison with Thee?

5 My flesh is hastening to decay,
   Soon shall the world have passed away;
   And what can mortal friends avail,
   When heart and strength and life shall fail;

6 But O, be Thou, my Saviour, nigh,
   And I will triumph while I die;
   My strength, my portion, is divine,
   And Jesus is forever mine.
Josiah Conder. (1789—1855.) 1836.

803   *"Befiehl du deine Wege."*   S. M.

1 GIVE to the winds thy fears;
   Hope, and be undismayed;
   God hears thy sighs and counts thy tears;
   God shall lift up thy head.

2 Through waves and clouds and storms,
   He gently clears thy way;
   Wait thou His time, so shall this night
   Soon end in joyous day.

3 What though thou rulest not,
   Yet heaven and earth and hell
   Proclaim, God sitteth on the throne,
   And ruleth all things well.

4 Far, far above thy thought
   His counsel shall appear,

When fully He the work hath wrought
   That caused thy needless fear.

5 Thou seest our weakness, Lord,
   Our hearts are known to Thee;
   O lift Thou up the sinking hand,
   Confirm the feeble knee.

6 Let us, in life, in death,
   Thy steadfast truth declare,
   And publish with our latest breath
   Thy love and guardian care.
Rev. Paul Gerhardt. (1606—1676.) 1653.
Tr. by Rev. John Wesley. (1703—1791.) 1739. ab.

804   *"All-sufficient Grace."*   S. M.

1 JESUS, my Lord, my God,
   Thy promise I embrace;
   And hail, beneath the Father's rod,
   Thy all-sufficient grace.

2 My oft-repeated prayer
   The kindest answer gains,
   When, by Thy gracious aid, I bear
   Life's keen and varied pains.

3 Should dread of want distress,
   And men or fiends assail,
   Infirmities my frame oppress,
   And earthly comforts fail,

4 Still may I trust in Thee,
   And calm each rising fear;
   For none of these can injure me
   While Thou, O Christ, art near.

5 My faith as gold refine;
   Each grace and virtue prove;
   That in my spotless life may shine
   The light of perfect love.
Unknown Author. ab.

805   *Help in Sorrow.*   S. M.

1 FEAR not, poor, weary one;
   But struggle bravely yet;
   Toil on until thy task is done,
   Until thy sun is set.

2 Though many are thy cares,
   And many are thy fears,
   The loving Christ thy burden shares,
   And wipes away thy tears.

3 No distant Christ is He,
   And one that doth not know;
   But watches close and constantly
   The path which thou dost go.

4 'Tis when thy heart is tried,
   'Tis in thine hour of grief,
   He standeth ever at thy side,
   And ever brings relief.
   Rev. Thomas Cogswell Upham. (1799—1872.) 1872.

806   *"My Times are in Thy Hand."*   **C. M.**
   Ps. xxxi. 15.

1 FATHER, I know that all my life
   Is portioned out for me;
   The changes that will surely come
   I do not fear to see:
   I ask Thee for a present mind,
   Intent on pleasing Thee.

2 I ask Thee for a thoughtful love,
   Through constant watching wise,
   To meet the glad with joyful smiles,
   And wipe the weeping eyes;
   A heart at leisure from itself,
   To soothe and sympathize.

3 I would not have the restless will
   That hurries to and fro,
   Seeking for some great thing to do,
   Or secret thing to know:
   I would be treated as a child,
   And guided where I go.

4 Wherever in the world I am,
   In whatsoe'er estate,
   I have a fellowship with hearts,
   To keep and cultivate;
   A work of lowly love to do
   For Him on whom I wait.

5 I ask Thee for the daily strength,
   To none that asked denied,
   A mind to blend with outward life,
   While keeping at Thy side;
   Content to fill a little space,
   If Thou be glorified.

6 And if some things I do not ask
   Among my blessings be,
   I'd have my spirit filled the more
   With grateful love to Thee;
   More careful, not to serve Thee much,
   But please Thee perfectly.

7 Briars and thorns beset our path
   That call for patient care;
   There is a cross in every lot,
   And earnest need for prayer;

   But lowly hearts, that lean on Thee,
   Are happy anywhere.

8 In service which Thy will appoints
   There are no bonds for me;
   My inmost heart is taught the truth
   That makes Thy children free;
   A life of self-renouncing love
   Is one of liberty.
   Miss Anna Laetitia Waring. 1850. alt.

807   *What is Prayer?*   **C. M.**

1 PRAYER is the breath of God in man,
   Returning whence it came;
   Love is the sacred fire within,
   And prayer the rising flame.

2 It gives the burdened spirit ease,
   And soothes the troubled breast;
   Yields comfort to the mourners here,
   And to the weary rest.

3 When God inclines the heart to pray,
   He hath an ear to hear;
   To Him there's music in a groan,
   And beauty in a tear.

4 The humble suppliant cannot fail
   To have his wants supplied,
   Since He for sinners intercedes,
   Who once for sinners died.
   Rev. Benjamin Beddome. (1717—1795.) 1787.

808   *What is Prayer?*   **C. M.**
   Acts. ix. 11.

1 PRAYER is the soul's sincere desire,
   Uttered or unexpressed,
   The motion of a hidden fire
   That trembles in the breast.

2 Prayer is the burden of a sigh,
   The falling of a tear,
   The upward glancing of an eye,
   When none but God is near.

3 Prayer is the simplest form of speech
   That infant lips can try;
   Prayer the sublimest strains that reach
   The Majesty on high.

4 Prayer is the contrite sinner's voice
   Returning from his ways,
   While angels in their songs rejoice,
   And cry, "Behold he prays!"

5 Prayer is the Christian's vital breath,
   The Christian's native air,
   His watchword at the gates of death ;
   He enters heaven with prayer.

6 O Thou, by whom we come to God,
   The Life, the Truth, the Way,
   The path of prayer Thyself hast trod ;
   Lord, teach us how to pray.
   James Montgomery. (1771—1854.) 1819, 1853. ab.

5 Author, and Guardian of my life,
   Sweet Source of love Divine,
   And, all harmonious names in one,
   My Saviour, Thou art mine !

6 What thanks I owe Thee, and what love,
   A boundless, endless store,
   Shall echo through the realms above
   When time shall be no more !
   William Cowper. (1731—1800.) 1779.

809 *Sins and Sorrows spread before God.* C. M.
Eph. ii. 13, 18.

1 O THAT I knew the secret place
   Where I might find my God !
   I'd spread my wants before His face,
   And pour my woes abroad.

2 I'd tell Him how my sins arise,
   What sorrows I sustain ;
   How grace decays, and comfort dies,
   And leaves my heart in pain.

3 He knows what arguments I'd take
   To wrestle with my God :
   I'd plead for His own mercy's sake,
   And for my Saviour's blood.

4 Arise, my soul, from deep distress,
   And banish every fear ;
   He calls thee to His throne of grace,
   To spread thy sorrows there.
   Rev. Isaac Watts. (1674—1748.) 1709. ab.

810 *Retirement* C. M.

1 FAR from the world, O Lord, I flee,
   From strife and tumult far ;
   From scenes where Satan wages still
   His most successful war.

2 The calm retreat, the silent shade,
   With prayer and praise agree,
   And seem by Thy sweet bounty made
   For those who follow Thee.

3 There, if Thy Spirit touch the soul,
   And grace her mean abode,
   O with what peace, and joy, and love,
   She communes with her God !

4 There, like the nightingale, she pours
   Her solitary lays ;
   Nor asks a witness of her song,
   Nor thirsts for human praise.

811 *Mounting up to God.* C. M.
Ps. lv. 6.

1 THE bird let loose in Eastern skies,
   When hastening fondly home,
   Ne'er stoops to earth her wing, nor flies
   Where idle warblers roam.

2 But high she shoots, through air and light,
   Above all low delay,
   Where nothing earthly bounds her flight,
   Nor shadow dims her way.

3 So grant me, Lord, from every care
   And stain of passion free,
   Aloft, through virtue's purer air,
   To hold my course to Thee.

4 No sin to cloud, no lure to stay
   My soul, as home she springs ;
   Thy sunshine on her joyful way,
   Thy freedom in her wings.
   Thomas Moore. (1779—1852.) 1816.

812 *To move the Hand which moves the World* C. M.

1 THERE is an eye that never sleeps
   Beneath the wing of night ;
   There is an ear that never shuts,
   When sink the beams of light.

2 There is an arm that never tires,
   When human strength gives way ;
   There is a love that never fails,
   When earthly loves decay.

3 That eye is fixed on seraph throngs ;
   That arm upholds the sky ;
   That ear is filled with angel songs ;
   That love is throned on high.

4 But there's a power which man can wield,
   When mortal aid is vain,
   That eye, that arm, that love to reach,
   That listening ear to gain.

5 That power is prayer, which soars on high,
   Through Jesus, to the throne,
And moves the hand which moves the world,
   To bring salvation down.
   Rev. John Aikman Wallace. (1802—1870.) 1839. ab.

813 *Blest Hour of Prayer.* L. M.

1 BLEST hour, when mortal man retires
   To hold communion with His God ;
   To send to Heaven his warm desires,
   And listen to the sacred word.

2 Blest hour, when God Himself draws nigh,
   Well pleased His people's voice to hear;
   To hush the penitential sigh,
   And wipe away the mourner's tear.

3 Blest hour, for where the Lord resorts
   Foretastes of future bliss are given;
   And mortals find His earthly courts
   The house of God, the gate of heaven.

4 Hail, peaceful hour, supremely blest
   Amid the hours of worldly care;
   The hour that yields the spirit rest,
   That sacred hour, the hour of prayer.

5 And when my hours of prayer are past,
   And this frail tenement decays,
   Then may I spend in heaven at last
   A never-ending hour of praise.
   Rev. Thomas Raffles. (1788—1863.) 1828. ab.

814 *Retirement and Meditation* L. M.
   Titus ii. 12

1 MY God, permit me not to be
   A stranger to myself and Thee ;
   Amidst a thousand thoughts I rove,
   Forgetful of my highest Love.

2 Why should my passions mix with earth,
   And thus debase my heavenly birth?
   Why should I cleave to things below,
   And let my God, my Saviour, go?

3 Call me away from flesh and sense,
   One sovereign word can draw me thence :
   I would obey the voice divine,
   And all inferior joys resign.

4 Be earth, with all her scenes, withdrawn ;
   Let noise and vanity be gone ;
   In secret silence of the mind
   My heaven, and there my God, I find.
   Rev. Isaac Watts. (1674—1748.) 1709.

815 *God with us in Solitude* L. M.

1 'TIS thus in solitude I roam
   O'er many a land and tossing sea;
   And yet, afar from friends and home,
   I find, O God, a home in Thee.

2 I pass from things of space and time,
   The finite meets or leaves my sight;
   But God expands o'er every clime,
   The clothing of the infinite.

3 He walks the earth, He rides the air;
   The lightning's speed He leaves behind.
   His name is Love. And tell me, where
   Is sea or land He cannot find?

4 O, long I've known Him. Could it be
   That if He did not hold me dear,
   He thus would travel land and sea,
   And throw His arms around me here?

5 I could not leave Him, if I would;
   I would not, if the power were given;
   'T would be to leave the True and Good,
   The soul's Repose, the spirit's Heaven.
   Rev. Thomas Cogswell Upham. (1799—1872.) 1855. ab.

816 *Exhortation to Prayer.* L. M.
   Col. iv. 2.

1 WHAT various hindrances we meet,
   In coming to a mercy-seat !
   Yet who that knows the worth of prayer,
   But wishes to be often there ?

2 Prayer makes the darkened cloud withdraw,
   Prayer climbs the ladder Jacob saw,
   Gives exercise to faith and love,
   Brings every blessing from above.

3 Restraining prayer, we cease to fight ;
   Prayer makes the Christian's armor bright ;
   And Satan trembles when he sees
   The weakest saint upon his knees.

4 Have you no words? Ah, think again,
   Words flow apace when you complain,
   And fill your fellow creature's ear
   With the sad tale of all your care.

5 Were half the breath thus vainly spent,
   To heaven in supplication sent,
   Our cheerful song would oftener be,
   "Hear what the Lord has done for me."
   William Cowper. (1731—1800.) 1779. ab.

PRAYER.

817 *Breathing after God.* L. M.

1 WHERE is my God? does He retire
  Beyond the reach of humble sighs?
  Are these weak breathings of desire
  Too languid to ascend the skies?

2 Look up, my soul, with cheerful eye,
  See where the great Redeemer stands,
  The glorious Advocate on high,
  With precious incense in His hands.

3 He sweetens every humble groan,
  He recommends each broken prayer:
  Recline thy hope on Him alone
  Whose power and love forbid despair.
  Miss Anne Steele. (1717—1778.) 1760, ab.

818 *"Prayer of the Heart and Lips."* L. M.

1 O BLESSED God, to Thee I raise
  My voice in thankful hymns of praise;
  And when my voice shall silent be,
  My silence shall be praise to Thee.

2 For voice and silence both impart
  The filial homage of my heart;
  And both alike are understood
  By Thee, Thou Parent of all good,

3 Whose grace is all unsearchable,
  Whose care for me no tongue can tell,
  Who loves my loudest praise to hear,
  And loves to bless my voiceless prayer.
  From the Greek. Sabbath Hymn Book. 1858.

819 *Watching and Praying.* L. M.

1 THEY pray the best who pray and watch,
  They watch the best who watch and pray,
  They hear Christ's fingers on the latch,
  Whether He comes by night, or day.

2 Whether they guard the gates and watch,
  Or, patient, toil for Him, and wait,
  They hear His fingers on the latch,
  If early He doth come, or late.

3 With trembling joy they hail their Lord,
  And haste His welcome feet to kiss,
  While He, well pleased, doth speak the word
  That thrills them with unending bliss:

4 "Well done, My servants, now receive,
  For faithful work, reward and rest,
  And wreaths which busy angels weave
  To crown the men who serve Me best."
  Rev. Edward Hopper. (1818—) 1873.

820 *Morning Prayer.* S. M.
Luke. vi. 12.

1 How sweet the melting lay
  Which breaks upon the ear,
  When at the hour of rising day
  Christians unite in prayer.

2 The breezes waft their cries
  Up to Jehovah's throne;
  He listens to their humble sighs,
  And sends His blessings down.

3 So Jesus rose to pray
  Before the morning light;
  Once on the chilling mount did stay,
  And wrestle all the night.

4 So Jesus still doth pray
  Before the morning bright,
  On heavenly mountains far away,
  While we toil here in night.

5 Leave, Lord, Thy vigil there,
  Descend upon life's wave;
  Come to the bark through midnight air,
  The storm shall cease to rave.
  Mrs. Phoebe Hinsdale Brown. (1783—1861.) 1835.

821 *At Morning, Noon, and Night.* S. M.
Ps. lv. 17.

1 COME at the morning hour,
  Come, let us kneel and pray;
  Prayer is the Christian pilgrim's staff
  To walk with God all day.

2 At noon, beneath the Rock
  Of ages, rest and pray;
  Sweet is that shelter from the sun
  In weary heat of day.

3 At evening, in thy home,
  Around its altar, pray;
  And finding there the house of God,
  With heaven then close the day.

4 When midnight veils our eyes,
  O, it is sweet to say,
  I sleep, but my heart waketh, Lord,
  With Thee to watch and pray.
  James Montgomery. (1771—1854.) 1853. alt.

822 *"Pray without ceasing."* S. M.
1 Thess. v. 17.

1 PRAY, without ceasing, pray,
  Your Captain gives the word:
  His summons cheerfully obey,
  And call upon the Lord.

PRAYER. THE HOLY SPIRIT.

2 To God your every want
  In instant prayer display;
  Pray always; pray, and never faint;
  Pray, without ceasing, pray.

3 His mercy now implore,
  And now show forth His praise;
  In shouts, or silent awe, adore
  His miracles of grace.

4 From strength to strength go on;
  Wrestle, and fight, and pray;
  Tread all the powers of darkness down,
  And win the well-fought day.

5 Still let the Spirit cry,
  In all His soldiers —"Come,"
  Till Christ the Lord descends from high,
  And takes the conquerors home.
        Rev. Charles Wesley. (1708—1788.) 1749. ab.

823   *"Ask what I shall give thee."*   S. M.
              1 Kings iii. 5.

1 BEHOLD the throne of grace,
  The promise calls me near;
  There Jesus shows a smiling face,
  And waits to answer prayer.

2 That rich atoning blood,
  Which sprinkled round I see,
  Provides for those who come to God
  An all-prevailing plea.

3 My soul, ask what thou wilt,
  Thou canst not be too bold;
  Since His own blood for thee He spilt,
  What else can He withhold?

4 Thine image, Lord, bestow,
  Thy presence and Thy love;
  I ask to serve Thee here below,
  And reign with Thee above.

5 Teach me to live by faith,
  Conform my will to Thine,
  Let me victorious be in death,
  And then in glory shine.
        Rev. John Newton. (1725—1807.) 1779. ab.

824   *In a Hurry of Business.*   S. M.
              Is. xxvi. 3.

1 THE praying spirit breathe,
  The watching power impart,
  From all entanglements beneath
  Call off my anxious heart.

2 My feeble mind sustain,
  By worldly thoughts opprest;
  Appear, and bid me turn again
  To my eternal rest.

3 Swift to my rescue come,
  Thine own this moment seize;
  Gather my wandering spirit home,
  And keep in perfect peace.

4 Suffered no more to rove
  O'er all the earth abroad,
  Arrest the prisoner of Thy love,
  And shut me up in God.
        Rev. Charles Wesley. 1749. ab.

825   *Importunacy in Prayer.*   S. M.
              Luke xviii. 1—7.

1 OUR Lord, who knows full well
  The heart of every saint,
  Invites us all our griefs to tell,
  To pray, and never faint.

2 He bows His gracious ear,
  We never plead in vain;
  Yet we must wait till He appear,
  And pray, and pray again.

3 Jesus the Lord will hear
  His chosen when they cry;
  Yes, though He may a while forbear,
  He'll help them from on high.

4 His nature, truth, and love,
  Engage Him on their side;
  When they are grieved, His mercies move,
  And can they be denied?

5 Then let us earnest be,
  And never faint in prayer;
  He loves our importunity,
  And makes our cause His care.
        Rev. John Newton. 1779. ab. and alt.

826   *The Spirit asked for.*   H. M.

1 O THOU that hearest prayer,
  Attend our humble cry;
  And let Thy servants share
  Thy blessing from on high:
  We plead the promise of Thy word;
  Grant us Thy Holy Spirit, Lord.

2 If earthly parents hear
  Their children when they cry,

If they, with love sincere,
  Their children's wants supply;
Much more wilt Thou Thy love display,
And answer when Thy children pray.

3 Our Heavenly Father, Thou!
  We, children of Thy grace:
  O let Thy Spirit now
  Descend, and fill the place:
So shall we feel the heavenly flame,
And all unite to praise Thy name.

4 O send Thy Spirit down
  On all the nations, Lord,
With great success to crown
  The preaching of Thy word,
Till heathen lands shall own Thy sway,
And cast their idol-gods away.
                    John Burton. (1803—) 1824. ab

827   *The Living Stone.*   H. M.
          1 Pet. ii. 4, 5.

1 WITH ecstasy of joy
    Extol His glorious name,
  Who raised the spacious earth,
    And raised our ruined frame:
  He built the Church who built the sky;
  Shout, and exalt His honors high.

2 See the foundation laid
    By power and love divine;
  Jesus His first-born Son,
    How bright His glories shine!
  Low He descends, in dust He lies,
  That from His tomb a Church might rise.

3 But He for ever lives,
    Nor for Himself alone;
  Each saint new life derives
    From this mysterious Stone;
  His influence darts through every soul,
  And in one house unites the whole.

4 To Him with joy we move,
    In Him cemented stand;
  The living temple grows,
    And owns the Founder's hand.
  That structure, Lord, still higher raise,
  Louder to sound its Builder's praise.

5 Descend, and shed abroad
    The tokens of Thy grace,
  And, with more radiant beams,
    Let glory fill the place;
Our joyful souls shall prostrate fall,
And own, our God is All in all.
                    Rev. Philip Doddridge. (1702—1751.) 1755.

828   "Angulare Fundamentum."

1 CHRIST is our Corner-stone,
    On Him alone we build;
  With His true saints alone
    The courts of heaven are filled:
On His great love | Of present grace,
Our hopes we place | And joys above.

2 O then with hymns of praise
    These hallowed courts shall ring;
  Our voices we will raise
    The Three in One to sing;
And thus proclaim | Both loud and long,
In joyful song, | That glorious Name.

3 Here, gracious God, do Thou
    Forevermore draw nigh;
  Accept each faithful prayer,
    And mark each suppliant sigh;
In copious shower | Each holy day,
On all who pray, | Thy blessings pour.

4 Here may we gain from Heaven
    The grace which we implore;
  And may that grace, once given,
    Be with us evermore,
Until that day | To endless rest
When all the blest | Are called away.
                    Unknown Author of the 8th century.
                    Tr. by Rev. John Chandler (1806—) 1837.

829   "One Lord, one Faith, one Baptism."   H. M.
          Eph. iv. 5.

1 ONE sole baptismal sign,
    One Lord below, above,
  Zion, one faith is thine,
    One only watchword, love:
  From different temples though it rise,
  One song ascendeth to the skies.

2 Our Sacrifice is one;
    One Priest before the throne,
  The slain, the risen Son,
    Redeemer, Lord alone:
  Thou who didst raise Him from the dead,
  Unite Thy people in their Head.

3 O may that holy prayer,
    His tenderest and His last,

His constant, latest care
Ere to His throne He passed,
No longer unfulfilled remain,
The world's offence, His people's stain!

4 Head of Thy church beneath,
The catholic, the true,
On all her members breathe,
Her broken frame renew:
Then shall Thy perfect will be done,
When Christians love and live as one.
George Robinson. 1842.

830 *God's Tabernacle with Men.* **8, 7. D.**
Ezek. xxxvii. 27.

1 PRAISE the Rock of our salvation,
Laud His Name from zone to zone;
On that Rock the Church is builded,
Christ Himself the Corner-Stone;
Vain against our rock-built Zion
Winds and waters, fire and hail,
Christ is in her midst; against her
Sin and hell shall not prevail.

2 Framed of living stones, cemented
By the Spirit's unity,
Based on Prophets and Apostles,
Firm in faith, and stayed on Thee,
May Thy Church, O Lord Incarnate,
Grow in grace, in peace, in love;
Emblem of the heavenly Zion,
The Jerusalem above.

3 Stands four-square that heavenly City;
Paved with gold like crystal bright;
Gates of pearl, and walls of jasper,
Emerald and chrysolyte;
Broad and lofty tower its ramparts;
At its gates twelve angels stand;
On its walls twelve names are graven,
Of the Apostles' chosen band.

4 Where Thou reignest, King of glory,
Throned in everlasting light,
Midst Thy saints, no more is needed
Sun by day, nor moon by night:
Soon may we those portals enter
When this earthly strife is o'er,
There to dwell with saints and angels
In Thy presence evermore.
Rev. Benjamin Webb. 1872. ab.

831 *The City of God.* **8, 7. D.**
Is. xxxiii. 20, 21.

1 GLORIOUS things of thee are spoken,
Zion, city of our God:
He whose word cannot be broken,
Formed thee for His own abode:
On the Rock of ages founded.
What can shake thy sure repose?
With salvation's walls surrounded,
Thou mayest smile at all thy foes.

2 See, the streams of living waters,
Springing from eternal love,
Well supply thy sons and daughters,
And all fear of want remove:
Who can faint, while such a river
Ever flows their thirst t' assuage?
Grace, which, like the Lord, the Giver,
Never fails from age to age.

3 Round each habitation hovering,
See the cloud and fire appear,
For a glory and a covering,
Showing that the Lord is near:
Thus deriving from their banner
Light by night, and shade by day,
Safe they feed upon the manna
Which He gives them when they pray.
Rev. John Newton. (1725—1807.) 1779.

832 *The Blessedness of the Saints.* **8, 7. D.**

1 BLEST inhabitants of Zion,
Washed in the Redeemer's blood,
Jesus, whom their souls rely on,
Makes them kings and priests to God:
'Tis His love His people raises
Over self to reign as kings;
And as priests, His solemn praises
Each for a thank-offering brings.

2 Saviour, if of Zion's city
I through grace a member am,
Let the world deride or pity,
I will glory in Thy name:
Fading is the worldling's pleasure,
All his boasted pomp and show;
Solid joys and lasting treasure
None but Zion's children know.
Rev. John Newton. 1779.

833 *"Angulare Fundamentum."* **8, 7.**

1 CHRIST is made the sure foundation,
Christ the Head and Corner-Stone,

THE CHURCH.

Chosen of the Lord, and precious,
  Binding all the Church in one,
Holy Zion's help forever,
  And her confidence alone.

2 All that dedicated city,
  Dearly loved of God on high,
In exultant jubilation
  Pours perpetual melody;
God the One in Three adoring
  In glad hymns eternally.

3 To this temple, where we call Thee,
  Come, O Lord of hosts, to-day:
With Thy wonted loving-kindness,
  Hear Thy servants as they pray;
And Thy fullest benediction
  Shed within its walls alway.

4 Here vouchsafe to all Thy servants
  What they ask of Thee to gain,
What they gain from Thee for ever
  With the blessèd to retain,
And hereafter in Thy glory
  Evermore with Thee to reign.

Unknown Author of the 6th century.
Tr. by Rev. John Mason Neale (1818—1866.) 1851. ab. alt.

834   *Zion secure.*   8, 7.
    Ps. cxxv. 2.

1 ZION stands by hills surrounded,
  Zion kept by power divine;
All her foes shall be confounded,
  Though the world in arms combine.
    Happy Zion!
  What a favored lot is thine!

2 Every human tie may perish;
  Friend to friend unfaithful prove;
Mothers cease their own to cherish;
  Heaven and earth at last remove;
    But no changes
  Can attend Jehovah's love.

3 In the furnace God may prove thee,
  Thence to bring thee forth more bright,
But can never cease to love thee;
  Thou art precious in His sight:
    God is with thee,
  God thine everlasting light.

Rev. Thomas Kelly. (1769—1855) 1806. ab.

835   *Love to the Church.*   S. M.
    Ps. cxxxvii.

1 I LOVE Thy kingdom, Lord,
  The house of Thine abode,
The church our blest Redeemer saved
  With His own precious blood.

2 I love Thy church, O God:
  Her walls before Thee stand,
Dear as the apple of Thine eye,
  And graven on Thy hand.

3 For her my tears shall fall,
  For her my prayers ascend;
To her my cares and toils be given,
  Till toils and cares shall end.

4 Beyond my highest joy
  I prize her heavenly ways,
Her sweet communion, solemn vows,
  Her hymns of love and praise.

5 Jesus, Thou Friend divine,
  Our Saviour and our King,
Thy hand from every snare and foe
  Shall great deliverance bring.

6 Sure as Thy truth shall last,
  To Zion shall be given
The brightest glories earth can yield,
  And brighter bliss of heaven.

Rev. Timothy Dwight. (1752—1817.) 1800. ab.

836   *The Beauty of the Church.*   S. M.
    Ps. xlviii.

1 FAR as Thy name is known,
  The world declares Thy praise;
Thy saints, O Lord, before Thy throne
  Their songs of honor raise.

2 With joy let Judah stand
  On Zion's chosen hill,
Proclaim the wonders of Thy hand,
  And counsels of Thy will.

3 Let strangers walk around
  The city where we dwell,
Compass and view Thy holy ground,
  And mark the building well;

4 The orders of Thy house,
  The worship of Thy court,
The cheerful songs, the solemn vows,
  And make a fair report.

5 How decent, and how wise!
  How glorious to behold!
Beyond the pomp that charms the eyes,
  And rites adorned with gold.

6 The God we worship now
    Will guide us, till we die;
    Will be our God, while here below,
    And ours above the sky.
            Rev. Isaac Watts. (1674—1748.) 1719.

837   *The Church the Safety of the Nation.*   S. M.
            Ps. xlvii.
1 GREAT is the Lord our God,
    And let His praise be great;
    He makes His churches His abode,
    His most delightful seat.

2 These temples of His grace,
    How beautiful they stand,
    The honors of our native place,
    And bulwarks of our land.

3 In Zion God is known,
    A Refuge in distress;
    How bright has His salvation shone
    Through all her palaces!

4 Oft have our fathers told,
    Our eyes have often seen,
    How well our God secures the fold,
    Where His own sheep have been.

5 In every new distress
    We'll to His house repair;
    We'll think upon His wondrous grace,
    And seek deliverance there.
            Rev. Isaac Watts. 1700. ab.

838   *"Come, Kingdom of our God."*   S. M.
1 COME, kingdom of our God,
    Sweet reign of light and love,
    Shed peace, and hope, and joy abroad,
    And wisdom from above.

2 Over our spirits first
    Extend thy healing reign;
    Then raise and quench the sacred thirst
    That never pains again.

3 Come, kingdom of our God,
    And make the broad earth thine;
    Stretch o'er her lands and isles the rod
    That flowers with grace divine.

4 Soon may all tribes be blest
    With fruit from life's glad tree;
    And in its shade, like brothers, rest,
    Sons of one family.

5 Come, kingdom of our God,
    And raise the glorious throne
    In worlds by the undying trod,
    When God shall bless His own.
            Rev. Henry D. Johns. 1853.

839   *The Pilgrim Church.*   S. M.
1 FAR down the ages now,
    Much of her journey done,
    The pilgrim church pursues her way,
    Until her crown be won.

2 The story of the past
    Comes up before her view;
    How well it seems to suit her still,
    Old, and yet ever new.

3 'Tis the same story still
    Of sin and weariness,
    Of grace and love yet flowing down
    To pardon and to bless.

4 No wider is the gate,
    No broader is the way,
    No smoother is the ancient path,
    That leads to light and day.

5 No sweeter is the cup,
    Nor less our lot of ill:
    'Twas tribulation ages since,
    'Tis tribulation still.

6 No slacker grows the fight,
    No feebler is the foe,
    Nor less the need of armor tried,
    Of shield and spear and bow.

7 Thus onward still we press
    Through evil and through good,
    Through pain and poverty and want,
    Through peril and through blood.

8 Still faithful to our God,
    And to our Captain true,
    We follow where He leads the way,
    The kingdom in our view.
            Rev. Horatius Bonar. (1808—) 1857. ab.

840   *"Walk about Zion."*   11, 9.
            Ps. xlvii.
1 O GREAT is Jehovah, and great be His praise;
    In the city of God He is King:
    Proclaim ye His triumphs in jubilant lays;
    On the mount of His holiness sing.

2 The joy of the earth, from her beautiful
   height,
  Is Zion's impregnable hill;
  The Lord in her temple still taketh delight;
  God reigns in her palaces still.

3 Go, walk about Zion, and measure the
   length,
  Her walls and her bulwarks mark well;
  Contemplate her palaces, glorious in
   strength,
  Her towers and their pinnacles tell.

4 Then say to your children, "Our stronghold is tried;
  This God is our God to the end;
  His people forever His counsels shall guide,
  His arm shall forever defend."
        James Montgomery. (1771—1854.) 1822. ab.

841   *"Make a joyful Noise."*   11, 9.

1 BE joyful in God, all ye lands of the earth;
  O serve Him with gladness and fear;
  Exult in His presence with music and mirth,
  With love and devotion draw near.

2 Jehovah is God, and Jehovah alone,
  Creator and Ruler o'er all;
  And we are His people, His sceptre we own;
  His sheep, and we follow His call.

3 O enter His gates with thanksgiving and
   song,
  Your vows in His temple proclaim;
  His praise with melodious accordance prolong,
  And bless His adorable name.

4 For good is the Lord, inexpressibly good,
  And we are the work of His hand;
  His mercy and truth from eternity stood,
  And shall to eternity stand.
        James Montgomery. 1822.

842   *"Ein fest Burg ist unser Gott."*   P. M.

1 A SAFE stronghold our God is still,
  A trusty shield and weapon;
  He'll help us clear from all the ill
   That hath us now o'ertaken.
  The ancient Prince of hell
  Hath risen with purpose fell;
  Strong mail of craft and power
  He weareth in this hour,
  On earth is not his fellow.

2 With force of arms we nothing can,
   Full soon were we down-ridden;
  But for us fights the proper Man,
   Whom God himself hath bidden.
  Ask ye, who is this same?
  Christ Jesus is His name,
  The Lord Sabaoth's Son,
  He and no other one
  Shall conquer in the battle.

3 And were this world all devils o'er,
   And watching to devour us,
  We lay it not to heart so sore,
   Not they can overpower us.
  And let the Prince of ill
  Look grim as e'er he will,
  He harms us not a whit:
  For why? His doom is writ,
  One little word shall slay him.

4 That word, for all their craft and force,
   One moment will not linger,
  But, spite of hell, shall have its course,
   'T is written by His finger.
  And though they take our life,
  Goods, honor, children, wife,
  Yet is their profit small;
  These things shall vanish all,
  The Kingdom ours remaineth.
        Martin Luther. (1483—1546.) 1529.
        Tr. by Thomas Carlyle. (1795—1881.) 1831. sl. alt.

843   *The great Commission.*   L. M.
     Mark xvi. 15.

1 "Go preach My gospel," saith the Lord,
  Bid the whole earth My grace receive;
  He shall be saved that trusts my word,
  He shall be damned that won't believe.

2 I'll make your great commission known;
   And ye shall prove My gospel true,
  By all the works that I have done,
  By all the wonders ye shall do.

3 Go, heal the sick; go, raise the dead;
  Go, cast out devils in My name;
  Nor let My prophets be afraid,
  Though Greeks reproach, and Jews blaspheme.

4 Teach all the nations My commands,
    I'm with you till the world shall end;
  All power is trusted to My hands,
    I can destroy, and I defend."

5 He spake, and light shone round His head;
  On a bright cloud to heaven He rode:
  They to the farthest nations spread
    The grace of their ascended God.
              Rev. Isaac Watts. (1674—1748.) 1709.

844   Prayer for Ministers.   L. M.

1 FATHER of mercies, bow Thine ear,
    Attentive to our earnest prayer;
  We plead for those who plead for Thee:
    Successful pleaders may they be.

2 How great their work, how vast their charge!
  Do Thou their anxious souls enlarge;
  To them Thy sacred truth reveal,
    Suppress their fear, inflame their zeal.

3 Teach them aright to sow the seed,
  Teach them Thy chosen flock to feed,
  Teach them immortal souls to gain,
    Nor let them labor, Lord, in vain.

4 Let thronging multitudes around
  Hear from their lips the joyful sound,
  In humble strains Thy grace adore,
    And feel Thy new-creating power.
              Rev. Benjamin Beddome. (1717—1795.) 1787, ab.

845   For a Meeting of Ministers.   L. M.

1 POUR out Thy Spirit from on high;
    Lord, Thine assembled servants bless:
  Graces and gifts to each supply,
    And clothe Thy priests with righteousness.

2 Within Thy temple, when we stand
    To teach the truth as taught by Thee,
  Saviour, like stars in Thy right hand,
    The angels of the churches be.

3 Wisdom, and zeal, and faith impart,
    Firmness with meekness from above,
  To bear Thy people on our heart,
    And love the souls whom Thou dost love:

4 To watch, and pray, and never faint;
    By day and night strict guard to keep;
  To warn the sinner, cheer the saint
    Nourish Thy lambs, and feed Thy sheep.

5 Then, when our work is finished here,
    In humble hope our charge resign;
  When the chief Shepherd shall appear,
    O God, may they and we be Thine.
              James Montgomery. (1771—1854.) 1825.

846   A Pastor sought of God.   L. M.
              Ezk. viii. 21.

1 SHEPHERD of Israel, bend Thine ear,
  Thy servants' prayers indulgent hear;
  Perplexed, distressed, to Thee we cry,
  And seek the guidance of Thine eye.

2 With longing eyes, behold, we wait,
  A suppliant band, at mercy's gate;
  Our drooping hearts, O God, sustain:
  Shall Israel seek Thy face in vain?

3 O Lord, in ways of peace return,
  Nor let Thy flock neglected mourn;
  May our blest eyes a shepherd see,
  Dear to our souls, and dear to Thee.

4 Fed by his care, our tongues shall raise
  A cheerful tribute to Thy praise,
  Our children learn the grateful song,
  And theirs the cheerful notes prolong.
              Rev. Philip Doddridge. (1702—1751.) 1755, ab. and alt.

847   Ordination of a Minister.   L. M.

1 FATHER of mercies, in Thy house,
  Smile on our homage, and our vows;
  While, with a grateful heart, we share
  These pledges of our Father's care.

2 The Saviour, when to heaven He rose,
  In splendid triumph o'er His foes,
  Scattered His gifts on men below,
  And wide His royal bounties flow.

3 Hence sprung th' apostles' honored name,
  Sacred beyond heroic fame;
  In lowlier forms, to bless our eyes,
  Pastors from hence, and teachers rise.

4 So shall the bright succession run,
  Through the last courses of the sun;
  While unborn churches, by their care,
  Shall rise and flourish, large and fair.

5 Jesus, our Lord, their hearts shall know,
  The Spring whence all these blessings flow;
  Pastors and people shout His praise,
  Through the long round of endless days.
                    Rev. Philip Doddridge. 1745. ab.

848   *A Pastor welcomed.*   L. M.

1 WE bid thee welcome, in the name
  Of Jesus, our exalted Head:
  Come as a servant; so He came,
  And we receive thee in His stead.

2 Come as a shepherd; guard and keep
  This fold from hell, and earth, and sin;
  Nourish the lambs, and feed the sheep,
  The wounded heal, the lost bring in.

3 Come as a teacher, sent from God,
  Charged His whole counsel to declare;
  Lift o'er our ranks the prophet's rod,
  While we uphold thy hands with prayer.

4 Come as a messenger of peace,
  Filled with the Spirit, fired with love;
  Live to behold our large increase,
  And die to meet us all above.
                    James Montgomery. 1825.

849   *"Come, Sacred Spirit!"*   L. M.
           Ezek. xxxvi. 37.

1 COME, Sacred Spirit, from above,
  And fill the coldest heart with love;
  Soften to flesh the rugged stone,
  And let Thy godlike power be known.

2 Speak Thou, and, from the haughtiest eyes,
  Shall floods of pious sorrow rise;
  While all their glowing souls are borne
  To seek that grace, which now they scorn.

3 O let a holy flock await,
  Numerous around Thy temple-gate,
  Each pressing on with zeal to be
  A living sacrifice to Thee.
                    Rev. Philip Doddridge. 1755. ab.

850   *"Come, Jesus, come!"*   L. M.

1 O SAVIOUR, is Thy promise fled?
  Nor longer might Thy grace endure
  To heal the sick, and raise the dead,
  And preach the gospel to the poor?

2 Come, Jesus, come, return again;
  With brighter beam Thy servants bless,
  Who long to feel Thy perfect reign,
  And share Thy kingdom's happiness.

3 Come, Jesus, come, and as of yore
  The prophet went to clear Thy way,
  A harbinger Thy feet before,
  A dawning to Thy brighter day:

4 So now may grace, with heavenly shower,
  Our stony hearts for truth prepare;
  Sow in our souls the seed of power,
  Then come and reap Thy harvest there.
                    Bp. Reginald Heber. (1783—1826) 1811. ab.

851   *The Blessedness of Gospel-times.*   S. M.
           Is. lii. 7—9. Matt. xiii. 16, 17.

1 How beauteous are their feet
  Who stand on Zion's hill,
  Who bring salvation on their tongues,
  And words of peace reveal!

2 How charming is their voice,
  How sweet the tidings are!
  "Zion, behold Thy Saviour King;
  He reigns and triumphs here."

3 How happy are our ears,
  That hear this joyful sound,
  Which kings and prophets waited for,
  And sought, but never found!

4 How blessèd are our eyes,
  That see this heavenly light!
  Prophets and kings desired it long,
  But died without the sight.

5 The watchmen join their voice,
  And tuneful notes employ;
  Jerusalem breaks forth in songs,
  And deserts learn the joy.

6 The Lord makes bare His arm
  Through all the earth abroad;
  Let every nation now behold
  Their Saviour and their God.
                    Rev. Isaac Watts. 1709.

852   *The Standard lifted up.*   S. M.

1 HARK, how the watchmen cry!
  Attend the trumpet's sound;
  Stand to your arms, the foe is nigh,
  The powers of hell surround.

2 See on the mountain's top
  The standard of your God;
  In Jesus' name 'tis lifted up,
  All stained with hallowed blood.

3 His standard-bearers now
   To all the nations call;
   To Jesus' cross, ye nations, bow;
   He bore the cross for all.
Rev. Charles Wesley. (1708—1788.) 1749. ab. and alt.

853 *Sowing beside all Waters.* S. M.
Is. xxxii. 20.

1 Sow in the morn thy seed,
   At eve hold not thy hand;
   To doubt and fear give thou no heed,
   Broadcast it o'er the land.

2 Beside all waters sow,
   The highway furrows stock,
   Drop it where thorns and thistles grow,
   Scatter it on the rock.

3 The good, the fruitful ground
   Expect not here nor there;
   O'er hill and dale alike 't is found;
   Go forth, then, everywhere.

4 And duly shall appear,
   In verdure, beauty, strength,
   The tender blade, the stalk, the ear,
   And the full corn at length.

5 Thou canst not toil in vain;
   Cold, heat, the moist and dry,
   Shall foster and mature the grain
   For garners in the sky.

6 Then, when the glorious end,
   The day of God, shall come,
   The angel-reapers shall descend,
   And heaven sing, "Harvest home!"
James Montgomery. (1771—1854.) 1825. ab.

854 *The watchful Servant.* S. M.
Luke xii. 35—38.

1 YE servants of the Lord,
   Each in His office wait,
   Observant of His heavenly word,
   And watchful at His gates.

2 Let all your lamps be bright,
   And trim the golden flame;
   Gird up your loins as in His sight,
   For awful is His name.

3 Watch! 't is your Lord's command;
   And while we speak, He's near:
   Mark the first signal of His hand,
   And ready all appear.

4 O happy servant he,
   In such a posture found!
   He shall his Lord with rapture see,
   And be with honor crowned.

5 Christ shall the banquet spread
   With His own royal hand,
   And raise that faithful servant's head
   Amid the angelic band.
Rev. Philip Doddridge. (1702—1751.) 1755. sl. alt.

855 *For more Laborers.* S. M.

1 LORD of the harvest, hear
   Thy needy servants cry;
   Answer our faith's effectual prayer,
   And all our wants supply.

2 On Thee we humbly wait,
   Our wants are in Thy view;
   The harvest truly, Lord, is great,
   The laborers are few.

3 Convert and send forth more
   Into Thy church abroad,
   And let them speak Thy word of power,
   As workers with their God.

4 O let them spread Thy name,
   Their mission fully prove;
   Thy universal grace proclaim,
   Thine all-redeeming love.
Rev. Charles Wesley. 1742. ab.

856 *Ordination of Missionaries.* S. M.

1 YE messengers of Christ,
   His sovereign voice obey;
   Arise, and follow where He leads,
   And peace attend your way.

2 The Master whom you serve
   Will needful strength bestow;
   Depending on His promised aid,
   With sacred courage go.

3 Mountains shall sink to plains,
   And hell in vain oppose;
   The cause is God's, and must prevail
   In spite of all His foes.

4 Go, spread a Saviour's fame,
   And tell His matchless grace,
   To the most guilty and depraved
   Of Adam's numerous race.
Mrs. Voke. 1806.

THE CHRISTIAN MINISTRY. BAPTISM.

857 *Sowing in Tears, Reaping in Joy.* S. M.
Ps. cxxvi

1 THE harvest dawn is near,
   The year delays not long;
And he who sows with many a tear,
   Shall reap with many a song.

2 Sad to his toil he goes,
   His seed with weeping leaves;
But he shall come at twilight's close,
   And bring his golden sheaves.

Bp. George Burgess. (1809—1866.) 1840.

858 *The different Success of the Gospel.* C. M.
1 Cor. i 23, 24.

1 CHRIST and His cross are all our theme;
   The mysteries that we speak
Are scandal in the Jew's esteem,
   And folly to the Greek.

2 But souls enlightened from above
   With joy receive the word;
They see what wisdom, power, and love,
   Shine in their dying Lord.

3 The vital savor of His name
   Restores their fainting breath;
But unbelief perverts the same
   To guilt, despair, and death.

4 Till God diffuse His graces down,
   Like showers of heavenly rain,
In vain Apollos sows the ground,
   And Paul may plant in vain.

Rev. Isaac Watts. (1674—1748.) 1709.

859 *For the Ordination of a Minister.* C. M.

1 LET Zion's watchmen all awake,
   And take the alarm they give;
Now let them from the mouth of God
   Their solemn charge receive.

2 'Tis not a cause of small import
   The pastor's care demands,
But what might fill an angel's heart,
   And filled a Saviour's hands.

3 They watch for souls for which the Lord
   Did heavenly bliss forego,
For souls that must forever live
   In raptures or in woe.

4 All to the great tribunal haste,
   The account to render there;
And shouldst Thou strictly mark our faults,
   Lord, how shall we appear?

5 May they that Jesus, whom they preach,
   Their own Redeemer see;
And watch Thou daily o'er their souls,
   That they may watch for Thee.

Rev. Philip Doddridge. 1736

860 *Christ's Call.* C. M.

1 LORD, Thou hast taught our hearts to glow
   With love's undying flame;
But more of Thee we long to know,
   And more would love Thy name.

2 Thy life, Thy death, inspire our song,
   Thy Spirit breathes through all;
And here our feet would linger long,
   But we obey Thy call.

3 Thou bid'st us go, with Thee to stand
   Against hell's marshalled powers;
And heart to heart, and hand to hand,
   To make Thine honor ours.

4 With Thine own pity, Saviour, see
   The thronged and darkening way;
We go to win the lost to Thee,
   O help us, Lord, we pray.

5 Teach Thou our lips of Thee to speak,
   Of Thy sweet love to tell;
Till they who wander far shall seek
   And find and serve Thee well.

6 O'er all the world Thy Spirit send,
   And make Thy goodness known,
Till earth and heaven together blend
   Their praises at Thy throne.

Rev. Ray Palmer. (1808—) 1869.

861 *Christ's Regard for Children.* C. M.
Mark x. 13—16.

1 SEE, Israel's gentle Shepherd stands,
   With all-engaging charms;
Hark, how He calls the tender lambs,
   And fold them in His arms!

2 "Permit them to approach," He cries,
   "Nor scorn their humble name;
For 't was to bless such souls as these,
   The Lord of angels came."

3 We bring them, Lord, in thankful hands,
   And yield them up to Thee;
Joyful that we ourselves are Thine,
   Thine let our offspring be.

BAPTISM.

4 Ye little flock, with pleasure hear;
   Ye children, seek His face;
And fly, with transport, to receive
   The blessings of His grace.
      Rev. Philip Doddridge. (1702—1751.) 1755. ab.

862 *"Unto thee, and to thy Seed after thee."* **C. M.**
      Gen. xvii. 7.

1 How large the promise, how divine,
   To Abraham and his seed:
"I'll be a God to thee and thine,
   Supplying all their need."

2 Jesus the ancient faith confirms,
   To our great fathers given;
He takes young children to His arms,
   And calls them heirs of heaven.

3 Our God, how faithful are His ways!
   His love endures the same;
Nor from the promise of His grace
   Blots out the children's name.
      Rev. Isaac Watts. (1674—1748.) 1709. ab.

863 *Baptism of Adults.* **C. M.**

1 WE long to move and breathe in Thee,
   Inspired with Thine own breath,
To live Thy life, O Lord, and be
   Baptized into Thy death.

2 Thy death to sin we die below,
   But we shall rise in love;
We here are planted in Thy woe,
   But we shall bloom above.

3 Above we shall Thy glory share,
   As we Thy cross have borne;
E'en we shall crowns of honor wear,
   When we the thorns have worn.

4 Thy crown of thorns is all our boast,
   While now we fall before
The Father, Son, and Holy Ghost,
   And tremble, love, adore.
      Unknown Author.

864 *Profession and Covenant.* **C. M.**

1 WITNESS, ye men and angels, now,
   Before the Lord we speak;
To Him we make our solemn vow,
   A vow we dare not break:—

2 That long as life itself shall last,
   Ourselves to Christ we yield;
Nor from His cause will we depart,
   Or ever quit the field.

3 We trust not in our native strength
   But on His grace rely,
That, with returning wants, the Lord
   Will all our need supply.

4 O guide our doubtful feet aright,
   And keep us in Thy ways;
And, while we turn our vows to prayers,
   Turn Thou our prayers to praise.
      Rev. Benjamin Beddome. (1717—1795.) 1818.

865 *"Lent unto the Lord."* **L. M.**
      1 Sam. i. 28.

1 GOD of that glorious gift of grace
By which Thy people seek Thy face,
When in Thy presence we appear,
Vouchsafe us faith to venture near.

2 Confiding in Thy truth alone,
Here, on the steps of Jesus' throne,
We lay the treasure Thou hast given
To be received and reared for heaven.

3 Lent to us for a season, we
Lend *him* forever, Lord, to Thee:
Assured, that, if to Thee *he* live,
We gain in what we seem to give.

4 Large and abundant blessings shed,
Warm as these prayers, upon *his* head:
And on *his* soul the dews of grace,
Fresh as these drops upon *his* face.

5 Make *him* and keep *him* Thine own child,
Meek follower of the Undefiled;
Possessor here of grace and love,
Inheritor of heaven above.
      Rev. John Samuel Bewley Monsell. (1811—) 1837.

866 *Let little Children come to Me.* **L. M.**

1 A LITTLE child the Saviour came,
The mighty God was still His name,
And angels worshipped, as He lay,
The seeming infant of a day.

2 He who, a little child, began
The life divine to show to man,
Proclaims from heaven the message free,
"Let little children come to Me."

3 We bring them, Lord, and with the sign
Of sprinkled water name them Thine;
Their souls with saving grace endow,
Baptize them with Thy Spirit now.

BAPTISM.

4 O give Thine angels charge, good Lord,
   Them safely in Thy way to guard;
   Thy blessing on their lives command,
   And write their names upon Thy hand.

5 O Thou, who by an infant's tongue
   Dost hear Thy perfect glory sung,
   May these with all the heavenly host
   Praise Father, Son, and Holy Ghost.
        Rev. William Robertson. (—1743.) 1751. ab.

867   *Prayer for the Children of the Church.* **L. M.**

1 DEAR Saviour, if these lambs should stray
   From Thy secure enclosure's bound,
   And, lured by worldly joys away,
   Among the thoughtless crowd be found;

2 Remember still that they are Thine,
   That Thy dear sacred name they bear;
   Think that the seal of love divine,
   The sign of covenant grace, they wear.

3 In all their erring, sinful years,
   O let them ne'er forgotten be;
   Remember all the prayers and tears
   Which made them consecrate to Thee.

4 And when these lips no more can pray,
   These eyes can weep for them no more,
   Turn Thou their feet from folly's way,
   The wanderers to Thy fold restore.
        Mrs. Ann Beadley Hyde. (—1872.) 1824.

868   *Prayer for Adoption* **L. M.**

1 FATHER, in these reveal Thy Son,
   In these for whom we seek Thy face;
   Adopt and seal them as Thine own,
   By Thy regenerating grace.

2 Jesus, with us Thou always art,
   Now ratify the sacred sign,
   The gift unspeakable impart,
   And bless Thy sacrament divine.

3 Come, Holy Spirit, from on high,
   Baptizer of our spirits, Thou!
   The purifying grace apply
   And witness with the water now.

4 Pour forth Thine energy divine,
   And sprinkle the atoning blood;
   May Father, Son, and Spirit join
   To seal each child a child of God.
        Rev. Charles Wesley. (1708—1788.) 1749. ab. and alt.

869   *Prayer for Cleansing.* **L. M.**

1 O LORD, encouraged by Thy grace,
   We bring our infant to Thy throne;
   Give it within Thy heart a place,
   Let it be Thine, and Thine alone.

2 Wash it from every stain of guilt,
   And let this child be sanctified;
   Lord, Thou canst cleanse it, if Thou wilt,
   And all its native evils hide.

3 We ask not for it earthly bliss,
   Or earthly honors, wealth or fame;
   The sum of our request is this,
   That it may love and fear Thy name.
        Miss Anne Steele. (1717—1778.) 1780. ab.

870   *"The gentle Saviour calls."* **S. M.**

1 THE gentle Saviour calls
   Our children to His breast;
   He folds them in His gracious arms,
   Himself declares them blest.

2 "Let them approach," He cries,
   "Nor scorn their humble claim;
   The heirs of heaven are such as these,
   For such as these I came."

3 Gladly we bring them, Lord,
   Devoting them to Thee,
   Imploring that, as we are Thine,
   Thine may our offspring be.
        Bp. Henry Ustick Onderdonk. (1789—1858.) 1826.

871   *Committed to the Shepherd's Care.* **8, 7**

1 SAVIOUR, who Thy flock art feeding,
   With the shepherd's kindest care,
   All the feeble gently leading,
   While the lambs Thy bosom share;

2 Now, these little ones receiving,
   Fold them in Thy gracious arm;
   There, we know, Thy word believing,
   Only there, secure from harm.

3 Never, from Thy pasture roving,
   Let them be the lion's prey;
   Let Thy tenderness, so loving,
   Keep them all life's dangerous way.

4 Then, within Thy fold eternal,
   Let them find a resting-place;
   Feed in pastures ever vernal,
   Drink the rivers of Thy grace.
        Rev. William Augustus Muhlenburg. (1796—) 1826.

CONFESSION OF FAITH.

872 *Rejoicing in our Covenant-Engagements.* L. M.
2 Chron. xv. 15.

1 O HAPPY day, that fixed my choice
  On Thee, my Saviour and my God;
Well may this glowing heart rejoice,
  And tell its raptures all abroad.

2 O happy bond, that seals my vows
  To Him who merits all my love;
Let cheerful anthems fill His house,
  While to that sacred shrine I move.

3 'T is done; the great transaction's done;
  I am my Lord's, and He is mine;
He drew me, and I followed on,
  Charmed to confess the voice divine.

4 Now rest, my long divided heart,
  Fixed on this blissful centre, rest;
With ashes who would grudge to part,
  When called on angels' bread to feast?

5 High heaven, that heard the solemn vow,
  That vow renewed shall daily hear,
Till in life's latest hour I bow,
  And bless in death a bond so dear.
  Rev. Philip Doddridge. (1702—1751.) 1755.

873 *Giving ourselves away.* L. M.

1 O, SWEETLY breathe the lyres above,
  When angels touch the quivering string,
And wake, to chant Immanuel's love,
  Such strains as angel-lips can sing.

2 And sweet on earth the choral swell,
  From mortal tongues, of gladsome lays,
When pardoned souls their raptures tell,
  And, grateful, hymn Immanuel's praise.

3 Jesus, Thy name our souls adore;
  We own the bond that makes us Thine;
And carnal joys, that charmed before,
  For Thy dear sake we now resign.

4 Our hearts, by dying love subdued,
  Accept Thine offered grace to-day;
Beneath the cross, with blood bedewed,
  We bow and give ourselves away.

5 In Thee we trust, on Thee rely;
  Though we are feeble, Thou art strong;
O keep us till our spirits fly
  To join the bright, immortal throng.
  Rev. Ray Palmer. (1808—) 1843.

874 *"Lord, I am Thine."* L. M.

1 LORD, I am Thine, entirely Thine,
  Purchased and saved by blood divine;
With full consent Thine I would be,
  And own Thy sovereign right in me.

2 Grant one poor sinner more a place,
  Among the children of Thy grace;
A wretched sinner, lost to God,
  But ransomed by Immanuel's blood.

3 Thine would I live, Thine would I die,
  Be Thine through all eternity;
The vow is past beyond repeal;
  Now will I set the solemn seal.

4 Here, at that cross where flows the blood
  That bought my guilty soul for God,
Thee my new Master now I call,
  And consecrate to Thee my all.

5 Do Thou assist a feeble worm
  The great engagement to perform;
Thy grace can full assistance lend,
  And on that grace I dare depend.
  Rev. Samuel Davies (1724—1761.) 1769.

875 *"Arm these Thy Soldiers."* L. M.

1 ARM these Thy soldiers, mighty Lord,
  With shield of faith and Spirit's sword;
Forth to the battle may they go,
  And boldly fight against the foe,
With banner of the cross unfurled,
  And by it overcome the world;
And so at last receive from Thee
  The palm and crown of victory.

2 Come, ever-blessed Spirit, come,
  And make Thy servants' hearts Thy home;
May each a living temple be,
  Hallowed for ever, Lord, to Thee;
Enrich that temple's holy shrine
  With sevenfold gifts of grace divine;
With wisdom, light, and knowledge bless,
  Strength, counsel, fear, and godliness.
  Bp. Christopher Wordsworth. (1807—) 1863. ab.

876 *"Come in!"* L. M.
Gen. xxiv. 31.

1 COME in, thou blessèd of the Lord,
  Enter in Jesus' precious name;
We welcome thee with one accord,
  And trust the Saviour does the same.

2 Those joys, which earth cannot afford,
   We'll seek in fellowship to prove;
   Joined in one spirit to our Lord,
   Together bound by mutual love.
3 And, while we pass this vale of tears,
   We'll make our joys and sorrows known;
   We'll share each other's hopes and fears,
   And count a brother's case our own.
4 Once more our welcome we repeat,
   Receive assurance of our love;
   O may we all together meet,
   Around the throne of God above.
                Rev. Thomas Kelly. (1769—1855.) 1812. ab.

877   *"Forget Him not"*   L. M.
1 O THOU, my soul, forget no more
   The Friend who all thy sorrows bore,
   Let every idol be forgot,
   But O my soul, forget Him not.
2 Renounce thy works and ways with grief,
   And fly to this divine relief;
   Nor Him forget, who left His throne,
   And for thy life gave up His own.
3 Eternal truth and beauty shine
   In Him, and He Himself is thine:
   And canst thou, then, with sin beset,
   Such charms, such matchless charms forget?
4 O no: till life itself depart,
   His name shall cheer and warm my heart;
   And, lisping this, from earth I'll rise,
   And join the chorus of the skies.
                Krishnoo Pal 1801.
   Tr. by Rev. Joshua Marshman. (1797—1837.) 1801.

878   *Choosing the Portion of God's Heritage.* 7. D.
                Ruth i. 16, 17
1 PEOPLE of the living God,
   I have sought the world around,
   Paths of sin and sorrow trod,
   Peace and comfort nowhere found.
   Now to you my spirit turns,
   Turns, a fugitive unblessed;
   Brethren, where your altar burns,
   O receive me into rest.
2 Lonely I no longer roam,
   Like the cloud, the wind, the wave;
   Where you dwell shall be my home,
   Where you die shall be my grave;
   Mine the God whom you adore,
   Your Redeemer shall be mine;

Earth can fill my heart no more,
Every idol I resign.
                James Montgomery. (1771—1854.) 1819, 1853. ab.

879   *The burdened Pilgrim welcomed.*   7.
1 PILGRIM, burdened with thy sin,
   Come the way to Zion's gate:
   There, till mercy lets thee in,
   Knock, and weep, and watch, and wait.
   Knock—He knows the sinner's cry;
   Weep—He loves the mourner's tears;
   Watch, for saving grace is nigh;
   Wait, till heavenly light appears.
2 Hark, it is the Bridegroom's voice:
   "Welcome, pilgrim, to thy rest!"
   Now within the gate rejoice,
   Safe, and sealed, and bought and blest:
   Safe, from all the lures of vice;
   Sealed, by signs the chosen know;
   Bought by love, and life the price;
   Blest, the mighty debt to owe.
3 Holy pilgrim, what for thee
   In a world like this remain?
   From thy guarded breast shall flee
   Fear, and shame, and doubt, and pain;
   Fear, the hope of heaven shall fly;
   Shame, from glory's view retire;
   Doubt, in certain rapture die;
   Pain, in endless bliss expire.
                Rev. George Crabbe. (1754—1832.) 1807. ab.

880   *"Thine for ever."*   7.
1 THINE for ever!—God of love,
   Hear us from Thy throne above;
   Thine for ever may we be,
   Here and in eternity.
   Thine for ever!—Lord of life,
   Shield us through our earthly strife;
   Thou, the Life, the Truth, the Way,
   Guide us to the realms of day.
2 Thine for ever!—Saviour, keep
   These Thy frail and trembling sheep;
   Safe alone beneath Thy care,
   Let us all Thy goodness share.
   Thine for ever!—Thou our Guide,
   All our wants by Thee supplied,
   All our sins by Thee forgiven,
   Lead us, Lord, from earth to heaven.
                Mrs. Mary Fawler Maude. 1845. ab.

881
"Lovest thou Me?" 7.

1 HARK, my soul, it is the Lord;
'Tis thy Saviour, hear His word;
Jesus speaks, and speaks to thee:
" Say, poor sinner, lovest thou me?

2 " I delivered thee, when bound,
And, when wounded, healed Thy wound;
Sought thee wandering, set thee right,
Turned thy darkness into light.

3 " Can a woman's tender care
Cease towards the child she bare?
Yes, she may forgetful be,
Yet will I remember thee.

4 " Mine is an unchanging love,
Higher than the heights above,
Deeper than the depths beneath,
Free and faithful, strong as death.

5 " Thou shalt see My glory soon,
When the work of grace is done;
Partner of My throne shalt be;
Say, poor sinner, lovest thou Me?"

6 Lord, it is my chief complaint,
That my love is weak and faint;
Yet I love Thee, and adore;
O for grace to love Thee more.
William Cowper. (1731—1800.) 1779.

882
Redeeming Love. 7.

1 SWEET the time, exceeding sweet,
When the saints together meet;
When the Saviour is the theme,
When they join to sing of Him.

2 Sing we then eternal love,
Such as did the Father move:
He beheld the world undone,
Loved the world, and gave His Son.

3 Sing the Son's amazing love:
How He left the realms above,
Took our nature and our place,
Lived and died to save our race.

4 Sing we, too, the Spirit's love:
With our wretched hearts He strove,
Took the things of Christ, and showed
How to reach His blest abode.

5 Sweet the place, exceeding sweet,
Where the saints in glory meet;
Where the Saviour's still the theme,
Where they see, and sing of Him.
Rev. George Burder. (1752—1832.) 1779. alt.

883
"Digname, O Jesu, roga te." 7.

1 JESUS, grant me this, I pray,
Ever in Thy heart to stay;
Let me evermore abide
Hidden in Thy wounded side.

2 If the evil one prepare,
Or the world, a tempting snare,
I am safe, when I abide
In Thy heart and wounded side.

3 If the flesh, more dangerous still,
Tempt my soul to deeds of ill,
Naught I fear, when I abide
In Thy heart and wounded side.

4 Death will come one day to me;
Jesus, cast me not from Thee;
Dying, let me still abide
In Thy heart and wounded side.
Of unknown authorship and date.
Tr. by Rev. Sir Henry Williams Baker. (1821—) 1861.

884
The Supper instituted.
1 Cor. xi. 23. L. M.

1 'TWAS on that dark, that doleful night,
When powers of earth and hell arose
Against the Son of God's delight,
And friends betrayed Him to His foes:

2 Before the mournful scene began,
He took the bread, and blessed, and brake:
What love through all His actions ran,
What wondrous words of grace He spake.

3 " This is My body, broke for sin;
Receive and eat the living food:"
Then took the cup, and blessed the wine,
"'T is the new covenant in My blood."

4 " Do this," He cried, " till time shall end
In memory of your dying Friend;
Meet at My table, and record
The love of your departed Lord."

5 Jesus, Thy feast we celebrate;
We show Thy death, we sing Thy name,
Till Thou return, and we shall eat
The marriage supper of the Lamb.
Rev. Isaac Watts. (1674—1748.) 1709. ab.

885 *Glorying in the Cross.* L. M.

1 AT Thy command, our dearest Lord,
    Here we attend Thy dying feast;
    Thy blood, like wine, adorns Thy board,
    And Thine own flesh feeds every guest.

2 Our faith adores Thy bleeding love,
    And trusts for life in One that died;
    We hope for heavenly crowns above,
    From a Redeemer crucified.

3 Let the vain world pronounce it shame,
    And fling their scandals on Thy cause;
    We come to boast our Saviour's name,
    And make our triumphs in His cross.

4 With joy we tell the scoffing age,
    He that was dead has left His tomb;
    He lives above their utmost rage,
    And we are waiting till He come.
            Rev. Isaac Watts. 1709.

886 *"Liebe die du mich so milde."* L. M.

1 O LOVE, who formedst me to wear
    The image of Thy God-head here;
    O Love, I give myself to Thee,
    Thine ever, only Thine to be.

2 O Love, of whom is truth and light,
    Whose heart was bared to them that smite;
    O love, I give myself to Thee,
    Thine ever, only Thine to be.
            Johann Angelus Silesius (1624—1677) 1657.
            Tr. by Miss Catherine Winkworth. (1829—) 1858. ab.

887 *Prayer for helping Grace.* L. M.

1 O JESUS, bruised and wounded more
    Than bursted grape, or bread of wheat,
    The Life of life within our souls,
    The Cup of our salvation sweet:

2 We come to show Thy dying hour,
    Thy streaming vein, Thy broken flesh;
    And still the blood is warm to save,
    And still the fragrant wounds are fresh.

3 O Heart, that, with a double tide
    Of blood and water, maketh pure;
    O Flesh, once offered on the cross,
    The gift that makes our pardon sure:

4 Let never more our sinful souls
    The anguish of Thy cross renew;
    Nor forge again the cruel nails
    That pierced Thy victim body through.
            Mrs. Cecil Frances Alexander. 1859.

888 *"Jesu, Dulcedo cordium."* L. M.

1 JESUS, Thou Joy of loving hearts,
    Thou Fount of life, Thou Light of men,
    From the best bliss that earth imparts,
    We turn unfilled to Thee again.

2 Thy truth unchanged hath ever stood;
    Thou savest those that on Thee call;
    To them that seek Thee, Thou art good,
    To them that find Thee, All in all.

3 We taste Thee, O thou living Bread,
    And long to feast upon Thee still;
    We drink of Thee, the Fountain Head,
    And thirst, our souls from Thee to fill.

4 Our restless spirits yearn for Thee,
    Where'er our changeful lot is cast;
    Glad, when Thy gracious smile we see,
    Blest, when our faith can hold Thee fast.

5 O Jesus, ever with us stay;
    Make all our moments calm and bright;
    Chase the dark night of sin away;
    Shed o'er the world Thy holy light.
            Bernard of Clairvaux. (1011—1153) 1140.
            Tr. by Rev. Ray Palmer (1808—) 1858.

889 *Trusting the Merits of Christ.*
Phil. III 7—9. L. M.

1 No more, my God, I boast no more
    Of all the duties I have done;
    I quit the hopes I held before,
    To trust the merits of Thy Son.

2 Now for the love I bear His name,
    What was my gain I count my loss;
    My former pride I call my shame,
    And nail my glory to His cross.

3 Yes, and I must and will esteem
    All things but loss for Jesus' sake;
    O may my soul be found in Him,
    And of His righteousness partake.

4 The best obedience of my hands
    Dares not appear before Thy throne;
    But faith can answer Thy demands,
    By pleading what my Lord has done.
            Rev. Isaac Watts. 1709.

890 *The Wonders of the Cross.* L. M.

1 O THE sweet wonders of that cross
    Where my Redeemer loved and died;
    Her noblest life my spirit draws   [side.
    From His dear wounds, and bleeding

THE LORD'S SUPPER.

2 I would forever speak His name
   In sounds to mortal ears unknown;
With angels join to praise the Lamb,
   And worship at His Father's throne.
Rev. Isaac Watts. (1674—1748.) 1709. ab.

891   *"This do in Remembrance of Me."*   L. M.
               Luke xxii. 19.

1 DRAW near, O Holy Dove, draw near,
   With peace and gladness on Thy wing;
Reveal the Saviour's presence here,
   And light, and life, and comfort bring.

2 "Eat, O my friends, drink, O beloved!"
   We hear the Master's voice exclaim:
Our hearts with new desire are moved,
   And kindled with a heavenly flame.

3 No room for doubt, no room for dread,
   Nor tears, nor groans, nor anxious sighs;
We do not mourn a Saviour dead,
   But hail Him living in the skies.

4 While this we do, remembering Thee,
   Dear Saviour, let our graces prove
We have Thy blessed company,
   Thy banner over us is love.
Rev. Aaron Roberts Wolfe. (1821—) 1852.

892   *"Bid us go in Peace."*   7, 6.

1 LAMB of God, whose bleeding love
   We now recall to mind,
Send the answer from above,
   And let us mercy find;
Think on us who think on Thee;
   Every struggling soul release;
O remember Calvary,
   And bid us go in peace.

2 By Thine agonizing pain
   And bloody sweat, we pray,
By Thy dying love to man,
   Take all our sins away;
Burst our bonds and set us free,
   From iniquity release;
O remember Calvary,
   And bid us go in peace.

3 Let Thy blood, by faith applied,
   The sinner's pardon seal;
Speak us freely justified,
   And all our sickness heal;
By Thy passion on the tree,
   Let our griefs and troubles cease;
O remember Calvary,
   And bid us go in peace.
Rev. Charles Wesley. (1708—1788.) 1745. ab. and sl. alt.

893   *"Bread of the World."*   9, 8.

1 BREAD of the world, in mercy broken,
   Wine of the soul, in mercy shed,
By whom the words of life were spoken,
   And in whose death our sins are dead;

2 Look on the heart by sorrow broken,
   Look on the tears by sinners shed;
And be Thy feast to us the token
   That by Thy grace our souls are fed.
Bp. Reginald Heber. (1783—1826.) 1827.

894   *"Ermuntert euch, ihr Frommen."*   7, 6.

1 REJOICE, rejoice, believers,
   And let your lights appear;
The evening is advancing,
   And darker night is near.
The Bridegroom is arising,
   And soon He will draw nigh:
Up, pray, and watch, and wrestle,
   At midnight comes the cry.

2 See that your lamps are burning,
   Replenish them with oil;
Look now for your salvation,
   The end of sin and toil.
The watchers on the mountain
   Proclaim the Bridegroom near,
Go meet Him as He cometh,
   With hallelujahs clear.

3 O wise and holy virgins,
   Now raise your voices higher,
Till, in your jubilations
   Ye meet the angel choir.
The marriage-feast is waiting,
   The gates wide open stand;
Up, up, ye heirs of glory,
   The Bridegroom is at hand.

4 Our hope and expectation,
   O Jesus, now appear;
Arise, thou Sun so longed for,
   O'er this benighted sphere.
With hearts and hands uplifted,
   We plead, O Lord, to see
The day of earth's redemption,
   And ever be with Thee.
Laurentius Laurenti. (1660—1722.)
Tr. by Miss Jane Borthwick. 1853. ab. and sl. alt.

THE LORD'S SUPPER.

395   "O Esca viatorum."   7, 6.

1 O BREAD to pilgrims given,
    O Food that angels eat,
  O Manna sent from heaven,
    For heaven-born natures meet:
  Give us, for Thee long pining,
    To eat till richly filled;
  Till, earth's delights resigning,
    Our every wish is stilled.

2 O Water, life bestowing,
    From out the Saviour's heart,
  A fountain purely flowing,
    A fount of love Thou art:
  O let us, freely tasting,
    Our burning thirst assuage;
  Thy sweetness, never wasting,
    Avails from age to age.

3 Jesus, this feast receiving,
    We Thee unseen adore;
  Thy faithful word believing,
    We take, and doubt no more:
  Give us, Thou true and loving,
    On earth to live in Thee;
  Then, death the veil removing,
    Thy glorious face to see.
            Unknown mediaeval Author.
        Tr. by Rev. Ray Palmer. (1808—) 1858.

396   "O Esca viatorum." 7, 7, 6, 7, 7, 8.

1 O BREAD of Life from heaven
    To saints and angels given,
        O Manna from above:
  The souls that hunger feed Thou,
  The hearts that seek Thee lead Thou,
        To Thy most sweet and tender love.

2 O Fount of grace redeeming,
  O River ever streaming
        From Jesus' wounded side:
  Come Thou, Thyself bestowing
  On thirsting souls, and flowing
        Till all their wants are satisfied.

3 Jesus, this feast receiving,
  Thy word of truth believing,
        We Thee unseen adore;
  Grant, when our race is ended,
  That we, to heaven ascended,
        May see Thy glory ever more.
            Unknown mediaeval Author.
        Tr. by Rev. Philip Schaff. (1819—) 1869, 1873.

897   "Till He come."   7. 6l.
                1 Cor. xi. 26.

1 TILL He come, O let the words
  Linger on the trembling chords:
  Let the little while between
  In their golden light be seen;
  Let us think how heaven and home
  Lie beyond that, *Till He come*.

2 When the weary ones we love
  Enter on their rest above,
  Seems the earth so poor and vast,
  All our life-joy overcast?
  Hush, be every murmur dumb:
  It is only, *Till He come*.

3 See, the feast of love is spread,
  Drink the wine, and break the bread:
  Sweet memorials,—till The Lord
  Call us round His heavenly board;
  Some from earth, from glory some,
  Severed only, *Till He come*.
        Rev. Edward Henry Bickersteth. (1825—) 1861. ab.

898   "Bread of Heaven."   7. 6l.

1 BREAD of heaven, on Thee I feed,
  For Thy flesh is meat indeed;
  Ever may my soul be fed
  With this true and living bread;
  Day by day with strength supplied,
  Through the life of Him who died.

2 Vine of heaven, Thy blood supplies
  This blest cup of sacrifice;
  'Tis Thy wounds my healing give;
  To Thy cross I look and live.
  Thou my life, O let me be
  Rooted, grafted, built on Thee.
            Josiah Conder (1789—1855.) 1824.

899   "Ad regias Agni dapes."   7.

1 AT the Lamb's high feast we sing
  Praise to our victorious King,
  Who hath washed us in the tide,
  Flowing from His pierced side.

2 Praise we Him, whose love divine
  Gives His sacred blood for wine,
  Gives His body for the feast:
  Christ the Victim, Christ the Priest.

3 Where the paschal blood is poured,
  Death's dark angel sheathes his sword;
  Israel's hosts triumphant go
  Through the wave that drowns the foe.

4 Praise we Christ, whose blood was shed,
   Paschal Victim, paschal Bread;
   With sincerity and love,
   Eat we manna from above.

5 Mighty Victim from the sky,
   Hell's fierce powers beneath Thee lie;
   Thou hast conquered in the fight,
   Thou has brought us life and light.

6 Hymns of glory and of praise,
   Risen Lord, to Thee we raise;
   Holy Father, praise to Thee,
   With the Spirit, ever be!
   Roman Breviary.
   Tr. by Robert Campbell. (—1868.) 1850.

900 *"To him that overcometh."*
Rev. iii. 21.

1 JESUS, once for sinners slain,
   From the dead was raised again;
   And in heaven is now set down
   With his Father in His throne.

2 There He reigns a King supreme;
   We shall also reign with Him:
   Feeble souls, be not dismayed,
   Trust in His almighty aid.

3 He has made an end of sin,
   And His blood has washed us clean:
   Fear not, He is ever near,
   Now, e'en now, He's with us here.

4 Thus assembling, we by faith,
   Till He come, show forth His death:
   Of His body bread's the sign,
   And we drink His blood in wine.

5 Saints on earth with saints above
   Celebrate His dying love;
   And let every ransomed soul
   Sound His praise from pole to pole.
   Rev. Joseph Hart. (1712—1768.) 1762. ab.

901 *At the Table.* C. M.

1 How sweet and awful is the place,
   With Christ within the doors,
   While everlasting love displays
   The choicest of her stores.

2 While all our hearts, and all our songs,
   Join to admire the feast,
   Each of us cry, with thankful tongues,
   "Lord, why was I a guest?"

3 "Why was I made to hear Thy voice,
   And enter while there's room,
   When thousands make a wretched choice,
   And rather starve than come?"

4 'Twas the same love that spread the feast,
   That sweetly forced us in;
   Else we had still refused to taste,
   And perished in our sin.

5 Pity the nations, O our God;
   Constrain the earth to come;
   Send Thy victorious word abroad,
   And bring the strangers home.

6 We long to see Thy churches full,
   That all the chosen race
   May, with one voice, and heart, and soul,
   Sing Thy redeeming grace.
   Rev. Isaac Watts. (1674—1748.) 1709.

902 *The Farewell.* C. M.
Matt. xxvi. 29.

1 THE hour is come; the feast is spread;
   Behold My body given;
   Behold My life-blood freely shed
   To ransom souls for heaven.

2 When of this cup I drink again,
   In glory and with you,
   No tears its perfect joy shall stain,
   A joy forever new.

3 Ere then ten thousand thousand times
   My table shall be spread,
   And countless souls in distant climes
   Be comforted and fed.

4 Grace, mercy, peace, be multiplied
   To those who commune there;
   While seated by My Father's side
   Their mansion I prepare.

5 But now these lips a different cup
   For you must taste and drain,
   And unrepiningly drink up
   The dregs of bitter pain.

6 The griefs ye know not that are Mine,
   Nor yet My glories see;
   But break the bread and drink the wine,
   And thus remember Me.
   Rev. Edward Henry Bickersteth. (1825—) 1870.

THE LORD'S SUPPER.

903 *The Body and Blood of Christ.* C. M.

1 HERE at Thy table, Lord, we meet,
  To feed on food divine;
Thy body is the bread we eat,
  Thy precious blood the wine.

2 He, that prepares this rich repast,
  Himself comes down, and dies;
And then invites us thus to feast
  Upon the sacrifice.

3 Sure, there was never love so free,
  Dear Saviour, so divine;
Well Thou may'st claim that heart of me,
  Which owes so much to Thine.
Rev. Samuel Stennett. (1727—1795.) 1787. ab.

904 *Grateful and tender Remembrance.* C. M.

1 IF human kindness meets return,
  And owns the grateful tie;
If tender thoughts within us burn,
  To feel a friend is nigh;

2 O shall not warmer accents tell
  The gratitude we owe
To Him, who died, our fears to quell,
  Our more than orphan's woe?

3 While yet His anguished soul surveyed
  Those pangs He would not flee,
What love His latest words displayed,
  "Meet, and remember Me."

4 Remember Thee, Thy death, Thy shame,
  Our sinful hearts to share!
O memory, leave no other name
  But His recorded there.
Hon. and Rev. Gerard Thomas Noel. (1782—1851.) 1813.

905 *Remembrance Pledged.* C. M.

1 ACCORDING to Thy gracious word,
  In meek humility,
This will I do, my dying Lord,
  I will remember Thee.

2 Thy body, broken for my sake,
  My bread from heaven shall be;
Thy testamental cup I take,
  And thus remember Thee.

3 Gethsemane can I forget?
  Or there Thy conflict see,
Thine agony and bloody sweat,
  And not remember Thee?

4 When to the cross I turn mine eyes,
  And rest on Calvary,
O Lamb of God, my sacrifice,
  I must remember Thee:

5 Remember Thee and all Thy pains,
  And all Thy love to me;
Yea, while a breath, a pulse remains,
  Will I remember Thee.

6 And when these failing lips grow dumb,
  And mind and memory flee,
When Thou shalt in Thy kingdom come,
  Jesus, remember me.
James Montgomery. (1771—1854.) 1825.

906 *Prayer for constant Nourishment.* C. M.

1 SHEPHERD of souls, refresh and bless
  Thy chosen pilgrim flock,
With manna in the wilderness,
  With water from the rock.

2 Hungry and thirsty, faint and weak,
  As Thou when here below,
Our souls the joys celestial seek
  Which from Thy sorrows flow.

3 We would not live by bread alone,
  But by that word of grace,
In strength of which we travel on
  To our abiding place.

4 Be known to us in breaking bread,
  But do not then depart;
Saviour, abide with us, and spread
  Thy table in our heart.

5 Lord, sup with us in love divine;
  Thy body and Thy blood,
That living bread, that heavenly wine,
  Be our immortal food.
James Montgomery. 1825, 1849.

907 *In Remembrance of Christ.* 8, 7. D.

1 JESUS spreads His banner o'er us,
  Cheers our famished souls with food;
He the banquet spreads before us
  Of His mystic flesh and blood.
Precious banquet; bread of heaven;
  Wine of gladness, flowing free:
May we taste it, kindly given,
  In remembrance, Lord, of Thee.

2 In Thy holy incarnation,
  When the angels sang Thy birth;
 In Thy fasting and temptation;
 In Thy labors on the earth;
 In Thy trial, and rejection;
 In Thy sufferings on the tree;
 In Thy glorious resurrection;
  May we, Lord, remember Thee.
    Rev. Roswell Park. (1807—1869.) 1836.

908 *Showing the Lord's Death.* 8, 7. D.
  1 Cor. xi. 26.

1 WHILE in sweet communion feeding
  On this earthly bread and wine,
 Saviour, may we see Thee bleeding
  On the cross, to make us Thine.
 Now our eyes for ever closing
  To this fleeting world below,
 On Thy gentle breast reposing,
  Teach us, Lord, Thy grace to know.

2 Though unseen, be ever near us,
  With the still small voice of love;
 Whispering words of peace to cheer us,
  Every doubt and fear remove.
 Bring before us all the story
  Of Thy life and death of woe,
 And, with hopes of endless glory,
  Wean our hearts from all below.
    Sir Edward Denny. (1796—) 1839.

909 *"Closer than a Brother."* 8, 7. D.
  (Abridged form.)

1 ONE there is, above all others,
  Well deserves the name of Friend;
 His is love beyond a brother's,
  Costly, free, and knows no end.
 Which of all our friends, to save us,
  Could or would have shed his blood?
 But our Jesus died to have us
  Reconciled in Him to God.

2 When He lived on earth abased,
  Friend of sinners was His name;
 Now above all glory raised,
  He rejoices in the same.
 O for grace our hearts to soften;
  Teach us, Lord, at length to love;
 We, alas, forget too often
  What a Friend we have above.
    Rev. John Newton. (1725—1807.) 1779 ab.

910 *Giving the Heart.* 8, 7. D.

1 TAKE my heart, O Father, take it;
  Make and keep it all Thine own;
 Let Thy Spirit melt and break it,
  This proud heart of sin and stone.
 Father, make it pure and lowly,
  Fond of peace, and far from strife;
 Turning from the paths unholy
  Of this vain and sinful life.

2 Ever let Thy grace surround it;
  Strengthen it with power divine,
 Till Thy cords of love have bound it:
  Make it to be wholly Thine.
 May the blood of Jesus heal it,
  And its sins be all forgiven;
 Holy Spirit, take and seal it,
  Guide it in the path to heaven.
    Sabbath Hymn Book. 1858.

911 *"Igjennem Nat og Traengsel."* 8, 7. D.

1 THROUGH the night of doubt and sorrow,
  Onward goes the pilgrim band,
 Singing songs of expectation,
  Marching to the Promised Land.
 And before us through the darkness
  Gleaming clear the guiding Light;
 Brother clasps the hand of brother,
  And steps fearless through the night.

2 One the light of God's dear presence,
  Never in its work to fail,
 Which illumes the wild rough places
  Of this gloomy haunted vale.
 One the object of our journey,
  One the faith which never tires,
 One the earnest looking forward,
  One the hope our God inspires.

3 One the strain which mouths of thousands
  Lift as from the heart of one;
 One the conflict, one the peril,
  One the march in God begun,
 One the gladness of rejoicing
  On the Resurrection shore,
 With One Father o'er us shining
  In His love for evermore.

4 Go we onward, pilgrim brothers,
  Visit first the cross and grave,
 Where the cross its shadow flingeth,
  Where the boughs of cypress wave.

Then, a shaking as of earthquakes,
Then, a rending of the tomb,
Then, a scattering of all shadows,
And an end of toil and gloom.
  Bernhardt Severin Ingemann. (1789—1862.)
  Tr. by Rev. Sabine Baring Gould. (1834—) 1867.

912 *Prayer for Union.* 8, 7. D.

1 HAIL, Thou God of grace and glory,
   Who Thy name hast magnified,
 By redemption's wondrous story,
   By the Saviour crucified;
 Thanks to Thee for every blessing,
   Flowing from the Fount of love;
 Thanks for present good unceasing,
   And for hopes of bliss above.

2 Hear us, as thus bending lowly,
   Near Thy bright and burning throne,
 We invoke Thee, God most holy,
   Through Thy well-beloved Son;
 Send the baptism of Thy Spirit,
   Shed the pentecostal fire;
 Let us all Thy grace inherit,
   Waken, crown each good desire.

3 Bind Thy people, Lord, in union,
   With the sevenfold cord of love;
 Breathe a spirit of communion
   With the glorious hosts above;
 Let Thy work be seen progressing;
   Bow each heart, and bend each knee,
 Till the world, Thy truth possessing,
   Celebrates its jubilee.
     Rev. Thomas William Aveling. (1815—) 1844.

913 *"Knit together in Love."* C. M.
       Col. ii. 2.

1 OUR souls, by love together knit,
   Cemented, mixed in one,
 One hope, one heart, one mind, one voice,
   'T is heaven on earth begun.

2 Our hearts have often burned within,
   And glowed with sacred fire,
 While Jesus spoke, and fed and blessed,
   And filled th' enlarged desire.

3 The little cloud increases still,
   The heavens are big with rain;
 We haste to catch the teeming shower,
   And all its moisture drain.

4 A rill, a stream, a torrent flows;
   But pour a mighty flood:
 O sweep the nations, shake the earth,
   Till all proclaim Thee God.

5 And when Thou mak'st Thy jewels up,
   And sett'st Thy starry crown,
 When all Thy sparkling gems shall shine,
   Proclaimed by Thee Thine own;

6 May we, a little band of love,
   We sinners, saved by grace,
 From glory unto glory changed,
   Behold Thee face to face.
     Rev. William Edward Miller. (1766—1839.) 1800.

914 *"The golden Chain."* C. M.

1 How sweet, how heavenly is the sight,
   When those who love the Lord
 In one another's peace delight,
   And so fulfil His word.

2 When each can feel his brother's sigh,
   And with him bear a part:
 When sorrow flows from eye to eye,
   And joy from heart to heart;

3 When, free from envy, scorn, and pride,
   Our wishes all above,
 Each can his brother's failings hide,
   And show a brother's love;

4 When love, in one delightful stream,
   Through every bosom flows;
 When union sweet, and dear esteem,
   In every action glows.

5 Love is the golden chain that binds
   The happy souls above;
 And he's an heir of heaven that finds
   His bosom glow with love.
     Rev. Joseph Swain. (1761—1796.) 1792.

915 *The Sacrament a Pledge of Heaven.* C. M.

1 HAPPY the souls to Jesus joined,
   And saved by grace alone;
 Walking in all Thy ways, we find
   Our heaven on earth begun.

2 The Church triumphant in Thy love,
   Their mighty joys we know;
 They sing the Lamb in hymns above,
   And we in hymns below.

3 Thee, in Thy glorious realm, they praise,
   And bow before Thy throne;
   We, in the kingdom of Thy grace:
   The kingdoms are but one.

4 The holy to the holiest leads;
   From hence our spirits rise;
   And he that in Thy statutes treads
   Shall meet Thee in the skies.
        Rev. Charles Wesley. (1708—1788.) 1745.

916   *One Church, one Army.*   C. M.

1 COME, let us join our friends above
   That have obtained the prize,
   And on the eagle wings of love,
   To joy celestial rise.

2 Let saints below in concert sing
   With those to glory gone;
   For all the servants of our King
   In earth and heaven are one.

3 One family, we dwell in Him,
   One Church above, beneath,
   Though now divided by the stream,
   The narrow stream of death.

4 One army of the living God,
   To His command we bow;
   Part of the host have crossed the flood,
   And part are crossing now.

5 E'en now to their eternal home
   Some happy spirits fly;
   And we are to the margin come,
   And soon expect to die.

6 Dear Saviour, be our constant Guide;
   Then, when the word is given,
   Bid Jordan's narrow stream divide,
   And land us safe in heaven.
        Rev. Charles Wesley. 1759. ab. and alt.

917 *The Church militant learning the Church triumphant's Song.* C. M.

1 SING we the song of those who stand
   Around the eternal throne,
   Of every kindred, clime, and land,
   A multitude unknown.

2 Life's poor distinctions vanish here;
   To-day, the young, the old,
   Our Saviour and His flock appear
   One Shepherd and one fold.

3 Toil, trial, suffering, still await
   On earth the pilgrim-throng;
   Yet learn we, in our low estate,
   The Church triumphant's song.

4 "Worthy the Lamb for sinners slain,"
   Cry the redeemed above.
   "Blessing and honor to obtain,
   And everlasting love."

5 "Worthy the Lamb, on earth we sing,
   "Who died our souls to save;
   Henceforth, O Death, where is thy sting?
   Thy victory, O Grave?"

6 Then, hallelujah, power and praise
   To God in Christ be given;
   May all who now this anthem raise,
   Renew the strain in heaven.
        James Montgomery. (1771—1854.) 1825, 1853.

918   *At Parting.*   C. M.

1 BLEST be the dear, uniting love,
   That will not let us part;
   Our bodies may far off remove,
   We still are joined in heart.

2 Joined in one spirit to our Head,
   Where He appoints we go,
   And still in Jesus' footsteps tread,
   And do His work below.

3 Partakers of the Saviour's grace,
   The same in mind and heart,
   Nor joy, nor grief, nor time, nor place,
   Nor life, nor death can part.
        Rev. Charles Wesley. 1742. ab.

919   *"The Saints above."*   C. M.

1 GIVE me the wings of faith, to rise
   Within the veil, and see
   The saints above, how great their joys,
   How bright their glories be.

2 Once they were mourning here below,
   And wet their couch with tears;
   They wrestled hard, as we do now,
   With sins, and doubts, and fears.

3 I ask them, from whence their victory came?
   They, with united breath,
   Ascribe their conquest to the Lamb,
   Their triumph to His death.

THE COMMUNION OF SAINTS.

4 They marked the footsteps that He trod;
   His zeal inspired their breast;
   And following their incarnate God,
   Possess the promised rest.

5 Our glorious Leader claims our praise,
   For His own pattern given,
   While the long cloud of witnesses
   Show the same path to heaven.
        Rev. Isaac Watts. (1674—1748.) 1709.

920   *The ancient Worthies.*   C. M.

1 RISE, O my soul, pursue the path,
   By ancient worthies trod;
   Aspiring, view those holy men
   Who lived and walked with God.

2 Though dead, they speak in reason's ear,
   And in example live;
   Their faith, and hope, and mighty deeds,
   Still fresh instruction give.

3 'T was through the Lamb's most precious
   They conquered every foe;   [blood,
   And to His power and matchless grace
   Their crowns and honors owe.

4 Lord, may I ever keep in view
   The patterns Thou hast given;
   And ne'er forsake the blessed path
   Which led them safe to heaven.
        Rev. John Needham 1768.

921   *The March to Canaan.*   C. M.

1 FORTH to the Land of Promise bound,
   Our desert path we tread;
   God's fiery pillar for our guide,
   His Captain at our head.

2 E'en now we faintly trace the hills,
   And catch their distant blue;
   And the bright city's gleaming spires
   Rise dimly on our view.

3 Soon, when the desert shall be crossed,
   The flood of death past o'er,
   Our pilgrim hosts shall safely land
   On Canaan's peaceful shore.

4 There love shall have its perfect work,
   And prayer be lost in praise;
   And all the servants of our God
   Their endless anthems raise.
        Rev. Henry Alford (1810—1871.) 1823

922   *The Dead in Christ.*   7. 6l.

1 THEY whose course on earth is o'er,
   Think they of their brethren more?
   They before the Throne who bow,
   Feel they for their brethren now?

2 Yea, the dead in Christ have still
   Part in all our joy and ill;
   Keeping all our steps in view,
   Guiding them, it may be, too.

3 We, by enemies distrest,
   They, in Paradise at rest;
   We the captives, they the freed,
   We and they are one indeed.

4 One in all we seek or shun;
   One, because our Lord is One;
   One in heart, and one in love:
   We below, and they above.
        Rev. John Mason Neale (1818—1866.) 1844.

923   *The Saints on Earth all one.*   7. 6l.
       (Second part of the preceding hymn.)

1 THOSE whom many a land divides,
   Many mountains, many tides,
   Have they with each other part?
   Have they fellowship in heart?

2 Each to each may be unknown,
   Wide apart their lots be thrown;
   Differing tongues their lips may speak,
   One be strong, and one be weak:

3 Yet in sacrament and prayer
   Each with other hath a share;
   Hath a share in tear and sigh,
   Watch, and fast, and litany.

4 With each other join they here
   In affliction, doubt, and fear;
   That hereafter they may be
   Joined, O Lord, in bliss with Thee.

5 So with them our hearts we raise,
   Share their work and join their praise;
   Rendering worship, thanks, and love,
   To the Trinity above.
        Rev. John Mason Neale. 1844.

924   *Brotherly Love.*   7. 6l.
       Ps. cxxxiii.

1 'TIS a pleasant thing to see
   Brethren in the Lord agree,
   Children of a God of love

THE COMMUNION OF SAINTS.

Live as they shall live above,
Acting each a Christian part,
One in lip, and one in heart.

2 As the precious ointment, shed
Upon Aaron's hallowed head,
Downward through his garments stole,
Spreading odor o'er the whole ;
So from our High Priest above
To His Church flows heavenly love.

3 Gently as the dews distil
Down on Zion's holy hill,
Dropping gladness where they fall,
Brightening and refreshing all ;
Such is Christian union, shed
Through the members from the Head.

4 Where divine affection lives,
There the Lord His blessing gives,
There His will on earth is done ;
There His heaven is half begun.
Lord, our great example prove,
Teach us all like Thee to love.
Rev. Henry Francis Lyte. (1793—1847.) 1834.

925 *Brotherly Love.* S. M.

1 BLEST be the tie that binds
Our hearts in Christian love :
The fellowship of kindred minds
Is like to that above.

2 Before our Father's throne
We pour our ardent prayers ;
Our fears, our hopes, our aims are one,
Our comforts and our cares.

3 We share our mutual woes ;
Our mutual burdens bear ;
And often for each other flows
The sympathizing tear.

4 When we asunder part,
It gives us inward pain ;
But we shall still be joined in heart,
And hope to meet again.

5 This glorious hope revives
Our courage by the way ;
While each in expectation lives,
And longs to see the day.

6 From sorrow, toil, and pain,
And sin we shall be free ;
And perfect love and friendship reign
Through all eternity.
Rev. John Fawcett. (1739—1817.) 1772.

926 *Grateful Commemoration.* S. M.

1 FOR all Thy saints, O Lord,
Who strove in Thee to live,
Who followed Thee, obeyed, adored,
Our grateful hymn receive.

2 For all Thy saints, O Lord,
Accept our thankful cry,
Who counted Thee their great reward,
And strove in Thee to die.

3 They all in life and death,
With Thee, their Lord, in view,
Learned from Thy Holy Spirit's breath
To suffer and to do.

4 For this Thy name we bless,
And humbly pray that we
May follow them in holiness,
And live and die in Thee.
Bp. Richard Mant. (1776—1848.) 1837. ab.

927 *Cross and Crown.* S. M.

1 O WHAT, if we are Christ's,
Is earthly shame or loss ?
Bright shall the crown of glory be,
When we have borne the cross.

2 Keen was the trial once,
Bitter the cup of woe,
When martyred saints, baptized in blood,
Christ's sufferings shared below.

3 Bright is their glory now,
Boundless their joy above,
Where, on the bosom of their God,
They rest in perfect love.

4 Lord, may that grace be ours,
Like them in faith to bear
All that of sorrow, grief, or pain
May be our portion here.

5 Enough, if Thou at last
The word of blessing give,
And let us rest beneath Thy feet,
Where saints and angels live.
Rev. Sir Henry Williams Baker. (1821—) 1852.

928 The Fellowship of all the Saints. 10.

1 FOR all the saints, who from their labors rest,
Who Thee by faith before the world confest,
Thy name, O Jesus, be forever blest,
    Alleluia.

2 Thou wast their Rock, their Fortress and their Light;
Thou, Lord, their Captain in the well-fought fight;
Thou, in the darkness drear, their Light of light.
    Alleluia.

3 O may Thy soldiers, faithful, true, and bold,
Fight as the saints who nobly fought of old,
And win with them the victors' crown of gold.
    Alleluia.

4 O blest Communion, fellowship divine!
We feebly struggle, they in glory shine;
Yet all are one in Thee, for all are Thine.
    Alleluia.

5 And when the strife is fierce, the warfare long,
Steals on the ear the distant triumph-song,
And hearts are brave again, and arms are strong.
    Alleluia.

6 The golden evening brightens in the west;
Soon, soon to faithful warriors comes the rest;
Sweet is the calm of Paradise the blest.
    Alleluia.

7 But lo, there breaks a yet more glorious day;
The saints triumphant rise in bright array:
The King of Glory passes on His way.
    Alleluia.

8 From earth's wide bounds, from ocean's farthest coast,
Through gates of pearl streams in the countless host,
Singing to Father, Son, and Holy Ghost.
    Alleluia.

Rev. William Walsham How. (—1823.) 1854.

929 Christ the Corner-Stone. 7, 6. D.
Eph. ii. 20.

1 THE Church's one foundation
Is Jesus Christ her Lord;
She is His new creation
By water and the word:
From heaven He came and sought her
To be His holy bride;
With His own blood He bought her,
And for her life He died.

2 Elect from every nation,
Yet one o'er all the earth,
Her charter of salvation
One Lord, one faith, one birth;
One holy Name she blesses,
Partakes one holy food,
And to one hope she presses,
With every grace endued.

3 Though with a scornful wonder,
Men see her sore opprest,
By schisms rent asunder,
By heresies distrest;
Yet saints their watch are keeping,
Their cry goes up, "How long?"
And soon the night of weeping
Shall be the morn of song.

4 'Mid toil and tribulation,
And tumult of her war,
She waits the consummation
Of peace for evermore;
Till with the vision glorious
Her longing eyes are blest,
And the great Church victorious
Shall be the Church at rest.

5 Yet she on earth hath union
With God the Three in One,
And mystic sweet communion
With those whose rest is won:
O happy ones and holy!
Lord, give us grace that we
Like them, the meek and lowly,
On high may dwell with Thee.

Rev. Samuel John Stone. 1866. ab. and sl. alt.

930 "And there shall be one Fold and one Shepherd." 7, 6. D.
John x. 16.

1 AND is the time approaching,
By prophets long foretold,
When all shall dwell together,
One Shepherd and one fold?

  Shall every idol perish,
   To moles and bats be thrown,
  And every prayer be offered
   To God in Christ alone?

2 Shall Jew and Gentile, meeting
  From many a distant shore,
  Around one altar kneeling,
   One common Lord adore?
  Shall all that now divides us
   Remove and pass away,
  Like shadows of the morning
   Before the blaze of day?

3 Shall all that now unites us
  More sweet and lasting prove,
  A closer bond of union,
   In a blest land of love?
  Shall war be learned no longer,
   Shall strife and tumult cease,
  All earth His blessed kingdom,
   The Lord and Prince of Peace?

4 O long-expected dawning,
  Come with thy cheering ray:
  When shall the morning brighten,
   The shadows flee away?
  O sweet anticipation,
   It cheers the watchers on,
  To pray, and hope, and labor,
   Till the dark night be gone.
     Miss Jane Borthwick. 1863.

931   *"The Day which the Lord hath made."*   7, 6.
    Ps. cxviii. 24.

1 O DAY of rest and gladness,
  O day of joy and light,
  O balm of care and sadness,
   Most beautiful, most bright:
  On thee, the high and lowly,
   Through ages joined in tune,
  Sing holy, holy, holy,
   To the Great God Triune.

2 On thee, at the creation,
  The light first had its birth;
  On thee, for our salvation,
   Christ rose from depths of earth;
  On thee our Lord, victorious,
   The Spirit sent from heaven,
  And thus on thee, most glorious,
   A triple light was given.

3 To-day on weary nations
  The heavenly manna falls;
  To holy convocations
   The silver trumpet calls,
  Where gospel light is glowing
   With pure and radiant beams,
  And living water flowing
   With soul-refreshing streams.

4 New graces ever gaining
  From this our day of rest,
  We reach the rest remaining
   To spirits of the blest;
  To Holy Ghost be praises,
   To Father, and to Son;
  The Church her voice upraises
   To Thee, blest Three in One.
  Bp. Christopher Wordsworth. (1807—) 1862. ab. and alt.

932   *Delighting in God's Day.*   7, 6.

1 THY holy day's returning
  Our hearts exult to see;
  And with devotion burning,
   Ascend, O God, to Thee.
  To-day with purest pleasure,
   Our thoughts from earth withdraw;
  We search for heavenly treasure,
   We learn Thy holy law.

2 We join to sing Thy praises,
  Lord of the Sabbath day;
  Each voice in gladness raises
   Its loudest, sweetest lay.
  Thy richest mercies sharing,
   Inspire us with Thy love,
  By grace our souls preparing
   For nobler praise above.
     Rev. Ray Palmer. (1808—) 1834.

933   Ἀναστάσεως ἡμέρα.   7, 6.

1 THE day of resurrection,
  Earth, tell it out abroad:
  The Passover of gladness,
   The Passover of God.
  From death to life eternal,
   From earth unto the sky,
  Our Christ hath brought us over,
   With hymns of victory.

2 Our hearts be pure from evil,
  That we may see aright
  The Lord in rays eternal
   Of resurrection-light;

And, listening to His accents,
  May hear, so calm and plain,
His own "All hail!" and, hearing,
  May raise the victor-strain.

3 Now let the heavens be joyful;
  Let earth her song begin;
Let the round world keep triumph,
  And all that is therein;
Invisible and visible,
  Their notes let all things blend,
For Christ the Lord hath risen,
  Our Joy that hath no end.
            John of Damascus. (—c. 780.)
  Tr. by Rev. John Mason Neale. (1818—1866.) 1862.

934 *The Lord's Day welcomed.* S. M.

1 WELCOME, sweet day of rest,
  That saw the Lord arise;
Welcome to this reviving breast,
  And these rejoicing eyes.

2 The King Himself comes near,
  And feasts His saints to-day;
Here we may sit, and see Him here,
  And love, and praise, and pray.

3 One day amidst the place
  Where my dear God hath been,
Is sweeter than ten thousand days
  Of pleasurable sin.

4 My willing soul would stay
  In such a frame as this,
And sit, and sing herself away
  To everlasting bliss.
            Rev. Isaac Watts. (1674—1748.) 1709.

935 *The Sweetness of the Sabbath.* S. M.
              Ps. xcii.

1 SWEET is the work, O Lord,
  Thy glorious acts to sing,
To praise Thy name, and hear Thy word,
  And grateful offerings bring.

2 Sweet, at the dawning light,
  Thy boundless love to tell;
And, when approach the shades of night,
  Still on the theme to dwell.

3 Sweet, on this day of rest,
  To join in heart and voice
With those who love and serve Thee best,
  And in Thy name rejoice.

4 To songs of praise and joy
  Be every Sabbath given,
That such may be our blest employ
  Eternally in heaven.
            Miss Harriet Auber. (1773—1862.) 1829. alt.

936 *Given in Mercy to our Fathers.* S. M.
              Ps. lxxxi.

1 SING to the Lord, our Might,
  With holy fervor sing;
Let hearts and instruments unite
  To praise our heavenly King.

2 This is His holy house,
  And this His festal day,
When He accepts the humblest vows
  That we sincerely pay.

3 The Sabbath to our sires
  In mercy first was given;
The Church her Sabbaths still requires
  To speed her on to heaven.

4 We still, like them of old,
  Are in the wilderness;
And God is still as near His fold,
  To pity and to bless.

5 Then let us open wide
  Our hearts for Him to fill;
And He that Israel then supplied,
  Will help His Israel still.
            Rev. Henry Francis Lyte. (1793—1847.) 1834.

937 *The Pleasures of Worship.* S. M.

1 HOW charming is the place,
  Where my Redeemer God
Unveils the beauties of His face,
  And sheds His love abroad.

2 Not the fair palaces,
  To which the great resort,
Are once to be compared with this,
  Where Jesus holds His court.

3 Here, on the mercy-seat,
  With radiant glory crowned,
Our joyful eyes behold Him sit,
  And smile on all around.

4 To Him their prayers and cries
  Each humble soul presents:
He listens to their broken sighs,
  And grants them all their wants.

THE LORD'S DAY AND WORSHIP.

5 To them His sovereign will
   He graciously imparts;
   And in return accepts, with smiles,
   The tribute of their hearts.

6 Give me, O Lord, a place
   Within Thy blest abode,
   Among the children of Thy grace,
   The servants of my God.
   Rev. Samuel Stennett. (1727—1795.) 1778.

938 *God's Sabbath.* S. M.

1 HAIL to the Sabbath day:
   The day divinely given;
   When men to God their homage pay,
   And earth draws near to heaven.

2 Lord, in this sacred hour
   Within Thy courts we bend,
   And bless Thy love, and own Thy power,
   Our Father and our Friend.

3 But Thou art not alone
   In courts by mortals trod;
   Nor only is the day Thine own
   When man draws near to God.

4 Thy temple is the arch
   Of yon unmeasured sky;
   Thy Sabbath, the stupendous march
   Of grand eternity.

5 Lord, may that holier day
   Dawn on Thy servants' sight;
   And purer worship may we pay
   In heaven's unclouded light.
   Rev. Stephen Greenleaf Bulfinch. (1809—1870.) 1832.

939 *The Lord's Day.* S. M.
         Ps. cxviii.

1 SEE what a living stone
   The builders did refuse;
   Yet God has built His Church thereon,
   In spite of envious Jews.

2 The scribe and angry priest
   Reject Thine only Son;
   Yet on this rock shall Zion rest
   As the chief corner-stone.

3 The work, O Lord, is Thine,
   And wondrous in our eyes;
   This day declares it all divine,
   This day did Jesus rise.

4 This is the glorious day
   That our Redeemer made:
   Let us rejoice, and sing, and pray,
   Let all the Church be glad.

5 Hosanna to the King
   Of David's royal blood:
   Bless Him, ye saints, He comes to bring
   Salvation from your God.

6 We bless Thy holy word,
   Which all this grace displays;
   And offer on Thine altar, Lord,
   Our sacrifice of praise.
   Rev. Isaac Watts. (1674—1748.) 1719.

940 *The Day of holy Rest.* L. M.

1 ANOTHER six days' work is done,
   Another Sabbath is begun:
   Return my soul, enjoy thy rest,
   Improve the day thy God hath blest.

2 Come, bless the Lord, whose love assigns
   So sweet a rest to wearied minds;
   Provides an antepast of heaven,
   And gives this day the food of seven.

3 O that our thoughts and thanks may rise,
   As grateful incense, to the skies;
   And draw from heaven that sweet repose,
   Which none but he that feels it knows.

4 This heavenly calm within the breast
   Is the dear pledge of glorious rest,
   Which for the Church of God remains,
   The end of cares, the end of pains.

5 In holy duties let the day,
   In holy pleasures, pass away;
   How sweet a Sabbath thus to spend,
   In hope of one that ne'er shall end.
   Rev. Joseph Stennett. (1663—1713.) 1732. ab. and much alt.

941 *"Morning of Hope."* L. M.

1 HAIL, morning known among the blest,
   Morning of hope, and joy, and love,
   Of heavenly peace, and holy rest,
   Pledge of the endless rest above!

2 Blest be the Father of our Lord,
   Who from the dead hath brought His Son;
   Hope to the lost was then restored,
   And everlasting glory won.

THE LORD'S DAY AND WORSHIP.

3 Mercy looked down, with smiling eye,
  When our Immanuel left the dead;
  Faith marked His bright ascent on high;
  And hope, with gladness, raised her head.

4 Descend, O Spirit of the Lord:
  Thy fire to every bosom bring;
  Then shall our ardent hearts accord,
  And teach our lips God's praise to sing.
  Rev. Ralph Wardlaw. (1779—1853.) 1817. ab.

942 *Delight in Worship.* L. M.

1 FAR from my thoughts, vain world, be gone;
  Let my religious hours alone;
  Fain would mine eyes my Saviour see:
  I wait a visit, Lord, from Thee.

2 My heart grows warm with holy fire,
  And kindles with a pure desire;
  Come, my dear Jesus, from above,
  And feed my soul with heavenly love.

3 Blest Jesus, what delicious fare,
  How sweet Thine entertainments are:
  Never did angels taste above
  Redeeming grace, and dying love.

4 Hail, great Immanuel, all-divine,
  In Thee Thy Father's glories shine:
  Thou brightest, sweetest, fairest One,
  That eyes have seen, or angels known.
  Rev. Isaac Watts. 1709. ab.

943 *The Peace of God.* L. M.

1 THE peace which God alone reveals,
  And by His word of grace imparts,
  Which only the believer feels,
  Direct, and keep, and cheer our hearts.

2 And may the holy Three in One,
  The Father, Word, and Comforter,
  Pour an abundant blessing down
  On every soul assembled here.
  Rev. John Newton. (1725—1807.) 1779. sl. alt.

944 *A Psalm for the Lord's Day.* L. M.
  Ps. xcii.

1 SWEET is the work, my God, my King,
  To praise Thy name, give thanks, and sing;
  To show Thy love by morning light,
  And talk of all Thy truth at night.

2 Sweet is the day of sacred rest;
  No mortal cares shall seize my breast;
  O may my heart in tune be found,
  Like David's harp of solemn sound.

3 My heart shall triumph in my Lord,
  And bless His works, and bless His word;
  Thy works of grace, how bright they shine,
  How deep Thy counsels, how divine.

4 Lord, I shall share a glorious part,
  When grace hath well refined my heart,
  And fresh supplies of joy are shed,
  Like holy oil, to cheer my head.

5 Then shall I see, and hear, and know
  All I desired or wished below;
  And every power find sweet employ,
  In that eternal world of joy.
  Rev. Isaac Watts. 1719. ab. and sl. alt.

945 *The precious Day.* L. M.

1 DEAR is the hallowed morn to me,
  When Sabbath bells awake the day,
  And, by their sacred minstrelsy,
  Call me from earthly cares away.

2 And dear to me the wingèd hour
  Spent in Thy hallowed courts, O Lord:
  To feel devotion's soothing power,
  And catch the manna of Thy word.

3 And dear to me the loud Amen
  Which echoes through the blest abode,
  Which swells, and sinks, and swells again,
  Dies on the walls, but lives to God.

4 Oft when the world, with iron hands,
  Has bound me in its six days' chain,
  This bursts them, like the strong man's bands,
  And lets my spirit loose again.

5 Then dear to me the Sabbath morn,
  The village bells, the shepherd's voice:
  These oft have found my heart forlorn,
  And always bid that heart rejoice.
  Rev. John William Cunningham. (1780—1861.) 1822. alt.

946 *"To-day, if ye will hear His Voice."* L. M.
  Ps. xcv.

1 COME, let our voices join to raise
  A sacred song of solemn praise:
  God is a sovereign King, rehearse
  His honors in exalted verse.

2 Come, let our souls address the Lord,
  Who framed our natures with His word;
  He is our Shepherd, we the sheep
  His mercy choose, His pastures keep.

3 Come, let us hear His voice to-day,
　The counsels of His love obey;
　Nor let our hardened hearts renew
　The sins and plagues that Israel knew.

4 Look back, my soul, with holy dread,
　And view those ancient rebels dead;
　Attend the offered grace to-day,
　Nor lose the blessing by delay.

5 Seize the kind promise, while it waits,
　And march to Zion's heavenly gates;
　Believe, and take the promised rest;
　Obey, and be for ever blest.
　　　　　Rev. Isaac Watts. (1674—1748.) 1719. ab.

947　　　*Sabbath Morning.*　　H. M.

1 WELCOME, delightful morn,
　　Thou day of sacred rest:
　I hail thy kind return;
　　Lord, make these moments blest;
　From the low train of mortal toys,
　I soar to reach immortal joys.

2 Now may the King descend,
　　And fill His throne of grace:
　Thy sceptre, Lord, extend,
　　While saints address Thy face;
　Let sinners feel Thy quickening word,
　And learn to know and fear the Lord.

3 Descend, celestial Dove,
　　With all Thy quickening powers,
　Disclose a Saviour's love,
　　And bless these sacred hours;
　Then shall my soul new life obtain,
　Nor Sabbaths e'er be spent in vain.
　　　　　Hayward. John Dobell's Collection. 1806.

948　　　*Sabbath Morning.*　　H. M.

1 AWAKE, our drowsy souls,
　　Shake off each slothful band;
　The wonders of this day
　　Our noblest songs demand:
　Auspicious morn, thy blissful rays
　Bright seraphs hail, in songs of praise.

2 At thy approaching dawn,
　　Reluctant death resigned
　The glorious Prince of life,
　　In dark domains confined:
　Th' angelic host around Him bends,
　And midst their shouts the God ascends.

3 All hail, triumphant Lord;
　　Heaven with hosannas rings;
　While earth, in humbler strains,
　　Thy praise responsive sings:
　"Worthy art Thou, who once wast slain,
　Through endless years to live and reign."

4 Gird on, great God, Thy sword,
　　Ascend Thy conquering car,
　While justice, truth, and love
　　Maintain the glorious war;
　Victorious, Thou Thy foes shalt tread,
　And sin and hell in triumph lead.

5 Make bare Thy potent arm,
　　And wing th' unerring dart,
　With salutary pangs,
　　To each rebellious heart;
　Then dying souls for life shall sue,
　Numerous as drops of morning dew.
　　　　　Miss Elizabeth Scott. 1763.
　　　　　John Dobell's Collection. 1806. ab.

949　　　*"Take up the Strain."*　　H. M.

1 SHALL hymns of grateful love
　　Through heaven's high arches ring,
　And all the hosts above
　　Their songs of triumph sing;
　And shall not we take up the strain,
　And send the echo back again?

2 Shall they adore the Lord,
　　Who bought them with His blood,
　And all the love record
　　That led them home to God;
　And shall not we take up the strain,
　And send the echo back again?

3 O spread the joyful sound,
　　The Saviour's love proclaim,
　And publish all around
　　Salvation through His name;
　Till all the world take up the strain,
　And send the echo back again.
　　　　　Rev. James J. Cummins. (—1867.) 1849. ab.

950　　*Longing for the House of God.*　H. M.
　　　　　Ps. lxxxiv.

1 LORD of the worlds above,
　　How pleasant and how fair
　The dwellings of Thy love,
　　Thine earthly temples are:
　To thine abode　│　With warm desires,
　My heart aspires,　│　To see my God.

2 The sparrow for her young
    With pleasure seeks a nest;
    And wandering swallows long
    To find their wonted rest:
My spirit faints | To rise and dwell
With equal zeal | Among Thy saints.

3 O happy souls that pray
    Where God appoints to hear;
    O happy men that pay
    Their constant service there:
They praise Thee still; | That love the way
And happy they | To Zion's hill.

4 They go from strength to strength,
    Through this dark vale of tears,
    Till each arrives at length,
    Till each in heaven appears:
O glorious seat, | Shall thither bring
When God our King | Our willing feet!
    Rev. Isaac Watts. 1719.

951 *Longing for the House of God.* H. M.
Ps. lxxxiv.

1 TO spend one sacred day,
    Where God and saints abide,
    Affords diviner joy
    Than thousand days beside:
Where God resorts, | To keep the door,
I love it more | Than shine in courts.

2 God is our sun and shield,
    Our light and our defence;
    With gifts His hands are filled,
    We draw our blessings thence:
He will bestow | Peculiar grace,
On Jacob's race | And glory too.

3 The Lord His people loves;
    His hand no good withholds
    From those His heart approves,
    From pure and pious souls:
Thrice happy he, | Whose spirit trusts
O God of hosts, | Alone in Thee.
    Rev. Isaac Watts. 1719.

952 *A general Song of Praise.* H. M.
Ps. c.

1 SING to the Lord most high;
    Let every land adore;
    With grateful voice make known
    His goodness and His power.
Let cheerful songs | And let His praise
Declare His ways, | Inspire your tongues.

2 Enter His courts with joy;
    With fear address the Lord;
    He formed us with His hand,
    And quickened by His word.
With wide command | O'er every sea,
He spreads His sway | And every land.

3 His hands provide our food,
    And every blessing give;
    We feed upon His care,
    And in His pastures live.
With cheerful songs | And let His praise
Declare His ways, | Inspire our tongues.

4 Good is the Lord our God,
    His truth and mercy sure;
    While earth and heaven shall last,
    His promises endure.
With bounteous hand | O'er every sea,
He spreads His sway | And every land.
    Rev. Timothy Dwight. (1752–1817.) 1800.

953 *"Safely, through another Week."* 7. 6 l.

1 SAFELY, through another week,
    God has brought us on our way;
    Let us now a blessing seek,
    Waiting in His courts to-day:
Day of all the week the best,
Emblem of eternal rest.

2 While we pray for pardoning grace,
    Through the dear Redeemer's name;
    Show Thy reconciled face,
    Take away our sin and shame;
From our worldly cares set free,
May we rest this day in Thee.

3 Here we come Thy name to praise;
    May we feel Thy presence near:
    May Thy glory meet our eyes,
    While we in Thy house appear:
Here afford us, Lord, a taste
Of our everlasting feast.

4 May Thy gospel's joyful sound
    Conquer sinners, comfort saints;
    Make the fruits of grace abound,
    Bring relief for all complaints:
Thus may all our Sabbaths prove,
Till we join the Church above.
    Rev. John Newton. (1725–1807.) 1779.

954 *Creator, Saviour, Comforter.* 7. 6 l.

1 GREAT Creator, who this day
   From Thy perfect work didst rest,
 By the souls that own Thy sway
   Hallowed be its hours and blest:
 Cares of earth aside be thrown,
 This day given to heaven alone.

2 Saviour, who this day didst break
   The dark prison of the tomb,
 Bid my slumbering soul awake,
   Shine through all its sin and gloom:
 Let me, from my bonds set free,
 Rise from sin, and live to Thee.

3 Blessed Spirit, Comforter,
   Sent this day from Christ on high,
 Lord, on me Thy gifts confer,
   Cleanse, illumine, sanctify;
 All Thine influence shed abroad,
 Lead me to the truth of God.
      Mrs. Julia Anne Elliott. (—1841.) 1835.

955 *Rest here, and above.* 7. 6 l.

1 HAIL, thou bright and sacred morn,
   Risen with gladness in thy beams:
 Light, which not of earth is born,
   From thy dawn in glory streams;
 Airs of heaven are breathed around,
 And each place is holy ground.

2 Sad and weary were our way,
   Fainting oft beneath our load,
 But for thee, thou blessed day,
   Resting-place on life's rough road:
 Here flow forth the streams of grace,
 Strengthened hence we run our race.

3 Soon, too soon, the sweet repose
   Of this day of God will cease;
 Soon this glimpse of heaven will close,
   Vanish soon the hours of peace;
 Soon return the toil, the strife,
 All the weariness of life.

4 But the rest which yet remains
   For Thy people, Lord, above,
 Knows nor change, nor fears, nor pains,
   Endless as their Saviour's love:
 O may every Sabbath here
 Bring us to that rest more near.
      Mrs. Julia Anne Elliott. 1835.

956 *Prayer for Light and Enlargement.* 7. 6 l.
      Ps. lxvii.

1 GOD of mercy, God of grace,
   Show the brightness of Thy face;
 Shine upon us, Saviour, shine,
   Fill Thy Church with light divine;
 And Thy saving health extend
 Unto earth's remotest end.

2 Let the people praise Thee, Lord,
   Be by all that live adored:
 Let the nations shout and sing,
   Glory to their Saviour-King;
 At Thy feet their tributes pay,
 And Thy holy will obey.

3 Let the people praise Thee, Lord,
   Earth shall then her fruits afford:
 God to man His blessing give,
   Man to God devoted live;
 All below, and all above,
 One in joy, and light, and love.
      Rev. Henry Francis Lyte. (1793—1847.) 1834.

957 *"Morgenglanz der Ewigkeit."* 7. 6 l.
      Ps. v. 3.

1 JESUS, Sun of righteousness,
   Brightest beam of love divine,
 With the early morning rays,
   Do Thou on our darkness shine,
 And dispel, with purest light,
 All our long and gloomy night.

2 Like the sun's reviving ray,
   May Thy love, with tender glow,
 All our coldness melt away,
   Warm and cheer us, forth to go;
 Gladly serve Thee and obey,
 All our life's short earthly day.

3 Thou, our only hope and guide,
   Never leave us nor forsake;
 Keep us ever at Thy side,
   Till th' eternal morning break;
 Moving on to Zion's hill,
 Onward, upward, homeward still.
      Christian Knorr von Rosenroth. 1664.
      Tr. by Miss Jane Borthwick, ab. and alt.

958 *Morning Hymn.* 7. 6 l.

1 CHRIST, whose glory fills the skies,
   Christ, the true, the only Light,
 Sun of righteousness, arise,
   Triumph o'er the shades of night:

Dayspring from on high, be near;
Daystar, in my heart appear.

2 Dark and cheerless is the morn,
  Unaccompanied by Thee;
  Joyless is the day's return,
  Till Thy mercy's beams I see:
  Till they inward light impart,
  Glad my eyes, and warm my heart.

3 Visit then this soul of mine,
  Pierce the gloom of sin and grief;
  Fill me, Radiancy divine,
  Scatter all my unbelief:
  More and more Thyself display,
  Shining to the perfect day.
        Rev. Charles Wesley. (1708—1788.) 1740.

959   *Cause Thy Face to shine.* 7. 61.
          Ps. lxvii.

1 On Thy Church, O Power divine,
  Cause Thy glorious face to shine;
  Till the nations, from afar,
  Hail her as their guiding star;
  Till her sons, from zone to zone,
  Make Thy great salvation known.

2 Then shall God, with lavish hand,
  Scatter blessings o'er the land;
  Earth shall yield her rich increase,
  Every breeze shall whisper peace,
  And the world's remotest bound
  With the voice of praise resound.
        Miss Harriet Auber. (1773—1862.) 1829.

960   *Going to Church.*   S. P. M.
          Ps. cxxii.

1 How pleased and blest was I,
  To hear the people cry,
  "Come, let us seek our God to-day!"
  Yes, with a cheerful zeal,
  We haste to Zion's hill,
  And there our vows and honors pay.

2 Zion, thrice happy place,
  Adorned with wondrous grace,
  And walls of strength embrace thee round:
  In thee our tribes appear,
  To pray, and praise, and hear
  The sacred gospel's joyful sound.

3 There David's greater Son
  Has fixed His royal throne;
  He sits for grace and judgment there.

He bids the saints be glad;
He makes the sinner sad;
And humble souls rejoice with fear.

4 May peace attend thy gate,
  And joy within thee wait,
  To bless the soul of every guest:
  The man that seeks thy peace,
  And wishes thine increase,
  A thousand blessings on him rest!

5 My tongue repeats her vows,
  "Peace to this sacred house!"
  For there my friends and kindred dwell;
  And since my glorious God
  Makes thee His blest abode,
  My soul shall ever love thee well.
        Rev. Isaac Watts. (1674—1748.) 1719.

961   *"Heaven begun below."*   S. P. M.

1 'Tis heaven begun below
  To hear Christ's praises flow
  In Zion, where His name is known:
  What will it be above
  To sing redeeming love,
  And cast our crowns before His throne!

2 When we adore Him there,
  We shall be void of fear,
  Nor faith, nor hope, nor patience need:
  Love will absorb us quite,
  Love, in the midst of light,
  On God's eternal love shall feed.

3 O what sweet company
  We then shall hear and see,
  What harmony will there abound,
  When souls unnumbered sing
  The praise of Zion's King,
  Nor one dissenting voice is found!

4 With everlasting joy,
  Such as will never cloy,
  We shall be filled, nor wish for more;
  Bright as meridian day,
  Calm as the evening ray,
  Full as a sea without a shore.

5 Till that blest period come,
  Zion shall be my home;
  And may I never thence remove,
  Till from the Church below
  To that on high I go,
  And there commune in perfect love.
        Rev. Joseph Swain. (1761—1796.) 1792. sl. alt.

962 "Speak, for Thy Servant heareth." 8, 7, 4.
1 Sam. iii. 10

1 IN Thy name, O Lord, assembling,
  We, Thy people, now draw near;
  Teach us to rejoice with trembling;
    Speak, and let Thy servants hear,
      Hear with meekness,
    Hear Thy word with godly fear.

2 While our days on earth are lengthened,
  May we give them, Lord, to Thee;
  Cheered by hope, and daily strengthened,
    May we run, nor weary be,
      Till Thy glory
    Without clouds in heaven we see.

3 There in worship purer, sweeter,
  Thee Thy people shall adore;
  Tasting of enjoyment greater
    Far than thought conceived before;
      Full enjoyment,
    Full, unmixed, and evermore.
      Rev. Thomas Kelly. (1769—1855.) 1815.

963 Dismission. 8, 7, 4.

1 LORD, dismiss us with Thy blessing,
  Fill our hearts with joy and peace;
  Let us each, Thy love possessing,
    Triumph in redeeming grace:
      O refresh us,
    Traveling through this wilderness.

2 Thanks we give, and adoration,
  For Thy gospel's joyful sound:
  May the fruits of Thy salvation
    In our hearts and lives abound;
      May Thy presence
    With us evermore be found.

3 So, whene'er the signal's given,
  Us from earth to call away,
  Borne on angels' wings to heaven,
    Glad the summons to obey,
      May we ever
    Reign with Christ in endless day.
      Hon. and Rev. Walter Shirley. (1725—1786.) 1774.

964 For the great Congregation. 8, 7, 4.
Hab. ii. 20

1 GOD is in His holy temple,
  All the earth, keep silence here;
  Worship Him in truth and spirit,
    Reverence Him with godly fear;
      Holy, holy,
    Lord of hosts, our Lord, appear.

2 God in Christ reveals His presence,
  Throned upon the mercy-seat:
  Saints, rejoice, and sinners, tremble;
    Each prepare his God to meet;
      Lowly, lowly
    Bow adoring at His feet.

3 Hail Him here with songs of praises,
  Him with prayers of faith surround;
  Hearken to His glorious gospel,
    While the preacher's lips expound;
      Blessed, blessed,
    They who know the joyful sound.
      James Montgomery. (1771—1854.) 1855. ab.

965 God giveth the Increase. 8, 7, 4.
1 Cor. iii. 7

1 COME, Thou soul-transforming Spirit,
  Bless the sower and the seed;
  Let each heart Thy grace inherit;
    Raise the weak, the hungry feed:
      From the gospel,
    Now supply Thy people's need.

2 O may all enjoy the blessing
  Which Thy word's designed to give;
  Let us all, Thy love possessing,
    Joyfully the truth receive;
      And for ever
    To Thy praise and glory live.
      Rev. Jonathan Evans. (1749–1809.) 1784.

966 "Most calm, most bright." C. M.

1 BLEST day of God, most calm, most bright,
    The first and best of days;
  The laborer's rest, the saints delight,
    A day of mirth and praise.

2 My Saviour's face did make thee shine,
    His rising did thee raise:
  This made thee heavenly and divine
    Beyond the common days.

3 The first-fruits do a blessing prove
    To all the sheaves behind;
  And they that do a Sabbath love
    A happy week shall find.

4 My Lord on thee His name did fix,
    Which makes thee rich and gay;
  Amid His golden candlesticks
    My Saviour walks this day.

THE LORD'S DAY AND WORSHIP.

5 This day must I fore God appear,
 For, Lord, the day is Thine:
 O let me spend it in Thy fear,
 Then shall the day be mine.
    Rev. John Mason. (—1694.) 1683.

967 *Yearning for Rest.* C. M.

1 WHEN the worn spirit wants repose,
 And sighs for God to seek,
 How sweet to hail the evening's close
 That ends the weary week.

2 How sweet will be the early dawn
 That opens on the sight,
 When first the soul-reviving morn
 Shall shed new rays of light.

3 Blest day, thine hours too soon will cease,
 Yet, while they gently roll,
 Breathe, heavenly Spirit, source of peace,
 A Sabbath o'er my soul.

4 When will my pilgrimage be done,
 The world's long week be o'er,
 That Sabbath dawn which needs no sun,
 That day which fades no more?
    James Edmeston. (1791—1867.) 1820.

968 *Sweet Rest.* C. M.

1 MY Lord, my Love, was crucified,
 He all the pains did bear;
 But in the sweetness of His rest
 He makes His servants share.

2 How sweetly rest Thy saints above
 Which in Thy bosom lie;
 The Church below doth rest in hope
 Of that felicity.

3 Thou, Lord, who daily feed'st Thy sheep,
 Mak'st them a weekly feast;
 Thy flocks meet in their several folds
 Upon this day of rest.

4 Welcome and dear unto my soul
 Are these sweet feasts of love;
 But what a Sabbath shall I keep
 When I shall rest above!

5 I bless Thy wise and wondrous love,
 Which binds us to be free;
 Which makes us leave our earthly snares,
 That we may come to Thee.

6 I come, I wait, I hear, I pray,
 Thy footsteps, Lord, I trace;
 I sing to think this is the way
 Unto my Saviour's face.
    Rev. John Mason. 1683. ab.

969 *"The Day the Lord hath made."* C. M.
     Ps. cxviii.

1 THIS is the day the Lord hath made,
 He calls the hours His own;
 Let heaven rejoice, let earth be glad,
 And praise surround the throne.

2 To-day He rose and left the dead,
 And Satan's empire fell;
 To-day the saints His triumphs spread,
 And all His wonders tell.

3 Hosanna to th' anointed King,
 To David's holy Son;
 Help us, O Lord, descend and bring
 Salvation from the throne.

4 Blest be the Lord, who comes to men
 With messages of grace;
 Who comes in God His Father's name,
 To save our sinful race.

5 Hosanna, in the highest strains
 The Church on earth can raise;
 The highest heavens, in which He reigns,
 Shall give Him nobler praise.
    Rev. Isaac Watts. (1674—1748.) 1719.

970 *"We hail the sacred Day."* C. M.
     Ps. cxxii.

1 WITH joy we hail the sacred day,
 Which God has called His own;
 With joy the summons we obey
 To worship at His throne.

2 Thy chosen temple, Lord, how fair,
 Where willing votaries throng,
 To breathe the humble, fervent prayer,
 And pour the choral song.

3 Spirit of grace, O deign to dwell
 Within Thy Church below;
 Make her in holiness excel,
 With pure devotion glow.

4 Let peace within her walls be found;
 Let all her sons unite,
 To spread with grateful zeal around
 Her clear and shining light.
    Miss Harriet Auber. (1773—1862.) 1829.

971 Christ's Triumph. C. M.

1 AGAIN the Lord of life and light
Awakes the kindling ray,
Unseals the eyelids of the morn,
And pours increasing day.

2 O what a night was that which wrapt
The heathen world in gloom;
O what a sun which broke this day
Triumphant from the tomb.

3 Ten thousand differing lips shall join
To hail this welcome morn,
Which scatters blessings from its wings
To nations yet unborn.

4 Jesus, the Friend of human-kind,
With strong compassion moved,
Descended like a pitying God,
To save the souls He loved.

5 And now His conquering chariot wheels
Ascend the lofty skies;
While, broke beneath His powerful cross,
Death's iron sceptre lies.

6 Exalted high at God's right hand,
The Lord of all below,
Through Him is pardoning love dispensed,
And boundless blessings flow.

Mrs. Anna Laetitia Barbauld. (1743—1825.) 1773; 1825. ab.

972 For the Lord's Day Morning. C. M.
Ps. v.

1 LORD, in the morning Thou shalt hear
My voice ascending high;
To Thee will I direct my prayer,
To Thee lift up mine eye:

2 Up to the hills, where Christ is gone
To plead for all His saints,
Presenting, at His Father's throne,
Our songs and our complaints.

3 Thou art a God, before whose sight
The wicked shall not stand;
Sinners shall ne'er be Thy delight,
Nor dwell at Thy right hand.

4 But to Thy house will I resort,
To taste Thy mercies there;
I will frequent Thy holy court,
And worship in Thy fear.

5 O may Thy Spirit guide my feet
In ways of righteousness;
Make every path of duty straight,
And plain before my face.

Rev. Isaac Watts. (1674—1748.) 1719.

973 The Resurrection of Christ. C. M.

1 BLEST morning, whose young dawning rays
Beheld our rising God;
That saw Him triumph o'er the dust,
And leave His dark abode.

2 In the cold prison of a tomb
The dead Redeemer lay,
Till the revolving skies had brought
The third, th' appointed day.

3 Hell and the grave unite their force
To hold our God, in vain;
The sleeping Conqueror arose,
And burst their feeble chain.

4 To Thy great name, almighty Lord,
These sacred hours we pay;
And loud hosannas shall proclaim
The triumph of the day.

5 Salvation, and immortal praise,
To our victorious King;
Let heaven and earth, and rocks and seas,
With glad hosannas ring.

Rev. Isaac Watts. 1709.

974 The Church our Delight and Safety. C. M.
Ps. xxvii.

1 THE Lord of glory is my light,
And my salvation too;
God is my strength, nor will I fear
What all my foes can do.

2 One privilege my heart desires:
O grant me an abode
Among the churches of Thy saints,
The temples of my God.

3 There shall I offer my requests,
And see Thy beauty still;
Shall hear Thy messages of love,
And there inquire Thy will.

4 When troubles rise, and storms appear,
There may His children hide;
God has a strong pavilion, where
He makes my soul abide.

5 Now shall my head be lifted high
   Above my foes around;
   And songs of joy and victory
   Within Thy temple sound.
   Rev. Isaac Watts. 1719.

975
Going to Church. C. M.
Ps. cxxii.

1 How did my heart rejoice to hear
   My friends devoutly say,
   In Zion let us all appear,
   And keep the solemn day!"

2 I love her gates, I love the road;
   The Church, adorned with grace,
   Stands like a palace built for God,
   To show His milder face.

3 Up to her courts, with joys unknown,
   The holy tribes repair;
   The Son of David holds His throne,
   And sits in judgment there.

4 He hears our praises, and complaints;
   And while His awful voice
   Divides the sinners from the saints,
   We tremble and rejoice.

5 Peace be within this sacred place,
   And joy a constant guest;
   With holy gifts and heavenly grace,
   Be her attendants blest.

6 My soul shall pray for Zion still,
   While life or breath remains;
   There my best friends, my kindred dwell,
   There God, my Saviour, reigns.
   Rev. Isaac Watts. 1719.

976
"To the Temple haste!" C. M.
Ps. cxxii.

1 O 'TWAS a joyful sound, to hear
   Our tribes devoutly say,
   "Up, Israel, to the temple haste,
   And keep your festal day!"

2 At Salem's courts we must appear,
   With our assembled powers,
   In strong and beauteous order ranged,
   Like her united towers.

3 O ever pray for Salem's peace;
   For they shall prosperous be,
   Thou holy City of our God,
   Who bear true love to thee.
   Tate and Brady 1696. ab. and sl. alt.

977
The Morning of a Lord's Day. C. M.
Ps. lxiii.

1 EARLY, my God, without delay,
   I haste to seek Thy face;
   My thirsty spirit faints away,
   Without Thy cheering grace.

2 So pilgrims on the scorching sand,
   Beneath a burning sky,
   Long for a cooling stream at hand,
   And they must drink or die.

3 I've seen Thy glory and Thy power
   Through all Thy temple shine:
   My God repeat that heavenly hour,
   That vision so divine.

4 Not all the blessings of a feast
   Can please my soul so well,
   As when Thy richer grace I taste,
   And in Thy presence dwell.

5 Not life itself, with all its joys,
   Can my best passions move;
   Or raise so high my cheerful voice,
   As Thy forgiving love.

6 Thus, till my last expiring day,
   I'll bless my God and King;
   Thus will I lift my hands to pray,
   And tune my lips to sing.
   Rev. Isaac Watts. 1719. sl. alt.

978
A Day in the Lord's Courts. 7

1 To Thy temple I repair;
   Lord, I love to worship there,
   When within the veil I meet
   Christ before the mercy-seat.

2 Thou through Him art reconciled,
   I through Him become Thy child;
   Abba, Father, give me grace
   In Thy courts to seek Thy face.

3 While Thy glorious praise is sung,
   Touch my lips, unloose my tongue,
   That my joyful soul may bless
   Thee, the Lord my Righteousness.

4 While the prayers of saints ascend,
   God of love, to mine attend;
   Hear me, for Thy Spirit pleads,
   Hear, for Jesus intercedes.

5 While I hearken to Thy law,
   Fill my soul with humble awe,
   Till Thy gospel bring to me
   Life and immortality.

6 While Thy ministers proclaim
   Peace and pardon in Thy Name,
   Through their voice, by faith, may I
   Hear Thee speaking from the sky.

7 From Thy house when I return,
   May my heart within me burn;
   And at evening let me say,
   I have walked with God to-day.
   James Montgomery. (1771—1854.) 1825.

979 "*Ask what I shall give thee.*" 7.
1 Kings iii. 5.

1 COME, my soul, thy suit prepare,
   Jesus loves to answer prayer;
   He Himself has bid thee pray,
   Therefore will not say thee nay.

2 Thou art coming to a King,
   Large petitions with thee bring;
   For His grace and power are such,
   None can ever ask too much.

3 With my burden I begin,
   Lord, remove this load of sin;
   Let Thy blood, for sinners spilt,
   Set my conscience free from guilt.

4 Lord, I come to Thee for rest,
   Take possession of my breast;
   There Thy blood-bought right maintain,
   And without a rival reign.

5 While I am a pilgrim here,
   Let Thy love my spirit cheer;
   As my Guide, my Guard, my Friend,
   Lead me to my journey's end.

6 Show me what I have to do,
   Every hour my strength renew;
   Let me live a life of faith,
   Let me die Thy people's death.
   Rev. John Newton. (1725—1807.) 1779. ab.

980 *With Angels.* 7.

1 THEE to laud in songs divine
   Angels and archangels join:
   We with them our voices raise,
   Echo Thine eternal praise.

2 Holy, holy, holy Lord,
   Live, by heaven and earth adored;
   Full of Thee, they ever cry,
   "Glory be to God on high!"
   Rev. Charles Wesley. (1708—1788.) 1739. ab.

981 "*Ye shall seek Me, and find Me.*" 7.
Jer. xxix. 13.

1 LORD, we come before Thee now,
   At Thy feet we humbly bow;
   O do not our suit disdain,
   Shall we seek Thee, Lord, in vain?

2 Lord, on Thee our souls depend
   In compassion, now descend;
   Fill our hearts with Thy rich grace,
   Tune our lips to sing Thy praise.

3 In Thine own appointed way,
   Now we seek Thee, here we stay:
   Lord, we know not how to go,
   Till a blessing Thou bestow.

4 Send some message from Thy word,
   That may joy and peace afford;
   Let Thy Spirit now impart
   Full salvation to each heart.

5 Comfort those who weep and mourn,
   Let the time of joy return:
   Those that are cast down lift up,
   Strong in faith, in love, and hope.

6 Grant that those who seek may find
   Thee a God sincere and kind;
   Heal the sick, the captive free,
   Let us all rejoice in Thee.
   Rev. William Hammond. (—1783.) 1745. ab.

982 "*Let us sing unto the Lord.*" 7.
Ps. xcv. 1.

1 JOYFUL be the hours to-day;
   Joyful let the season be;
   Let us sing, for well we may:
   Jesus, we will sing of Thee.

2 Should Thy people silent be,
   Then the very stones would sing.
   What a debt we owe to Thee,
   Thee our Saviour, Thee our King.

3 Meet it is that we should own
   What Thy grace has done for us;
   Saved we are by grace alone,
   And we joy to have it thus.

4 'Tis Thy grace alone can save;
   Every blessing comes from Thee:
   All we have, and hope to have,
   All we are, and hope to be.

5 Thine the Name to sinners dear,
   Thine the Name all names before:
   Blessèd here and everywhere;
   Blessèd now and evermore.
       Rev. Thomas Kelly. (1769—1855.) 1853.

983   *Delight in God's House.*   7.

1 LORD of hosts, how bright, how fair,
   E'en on earth, Thy temples are:
   Here Thy waiting people see
   Much of heaven, and much of Thee.

2 From Thy gracious presence flows
   Bliss that softens all our woes;
   While Thy Spirit's holy fire
   Warms our hearts with pure desire.

3 Here we supplicate Thy throne;
   Here Thou mak'st Thy glories known;
   Here we learn Thy righteous ways,
   Taste Thy love, and sing Thy praise.

4 Thus with sacred songs of joy,
   We our happy lives employ:
   Love, and long to love Thee more,
   Till from earth to heaven we soar.
       Rev. Daniel Turner. (1710—1798.) 1787. alt.

984   *God and His Church.*   L. M.
       Ps. lxxxiv.

1 GREAT God, attend while Zion sings
   The joy that from Thy presence springs:
   To spend one day with Thee on earth,
   Exceeds a thousand days of mirth.

2 Might I enjoy the meanest place
   Within Thy house, O God of grace,
   Not tents of ease, nor thrones of power,
   Should tempt my feet to leave Thy door.

3 God is our Sun, He makes our day;
   God is our Shield, He guards our way
   From all the assaults of hell and sin,
   From foes without and foes within.

4 All needful grace will God bestow,
   And crown that grace with glory too;
   He gives us all things, and withholds
   No real good from upright souls.

5 O God, our King, whose sovereign sway
   The glorious hosts of heaven obey,
   And devils at Thy presence flee;
   Blest is the man that trusts in Thee.
       Rev. Isaac Watts. (1674—1748.) 1719.

985   *The Church the Birth-place of the Saints.* L. M.
       Ps. lxxxvii.

1 GOD in His earthly temple lays
   Foundations for His heavenly praise;
   He likes the tents of Jacob well,
   But still in Zion loves to dwell.

2 His mercy visits every house
   That pays its night and morning vows;
   But makes a more delightful stay
   Where churches meet to praise and pray.

3 What glories were described of old,
   What wonders are of Zion told!
   Thou City of our God below,
   Thy fame shall Tyre and Egypt know.

4 Egypt and Tyre, and Greek and Jew,
   Shall there begin their lives anew;
   Angels and men shall join to sing
   The hill where living waters spring.

5 When God makes up His last account
   Of natives in His holy mount,
   'Twill be an honor to appear
   As one new-born or nourished there.
       Rev. Isaac Watts. 1719.

986   *Universal Worship.*   L. M.
       John iv. 21—23.

1 O THOU to whom, in ancient time,
   The lyre of Hebrew bards was strung,
   Whom kings adored in songs sublime,
   And prophets praised with glowing tongue;

2 Not now on Zion's height alone
   Thy favored worshipper may dwell;
   Nor where, at sultry noon, Thy Son
   Sat weary by the patriarch's well.

3 From every place below the skies,
   The grateful song, the fervent prayer,
   The incense of the heart, may rise
   To heaven, and find acceptance there.

4 O Thou to whom, in ancient time,
   The lyre of prophet-bards was strung,
   To Thee, at last, in every clime,
   Shall temples rise, and praise be sung.
       Rev. John Pierpont. (1785—1866.) 1824.

987 *The Pleasures of public Worship.* L. M.
Ps. lxxxiv.

1 How pleasant, how divinely fair,
  O Lord of hosts, Thy dwellings are;
  With long desire my spirit faints,
  To meet th' assemblies of Thy saints.

2 My flesh would rest in Thine abode,
  My panting heart cries out for God;
  My God, my King, why should I be
  So far from all my joys and Thee?

3 Blest are the saints who sit on high,
  Around Thy throne of majesty;
  Thy brightest glories shine above,
  And all their work is praise and love.

4 Blest are the souls who find a place
  Within the temple of Thy grace;
  There they behold Thy gentler rays,
  And seek Thy face, and learn Thy praise.

5 Blest are the men whose hearts are set
  To find the way to Zion's gate;
  God is their strength, and, through the road,
  They lean upon their helper, God.

6 Cheerful they walk with growing strength,
  Till all shall meet in heaven at length;
  Till all before Thy face appear,
  And join in nobler worship there.
  Rev. Isaac Watts. (1674—1748.) 1719. ab.

988 *Christ's Promise.* L. M.
Matt. xviii. 20.

1 How sweet to leave the world awhile,
  And seek the presence of our Lord;
  Dear Saviour, on Thy people smile,
  And come according to Thy word.

2 From busy scenes we now retreat,
  That we may here converse with Thee;
  Ah, Lord, behold us at Thy feet;
  Let this the gate of heaven be.

3 Chief of ten thousand, now appear,
  That we by faith may see Thy face;
  O speak, that we Thy voice may hear,
  And let Thy presence fill this place.
  Rev. Thomas Kelly. (1769—1855.) 1809. ab.

989 *"Where two or three."* L. M.
Matt. xviii. 20.

1 "Where two or three, with sweet accord,
  Obedient to their sovereign Lord,
  Meet to recount His acts of grace,
  And offer solemn prayer and praise;

2 "There," says the Saviour, "will I be,
  Amid this little company;
  To them unveil My smiling face,
  And shed My glories round the place."

3 We meet at Thy command, dear Lord,
  Relying on Thy faithful word:
  Now send Thy Spirit from above;
  Now fill our hearts with heavenly love.
  Rev. Samuel Stennett. (1727—1795.) 1778.

990 *The Love of God shed abroad in the Heart.* L. M.
Eph. iii. 16.

1 Come, dearest Lord, descend and dwell,
  By faith and love, in every breast;
  Then shall we know, and taste, and feel,
  The joys that cannot be exprest.

2 Come, fill our hearts with inward strength,
  Make our enlargèd souls possess,
  And learn the height and breadth and length
  Of Thine unmeasurable grace.

3 Now to the God whose power can do
  More than our thoughts or wishes know,
  Be everlasting honors done,
  By all the Church, thro' Christ, His Son.
  Rev. Isaac Watts. 1709.

991 *Flying to the Shadow of the Altar.* L. M.

1 Forth from the dark and stormy sky,
  Lord, to Thine altar's shade we fly;
  Forth from the world, its hope and fear,
  Saviour, we seek Thy shelter here:
  Weary and weak, Thy grace we pray;
  Turn not, O Lord, Thy guests away.

2 Long have we roamed in want and pain,
  Long have we sought Thy rest in vain;
  Wildered in doubt, in darkness lost,
  Long have our souls been tempest-tost:
  Low at Thy feet our sins we lay;
  Turn not, O Lord, Thy guests away.
  Bp. Reginald Heber. (1783—1826.) 1825.

992 *"Gott ist gegenwärtig: O lasst uns anbeten."* L. M.

1 Lo, God is here: let us adore,
  And own, how dreadful is this place.
  Let all within us feel His power,
  And silent bow before His face.
  Who know His power, His grace who prove,
  Serve Him with awe, with reverence love.

2 Lo, God is here: Him day and night
  Th' united choirs of angels sing;

To Him, enthroned above all height,
  Heaven's host their noblest praises bring.
Disdain not, Lord, our meaner song,
  Who praise Thee with a stammering tongue.

2 Gladly the toys of earth we leave,
  Wealth, pleasure, fame, for Thee alone;
To Thee our will, soul, flesh, we give;
  O take, O seal them for Thine own.
Thou art the God, Thou art the Lord;
  Be Thou by all Thy works adored.

4 Being of beings, may our praise
  Thy courts with grateful fragrance fill;
Still may we stand before Thy face,
  Still hear and do Thy sovereign will;
To Thee may all our thoughts arise,
  Ceaseless, accepted sacrifice.

Gerhard Tersteegen. (1697—1769.) 1731.
Tr. by Rev. John Wesley. (1703—1791.) 1739. ab.

993   *Lord's Day.*   L. M.
Num. x. 2.

1 THE day of rest once more comes round,
  A day to all believers dear;
The silver trumpets seem to sound,
  That call the tribes of Israel near;
Ye people all, obey the call,
  And in Jehovah's courts appear.

2 Obedient to Thy summons, Lord,
  We to Thy sanctuary come;
Thy gracious presence here afford,
  And send Thy people joyful home;
Of Thee our King O may we sing,
  And none with such a theme be dumb.

3 O hasten, Lord, the day when those
  Who know Thee here shall see Thy face:
When suffering shall forever close,
  And they shall reach their destined place;
Then shall they rest, supremely blest,
  Eternal debtors to Thy grace.

Rev. Thomas Kelly. 1806.

994   *"The festal Morn is come."*   C. P. M.
Ps. cxxii.

1 THE festal morn, my God, is come,
  That calls me to Thy sacred dome,
    Thy presence to adore:
My feet the summons shall attend,
With willing steps Thy courts ascend,
    And tread the hallowed floor.

2 With holy joy I hail the day,
  That warns my thirsting soul away;
    What transports fill my breast;
For lo, my great Redeemer's power
Unfolds the everlasting door,
    And leads me to His rest.

3 E'en now, to my expecting eyes,
  The heaven-built towers of Salem rise;
    E'en now, with glad survey,
I view her mansions, that contain
Th' angelic forms, an awful train,
    And shine with cloudless day.

4 Hither, from earth's remotest end,
  Lo, the redeemed of God ascend,
    Their tribute hither bring;
Here, crowned with everlasting joy,
In hymns of praise their tongues employ,
    And hail th' immortal King.

5 Mother of cities, o'er thy head
  Bright peace, with healing wings outspread,
    For evermore shall dwell:
Let me, blest seat, my name behold
Among thy citizens enrolled,
    And bid the world farewell.

Rev. James Merrick. (1720—1769.) 1765. ab. and alt.

995   *"Welcome, sweet Day."*   C. P. M.

1 WELCOME, sweet day, of days the best,
  The time of holy mirth and rest:
    To God's own house repair,
To hear His word and see His face,
To learn His will and sing His grace,
    To join in praise and prayer.

2 This is employment all divine;
  My soul, the blest assembly join,
    And from the world retire;
Go, bow before thy Maker's throne,
Thy risen Saviour's glories own,
    And fan devotion's fire.

3 Forget the trifles here below,
  The shining heap, the gaudy show,
    Vain mirth and worldly cares:
On wings of strong devotion rise,
Pass every cloud, pass all the skies,
    And soar above the stars.

4 To God direct thy steady flight,
  Great Fund of bliss, and Source of light,
    And there delight thine eyes;
View every shining wonder o'er,
With glad transported heart adore,
    And feast in paradise.

Rev. Simon Browne. (1680—1732.) 1720. alt.

THE LORD'S DAY AND WORSHIP.

996 *"Hosanna to the living Lord."* L. M.

1 HOSANNA to the living Lord,
Hosanna to th' incarnate Word:
To Christ, Creator, Saviour, King,
Let earth, let heaven, Hosanna sing.

2 "Hosanna, Lord!" Thine angels cry,
"Hosanna, Lord!" Thy saints reply;
Above, beneath us, and around,
The dead and living swell the sound.

3 O Saviour, with protecting care,
Return to this, Thy house of prayer,
Assembled in Thy sacred name,
Where we Thy parting promise claim.

4 But chiefest in our cleansèd breast,
Eternal, bid Thy Spirit rest,
And make our secret soul to be
A temple pure, and worthy Thee.

5 So, in the last and dreadful day,
When earth and heaven shall melt away,
Thy flock, redeemed from sinful stain,
Shall swell the sound of praise again.
Bp. Reginald Heber. (1783—1826.) 1811.

997 *"Gott ist gegenwärtig: O lasset uns anbeten."* (Abridged form.) L. M.

1 LO, God is here: let us adore,
And own how dreadful is this place;
Let all within us feel His power,
And silent bow before His face.

2 Lo, God is here: Him day and night
United choirs of angels sing;
To Him, enthroned above all height,
Let saints their humble worship bring.

3 Lord God of hosts, O may our praise
Thy courts with grateful incense fill;
Still may we stand before Thy face,
Still hear and do Thy sovereign will.
Gerhard Tersteegen. (1697—1769.) 1731.
Tr. by Rev. John Wesley. (1703—1791.) 1739. ab. and alt.

998 *Praise waiting in Zion.* Ps. lxv. L. M.

1 PRAISE, Lord, for Thee in Zion waits;
Prayer shall besiege Thy temple gates;
All flesh shall to Thy throne repair,
And find, through Christ, salvation there.

2 Our spirits faint; our sins prevail;
Leave not our trembling hearts to fail;
O Thou that hearest prayer, descend,
And still be found the sinner's Friend.

3 How blest Thy saints, how safely led,
How surely kept, how richly fed;
Saviour of all in earth and sea,
How happy they who rest in Thee.

4 Lord, on our souls Thy spirit pour;
The moral waste within restore;
O let Thy love our spring-tide be,
And make us all bear fruit to Thee.
Rev. Henry Francis Lyte. (1793—1847.) 1834. ab.

999 *"O luce qui mortalibus."* L. M.

1 GREAT God, who, hid from mortal sight,
Dost dwell in unapproached light,
Before whose presence angels bow
With faces veiled, in homage low;

2 Awhile in darkness we remain,
And round us yet are sin and pain;
But soon the everlasting day
Shall chase our shades of night away.

3 Then, from its fleshly bonds set free,
The soul shall fly, O God, to Thee;
To see Thee, love Thee, and adore,
Her blissful task for evermore.
Prof. Charles Coffin. (1676—1749.) 1736.
Tr. by Rev. Sir Henry Williams Baker. (1821—1877.) alt.

1000 *Peace at the Mercy-Seat.* L. M.

1 FROM every stormy wind that blows,
From every swelling tide of woes,
There is a calm, a sure retreat;
'T is found beneath the mercy-seat.

2 There is a place where Jesus sheds
The oil of gladness on our heads:
A place than all besides more sweet:
It is the blood-bought mercy-seat.

3 There is a spot where spirits blend,
Where friend holds fellowship with friend:
Though sundered far, by faith they meet
Around one common mercy-seat.

4 There, there, on eagle wings we soar,
And time and sense seem all no more;
And heaven comes down our souls to greet,
And glory crowns the mercy-seat.

5 O may my hand forget her skill,
My tongue be silent, cold, and still,
This bounding heart forget to beat,
If I forget the mercy-seat.
Rev. Hugh Stowell. (1799—1865.) 1832. ab.

1001 "O quam juvat fratres, Deus." L. M.

1 O LORD, how joyful 'tis to see
The brethren join in love to Thee:
On Thee alone their heart relies;
Their only strength Thy grace supplies.

2 How sweet, within Thy holy place,
With one accord to sing Thy grace,
Besieging Thine attentive ear
With all the force of fervent prayer.

3 O may we love the house of God,
Of peace and joy the blest abode;
O may no angry strife destroy
That sacred peace, that holy joy.

4 The world without may rage, but we
Will only cling more close to Thee,
With hearts to Thee more wholly given,
More weaned from earth, more fixed on heaven.

5 Lord, shower upon us from above
The sacred gift of mutual love;
Each other's wants may we supply,
And reign together in the sky.

Santolius Victorinus. (1630—1697.) 1736.
Tr. by Rev. John Chandler. (1800—) 1837.

1002 On entering a new Place of Worship. L. M.

1 JESUS, where'er Thy people meet,
There they behold Thy mercy-seat;
Where'er they seek Thee, Thou art found,
And every place is hallowed ground.

2 For Thou, within no walls confined,
Inhabitest the humble mind;
Such ever bring Thee where they come,
And going, take Thee to their home.

3 Dear Shepherd of Thy chosen few,
Thy former mercies here renew;
Here to our waiting hearts proclaim
The sweetness of Thy saving name.

4 Here may we prove the power of prayer
To strengthen faith, and sweeten care,
To teach our faint desires to rise,
And bring all heaven before our eyes.

5 Lord, we are few, but Thou art near:
Nor short Thine arm, nor deaf Thine ear:
O rend the heavens, come quickly down,
And make a thousand hearts Thine own.

William Cowper. (1731—1800.) 1769 ab.

1003 The Pleasures of public Worship. 7. D.
Ps. lxxxiv.

1 PLEASANT are Thy courts above,
In the land of light and love;
Pleasant are Thy courts below,
In this land of sin and woe.
O, my spirit longs and faints
For the converse of Thy saints,
For the brightness of Thy face,
King of glory, God of grace.

2 Happy birds, that sing and fly
Round Thy altars, O Most High;
Happier souls, that find a rest
In a Heavenly Father's breast:
Like the wandering dove, that found
No repose on earth around,
They can to their ark repair,
And enjoy it ever there.

3 Happy souls, their praises flow
Even in this vale of woe;
Waters in the desert rise,
Manna feeds them from the skies:
On they go from strength to strength,
Till they reach Thy throne at length;
At Thy feet adoring fall,
Who hast led them safe through all.

4 Lord be mine this prize to win;
Guide me through a world of sin;
Keep me by Thy saving grace;
Give me at Thy side a place.
Sun and Shield alike Thou art;
Guide and guard my erring heart;
Grace and glory flow from Thee,
Shower, O shower them, Lord, on me.

Rev. Henry Francis Lyte. 1834.

1004 "It is good to give Thanks." 7. D.
Ps. xcii.

1 THOU who art enthroned above,
Thou in whom we live and move,
Good it is with joyful tongue
To resound Thy praise in song:
When the morning paints the skies,
When the sparkling stars arise,
All Thy favors to rehearse,
And give thanks in grateful verse.

2 Sweet the day of sacred rest,
When devotion fires the breast;
When we dwell within Thy house,
Hear Thy gospel, pay our vows,

Songs to heaven's high mansion raise,
Fill Thy courts with songs of praise,
And in psalms and hymns proclaim
Honors to Thy glorious Name.

3 From Thy works our joys arise,
O Thou only good and wise:
Who Thy wonders can express?
All Thy thoughts are fathomless.
Warm our hearts with sacred fire,
And with songs of praise inspire;
All our powers with all their might
Ever in Thy praise unite.
George Sandys. (1577—1643.) 1638. alt.

1005   "*Part in Peace.*"   7. D.

1 PART in peace, Christ's life was peace;
Let us live our life in Him:
Part in peace, Christ's death was peace;
Let us die our death in Him.
Part in peace, Christ promise gave
Of a life beyond the grave,
Where all mortal partings cease:
Brethren, sisters, part in peace.
Mrs. Sarah Flower Adams. (1805—1848.) 1841. alt.

1006   "*Let not your Heart be troubled.*"   7. D.
John xiv. 1.

1 CALMER of the troubled heart,
Bid my unbelief depart;
Speak, and all my sorrows cease,
Speak, and all my soul is peace;
Comfort me, whene'er I mourn,
With the hope of Thy return;
And till I Thy glory see,
Bid me still believe in Thee.
Rev. Charles Wesley. (1708—1788.) 1762.

1007   Sabbath Evening.   7.

1 ERE another Sabbath's close,
Ere again we seek repose,
Lord, our song ascends to Thee;
At Thy feet we bow the knee.

2 For the mercies of the day,
For this rest upon our way,
Thanks to Thee alone be given,
Lord of earth and King of Heaven.

3 Cold our services have been,
Mingled every prayer with sin;
But Thou canst and wilt forgive:
By Thy grace alone we live.

4 Whilst this thorny path we tread,
May Thy love our footsteps lead;
When our journey here is past,
May we rest with Thee at last.

5 Let these earthly Sabbaths prove
Foretastes of our joys above;
While their steps Thy pilgrims bend
To the rest, which knows no end.
Unknown. Rev. Baptist Wriothesley Noel's Selection. 1832.

1008   Sabbath Evening.   7.

1 SOFTLY fades the twilight ray
Of the holy Sabbath day;
Gently as life's setting sun,
When the Christian's course is run.

2 Night her solemn mantle spreads
O'er the earth as daylight fades;
All things tell of calm repose,
At the holy Sabbath's close.

3 Peace is on the world abroad;
'T is the holy peace of God,
Symbol of the peace within
When the spirit rests from sin.

4 Still the Spirit lingers near,
Where the evening worshipper
Seeks communion with the skies,
Pressing onward to the prize.

5 Saviour, may our Sabbaths be
Days of joy and peace in Thee,
Till in heaven our souls repose,
Where the Sabbath ne'er shall close.
Rev. Samuel Francis Smith. (1805—) 1843.

1009   God our Portion.   L. M.
Ps. lxiii.

1 O LORD, within Thy sacred gate,
Where we so oft have sought for Thee,
Again our longing spirits wait,
The fulness of delight to see.

2 In blessing Thee with thankful songs,
Our happy lives shall glide away;
The praise that to Thy name belongs,
With lifted hands we'll daily pay.

3 Abundant sweetness, while we sing
Thy love, our favored souls o'erflows;
Secure in Thee, our God, our King,
Of glory that no period knows.

4 More dear than life itself, Thy love
    Our hearts and tongues shall still employ;
    Thy love to sing, Thy grace to prove,
    Be this our glory, peace, and joy.
5 O Father, Son, and Holy Ghost,
    The God, Whom heaven and earth adore,
    To Thee from men and heaven's bright host
    Be praise and glory evermore.
Unknown Spanish Author.
Tr. by Rev. John Wesley. (1703—1791.) 1738. much alt.

1010   *Longing after God.*   L. M.
        Ps. lxiii.

1 GREAT God, indulge my humble claim,
    Thou art my hope, my joy, my rest;
    The glories that compose Thy name
    Stand all engaged to make me blest.
2 Thou great and good, Thou just and wise,
    Thou art my Father and my God;
    And I am Thine by sacred ties,
    Thy son, Thy servant bought with blood.
3 With heart and eyes, and lifted hands,
    For Thee I long, to Thee I look;
    As travelers in thirsty lands
    Pant for the cooling waterbrook.
4 With early feet I love t'appear
    Among Thy saints, and seek Thy face;
    Oft have I seen Thy glory there,
    And felt the power of sovereign grace.
5 I'll lift my hands, I'll raise my voice,
    While I have breath to pray or praise;
    This work shall make my heart rejoice,
    And spend the remnant of my days.
Rev. Isaac Watts. (1671—1748.) 1719. ab.

1011   *Delight in God's House.*   L. M.
        Ps. cxxii.

1 SWEET is the solemn voice that calls
    The Christian to the house of prayer;
    I love to stand within its walls,
    For Thou, O Lord, art present there.
2 I love to tread the hallowed courts,
    Where two or three for worship meet;
    For thither Christ Himself resorts,
    And makes the little band complete.
3 'T is sweet to raise the common song,
    To join in holy praise and love;
    And imitate the blessèd throng
    That mingle hearts and songs above.

4 Within these walls may peace abound,
    May all our hearts in one agree;
    Where brethren meet, where Christ is found,
    May peace and concord ever be.
Rev. Henry Francis Lyte. (1793—1847.) 1834.

1012   *The eternal Sabbath.*   L. M.
        Heb. iv. 9

1 LORD of the Sabbath, hear our vows,
    On this Thy day, in this Thy house;
    And own as grateful sacrifice
    The songs which from the desert rise.
2 Thine earthly Sabbaths, Lord, we love;
    But there's a nobler rest above;
    To that our laboring souls aspire
    With ardent hope and strong desire.
3 No more fatigue, no more distress,
    Nor sin, nor hell, shall reach the place;
    No groans to mingle with the songs
    Which warble from immortal tongues.
4 No rude alarms of raging foes;
    No cares to break the long repose;
    No midnight shade, no clouded sun,
    But sacred, high, eternal noon.
5 O long-expected day, begin;
    Dawn on these realms of woe and sin;
    Fain would we leave this weary road,
    And sleep in death, to rest with God.
Rev. Philip Doddridge. (1702—1751.) 1755. alt.

1013   *Sabbath Evening.*   L. M.

1 SWEET is the light of Sabbath eve,
    And soft the sunbeams lingering there;
    For these blest hours the world I leave,
    Wafted on wings of faith and prayer.
2 The time how lovely and how still,
    Peace shines and smiles on all below;
    The plain, the stream, the wood, the hill,
    All fair with evening's setting glow.
3 Season of rest, the tranquil soul
    Feels the sweet calm, and melts to love;
    And while these sacred moments roll,
    Faith sees a smiling heaven above.
4 Nor will our days of toil be long;
    Our pilgrimage will soon be trod,
    And we shall join the ceaseless song,
    The endless Sabbath of our God.
James Edmeston. (1791—1867.) 1820. ab.

1014 *"Now we part."* L. M.

1 LORD, now we part in Thy blest name,
   In which we here together came;
   Grant us, our few remaining days,
   To work Thy will, and spread Thy praise.

2 Teach us in life and death to bless
   Thee, Lord, our strength and righteousness;
   Grant that we all may meet above,
   Where we shall better sing Thy love.

3 To God the Father, God the Son,
   And God the Spirit, Three in One,
   Be honor, praise, and glory given,
   By all on earth, and all in heaven.
   Rev. John Dracup. (—1795.) 1787. alt.

1015 *At Dismission.* L. M.

1 DISMISS us with Thy blessing, Lord;
   Help us to feed upon Thy word;
   All that has been amiss forgive,
   And let Thy truth within us live.

2 Though we are guilty, Thou art good;
   Wash all our works in Jesus' blood;
   Give every fettered soul release,
   And bid us all depart in peace.
   Rev. Joseph Hart. (1712—1768.) 1762.

1016 *The endless Sabbath anticipated.* C. M.

1 FREQUENT the day of God returns
   To shed its quickening beams;
   And yet how slow devotion burns,
   How languid are its flames.

2 Accept our faint attempts to love,
   Our frailties, Lord, forgive;
   We would be like Thy saints above,
   And praise Thee while we live.

3 Increase, O Lord, our faith and hope,
   And fit us to ascend
   Where the assembly ne'er breaks up,
   The Sabbath ne'er will end;

4 Where we shall breathe in heavenly air,
   With heavenly lustre shine;
   For ever feed on heavenly fare,
   And feast on love divine;

5 Where we, in high seraphic strains,
   Shall all our powers employ,
   Delighted range th' ethereal plains,
   And take our fill of joy.
   Rev. Simon Browne. (1680—1732.) 1720. ab. and alt.

1017 *The Blessedness of God's Service.* C. M.
Ps. lxxxiv.

1 How lovely are Thy dwellings fair,
   O Lord of hosts, how dear
   The pleasant tabernacles are,
   Where Thou dost dwell so near.

2 My soul doth long and almost die
   Thy courts, O Lord, to see;
   My heart and flesh aloud do cry,
   O living God, for Thee.

3 Happy, who in Thy house reside,
   Where Thee they ever praise;
   Happy, whose strength in Thee doth bide,
   And in their hearts Thy ways.

4 They journey on from strength to strength
   With joy and gladsome cheer,
   Till all before our God at length
   In Zion do appear.
   John Milton. (1608—1674.) 1648. ab.

1018 *Evening Hymn.*

1 GOD of the sun-light hours, how sad
   Would evening shadows be,
   Or night, in deeper sable clad,
   If aught were dark to Thee.

2 How mournfully that golden gleam
   Would touch the thoughtful heart,
   If with its soft, retiring beam,
   We saw Thy love depart.

3 But though the gathering gloom may hide
   Those gentle rays awhile,
   Yet they who in Thy house abide,
   Shall ever share Thy smile.

4 Then let creation's volume close,
   Though every page be bright;
   On Thine, still open, we repose
   With more intense delight.
   Mrs. Maria Grace Saffery. (1773—1858.) 1834. alt.

1019 *"But then Face to Face."*
1 Cor. xiii. 12.

1 WHEN, O dear Jesus, when shall I
   Behold Thee all-serene,
   Blest in perpetual Sabbath-day,
   Without a veil between?

2 Thy Spirit, O my Father, give,
   To be my guide and friend,
   To light my path to ceaseless joys,
   To Sabbaths without end.
                Rev. John Cennick. (1717—1755.) 1741. ab.

1020 "*The Day is far spent.*" S. M.
          Luke xxiv. 29.

1 THE day, O Lord, is spent,
   Abide with us, and rest;
   Our hearts' desires are fully bent
   On making Thee our guest.

2 We have not reached that land,
   That happy land, as yet,
   Where holy angels round Thee stand,
   Whose sun can never set.

3 Our sun is sinking now,
   Our day is almost o'er;
   O Sun of Righteousness, do Thou
   Shine on us evermore.
                Rev. John Mason Neale. (1818—1866.) 1854.

1021 *The Worship that never ceases.* S. M.

1 OUR day of praise is done;
   The evening shadows fall;
   Yet pass not from us with the sun,
   True light that lightenest all.

2 Around the throne on high
   Where night can never be,
   The white-robed harpers of the sky
   Bring ceaseless hymns to Thee.

3 Too faint our anthems here;
   Too soon of praise we tire;
   But, O the strains, how full and clear,
   Of that eternal choir.

4 Yet, Lord, to Thy dear will
   If Thou attune the heart,
   We in Thine angels' music still
   May bear our lower part.

5 'T is Thine each soul to calm,
   Each wayward thought reclaim,
   And make our daily life a psalm
   Of glory to Thy name.

6 A little while, and then
   Shall come the glorious end;
   And songs of angels and of men
   In perfect praise shall blend.
                Rev. John Ellerton. (1826—) 1867.

1022 *At Dismission.* S. M.

1 ONCE more, before we part,
   O bless the Saviour's name;
   Let every tongue and every heart
   Adore and praise the same.

2 Lord, in Thy grace we came,
   That blessing still impart;
   We met in Jesus' sacred name,
   In Jesus' name we part.

3 Still on Thy holy word
   Help us to feed, and grow,
   Still to go on to know the Lord,
   And practise what we know.

4 Now, Lord, before we part,
   Help us to bless Thy name:
   Let every tongue and every heart
   Adore and praise the same.
                Rev. Joseph Hart. 1762. much alt.

1023 *Praise to God from all Nations.* S. M.
          Ps. cxvii.

1 THY name, Almighty Lord,
   Shall sound through distant lands;
   Great is Thy grace, and sure Thy word;
   Thy truth forever stands.

2 Far be Thine honor spread,
   And long Thy praise endure,
   Till morning light and evening shade
   Shall be exchanged no more.
                Rev. Isaac Watts. (1674—1748.) 1719.

1024 *The Eventide of Life.* 10.

1 ABIDE with me: fast falls the eventide;
   The darkness deepens: Lord, with me abide;
   When other helpers fail, and comforts flee,
   Help of the helpless, O abide with me.

2 Swift to its close ebbs out life's little day;
   Earth's joys grow dim, its glories pass away;
   Change and decay in all around I see;
   O Thou, who changest not, abide with me.

3 Not a brief glance I beg, a passing word;
   But, as Thou dwell'st with Thy disciples, Lord,
   Familiar, condescending, patient, free,
   Come, not to sojourn, but abide, with me.

4 Come not in terrors, as the King of kings;
   But kind and good, with healing in Thy wings;
   Tears for all woes, a heart for every plea;
   Come, Friend of sinners, thus abide with me.

5 Thou on my head in early youth didst smile;
And, though rebellious and perverse meanwhile,
Thou hast not left me, oft as I left Thee.
On to the close, O Lord, abide with me.

6 I need Thy presence every passing hour:
What but Thy grace can foil the tempter's power?
Who like Thyself my guide and stay can be?
Through cloud and sunshine, O abide with me.

7 I fear no foe, with Thee at hand to bless;
Ills have no weight, and tears no bitterness;
Where is death's sting? where, grave, thy victory?
I triumph still, if Thou abide with me.

8 Hold Thou Thy cross before my closing eyes;
Shine thro' the gloom and point me to the skies;
Heaven's morning breaks, and earth's vain shadows flee;
In life, in death, O Lord, abide with me.

Rev. Henry Francis Lyte. (1793–1847.) 1847.

1025 *Parting Hymn.* 10.

1 SAVIOUR, again to Thy dear name we raise,
With one accord, our parting hymn of praise;
We stand to bless Thee ere our worship cease,
Then, lowly kneeling, wait Thy word of peace.

2 Grant us Thy peace upon our homeward way;
With Thee began, with Thee shall end the day;
Guard Thou the lips from sin, the hearts from shame,
That in this house have called upon Thy Name.

3 Grant us Thy peace, Lord, through the coming night,
Turn Thou for us its darkness into light;
From harm and danger keep Thy children free,
For dark and light are both alike to Thee.

4 Grant us Thy peace throughout our earthly life,
Our balm in sorrow, and our stay in strife;
Then, when Thy voice shall bid our conflict cease,
Call us, O Lord, to Thine eternal peace.

Rev. John Ellerton. (1826—) 1866.

1026 "*Fading, still fading.*" P. M.

1 FADING, still fading, the last beam is shining,
Father in heaven, the day is declining,
Safety and innocence fly with the light,
Temptation and danger walk forth with the night;
From the fall of the shade till the morning-bells chime,
Shield me from danger, save me from crime.
Father, have mercy, through Jesus Christ our Lord.

2 Father in heaven, O hear when we call,
Hear, for Christ's sake, who is Saviour of all:
Feeble and fainting we trust in Thy might;
In doubting and darkness Thy love be our light;
Let us sleep on Thy breast while the night taper burns,
Wake in Thy arms when morning returns.
Father, have mercy, &c.

Unknown Author. 1730.

1027 "*Morgenglanz der Ewigkeit.*" P. M.

1 DAYSPRING of Eternity.
Brightness of the Father's glory,
Dawn on us, that we may see
Clouds and darkness flee before Thee;
Drive afar, with conquering might,
All our night.

2 Let Thy grace, like morning dew,
Fall on hearts in Thee confiding,
Thy sweet comfort, ever new,
Fill our souls with strength abiding;
And Thy quickening eyes behold
Thy dear fold.

3 Give the flame of love, to burn
Till the bands of sin it breaketh,
Till, at each new day's return
Purer light my soul awaketh;
O, ere twilight come, let me
Rise to Thee.

4 Thou that hast gone up on high,
Grant that when Thy trumpet soundeth,
When with glory, in the sky,
Thee the cloud of saints surroundeth,
We may stand among Thine own,
Round Thy throne.

5 Lead us to the golden shore,
  O Thou rising Sun of Morning,
  Lead where tears shall flow no more,
  Where all sighs to songs are turning,
    Where Thy glory sheds alway
      Perfect day.
  Christian Knorr von Rosenroth. (1636—1689.) 1684.
  Tr. by Miss Catherine Winkworth. (1829—) 1863.

1028 *"Three in One, and One in Three."* 7,7,7,5.

1 THREE in One, and One in Three,
  Ruler of the earth and sea,
  Hear us, while we lift to Thee
      Holy chant and psalm.

2 Light of lights, with morning, shine:
  Lift on us Thy light divine;
  And let charity benign
      Breathe on us her balm.

3 Light of lights, when falls the even,
  Let it close on sin forgiven;
  Fold us in the peace of heaven,
      Shed a holy calm.

4 Three in One, and One in Three,
  Dimly here we worship Thee:
  With the saints hereafter we
      Hope to bear the palm.
  Rev. Gilbert Rorison. (1821—1869.) 1850. alt.

1029 *"Abide with us."* Luke xxiv. 29. L. M.

1 SUN of my soul, Thou Saviour dear,
  It is not night if Thou be near:
  O may no earth-born cloud arise
  To hide Thee from Thy servant's eyes.

2 When the soft dews of kindly sleep,
  My wearied eyelids gently steep,
  Be my last thought, how sweet to rest
  Forever on my Saviour's breast.

3 Abide with me from morn till eve,
  For without Thee I cannot live;
  Abide with me when night is nigh,
  For without Thee I dare not die.

4 If some poor wandering child of Thine
  Have spurned, to-day, the voice divine,
  Now, Lord, the gracious work begin;
  Let Him no more lie down in sin.

5 Watch by the sick; enrich the poor
  With blessings from Thy boundless store;
  Be every mourner's sleep to-night,
  Like infant's slumbers, pure and light.

6 Come near and bless us when we wake,
  Ere through the world our way we take;
  Till, in the ocean of Thy love,
  We lose ourselves in heaven above.
  Rev. John Keble. (1792—1866.) 1827. ab.

1030 *The Lord's Day Evening.* L. M.

1 SWEET Saviour, bless us ere we go;
  Thy word into our minds instil;
  And make our lukewarm hearts to glow
  With lowly love and fervent will.

2 The day is done, its hours have run;
  And Thou hast taken count of all,
  The scanty triumphs grace hath won,
  The broken vow, the frequent fall.

3 Grant us, dear Lord, from evil ways
  True absolution and release;
  And bless us, more than in past days,
  With purity and inward peace.

4 Do more than pardon: give us joy,
  Sweet fear, and sober liberty,
  And loving hearts without alloy
  That only long to be like Thee.

5 For all we love, the poor, the sad,
  The sinful, unto Thee we call;
  O let Thy mercy make us glad;
  Thou art our Jesus, and our All.
  Rev. Frederick William Faber. (1814—1863.) 1849. ab.

1031 *Evening Song for the Lord's Day.* L. M.

1 MILLIONS within Thy courts have met,
  Millions this day before Thee bowed;
  Their faces Zion-ward were set,
  Vows with their lips to Thee they vowed.

2 Soon as the light of morning broke
  O'er island, continent, or deep,
  Thy far-spread family awoke,
  Sabbath all round the world to keep.

3 And not a prayer, a tear, a sigh,
  Hath failed this day some suit to gain;
  To those in trouble Thou wert nigh:
  Not one hath sought Thy face in vain.

4 Yet one prayer more, and be it one,
  In which both heaven and earth accord:
  Fulfil Thy promise to Thy Son;
  Let all that breathe call Jesus Lord.
  James Montgomery. (1771—1854.) 1853. ab. and al. alt.

DEDICATING PLACES OF WORSHIP.

1032 *Laying a Corner-stone.* L. M.
2 Chron. vi. 18.

1 THIS stone to Thee in faith we lay,
  We build the temple, Lord, to Thee;
  Thine eye be open night and day
  To guard this house and sanctuary.

2 Here, when Thy people seek Thy face,
  And dying sinners pray to live,
  Hear Thou in heaven, Thy dwelling-place,
  And when Thou hearest, O forgive.

3 Here, when Thy messengers proclaim
  The blessèd gospel of Thy Son,
  Still by the power of His great name
  Be mighty signs and wonders done.

4 Hosanna! to their heavenly King,
  When children's voices raise that song,
  Hosanna! let their angels sing,
  And heaven with earth the strain prolong.

5 But will, indeed, Jehovah deign
  Here to abide, no transient guest?
  Here will the world's Redeemer reign?
  And here the Holy Spirit rest?

6 That glory never hence depart;
  Yet choose not, Lord, this house alone:
  Thy kingdom come to every heart,
  In every bosom fix Thy throne.
  James Montgomery. (1771–1854.) 1825.

1033 *Thankfulness for the House.* L. M.

1 SING to the Lord with heart and voice,
  Ye children of His sovereign choice;
  The work achieved, the temple raised,
  Now be our God devoutly praised.

2 For all the treasure freely brought,
  For all the toil in gladness wrought,
  For warmth of zeal, and purpose strong,
  Wake we to-day the thankful song.

3 Lord of the temple, once disowned,
  But now in worlds of light enthroned;
  Thy glory let Thy servants see,
  Who dedicate this house to Thee.

4 Be Thy dear name, like ointment, shed
  O'er every soul, on every head;
  Make glorious, O our Saviour King,
  The place where thus Thy chosen sing.

5 More grand the temple, and the strain
  More sweet, when we Thy heaven shall gain,
  And bid, for realms where angels dwell,
  Thy courts on earth a glad farewell.
  Joseph Tritton. 1861.

1034 *God's Temple.* L. M.

1 THE perfect world, by Adam trod,
  Was the first temple, built by God;
  His fiat laid the corner-stone,
  And heaved its pillars one by one.

2 He hung its starry roof on high,
  The broad, illimitable sky;
  He spread its pavement, green and bright,
  And curtained it with morning light.

3 The mountains in their places stood,
  The sea, the sky, and "all was good;"
  And when its first pure praises rang,
  The "morning stars together sang."

4 Lord, 'tis not ours to make the sea,
  And earth, and sky, a house for Thee;
  But in Thy sight our offering stands,
  A humbler temple, "made with hands."
  Nathaniel Parker Willis. (1807–1867.) 1826. ab.

1035 *On opening a Place for Worship.* 7.

1 LORD of hosts, to Thee we raise
  Here a house of prayer and praise:
  Thou Thy people's hearts prepare
  Here to meet for praise and prayer.

2 Let the living here be fed
  With Thy word, the heavenly bread;
  Here in hope of glory blest,
  May the dead be laid to rest.

3 Here to Thee a temple stand,
  While the sea shall gird the land;
  Here reveal Thy mercy sure,
  While the sun and moon endure.

4 Hallelujah! earth and sky
  To the joyful sound reply;
  Hallelujah! hence ascend
  Prayer and praise till time shall end.
  James Montgomery. 1825.

1036 *Prayer of Dedication.* C. M.
Ps. cxxxii.

1 ARISE, O King of grace, arise,
  And enter to Thy rest;
  Lo, Thy church waits with longing eyes,
  Thus to be owned and blest.

2 Enter with all Thy glorious train,
  Thy Spirit and Thy word;
  All that the ark did once contain
  Could no such grace afford.

3 Here, mighty God, accept our vows,
  Here let Thy praise be spread;
  Bless the provisions of Thy house,
  And fill Thy poor with bread.

4 Here let the Son of David reign,
  Let God's Anointed shine,
  Justice and truth His court maintain,
  With love and power divine,

5 Here let Him hold a lasting throne,
  And as His kingdom grows,
  Fresh honors shall adorn His crown,
  And shame confound His foes.
  Rev. Isaac Watts. (1674—1748.) 1719.

1037 *God's Blessing invoked.* C. M.

1 O THOU, whose own vast temple stands,
  Built over earth and sea,
  Accept the walls that human hands
  Have raised to worship Thee.

2 Lord, from Thine inmost glory send,
  Within these walls t' abide,
  The peace that dwelleth without end
  Serenely by Thy side.

3 May erring minds, that worship here,
  Be taught the better way;
  And they who mourn, and they who fear,
  Be strengthened as they pray,

4 May faith grow firm, and love grow warm,
  And pure devotion rise,
  While round these hallowed walls the storm
  Of earth-born passion dies.
  William Cullen Bryant. (1794—) 1835.

1038 *Christ's Beneficence a Pattern for us.* L. M.
Acts x. 38.

1 WHEN Jesus dwelt in mortal clay,
  What were His works from day to day,
  But miracles of power and grace,
  That spread salvation through our race?

2 Teach us, O Lord, to keep in view
  Thy pattern, and Thy steps pursue;
  Let alms bestowed, let kindness done,
  Be witnessed by each rolling sun.

3 That man may last, but never lives,
  Who much receives, but nothing gives,
  Whom none can love, whom none can thank,
  Creation's blot, creation's blank;

4 But he who marks from day to day
  In generous acts his radiant way,
  Treads the same path the Saviour trod,
  The path to glory and to God.
  Rev. Thomas Gibbons. (1720—1785.) 1784

1039 *The useful Life.* L. M.

1 Go, labor on; spend and be spent,
  Thy joy to do the Father's will:
  It is the way the Master went;
  Should not the servant tread it still?

2 Go, labor on; 'tis not for naught;
  Thine earthly loss is heavenly gain:
  Men heed thee, love thee, praise thee not;
  The Master praises,—what are men?

3 Go, labor on; enough, while here,
  If He shall praise thee, if He deign
  Thy willing heart to mark and cheer:
  No toil for Him shall be in vain.

4 Toil on, and in thy toil rejoice;
  For toil comes rest, for exile home;
  Soon shalt thou hear the Bridegroom's voice,
  The midnight peal: "Behold, I come!"
  Rev. Horatius Bonar. (1808—) 1857. ab.

1040 *The Christian Graces.* L. M.
1 Cor. xiii. 13.

1 FAITH, hope, and charity, these three,
  Yet is the greatest charity:
  Father of lights, these gifts impart
  To mine and every human heart.

2 Faith, that in prayer can never fail;
  Hope, that o'er doubting must prevail;
  And charity, whose name above
  Is God's own name, for "God is love."

3 The morning star is lost in light,
  Faith vanishes at perfect sight,
  The rainbow passes with the storm,
  And hope with sorrow's fading form;

4 But charity, serene, sublime,
  Beyond the range of death and time,
  Like the blue sky's all-'bounding space,
  Holds heaven and earth in its embrace.
  James Montgomery. 1852.

1041   *Charity.*   L. M.

1 ONE cup of healing oil and wine,
One offering laid on mercy's shrine,
Is thrice more grateful, Lord, to Thee,
Than lifted eye or bended knee.

2 In true and inward faith we trace
The source of every outward grace;
Within the pious heart it plays,
A living fount of joy and praise.

3 Kind deeds of peace and love betray
Where'er the stream has found its way;
But, where these spring not rich and fair,
The stream has never wandered there.
Rev. William Hamilton Drummond. (1772—1856.) 1818. ab.

1042   *Charitable Collections.*   L. M.

1 O LORD of heaven, and earth, and sea,
To Thee all praise and glory be;
How shall we show our love to Thee,
    Who givest all?

2 Thou didst not spare Thine only Son,
But gav'st Him for a world undone,
And freely with that Blessèd One
    Thou givest all.

3 Thou giv'st the Spirit's blessèd dower,
Spirit of life, and love, and power,
And dost His sevenfold graces shower
    Upon us all.

4 For souls redeemed, for sins forgiven,
For means of grace and hopes of heaven,
What can to Thee, O Lord, be given,
    Who givest all?
Bp. Christopher Wordsworth (1807—) 1863. ab. and alt.

1043   *Care of the Poor.*   L. M.
    Ps. xli.

1 BLEST is the man whose spirit shares
A suffering brother's wants and cares:
The Lord will visit him in grief,
And bring his trials sweet relief.

2 The sinner's Friend delights to see
His people kind and good as He;
And bids them each with each unite
To make their common burden light.

3 That burden well the Saviour knows;
He bore on earth our sins and woes;
By friends betrayed, by foes assailed,
Yet love divine o'er all prevailed.

4 That love, O Lord, still let us share,
Still lead us on through foe and snare,
Till we Thy face unclouded see,
And lose ourselves and earth in Thee.
Rev. Henry Francis Lyte. (1793—1847.) 1834

1044   *Liberality.*   L. M.

1 O WHAT stupendous mercy shines
Around the Majesty of heaven:
Rebels He deigns to call His sons,
Their souls renewed, their sins forgiven.

2 Go, imitate the grace divine,
The grace that blazes like a sun;
Hold forth your fair though feeble light;
Through all your lives let mercy run.

3 Upon your bounty's willing wings
Swift fly your gifts and charity;
The hungry feed, the naked clothe,
To pain and sickness health apply.

4 Pity the weeping widow's woe,
And be her counsellor and stay;
Adopt the fatherless, and smooth
To useful, happy life, his way.

5 When all is done, renounce your deeds,
Renounce self-righteousness with scorn;
Thus will you glorify your God,
And thus the Christian name adorn.
Rev. Thomas Gibbons. (1720—1785.) 1784. ab. and alt.

1045   *"Ye have done it unto Me."*   C. M.
    Matt. xxv. 40.

1 JESUS, my Lord, how rich Thy grace,
Thy bounties how complete:
How shall I count the matchless sum,
How pay the mighty debt.

2 High on a throne of radiant light
Dost Thou exalted shine;
What can my poverty bestow,
When all the worlds are Thine?

3 But Thou hast brethren here below,
The partners of Thy grace,
And wilt confess their humble names
Before Thy Father's face.

4 In them Thou mayest be clothed and fed,
And visited and cheered;
And in their accents of distress
My Saviour's voice is heard.

5 Thy face, with reverence and with love,
   I in Thy poor would see ;
   O rather let me beg my bread
   Than hold it back from Thee.
   Rev. Philip Doddridge. (1702—1751.) 1755.

1046 "*The Poor always with you.*" C. M.
   Matt. xxvi. 11.

1 LORD, lead the way the Saviour went,
   By lane and cell obscure,
   And let our treasures still be spent,
   Like His, upon the poor.

2 Like Him, through scenes of deep distress,
   Who bore the world's sad weight,
   We, in their crowded loneliness,
   Would seek the desolate.

3 For Thou hast placed us side by side
   In this wide world of ill ;
   And that Thy followers may be tried,
   The poor are with us still.

4 Mean are all offerings we can make ;
   But Thou hast taught us, Lord,
   If given for the Saviour's sake,
   They lose not their reward.
   Rev. William Croswell. (1804—1851.) 1831.

1047 *Following Christ.* C. M.

1 O THOU, great Teacher from the skies,
   Who lived and died for men ;
   Teach us with Thee to sympathize,
   And be as Thou wast then.

2 It was the glory of Thy heart,
   Whate'er Thou hadst to give ;
   For others' sufferings to impart,
   For others' good to live.

3 Be Thou in us a living soul ;
   Be Thou our spirit's power ;
   Its secret thought, its life's control,
   To guide it every hour.

4 We need like Thee a spirit true,
   A just and generous mind,
   Which seeks, in all it has to do,
   The good of all mankind.
   Rev. Thomas Cogswell Upham. (1799—1872.) 1872.

1048 "*A Treasure in the Heavens.*" C. M.
   Luke xii. 33.

1 THE seeds, which piety and love
   Have scattered here below,
   In the fair fertile fields above
   To ample harvests grow.

2 The mite my willing hands can give
   At Jesus' feet I lay ;
   Grace shall the humble gift receive,
   And heaven at large repay.
   Rev. Philip Doddridge. 1755. ab.

1049 *Loving one another.* C. M.
   1 John iv. 11.

1 How shall we show our love to Thee,
   Thou living God most high,
   But loving this Thy family,
   For which Thou deign'dst to die ?

2 If Thou for me such love didst bear,
   Shall I not love again ?
   For all are objects of Thy care ;
   Thy love doth all sustain.

3 If we have love for Thee in heaven,
   'Tis seen by love on earth ;
   Love only, love which God hath given,
   Doth prove our heavenly birth.

4 Love is of life the only sign,
   Love is our vital breath ;
   Love only shows the child divine,
   Love only conquers death.

5 Whate'er we do, where'er we go,
   Let love our sonship prove :
   Our lives the fire celestial show,
   Our thoughts and words be love.
   Rev. Isaac Williams. (1802—1865.) 1842. ab. and alt.

1050 *Waiting for Light.* C. M.

1 O VERY God of very God,
   And very Light of Light,
   Whose feet this earth's dark valley trod,
   That so it might be bright ;

2 Our hopes are weak, our fears are strong,
   Thick darkness blinds our eyes ;
   Cold is the night, and O we long
   That Thou, our Sun, wouldst rise.

3 And even now, though dull and grey,
   The east is brightening fast,
   And kindling to the perfect day,
   That never shall be past.

4 O guide us till our path is done,
   And we have reached the shore
   Where Thou, our everlasting Sun,
   Art shining evermore.

5 We wait in faith, and turn our face
    To where the daylight springs,
  Till Thou shalt come our gloom to chase,
    With healing on Thy wings.
      Rev. John Mason Neale. (1818—1866.) 1854. ab.

1051   *The winning Side.*   **C. M.**

1 WORKMAN of God, O lose not heart,
    But learn what God is like;
  And in the darkest battle-field
    Thou shalt know where to strike.

2 Thrice blest is he to whom is given
    The instinct that can tell
  That God is on the field, when He
    Is most invisible.

3 Blest too is he who can divine,
    Where real right doth lie,
  And dares to take the side that seems
    Wrong to man's blindfold eye.

4 Then learn to scorn the praise of men,
    And learn to lose with God;
  For Jesus won the world through shame,
    And beckons thee His road.

5 For right is right, since God is God;
    And right the day must win;
  To doubt would be disloyalty,
    To falter would be sin.
      Rev. Frederick William Faber. (1814—1863.) 1849. ab.

1052   *"It is more blessed to give than to receive." Acts xx. 35.*   **8, 7. 8l.**

1 LORD of glory, who hast bought us
    With Thy life-blood as the price,
  Never grudging from the lost ones
    That tremendous sacrifice,
  And with that hast freely given
    Blessings countless as the sand,
  To th' unthankful and the evil,
    With Thine own unsparing hand;

2 Wondrous honor hast Thou given
    To our humblest charity;
  In Thine own mysterious sentence,
    "Ye have done it unto Me."
  Can it be, O gracious Master,
    Thou dost deign for alms to sue,
  Saying, by Thy poor and needy,
    "Give, as I have given to you?"

3 Yes: the sorrow and the suffering,
    Which on every hand we see,
  Channels are for tithes and offerings,
    Due by solemn right to Thee;
  Right of which we may not rob Thee;
    Debt we may not choose but pay,
  Lest that Face of love and pity
    Turn from us another day.

4 Lord of glory, who hast bought us
    With Thy life-blood as the price,
  Never grudging for the lost ones
    That tremendous sacrifice,
  Give us faith, to trust Thee boldly,
    Hope to stay our souls on Thee;
  But, O best of all Thy graces,
    Give us Thine own charity.
      Mrs. Alderson. 1868. ab.

1053   *Honoring the Lord with our Substance. Prov. iii. 9.*   **8, 7.**

1 PRAISE the Saviour, all ye nations,
    Praise Him, all ye hosts above;
  Shout with joyful acclamations,
    His divine victorious love.
  Be His kingdom now promoted,
    Let the earth her Monarch know;
  Be my all to Him devoted,
    To my Lord my all I owe.

2 With my substance I will honor
    My Redeemer and my Lord;
  Were ten thousand worlds my manor,
    All were nothing to His word.
  While the heralds of salvation,
    His abounding grace proclaim,
  Let His friends of every station
    Gladly join to spread His fame.
      Rev. Benjamin Francis. (1734—1799.) 1787. ab.

1054   *"Cast thy Bread upon the Waters." Eccl. xi. 1.*   **8, 7.**

1 CAST thy bread upon the waters,
    Thinking not 't is thrown away;
  God Himself saith, thou shalt gather
    It again some future day.

2 Cast thy bread upon the waters;
    Wildly though the billows roll,
  They but aid thee as thou toilest
    Truth to spread from pole to pole.

3 As the seed, by billows floated,
    To some distant island lone,
  So to human souls benighted,
    That thou flingest may be borne.

4 Cast thy bread upon the waters;
   Why wilt thou still doubting stand?
   Bounteous shall God send the harvest,
   If thou sow'st with liberal hand.
   Mrs. J. H. Hanaford. 1852. ab. and alt.

1055   *Nothing our own.*   S. M.

1 WE give Thee but Thine own,
   Whate'er the gift may be:
   All that we have is Thine alone,
   A trust, O Lord, from Thee.

2 May we Thy bounties thus
   As stewards true receive,
   And gladly, as Thou blessest us,
   To Thee our first-fruits give.

3 O, hearts are bruised and dead,
   And homes are bare and cold,
   And lambs, for whom the Shepherd bled,
   Are straying from the fold.

4 To comfort and to bless,
   To find a balm for woe,
   To tend the lone and fatherless,
   Is angels' work below.

5 The captive to release,
   To God the lost to bring,
   To teach the way of life and peace,
   It is a Christ-like thing.

6 And we believe Thy word,
   Though dim our faith may be;
   Whate'er for Thine we do, O Lord,
   We do it unto Thee.
   Rev. William Walsham How. (1823—) 1854.

1056   *"Bear ye one another's Burdens."*   S. M.
   Gal. vi. 2

1 O PRAISE our God to-day,
   His constant mercy bless,
   Whose love hath helped us on our way,
   And granted us success.

2 His arm the strength imparts
   Our daily toil to bear;
   His grace alone inspires our hearts,
   Each other's load to share.

3 O happiest work below,
   Earnest of joy above,
   To sweeten many a cup of woe,
   By deeds of holy love!

4 Lord, may it be our choice
   This blessed rule to keep,
   "Rejoice with them that do rejoice,
   And weep with them that weep."

5 God of the widow, hear;
   Our work of mercy bless,
   God of the fatherless, be near,
   And grant us good success.
   Rev. Sir Henry Williams Baker. (1821—) 1861.

1057   *Obedience.*   S. M.

1 HAPPY the man, who knows
   His Master to obey;
   Whose life of care and labor flows,
   Where God points out the way.

2 He riseth to his task,
   Soon as the word is given;
   Nor waits, nor doth a question ask,
   When orders come from heaven.

3 Nothing he calls his own;
   Nothing he hath to say;
   His feet are shod for God alone,
   And God alone obey.

4 Give us, O God, this mind,
   Which waits for Thy command,
   And doth its highest pleasure find
   In Thy great work to stand.
   Rev. Thomas Cogswell Upham. (1799—1872.) 1872.

1058   *God entreated for Zion.*   L. M.
   Is. lxii. 6, 7.

1 INDULGENT Sovereign of the skies,
   And wilt Thou bow Thy gracious ear?
   While feeble mortals raise their cries,
   Wilt Thou, the great Jehovah, hear?

2 How shall Thy servants give Thee rest,
   Till Zion's mouldering walls Thou raise?
   Till Thine own power shall stand confest,
   And make Jerusalem a praise?

3 Look down, O God, with pitying eye,
   And view the desolation round;
   See what wide realms in darkness lie,
   And cast their idols to the ground.

4 Loud let the gospel trumpet blow,
   And call the nations from afar;
   Let all the isles their Saviour know,
   And earth's remotest ends draw near.

5 On all our souls let grace descend,
   Like heavenly dew, in copious showers;
   That we may call our God our Friend,
   That we may hail salvation ours.
   Rev. Philip Doddridge. (1702—1751.) 1755. ab.

1059 *Israel in Captivity.* L. M.
Ps. cxxxvii.

1 WHEN we, our wearied limbs to rest,
   Sat down by proud Euphrates' stream,
   We wept, with doleful thoughts opprest,
   And Zion was our mournful theme.

2 Our harps that, when with joy we sung,
   Were wont their tuneful parts to bear,
   With silent strings neglected hung
   On willow trees that withered there.

3 How shall we tune our voice to sing,
   Or touch our harps with skilful hands?
   Shall hymns of joy, to God our King,
   Be sung by slaves in foreign lands?

4 O Salem, our once happy seat,
   When I of thee forgetful prove,
   Let then my trembling heart forget
   The tuneful strings with art to move.

5 If I to mention thee forbear,
   Eternal silence seize my tongue;
   Or if I sing one cheerful air,
   Till thy deliverance is my song.
   Tate and Brady. 1696. ab.

1060 *"For God is able to graff them in again."* L. M.
Rom. xi. 23.

1 O WHY should Israel's sons, once blest,
   Still roam the scorning world around,
   Disowned by heaven, by man opprest,
   Outcasts from Zion's hallowed ground?

2 Lord, visit Thy forsaken race;
   Back to Thy fold the wanderers bring;
   Teach them to seek Thy slighted grace;
   To hail in Christ their promised King.

3 The veil of darkness rend in twain,
   Which hides their Shiloh's glorious light;
   The severed olive-branch again
   Firm to its parent stock unite.

4 Haste, glorious day, expected long,
   When Jew and Greek one pray'r shall pour,
   With eager feet one temple throng,
   One God with grateful heart adore.
   Rev. James Joyce. (1781—1850.) 1809. ab. and alt.

1061 *Grief for the Sins of Men.* L. M.
Ps. cxix. 136, 158.

1 ARISE, my tenderest thoughts, arise,
   To torrents melt my streaming eyes;
   And thou, my heart, with anguish feel
   Those evils which thou canst not heal.

2 See human nature sunk in shame;
   See scandals poured on Jesus' name;
   The Father wounded through the Son;
   The world abused, the soul undone.

3 See the short course of vain delight
   Closing in everlasting night;
   In flames that no abatement know,
   Though briny tears for ever flow.

4 My God, I feel the mournful scene;
   My bowels yearn o'er dying men:
   And fain my pity would reclaim,
   And snatch the firebrands from the flame.

5 But feeble my compassion proves,
   And can but weep where most it loves;
   Thy own all-saving arm employ,
   And turn these drops of grief to joy.
   Rev. Philip Doddridge. 1755.

1062 *The Vision of dry Bones.* L. M.
Ezek. xxxvii. 3.

1 LOOK down, O Lord, with pitying eye;
   See Adam's race in ruin lie;
   Sin spreads its trophies o'er the ground,
   And scatters slaughtered heaps around.

2 And can these mouldering corpses live?
   And can these perished bones revive?
   That, mighty God, to Thee is known;
   That wondrous work is all Thine own.

3 Thy ministers are sent in vain
   To prophesy upon the slain;
   In vain they call, in vain they cry,
   Till Thine almighty aid is nigh.

4 But if Thy Spirit deign to breathe,
   Life spreads through all the realms of death;
   Dry bones obey Thy powerful voice;
   They move, they waken, they rejoice.

5 So when Thy trumpet's awful sound
   Shall shake the heav'ns and rend the ground,
   Dead saints shall from their tombs arise,
   And spring to life beyond the skies.
   Rev. Philip Doddridge. 1755.

1063 *Hoping for a Revival.* L. M.

1 WHILE I to grief my soul gave way,
    To see the work of God decline,
  Methought I heard the Saviour say,
    "Dismiss thy fears, the ark is Mine.

2 Though for a time I hide My face,
    Rely upon My love and power;
  Still wrestle at a throne of grace,
    And wait for a reviving hour.

3 Take down the long-neglected harp,
    I've seen thy tears and heard thy prayer;
  The winter season has been sharp,
    But spring shall all its wastes repair."

4 Lord, I obey; my hopes revive;
    Come, join with me, ye saints, and sing;
  Our foes in vain against us strive,
    For God will help and triumph bring.
        Rev. John Newton. (1725—1807.) 1779. ab. and sl. alt.

1064 *Prayer for Home Missions.* L. M.

1 LOOK from Thy sphere of endless day,
    O God of mercy and of might;
  In pity look on those who stray,
    Benighted, in this land of light.

2 In peopled vale, in lonely glen,
    In crowded mart, by stream or sea,
  How many of the sons of men
    Hear not the message sent from Thee.

3 Send forth Thy heralds, Lord, to call
    The thoughtless young, the hardened old;
  A scattered, homeless flock, till all
    Be gathered to Thy peaceful fold.

4 Send them Thy mighty word to speak,
    Till faith shall dawn, and doubt depart,
  To awe the bold, to stay the weak,
    And bind and heal the broken heart.

5 Then all these wastes, a dreary scene,
    That make us sadden as we gaze,
  Shall grow with living waters green,
    And lift to heaven the voice of praise.
        William Cullen Bryant. (1794—) 1840.

1065 *Zion rejoicing.* L. M.

1 WHY, on the bending willows hung,
    Israel, still sleeps thy tuneful string?
  Still mute remains thy sullen tongue,
    And Zion's song declines to sing?

2 Awake, thy sweetest raptures raise;
    Let heart and voice unite their strains;
  Thy promised King His sceptre sways;
    And Jesus, Thy Messiah, reigns.

3 No taunting foes the song require;
    No stranger mocks thy captive chain;
  But friends invite the silent lyre,
    And brethren ask the holy strain.

4 Nor fear thy Salem's hill to wrong,
    If other lands thy triumph share:
  A heavenly city claims thy song,
    A brighter Salem rises there.

5 By foreign streams no longer roam,
    Nor, weeping, think of Jordan's flood;
  In every clime behold a home,
    In every temple see thy God.
        Rev. James Joyce. (1781—1850.) 1809.

1066 *The Church in the Desert.* L. M.
Ps. lxxx.

1 GREAT Shepherd of Thine Israel,
    Who didst between the cherubs dwell,
  And lead the tribes, Thy chosen sheep,
    Safe through the desert and the deep;

2 Thy Church is in the desert now:
    Shine from on high, and guide us through;
  Turn us to Thee, Thy love restore;
    We shall be saved, and sigh no more.

3 Hast Thou not planted with Thy hand
    A lovely vine in this our land?
  Did not Thy power defend it round,
    And heavenly dew enrich the ground?

4 How did the spreading branches shoot,
    And bless the nations with their fruit!
  But now, O Lord, look down and see
    Thy mourning vine, that lovely tree.

5 Return, Almighty God, return,
    Nor let Thy bleeding vineyard mourn:
  Turn us to Thee, Thy love restore;
    We shall be saved, and sigh no more.
        Rev. Isaac Watts. (1674—1748.) 1719. ab. and alt.

1067 *The Spirit accompanying the Word of God.* L. M.

1 O SPIRIT of the living God,
    In all Thy plenitude of grace,
  Where'er the foot of man hath trod,
    Descend on our apostate race.

2 Give tongues of fire, and hearts of love,
   To preach the reconciling word;
   Give power and unction from above,
   Whene'er the joyful sound is heard.

3 Be darkness, at Thy coming, light,
   Confusion, order in Thy path;
   Souls without strength inspire with might;
   Bid mercy triumph over wrath.

4 O Spirit of the Lord, prepare
   All the round earth her God to meet;
   Breathe Thou abroad like morning air,
   Till hearts of stone begin to beat.

5 Baptize the nations; far and nigh
   The triumphs of the cross record;
   The name of Jesus glorify,
   Till every kindred call Him Lord.
   James Montgomery (1771—1854.) 1825. ab.

1068 *Zion's favored Hour.* L. M.

1 SOVEREIGN of worlds, display Thy power;
   Be this Thy Zion's favored hour;
   O bid the morning star arise;
   O point the heathen to the skies.

2 Set up Thy throne where Satan reigns,
   In western wilds and eastern plains;
   Far let the gospel's sound be known;
   Make Thou the universe Thine own.

3 Speak, and the world shall hear Thy voice;
   Speak, and the desert shall rejoice:
   Dispel the gloom of heathen night;
   Bid every nation hail the light.
   Mrs. Voke. 1816.

1069 *"Awake, awake."* L. M.
   Is. li. 9.

1 ARM of the Lord, awake, awake;
   Put on Thy strength, the nations shake;
   And let the world, adoring, see
   Triumphs of mercy wrought by Thee.

2 Say to the heathen from Thy throne,
   "I am Jehovah, God alone!"
   Thy voice their idols shall confound,
   And cast their altars to the ground.

3 No more let human blood be spilt,
   Vain sacrifice for human guilt;
   But to each conscience be applied
   The blood that flowed from Jesus' side.

4 Almighty God, Thy grace proclaim
   In every clime, of every name,
   Till adverse powers before Thee fall,
   And crown the Saviour, Lord of all.
   William Shrubsole, Jr. (1759—1829.) 1795. ab.

1070 *Prayer for speedy Triumph.* L. M.

1 SOON may the last glad song arise
   Through all the millions of the skies,
   That song of triumph, which records
   That all the earth is now the Lord's.

2 Let thrones, and powers, and kingdoms be
   Obedient, mighty God, to Thee;
   And over land, and stream, and main,
   Wave Thou the sceptre of Thy reign.

3 O that the anthem now might swell,
   And host to host the triumph tell,
   That not one rebel heart remains,
   But over all the Saviour reigns.
   Mrs. Voke. 1816.

1071 *"O Lord our God, arise."* S. M.

1 O LORD our God, arise,
   The cause of truth maintain;
   And wide o'er all the peopled world
   Extend her blessed reign.

2 Thou Prince of life, arise,
   Nor let Thy glory cease;
   Far spread the conquests of Thy grace,
   And bless the earth with peace.

3 Thou Holy Ghost, arise,
   Expand Thy quickening wing,
   And o'er a dark and ruined world
   Let light and order spring.

4 All on the earth, arise,
   To God the Saviour sing;
   From shore to shore, from earth to heaven,
   Let echoing anthems ring.
   Rev. Ralph Wardlaw. (1779—1853.) 1803.

1072 *The Majesty of Christ's Kingdom.* S. M.
   Ps. xlv.

1 MY Saviour and my King,
   Thy beauties are divine;
   Thy lips with blessings overflow,
   And every grace is Thine.

2 Now make Thy glory known;
   Gird on Thy dreadful sword,

And ride in majesty, to spread
The conquests of Thy word.

3 Strike through Thy stubborn foes,
Or make their hearts obey;
While justice, meekness, grace and truth,
Attend Thy glorious way.

4 Thy laws, O God, are right;
Thy throne shall ever stand;
And Thy victorious gospel prove
A sceptre in Thy hand.

Rev. Isaac Watts. (1674—1748.) 1719. ab. and sl. alt.

1073 *Hebrew Missionaries.* S. M.
Is. lxvi. 19, 20.

1 ALMIGHTY God of love,
Set up th' attracting sign,
And summon whom Thou dost approve
For messengers divine.

2 From Abrah'm's favored seed
Thy new apostles choose,
In isles and continents to spread
The dead-reviving news.

3 We know it must be done,
For God hath spoke the word;
All Israel shall their Saviour own,
To their first state restored.

4 Send, then, Thy servants forth
To call the Hebrews home;
From west and east, and south and north,
Let all the wanderers come.

5 With Israel's myriads sealed,
Let all the nations meet;
And show Thy mystery fulfilled,
Thy family complete.

Rev. Charles Wesley. (1708—1788.) 1762. ab.

1074 *Pleading for all Mankind.* S. M.

1 O GOD of sovereign grace,
We bow before Thy Throne;
And plead, for all the human race,
The merits of Thy Son.

2 Spread through the earth, O Lord,
The knowledge of Thy ways;
And let all lands with joy record
The great Redeemer's praise.

Melrose. In Nettleton's *Village Hymns*. 1824.

1075 *The Spirit creating all Things new.* C. M.

1 SPIRIT of power and might, behold
A world by sin destroyed;
Creator, Spirit, as of old,
Move on the formless void.

2 Give Thou the word: that healing sound
Shall quell the deadly strife,
And earth again, like Eden crowned,
Produce the tree of life.

3 If sang the morning stars for joy
When nature rose to view,
What strains will angel-harps employ
When Thou shalt all renew!

4 And if the sons of God rejoice
To hear a Saviour's name,
How shall the ransomed raise their voice,
To whom that Saviour came!

5 So every kindred, tongue, and tribe,
Assembling round the throne,
Thy new creation shall ascribe
To sovereign love alone.

James Montgomery. 1825, 1853.

1076 *The Gospel for all Nations.* C. M.
Mark xiii. 10.

1 GREAT God, the nations of the earth
Are by creation Thine;
And in Thy works, by all beheld,
Thy radiant glories shine.

2 But, Lord, Thy greater love has sent
Thy gospel to mankind,
Unveiling what rich stores of grace
Are treasured in Thy mind.

3 Lord, when shall these glad tidings spread
The spacious earth around,
Till every tribe, and every soul,
Shall hear the joyful sound?

4 Smile, Lord, on each divine attempt
To spread the gospel's rays,
And build on sin's demolished throne
The temples of Thy praise.

Rev. Thomas Gibbons. (1720—1785.) 1769. ab. and alt.

1077 *Watching for the Morning.* C. M.

1 LIGHT of the lonely pilgrim's heart,
Star of the coming day,
Arise, and, with Thy morning beams,
Chase all our griefs away.

2 Come, blessèd Lord, bid every shore
    And answering island sing
  The praises of Thy royal name,
    And own Thee as their King.

3 Bid the whole earth, responsive now
    To the bright world above,
  Break forth in rapturous strains of joy
    In memory of Thy love.

4 Lord, Lord, Thy fair creation groans,
    The air, the earth, the sea,
  In unison with all our hearts,
    And calls aloud for Thee.

5 Thine was the cross, with all its fruits
    Of grace and peace divine:
  Be Thine the crown of glory now,
    The palm of victory Thine.
        Sir Edward Denny. (1796—) 1839. ab.

1078 *"So shall He sprinkle many Nations."* 8, 7.
Is. lii. 15.

1 SAVIOUR, sprinkle many nations,
    Fruitful let Thy sorrows be;
  By Thy pains and consolations,
    Draw the Gentiles unto Thee:
  Of Thy Cross the wondrous story,
    Be it to the nations told;
  Let them see Thee in Thy glory,
    And Thy mercy manifold.

2 Far and wide, though all unknowing,
    Pants for Thee each mortal breast;
  Human tears for Thee are flowing,
    Human hearts in Thee would rest,
  Thirsting, as for dews of even,
    As the new-mown grass for rain;
  Thee, they seek, as God of heaven,
    Thee as Man for sinners slain.

3 Saviour, lo, the isles are waiting,
    Stretch'd the hand, and strained the sight,
  For Thy Spirit, new creating
    Love's pure flame and wisdom's light;
  Give the word, and of the preacher
    Speed the foot, and touch the tongue,
  Till on earth by every creature
    Glory to the Lamb be sung.
        Bp. Arthur Cleveland Coxe. (1818—) 1851.

1079 *The Lord makes bare His Arm.* 8, 7.
Is. lii. 10.

1 YES, we trust the day is breaking,
    Joyful times are near at hand,
  God, the mighty God, is speaking
    By His word, in every land.
      Mark His progress,
  Darkness flies at His command.

2 While the foe becomes more daring,
    While he "enters like a flood,"
  God the Saviour is preparing
    Means to spread His truth abroad;
      Every language
  Soon shall tell the love of God.

3 God of Jacob, high and glorious,
    Let Thy people see Thy hand;
  Let the gospel be victorious,
    Through the world in every land;
      Let the idols
  Perish, Lord, at Thy command.
        Rev. Thomas Kelly. (1769—1855) 1839. ab.

1080 *"A Light to lighten the Gentiles."* 8,
Luke ii. 32.

1 O'er the realms of pagan darkness
    Let the eye of pity gaze;
  See the thronging, wandering nations,
    Lost in sin's bewildering maze:
      Darkness brooding
  On the face of all the earth.

2 Light of them that sit in darkness,
    Rise and shine, Thy blessings bring:
  Light to lighten all the Gentiles,
    Rise with healing in Thy wing;
      To Thy brightness
  Let all kings and nations come.

3 May the millions now adoring
    Idol-gods of wood and stone,
  Come, and worshipping before Him,
    Serve the living God alone;
      Let Thy glory
  Fill the earth, as floods the sea.

4 Thou to whom all power is given,
    Speak the word; at Thy command
  Let the heralds of Thy mercy
    Spread Thy name from land to land;
      Lord, be with them,
  Always, to the end of time.
        Rev. Thomas Cotterill. (1779—1823) 1819. alt.

THY KINGDOM COME.

1081 *Light in the Darkness.* 8, 7, 4.
Matt. iv. 16.

O'ER the gloomy hills of darkness,
  Look, my soul, be still and gaze;
All the promises do travail
  With a glorious day of grace.
    Blessèd jubilee,
  Let thy glorious morning dawn.

2 Kingdoms wide that sit in darkness,
  Grant them, Lord, Thy glorious light,
And from eastern coast to western
  May the morning chase the night;
    And redemption,
  Freely purchased, win the day.

3 Fly abroad, eternal Gospel,
  Win and conquer, never cease:
May thy lasting wide dominions
  Multiply, and still increase;
    May thy sceptre
  Sway the enlightened world around.

      Rev. William Williams. (1717—1791.) 1772. ab. and alt.

1082 *The Heathen call us.* 8, 7, 4.

1 SOULS in heathen darkness lying,
  Where no light has broken through,
Souls that Jesus bought by dying,
  Whom His soul in travail knew:
    Thousand voices
  Call us, o'er the waters blue.

2 Christians, hearken: none has taught them
  Of His love so deep and dear;
Of the precious price that bought them;
  Of the nail, the thorn, the spear;
    Ye who know Him,
  Guide them from their darkness drear.

3 Haste, O haste, and spread the tidings
  Wide to earth's remotest strand;
Let no brother's bitter chidings
  Rise against us when we stand
    In the judgment,
  From some far, forgotten land.

4 Lo, the hills for harvest whiten,
  All along each distant shore;
Seaward far the islands brighten;
  Light of nations, lead us o'er;
    When we seek them,
  Let Thy Spirit go before.

      Mrs. Cecil Frances Alexander. 1850. alt.

1083 *"Cry aloud, spare not."* 8, 7, 4.
Is. lviii. 1.

1 MEN of God, go take your stations,
  Darkness reigns throughout the earth;
Go, proclaim among the nations
  Joyful news of heavenly birth:
    Bear the tidings
  Of the Saviour's matchless worth.

2 Of His gospel not ashamèd,
  As the power of God to save,
Go where Christ was never namèd,
  Publish freedom to the slave:
    Blessèd freedom,
  Freedom Zion's children have.

3 When exposed to fearful dangers,
  Jesus will His own defend:
Borne afar 'mid foes and strangers,
  Jesus will appear your Friend;
    And His presence
  Shall be with you to the end.

      Rev. Thomas Kelly. 1806. ab.

1084 *Call to missionary Work.* 6, 4.
Is. lviii. 1.

1 SOUND, sound the truth abroad,
  Bear ye the word of God
    Through the wide world:
  Tell what our Lord has done,
  Tell how the day is won,
  And from the lofty throne
    Satan is hurled.

2 Far over sea and land,
  'Tis our Lord's own command,
    Bear ye His name;
  Bear it to every shore,
  Regions unknown explore,
  Enter at every door;
    Silence is shame.

3 Speed on the wings of love,
  Jesus, who reigns above,
    Bids us to fly;
  They who His message bear
  Should neither doubt nor fear,
  He will their Friend appear,
    He will be nigh.

4 When on the mighty deep,
  He will their spirits keep,
    Stayed on His word;

THY KINGDOM COME.

When in a foreign land,
No other friend at hand,
Jesus will by them stand,
    Jesus, their Lord.

5 Ye who, forsaking all
At your loved Master's call,
    Comforts resign;
Soon will your work be done;
Soon will the prize be won;
Brighter than yonder sun
    Then shall ye shine.
        Rev. Thomas Kelly. (1769—1855.) 1820.

1085   *"Speed on Thy Word."*   6, 4.

1 LORD of all power and might,
Father of love and light,
    Speed on Thy word:
O let the gospel sound
All the wide world around,
Wherever man is found:
    God speed His word.

2 Hail, blessed Jubilee:
Thine, Lord, the glory be;
    Forevermore!
Thine was the mighty plan,
From Thee the work began;
Away with praise of man,
    Glory to God!

3 Lo, what embattled foes,
Stern in their hate, oppose
    God's holy word:
One for His truth we stand,
Strong in His own right hand,
Firm as a martyr-band:
    God shield His word.

4 Onward shall be our course,
Despite of fraud or force;
    God is before:
His word ere long shall run
Free as the noon-day sun;
His purpose must be done:
    God bless His word.
        Rev. Hugh Stowell. (1799—1865.) 1854. sl. alt.

1086   *"Christ for the World."*   6, 4.

1 CHRIST for the world we sing;
The world to Christ we bring,
    With loving zeal;

The poor, and them that mourn,
The faint and overborne,
Sin-sick and sorrow-worn,
    Whom Christ doth heal.

2 Christ for the world we sing;
The world to Christ we bring,
    With fervent prayer:
The wayward and the lost,
By restless passion tossed,
Redeemed, at countless cost,
    From dark despair.

3 Christ for the world we sing;
The world to Christ we bring,
    With one accord;
With us the work to share,
With us reproach to dare,
With us the cross to bear,
    For Christ our Lord.

4 Christ for the world we sing;
The world to Christ we bring,
    With joyful song;
The new-born souls, whose days,
Reclaimed from error's ways,
Inspired with hope and praise,
    To Christ belong.
        Rev. Samuel Wolcott. (1813—) 1869.

1087   *The Kingdom of Christ.*   H. M.
        Ps. cx. 3—5.

1 ALL hail, incarnate God:
    The wondrous things foretold
Of Thee, in sacred writ,
    With joy our eyes behold:
Still does Thine arm new trophies wear,
And monuments of glory rear.

2 O haste, victorious Prince,
    That glorious, happy day,
When souls, like drops of dew,
    Shall own Thy gentle sway:
O may it bless our longing eyes,
And bear our shouts beyond the skies.
        Miss Elizabeth Scott. 1763. ab.

1088   *Gird on Thy Sword.*   H. M.
        Ps. xlv.

1 GIRD on Thy conquering sword,
    Ascend Thy shining car,
And march, almighty Lord,
    To wage Thy holy war:

Before His wheels, in glad surprise,
Ye valleys, rise; and sink, ye hills.

2 Before Thine awful face
Millions of foes shall fall,
The captives of Thy grace,
That grace which conquers all:
The world shall know, great King of kings,
What wondrous things Thine arm can do.
Rev. Philip Doddridge. (1702—1751.) 1736. ab.

1089 *"The Voice of Jesus calling."* 8, 7. D.

1 HARK, the voice of Jesus calling,
Who will go and work to-day?
Fields are white, and harvests waiting,
Who will bear the sheaves away?
Loud and long the Master calleth,
Rich reward He offers free;
Who will answer, gladly saying,
"Here am I, send me, send me?"

2 Let none hear you idly saying,
"There is nothing I can do,"
While the souls of men are dying,
And the Master calls for you:
Take the task He gives you gladly;
Let His work your pleasure be;
Answer quickly when He calleth,
"Here am I, send me, send me."
Rev. Daniel March. (1816—) 1869. ab.

1090 *"Come over and help us."* 8, 7. D.
Acts xvi. 9.

1 HARK, what mean those lamentations,
Rolling sadly through the sky?
'T is the cry of heathen nations,
"Come and help us, or we die."
Lost and helpless and desponding,
Wrapt in error's night they lie;
To their cries your hearts responding,
Haste to help them ere they die.

2 Hark, again those lamentations
Rolling sadly through the sky;
Louder cry the heathen nations,
"Come and help us, or we die."
Hear the heathen's sad complaining;
Christians, hear their dying cry;
And the love of Christ constraining,
Join to help them ere they die.
Rev. John Cawood. (1775—1852.) 1819. alt.

1091 *Sowing and Reaping.* 8, 7. D.

1 HE that goeth forth with weeping,
Bearing precious seed in love,
Never tiring, never sleeping,
Findeth mercy from above:
Soft descend the dews of heaven,
Bright the rays celestial shine;
Precious fruits will thus be given,
Through an influence all divine.

2 Sow thy seed, be never weary,
Let no fears thy soul annoy;
Be the prospect ne'er so dreary,
Thou shalt reap the fruits of joy.
Lo, the scene of verdure brightening,
See the rising grain appear;
Look again: the fields are whitening,
For the harvest time is near.
Thomas Hastings. (1784—1872.)

1092 *The Call to Service.* 8, 7. D.

1 WE are living, we are dwelling,
In a grand and awful time,
In an age on ages telling;
To be living is sublime.
Hark, the waking up of nations,
Gog and Magog to the fray.
Hark, what soundeth? is creation
Groaning for its latter day?

2 Worlds are charging, heaven beholding.
Thou hast but an hour to fight;
Now the blazoned cross unfolding,
On, right onward for the right!
On! let all the soul within you
For the truth's sake go abroad.
Strike, let every nerve and sinew
Tell on ages, tell for God.
Bp. Arthur Cleveland Coxe. (1818—) 1840.

1093 *"I love to tell the Story."* 7, 6. D.

1 I LOVE to tell the story,
Of unseen things above,
Of Jesus and His glory,
Of Jesus and His love.
I love to tell the story,
Because I know 't is true;
It satisfies my longings,
As nothing else can do.
Cho.—I love to tell the story,
'T will be my theme in glory,

To tell the old, old story
Of Jesus and His love.

2 I love to tell the story;
'Tis pleasant to repeat
What seems, each time I tell it,
More wonderfully sweet.
I love to tell the story;
For some have never heard
The message of salvation
From God's own holy word.—*Cho.*

3 I love to tell the story:
For those who know it best
Seem hungering and thirsting
To hear it like the rest.
And when, in scenes of glory,
I sing the new, new song,
'Twill be the old, old story
That I have loved so long.—*Cho.*
Miss Kate Hankey. 1865. ab.

1094 *"Uplift the Blood-red Banner."* 7, 6. D.

1 UPLIFT the blood-red banner,
And shout, with trumpet's sound,
Deliverance to the captive,
And freedom to the bound;
Earth's jubilee of glory,
The year of full release:
O tell the wondrous story,
Go forth and publish peace.

2 Go forth, Confessors, Martyrs,
With zeal and love unpriced,
And preach the blood of sprinkling,
And live, or die, for Christ;
For Christ claim every nation,
Your banner wide unfurled;
Go forth and preach salvation,
Salvation for the world.
Benjamin Gough. (1805–) 1865. ab.

1095 *"The Salvation of Israel."* 6. D.
Ps. xiv.

1 O THAT the Lord's salvation
Were out of Zion come,
To heal His ancient nation,
To lead His outcast home.
How long the holy city
Shall heathen feet profane?
Return, O Lord, in pity;
Rebuild her walls again.

2 Let fall Thy rod of terror,
Thy saving grace impart;
Roll back the veil of error,
Release the fettered heart.
Let Israel, home returning,
Her lost Messiah see;
Give oil of joy for mourning,
And bind Thy Church to Thee.
Rev. Henry Francis Lyte. (1793–1847.) 1834.

1096 *"Soldiers of the Cross, arise."* 7. D

1 SOLDIERS of the cross, arise,
Gird you with your armor bright;
Mighty are your enemies,
Hard the battle ye must fight.
O'er a faithless fallen world
Raise your banner in the sky,
Let it float there wide unfurled,
Bear it onward, lift it high.

2 'Mid the homes of want and woe,
Strangers to the living Word,
Let the Saviour's herald go,
Let the voice of hope be heard.
Where the shadows deepest lie,
Carry truth's unsullied ray;
Where are crimes of blackest dye,
There the saving sign display.

3 To the weary and the worn
Tell of realms where sorrows cease:
To the outcast and forlorn
Speak of mercy and of peace.
Guard the helpless, seek the strayed,
Comfort trouble, banish grief;
With the Spirit's sword arrayed,
Scatter sin and unbelief.

4 Be the banner still unfurled,
Bear it bravely still abroad,
Till the kingdoms of the world
Are the kingdoms of the Lord,
Praise with songs of holy glee,
Saints of earth and Heavenly Host,
Godhead One in Persons Three,
Father, Son, and Holy Ghost.
Rev. William Walsham How. (1823–) 1854

1097 *"Go, ye Messengers of God."* 7. D.

1 GO, ye messengers of God,
Like the beams of morning fly

Take the wonder-working rod,
  Wave the banner-cross on high,
Where the lofty minaret
  Gleams along the morning skies,
Wave it till the crescent set,
  And the "Star of Jacob" rise.

2 Go to many a tropic isle,
  In the bosom of the deep,
Where the skies for ever smile,
  And th' oppressed for ever weep.
O'er the negro's night of care
  Pour the living light of heaven;
Chase away the fiend despair,
  Bid him hope to be forgiven.

3 Where the golden gates of day
  Open on the palmy East,
Wide the bleeding cross display,
  Spread the gospel's richest feast.
Bear the tidings round the ball,
  Visit every soil and sea;
Preach the cross of Christ to all,
  Christ, whose love is full and free.
    Rev. Joshua Marsden. 1812.

1098 *"Jesus' Love the Nations fires."* 7. D.

1 SEE, how great a flame aspires,
  Kindled by a spark of grace:
Jesus' love the nations fires,
  Sets the kingdoms on a blaze.
Fire to bring on earth He came;
  Kindled in some hearts it is;
O that all might catch the flame,
  All partake the glorious bliss.

2 When He first the work begun,
  Small and feeble was His day;
Now the word doth swiftly run,
  Now it wins its widening way;
More and more it spreads and grows,
  Ever mighty to prevail;
Sin's strongholds it now o'erthrows,
  Shakes the trembling gates of hell.

3 Sons of God, your Saviour praise;
  He the door hath opened wide,
He hath given the word of grace;
  Jesus' word is glorified:
Jesus, mighty to redeem,
  He alone the work hath wrought;
Worthy is the work of Him,
  Him who spake a world from naught.

4 Saw ye not the cloud arise,
  Little as a human hand?
Now it spreads along the skies,
  Hangs o'er all the thirsty land.
Lo, the promise of a shower,
  Drops already from above;
But the Lord shall shortly pour
  All the riches of His love.
    Rev. Charles Wesley. (1708–1788.) 1749. sl. alt.

1099 *Zion enlarged.* 7. D.

1 "GIVE us room, that we may dwell,"
  Zion's children cry aloud:
See her numbers, how they swell,
  How they gather like a cloud.

2 O how bright the morning seems,
  Brighter, from so dark a night;
Zion is like one that dreams,
  Filled with wonder and delight.

3 Lo, thy sun goes down no more,
  God himself will be thy light;
All that caused thee grief before
  Buried lies in endless night.

4 Zion, now arise and shine,
  Lo, thy light from heaven is come;
These that crowd from far are thine,
  Give thy sons and daughters room.
    Rev. Thomas Kelly. (1769–1855.) 1806. ab. and sl. alt.

1100 *"Go ye into all the World."* L. M.
          Mark xvi. 15.

1 YE Christian heralds, go, proclaim
Salvation through Immanuel's name;
To distant climes the tidings bear,
And plant the Rose of Sharon there.

2 He'll shield you with a wall of fire,
With flaming zeal your breast inspire,
Bid raging winds their fury cease,
And hush the tempest into peace.

3 And when our labors all are o'er,
Then we shall meet to part no more;
Meet, with the blood-bought throng to fall,
And crown our Jesus Lord of all.
    Mrs. Voke. 1816.

1101 *"Fling out the Banner."* L. M.

1 FLING out the banner; let it float
  Skyward and seaward, high and wide;
The sun, that lights its shining folds,
  The cross, on which the Saviour died.

2 Fling out the banner: angels bend
   In anxious silence o'er the sign,
   And vainly seek to comprehend
   The wonder of the Love Divine.

3 Fling out the banner: heathen lands
   Shall see from far the glorious sight;
   And nations, crowding to be born,
   Baptize their spirits in its light.

4 Fling out the banner: sin-sick souls,
   That sink and perish in the strife,
   Shall touch in faith its radiant hem,
   And spring immortal into life.

5 Fling out the banner: let it float
   Skyward and seaward, high and wide:
   Our glory only in the cross,
   Our only hope, the Crucified.

6 Fling out the banner: wide and high,
   Seaward and skyward let it shine;
   Nor skill, nor might, nor merit ours:
   We conquer only in that sign.

   Bp. George Washington Doane. (1799—1859.) 1824.

1102 *The Glory of the Church.* L. M.

1 ZION, awake, thy strength renew,
   Put on thy robes of beauteous hue;
   And let th' admiring world behold
   The King's fair daughter clothed in gold.

2 Church of our God, arise and shine,
   Bright with the beams of truth divine:
   Then shall thy radiance stream afar,
   Wide as the heathen nations are.

3 Gentiles and kings thy light shall view:
   All shall admire and love thee too;
   Shall come like clouds across the sky,
   Or doves that to their windows fly.

   William Shrubsole, Jr. (1759—1829.) 1796.

1103 *Light for those that sit in Darkness.* L. M.
   Is. ix. 2.

1 THOUGH now the nations sit beneath
   The darkness of o'erspreading death;
   God will arise with light divine,
   On Zion's holy towers to shine.

2 That light shall shine on distant lands,
   And wandering tribes, in joyful bands,
   Shall come Thy glory, Lord, to see,
   And in Thy courts to worship Thee.

3 O light of Zion, now arise,
   Let the glad morning bless our eyes:
   Ye nations, catch the kindling ray,
   And hail the splendors of the day.

   Rev. Leonard Bacon. (1802—) 1845.

1104 *The Missionary's Farewell.* 8, 7.

1 YES, my native land, I love thee;
   All thy scenes, I love thee well:
   Friends, connections, happy country,
   Can I bid you all farewell?
      Can I leave you,
   Far in heathen lands to dwell?

2 Scenes of sacred peace and pleasure,
   Holy days and Sabbath bell,
   Richest, brightest, sweetest treasure,
   Can I say a last farewell?
      Can I leave you,
   Far in heathen lands to dwell?

3 Yes, I hasten from you gladly,
   From the scenes I loved so well:
   Far away, ye billows, bear me;
   Lovely, native land, farewell:
      Pleased I leave thee,
   Far in heathen lands to dwell.

4 Bear me on, thou restless ocean;
   Let the winds my canvas swell:
   Heaves my heart with warm emotion,
   While I go far hence to dwell:
      Glad I bid thee,
   Native land, farewell, farewell.

   Rev. Samuel Francis Smith. (1808—) 1833. ab.

1105 *Prayer for departing Missionaries.* 8, 7.

1 SPEED Thy servants, Saviour, speed them,
   Thou art Lord of winds and waves
   They are bound, but Thou hast freed them;
   Now they go to free the slaves:
      Be Thou with them,
   'Tis Thine arm alone that saves.

2 When they reach the land of strangers,
   And the prospect dark appears,
   Nothing seen but toil and dangers,
   Nothing felt but doubts and fears;
      Be Thou with them:
   Hear their sighs, and count their tears.

3 When they think of home, now dearer
   Than it ever seemed before,

Bring the promised glory nearer;
　Let them see that peaceful shore,
　Where Thy people
　Rest from toil, and weep no more:—

4 There to reap, in joy forever,
　Fruit that grows from seed here sown,
　There to be with Him who never
　　Ceases to preserve His own,
　　And with gladness
　Give the praise to Him alone.
　　　　　　Rev. Thomas Kelly. (1769—1855.) 1836. ab.

1106　*God praised for His Gospel.*　C. M.
　　　　Is. xlii. 10—12.

1 O CITY of the Lord, begin
　The universal song;
　And let the scattered villages
　The joyful notes prolong.

2 Let Kedar's wilderness afar
　Lift up the lonely voice;
　And let the tenants of the rock,
　With accent rude, rejoice.

3 O from the streams of distant lands,
　Unto Jehovah sing;
　And joyful from the mountain-tops
　Shout to the Lord, the King.

4 Let all combined, with one accord,
　The Saviour's glories raise;
　Till, in the earth's remotest bounds,
　The nations sound His praise.
　　　　　　Michael Bruce. (1746—1767.) 1781. ab.

1107　*The Millennium.*　C. M.
　　　　Micah iv. 1, 2. Is. ii. 1—4.

1 BEHOLD, the Mountain of the Lord
　In latter days shall rise,
　Above the mountains and the hills,
　And draw the wondering eyes.

2 To this the joyful nations round,
　All tribes and tongues shall flow;
　Up to the hill of God they'll say,
　And to His house we'll go.

3 The beam that shines on Zion's hill
　Shall lighten every land;
　The King who reigns in Zion's towers
　Shall all the world command.

4 No strife shall vex Messiah's reign,
　Or mar the peaceful years;
　To ploughshares soon they beat their swords,
　To pruning-hooks their spears.

5 No longer hosts encountering hosts
　Their millions slain deplore;
　They hang the trumpet in the hall,
　And study war no more.

6 Come, then, O come from every land,
　To worship at His shrine;
　And, walking in the light of God,
　With holy beauties shine.
　　　　　　Michael Bruce. 1781.

1108　*The Restoration of Israel.*　C. M.

1 DAUGHTER of Zion, from the dust
　Exalt thy fallen head;
　Again in thy Redeemer trust:
　He calls thee from the dead.

2 Awake, awake, put on thy strength,
　Thy beautiful array;
　The day of freedom dawns at length,
　The Lord's appointed day.

3 Rebuild thy walls, thy bounds enlarge,
　And send thy heralds forth;
　Say to the South, "Give up thy charge,
　And keep not back, O North."

4 They come, they come: thine exiled bands,
　Where'er they rest or roam,
　Have heard thy voice in distant lands,
　And hasten to their home.

5 Thus, though the universe shall burn,
　And God His works destroy,
　With songs the ransomed shall return,
　And everlasting joy.
　　　　　　James Montgomery. (1771—1854.) 1825. 1853.

1109　*Prayer heard, and Zion restored.*　C. M.
　　　　Ps. cii. 13—21.

1 LET Zion and her sons rejoice;
　Behold the promised hour:
　Her God hath heard her mourning voice,
　And comes t' exalt His power.

2 Her dust and ruins that remain
　Are precious in our eyes;
　Those ruins shall be built again,
　And all that dust shall rise.

3 The Lord will raise Jerusalem,
    And stand in glory there;
  Nations shall bow before His name,
    And kings attend with fear.

4 He sits a sovereign on His throne,
    With pity in His eyes;
  He hears the dying prisoners groan,
    And sees their sighs arise.

5 He frees the souls condemned to death,
    Nor when His saints complain,
  Shall it be said, that praying breath
    Was ever spent in vain.

6 This shall be known when we are dead,
    And left on long record,
  That ages yet unborn may read,
    And trust and praise the Lord.
           Rev. Isaac Watts. (1674—1748.) 1719.

1110   *Prayer for Home Missions.*   C. M.

1 On Zion and on Lebanon,
    On Carmel's blooming height,
  On Sharon's fertile plains, once shone
    The glory, pure and bright.

2 From thence its mild and cheering ray
    Streamed forth from land to land;
  And empires now behold its day;
    And still its beams expand.

3 But ah, our deserts deep and wild
    See not this heavenly light;
  No sacred beams, no radiance mild,
    Dispel their dreary night.

4 Thou, who didst lighten Zion's hill,
    On Carmel who didst shine,
  Our deserts let Thy glory fill,
    Thy excellence divine.
       Bp. Henry Ustick Onderdonk. (1789—1858.) 1826. ab.

1111   *The Glory of the latter Days.*   C. M.

1 Our God, our God, Thou shinest here,
    Thine own this latter day;
  To us Thy radiant steps appear:
    We watch Thy glorious way.

2 Thou tookest once our flesh; Thy face
    Once on our darkness shone;
  Yet through each age new births of grace
    Still make Thy glory known.

3 Not only olden ages felt
    The presence of the Lord;
  Not only with the fathers dwelt
    Thy Spirit and Thy word.

4 Doth not the Spirit still descend,
    And bring the heavenly fire?
  Doth not He still Thy Church extend,
    And waiting souls inspire?

5 Come, Holy Ghost, in us arise;
    Be this Thy mighty hour;
  And make Thy willing people wise
    To know Thy day of power.
           Thomas Hornblower Gill. (1819—) 1860. ab.

1112   *The Kingdom of Christ.*   L. M.
              Ps. lxxii.

1 Great God, whose universal sway
  The known and the unknown worlds obey,
  Now give the kingdom to Thy Son,
  Extend His power, exalt His throne.

2 Thy sceptre well becomes His hands,
  All heaven submits to His commands;
  His justice shall avenge the poor,
  And pride and rage prevail no more.

3 As rain on meadows newly mown,
  So shall He send His influence down;
  His grace on fainting souls distils,
  Like heavenly dew on thirsty hills.

4 The heathen lands, that lie beneath
  The shades of overspreading death,
  Revive at His first dawning light,
  And deserts blossom at the sight.

5 The saints shall flourish in His days,
  Dressed in the robes of joy and praise;
  Peace, like a river, from His throne
  Shall flow to nations yet unknown.
           Rev. Isaac Watts. 1719. ab.

1113   *The approaching Triumph.*   L. M.

1 Eternal Father, Thou hast said,
  That Christ all glory shall obtain;
  That He who once a sufferer bled
  Shall o'er the world a conqueror reign.

2 We wait Thy triumph, Saviour King:
  Long ages have prepared Thy way;
  Now all abroad Thy banner fling,
  Set time's great battle in array.

3 Thy hosts are mustered to the field;
   "The Cross! the Cross!" the battle-call;
   The old grim towers of darkness yield,
   And soon shall totter to their fall.

4 On mountain tops the watch-fires glow,
   Where scatter'd wide the watchmen stand;
   Voice echoes voice, and onward flow
   The joyous shouts from land to land.

5 O fill Thy church with faith and power;
   Bid her long night of weeping cease;
   To groaning nations haste the hour
   Of life and freedom, light and peace.

6 Come, Spirit, make Thy wonders known,
   Fulfil the Father's high decree;
   Then earth, the might of hell o'erthrown,
   Shall keep her last great jubilee.
   Rev. Ray Palmer. (1805—) 1860.

3 People and realms of every tongue
   Dwell on His love with sweetest song;
   And infant voices shall proclaim
   Their early blessings on His Name.

4 Blessings abound where'er He reigns;
   The prisoner leaps to loose his chains;
   The weary find eternal rest,
   And all the sons of want are blest.

5 Where He displays His healing power,
   Death and the curse are known no more;
   In Him the tribes of Adam boast
   More blessings than their father lost.

6 Let every creature rise and bring
   Peculiar honors to our King;
   Angels descend with songs again,
   And earth repeat the loud Amen.
   Rev. Isaac Watts. 1719. ab. and sl. alt.

1114 *For a Missionary Meeting.*

1 ASSEMBLED at Thy great command,
   Before Thy face, dread King, we stand;
   The voice that marshaled every star,
   Has called Thy people from afar.

2 We meet, through distant lands to spread
   The truth for which the martyrs bled;
   Along the line, to either pole,
   The thunder of Thy praise to roll.

3 Our prayers assist, accept our praise,
   Our hopes revive, our courage raise,
   Our counsels aid; and O impart
   The single eye, the faithful heart.

4 Forth with Thy chosen heralds come,
   Recall the wandering spirits home;
   From Zion's mount send forth the sound,
   To spread the spacious earth around.
   Rev. William Bengo Collyer. (1782—1854.) 1812. ab.

1116 *The holy City purified and guarded.* L. M.
Is. lx. 1, 2.

1 TRIUMPHANT Zion, lift thy head
   From dust, and darkness, and the dead;
   Though humbled long, awake at length,
   And gird thee with thy Saviour's strength.

2 Put all thy beauteous garments on,
   And let thy various charms be known:
   The world thy glories shall confess,
   Decked in the robes of righteousness.

3 No more shall foes unclean invade,
   And fill thy hallow'd walls with dread;
   No more shall hell's insulting host
   Their victory and thy sorrows boast.

4 God from on high thy groans will hear;
   His hand thy ruins shall repair;
   Nor will thy watchful Monarch cease
   To guard thee in eternal peace.
   Rev. Philip Doddridge. (1702—1751.) 1755. ab. and sl. alt.

1115 *Christ's Dominion.* L. M.
Ps. lxxii.

1 JESUS shall reign where'er the sun
   Does his successive journeys run;
   His kingdom stretch from shore to shore,
   Till moons shall wax and wane no more.

2 To Him shall endless prayer be made,
   And princes throng to crown His head;
   His Name, like sweet perfume, shall rise
   With every morning sacrifice.

1117 *Prayer for the Millennium.* L. M.

1 JESUS, we bow before Thy throne,
   We lift our eyes to seek Thy face;
   To bleeding hearts Thy love make known,
   On contrite souls bestow Thy grace.

2 See, spread beneath Thy gracious eye,
   A world o'erwhelmed in guilt and tears,
   Where deathless souls in ruin lie
   And no kind voice dispels their fears.

3 Lord, arm Thy truth with power divine,
   Its conquests spread from shore to shore,
Till suns and stars forget to shine,
   And earth and skies shall be no more.
Rev. Nathan Sidney Smith Beman. (1786—1871.) 1832. ab.

1118 *The Coming of Christ's Kingdom.*   L. M.

1 ASCEND Thy throne, almighty King,
   And spread Thy glories all abroad;
Let Thine own arm salvation bring,
   And be Thou known the gracious God.

O let the kingdoms of the world
   Become the kingdoms of the Lord;
Let saints and angels praise Thy name,
   Be Thou through heaven and earth adored.
Rev. Benjamin Beddome. (1717—1795.) 1818. ab.

1119 *"From Greenland's icy Mountains."*   7, 6. D.

1 FROM Greenland's icy mountains,
   From India's coral strand,
Where Afric's sunny fountains
   Roll down their golden sand:
From many an ancient river,
   From many a palmy plain,
They call us to deliver
   Their land from error's chain.

2 What though the spicy breezes
   Blow soft o'er Ceylon's isle,
Though every prospect pleases,
   And only man is vile:
vain with lavish kindness
   The gifts of God are strown,
The heathen in his blindness
   Bows down to wood and stone.

3 Can we, whose souls are lighted
   With wisdom from on high,
Can we to men benighted
   The lamp of life deny?
Salvation, O salvation!
   The joyful sound proclaim,
Till each remotest nation
   Has learnt Messiah's name.

4 Waft, waft, ye winds, His story,
   And you, ye waters, roll,
Till, like a sea of glory,
   It spreads from pole to pole;

Till o'er our ransomed nature,
   The Lamb for sinners slain,
Redeemer, King, Creator,
   In bliss returns to reign.
Bp. Reginald Heber. (1783—1826.) 1819.

1120 *Prayer for the Safety of Missionaries.*   7, 6. D.

1 ROLL on, thou mighty ocean;
   And, as thy billows flow,
Bear messengers of mercy
   To every land below;
Arise, ye gales, and waft them
   Safe to the destined shore;
That man may sit in darkness
   And death's black shade no more.

2 O Thou eternal Ruler,
   Who holdest in Thine arm
The tempests of the ocean,
   Protect them from all harm:
Thy presence e'er be with them,
   Wherever they may be;
Though far from those who love them,
   Still let them be with Thee.
James Edmeston. (1791—1867.) 1822.

1121 *The final Reign of Christ.*   7, 6. D.

1 WHEN shall the voice of singing
   Flow joyfully along,
When hill and valley, ringing
   With one triumphant song,
Proclaim the contest ended,
   And Him, who once was slain,
Again to earth descended,
   In righteousness to reign?

2 Then from the craggy mountains
   The sacred shout shall fly;
And shady vales and fountains
   Shall echo the reply:
High tower and lowly dwelling
   Shall send the chorus round,
All hallelujah swelling
   In one eternal sound.
James Edmeston. 1822. alt.

1122 *"Daily shall He be praised."*   7, 6. D.
   Ps. lxxii. 15.

1 HAIL to the Lord's Anointed,
   Great David's greater Son;
Hail, in the time appointed,
   His reign on earth begun.

    He comes to break oppression,
      To set the captive free;
    To take away transgression,
      And rule in equity.

2 He comes with succor speedy
      To those who suffer wrong;
    To help the poor and needy,
      And bid the weak be strong;
    To give them songs for sighing,
      Their darkness turn to light,
    Whose souls, condemned and dying,
      Were precious in His sight.

3 He shall come down like showers
      Upon the fruitful earth;
    And love, joy, hope, like flowers,
      Spring in His path to birth:
    Before Him on the mountains
      Shall peace, the herald, go;
    And righteousness, in fountains,
      From hill to valley flow.

4 For Him shall prayer unceasing
      And daily vows ascend;
    His kingdom still increasing,
      A kingdom without end:
    The mountain dews shall nourish
      A seed in weakness sown,
    Whose fruit shall spread, and flourish,
      And shake like Lebanon.

5 O'er every foe victorious
      He on His throne shall rest,
    From age to age more glorious,
      All-blessing and all-blest:
    The tide of time shall never
      His covenant remove;
    His name shall stand forever,
      That name to us is Love.
          James Montgomery. (1771–1854.) 1822. al.

1123   "*The Gospel Banner.*"   7, 6. D.

1 Now be the Gospel banner
      In every land unfurled,
    And be the shout, "Hosanna!"
      Reechoed through the world:
    Till every isle and nation,
      Till every tribe and tongue,
    Receive the great salvation,
      And join the happy throng.

2 What though th' embattled legions
      Of earth and hell combine?
    His power, throughout their regions,
      Shall soon resplendent shine:
    Ride on, O Lord, victorious,
      Immanuel, Prince of peace;
    Thy triumph shall be glorious,
      Thine empire still increase.

3 Yes, Thou shalt reign for ever,
      O Jesus, King of kings:
    Thy light, Thy love, Thy favor,
      Each ransomed captive sings.
    The isles for Thee are waiting,
      The deserts learn Thy praise,
    The hills and valleys greeting,
      The song responsive raise.
          Thomas Hastings. (1784–1872.) 1830.

1124   "*The Prince of Salvation.*"   12, 11, 8.

1 THE Prince of Salvation in triumph is riding,
    And glory attends Him along His bright
      way;
    The tidings of grace on the breezes are
      gliding,
    And nations are owning His sway.

2 Ride on in Thy greatness, Thou conquer-
      ing Saviour;
    Let thousands of thousands submit to
      Thy reign,
    Acknowledge Thy goodness, entreat for
      Thy favor,
    And follow Thy glorious train.

3 Then loud shall ascend, from each sancti-
      fied nation,
    The voice of thanksgiving, the chorus
      of praise;
    And heaven shall reecho the song of sal-
      vation
    In rich and melodious lays.
          Rev. Samuel Francis Smith. (1808–) 1832.

1125   *Gentiles coming into the Church.*   10.

1 RISE, crowned in light, imperial Salem, rise:
    Exalt thy towering head, and lift thine eyes;
    See heaven its sparkling portals wide display
    And break upon thee in a flood of day.

2 See a long race thy spacious courts adorn,
    See future sons and daughters yet unborn

In crowding ranks on every side arise,
Demanding life, impatient for the skies.

3 See barbarous nations at thy gates attend,
Walk in thy light, and in thy temple bend;
See thy bright altars thronged with prostrate kings,
While every land its joyful tribute brings.

4 The seas shall waste, the skies to smoke decay,
Rocks fall to dust, and mountains melt away;
But fixed His word His saving power remains;
Thy realm shall last, thy own Messiah reigns.

Alexander Pope. (1688—1744.) 1712. ab. and alt.

1126　　*The Latter Day.*　　11, 10.

1 HAIL to the brightness of Zion's glad morning;
Joy to the lands that in darkness have lain;
Hushed be the accents of sorrow and mourning;
Zion in triumph begins her mild reign.

2 Hail to the brightness of Zion's glad morning,
Long by the prophets of Israel foretold;
Hail to the millions from bondage returning;
Gentiles and Jews the blest vision behold.

3 Lo, in the desert rich flowers are springing;
Streams ever copious are gliding along;
Loud from the mountain-tops echoes are ringing;
Wastes rise in verdure, and mingle in song.

4 See, from all lands, from the isles of the ocean,
Praise to Jehovah ascending on high;
Fallen are the engines of war and commotion;
Shouts of salvation are rending the sky.

Thomas Hastings. (1782—1872.) 1830.

1127　　*The Church victorious.*　　11, 10.

1 DAUGHTER of Zion, awake from thy sadness;
Wake, for thy foes shall oppress thee no more;

Bright o'er thy hills dawns the day-star of gladness;
Rise, for the night of thy sorrow is o'er.

2 Strong were thy foes; but the arm that subdued them,
And scattered their legions, was mightier far;
They fled like the chaff from the scourge that pursued them;
Vain were their steeds and their chariots of war.

3 Daughter of Zion, the power that hath saved thee
Extolled with the harp and the timbrel should be;
Shout, for the foe is destroyed that enslaved thee;
Th' oppressor is vanquished, and Zion is free.

Fitzgerald's Collection. 1830.

1128　　*Good Tidings to Zion.*　　8, 7, 4.
Is. lii. 7.

1 ON the mountain's top appearing,
Lo, the sacred herald stands,
Welcome news to Zion bearing,
Zion long in hostile lands:
　　Mourning captive,
God Himself will loose thy bands.

2 Has thy night been long and mournful?
Have thy friends unfaithful proved?
Have thy foes been proud and scornful,
By thy sighs and tears unmoved?
　　Cease thy mourning;
Zion still is well beloved.

3 God, thy God, will now restore thee;
He Himself appears thy Friend;
All Thy foes shall flee before thee;
Here their boasts and triumphs end:
　　Great deliverance
Zion's King vouchsafes to send.

4 Enemies no more shall trouble;
All thy wrongs shall be redressed;
For Thy shame thou shalt have double,
In thy Maker's favor blessed;
　　All thy conflicts
End in everlasting rest.

Rev. Thomas Kelly. (1769—1855.) 1806.

THY KINGDOM COME.

1129 *"A Fountain opened."* 8, 7, 4.
Zech. xiii. 1.

1 SEE, from Zion's sacred mountain
Streams of living water flow;
God has opened there a fountain,
That supplies the world below:
   They are blesséd,
Who its sovereign virtues know.

2 Through ten thousand channels flowing,
Streams of mercy find their way;
Life, and health, and joy bestowing,
Making all around look gay:
   O ye nations,
Hail the long-expected day.
Rev. Thomas Kelly. 1809. ab.

1130 *For the Outpouring of the Spirit.* 8, 7, 4.

1 WHO but Thou, almighty Spirit,
Can the heathen world reclaim?
Men may preach, but till Thou favor,
Heathens still will be the same:
   Mighty Spirit,
Witness to the Saviour's name.

2 Thou hast promised by the prophets
Glorious light in latter days:
Come, and bless bewildered nations;
Change our prayers and tears to praise:
   Promised Spirit,
Round the world diffuse Thy rays.

3 All our hopes, and prayers, and labors,
Must be vain without Thy aid;
But Thou wilt not disappoint us;
All is true that Thou hast said:
   Gracious Spirit,
O'er the world Thy influence shed.
"Priphas," Evangelical Magazine. 1821.

1131 *Christ's Coming and Kingdom.* 8, 7, 4.

1 LIFT your heads, ye friends of Jesus,
Partners in His patience here:
Christ, to all believers precious,
Lord of lords, shall soon appear:
   Mark the tokens
Of His heavenly kingdom near.

2 Lo, 'tis He: our hearts' Desire,
Come for His espoused below;
Come to join us with His choir,
Come to make our joys o'erflow:
   Palms of victory,
Crowns of glory, to bestow.
Rev. Charles Wesley. (1708—1788.) 1750. ab.

1132 *Success of the Gospel.* 7, 6. D.

1 THE morning light is breaking;
The darkness disappears;
The sons of earth are waking
To penitential tears:
Each breeze that sweeps the ocean
Brings tidings from afar
Of nations in commotion,
Prepared for Zion's war.

2 See heathen nations bending
Before the God we love,
And thousand hearts ascending,
In gratitude above;
While sinners, now confessing,
The gospel call obey,
And seek the Saviour's blessing,
A nation in a day.

3 Blest river of salvation,
Pursue thine onward way;
Flow thou to every nation,
Nor in thy riches stay;
Stay not, till all the lowly
Triumphant reach their home;
Stay not, till all the holy
Proclaim, "The Lord is come."
Rev. Samuel Francis Smith. (1808—) 1831. ab.

1133 *The coming Millennium.* 7, 6. D.

1 AWAKE, awake, O Zion,
Put on thy strength divine,
Thy garments bright in beauty,
The bridal dress be thine:
Jerusalem the holy,
To purity restored;
Meek Bride, all fair and lowly,
Go forth to meet thy Lord.

2 The Lamb who bore our sorrows
Comes down to earth again;
No Sufferer now, but Victor,
For evermore to reign;
To reign in every nation,
To rule in every zone:
O wide-world coronation,
In every heart a throne.

3 Awake, awake, O Zion,
   The bridal day draws nigh,
 The day of signs and wonders,
   And marvels from on high:
 Thy sun uprises slowly,
   But keep thou watch and ward;
 Fair Bride, all pure and lowly,
   Go forth to meet thy Lord.
         Benjamin Gough. (1805—) 1865. ab.

1134   *The good Tidings.*   7, 6. D.

1 HOW beauteous on the mountains,
    The feet of him that brings,
  Like streams from living fountains,
    Good tidings of good things;
  That publisheth salvation,
    And jubilee release,
  To every tribe and nation,
    God's reign of joy and peace.

2 Lift up thy voice, O watchman,
    And shout from Zion's towers
  Thy hallelujah chorus,
    "The victory is ours!"
  The Lord shall build up Zion
    In glory and renown,
  And Jesus, Judah's Lion,
    Shall wear His rightful crown.
         Benjamin Gough. 1865. ab. and sl. alt.

1135   *Prayer for a Revival of Religion.*   7.

1 COME, divine Emmanuel, come,
  Take possession of Thy home;
  Now Thy mercy's wings expand,
  Stretch throughout the happy land.

2 Carry on Thy victory,
  Spread Thy rule from sea to sea;
  Rescue all Thy ransomed race,
  Save us, save us, Lord, by grace.

3 Take the purchase of Thy blood,
  Bring us to a pardoning God;
  Give us eyes to see our day,
  Hearts the gospel truth to obey:

4 Ears to hear the gospel sound;
  Grace doth more than sin abound;
  God appeased, and man forgiven,
  Peace on earth, and joy in heaven.

5 O that every soul might be
  Perfectly subdued to Thee;
  O that all in Thee might know
  Everlasting life below.

6 Now Thy mercy's wings expand,
  Stretch throughout the happy land:
  Take possession of Thy home;
  Come, divine Emmanuel, come.
         Rev. Charles Wesley. (1708—1788.) 1749. alt.

1136   *Thanksgiving for a Revival of Religion.*   7.

1 FOUNT of everlasting love,
    Rich Thy streams of mercy are;
  Flowing purely from above,
    Beauty marks their course afar.

2 Lo, Thy Church, athirst and faint,
    Drinks the full, refreshing tide;
  Thou hast heard her sad complaint,
    Floods of grace are sweeping wide.

3 God of mercy, to Thy throne
    Now our fervent thanks we bring;
  Thine the glory, Thine alone,
    Joyous praise to Thee we sing.

4 While we lift our grateful song,
    Let Thy Spirit still descend;
  Roll the tide of grace along,
    Widening, deepening, to the end.
         Rev. Ray Palmer. (1802—) 1832, 1865.

1137   *Zion enlarge.*   7.

1 WHO are these that come from far,
  Led by Jacob's rising star?
  Strangers now to Zion come,
  There to seek a peaceful home.

2 Lo, they gather like a cloud,
  Or as doves their windows crowd:
  Zion wonders at the sight,
  Zion feels a strange delight.

3 Zion now no more shall sigh,
  God will raise her glory high;
  He will send a large increase,
  He will give His people peace.

4 Sons of Zion, sing aloud;
  See her sky without a cloud:
  God will make her joy complete;
  Zion's sun shall never set.
         Rev. Thomas Kelly. (1769—1855) 1816. ab. and alt.

1138 *Missionary Success.* 7.

1 HARK, the distant isles proclaim
  Glory to Messiah's name;
  Hymns of praise unheard before
  Echo from the farthest shore.

2 Hearts that once were taught to own
  Idol gods of wood and stone,
  Now to light and life restored,
  Honor Jesus as their Lord.

3 Blessèd Saviour, still proceed;
  Bid the glorious conquest speed;
  Let this first refreshing ray
  Brighten to a perfect day.

  Rev. William Hiley Bathurst. (1796—) 1831. ab.

1139 *The Victory anticipated.* 7. D.
Ps. lxxii.

1 HASTEN, Lord, the glorious time,
  When, beneath Messiah's sway,
  Every nation, every clime,
  Shall the gospel call obey.
  Mightiest kings His power shall own,
  Heathen tribes His name adore;
  Satan and his host o'erthrown,
  Bound in chains, shall hurt no more.

2 Then shall wars and tumults cease,
  Then be banished grief and pain;
  Righteousness, and joy, and peace,
  Undisturbed shall ever reign.
  Time shall sun and moon obscure,
  Seas be dried, and rocks be riven,
  But His reign shall still endure,
  Endless as the days of Heaven.

  Miss Harriet Auber. (1773—1862.) 1829. ab.

1140 *Christ reigning over all the Earth.* 7.

1 WAKE the song of jubilee;
  Let it echo o'er the sea:
  Now is come the promised hour;
  Jesus reigns with glorious power.

2 All ye nations, join and sing,
  Praise your Saviour, praise your King;
  Let it sound from shore to shore,
  "Jesus reigns for evermore!"

3 Hark, the desert lands rejoice;
  And the islands join their voice:
  Joy! the whole creation sings,
  "Jesus is the King of kings!"

  Rev. Leonard Bacon. (1802—) 1823.

1141 *"The Song of Jubilee."* 7. D.

1 HARK, the song of jubilee,
  Loud as mighty thunders roar,
  Or the fulness of the sea,
  When it breaks upon the shore:
  Hallelujah! for the Lord
  God Omnipotent shall reign;
  Hallelujah! let the word
  Echo round the earth and main.

2 Hallelujah! hark, the sound,
  From the centre to the skies,
  Wakes above, beneath, around,
  All creation's harmonies.
  See Jehovah's banners furled,
  Sheathed His sword: He speaks; 'tis done,
  And the kingdoms of this world
  Are the kingdoms of His Son.

3 He shall reign from pole to pole
  With illimitable sway;
  He shall reign, when like a scroll
  Yonder heavens have passed away
  Then the end; beneath His rod
  Man's last enemy shall fall:
  Hallelujah! Christ in God,
  God in Christ, is All in all.

  James Montgomery. (1771—1854.) 1819, 1825.

1142 *"For those in Peril."* L. M. 6L.

1 ETERNAL Father, strong to save,
  Whose arm doth bind the restless wave,
  Who bidd'st the mighty ocean deep
  Its own appointed limits keep;
  O hear us when we cry to Thee
  For those in peril on the sea.

2 O Saviour, whose almighty word
  The winds and waves submissive heard,
  Who walkedst in the foaming deep,
  And calm amid its rage didst sleep;
  O hear us when we cry to Thee
  For those in peril on the sea.

3 O Sacred Spirit, who didst brood
  Upon the chaos dark and rude,
  Who bad'st its angry tumult cease,
  And gavest light, and life, and peace;
  O hear us when we cry to Thee
  For those in peril on the sea.

4 O Trinity of love and power,
  Our brethren shield in danger's hour;

From rock and tempest, fire and foe,
Protect them wheresoe'er they go;
And ever let there rise to Thee
Glad hymns of praise from land and sea.
William Whiting. (1825—) 1860.

1143 *Prayer for Mariners.* L. M.

1 WHILE o'er the deep Thy servants sail,
Send Thou, O Lord, the prosperous gale;
And on their hearts where'er they go,
O let Thy heavenly breezes blow.

2 If on the morning's wings they fly,
They will not pass beyond Thine eye:
The wanderer's prayer Thou bend'st to hear,
And faith exults to know Thee near.

3 When tempests rock the groaning bark,
O hide them safe in Jesus' ark;
When in the tempting port they ride,
O keep them safe at Jesus' side.

4 If life's wide ocean smile or roar,
Still guide them to the heavenly shore;
And grant their dust in Christ may sleep,
Abroad, at home, or in the deep.
Bp. George Burgess. (1809—1866.) 1840

1144 *For Seamen.* L. M.
Ps. cvii. 23—30.

1 O GOD, Who metest in Thy Hand
 The waters of the mighty sea,
And barrest ocean with the sand
 By Thy perpetual decree;

2 When they who to the sea go down,
 And in the waters ply their toil,
Are lifted on the surge's crown,
 And plunged where seething eddies boil;

3 Rule then, O Lord, the ocean's wrath,
 And bind the tempest with Thy will;
Tread, as of old, the water's path,
 And speak Thy bidding, "Peace, be still."

4 And when there shall be sea no more,
 Save that of mingled flame and glass,
Where goes no galley sped by oar,
 Where gallant ships no longer pass;

5 When dawns the Resurrection morn,
 Upon that shore, O Jesus, stand,
And give Thy pilgrims, faint and worn,
 Their welcome to the Happy Land.
Rev. Richard Frederick Littledale. (1833—) 1867. ab.

1145 *"Save, Lord, or we perish."* 12.
Matt. viii. 25.

1 WHEN thro' the torn sail the wild tempest is
 streaming,
When o'er the dark wave the red lightning
 is gleaming,
Nor hope lends a ray the poor sailors to
 cherish,
They fly to their Master, "Save, Lord, or we
 perish."

2 O Jesus, once rocked on the breast of the
 billow,
Aroused by the shriek of despair from Thy
 pillow,
Now seated in glory, the poor sinner cherish,
Who cries in his anguish, "Save, Lord, or
 we perish."
Bp. Reginald Heber. (1783—1826.) 1820. ab. and alt.

1146 *The guiding Star.* 8, 7, 4.

1 STAR of peace, to wanderers weary,
 Bright the beams that smile on me;
Cheer the pilot's vision dreary,
 Far, far at sea.

2 Star of hope, gleam on the billow,
 Bless the soul that sighs for thee;
Bless the sailor's lonely pillow,
 Far, far at sea.

3 Star of faith, when winds are mocking
 All his toil, he flies to thee;
Save him on the billows rocking,
 Far, far at sea.

4 Star divine, O safely guide him,
 Bring the wanderer home to thee;
Sore temptations long have tried him,
 Far, far at sea.
Mrs. Jane Cross Bell Simpson. 1830. ab.

1147 *Christ on the Lake of Galilee.* 8, 7. D.
Mark iv. 38.

1 TOSSED upon life's raging billow,
 Sweet it is, O Lord, to know,
Thou didst press a sailor's pillow,
 And canst feel a sailor's woe.
Never slumbering, never sleeping,
 Though the night be dark and drear,
Thou the faithful watch art keeping,
 "All, all's well," Thy constant cheer.

2 And though loud the wind is howling,
   Fierce though flash the lightnings red;
  Darkly though the storm-cloud's scowling
   O'er the sailor's anxious head;
  Thou canst calm the raging ocean,
   All its noise and tumult still,
  Hush the tempest's wild commotion,
   At the bidding of Thy will.

3 Thus my heart the hope will cherish,
   While to Thee I lift mine eye,
  Thou wilt save me ere I perish,
   Thou wilt hear the sailor's cry;
  And though mast and sail be riven,
   Life's short voyage will soon be o'er;
  Safely moored in Heaven's wide haven,
   Storms and tempests vex no more.
  Rev. George Washington Bethune. (1805–1862.) 1830. alt.

1148   *Wreck and Rescue.*   8, 7. D.

1 WRECKED and struggling in mid-ocean,
   Clinging to a broken spar,
  Darkness round me, billows o'er me,
   Not the glimmer of a star:
  Billows o'er me, and no mercy,
   Gasping as I was for breath;
  Night upon me, and the coming
   Of the darker night of death.

2 All the evils of a life-time
   Bearing down on my dark path,
  And I sinking,—O I tremble,
   Thinking of the night of wrath!
  Cast away, and lost, and sinking,
   Clinging to a broken spar;
  Suddenly a light from heaven
   Burst upon me like a star.

3 And a voice spoke to me cheerly,
   Spoke as from that burning star,
  "Trust to me, and I will save you;
   Cling not to a broken spar."
  Trembling, yet believing, hoping,
   I was borne above the wave;
  And I live to tell how Jesus
   Did a poor lost sinner save.
  Rev. Edward Hopper. (1818–) 1870, 1873.

1149   *"Nun danket all' Gott."*   7, 6, 6.

1 NOW thank we all our God,
   With heart and hand and voices
  Who wondrous things hath done,
   In whom this world rejoices;
  Who from our mother's arms
   Hath blessed us on our way
  With countless gifts of love
   And still is ours to-day.

2 O may this bounteous God,
   Through all our life be near us,
  With ever joyful hearts
   And blessed peace to cheer us;
  And keep us in His grace,
   And guide us when perplext,
  And free us from all ills
   In this world and the next.
  Rev. Martin Rinkart (1586–1649.) 1644.
  Tr. by Miss Catherine Winkworth. (1829–) 1858. ab.

1150   *"Herr Gott, wir danken Dir."*   7, 6, 6.

1 LORD God, we worship Thee:
   In loud and happy chorus
  We praise Thy love and power,
   Whose goodness reigneth o'er us
  To heaven our song shall soar,
   For ever shall it be
  Resounding o'er and o'er,
   Lord God, we worship Thee.

2 Lord God, we worship Thee:
   For Thou our land defendest;
  Thou pourest down Thy grace,
   And strife and war Thou endest.
  Since golden peace, O Lord,
   Thou grantest us to see,
  Our land with one accord,
   Lord God, gives thanks to Thee.

3 Lord God, we worship Thee:
   Thou didst indeed chastise us,
  Yet still Thy anger spares,
   And still Thy mercy tries us:
  Once more our Father's hand
   Doth bid our sorrows flee,
  And peace rejoice our land:
   Lord God, we worship Thee.
  Johann Frank. (1618–1677.) 1653.
  Tr. by Miss Catherine Winkworth. 1863. ab.

1151   *Thanksgiving.*   6, 7, 6.
        Ps. xxvi; cii.

1 TO Thee, O God, we raise
   Our voice, in choral singing;

We come, with prayer and praise,
  Our hearts' oblations bringing,
Thou art our fathers' God,
  And ever shalt be ours:
Our lips and lives shall laud
  Thy name, with all our powers.

2 Thy goodness, like the dew
    On Hermon's hill descending,
  Is every morning new,
    And tells of love unending.
  We bless Thy tender care
    That led our wayward feet,
  Past every fatal snare,
    To streams and pastures sweet.

3 We bless Thy Son, who bore
    The cross, for sinners dying;
  Thy Spirit we adore,
    The precious blood applying.
  Let work and worship send
    Their incense unto Thee,
  Till song and service blend,
    Beside the crystal sea.
        Rev. Arthur Tappan Pierson. (1836—) 1873.

1152 *National Blessings recounted.* 7.

1 SWELL the anthem, raise the song,
    Praises to our God belong;
  Saints and angels, join to sing
    Praise to heaven's almighty King.

2 Blessings from His liberal hand
    Pour around this happy land:
  Let our hearts, beneath His sway,
    Hail the bright, triumphant day.

3 Now to Thee our joys ascend,
    Thou hast been our heavenly Friend:
  Guarded by Thy mighty power,
    Peace and freedom bless our shore.

4 Here, beneath a virtuous sway,
    Lawful rulers we obey;
  Here we feel no tyrant's rod,
    Here we own and worship God.

5 Hark, the voice of nature sings
    Praises to the King of kings;
  Let us join the choral song,
    And the heavenly notes prolong.
        Rev. Nathan Strong. (1748—1816.) 1799.

1153 "*Give Thanks unto the Lord.*" 7.
        Ps. cxxxvi.

1 PRAISE, O praise our God and King,
  Hymns of adoration sing;
  For His mercies still endure
  Ever faithful, ever sure.

2 Praise Him that He made the sun
  Day by day his course to run;
  And the silver moon by night,
  Shining with her gentle light.

3 Praise Him that He gave the rain
  To mature the swelling grain;
  And hath bid the fruitful field
  Crops of precious increase yield.

4 Praise Him for our harvest-store,
  He hath filled the garner-floor;
  And for richer food than this,
  Pledge of everlasting bliss.

5 Glory to our bounteous King;
  Glory let Creation sing;
  Glory to the Father, Son,
  And blest Spirit, Three in One.
        Rev. Sir Henry Williams Baker. (1821—) 1861. ab.

1154 "*Praise waiteth for Thee, O God.*" 7.
        Ps. lxv.

1 PRAISE to God, immortal praise,
  For the love that crowns our days!
  Bounteous Source of every joy,
  Let Thy praise our tongues employ.

2 For the blessings of the field,
  For the stores the gardens yield;
  For the fruits in full supply,
  Ripened 'neath the summer sky;

3 Flocks that whiten all the plain;
  Yellow sheaves of ripened grain;
  Clouds that drop their fattening dews;
  Suns that temperate warmth diffuse;

4 All that spring with bounteous hand
  Scatters o'er the smiling land;
  All that liberal autumn pours
  From her rich o'erflowing stores:

5 These to Thee, my God, we owe,
  Source whence all our blessings flow;
  And for these my soul shall raise
  Grateful vows and solemn praise.
        Mrs. Anna Lætitia Barbauld. (1743—1825.) 1773. ab. and alt.

1155 *Harvest Hymn.* 7. D.

1 COME, ye thankful people, come,
  Raise the song of Harvest-home:
  All is safely gathered in,
  Ere the winter storms begin;
  God, our Maker, doth provide
  For our wants to be supplied:
  Come to God's own temple, come,
  Raise the song of Harvest-home.

2 All the world is God's own field,
  Fruit unto His praise to yield;
  Wheat and tares together sown,
  Unto joy or sorrow grown;
  First the blade, and then the ear,
  Then the full corn shall appear:
  Lord of Harvest, grant that we
  Wholesome grain and pure may be.

3 For the Lord our God shall come,
  And shall take His harvest home;
  From His field shall in that day
  All offences purge away;
  Give His angels charge at last
  In the fire the tares to cast;
  But the fruitful ears to store
  In His garner evermore.

4 Even so, Lord, quickly come
  To Thy final Harvest-home;
  Gather Thou Thy people in,
  Free from sorrow, free from sin;
  There, forever purified,
  In Thy presence to abide :
  Come, with all Thine angels, come,
  Raise the glorious Harvest-home.
    Rev. Henry Alford. (1810—1871.) 1845.

1156 *Thanksgiving or Fast.* 7. D.

1 CHRIST, by heavenly hosts adored,
  Gracious, mighty, sovereign Lord,
  God of nations, King of kings,
  Head of all created things,
  By the Church with joy confest,
  God o'er all forever blest;
  Pleading at Thy throne we stand,
  Save Thy people, bless our land.

2 On our fields of grass and grain
  Drop, O Lord, the kindly rain;
  O'er our wide and goodly land
  Crown the labors of each hand;
  Let Thy kind protection be
  O'er our commerce on the sea;
  Open, Lord, Thy bounteous hand,
  Bless Thy people, bless our land.

3 Let our rulers ever be
  Men that love and honor Thee;
  Let the powers by Thee ordained,
  Be in righteousness maintained :
  In the people's hearts increase
  Love of piety and peace;
  Thus, united we shall stand
  One wide, free, and happy land.
    Rev. Henry Harbaugh. (1818—1867.) 1860. ab. and alt.

1157 *God's Dealings with our Fathers.* C. M.
  Ps. xlv.

1 O LORD, our fathers oft have told,
    In our attentive ears,
  Thy wonders in their days performed,
    And elder times than theirs.

2 For not their courage, not their sword,
    To them salvation gave;
  Nor strength that from unequal force
    Their fainting troops could save.

3 But Thy right hand and powerful arm,
    Whose succor they implored;
  Thy presence with the chosen race,
    Who Thy great name adored.

4 As Thee their God our fathers owned,
    Thou art our sovereign King:
  O therefore, as Thou didst to them,
    To us deliverance bring.

5 To Thee the triumph we ascribe,
    From whom the conquest came;
  In God we will rejoice all day,
    And ever bless Thy name.
        Tate and Brady. 1696. ab. and alt.

1158 *The Story handed down.* C. M.
  Ps. lxxviii.

1 LET children hear the mighty deeds,
    Which God performed of old;
  Which in our younger years we saw,
    And which our fathers told.

2 He bids us make His glories known,
    His works of power and grace;
  And we 'll convey His wonders down
    Through every rising race.

3 Our lips shall tell them to our sons,
   And they again to theirs,
   That generations yet unborn
   May teach them to their heirs.

4 Thus shall they learn, in God alone
   Their hope securely stands ;
   That they may ne'er forget His works,
   But practice His commands.
                Rev. Isaac Watts. (1674—1748.) 1719.

1159   *The Nation prospered, and the Church increased.*
                Ps. lxvii.   C. M.

1 SHINE on our land, Jehovah, shine,
   With beams of heavenly grace ;
   Reveal Thy power through all our coasts,
   And show Thy smiling face.

2 When shall Thy name, from shore to shore,
   Sound all the earth abroad,
   And distant nations know and love
   Their Saviour and their God?

3 Sing to the Lord, ye distant lands,
   Sing loud with solemn voice ;
   Let thankful tongues exalt His praise,
   And thankful hearts rejoice.

4 He, the great Lord, the sovereign Judge,
   That sits enthroned above,
   Wisely commands the worlds He made,
   In justice and in love.

5 Earth shall confess her Maker's hand,
   And yield a full increase ;
   Our God will crown His chosen land
   With fruitfulness and peace.

6 God, the Redeemer, scatters round
   His choicest favors here ;
   While the creation's utmost bound
   Shall see, adore and fear.
                Rev. Isaac Watts. 1719. ab. and alt.

1160 *Deliverance from national Judgments implored.*   L. M.

1 WHILE o'er our guilty land, O Lord,
   We view the terrors of Thy sword,
   O whither shall the helpless fly ?
   To whom but Thee direct their cry ?

2 On Thee, our guardian God, we call ;
   Before Thy throne of grace we fall ;
   And is there no deliverance there ?
   And must we perish in despair ?

3 See, we repent, we weep, we mourn,
   To our forsaken God we turn ;
   O spare our guilty country, spare
   The Church which Thou hast planted here.

4 We plead Thy grace, indulgent God,
   We plead Thy Son's atoning blood,
   We plead Thy gracious promises ;
   And are they unavailing pleas ?

5 These pleas, presented at Thy throne,
   Have brought ten thousand blessings down
   On guilty lands in helpless woe ;
   Let them prevail and help us too.
                Rev. Samuel Davies. (1724—1761.) 1759.

1161   *Humble Confession of Sin.*   L. M.

1 IN prayer together let us fall,
   And cry for mercy, one and all,
   And weep before the Judge, and say,
   O turn from us Thy wrath away.

2 Thy grace have we offended sore
   By sins, O God, which we deplore ;
   Pour down upon us from above
   The riches of Thy pardoning love.

3 Remember, Lord, though frail we be,
   That yet Thy handiwork are we ;
   Nor let the honor of Thy Name
   Be by another put to shame.

4 Forgive the sin that we have wrought,
   Increase the good that we have sought ;
   That we at length, our wanderings o'er,
   May please Thee here and evermore.

5 Blest Three in One and One in Three,
   Almighty God, we pray to Thee,
   That Thou wouldst now vouchsafe to bless
   Our fast with fruits of righteousness.
                Rev. John Mason Neale, (1818—1866.) 1851. alt.
                Rev. Sir Henry Williams Baker. (1821—) 1861.

1162   *Forefathers' Day.*   L. M.

1 O GOD, beneath Thy guiding hand,
   Our exiled fathers crossed the sea ;
   And when they trod the wintry strand,
   With prayer and psalm they worshipped
       Thee.

2 Thou heard'st, well pleased, the song, the
       prayer :
   Thy blessing came ; and still its power

FESTIVALS AND FASTS.

Shall onward through all ages bear
  The memory of that holy hour.
3 Laws, freedom, truth, and faith in God
  Came with those exiles o'er the waves;
  And where their pilgrim feet have trod,
  The God they trusted guards their graves.
4 And here Thy name, O God of love,
  Their children's children shall adore,
  Till these eternal hills remove,
  And spring adorns the earth no more.
      Rev. Leonard Bacon. (1802—) 1838, 1845. ab.

1163   *Prayer for Peace.*   11, 10, 9.
1 GOD, the All-Terrible, Thou who ordainest
  Thunder Thy clarion, and lightning Thy sword;
  Show forth Thy pity on high where Thou reignest;
  Give to us peace in our time, O Lord.
2 God, the Omnipotent, Mighty Avenger,
  Watching invisible, judging unheard;
  Save us in mercy, O save us from danger;
  Give to us peace in our time, O Lord.
3 God, the All-Merciful, earth hath forsaken
  Thy ways all holy, and slighted Thy word;
  Let not Thy wrath in its terror awaken;
  Give to us pardon and peace, O Lord.
4 So will Thy people, with thankful devotion,
  Praise Him who saved them from peril and sword,
  Shouting in chorus, from ocean to ocean,
  Peace to the nations, and praise to the Lord.
      Henry Fothergill Chorley. (1808—1872.)

1164   *Prayer for Protection.*   8, 8, 8, 6.
1 FROM foes that would the land devour;
  From guilty pride, and lust of power;
  From wild sedition's lawless hour;
    From yoke of slavery;
2 From blinded zeal, by faction led;
  From giddy change, by fancy bred;
  From poisoned error's serpent head,
    Good Lord, preserve us free.
3 Defend, O God, with guardian hand,
  The laws and rulers of our land,

And grant Thy churches grace to stand
  In faith and unity.
4 Thy Spirit's help of Thee we crave,
  That Thy Messiah, sent to save,
  Returning to the world, might have
    A people serving Thee.
      Bp. Reginald Heber. (1783—1826.) 1827. alt.

1165   *National Hymn.*   6, 4.
1 MY country 'tis of Thee,
  Sweet land of liberty,
    Of thee I sing;
  Land where my fathers died,
  Land of the pilgrim's pride,
  From every mountain side
    Let freedom ring.
2 My native country, thee,
  Land of the noble, free,
    Thy name I love;
  I love thy rocks and rills,
  Thy woods and templed hills;
  My heart with rapture thrills
    Like that above.
3 Let music swell the breeze,
  And ring from all the trees
    Sweet freedom's song;
  Let mortal tongues awake,
  Let all that breathe partake,
  Let rocks their silence break,
    The sound prolong.
4 Our fathers' God, to Thee,
  Author of liberty,
    To Thee we sing;
  Long may our land be bright
  With freedom's holy light;
  Protect us by Thy might,
    Great God, our King.
      Rev. Samuel Francis Smith. (1808—) 1832.

1166   *"God save the State."*   6, 4.
1 GOD bless our native land;
  Firm may she ever stand,
    Through storm and night;
  When the wild tempests rave,
  Ruler of wind and wave,
  Do Thou our country save
    By Thy great might.

2 For her our prayer shall rise
  To God, above the skies;
  On Him we wait;
  Thou who art ever nigh,
  Guarding with watchful eye,
  To Thee aloud we cry,
  God save the State.
  Rev. John Sullivan Dwight. (1812—) 1844.

1167   *Thanksgiving for Harvest.*   6, 4.

1 THE God of harvest praise,
  In loud thanksgivings, raise
    Hand, heart, and voice;
  The valleys laugh and sing,
  Forests and mountains ring,
  The plains their tribute bring,
    The streams rejoice.

2 Yea, bless His holy name,
  And joyous thanks proclaim
    Through all the earth;
  To glory in your lot
  Is comely; but be not
  God's benefits forgot
    Amidst your mirth.

3 The God of harvest praise;
  Hands, hearts, and voices raise
    With one accord;
  From field to garner throng,
  Bearing your sheaves along,
  And in your harvest song
    Bless ye the Lord.
  James Montgomery. (1771—1854.) 1822. ab. and alt.

1168   *Wedding Hymn.*   S. M.
              John ii. 2.

1 HOW welcome was the call,
    And sweet the festal lay,
  When Jesus deigned in Cana's hall
    To bless the marriage day.

2 And happy was the bride,
    And glad the bridegroom's heart,
  For He who tarried at their side
    Bade grief and ill depart.

3 His gracious power divine
    The water vessels knew;
  And plenteous was the mystic wine
    The wondering servants drew.

4 O Lord of life and love,
    Come Thou again to-day;
  And bring a blessing from above
    That ne'er shall pass away.

5 O bless, as erst of old,
    The bridegroom and the bride;
  Bless with the holier stream that flowed
    Forth from Thy pierced side.

6 Before Thine altar-throne
    This mercy we implore;
  As Thou dost knit them, Lord, in one,
    So bless them evermore.
  Rev. Sir Henry Williams Baker. (1821—) 1861.

1169   *Love and Worship in a Family.*   S. M.
              Ps. cxxxiii.

1 BLEST are the sons of peace,
    Whose hearts and hopes are one;
  Whose kind designs to serve and please,
    Through all their actions run.

2 Blest is the pious house,
    Where zeal and friendship meet;
  Their songs of praise, their mingled vows
    Make their communion sweet.

3 Thus when on Aaron's head
    They poured the rich perfume,
  The oil through all his raiment spread,
    And pleasure filled the room.

4 Thus on the heavenly hills
    The saints are blest above;
  Where joy, like morning dew, distils,
    And all the air is love.
  Rev. Isaac Watts. (1674—1748.) 1719.

1170   *The Lord's Prayer.*   S. M.

1 OUR heavenly Father, hear
    The prayer we offer now;
  Thy name be hallowed far and near;
    To Thee all nations bow.

2 Thy kingdom come; Thy will
    On earth be done in love,
  As saints and seraphim fulfil
    Thy perfect law above.

3 Our daily bread supply,
    While by Thy word we live;
  The guilt of our iniquity
    Forgive, as we forgive.

4 From dark temptation's power,
   From Satan's wiles defend;
   Deliver in the evil hour,
   And guide us to the end.

5 Thine then forever be
   Glory and power divine;
   The sceptre, throne, and majesty
   Of heaven and earth are Thine.
                    James Montgomery. 1825. ab.

1171   *Dedication of a Home.*   C. M.
           Gen. xii. 7. 2 Cor. v. 1.

1 STRANGERS and pilgrims here below,
   To Thee our prayers we send;
   O God, from danger and from woe
   This dwelling-place defend.

2 Here let Thy peace, O Saviour, rest;
   Here let Thy love abide;
   Make us a blessing, make us blest,
   In all that may betide.

3 Keep storm, and fire, and sickness hence,
   And danger and alarm;
   Nor let the son of violence
   Approach to do us harm.

4 Let our petitions when we meet,
   And every secret prayer,
   Come up before Thy mercy-seat,
   And find acceptance there.

5 Teach us, in life, with faith and love
   To do our Lord's commands;
   And give us, in Thy time, above,
   A house not made with hands.
            Rev. John Mason Neale. (1818—1866.) 1844. ab.

1172   *Jacob's Vow.*   C. M.
           Gen. xxviii. 20—22.

1 O GOD of Bethel, by whose hand
   Thy people still are fed;
   Who through this weary pilgrimage
   Hast all our fathers led:

2 Our vows, our prayers, we now present
   Before Thy throne of grace:
   God of our fathers, be the God
   Of their succeeding race.

3 Through each perplexing path of life
   Our wandering footsteps guide;
   Give us each day our daily bread,
   And raiment fit provide.

4 O spread Thy covering wings around,
   Till all our wanderings cease,
   And, at our Father's loved abode,
   Our souls arrive in peace.

5 Such blessings from Thy gracious hand
   Our humble prayers implore;
   And Thou shalt be our chosen God
   And portion evermore.
        Rev. Philip Doddridge. (1702—1751.) 1737.
        Michael Bruce. (1746—1767.) 1781. alt.

1173   *Christ's Presence in the House.*

1 DEAR Friend, whose presence in the house,
   Whose gracious word benign,
   Could once at Cana's wedding feast
   Turn water into wine:

2 Come visit us, and when dull work
   Grows weary, line on line,
   Revive our souls, and make us see
   Life's water glow as wine.

3 Gay mirth shall deepen into joy,
   Earth's hopes shall grow divine,
   When Jesus visits us, to turn
   Life's water into wine.

4 The social talk, the evening fire,
   The homely household shrine,
   Shall glow with angels' visits when
   The Lord pours out the wine.

5 For when self-seeking turns to love,
   Which knows not mine and thine,
   The miracle again is wrought,
   And water changed to wine.
            Rev. James Freeman Clarke. (1810—) 1856.

1174   *God's Blessing invoked.*   C. M.
           Ps. xc. 17.

1 SHINE on our souls, eternal God,
   With rays of beauty shine:
   O let Thy favor crown our days,
   And all their round be Thine.

2 Did we not raise our hands to Thee,
   Our hands might toil in vain;
   Small joy success itself could give,
   If Thou Thy love restrain.

3 With Thee let every week begin,
   With Thee each day be spent;
   For Thee each fleeting hour improved,
   Since each by Thee is lent.

4 Thus cheer us through this desert road,
   Till all our labors cease ;
   And Heaven refresh our weary souls
   With everlasting peace.
   <small>Rev. Philip Doddridge. (1702—1751.) 1755.</small>

1175 *The Shepherd of Israel.* **C. M.**
<small>Ps. lxxx. 1.</small>

1 SHEPHERD of Israel, from above
   Thy feeble flock behold ;
   And never let us lose Thy love,
   Nor wander from Thy fold.

2 Thou wilt not cast Thy lambs away ;
   Thy hand is ever near,
   To guide them lest they go astray,
   And keep them safe from fear.

3 Thy tender care supports the weak,
   And will not let them fall ;
   Then teach us, Lord, Thy praise to speak,
   And on Thy name to call.

4 We want Thy help, for we are frail;
   Thy light, for we are blind ;
   Let grace o'er all our doubts prevail,
   To prove that Thou art kind.

5 Guide us through life ; and when at last
   We enter into rest,
   Thy tender arms around us cast,
   And fold us to Thy breast.
   <small>Rev. William Hiley Bathurst. (1796—) 1831 ab.</small>

1176 *Christ a Pattern for Children.* **C. M.**
<small>Luke ii. 40.</small>

1 BY cool Siloam's shady rill
   How sweet the lily grows !
   How sweet the breath beneath the hill
   Of Sharon's dewy rose !

2 Lo, such the child whose early feet
   The paths of peace have trod ;
   Whose secret heart, with influence sweet,
   Is upward drawn to God.

3 By cool Siloam's shady rill,
   The lily must decay ;
   The rose that blooms beneath the hill
   Must shortly fade away.

4 And soon, too soon, the wintry hour
   Of man's maturer age
   Will shake the soul with sorrow's power,
   And stormy passion's rage.

5 O Thou, whose infant feet were found
   Within Thy Father's shrine,
   Whose years, with changeless virtue crowned,
   Were all alike divine ;

6 Dependent on Thy bounteous breath,
   We seek Thy grace alone,
   In childhood, manhood, age, and death,
   To keep us still Thine own.
   <small>Bp. Reginald Heber. (1783—1826.) 1812.</small>

1177 *Children recalling Christ's Example.* **C. M.**

1 WHEN Jesus left His Father's throne,
   He chose an humble birth ;
   Like us, unhonored and unknown,
   He came to dwell on earth.

2 Like Him, may we be found below
   In wisdom's path of peace ;
   Like Him, in grace and knowledge grow,
   As years and strength increase.

3 Sweet were His words, and kind His look,
   When mothers round Him pressed ;
   Their infants in His arms He took,
   And on His bosom blessed.

4 Safe from the world's alluring harms,
   Beneath His watchful eye,
   Thus in the circle of His arms
   May we forever lie.

5 When Jesus into Salem rode,
   The children sang around ;
   For joy they plucked the palms, and strowed
   Their garments on the ground.

6 Hosanna our glad voices raise,
   Hosanna to our King ;
   Should we forget our Saviour's praise,
   The stones themselves would sing.
   <small>James Montgomery. (1771—1854.) 1819, 1825 ab.</small>

1178 *The gentle Shepherd.* **C. M.**

1 THERE is a little lonely fold,
   Whose flock One Shepherd keeps,
   Through summer's heat and winter's cold,
   With eye that never sleeps.

2 By evil beast, or burning sky,
   Or damp of midnight air,
   Not one in all that flock shall die
   Beneath that Shepherd's care.

3 For if, unheeding or beguiled,
   In danger's path they roam,
   His pity follows through the wild,
   And guards them safely home.

4 O gentle Shepherd, still behold
   Thy helpless charge in me;
   And take a wanderer to Thy fold,
   That trembling turns to Thee.
   Mrs. Maria Grace Saffery. (1773—1858.), 1844.

4 Soon will our earthly race be run,
   Our mortal frame decay;
   Parents and children, one by one,
   Must die and pass away.

5 Great God, impress the serious thought,
   This day on every breast,
   That both the teachers and the taught,
   May enter to Thy rest.
   Miss Jane Taylor. (1783—1824.) 1809.

1179 *Christ dying to save us.* C. M.

1 THERE is a green hill far away,
   Without a city wall,
   Where the dear Lord was crucified,
   Who died to save us all.

2 We may not know, we cannot tell
   What pains He had to bear;
   But we believe it was for us
   He hung and suffered there.

3 He died that we might be forgiven,
   He died to make us good,
   That we might go at last to Heaven,
   Saved by His precious blood.

4 There was no other good enough
   To pay the price of sin;
   He only could unlock the gate
   Of Heaven, and let us in.

5 O, dearly, dearly has He loved,
   And we must love Him too,
   And trust in His redeeming blood,
   And try His works to do.
   Mrs. Cecil Frances Alexander. 1848.

1181 *Jesus watching over Children.* C. M.

1 DEAR Jesus, ever at my side,
   How loving must Thou be,
   To leave Thy home in heaven to guard
   A little child like me.

2 I cannot feel Thee touch my hand,
   With pressure light and mild,
   To check me as my mother did,
   When I was but a child.

3 But I have felt Thee in my thoughts,
   Rebuking sin for me;
   And, when my heart loves God, I know
   The sweetness is from Thee.

4 And when, dear Saviour, I kneel down,
   Morning and night, to prayer,
   Something there is within my heart
   Which tells me Thou art there.

5 Yes, when I pray, Thou prayest too;
   Thy prayer is all for me;
   But when I sleep, Thou sleepest not,
   But watchest patiently.
   Rev. Frederick William Faber. (1814—1863.) 1849. abridged.

1180 *Infant Tongues in Heaven.* C. M.

1 THERE is a glorious world of light
   Above the starry sky,
   Where saints departed, clothed in white,
   Adore the Lord most high.

2 And hark, amid the sacred songs
   Those heavenly voices raise,
   Ten thousand thousand infant tongues
   Unite in perfect praise.

3 Those are the hymns that we shall know,
   If Jesus we obey;
   That is the place where we shall go,
   If found in wisdom's way.

1182 *"Speak gently."* C. M.

1 SPEAK gently: it is better far
   To rule by love than fear;
   Speak gently: let no harsh word mar
   The good we may do here.

2 Speak gently to the little child:
   Its love be sure to gain;
   Teach it in accents soft and mild;
   It may not long remain.

3 Speak gently to the young: for they
   Will have enough to bear;
   Pass through this life as best they may,
   'T is full of anxious care.

4 Speak gently to the aged one,
　Grieve not the careworn heart:
　The sands of life are nearly run,
　Let them in peace depart.

5 Speak gently to the erring: know
　They must have toiled in vain;
　Perchance unkindness made them so;
　O win them back again.

6 Speak gently: 'tis a little thing,
　Dropped in the heart's deep well;
　The good, the joy, that it may bring,
　Eternity shall tell.
George Washington Hangford. 1841. ab.

1183　　*Humble Service.*　　C. M.

1 SCORN not the slightest word or deed,
　Nor deem it void of power;
　There's fruit in each wind-wafted seed,
　That waits its natal hour.

2 A whispered word may touch the heart,
　And call it back to life;
　A look of love bid sin depart,
　And still unholy strife.

3 No act falls fruitless; none can tell
　How vast its power may be,
　Nor what results infolded dwell
　Within it silently.

4 Work on, despair not, bring thy mite,
　Nor care how small it be;
　God is with all that serve the right,
　The holy, true, and free.
Unknown Author.

1184　　*The Little Travellers.*　　7.

1 LITTLE travellers Zionward,
　Each one entering into rest,
　In the kingdom of your Lord,
　In the mansions of the blest:
　There, to welcome, Jesus waits,
　Gives the crowns His followers win.
　Lift your heads, ye golden gates,
　Let the little travellers in.

2 Who are they whose little feet,
　Pacing life's dark journey through,
　Now have reached that heavenly seat
　They had ever kept in view?
　"I from Greenland's frozen land;"
　"I from India's sultry plain;"
　"I from Afric's barren sand;"
　"I from islands of the main."

3 All our earthly journey past,
　Every tear and pain gone by,
　Here together met at last
　At the portal of the sky:
　Each the welcome, "Come," awaits,
　Conquerors over death and sin;
　Lift your heads, ye golden gates,
　Let the little travellers in.
James Edmeston. (1791—1867.) 1846.

1185　　*Prayer for Humility.*　　7.

1 LORD, for ever at Thy side
　May my place and portion be;
　Strip me of the robe of pride,
　Clothe me with humility.
　Meekly may my soul receive
　All Thy Spirit hath revealed;
　Thou hast spoken: I believe,
　Though the prophecy were sealed.

2 Quiet as a weanèd child,
　Weaned from the mother's breast,
　By no subtlety beguiled,
　On Thy faithfulness I rest.
　Saints rejoicing evermore,
　In the Lord Jehovah trust;
　Him in all His ways adore,
　Wise, and wonderful, and just.
James Montgomery. (1771—1854.) 1819.

1186　　*Praise to Jesus.*　　7.

1 LET us sing, with one accord,
　Praise to Jesus Christ our Lord;
　He hath made us by His power,
　He hath kept us to this hour,
　He redeems us from the grave,
　He who died now lives to save;
　Hearts and voices let us raise,
　He is worthy whom we praise.

2 Angels praise Him, so will we,
　Sinful children though we be;
　Poor and weak, we'll sing the more,
　Jesus helps the weak and poor.
　Dear to Him is childhood's prayer,
　Children's hearts to Him are dear;
　Hearts and voices let us raise,
　He is worthy whom we praise.
Miss Dorothy Ann Thrupp. (1779—1847.) 1853. ab. and alt.

1187 *Child's Evening Prayer.* 8, 7.

1 JESUS, tender Shepherd, hear me,
    Bless Thy little lamb to-night;
Through the darkness be Thou near me,
    Keep me safe till morning light.

2 All this day Thy hand has led me,
    And I thank Thee for Thy care;
Thou hast clothed me, warmed and fed me,
    Listen to my evening prayer.

3 Let my sins be all forgiven,
    Bless the friends I love so well;
Take me when I die to heaven,
    Happy there with Thee to dwell.
        Mrs. Mary Lundie Duncan. (1814—1840.) 1839.

1188 *Christ's Example.* 8, 7.

1 JESUS Christ, my Lord and Saviour,
    Once became a child like me;
O that in my whole behavior,
    He my pattern still might be.

2 All my nature is unholy,
    Pride and passion dwell within;
But the Lord was meek and lowly,
    Pure and spotless, free from sin.

3 While I'm often vainly trying
    Some new pleasure to possess,
He was always self-denying,
    Patient in His worst distress.

4 Let me never be forgetful
    Of His precepts any more;
Idle, passionate, and fretful,
    As I've often been before.

5 Lord, though now Thou art in glory,
    We have Thine example still;
I can read Thy sacred story,
    And obey Thy holy will.

6 Help me by that rule to measure
    Every word and every thought,
Thinking it my greatest pleasure
    There to learn what Thou hast taught.
        Miss Jane Taylor. (1783—1824.) 1809.

1189 *Christian Children.* 8, 7.

1 WE are little Christian children;
    We can run, and talk, and play;
The great God of earth and heaven
    Made, and keeps us every day.

2 We are little Christian children;
    Christ, the Son of God Most High,
With His precious blood redeemed us,
    Dying that we might not die.

3 We are little Christian children;
    God the Holy Ghost is here,
Dwelling in our hearts, to make us
    Kind and holy, good and dear.

4 We are little Christian children,
    Saved by Him who loved us most;
We believe in God Almighty,
    Father, Son and Holy Ghost.
        Mrs. Cecil Frances Alexander. 1848.

1190 *Christ's great Love and Condescension.* 8, 7.

1 WHAT a strange and wondrous story,
    From the Book of God is read:
How the Lord of life and glory
    Had not where to lay His head.

2 How He left His throne in heaven,
    Here to suffer, bleed, and die,
That my soul might be forgiven,
    And ascend to God on high.

3 Father, let Thy Holy Spirit
    Still reveal a Saviour's love,
And prepare me to inherit
    Glory where He reigns above;

4 There, with saints and angels dwelling,
    May I that great love proclaim,
And with them be ever telling
    All the wonders of His name.
        Unknown Author.

1191 *Prayer for Guidance.* 3, 7, 4.

1 SAVIOUR, like a shepherd lead us,
    Much we need Thy tender care;
In Thy pleasant pastures feed us,
    For our use Thy folds prepare.
      Blessed Jesus,
Thou hast bought us, Thine we are.

2 We are Thine, do Thou befriend us,
    Be the guardian of our way;
Keep Thy flock, from sin defend us,
    Seek us when we go astray;
      Blessed Jesus,
Hear the children when they pray.

3 Thou hast promised to receive us,
  Poor and sinful though we be;
Thou hast mercy to relieve us,
  Grace to cleanse, and power to free;
    Blessèd Jesus,
  Let us early turn to Thee.

4 Early let us seek Thy favor,
  Early let us do Thy will;
Holy Lord, our only Saviour,
  With Thy grace our bosoms fill;
    Blessèd Jesus,
  Thou hast loved us, love us still.
        Miss Dorothy Ann Thrupp. 1838.

1192   *Working in the Vineyard.*   8, 7, 4.

1 In the vineyard of our Father
  Daily work we find to do;
Scattered gleanings we may gather,
  Though we are but young and few;
    Little clusters
  Help to fill the garners too.

2 Toiling early in the morning,
  Catching moments through the day,
Nothing small or lowly scorning,
  While we work, and watch, and pray;
    Gathering gladly
  Free-will offerings by the way.

3 Not for selfish praise or glory,
  Not for objects nothing worth,
But to send the blessèd story
  Of the gospel o'er the earth,
    Telling mortals
  Of our Lord and Saviour's birth.

4 Up and ever at our calling,
  Till in death our lips are dumb,
Or till, sin's dominion falling,
  Christ shall in His kingdom come,
    And His children
  Reach their everlasting home.

5 Steadfast, then, in our endeavor,
  Heavenly Father, may we be;
And for ever, and for ever,
  We will give the praise to Thee;
    Hallelujah
  Singing, all eternity.
        Thomas MacKellar. (1812—) 1849.

1193   Στόμιον πώλων ἀδαῶν.   6, 4.

1 SHEPHERD of tender youth,
  Guiding in love and truth
    Through devious ways;
  Christ our triumphant King,
  We come Thy name to sing;
    Hither our children bring
    To shout Thy praise.

2 Thou art our Holy Lord,
  The all-subduing Word,
    Healer of strife:
  Thou didst Thyself abase,
  That from sin's deep disgrace
  Thou mightest save our race,
    And give us life.

3 Thou art the great High Priest,
  Thou hast prepared the feast
    Of heavenly love;
  While in our mortal pain
  None calls on Thee in vain;
  Help Thou dost not disdain,
    Help from above.

4 Ever be Thou our Guide,
  Our Shepherd and our Pride,
    Our Staff and Song:
  Jesus, Thou Christ of God,
  By Thy perennial Word
  Lead us where Thou hast trod,
    Make our faith strong.

5 So now, and till we die,
  Sound we Thy praises high,
    And joyful sing:
  Infants, and the glad throng
  Who to Thy Church belong,
  Unite to swell the song
    To Christ our King.
        From Clement of Alexandria. (—220.)
  Tr. by Rev. Henry Martyn Dexter. (1821—) 1846, 1849.

1194   *Children around God's Throne.*   C. M.
           Rev. vii. 13.

1 AROUND the throne of God in heaven
    Thousands of children stand;
  Children whose sins are all forgiven,
    A holy, happy band,
Cho. Singing, Glory, glory,
    Glory be to God on high.

2 In flowing robes of spotless white
　　See every one arrayed;
　　Dwelling in everlasting light,
　　And joys that never fade. *Cho.*

3 What brought them to that world above,
　　That heaven so bright and fair,
　　Where all is peace, and joy, and love,
　　How came those children there? *Cho.*

4 Because the Saviour shed His blood,
　　To wash away their sin;
　　Bathed in that pure and precious flood,
　　Behold them white and clean. *Cho.*

5 On earth they sought the Saviour's grace,
　　On earth they loved His name;
　　So now they see His blessèd face,
　　And stand before the Lamb. *Cho.*

Mrs. Anne Houlditch Shepherd. (1809—1857.) 1841. ab.

1195　*The Children in the Temple.*　7, 6.
　　Matt. xxi. 15, 16.

1 WHEN, His salvation bringing,
　　To Zion Jesus came,
　　The children all stood singing
　　Hosanna to His name.
　　Nor did their zeal offend Him,
　　But as He rode along,
　　He let them still attend Him,
　　And smiled to hear their song.

2 And since the Lord retaineth
　　His love to children still,
　　Though now as King He reigneth
　　On Zion's heavenly hill;
　　We'll flock around His banner,
　　We'll bow before His throne,
　　And cry aloud, Hosanna
　　To David's royal Son.

3 For should we fail proclaiming
　　Our great Redeemer's praise,
　　The stones, our silence shaming,
　　Would their hosannas raise.
　　But shall we only render
　　The tribute of our words?
　　No; while our hearts are tender,
　　They too shall be the Lord's.

Rev. Joshua King. 1830.

1196　*"Mighty to save."*　7, 6.
　　Is. lxiii. 1.

1 HE comes in blood-stained garments;
　　Upon His brow a crown;
　　The gates of brass fly open,
　　The iron bands drop down;
　　From off the fettered captive
　　The chains of Satan fall,
　　While angels shout triumphant,
　　That Christ is Lord of all.

2 O Christ, His love is mighty,
　　Long-suffering is His grace;
　　And glorious is the splendor
　　That beameth from His face.
　　Our hearts up-leap in gladness
　　When we behold that love,
　　As we go singing onward
　　To dwell with Him above.

Mrs. Charitie Lees Bancroft. (1841—) 1860. ab.

1197　*A Morning Hymn.*　L. M.

1 AWAKE, my soul, and with the sun
　　Thy daily stage of duty run;
　　Shake off dull sloth, and joyful rise
　　To pay thy morning sacrifice.

2 Wake, and lift up thyself, my heart,
　　And with the angels bear thy part,
　　Who, all night long, unwearied sing
　　High praise to the eternal King.

3 All praise to Thee who safe hast kept,
　　And hast refreshed me whilst I slept;
　　Grant, Lord, when I from death shall wake,
　　I may of endless light partake.

4 Lord, I my vows to Thee renew;
　　Disperse my sins as morning dew;
　　Guard my first springs of thought and will,
　　And with Thyself my spirit fill.

5 Direct, control, suggest this day,
　　All I design, or do, or say;
　　That all my powers, with all their might,
　　In Thy sole glory may unite.

6 Praise God, from whom all blessings flow;
　　Praise Him, all creatures here below;
　　Praise Him above, ye heavenly host;
　　Praise Father, Son, and Holy Ghost.

Bp. Thomas Ken. (1637—1711.) 1697, 1709. ab.

FAMILY WORSHIP.

1198 *A Morning Hymn.* L. M.
Ps. xix. 5, 8; lxxiii. 24, 25.

1 GOD of the morning, at whose voice
The cheerful sun makes haste to rise,
And like a giant doth rejoice
To run his journey through the skies:

2 From the fair chambers of the east
The circuit of his race begins;
And, without weariness or rest,
Round the whole earth he flies and shines.

3 O like the sun may I fulfil
The appointed duties of the day;
With ready mind, and active will,
March on and keep my heavenly way.

4 But I shall rove, and lose the race,
If God my Sun should disappear,
And leave me in the world's wide maze,
To follow every wandering star.

5 Give me Thy counsel for my guide,
And then receive me to Thy bliss:
All my desires and hopes beside
Are faint and cold compared with this.
Rev. Isaac Watts. (1674—1748.) 1709. ab. and sl. alt.

1199 *New every Morning.* L. M.
Lam. iii. 22, 23.

1 NEW every morning is the love
Our wakening and uprising prove;
Through sleep and darkness safely brought,
Restored to life, and power, and thought.

2 New mercies, each returning day,
Hover around us while we pray;
New perils past, new sins forgiven,
New thoughts of God, new hopes of heaven.

3 If on our daily course our mind
Be set to hallow all we find,
New treasures still, of countless price,
God will provide for sacrifice.

4 The trivial round, the common task,
Will furnish all we ought to ask,—
Room to deny ourselves, a road
To bring us daily nearer God.

5 Only, O Lord, in Thy dear love
Fit us for perfect rest above;
And help us, this and every day,
To live more nearly as we pray.
Rev. John Keble. (1792—1866.) 1827. ab.

1200 *For Morning or Evening.* L. M.
Lam. iii 23; Is. xlv. 7.

1 My God, how endless is Thy love:
Thy gifts are every evening new;
And morning mercies from above
Gently distil like early dew.

2 Thou spread'st the curtains of the night,
Great Guardian of my sleeping hours;
Thy sovereign word restores the light,
And quickens all my drowsy powers.

3 I yield my powers to Thy command;
To Thee I consecrate my days;
Perpetual blessings from Thy hand
Demand perpetual songs of praise.
Rev. Isaac Watts. 1709.

1201 *Before Work.* L. M.

1 FORTH in Thy Name, O Lord, I go,
My daily labor to pursue;
Thee, only Thee, resolved to know
In all I think, or speak, or do.

2 The task Thy wisdom hath assigned
O let me cheerfully fulfil;
In all my works Thy presence find,
And prove Thy good and perfect will.

3 Thee may I set at my right hand,
Whose eyes my inmost substance see:
And labor on at Thy command,
And offer all my works to Thee.

4 Give me to bear Thine easy yoke,
And every moment watch and pray;
And still to things eternal look,
And hasten to Thy glorious day.

5 Fain would I still for Thee employ
Whate'er Thy bounteous grace hath given,
And run my course with even joy,
And closely walk with Thee to heaven.
Rev. Charles Wesley. (1708—1788.) 1749. ab. and alt.

1202 *"Splendor paterne glorie."* L. M.

1 O JESUS, Lord of light and grace,
Thou brightness of the Father's face,
Thou fountain of eternal light,
Whose beams disperse the shades of night:

2 Come holy Sun of heavenly love,
Come in Thy radiance from above,
And to our inward hearts convey
The Holy Spirit's cloudless ray.

3 May He our actions deign to bless,
    And loose the bonds of wickedness;
    From sudden falls our feet defend,
    And guide us safely to the end.
4 May faith, deep rooted in the soul,
    Subdue our flesh, our minds control;
    May guile depart, and discord cease,
    And all within be joy and peace.
5 O hallowed thus be every day;
    Let meekness be our morning ray,
    Our faith like noontide splendor glow,
    Our souls the twilight never know.
            Ambrose of Milan. (340—397.)
    Tr. by Rev. John Chandler. (1806—) 1837. ab. and alt.

1203   "*Aurora jam spargit polum.*"   L. M.
1 THE dawn is sprinkling in the east
    Its golden shower, as day flows in;
    Fast mount the pointed shafts of light:
    Farewell to darkness and to sin.
2 So, Lord, when that last morning breaks,
    Which shrouds in darkness earth and skies,
    May it on us, low bending here,
    Arrayed in joyful light arise.
            Ambrosian. 4th or 5th century.
    Tr. by Rev. Edward Caswall. (1814—) 1849. ab. and alt.

1204   *Morning Hymn.*   L. M.
1 IN sleep's serene oblivion laid,
    I safely passed the silent night;
    Again I see the breaking shade,
    I drink again the morning light.
2 New-born, I bless the waking hour;
    Once more, with awe, rejoice to be;
    My conscious soul resumes her power,
    And springs, my guardian God, to Thee.
3 O guide me through the various maze
    My doubtful feet are doomed to tread;
    And spread Thy shield's protecting blaze,
    When dangers press around my head.
4 A deeper shade will soon impend,
    A deeper sleep mine eyes oppress;
    Yet then Thy strength shall still defend,
    Thy goodness still delight to bless.
5 That deeper shade shall break away,
    That deeper sleep shall leave mine eyes;
    Thy light shall give eternal day,
    Thy love, the rapture of the skies.
            John Hawkesworth. (1715—1773.) 1773.

1205   *Morning Hymn.*   L. M.
1 LORD God of morning and of night,
    We thank Thee for Thy gift of light;
    As in the dawn the shadows fly
    We seem to find Thee now more nigh.
2 Fresh hopes have wakened in the heart,
    Fresh force to do our daily part;
    Thy thousand sleeps our strength restore,
    A thousand-fold to serve Thee more.
3 Yet whilst Thy will we would pursue,
    Oft what we would we cannot do;
    The sun may stand in zenith skies,
    But on the soul thick midnight lies.
4 O Lord of lights, 'tis Thou alone
    Canst make our darkened hearts Thine own;
    Though this new day with joy we see,
    O dawn of God, we cry for Thee.
5 Praise God, our Maker and our Friend;
    Praise Him through time, till time shall end;
    Till psalm and song His Name adore
    Through Heaven's great day of Evermore.
            Francis Turner Palgrave. (1824—) 1867.

1206   *A Morning Prayer.*   L. M.
1 O THOU great Ruler of the sky,
    Who art, and canst not cease to be,
    Whose power and greatness never die,
    We raise our morning prayer to Thee.
2 In the beginning of the day,
    With the bright rising of the sun,
    Direct the footsteps of our way,
    Nor leave us till the day is done.
3 As hour succeeds to passing hour,
    And duties every moment fill,
    Uphold us by Thy mighty power,
    And guide us by Thy heavenly will.
4 And thus, when all our days shall close,
    And suns for us no more shall shine,
    O may our souls in Thee repose,
    And life and joy be one in Thine.
            Rev. Thomas Cogswell Upham. (1799—1872.) 1872.

1207   *A Morning Song.*   C. M.
1 ONCE more, my soul, the rising day
    Salutes thy waking eyes;
    Once more, my voice, thy tribute pay
    To Him that rules the skies.

2 Night unto night His Name repeats,
　The day renews the sound;
Wide as the heaven on which He sits,
　To turn the seasons round.

3 'Tis He supports my mortal frame;
　My tongue shall speak His praise;
My sins would rouse His wrath to flame;
　And yet His wrath delays.

4 A thousand wretched souls are fled
　Since the last setting sun;
And yet Thou lengthenest out my thread,
　And yet my moments run.

5 Dear God, let all my hours be Thine,
　While I enjoy the light:
Then shall my sun in smiles decline,
　And bring a pleasant night.
　　　　Rev. Isaac Watts. (1674—1748.) 1709. ab.

1208　　"*Aeterna caeli gloria.*"　　C. M.

1 JESUS, be near us when we wake;
　And, at the break of day,
With Thy blest touch awake the soul,
　Her meed of praise to pay.

2 The star that heralds in the morn
　Is fading in the skies;
The darkness melts: O Thou true Light,
　Once more on us arise.

3 Steep all our senses in Thy beam;
　The world's false night expel;
Purge each defilement from the soul,
　And in our bosoms dwell.

4 Come, early Faith, fix in our hearts
　Thy root immovably;
Come, smiling Hope, and, greater still,
　Come, heaven-born Charity.

5 To God the Father glory be,
　And sole eternal Son:
And glory, Holy Ghost, to Thee,
　While endless ages run.
　　　　Ambrosian. 5th century.
　　Tr. by Rev. Edward Caswall. (1814—) 1849. ab.

1209　　"*Jam lucis orto sidere.*"　　C. M.

1 Now that the sun is gleaming bright,
　Implore we, bending low,
That He, the uncreated Light,
　May guide us as we go.

2 No sinful word, nor deed of wrong,
　Nor thoughts that idly rove;
But simple truth be on our tongue,
　And in our hearts be love.

3 And while the hours in order flow,
　O Christ, securely fence
Our gates, beleaguered by the foe,
　The gate of every sense.

4 And grant that to Thine honor, Lord,
　Our daily toil may tend;
That we begin it at Thy word,
　And in Thy favor end.

5 Now to our God, the Father, Son,
　And Holy Spirit, sing:
With praise to God, the Three in One,
　Let all creation ring.
　　　　Paris Breviary. 1736.
Tr. by Rev. John Henry Newman. (1801—) 1842. ab. and al.

1210　　*Angels watching over us.*　　L. M.

1 INSPIRER and hearer of prayer,
　Thou Shepherd and Guardian of Thine,
My all to Thy covenant care
　I, sleeping and waking, resign:
If Thou art my Shield and my Sun,
　The night is no darkness to me;
And, fast as my moments roll on,
　They bring me but nearer to Thee.

2 Thy ministering spirits descend,
　And watch while Thy saints are asleep;
By day and by night they attend,
　The heirs of salvation to keep:
Bright seraphs, despatched from the throne,
　Fly swift to their stations assigned,
And angels elect are sent down,
　To guard the redeemed of mankind.

3 Thy worship no interval knows;
　Their fervor is still on the wing;
And, while they protect my repose,
　They chant to the praise of my King:
I, too, at the season ordained,
　Their chorus for ever shall join;
And love and adore, without end,
　Their gracious Creator, and mine.
Rev. Augustus Montague Toplady. (1740—1778.) 1774. alt.

1211　　*Christ near us through the Night.*　　L. M.

1 WHAT, though my frail eye-lids refuse
　Continual watching to keep,

And, punctual as midnight renews,
  Demand the refreshment of sleep?
A sovereign Protector I have,
  Unseen, yet forever at hand;
Unchangeably faithful to save,
  Almighty to rule and command.

2 From evil secure, and its dread,
  I rest, if my Saviour is nigh;
And songs His kind presence, indeed,
  Shall in the night-season supply:
He smiles, and my comforts abound;
  His grace, as the dew, shall descend;
And walls of salvation surround
  The soul He delights to defend.

3 Kind Author, and Ground of my hope,
  Thee, Thee for my God I avow;
My glad Ebenezer set up,
  And own Thou hast helped me till now;
I muse on the years that are past,
  Wherein my defence Thou hast proved,
Nor wilt Thou relinquish, at last,
  A sinner so signally loved.
          Rev. Augustus Montague Toplady. 1774.

1212   "*Sweet Hour of Prayer.*"   L. M.

1 SWEET hour of prayer, sweet hour of prayer,
  That calls me from a world of care,
  And bids me, at my Father's throne,
  Make all my wants and wishes known:
  In seasons of distress and grief,
  My soul has often found relief,
  And oft escaped the tempter's snare,
  By thy return, sweet hour of prayer.

2 Sweet hour of prayer, sweet hour of prayer,
  Thy wings shall my petition bear
  To Him, whose truth and faithfulness
  Engage the waiting soul to bless:
  And since He bids me seek His face,
  Believe His word, and trust His grace,
  I'll cast on Him my every care,
  And wait for thee, sweet hour of prayer.

3 Sweet hour of prayer, sweet hour of prayer,
  May I thy consolation share,
  Till, from Mount Pisgah's lofty height,
  I view my home, and take my flight;
  This robe of flesh I'll drop, and rise,
  To seize the everlasting prize;
  And shout, while passing through the air,
  Farewell, farewell, sweet hour of prayer.
          Rev. W. W. Walford. 1845. ab.

1213   *At Home with God everywhere.*   L. M.

1 MY Lord, how full of sweet content,
  I pass my years of banishment:
  Where'er I dwell, I dwell with Thee,
  In heaven, in earth, or on the sea.
  To me remains nor place nor time;
  My country is in every clime:
  I can be calm and free from care
  On any shore, since God is there.

2 While place we seek, or place we shun,
  The soul finds happiness in none;
  But with a God to guide our way,
  'T is equal joy, to go or stay.
  Could I be cast where Thou art not,
  That were indeed a dreadful lot;
  But regions none remote I call,
  Secure of finding God in all.
          Madame J. B. de la Motte Guyon. (1648—1717.) 1702.
          Tr. by William Cowper. (1731—1800.) 1782. ab. and alt.

1214   *Evening Prayer for Healing.*   L. M.
          Mark i. 32.

1 AT even, ere the sun was set,
  The sick, O Lord, around Thee lay;
  O in what divers pains they met,
  O with what joy they went away.
  Once more 't is eventide, and we,
  Oppressed with various ills, draw near:
  What if Thy form we cannot see?
  We know and feel that Thou art here.

2 O Saviour Christ, our woes dispel;
  For some are sick, and some are sad,
  And some have never loved Thee well,
  And some have lost the love they had;
  And none, O Lord, have perfect rest,
  For none are wholly free from sin;
  And they who fain would serve Thee best,
  Are conscious most of wrong within.

3 O Saviour Christ, Thou too art Man;
  Thou hast been troubled, tempted, tried:
  Thy kind but searching glance can scan
  The very wounds that shame would hide;
  Thy touch has still its ancient power,
  No word from Thee can fruitless fall;
  Hear in this solemn evening hour,
  And in Thy mercy heal us all.
          Rev. Henry Twells. (1823—) 1868. ab.

1215 *A Morning Hymn.* 11,10,11,5.

1 BEHOLD, the shade of night is now receding,
Kindling with splendors fair the dawn is glowing,
With fervent hearts, O let us all implore Him,
Ruler Almighty:

2 That He, our God, will look on us in pity,
Send strength for weakness, grant us His salvation,
And with a Father's pure affection give us
Glory eternal.

3 This grace O grant us, Godhead ever-blessèd,
Of Father, Son, and Holy Ghost in union,
Whose praises be through earth's most distant regions
Ever resounding.

Gregory. (540—604.) Tr. by Rev. Ray Palmer. (1808—) 1871.

1216 *An Evening Hymn.* 11,10,11,5.

1 'MID evening shadows let us all be watching,
Ever in psalms our deep devotion waking,
And with one voice hymns to the Lord, the Saviour,
Sweetly be singing.

2 That to the Holy King our songs ascending,
We worthily, with all His saints, may enter
The heavenly temple, joyfully partaking
Life everlasting.

3 This grace O grant us, Godhead ever-blessèd,
Of Father, Son, and Holy Ghost in union,
Whose praises be through earth's most distant regions
Ever resounding.

Gregory. Tr. by Rev. Ray Palmer. 1871.

1217 *Evening Prayer.* 8,4,8,4,8,4.

1 GOD, that madest earth and heaven,
Darkness and light;
Who the day for toil hast given,
For rest the night:
May Thine angel-guards defend us,
Slumber sweet Thy mercy send us,
Holy dreams and hopes attend us,
This livelong night.

2 And when morn again shall call us
To run life's way,
May we still, whate'er befall us,
Thy will obey:
From the power of evil hide us,
In the narrow pathway guide us,
Nor Thy smile be e'er denied us,
The livelong day.

3 Guard us waking, guard us sleeping,
And when we die,
May we in Thy mighty keeping
All peaceful lie:
When the last dread call shall wake us,
Do not Thou our God forsake us,
But to reign in glory take us
With Thee on high.

Bp. Reginald Heber. (1783—1826.) 1827. v. 1.
Abp. Richard Whately. (1787—1863.) 1860. vs. 2, 3.

1218 *"Strangers and Pilgrims."* 9,11,10,10.
Heb. xi. 13.

1 I'M a pilgrim, and I'm a stranger;
I can tarry, I can tarry but a night;
Do not detain me, for I am going
To where the fountains are ever flowing:
I'm a pilgrim, etc.

2 There the glory is ever shining:
O, my longing heart, my longing heart is there;
Here in this country so dark and dreary,
I long have wandered forlorn and weary.

3 There's the city to which I journey;
My Redeemer, my Redeemer is its light;
There is no sorrow, nor any sighing,
Nor any tears there, nor any dying.

Mrs. Mary S. B. Dana. (1810—) 1840.

1219 *The Hour of Prayer.* 8,8,8,4.
Phil. iv. 6, 7.

1 MY God, is any hour so sweet,
From blush of morn to evening star,
As that which calls me to Thy feet,
The hour of prayer?

2 Blest is that tranquil hour of morn,
And blest that solemn hour of eve,
When, on the wings of prayer upborne,
The world I leave.

3 Then is my strength by Thee renewed;
Then are my sins by Thee forgiven,
Then dost Thou cheer my solitude
With hopes of heaven.

4 No words can tell what sweet relief
    Here for my every want I find;
    What strength for warfare, balm for grief,
    What peace of mind.

5 Hushed is each doubt, gone every fear;
    My spirit seems in heaven to stay;
    And e'en the penitential tear
    Is wiped away.

6 Lord, till I reach that blissful shore,
    No privilege so dear shall be
    As thus my inmost soul to pour
    In prayer to Thee.
        Miss Charlotte Elliott. (1789—1871.) 1834.

1220   *Prayer to Christ.*   8,8,8,4.

1 JESUS, my Saviour, look on me,
    For I am weary and opprest;
    I come to cast myself on Thee:
    Thou art my Rest.

2 Look down on me, for I am weak,
    I feel the toilsome journey's length;
    Thine aid omnipotent I seek:
    Thou art my Strength.

3 I am bewildered on my way,
    Dark and tempestuous is the night;
    O send Thou forth some cheering ray:
    Thou art my Light.

4 When Satan flings his fiery darts,
    I look to Thee: my terrors cease;
    Thy cross a hiding-place imparts:
    Thou art my Peace.

5 Standing alone on Jordan's brink,
    In that tremendous latest strife,
    Thou wilt not suffer me to sink:
    Thou art my Life.

6 Thou wilt my every want supply,
    E'en to the end, whate'er befall;
    Through life, in death, eternally,
    Thou art my All.
        Rev. John Robert Macduff. 1853.

1221   *"Thy Will be done."*   8,8,8,4.

1 MY God and Father, while I stray
    Far from my home, on life's rough way,
    O teach me from my heart to say,
    Thy will be done.

2 Renew my will from day to day;
    Blend it with Thine, and take away
    All that now makes it hard to say,
    Thy will be done.

3 Then when on earth I breathe no more,
    The prayer oft mixed with tears before
    I'll sing upon a happier shore:
    Thy will be done.
        Miss Charlotte Elliott. 1834. ab.

1222   *An Evening Hymn.*   L. M.

1 ALL praise to Thee, my God, this night,
    For all the blessings of the light;
    Keep me, O keep me, King of kings,
    Beneath Thine own almighty wings.

2 Forgive me, Lord, for Thy dear Son,
    The ill that I this day have done;
    That with the world, myself, and Thee,
    I, ere I sleep, at peace may be.

3 Teach me to live, that I may dread
    The grave as little as my bed;
    To die, that this vile body may
    Rise glorious at the awful day.

4 O may my soul on Thee repose,
    And may sweet sleep my eyelids close;
    Sleep, that shall me more vigorous make,
    To serve my God when I awake.

5 When in the night I sleepless lie,
    My soul with heavenly thoughts supply;
    Let no ill dreams disturb my rest,
    No powers of darkness me molest.

6 Praise God, from whom all blessings flow;
    Praise Him, all creatures here below;
    Praise Him above, ye heavenly host;
    Praise Father, Son, and Holy Ghost.
        Bp. Thomas Ken. (1637—1711.) 1695, 1709. ab.

1223   *An Evening Hymn.*   L. M.
        Ps. iv.

1 THUS far the Lord has led me on,
    Thus far His power prolongs my days;
    And every evening shall make known
    Some fresh memorial of His grace.

2 Much of my time has run to waste,
    And I perhaps am near my home;
    But He forgives my follies past,
    And gives me strength for days to come.

3 I lay my body down to sleep;
  Peace is the pillow for my head,
  While well-appointed angels keep
  Their watchful stations round my bed.

4 Faith in His name forbids my fear;
  O may Thy presence ne'er depart;
  And, in the morning, make me hear
  The love and kindness of Thy heart.

5 Thus, when the night of death shall come,
  My flesh shall rest beneath the ground;
  And wait Thy voice to rouse my tomb,
  With sweet salvation in the sound.
    Rev. Isaac Watts. (1674—1748.) 1709. ab.

1224   *An Evening Hymn.*   L. M.

1 GREAT God, to Thee my evening song
  With humble gratitude I raise;
  O let Thy mercy tune my tongue,
  And fill my heart with lively praise.

2 My days, unclouded as they pass,
  And every gently rolling hour,
  Are monuments of wondrous grace,
  And witness to Thy love and power.

3 And yet this thoughtless, wretched heart,
  Too oft regardless of Thy love,
  Ungrateful, can from Thee depart,
  And, fond of trifles, vainly rove.

4 Seal my forgiveness in the blood
  Of Jesus; His dear name alone
  I plead for pardon, gracious God,
  And kind acceptance at Thy throne.

5 Let this blest hope mine eyelids close;
  With sleep refresh my feeble frame;
  Safe in Thy care may I repose,
  And wake with praises to Thy name.
    Miss Anne Steele. (1717—1778.) 1760. ab.

1225   *"The Day-star from on high."*   S. M.

1 WE lift our hearts to Thee,
    Thou Day-star from on high;
  The sun itself is but Thy shade,
    Yet cheers both earth and sky.

2 O let Thy rising beams
    Dispel the shades of night;
  And let the glories of Thy love
    Come like the morning light.

3 How beauteous nature now,
    How dark and sad before:
  With joy we view the pleasing change
    And nature's God adore.

4 May we this life improve
    To mourn for errors past;
  And live, this short, revolving day,
    As if it were our last.
    Rev. John Wesley? (1703—1791.) 1741. ab. and alt.

1226   *"Still with Thee."*   S. M.

1 STILL, still with Thee, my God,
    I would desire to be:
  By day, by night, at home, abroad,
    I would be still with Thee.

2 With Thee, when dawn comes in,
    And calls me back to care,
  Each day returning to begin
    With Thee, my God, in prayer.

3 With Thee amid the crowd
    That throngs the busy mart,
  To hear Thy voice, 'mid clamor loud,
    Speak softly to my heart.

4 With Thee, when day is done,
    And evening calms the mind;
  The setting, as the rising, sun
    With Thee my heart would find.

5 With Thee, when darkness brings
    The signal of repose,
  Calm in the shadow of Thy wings,
    Mine eyelids I would close.

6 With Thee, in Thee, by faith
    Abiding I would be;
  By day, by night, in life, in death,
    I would be still with Thee.
    Rev. James Drummond Burns. (1823—1864.) 1856. sl. alt.

1227   *For a Lord's-Day Morning.*   S. M.
            Ps. xix.

1 BEHOLD, the morning sun
    Begins his glorious way;
  His beams through all the nations run,
    And life and light convey.

2 But where the Gospel comes,
    It spreads diviner light;
  It calls dead sinners from their tombs,
    And gives the blind their sight.

3 How perfect is Thy word,
　And all Thy judgments just;
　For ever sure Thy promise, Lord,
　And men securely trust.

4 My gracious God, how plain
　Are Thy directions given:
　O may I never read in vain,
　But find the path to heaven.

5 While with my heart and tongue
　I spread Thy praise abroad,
　Accept the worship and the song,
　My Saviour and my God.
　　　　　Rev. Isaac Watts. 1719. ab.

1228　　On going to Rest.　　S. M.

1 THE day is past and gone,
　The evening shades appear;
　O may I ever keep in mind,
　The night of death draws near.

2 I lay my garments by,
　Upon my bed to rest;
　So death will soon remove me hence,
　And leave my soul undressed.

3 Lord, keep me safe this night,
　Secure from all my fears;
　May angels guard me, while I sleep,
　Till morning light appears.

4 And when I early rise,
　To view th' unwearied sun,
　May I set out to win the prize,
　And after glory run:

5 That when my days are past,
　And I from time remove,
　Lord, I may in Thy bosom rest,
　The bosom of Thy love.
　　　　Rev. John Leland. (1754—1841.) 1799.

1229　"Hath not where to lay His Head."　S. M.
　　　　Luke ix. 58.

1 ALMIGHTY God, to-night
　To Thee for help we pray;
　To whom the darkness is as light,
　And midnight like the day.

2 Thy tender love and care
　Prepares our peaceful bed;
　But Thou, O Saviour, hadst not where
　To lay Thy blessed head.

3 O keep us now from harm,
　As Thou hast done before;
　And let Thine everlasting arm
　Be round us evermore.

4 Let holy angels stand
　About us every night,
　Until they bear us to the land
　Of everlasting light.

5 From men below the skies,
　And all the heavenly host,
　To God the Father praise arise,
　The Son and Holy Ghost.
　　　Rev. John Mason Neale. (1818—1866.) 1854

1230　　The final Rest.　　S. M.

1 THE day is past and gone,
　Great God, we bow to Thee;
　Again, as shades of night steal on,
　Unto Thy Side we flee.

2 O when shall that day come,
　Ne'er sinking in the west,
　That country and that happy home,
　Where none shall break our rest;

3 Where all things shall be peace,
　And pleasure without end,
　And golden harps, that never cease,
　With joyous hymns shall blend;

4 Where we, preserved beneath
　The shelter of Thy wing,
　For evermore Thy praise shall breathe,
　And of Thy mercy sing.

5 To God the Father praise,
　And to the Eternal Son,
　And to the Holy Ghost always,
　Co-equal Three in One.
　　　　Rev. William John Blew. 1849.

1231　　Evening Twilight.　　C. M.

1 I LOVE to steal awhile away
　From every cumbering care,
　And spend the hours of setting day
　In humble, grateful prayer.

2 I love, in solitude, to shed
　The penitential tear;
　And all His promises to plead
　Where none but God can hear.

3 I love to think on mercies past,
   And future good implore;
   And all my cares and sorrows cast
   On Him whom I adore.

4 I love, by faith, to take a view
   Of brighter scenes in heaven;
   The prospect doth my strength renew,
   While here by tempests driven.

5 Thus, when life's toilsome day is o'er,
   May its departing ray
   Be calm as this impressive hour,
   And lead to endless day.
             Mrs. Phœbe Hinsdale Brown. (1783—1861.) 1824.

1232   *Evening Twilight.*   C. M.

1 HAIL, tranquil hour of closing day,
   Begone, disturbing care;
   And look, my soul, from earth away
   To Him who heareth prayer.

2 How sweet the tear of penitence,
   Before His throne of grace,
   While, to the contrite spirit's sense,
   He shows His smiling face.

3 How sweet, thro' long-remembered years,
   His mercies to recall,
   And pressed with wants, and griefs, and fears,
   To trust His love for all.

4 How sweet to look, in thoughtful hope,
   Beyond this fading sky,
   And hear Him call His children up
   To His fair home on high.

5 Calmly the day forsakes our heaven
   To dawn beyond the west;
   So let my soul, in life's last even,
   Retire to glorious rest.
             Rev. Leonard Bacon. (1802—) 1845.

1233   *"He knoweth the Way that I take."*   C. M.
             Job xxiii. 10.

1 THE twilight falls, the night is near,
   I fold my work away,
   And kneel to One who bends to hear
   The story of the day.

2 The old, old story; yet I kneel
   To tell it at Thy call,
   And cares grow lighter as I feel
   That Jesus knows them all.

3 Thou knowest all: I lean my head;
   My weary eyelids close;
   Content and glad awhile to tread
   This path, since Jesus knows.

4 And He has loved me: All my heart
   With answering love is stirred,
   And every anguished pain and smart
   Finds healing in the word.

5 So here I lay me down to rest,
   As nightly shadows fall,
   And lean confiding on His breast
   Who knows and pities all.
             Unknown Author.

1234   *An Evening Psalm.*   C. M.
             Ps. iv.

1 LORD, Thou wilt hear me when I pray,
   I am forever Thine;
   I fear before Thee all the day,
   Nor would I dare to sin.

2 And while I rest my weary head,
   From cares and business free,
   'Tis sweet conversing on my bed
   With my own heart and Thee.

3 I pay this evening sacrifice;
   And when my work is done,
   Great God, my faith and hope relies
   Upon Thy grace alone.

4 Thus with my thoughts composed to peace,
   I'll give mine eyes to sleep;
   Thy hand in safety keeps my days,
   And will my slumbers keep.
             Rev. Isaac Watts. (1674—1748.) 1719.

1235   *An Evening Song.*   C. M.

1 DREAD Sovereign, let my evening song
   Like holy incense rise;
   Assist the offerings of my tongue
   To reach the lofty skies.

2 Through all the dangers of the day
   Thy hand was still my guard;
   And still to drive my wants away
   Thy mercy stood prepared.

3 Perpetual blessings from above
   Encompass me around;
   But O how few returns of love
   Hath my Creator found.

4 What have I done for Him that died
   To save my wretched soul?
   How are my follies multiplied,
   Fast as the minutes roll.

5 Lord, with this guilty heart of mine,
   To Thy dear cross I flee,
   And to Thy grace my soul resign
   To be renewed by Thee.

6 Sprinkled afresh with pardoning blood,
   I lay me down to rest,
   As in the embraces of my God,
   Or on my Saviour's breast.
   Rev. Isaac Watts. 1709.

1236 *Evening Worship.* C. M.

1 O LORD, another day is flown,
   And we, a lonely band,
   Are met once more before Thy throne,
   To bless Thy fostering hand.

2 And wilt Thou bend a listening ear
   To praises low as ours?
   Thou wilt, for Thou dost love to hear
   The song which meekness pours.

3 O let Thy grace perform its part,
   And let contention cease;
   And shed abroad in every heart
   Thine everlasting peace.

4 Thus chastened, cleansed, entirely Thine,
   A flock by Jesus led,
   The Sun of righteousness shall shine
   In glory on our head.

5 And Thou wilt turn our wandering feet,
   And Thou wilt bless our way;
   Till worlds shall fade, and faith shall greet
   The dawn of lasting day.
   Henry Kirke White. (1785—1806.) 1803. ab. and sl. alt.

1237 *Safety in God.* 8, 7.
   Ps. xci.

1 CALL Jehovah thy salvation,
   Rest beneath th' Almighty's shade,
   In His secret habitation
   Dwell, and never be dismayed.

2 There no tumult can alarm thee,
   Thou shalt dread no hidden snare;
   Guile nor violence can harm thee,
   In eternal safeguard there.

3 From the sword, at noonday wasting,
   From the noisome pestilence,
   In the depth of midnight, blasting,
   God shall be thy sure defence.

4 God shall charge His angel legions
   Watch and ward o'er thee to keep;
   Though thou walk through hostile regions,
   Though in desert wilds thou sleep.

5 Since, with pure and firm affection,
   Thou on God hast set thy love,
   With the wings of His protection
   He will shield thee from above.

6 Thou shalt call on Him in trouble,
   He will hearken, He will save;
   Here for grief reward thee double,
   Crown with life beyond the grave.
   James Montgomery. (1771—1854.) 1822. ab.

1238 *Our Need of God.* 8, 7.
   Ps. cxxvii.

1 VAINLY through night's weary hours,
   Keep we watch, lest foes alarm;
   Vain our bulwarks, and our towers,
   But for God's protecting arm.

2 Vain were all our toil and labor,
   Did not God that labor bless;
   Vain, without His grace and favor,
   Every talent we possess.

3 Vainer still the hope of heaven,
   That on human strength relies;
   But to Him shall help be given,
   Who in humble faith applies.

4 Seek we, then, the Lord's Anointed;
   He will grant us peace and rest;
   Ne'er was suppliant disappointed,
   Who through Christ his prayer addressed.
   Miss Harriet Auber. (1773—1862.) 1829.

1239 *An Evening Prayer.* 8, 7.

1 HEAR my prayer, O heavenly Father,
   Ere I lay me down to sleep;
   Bid Thine angels, pure and holy,
   Round my bed their vigil keep.

2 Great my sins are, but Thy mercy
   Far outweighs them every one;
   Down before Thy cross I cast them,
   Trusting in Thy help alone.

3 Keep me, through this night of peril,
   Underneath its boundless shade;
   Take me to Thy rest, I pray Thee,
   When my pilgrimage is made.

4 None shall measure out Thy patience
   By the span of human thought;
   None shall bound the tender mercies
   Which Thy holy Son has brought.

5 Pardon all my past transgressions;
   Give me strength for days to come;
   Guide and guard me with Thy blessing,
   Till Thine angels bid me home.
          Miss Harriet Parr. 1856. sl. alt.

1240   *Sacred Memories.*   8, 7.

1 SILENTLY the shades of evening
   Gather round my lowly door;
   Silently they bring before me
   Faces I shall see no more.

2 O the lost, the unforgotten,
   Though the world be oft forgot;
   O the shrouded and the lonely,
   In our hearts they perish not.

3 Living in the silent hours
   Where our spirits only blend;
   They, unlinked with earthly trouble,
   We, still hoping for its end.

4 How such holy memories cluster,
   Like the stars when storms are past;
   Pointing up to that far heaven
   We may hope to gain at last.
          C. C. Cox. 1848.

1241   *On going to Rest.*   8, 7.

1 SAVIOUR, breathe an evening blessing,
   Ere repose our spirits seal;
   Sin and want we come confessing,
   Thou canst save, and Thou canst heal.

2 Though destruction walk around us,
   Though the arrow past us fly,
   Angel-guards from Thee surround us,
   We are safe, if Thou art nigh.

3 Though the night be dark and dreary,
   Darkness cannot hide from Thee;
   Thou art He who, never weary,
   Watchest where Thy people be.

4 Should swift death this night o'ertake us,
   And our couch become our tomb,
   May the morn in heaven awake us,
   Clad in light and deathless bloom.
          James Edmeston. (1791—1867.) 1822.

1242   *Evening Shadows.*   8, 7.

1 TARRY with me, O my Saviour,
   For the day is passing by;
   See, the shades of evening gather,
   And the night is drawing nigh.

2 Deeper, deeper grow the shadows,
   Paler now the glowing west;
   Swift the night of death advances;
   Shall it be the night of rest?

3 Feeble, trembling, fainting, dying,
   Lord, I cast myself on Thee;
   Tarry with me through the darkness;
   While I sleep, still watch by me.

4 Tarry with me, O my Saviour;
   Lay my head upon Thy breast
   Till the morning, then awake me,—
   Morning of eternal rest.
          Mrs. Caroline Sprague Smith. 1855. ab.

1243   *Be ye also ready.*   8, 7.

1 DAYS and moments quickly flying
   Blend the living with the dead;
   Soon shall we who sing be lying
   Each within our narrow bed.

2 Jesus, infinite Redeemer,
   Maker of this mighty frame;
   Teach, O teach us to remember
   What we are, and whence we came.

3 Grant us grace, that whatsoever
   May befall us, we may be
   Ready for Thy solemn summons,
   And in joy to answer Thee.
          Rev. Edward Caswall. (1814—) 1849. ab. and alt.

1244   "*Te lucis ante terminum.*"   7.

1 ERE the waning light decay,
   God of all, to Thee we pray,
   Thee Thy healthful grace to send,
   Thee to guard us and defend.

2 Guard from dreams that may affright;
   Guard from terrors of the night;
   Guard from foes, without, within,
   Outward danger, inward sin.

3 Mindful of our only stay,
  Duly thus to Thee we pray;
  Duly thus to Thee we raise
  Trophies of our grateful praise.

4 Hear the prayer, almighty King;
  Hear Thy praises while we sing,
  Hymning with Thy heavenly host,
  Father, Son, and Holy Ghost.
              Ambrose of Milan. (340—397.)
        Tr. by Bp. Richard Mant. (1776—1848.) 1837.

1245   *"The Lord is Thy Keeper."*   7.
           Ps. cxxi. 5.

1 EVERY morning mercies new
  Fall as fresh as morning dew;
  Every morning let us pay
  Tribute with the early day;
  For Thy mercies, Lord, are sure;
  Thy compassion doth endure.

2 Still the greatness of Thy love
  Daily doth our sins remove;
  Daily, far as east from west,
  Lifts the burden from the breast;
  Gives unbought to those who pray
  Strength to stand in evil day.

3 Let our prayers each morn prevail,
  That these gifts may never fail;
  And, as we confess the sin
  And the tempter's power within,
  Feed us with the Bread of Life;
  Fit us for our daily strife.

4 As the morning light returns,
  As the sun with splendor burns,
  Teach us still to turn to Thee,
  Ever blessed Trinity,
  With our hands our hearts to raise,
  In unfailing prayer and praise.
              Rev. Horatius Bonar. (1808—) 1866.

1246   *The fading Light.*   7.

1 SOFTLY now the light of day
  Fades upon my sight away;
  Free from care, from labor free,
  Lord, I would commune with Thee.

2 Thou, whose all-pervading eye
  Naught escapes, without, within,
  Pardon each infirmity,
  Open fault, and secret sin.

3 Soon, for me, the light of day
  Shall forever pass away;

Then, from sin and sorrow free,
Take me, Lord, to dwell with Thee.

4 Thou who, sinless, yet hast known
  All of man's infirmity;
  Then, from Thine eternal throne,
  Jesus, look with pitying eye.
        Bp. George Washington Doane. (1799—1859.) 1824.

1247   *Morning Prayer.*   7. 6l.

1 IN this calm impressive hour,
    Let my prayer ascend on high;
  God of mercy, God of power,
    Hear me, when to Thee I cry:
  Hear me from Thy lofty throne,
  For the sake of Christ, Thy Son.

2 With the morning's early ray,
    While the shades of night depart,
  Let Thy beams of light convey
    Joy and gladness to my heart:
  Now o'er all my steps preside,
  And for all my wants provide.

3 O what joy that word affords,
    "Thou shalt reign o'er all the earth;"
  King of kings, and Lord of lords,
    Send Thy Gospel-heralds forth:
  Now begin Thy boundless sway,
  Usher in the glorious day.
              Thomas Hastings. (1784—1872.) 1831.

1248   *Evening Hymn.*   7. 6l.

1 Now from labor and from care
    Evening hours have set me free,
  In the work of praise and prayer,
    Lord, I would converse with Thee:
  O behold me from above,
  Fill me with a Saviour's love.

2 Sin and sorrow, guilt and woe
    Wither all my earthly joys;
  Naught can charm me here below,
    But my Saviour's melting voice:
  Lord, forgive, Thy grace restore,
  Make me Thine for evermore.

3 For the blessings of this day,
    For the mercies of this hour,
  For the gospel's cheering ray,
    For the Spirit's quickening power,
  Grateful notes to Thee I raise;
  O accept the song of praise.
              Thomas Hastings. 1831.

1249 Evening 7. 61.

1 FATHER, by Thy love and power,
   Comes again the evening hour;
   Light has vanished, labors cease,
   Weary creatures rest in peace:
   We to Thee ourselves resign,
   Let our latest thoughts be Thine.

2 Saviour, to Thy Father bear
   This our feeble evening prayer;
   Thou hast seen how oft to-day
   We, like sheep, have gone astray;
   Blessèd Saviour, we, through Thee,
   Pray that we may pardoned be.

3 Holy Spirit, Breath of balm,
   Fall on us in evening's calm;
   Yet awhile, before we sleep,
   We with Thee will vigil keep.
   Melt our spirits, mould our will,
   Soften, strengthen, comfort still.

4 Blessèd Trinity, be near
   Through the hours of darkness drear;
   Father, Son, and Holy Ghost,
   Round us set th' angelic host,
   Till the flood of morning rays
   Wake us to a song of praise.
   Prof. Joseph Anstice. (1808—1836.) 1836. ab. and alt.

1250 The Frailty of Life. C. M.

1 THEE we adore, Eternal Name,
   And humbly own to Thee
   How feeble is our mortal frame,
   What dying worms are we.

2 The year rolls round, and steals away
   The breath that first it gave;
   Whate'er we do, where'er we be,
   We're travelling to the grave.

3 Great God, on what a slender thread
   Hang everlasting things;
   The eternal state of all the dead
   Upon life's feeble strings.

4 Infinite joy, or endless woe,
   Attends on every breath;
   And yet how unconcerned we go
   Upon the brink of death.

5 Waken, O Lord, our drowsy sense,
   To walk this dangerous road;
   And if our souls are hurried hence,
   May they be found with God.
   Rev. Isaac Watts. (1674—1748.) 1709. ab.

1251 Let us awake. C. M.
Rom. xiii. 11.

1 AWAKE, ye saints, and raise your eyes
   And raise your voices high;
   Awake, and praise the sovereign love,
   That shows salvation nigh.

2 Swift on the wings of time it flies,
   Each moment brings it near;
   Then welcome, each declining day,
   Welcome, each closing year.

3 Not many years their round shall run,
   Not many mornings rise,
   Ere all its glories stand revealed
   To our admiring eyes.

4 Ye wheels of nature, speed your course,
   Ye mortal powers, decay,
   Fast as ye bring the night of death,
   Ye bring eternal day.
   Rev. Philip Doddridge. (1702—1751.) 1755.

1252 God in Nature. C. M.
Ps. lxv.

1 'TIS by Thy strength the mountains stand,
   God of eternal power;
   The sea grows calm at Thy command,
   And tempests cease to roar.

2 Thy morning light and evening shade
   Successive comforts bring;
   Thy plenteous fruits make harvest glad,
   Thy flowers adorn the spring.

3 Seasons and times, and moons and hours,
   Heaven, earth, and air are Thine;
   When clouds distil in fruitful showers,
   The author is divine.

4 Those wandering cisterns in the sky,
   Borne by the winds around,
   With watery treasures well supply
   The furrows of the ground.

5 The thirsty ridges drink their fill,
   And ranks of corn appear;
   Thy ways abound with blessings still,
   Thy goodness crowns the year.
   Rev. Isaac Watts. 1719.

1253   *Spring.*   C. M.

1 LORD, in Thy Name Thy servants plead,
   And Thou hast sworn to hear;
   Thine is the harvest, Thine the seed,
   The fresh and fading year.

2 Our hope, when autumn winds blew wild,
   We trusted, Lord, with Thee;
   And still, now spring has on us smiled,
   We wait on Thy decree.

3 The former and the latter rain,
   The summer sun and air,
   The green ear, and the golden grain,
   All Thine, are ours by prayer.

4 Thine too by right, and ours by grace,
   The wondrous growth unseen,
   The hopes that soothe, the fears that brace,
   The love that shines serene.

5 So grant the precious things brought forth
   By sun and moon below,
   That Thee, in Thy new heaven and earth,
   We never may forego.
       Rev. John Keble. (1792—1866.) 1857.

1254   *Winter and Spring.*   C. M.
       Ps. cxlvii.

1 WITH songs and honors sounding loud,
   Address the Lord on high:
   Over the heavens He spreads His cloud,
   And waters veil the sky.

2 He sends His showers of blessings down,
   To cheer the plains below;
   He makes the grass the mountains crown,
   And corn in valleys grow.

3 His steady counsels change the face
   Of the declining year;
   He bids the sun cut short his race,
   And wintry days appear.

4 His hoary frost, His fleecy snow,
   Descend and clothe the ground;
   The liquid streams forbear to flow,
   In icy fetters bound.

5 He sends His word and melts the snow,
   The fields no longer mourn;
   He calls the warmer gales to blow,
   And bids the spring return.

6 The changing wind, the flying cloud,
   Obey His mighty word:
   With songs and honors sounding loud,
   Praise ye the sovereign Lord.
       Rev. Isaac Watts. 1719. ab.

1255   *Seed-time and Harvest.*   C. M.

1 FOUNTAIN of mercy, God of love,
   How rich Thy bounties are;
   The rolling seasons, as they move,
   Proclaim Thy constant care.

2 When in the bosom of the earth
   The sower hid the grain,
   Thy goodness marked its secret birth,
   And sent the early rain.

3 The spring's sweet influence was Thine,
   The plants in beauty grew;
   Thou gav'st refulgent suns to shine,
   And mild refreshing dew.

4 These various mercies from above
   Matured the swelling grain;
   A yellow harvest crowns Thy love,
   And plenty fills the plain.

5 Seed-time and harvest, Lord, alone
   Thou dost on man bestow;
   Let him not then forget to own
   From whom his blessings flow.
       Mrs. Alice Flowerdew. (1759—1830.) 1811. ab.

1256   *For New Year's Day.*   L. M.
       Ps. lxv. 11.

1 ETERNAL Source of every joy,
   Well may Thy praise our lips employ,
   While in Thy temple we appear,
   Whose goodness crowns the circling year.

2 Wide as the wheels of nature roll,
   Thy hand supports and guides the whole;
   The sun is taught by Thee to rise,
   And darkness when to veil the skies.

3 The flowery spring, at Thy command,
   Perfumes the air and paints the land;
   The summer rays with vigor shine,
   To raise the corn and cheer the vine.

4 Thy hand in autumn richly pours
   Through all our coasts redundant stores;
   And winters, softened by Thy care,
   No more a face of horror wear.

5 Seasons, and months, and weeks, and days,
  Demand successive songs of praise;
  And be the grateful homage paid,
  With morning light and evening shade.

6 Here in Thy house let incense rise,
  And circling sabbaths bless our eyes;
  Till to those lofty heights we soar,
  Where days and years revolve no more.
  Rev. Philip Doddridge (1702—1751.) 1755. ab. and alt.

1257 *Help obtained of God.* L. M.
Acts xxvi. 22.

1 GREAT God, we sing that mighty hand
  By which supported still we stand;
  The opening year Thy mercy shows;
  Let mercy crown it till it close.

2 By day, by night, at home, abroad,
  Still we are guided by our God;
  By His incessant bounty fed,
  By His unerring counsel led.

3 With grateful hearts the past we own;
  The future, all to us unknown,
  We to Thy guardian care commit,
  And peaceful leave before Thy feet.

4 In scenes exalted or deprest,
  Be Thou our joy, and Thou our rest;
  Thy goodness all our hopes shall raise,
  Adored through all our changing days.
  Rev. Philip Doddridge. 1755 ab. and alt.

1258 *New Year.* L. M.

1 ANOTHER year, another year
  Hath sped its flight on silent wing;
  And all that marked its brief career
  Hath passed from mortal reckoning.

2 Lord, for Thy grace and patient love,
  Unwearied still, and still the same,
  For all our hopes of joy above,
  We laud and bless Thy Holy Name.

3 We bless Thee for each happy soul,
  Throughout another fleeting year,
  Or by Thy quickening grace made whole,
  Or parted in Thy faith and fear.

4 Still bear with us, and bless us still;
  And, while in this dark world we stay,
  O let us love Thy sacred will,
  O let us keep Thy narrow way.

5 So, when the rolling stream of time
  Hath opened to a boundless sea,
  Loud will we raise that song sublime,
  "All power and glory be to Thee."
  Rev. Richard Frederick Littledale. (1833—) 1867.

1259 *New Year's Day.* 11, 5.

1 COME, let us anew
  Our journey pursue,
  Roll round with the year,
And never stand still, till the Master appear.
  His adorable will
  Let us gladly fulfil,
  And our talents improve
By the patience of hope, and the labor of love.

2 Our life is a dream,
  Our time, as a stream,
  Glides swiftly away,
And the fugitive moment refuses to stay.
  The arrow is flown,
  The moment is gone,
  The millennial year
Rushes on to our view, and eternity's here.

3 O that each in the day
  Of His coming might say,
  "I have fought my way through,
"I have finished the work Thou didst give
    me to do."
  O that each from his Lord
  May receive the glad word,
  "Well and faithfully done,
"Enter into My joy, and sit down on My
    throne."
  Rev. Charles Wesley. (1708—1788.) 1750.

1260 *Speeding homeward.* 11, 5.

1 COME, let us anew
  Our journey pursue,
  With vigor arise,
And press to our permanent place in the skies.
  Of heavenly birth,
  Though wandering on earth,
  This is not our place,
But strangers and pilgrims ourselves we confess.

2 No longing we find
  For the country behind;
  But onward we move,
And still we are seeking a country abo

A country of joy
Without any alloy,
We thither repair ;
Our hearts and our treasure already are there.

3 The rougher our way,
The shorter our stay;
The troubles that come
Shall come to our rescue, and hasten us home.
The fiercer the blast,
The sooner 'tis past;
The tempests that rise
Shall serve but to hurry our souls to the skies.
Rev. Charles Wesley. 1749. ab. and alt.

1261 *Time how swift.* 7. D.

1 WHILE with ceaseless course the sun
 Hasted through the former year,
Many souls their race have run,
 Never more to meet us here :
Fixed in an eternal state,
They have done with all below;
We a little longer wait,
But how little none can know.

2 As the wingèd arrow flies
 Speedily the mark to find ;
As the lightning from the skies
 Darts, and leaves no trace behind;
Swiftly thus our fleeting days
Bear us down life's rapid stream:
Upward, Lord, our spirits raise,
All below is but a dream.

3 Thanks for mercies past receive;
 Pardon of our sins renew;
Teach us henceforth how to live
 With eternity in view:
Bless Thy word to young and old;
Fill us with a Saviour's love;
And when life's short tale is told,
May we dwell with Thee above.
Rev. John Newton. (1725—1807.) 1779.

1262 *The Close of the Year.* 7. D.

1 THOU who roll'st the year around,
 Crowned with mercies large and free,
Rich Thy gifts to us abound,
 Warm our thanks shall rise to Thee:
Kindly to our worship bow,
 While our grateful praises swell,
That, sustained by Thee, we now
 Bid the parting year farewell.

2 All its numbered days are sped,
 All its busy scenes are o'er,
All its joys for ever fled,
 All its sorrows felt no more :
Mingled with th' eternal past,
 Its remembrance shall decay ;
Yet to be revived at last
 At the solemn judgment-day.

3 All our follies, Lord, forgive ;
 Cleanse each heart and make us Thine ;
Let Thy grace within us live,
 As our future suns decline ;
Then, when life's last eve shall come,
 Happy spirits, let us fly
To our everlasting home,
 To our Father's house on high.
Rev. Ray Palmer. (1808—) 1832.

1263 *For New Year's Eve.* 7. D.

1 FOR Thy mercy and Thy grace,
 Faithful through another year,
Hear our songs of thankfulness,
 Father and Redeemer, hear.

2 In our weakness and distress,
 Rock of strength, be Thou our stay;
In the pathless wilderness
 Be our true and living way.

3 Who of us death's awful road
 In the coming year shall tread?
With Thy rod and staff, O God,
 Comfort Thou his dying bed.

4 Keep us faithful, keep us pure,
 Keep us evermore Thine own;
Help Thy servants to endure,
 Fit us for the promised crown.

5 So within Thy palace gate
 We shall praise, on golden strings,
Thee, the only Potentate,
 Lord of lords, and King of kings.
Rev. Henry Downton. (1818—) 1839. ab.

1264   *Jordan's Strand.*   8, 7.

1 My days are gliding swiftly by,
    And I, a pilgrim stranger,
Would not detain them, as they fly,
    Those hours of toil and danger:
Cho. For, O we stand on Jordan's strand;
    Our friends are passing over;
And just before the shining shore
    We may almost discover.

2 We'll gird our loins, my brethren dear,
    Our heavenly home discerning;
Our absent Lord has left us word,
    "Let every lamp be burning:" *Cho.*

3 Should coming days be cold and dark,
    We need not cease our singing;
That perfect rest nought can molest,
    Where golden harps are ringing: *Cho.*

4 Let sorrow's rudest tempest blow,
    Each cord on earth to sever;
Our King says, "Come!" and there's our home,
    Forever, O for ever. *Cho.*
        Rev. David Nelson. (1793—1844.) 1835.

1265   *Earth and Heaven.*   L. M.

1 How vain is all beneath the skies,
How transient every earthly bliss;
How slender all the fondest ties,
That bind us to a world like this.
The evening cloud, the morning dew,
The withering grass, the fading flower,
Of earthly hopes are emblems true,
The glory of a passing hour.

2 But though earth's fairest blossoms die,
And all beneath the skies is vain,
There is a land, whose confines lie
Beyond the reach of care and pain.
Then let the hope of joys to come
Dispel our cares, and chase our fears:
If God be ours, we're travelling home,
Though passing through a vale of tears.
        Rev. David Everard Ford. 1828.

1266   *A Pilgrim's Song.*   S. M.

1 A few more years shall roll,
    A few more seasons come,
And we shall be with those that rest
    Asleep within the tomb.
Cho. Then, O my Lord, prepare
    My soul for that great day;
O wash me in Thy precious blood,
    And take my sins away.

2 A few more storms shall beat
    On this wild, rocky shore;
And we shall be where tempests cease,
    And surges swell no more. *Cho.*

3 A few more struggles here,
    A few more partings o'er,
A few more toils, a few more tears,
    And we shall weep no more. *Cho.*

4 'Tis but a little while
    And He shall come again,
Who died that we might live, who lives
    That we with Him may reign. *Cho.*
        Rev. Horatius Bonar. (1808—) 1857. ab.

1267   *The Uncertainty of Life.*   S. M.
        James iv. 13—15.

1 To-morrow, Lord, is Thine,
    Lodged in Thy sovereign hand;
And if its sun arise and shine,
    It shines by Thy command.

2 The present moment flies,
    And bears our life away;
O make Thy servants truly wise,
    That they may live to-day.

3 Since on this winged hour
    Eternity is hung,
Waken, by Thine almighty power,
    The aged and the young.

4 One thing demands our care,
    O be it still pursued;
Lest, slighted once, the season fair
    Should never be renewed.

5 To Jesus may we fly,
    Swift as the morning light,
Lest life's young golden beams should die
    In sudden, endless night.
        Rev. Philip Doddridge. (1702—1751.) 1755.

1268   *"Make Haste to live."*   S. M.

1 Make haste, O man, to live,
    For thou so soon must die;
Time hurries past thee like the breeze,
    How swift its moments fly.

2 Make haste, O man, to do
   Whatever must be done;
   Thou hast no time to lose in sloth,
   Thy day will soon be gone.

3 Up then with speed, and work;
   Fling ease and self away;
   This is no time for thee to sleep,
   Up, watch, and work and pray.

4 Make haste, O man, to live,
   Thy time is almost o'er;
   O sleep not, dream not, but arise,
   The Judge is at the door.
           Rev. Horatius Bonar, 1857. ab.

1269 *The Brevity and Vanity of Life.* S. M.
           Ps. xxxix.

1 LORD, let me know mine end,
   My days, how brief their date,
   That I may timely comprehend
   How frail my best estate.

2 My life is but a span,
   Mine age is nought with Thee;
   What is the highest boast of man
   But dust and vanity?

3 Dumb at Thy feet I lie,
   For Thou hast brought me low;
   Remove Thy judgments, lest I die;
   I faint beneath Thy blow.

4 At Thy rebuke, the bloom
   Of man's vain beauty flies;
   And grief shall, like a moth, consume
   All that delights our eyes.

5 Have pity on my fears;
   Hearken to my request;
   Turn not in silence from my tears,
   But give the mourner rest.

6 O spare me yet, I pray;
   Awhile my strength restore,
   Ere I am summoned hence away,
   And seen on earth no more.
           James Montgomery. (1771-1854.) 1822. ab. and alt.

1270 *Our Fathers.* S. M.
           Zech. i. 5.

1 How swift the torrent rolls
   That bears us to the sea;
   The tide that hurries thoughtless souls
   To vast eternity.

2 Our fathers, where are they,
   With all they called their own?
   Their joys and griefs, and hopes and cares,
   And wealth and honor gone.

3 God of our fathers, hear,
   Thou everlasting Friend,
   While we, as on life's utmost verge,
   Our souls to Thee commend.

4 Of all the pious dead
   May we the footsteps trace,
   Till with them, in the land of light,
   We dwell before Thy face.
           Rev. Philip Doddridge 1755 ab. and alt.

1271 *Triumph over Death.* S. M.

1 AND must this body die,
   This mortal frame decay?
   And must these active limbs of mine
   Lie mouldering in the clay?

2 God, my Redeemer, lives,
   And ever from the skies
   Looks down and watches all my dust,
   Till He shall bid it rise.

3 Arrayed in glorious grace,
   Shall these vile bodies shine,
   And every shape and every face
   Look heavenly and divine.

4 These lively hopes we owe
   To Jesus' dying love;
   We would adore His grace below,
   And sing His power above.

5 Dear Lord, accept the praise
   Of these our humble songs,
   Till tunes of nobler sound we raise
   With our immortal tongues.
           Rev. Isaac Watts. (1674-1748.) 1709. ab. and alt.

1272 *At a Funeral.* C. M.

1 BENEATH our feet and o'er our head
   Is equal warning given;
   Beneath us lie the countless dead,
   Above us in the heaven.

2 Death rides on every passing breeze,
   And lurks in every flower;
   Each season has its own disease,
   Its peril every hour.

3 Our eyes have seen the rosy light
    Of youth's soft cheek decay;
  And fate descend in sudden night
    On manhood's middle day.

4 Our eyes have seen the steps of age
    Halt feebly to the tomb;
  And yet shall earth our hearts engage,
    And dreams of days to come?

5 Turn, mortal, turn, thy danger know;
    Where'er thy foot can tread,
  The earth rings hollow from below,
    And warns thee of her dead.

6 Turn, Christian, turn, thy soul apply
    To truths divinely given;
  The bones that underneath thee lie,
    Shall live for hell or heaven.
    Bp. Reginald Heber. (1783—1826.) 1812. ab. and sl. alt.

1273 *"Marching to the Tomb."* C. M.

1 THROUGH sorrow's night and danger's path,
    Amid the deepening gloom,
  We, soldiers of an injured King,
    Are marching to the tomb.

2 There, when the turmoil is no more,
    And all our powers decay,
  Our cold remains in solitude
    Shall sleep the years away.

3 Our labors done, securely laid
    In this our last retreat,
  Unheeded, o'er our silent dust
    The storms of life shall beat.

4 Yet not thus lifeless, thus inane,
    The vital spark shall lie;
  For o'er life's wreck that spark shall rise
    To seek its kindred sky.

5 These ashes too, this little dust,
    Our Father's care shall keep,
  Till the last angel rise and break
    The long and dreary sleep.

6 Then love's soft dew o'er every eye
    Shall shed its mildest rays,
  And the long-silent dust shall burst
    With shouts of endless praise.
    Henry Kirke White. (1785—1806.) 1806.

1274 *"The Bitterness of Death is past."* C. M.
    1 Sam. xv. 32.

1 WHEN bending o'er the brink of life
    My trembling soul shall stand,
  Waiting to pass death's awful flood,
    Great God, at Thy command;

2 O thou great Source of joy supreme,
    Whose arm alone can save,
  Dispel the darkness that surrounds
    The entrance to the grave.

3 Lay Thy supporting, gentle hand
    Beneath my sinking head,
  And, with a ray of love divine,
    Illume my dying bed.
    Rev. William Bengo Collyer. (1782—1854.) 1812. ab.

1275 *"How shall I appear?"* C. M.

1 WHEN rising from the bed of death,
    O'erwhelmed with guilt and fear,
  I see my Maker face to face,
    O how shall I appear?

2 If yet while pardon may be found,
    And mercy may be sought,
  My heart with inward horror shrinks,
    And trembles at the thought;

3 When Thou, O Lord, shalt stand disclosed
    In majesty severe,
  And sit in judgment on my soul,
    O how shall I appear?

4 But Thou hast told the troubled soul,
    Who does her sins lament,
  The timely tribute of her tears
    Shall endless woe prevent.

5 Then see the sorrows of my heart,
    Ere yet it be too late,
  And add my Saviour's dying groans
    To give those sorrows weight.

6 For never shall my soul despair
    Her pardon to procure,
  Who knows Thine only Son has died
    To make that pardon sure.
    Joseph Addison. (1672—1719.) 1712. sl. alt.

1276 *"To live is Christ, and to die is Gain."* C. M.
    Phil. i. 21.

1 LORD, it belongs not to my care
    Whether I die or live;
  To love and serve Thee is my share,
    And this Thy grace must give.

2 If life be long. I will be glad
  That I may long obey;
  If short, yet why should I be sad
  To soar to endless day?

3 Christ leads me through no darker rooms
  Than He went through before;
  He that unto God's kingdom comes
  Must enter by this door.

4 Come, Lord, when grace hath made me meet
  Thy blessèd face to see;
  For, if Thy work on earth be sweet,
  What will Thy glory be?

5 Then I shall end my sad complaints,
  And weary sinful days,
  And join with the triumphant saints
  That sing Jehovah's praise.

6 My knowledge of that life is small;
  The eye of faith is dim;
  But it's enough that Christ knows all,
  And I shall be with Him.
  Rev. Richard Baxter. (1615—1689.) 1681, ab. and alt.

1277 *Prepared to die.* C. M.
2 Tim. iv. 6, 7, 18.

1 DEATH may dissolve my body now,
  And bear my spirit home;
  Why do my minutes move so slow,
  Nor my salvation come?

2 With heavenly weapons, I have fought
  The battles of the Lord;
  Finished my course, and kept the faith,
  And wait the sure reward.

3 Jesus, the Lord, shall guard me safe
  From every ill design;
  And to His heavenly kingdom take
  This feeble soul of mine.

4 God is my everlasting aid,
  And hell shall rage in vain;
  To Him be highest glory paid,
  And endless praise. Amen!
  Rev. Isaac Watts. (1674—1748.) 1709. ab.

1278 *Dying Hymn.* C. M.

1 EARTH, with its dark and dreadful ills,
  Recedes and fades away;
  Lift up your heads, ye heavenly hills,
  Ye gates of death give way.

2 My soul is full of whispered song,
  My blindness is my sight;
  The shadows that I feared so long
  Are all alive with light.

3 The while my pulses faintly beat,
  My faith doth so abound,
  I feel grow firm beneath my feet
  The green, immortal ground.

4 That faith to me a courage gives,
  Low as the grave to go:
  I know that my Redeemer lives,
  That I shall live, I know.

5 The palace walls I almost see
  Where dwells my Lord and King;
  O grave, where is thy victory,
  O death, where is thy sting!
  Miss Alice Cary. (1820—1871.) 1870.

1279 *In Sickness.* C. M.

1 WHEN languor and disease invade
  This trembling house of clay,
  'T is sweet to look beyond the cage,
  And long to fly away.

2 Sweet to look inward, and attend
  The whispers of His love;
  Sweet to look upward to the place
  Where Jesus pleads above;

3 Sweet to look back, and see my name
  In life's fair book set down;
  Sweet to look forward, and behold
  Eternal joys my own;

4 Sweet on His faithfulness to rest,
  Whose love can never end;
  Sweet on His covenant of grace
  For all things to depend;

5 Sweet, in the confidence of faith,
  To trust His firm decrees;
  Sweet to lie passive in His hands,
  And know no will but His;

6 Sweet to rejoice in lively hope,
  That, when my change shall come,
  Angels will hover round my bed,
  And waft my spirit home.
  Rev. Augustus Montague Toplady. (1740—1778.) 1776. ab.

LIFE AND DEATH.

1280 *In Sickness.* C. M.
Ps. lxxxviii. 11, 12. Phil. i. 23.

1 O THOU, Who lov'st to send relief
In time of our distress,
Because Thyself didst bear our grief,
And feel our sicknesses;

2 Thy will be done, I still would say,
Whate'er that will may be;
And let this trial, day by day,
Fulfil its end in me.

3 O Lord, look down, O Lord, forgive,
O help me from on high;
Since no man to himself must live,
Nor to himself can die.

4 And when, through feebleness or pain,
My thoughts are far from Thee,
Though I forget Thee, Saviour, then,
O yet forget not me.

5 In Him that bore our griefs and pains
Shall they that suffer boast,
Who with the Father ever reigns,
And with the Holy Ghost.
Rev. John Mason Neale. (1818—1866.) 1854. ab.

1281 *Hymn by the Sick-bed of a Mother.* C. M.

1 O THOU, who, in the olive shade,
When the dark hour came on,
Didst, with a breath of heavenly aid,
Strengthen Thy suffering Son;

2 O by the anguish of that night,
Send us down blest relief;
Or to the chastened let Thy might
Hallow this whelming grief.

3 And Thou, that, when the starry sky
Saw the dread strife begun,
Didst teach adoring faith to cry,
Father, Thy will be done;

4 By Thy meek Spirit, Thou, of all
That e'er have mourned the chief,
Blest Saviour, if the stroke must fall,
Hallow this whelming grief.
Mrs. Felicia Dorothea Hemans. (1794—1835.) 1834. alt.

1282 *"He healeth the broken in Heart."* C. M.
Ps. cxlvii. 3.

1 O THOU, who driest the mourner's tear,
How dark this world would be,
If, when deceived and wounded here,
We could not fly to Thee.

2 But Thou wilt heal that broken heart,
Which, like the plants that throw
Their fragrance from the wounded part,
Breathes sweetness on our woe.

3 When joy no longer soothes or cheers,
And e'en the hope that threw
A moment's sparkle o'er our tears
Is dimmed and vanished too;

4 O who would bear life's stormy doom,
Did not Thy wing of love
Come, brightly wafting through the gloom
Our peace-branch from above?

5 Then sorrow, touched by Thee, grows bright
With more than rapture's ray;
As darkness shows us worlds of light
We never saw by day.
Thomas Moore. (1779—1852.) 1816. ab.

1283 *"Weep not."* C. M.
Luke vii. 13.

1 DEAR as thou wert, and justly dear,
We will not weep for thee:
One thought shall check the starting tear,
It is, that thou art free.

2 And thus shall faith's consoling power
The tears of love restrain:
O who that saw thy parting hour,
Could wish thee back again.

3 Triumphant in thy closing eye
The hope of glory shone;
Joy breathed in thine expiring sigh,
To think the fight was won.

4 Gently the passing spirit fled,
Sustained by grace divine;
O may such grace on me be shed,
And make my end like thine.
Rev. Thomas Dale. (1797—1870.) 1818.

1284 *Death of the Righteous.* C. M.

1 BEHOLD the western evening light!
It melts in deepening gloom:
So calmly Christians sink away,
Descending to the tomb.

2 The wind breathes low; the withering leaf
Scarce whispers from the tree:
So gently flows the parting breath,
When good men cease to be.

3 How beautiful on all the hills
  The crimson light is shed!
  'Tis like the peace the Christian gives
  To mourners round his bed.

4 How mildly on the wandering cloud
  The sunset beam is cast!
  'Tis like the memory left behind
  When loved ones breathe their last.

5 And now above the dews of night
  The yellow star appears:
  So faith springs in the hearts of those
  Whose eyes are bathed in tears.

6 But soon the morning's happier light
  Its glory shall restore;
  And eyelids that are sealed in death
  Shall wake to close no more.
  Rev. William Bourn Oliver Peabody. (1799—1847.) 1823.

1285 *"I would not live alway."* 11.

1 I WOULD not live alway; I ask not to stay
  Where storm after storm rises dark o'er the way;
  A few lurid mornings, that dawn on us here,
  Are enough for life's woes, full enough for its cheer.

2 I would not live alway, thus fettered by sin,
  Temptation without and corruption within;
  E'en the rapture of pardon is mingled with fears,
  And the cup of thanksgiving with penitent tears.

3 I would not live alway; no, welcome the tomb;
  Since Jesus hath lain there, I dread not its gloom;
  There sweet be my rest, till He bid me arise,
  To hail Him in triumph descending the skies.

4 Who, who would live alway, away from his God;
  Away from yon heaven, that blissful abode,
  Where the rivers of pleasure flow o'er the bright plains,
  And the noontide of glory eternally reigns?

5 Where the saints of all ages in harmony meet,
  Their Saviour and brethren transported to greet;

While the anthems of rapture unceasingly roll,
  And the smile of the Lord is the feast of the soul.
  Rev. William Augustus Muhlenberg. (1796—) 1823.

1286 *Longing for Rest.* 11.
  Ps. lv.

1 O HAD I, my Saviour, the wings of a dove,
  How soon would I soar to Thy presence above;
  How soon would I flee where the weary have rest,
  And hide all my cares in Thy sheltering breast.

2 I flutter, I struggle, I pant to get free;
  I feel me a captive while banished from Thee:
  A pilgrim and stranger, the desert I roam,
  And look on to heaven, and long to be home.

3 Ah, there the wild tempest for ever shall cease;
  No billow shall ruffle that haven of peace;
  Temptation and trouble alike shall depart,
  All tears from the eye, and all sin from the heart.

4 Soon, soon may this Eden of promise be mine;
  Rise, bright Sun of glory, no more to decline!
  Thy light, yet unrisen, the wilderness cheers;
  O what will it be when the fulness appears?
  Rev. Henry Francis Lyte. (1793—1847.) 1834.

1287 *Parting Words.* 8, 7. 6 l.
  Gen. xxxii. 26.

1 LET me go, the day is breaking,
  Dear companions, let me go;
  We have spent a night of waking
  In the wilderness below;
  Upward now I bend my way,
  Part we here at break of day.

2 Let me go, I may not tarry,
  Wrestling thus with doubts and fears;
  Angels wait my soul to carry,
  Where my risen Lord appears;
  Friends and kindred, weep not so,
  If you love me, let me go.

3 'Tis not darkness gathering round me,
  Which withdraws me from your sight;

LIFE AND DEATH.

Walls of flesh no more can bound me,
  But, translated into light,
Like the lark on mounting wing,
  Though unseen you hear me sing.

4 Heaven's broad day hath o'er me broken,
  Far beyond earth's span of sky;
Am I dead?—nay, by this token,
  Know that I have ceased to die;
Would you solve the mystery,
  Come up hither, come and see.
  James Montgomery. (1771—1854.) 1837. ab.

1288 "*It is even a Vapor.*" 8, 7. 6 l.
  James iv. 14.

1 WHAT is life? 'T is but a vapor,
    Soon it vanishes away;
  Life is like a dying taper,
    O my soul, why wish to stay?
  Why not spread Thy wings, and fly
  Straight to yonder world of joy?

2 See that glory, how resplendent!
    Brighter far than fancy paints;
  There, in majesty transcendent,
    Jesus reigns, the King of saints:
  Spread thy wings, my soul, and fly
  Straight to yonder world of joy.

3 Joyful crowds, His throne surrounding,
    Sing with rapture of His love;
  Through the heavens His praises sounding,
    Filling all the courts above;
  Spread thy wings, my soul, and fly
  Straight to yonder world of joy.

4 Go, and share His people's glory,
    Midst the ransomed crowd appear;
  Thine a joyful, wondrous story,
    One that angels love to hear:
  Spread thy wings, my soul, and fly
  Straight to yonder world of joy.
  Rev. Thomas Kelly. (1769—1855.) 1809.

1289 *Christ's Presence makes Death easy.* L. M.

1 WHY should we start and fear to die?
  What timorous worms we mortals are:
  Death is the gate of endless joy,
  And yet we dread to enter there.

2 The pains, the groans, and dying strife
  Fright our approaching souls away;
  Still we shrink back again to life,
  Fond of our prison and our clay.

3 O if my Lord would come and meet,
  My soul should stretch her wings in haste,
  Fly fearless through death's iron gate,
  Nor feel the terrors as she passed.

4 Jesus can make a dying bed
  Feel soft as downy pillows are,
  While on His breast I lean my head,
  And breathe my life out sweetly there.
  Rev. Isaac Watts. (1674—1748.) 1709.

1290 *Departing, to be with Christ.* L. M.
  Phil. i. 23.

1 WHILE on the verge of life I stand,
  And view the scenes on either hand,
  My spirit struggles with its clay,
  And longs to wing its flight away.

2 Where Jesus dwells my soul would be;
  It faints my much-loved Lord to see;
  Earth, twine no more about my heart,
  For 'tis far better to depart.

3 Come, ye angelic envoys, come,
  And lead the willing pilgrim home:
  Ye know the way to Jesus' throne,
  Source of my joys, and of your own.

4 That blessèd interview, how sweet,
  To fall transported at His feet:
  Raised in His arms, to view His face,
  Through the full beamings of His grace.

5 Yet, with these prospects full in sight,
  I'll wait Thy signal for my flight;
  For while Thy service I pursue,
  I find my heaven begun below.
  Rev. Philip Doddridge. (1702—1751.) 1755. ab.

1291 *Dying in the Lord.* L. M.

1 THE hour of my departure's come;
  I hear the voice that calls me home:
  At last, O Lord, let trouble cease,
  And let Thy servant die in peace.

2 The race appointed I have run,
  The combat's o'er, the prize is won;
  And now my witness is on high,
  And now my record's in the sky.

3 Not in mine innocence I trust;
  I bow before Thee in the dust;
  And through my Saviour's blood alone
  I look for mercy at Thy throne.

LIFE AND DEATH.

4 I leave the world without a tear,
   Save for the friends I held so dear;
   To heal their sorrows, Lord, descend,
   And to the friendless prove a Friend.

5 I come, I come, at Thy command,
   I give my spirit to Thy hand;
   Stretch forth Thine everlasting arms,
   And shield me in the last alarms.

6 The hour of my departure's come;
   I hear the voice that calls me home:
   Now, O my God, let trouble cease;
   Now let Thy servant die in peace.
          Michael Bruce. (1746—1767.) 1781.

1292   "*Asleep in Jesus.*"   L. M.

1 ASLEEP in Jesus: blessèd sleep,
   From which none ever wakes to weep,
   A calm and undisturbed repose,
   Unbroken by the last of foes.

2 Asleep in Jesus: O how sweet
   To be for such a slumber meet;
   With holy confidence to sing,
   That death hath lost his venomed sting.

3 Asleep in Jesus: peaceful rest,
   Whose waking is supremely blest;
   No fear, no woe, shall dim that hour
   That manifests the Saviour's power.

4 Asleep in Jesus: O for me
   May such a blissful refuge be;
   Securely shall my ashes lie,
   Waiting the summons from on high.

5 Asleep in Jesus: far from thee
   Thy kindred and their graves may be;
   But thine is still a blessèd sleep,
   From which none ever wakes to weep.
          Mrs. Margaret Mackay. 1832. ab.

1293   *The Death of the Righteous.*   L. M.
        Num. xxiii. 10.

1 How blest the righteous, when he dies,
   When sinks a weary soul to rest;
   How mildly beam the closing eyes,
   How gently heaves th' expiring breast.

2 So fades a summer cloud away:
   So sinks the gale, when storms are o'er;
   So gently shuts the eye of day;
   So dies a wave along the shore.

3 A holy quiet reigns around,
   A calm which life nor death destroys;
   And naught disturbs that peace profound,
   Which his unfettered soul enjoys.

4 Farewell, conflicting hopes and fears,
   Where lights and shades alternate dwell:
   How bright th' unchanging morn appears,
   Farewell, inconstant world, farewell.

5 Life's labor done, as sinks the clay,
   Light from its load the spirit flies;
   While heaven and earth combine to say,
   "How blest the righteous when he dies!"
   Mrs. Anna Laetitia Barbauld. (1743—1825.) 1773. ab. and alt.

1294   *Resting in Christ.*   L. M.

1 GENTLY, my Saviour, let me down,
   To slumber in the arms of death;
   I rest my soul on Thee alone,
   E'en till my last, expiring breath.

2 Soon will the storm of life be o'er,
   And I shall enter endless rest;
   There I shall live to sin no more,
   And bless Thy name, for ever blest.

3 Bid me possess sweet peace within;
   Let childlike patience keep my heart;
   Then shall I feel my heaven begin,
   Before my spirit hence depart.

4 O speed Thy chariot, God of love,
   And take me from this world of woe;
   I long to reach those joys above,
   And bid farewell to all below.

5 There shall my raptured spirit raise
   Still louder notes than angels sing,
   High glories to Immanuel's grace,
   My God, my Saviour, and my King.
       Rev. Rowland Hill. (1744—1833.) 1796.

1295 *The aged Christian's Prayer and Song*   C. M
        Ps. lxxi. 17—21.

1 GOD of my childhood, and my youth,
   The Guide of all my days,
   I have declared Thy heavenly truth,
   And told Thy wondrous ways.

2 Wilt Thou forsake my hoary hairs,
   And leave my fainting heart?
   Who shall sustain my sinking years
   If God, my Strength, depart?

3 Let me Thy power and truth proclaim
   Before the rising age,
   And leave a savour of Thy name
   When I shall quit the stage.

4 The land of silence and of death
   Attends my next remove;
   O may these poor remains of breath
   Teach the wide world Thy love.
   Rev. Isaac Watts. (1674—1748.) 1719.

1296 *"Cast me not off in old Age."* C. M.
Ps. lxxi. 5—9.

1 My God, my everlasting hope,
   I live upon Thy truth;
   Thy hands have held my childhood up,
   And strengthened all my youth.

2 Still has my life new wonders seen
   Repeated every year;
   Behold, my days that yet remain,
   I trust them to Thy care.

3 Cast me not off when strength declines,
   When hoary hairs arise;
   And round me let Thy glory shine,
   Whene'er Thy servant dies.

4 Then, in the history of my age,
   When men review my days,
   They'll read Thy love in every page,
   In every line Thy praise.
   Rev. Isaac Watts. 1719. ab.

1297 *Trust in Providence.* C. M.

1 Almighty Father of mankind,
   On Thee my hopes remain;
   And when the day of trouble comes,
   I shall not trust in vain.

2 In early days Thou wast my Guide,
   And of my youth the Friend;
   And as my days began with Thee,
   With Thee my days shall end.

3 I know the Power in whom I trust,
   The arm on which I lean;
   He will my Saviour ever be,
   Who has my Saviour been.

4 Thou wilt not cast me off, when age
   And evil days descend;
   Thou wilt not leave me in despair,
   To mourn my latter end.

5 Therefore in life I'll trust in Thee,
   In death I will adore;
   And after death will sing Thy praise,
   When time shall be no more.
   Michael Bruce. (1746—1767.) 1781. ab.

1298 *"Comfort one another."* C. M.
1 Thess. iv. 18.

1 Why should our tears in sorrow flow,
   When God recalls His own,
   And bids them leave a world of woe
   For an immortal crown?

2 Is not e'en death a gain to those
   Whose life to God was given?
   Gladly to earth their eyes they close,
   To open them in heaven.

3 Their toils are past, their work is done,
   And they are fully blest;
   They've fought the fight, the victory won,
   And entered into rest.

4 Then let our sorrows cease to flow,
   God has recalled His own;
   But let our hearts, in every woe,
   Still say, "Thy will be done!"
   Rev. William Hiley Bathurst. (1796—) 1829. ab.

1299 *Bereaved Parents comforted.* C. M.
Is. lvi. 4, 5.

1 Ye mourning saints, whose streaming tears
   Flow o'er your children dead,
   Say not, in transports of despair,
   That all your hopes are fled.

2 While cleaving to that darling dust,
   In fond distress ye lie,
   Rise, and with joy and reverence view
   A heavenly Parent nigh.

3 Though, your young branches torn away,
   Like withered trunks ye stand,
   With fairer verdure shall ye bloom,
   Touched by th' Almighty's hand.

4 "I'll give the mourner," saith the Lord,
   "In My own house a place;
   No names of daughters and of sons
   Could yield so high a grace."

5 We welcome, Lord, those rising tears,
   Through which Thy face we see;
   And bless those wounds which through our
   Prepare a way for Thee. |heart.
   Rev. Philip Doddridge. (1702—1751.) 1755. ab.

LIFE AND DEATH.

1300 *The Death of a Child.* C. M.

1 LIFE is a span, a fleeting hour,
  How soon the vapor flies,
Man is a tender, transient flower,
  That, e'en in blooming, dies.

2 The once loved form, now cold and dead,
  Each mournful thought employs;
And nature weeps her comforts fled,
  And withered all her joys.

3 Hope looks beyond the bounds of time,
  When what we now deplore
Shall rise in full, immortal prime,
  And bloom to fade no more.

4 Cease, then, fond nature, cease thy tears,
  Religion points on high;
There everlasting spring appears,
  And joys that cannot die.
      Miss Anne Steele. (1717—1778.) 1760. ab.

1301 *Infants taken to the Saviour's Bosom.* C. M.

1 WITH joy I see a thousand charms
  Spread o'er the Saviour's face;
While infants in His tender arms
  Receive His smiling grace.

2 "I take these little lambs," said He,
  "And lay them in My breast;
Protection they shall find in Me,
  In Me be ever blest.

3 Death may the bands of life unloose,
  But can't dissolve My love;
Millions of infant souls compose
  The family above."

4 His words, ye happy parents, hear,
  And shout with joys divine,
Dear Saviour, all we have and are
  Shall be forever Thine.
      Rev. Philip Doddridge. 1755. ab.

1302 *"Non ce n'est pas mourir."* 7,6,7,7,6.

1 No, no, it is not dying
    To go unto our God,
  This gloomy earth forsaking,
  Our journey homeward taking
    Along the starry road.

2 No, no, it is not dying
    Heaven's citizen to be;
  A crown immortal wearing,
  And rest unbroken sharing,
    From care and conflict free.

3 No, no, it is not dying
    To hear this gracious word,
  "Receive a Father's blessing,
  For evermore possessing
    The favor of Thy Lord."

4 No, no, it is not dying
    The Shepherd's voice to know;
  His sheep He ever leadeth,
  His peaceful flock He feedeth,
    Where living pastures grow.

5 No, no, it is not dying
    To wear a lordly crown;
  Among God's people dwelling,
  The glorious triumph swelling
    Of Him whose sway we own.

6 O no, this is not dying,
    Thou Saviour of mankind:
  There, streams of love are flowing,
  No hindrance ever knowing;
    Here, drops alone we find.
      Rev. Cæsar Henri Abraham Malan. (1787—1864.) 1841.
      Tr. by Prof. Robinson Potter Dunn. (1825—1867.) 1852.

1303 *"Guter Hirt, Du hast gestillt."* 7,8,7,8,7,7.

1 TENDER Shepherd, Thou hast stilled
    Now Thy little lamb's brief weeping;
  Ah, how peaceful, pale, and mild
    In its narrow bed 'tis sleeping,
  And no sigh of anguish sore
  Heaves that little bosom more.

2 In this world of care and pain,
    Lord, Thou wouldst no longer leave it;
  To the sunny heavenly plain
    Thou dost now with joy receive it;
  Clothed in robes of spotless white,
  Now it dwells with Thee in light.

3 Ah, Lord Jesus, grant that we
    Where it lives may soon be living,
  And the lovely pastures see,
    That its heavenly food are giving;
  Then the gain of death we prove,
  Though Thou take what most we love.
      Rev. Wilhelm Meinhold. (1707—1851.)
      Tr. by Miss Catherine Winkworth. (1829—) 1858. sl. alt.

LIFE AND DEATH.

1304 *For One departing.* 8, 7.

1 HAPPY soul, thy days are ended,
   All thy mourning days below;
   Go, by angel-guards attended,
   To the sight of Jesus, go.

2 Waiting to receive thy spirit,
   Lo, the Saviour stands above,
   Shows the purchase of His merit,
   Reaches out the crown of love.

3 Struggle through thy latest passion
   To thy dear Redeemer's breast,
   To His uttermost salvation,
   To His everlasting rest.

4 For the joy He sets before thee,
   Bear a momentary pain;
   Die, to live the life of glory,
   Suffer, with thy Lord to reign.
   Rev. Charles Wesley. (1708—1788.) 1749.

1305 *Consolation* 8, 7.
   Rev. xxi. 3, 4, 23, 25.

1 THINK, O ye, who fondly languish
   O'er the grave of those you love,
   While your bosoms throb with anguish,
   They are warbling hymns above.

2 While your silent steps are straying
   Lonely through night's deepening shade,
   Glory's brightest beams are playing
   Round the happy Christian's head.

3 Night, the face of nature veiling,
   Rears her sable throne no more
   'Mid those spirits pure, inhaling
   Life from Him whom they adore.

4 Light and peace at once deriving
   From the hand of God most high,
   In His glorious presence living,
   They shall never, never die.

5 Cease, then, mourner, cease to languish
   O'er the grave of those you love;
   Pain, and death, and night, and anguish,
   Enter not the world above.
   Rev. William Bengo Collyer. (1782—1854) 1812. ab.

1306 *"Alles schwindet: Herzen brechen."* 8, 7.

1 ALL is dying; hearts are breaking
   Which to ours were closely bound;
   And the lips have ceased from speaking,
   Which once uttered such sweet sound.

2 And the arms are powerless lying,
   Which were our support and stay;
   And the eyes are dim and dying,
   Which once watched us night and day

3 Everything we love and cherish
   Hastens onward to the grave;
   Earthly joys and pleasures perish,
   And whate'er the world e'er gave.

4 All is fading, all is fleeing;
   Earthly flames must cease to glow,
   Earthly beings cease from being,
   Earthly blossoms cease to blow.

5 Yet unchanged while all decayeth,
   Jesus stands upon the dust;
   Lean on Me alone, He sayeth;
   Hope and love, and firmly trust.

6 O abide, abide with Jesus,
   Who Himself forever lives,
   Who from death eternal frees us,
   Yea, who life eternal gives.
   Rev. Carl Johann Philipp Spitta. (1801—1859.) 1833.
   Tr. by Richard Massie. 1800. ab.

1307 *A Funeral Hymn.* 7.

1 BROTHER, though from yonder sky
   Cometh neither voice nor cry,
   Yet we know from thee to-day
   Every pain hath passed away.

2 Not for thee shall tears be given,
   Child of God and heir of heaven;
   For He gave thee sweet release;
   Thine the Christian's death of peace.

3 Well we know thy living faith
   Had the power to conquer death;
   As a living rose may bloom
   By the border of the tomb.

4 Brother, in that solemn trust
   We commend thee, dust to dust;
   In that faith we wait, till, risen
   Thou shalt meet us all in heaven.

5 While we weep as Jesus wept,
   Thou shalt sleep as Jesus slept;
   With thy Saviour Thou shalt rest,
   Crowned, and glorified, and blest.
   Rev. James Henry Bancroft. (1819—1844.) 1839.

1308 *Christian Burial.* 7.

1 BROTHER, now thy toils are o'er,
    Fought the battle, won the crown;
  On life's rough and barren shore
    Thou hast laid thy burden down.

2 Through death's valley, dim and dark,
    Jesus guide thee in the gloom,
  Show thee where His footprints mark
    Tracks of glory through the tomb.

3 Angels bear thee to the land
    Where the towers of Zion rise,
  Safely lead thee by the hand
    To the fields of Paradise.

4 White-robed at the golden gate
    Of the New Jerusalem,
  May the host of martyrs wait,
    Give thee part and lot with them.

5 Earth to earth, and dust to dust,
    Clay we give to kindred clay;
  In the sure and certain trust
    Of the Resurrection Day.

6 Christ the Sower sows thee here:
    When the eternal day shall dawn,
  He will gather in the ear
    On that Resurrection morn.
               Rev. Gerard Moultrie. 1867. ab.

1309 *Citizenship in Heaven.* 7.
           Ps. xv.

1 WHO, O Lord, when life is o'er,
  Shall to heaven's blest mansions soar?
  Who an ever-welcome guest,
  In Thy holy place shall rest?

2 He whose heart Thy love has warmed;
  He, whose will to Thine conformed,
  Bids his life unsullied run;
  He whose words and thoughts are one;

3 He who shuns the sinner's road,
  Loving those who love their God;
  Who, with hope and faith unfeigned,
  Treads the path by Thee ordained;

4 He who trusts in Christ alone,
  Not in aught himself hath done;
  He, great God, shall be Thy care,
  And Thy choicest blessings share.
               Rev. James Merrick. (1720—1769.) 1765. ah.

1310 *The Death of the Righteous.* 6,6,8,6,8,8.

1 THIS place is holy ground;
    World, with thy cares away:
  Silence and darkness reign around;
    But, lo, the break of day!
  What bright and sudden dawn appears,
  To shine upon this scene of tears.

2 'T is not the morning light,
    That wakes the lark to sing;
  'T is not a meteor of the night,
    Nor track of angel's wing:
  It is an uncreated beam,
  Like that which shone on Jacob's dream.

3 Behold the bed of death,
    This pale and lovely clay;
  Heard ye the sobs of parting breath?
    Marked ye the eyes' last ray?
  No; life so sweetly ceased to be,
  It lapsed in immortality.

4 Could tears revive the dead,
    Rivers should swell our eyes;
  Could sighs recall the spirit fled,
    We would not quench our sighs,
  Till love relumed this altered mein,
  And all th' embodied soul were seen.

5 Bury the dead; and weep
    In stillness o'er the loss;
  Bury the dead: in Christ they sleep,
    Who bore on earth His cross,
  And from the grave their dust shall rise,
  In His own image to the skies.
               James Montgomery. (1771—1854.) 1816. ab.

1311 *The Loss of Friends.* 6,6,8,6,8,8.

1 FRIEND after friend departs;
    Who hath not lost a friend?
  There is no union here of hearts,
    That finds not here an end;
  Were this frail world our only rest,
  Living or dying, none were blest.

2 Beyond the flight of time,
    Beyond this vale of death,
  There surely is some blessèd clime
    Where life is not a breath;
  Nor life's affections transient fire,
  Whose sparks fly upward to expire.

3 There is a world above,
  Where parting is unknown;
  A whole eternity of love,
  Formed for the good alone;
  And faith beholds the dying here
  Translated to that happier sphere.

4 Thus star by star declines
  Till all are passed away,
  As morning high and higher shines
  To pure and perfect day;
  Nor sink those stars in empty night;
  They hide themselves in heaven's own light.
        James Montgomery. (1771—1854.) 1810.

1312   *God the Light of His Saints.*   C. M.
            Is. lx. 19.

1 YE golden lamps of heaven, farewell,
  With all your feeble light;
  Farewell, thou ever changing moon,
  Pale empress of the night.

2 And thou, refulgent orb of day,
  In brighter flames arrayed;
  My soul, that springs beyond thy sphere,
  No more demands thine aid.

3 Ye stars are but the shining dust
  Of my divine abode,
  The pavement of those heavenly courts
  Where I shall reign with God.

4 The Father of eternal light
  Shall there His beams display,
  Nor shall one moment's darkness mix
  With that unvaried day.

5 No more the drops of piercing grief
  Shall swell into mine eyes;
  Nor the meridian sun decline
  Amid those brighter skies.

6 There all the millions of His saints
  Shall in one song unite,
  And each the bliss of all shall view
  With infinite delight.
        Rev. Philip Doddridge (1702—1751.) 1755.

1313   *The Promised Land.*   C. M.
            Is. xxxii. 17.

1 FAR from these narrow scenes of night
  Unbounded glories rise,
  And realms of infinite delight,
  Unknown to mortal eyes.

2 Fair distant land; could mortal eyes
  But half its joys explore,
  How would our spirits long to rise,
  And dwell on earth no more.

3 There pain and sickness never come,
  And grief no more complains;
  Health triumphs in immortal bloom,
  And endless pleasure reigns.

4 No cloud those blissful regions know,
  Forever bright and fair;
  For sin, the source of mortal woe,
  Can never enter there.

5 There no alternate night is known,
  Nor sun's faint sickly ray;
  But glory from the sacred Throne
  Spreads everlasting day.

6 Prepare us, Lord, by grace divine,
  For Thy bright courts on high;
  Then bid our spirit rise, and join
  The chorus of the sky.
        Miss Anne Steele. (1717—1778.) 1760. ab.

1314   *Yearning for Home.*   C. M.

1 MY soul, amid this stormy world,
  Is like some fluttered dove,
  And fain would be as swift of wing
  To flee to Him I love.

2 May not an exile, Lord, desire
  His own sweet land to see?
  May not a captive seek release,
  A prisoner, to be free?

3 A child, when far away, may long
  For home and kindred dear;
  And she, that waits her absent lord,
  May sigh till he appear.

4 I would, my Lord and Saviour, know
  That which no measure knows;
  Would search the mystery of Thy love,
  The depths of all Thy woes.

5 I fain would strike my harp divine
  Before the Father's throne,
  There cast my crown of Righteousness,
  And sing what grace has done.

6 Ah, leave me not in this base world,
  A stranger still to roam;
  Come, Lord, and take me to Thyself;
  Come, Jesus, quickly come.
        Robert Cleaver Chapman. 1837, 1852. ab.

1315 *Yearning for Heaven.* C. M.

1 THE roseate hues of early dawn,
  The brightness of the day,
  The crimson of the sunset sky;
    How fast they fade away.

2 O for the pearly gates of heaven,
    O for the golden floor;
  O for the Sun of Righteousness
    That setteth nevermore.

3 The highest hopes we cherish here,
    How fast they tire and faint;
  How many a spot defiles the robe
    That wraps an earthly saint.

4 O for a heart that never sins,
    O for a soul washed white;
  O for a voice to praise our King,
    Nor weary day or night.

5 Here faith is ours, and heavenly hope,
    And grace to lead us higher;
  But there are perfectness and peace
    Beyond our best desire.

6 O by Thy love and anguish, Lord,
    O by Thy life laid down,
  O that we fall not from Thy grace,
    Nor cast away our crown.
    Mrs. Cecil Frances Alexander. 1853.

1316 *A Funeral Hymn.* 6, 4.

1 LOWLY and solemn be
  Thy children's cry to Thee,
    Father divine:
  A hymn of suppliant breath;
  Owning that life and death
    Alike are Thine.

2 O Father, in that hour,
  When earth all succoring power
    Shall disavow;
  When spear, and shield, and crown,
  In faintness are cast down;
    Sustain us, Thou.

3 By Him who bowed to take
  The death-cup for our sake,
    The thorn, the rod;
  From whom the last dismay
  Was not to pass away;
    Aid us, O God.

4 Tremblers beside the grave,
  We call on Thee to save,
    Father divine:
  Hear, hear our suppliant breath,
  Keep us in life and death,
    Thine, only Thine.
    Mrs. Felicia Dorothea Hemans. (1794—1835.) 1832. ab.

1317 *The dying Believer to his Soul.* 7. D.

1 DEATHLESS spirit, now arise,
  Soar, thou native of the skies;
  Pearl of price, by Jesus bought,
  To His glorious likeness wrought,
  Go, to shine before His throne;
  Deck His mediatorial crown;
  Go, His triumphs to adorn;
  Made for God, to God return.

2 Lo, He beckons from on high,
  Fearless to His presence fly:
  Thine the merit of His Blood;
  Thine the Righteousness of God.
  Angels, joyful to attend,
  Hovering round thy pillow, bend;
  Wait to catch the signal given,
  And escort thee quick to heaven.

3 Shudder not to pass the stream;
  Venture all thy care on Him;
  Him, whose dying love and power
  Stilled its tossing, hushed its roar.
  Safe is the expanded wave,
  Gentle as a summer's eve;
  Not one object of His care
  Ever suffered shipwreck there.

4 See the haven full in view;
  Love divine shall bear thee through;
  Trust to that propitious gale;
  Weigh thy anchor, spread thy sail.
  Saints, in glory perfect made,
  Wait thy passage through the shade;
  Ardent for thy coming o'er,
  See, they throng the blissful shore.
    Rev. Augustus Montague Toplady. (1740—1778.) 1776. ab.
    and alt.

1318 *The House not made with Hands.* 7. D.
  2 Cor. v. 1.

1 SPIRIT, leave thy house of clay,
  Lingering dust, resign thy breath;
  Spirit, cast thy chains away;
  Dust, be thou dissolved in death:

LIFE AND DEATH.

Thus the mighty Saviour speaks,
　While the faithful Christian dies;
Thus the bonds of life He breaks,
　And the ransomed captive flies.

Prisoner, long detained below,
　Prisoner, now with freedom blest,
Welcome from a world of woe;
　Welcome to a land of rest:
Thus the choir of angels sing,
　As they bear the soul on high,
While with hallelujahs ring
　All the regions of the sky.

3 Grave, the guardian of our dust,
　Grave, the treasury of the skies,
Every atom of thy trust
　Rests in hope again to rise:
Hark, the judgment-trumpet calls,
　Soul, rebuild thy house of clay;
Immortality thy walls,
　And eternity thy day.
　　　　　James Montgomery. (1771—1854.) 1803.

1319　　*A Funeral Hymn.*　　7. D.

1 HARK, a voice divides the sky:
　Happy are the faithful dead,
In the Lord who sweetly die;
　They from all their toils are freed;
Them the Spirit hath declared
　Blest, unutterably blest;
Jesus is their great Reward,
　Jesus is their endless Rest.

2 Followed by their works, they go
　Where their Head hath gone before;
Reconciled by grace below,
　Grace hath opened mercy's door;
Justified through faith alone,
　Here they *knew* their sins forgiven;
Here they laid their burden down,
　Hallowed, and made fit for heaven.

3 Who can now lament the lot
　Of a saint in Christ deceased?
Let the world, who knows us not,
　Call us hopeless and unblest:
Jesus smiles and says, "Well done,
　Good and faithful servant thou !
Enter, and receive thy crown;
　Reign with Me triumphant now !"

4 Angels catch the approving sound,
　Bow, and bless the just award,
Hail the heir with glory crowned,
　Now rejoicing with his Lord;
Fuller joys ordained to know,
　Waiting for the general doom,
When the archangel's trump shall blow,
　"Rise, ye dead, to judgment come."
　　　　　Rev. Charles Wesley. (1708—1788.) 1742. ab.

1320　　*A Funeral Hymn.*　　7. D.

1 Lo, the prisoner is released,
　Lightened of his fleshly load;
Where the weary are at rest,
　He is gathered unto God:
Lo, the pain of life is past,
　All his warfare now is o'er,
Death and hell behind are cast,
　Grief and suffering are no more.

2 Yes, the Christian's course is run,
　Ended is the glorious strife;
Fought the fight, the work is done,
　Death is swallowed up of life;
Borne by angels on their wings,
　Far from earth the spirit flies,
Finds his God, and sits and sings,
　Triumphing in Paradise.

3 Blessing, honor, thanks, and praise,
　Pay we, gracious God, to Thee;
Thou, in Thine abundant grace,
　Givest us the victory:
True and faithful to Thy word,
　Thou hast glorified Thy Son;
Jesus Christ, our dying Lord,
　He for us the fight hath won.
　　　　　Rev. Charles Wesley. 1742. ab. and sl. alt.

1321　　*The Death and Burial of a Saint.*　　C. M.

1 WHY do we mourn departing friends,
　Or shake at death's alarms?
'T is but the voice that Jesus sends,
　To call them to His arms.

2 Are we not tending upward, too,
　As fast as time can move?
Nor would we wish the hours more slow,
　To keep us from our love.

3 Why should we tremble to convey
　Their bodies to the tomb?

There the dear flesh of Jesus lay,
And left a long perfume.
4 The graves of all His saints He blessed,
And softened every bed;
Where should the dying members rest
But with the dying Head?
5 Thence He arose, ascending high,
And showed our feet the way;
Up to the Lord our flesh shall fly,
At the great rising-day.
6 Then let the last loud trumpet sound,
And bid our kindred rise;
Awake, ye nations under ground;
Ye saints, ascend the skies.
Rev. Isaac Watts. (1674—1748.) 1709.

1322 *The Blessedness of dying Saints.* **C. M.**
Rev. xiv. 13.

1 HEAR what the voice from heaven proclaims
For all the pious dead;
Sweet is the savour of their names,
And soft their sleeping bed.
2 They die in Jesus, and are blessed;
How kind their slumbers are:
From sufferings and from sins released,
And freed from every snare.
3 Far from this world of toil and strife,
They're present with the Lord;
The labors of their mortal life
End in a large reward.
Rev. Isaac Watts. 1709.

1323 *"Sorrow not."* **C. M.**
1 Thess. iv. 13.

1 As Jesus died, and rose again
Victorious from the dead,
So His disciples rise, and reign
With their triumphant Head.
2 The time draws nigh, when from the clouds
Christ shall with shouts descend;
And the last trumpet's awful voice
The heavens and earth shall rend.
3 Then they who live shall changed be,
And they who sleep shall wake;
The graves shall yield their ancient charge,
And earth's foundations shake.
4 The saints of God, from death set free,
With joy shall mount on high;
The heavenly host, with praises loud,
Shall meet them in the sky.

5 Together to their Father's house
With joyful hearts they go;
And dwell for ever with the Lord,
Beyond the reach of woe.
6 A few short years of evil past,
We reach the happy shore,
Where death-divided friends at last
Shall meet, to part no more.
Michael Bruce. (1746—1767.) 1781. ab.

1324 *At the Interment of a Body.* **L. M.**

1 UNVEIL, thy bosom, faithful tomb;
Take this new treasure to thy trust,
And give these sacred relics room
To seek a slumber in the dust.
2 Nor pain, nor grief, nor anxious fear
Invade thy bounds. No mortal woes
Can reach the peaceful sleeper here,
While angels watch the soft repose.
3 So Jesus slept: God's dying Son
Passed thro' the grave, and blest the bed;
Rest here, blest saint, till from His throne
The morning break, and pierce the shade.
4 Break from His throne, illustrious morn;
Attend, O earth, His sovereign word;
Restore thy trust: a glorious form
Shall then ascend to meet the Lord.
Rev. Isaac Watts. 1734.

1325 *Death not the End of our Being.* **L. M.**
Ps. lxxvii.

1 SHALL man, O God of light and life,
For ever moulder in the grave?
Canst Thou forget Thy glorious work,
Thy promise, and Thy power to save?
2 In those dark silent realms of night,
Shall peace and hope no more arise?
No future morning light the tomb,
No day-star gild the darksome skies?
3 Cease, cease, ye vain desponding fears:
When Christ, our Lord, from darkness sprang,
Death, the last foe, was captive led,
And heaven with praise and wonder rang.
4 Faith sees the bright eternal doors
Unfold to make His children way;
They shall be clothed with endless life,
And shine in everlasting day.
Rev. Timothy Dwight. (1752—1817.) 1800. ab. and sl. alt.

LIFE AND DEATH.

1326 *Death swallowed up in Victory.* L. M.

1 WE sing His love who once was slain,
Who soon o'er death revived again,
That all His saints through Him might have
Eternal conquests o'er the grave.

2 The saints who now in Jesus sleep,
His own almighty power shall keep,
Till dawns the bright illustrious day,
When death itself shall die away.

3 When Jesus we in glory meet,
Our utmost joys shall be complete;
When landed on that heavenly shore,
Death and the curse will be no more.

4 Hasten, dear Lord, the glorious day,
And this delightful scene display:
When all Thy saints from death shall ri
Raptured in bliss beyond the skies.

Rev. Rowland Hill. (1744—1833.) 1796. ab

1327 *At a Funeral.* 13,11,12,12.

1 THOU art gone to the grave; but we will not deplore thee,
  Though sorrows and darkness encompass the tomb;
Thy Saviour has passed through the portal before thee,
  And the lamp of His love is thy guide through the gloom.

2 Thou art gone to the grave; we no longer behold thee,
  Nor tread the rough path of the world by thy side:
But the wide arms of mercy are spread to enfold thee,
  And sinners may die, for the Sinless hath died.

3 Thou art gone to the grave; and, its mansion forsaking,
  Perchance thy weak spirit in fear lingered long;
But the mild rays of Paradise beamed on thy waking,
  And the sound which thou heardst was the seraphim's song.

4 Thou art gone to the grave; but we will not deplore thee;
  Whose God was thy Ransom, thy Guardian and Guide:
He gave thee, He took thee, and He will restore thee;
  And death has no sting, for the Saviour has died.

Bp. Reginald Heber. (1783—1826.) 1812.

1328 *"The Lord is my Portion."* 13,11,12,12.
    Lam. iii. 24.

1 WHILE Thou, O my God, art my Help and Defender,
  No cares can o'erwhelm me, no terrors appall;
The wiles and the snares of this world will but render
  More lively my hope in my God and my All.

2 To Thee, dearest Lord, will I turn without ceasing,
  Though grief may oppress me, or sorrow befall,
And love Thee till death, my blest spirit releasing,
  Secures to me Jesus, my God and my all.

Rev. William Young. (—1757.) ab.

1329 *For a Minister cut off in his Usefulness.* 11,10,11,10,9,10.

1 Go to the grave in all thy glorious prime,
    In full activity of zeal and power;
  A Christian cannot die before his time,
    The Lord's appointment is the servant's hour.
      Cho. Servant of Jesus, pass to thy rest:
        Soldier of Jesus, go dwell among the blest.

2 Go to the grave; at noon from labor cease;
   Rest on thy sheaves, thy harvest-task is done;
   Come from the heat of battle, and in peace,
   Soldier, go home; with thee the fight is won. *Cho.*
3 Go to the grave, which, faithful to its trust,
   The germ of immortality shall keep;
   While, safe as watched by cherubim, thy dust
   Shall to the judgment-day in Jesus sleep. *Cho.*
4 Go to the grave, for there thy Saviour lay
   In death's embraces, ere He rose on high;
   And all the ransomed, by that narrow way,
   Pass to eternal life beyond the sky. *Cho.*
   James Montgomery. (1771—1854.) 1825. ab. and Cho. added.

1330　　"*The Pilgrims of the Night.*"　　11,10,11,10,9,10.
1 HARK, hark, my soul: angelic songs are swelling
   O'er earth's green fields and ocean's wave-beat shore;
   How sweet the truth those blessèd strains are telling
   Of that new life when sin shall be no more.
   Chorus. Angels of Jesus, angels of light,
      Singing to welcome the pilgrims of the night.
2 Angels, sing on, your faithful watches keeping,
   Sing us sweet fragments of the songs above;
   Till morning's joy shall end the night of weeping,
   And life's long shadows break in cloudless love. *Cho.*
   Rev. Frederick William Faber. (1814—1863.) 1849. ab. and alt.

1331　*On the Death of a Minister.*　S. M. D.
1 SERVANT of God, well done,
   Rest from thy loved employ;
   The battle fought, the victory won,
   Enter thy Master's joy.
   The voice at midnight came,
   He started up to hear;
   A mortal arrow pierced his frame,
   He fell, but felt no fear.
2 At midnight came the cry,
   "To meet thy God prepare!"
   He woke, and caught his Captain's eye;
   Then, strong in faith and prayer,
   His spirit with a bound
   Left its encumbering clay;
   His tent, at sunrise, on the ground,
   A darkened ruin lay.
3 The pains of death are past,
   Labor and sorrow cease,
   And, life's long warfare closed at last,
   His soul is found in peace.
   Soldier of Christ, well done,
   Praise be thy new employ;
   And, while eternal ages run,
   Rest in thy Saviour's joy.
   James Montgomery. (1771—1854.) 1825. ab.

1332　　"*Non, ce n'est pas mourir.*"　　S. M. D.
1 IT is not death to die,
   To leave this weary road,
   And, 'midst the brotherhood on high,
   To be at home with God.
   It is not death to close
   The eye long dimmed by tears,
   And wake in glorious repose,
   To spend eternal years.
2 It is not death to bear
   The wrench that sets us free
   From dungeon-chain, to breathe the air
   Of boundless liberty.
   Jesus, Thou Prince of Life,
   Thy chosen cannot die;
   Like Thee, they conquer in the strife,
   To reign with Thee on high.
   Rev. Cæsar Henri Abraham Malan. (1787—1864.) 1841
   Tr. by Rev. George Washington Bethune. (1805—1862.) *

LIFE AND DEATH.

1333 *The Death of the Righteous.* S. M. D.

1 O FOR the death of those
   Who slumber in the Lord:
O be like theirs my last repose,
   Like theirs my last reward.
Their bodies, in the ground,
   In silent hope may lie,
Till the last trumpet's joyful sound
   Shall call them to the sky.

2 Their ransomed spirits soar
   On wings of faith and love,
To meet the Saviour they adore,
   And reign with Him above.
With us their names shall live
   Through long succeeding years,
Embalmed with all our hearts can give,
   Our praises and our tears.
Rev. Samuel Francis Smith. (1808—) 1831.

1334 *"For ever with the Lord."* S. M.

1 FOR ever with the Lord:
   Amen, so let it be;
Life from the dead is in that word,
   'T is immortality.

2 Here in the body pent,
   Absent from Him I roam,
Yet nightly pitch my moving tent
   A day's march nearer home.

3 My Father's house on high,
   Home of my soul, how near,
At times, to faith's foreseeing eye,
   Thy golden gates appear.

4 Ah, then my spirit faints
   To reach the land I love,
The bright inheritance of saints,
   Jerusalem above.

5 "For ever with the Lord!"
   Father, if 'tis Thy will,
The promise of that faithful word
   E'en here to me fulfil.
James Montgomery. (1771—1854.) 1835. ab.

1335 *The Flesh resting in Hope.* S. M.

1 REST for the toiling hand,
   Rest for the anxious brow,
Rest for the weary, way-sore feet,
   Rest from all labor now.

2 Rest for the fevered brain,
   Rest for the throbbing eye;
Through these parched lips of thine no more
   Shall pass the moan or sigh.

3 Soon shall the trump of God
   Give out the welcome sound,
That shakes thy silent chamber-walls,
   And breaks the turf-sealed ground.

4 Ye dwellers in the dust,
   Awake, come forth and sing;
Sharp has your frost of winter been,
   But bright shall be your spring.

5 'T was sown in weakness here,
   'T will then be raised in power:
That which was sown an earthly seed,
   Shall rise a heavenly flower.
Rev. Horatius Bonar. (1808—) 1857. ab.

1336 *Our House above.* S. M.

1 WE have a house above,
   Not made with mortal hands;
And firm as our Redeemer's love,
   That heavenly fabric stands.

2 It stands securely high,
   Indissolubly sure;
Our glorious mansion in the sky
   Shall evermore endure.

3 Beneath our earthly load
   We labor now and groan,
And hasten toward that house of God,
   And struggle to be gone.

4 Full of immortal hope,
   We urge the restless strife,
And hasten to be swallowed up
   Of everlasting life.

5 Thy grace with glory crown,
   Who hast the earnest given,
And then triumphantly come down
   And take us up to heaven.
Rev. Charles Wesley. (1708—1788.) 1759. ab. and sl. alt.

1337 *"Surely I come quickly."* 8, 7, 4.
   Rev. xxii. 20.

1 O'ER the distant mountains breaking,
   Comes the reddening dawn of day;
Rise, my soul, from sleep awaking,
   Rise, and sing, and watch, and pray:
     'T is thy Saviour,
   On His bright, returning way.

2 O Thou long expected, weary
   Waits my anxious soul for Thee;
   Life is dark, and earth is dreary
   Where Thy light I do not see:
     O my Saviour,
   When wilt Thou return to me?

3 Long, too long, in sin and sadness,
   Far away from Thee I pine;
   When, O when, shall I the gladness
   Of Thy Spirit feel in mine?
     O my Saviour,
   When shall I be wholly Thine?

4 Nearer is my soul's salvation,
   Spent the night, the day at hand;
   Keep me in my lowly station,
   Watching for Thee, till I stand,
     O my Saviour,
   In Thy bright and promised land.

5 With my lamp well-trimmed and burning,
   Swift to hear, and slow to roam,
   Watching for Thy glad returning
   To restore me to my home,
     Come, my Saviour,
   O my Saviour, quickly come.
      Rev. John Samuel Bewley Monsell. (1811—) 1863.

1338   *"Dies iræ, dies illa."*   8, 7, 4.

1 Lo, He cometh: countless trumpets
   Blow to raise the sleeping dead;
   Midst ten thousand saints and angels,
   See their great exalted Head:
     Hallelujah!
   Welcome, welcome, Son of God.

2 Full of joyful expectation,
   Saints, behold the Judge appear;
   Truth and justice go before Him;
   Now the royal sentence hear:
     Hallelujah!
   Welcome, welcome, Judge divine.

3 "Come, ye blessèd of my Father,
   Enter into life and joy;
   Banish all your fears and sorrows;
   Endless praise be your employ:"
     Hallelujah!
   Welcome, welcome, to the skies.
      Rev. John Cennick. (1717—1755.) 1749. ab.

1339   *"The Judgment Trumpet."*   8, 7, 4.

1 Hark, the judgment-trumpet sounding
   Rends the skies and shakes the poles;
   Lo, the day, with wrath abounding,
   Breaks upon astonished souls:
     Every creature
   Now the awful Judge beholds.

2 Jesus, Captain of salvation,
   Leads His armies down the skies,
   Every kindred, tribe and nation,
   From the sleep of death, arise:
     Heaven's loud summons
   Fills the world with dread surprise.

3 Zion's King, His throne ascending,
   Calls His saints before His face:
   Crowns, with glory never-ending,
   All the children of His grace:
     Heaven shall echo;
   Songs of triumph fill the place.
      Rev. Nathan Sidney Smith Beman. (1786—1871.) 1832. ab

1340   *Christ's Second Coming.*   8, 7, 4.

1 Lo, He comes, with clouds descending,
   Once for favored sinners slain;
   Thousand thousand saints attending
   Swell the triumph of His train:
     Hallelujah!
   God appears on earth to reign.

2 Every eye shall now behold Him,
   Robed in dreadful majesty;
   Those who set at nought and sold Him,
   Pierced and nailed Him to the tree,
     Deeply wailing,
   Shall the true Messiah see.

3 Every island, sea, and mountain,
   Heaven and earth, shall flee away;
   All who hate Him must, confounded,
   Hear the trump proclaim the day;
     Come to judgment,
   Come to judgment, come away.

4 Now redemption, long expected,
   See in solemn pomp appear;
   All His saints, by men rejected,
   Now shall meet Him in the air:
     Hallelujah!
   See the day of God appear.

5 Yea, amen; let all adore Thee,
   High on Thine eternal throne:
   Saviour, take the power and glory;
   Claim the kingdom for Thine own:
   O come quickly,
   Hallelujah! come, Lord, come.
      Rev. Charles Wesley. (1708—1788.) 1758.
      Rev. Martin Madan. (1726—1790.) 1760. ab.

1341 *The Day of Judgment.* 8, 7, 4.

1 DAY of judgment, day of wonders,
   Hark, the trumpet's awful sound,
   Louder than a thousand thunders,
   Shakes the vast creation round:
   How the summons
   Will the sinner's heart confound.

2 See the Judge, our nature wearing,
   Clothed in majesty divine:
   You who long for His appearing
   Then shall say, "This God is mine:"
   Gracious Saviour,
   Own me in that day for Thine.

3 At His call the dead awaken,
   Rise to life from earth and sea;
   All the powers of nature, shaken
   By His looks, prepare to flee:
   Careless sinner,
   What will then become of thee?

4 But to those who have confessed,
   Loved and served the Lord below,
   He will say, "Come near, ye blessed,
   See the kingdom I bestow;
   You for ever
   Shall My love and glory know."
      Rev. John Newton. (1725—1807.) 1779. ab.

1342 *Christ in us the Hope of Glory.* 7,6,7,4. D.
   Col i 27.

1 IN us the hope of glory,
   O risen Lord, art Thou;
   The first-fruits of the Spirit
   Are in us now.
   Yet still in dust and ashes
   Before Thy throne we kneel;
   And in our hearts is hidden
   Thy living seal.

2 The whole creation groaneth
   In prison chains for Thee:
   O rend the veil asunder,
   And set us free.
   Raise up Thy holy sleepers,
   And change Thy saints on earth,
   In all, as one, revealing
   The second birth.

3 O come in all Thy glory,
   Our great Immanuel;
   Come forth, our Prince and Saviour,
   With us to dwell.
   Bring Thine eternal Sabbath,
   Bring Thine eternal day,
   And cause all grief and sighing
   To flee away.
      Unknown Author.

1343   Ἰδοὺ ὁ Νυμφίος ἔρχεται.   14.

1 BEHOLD, the Bridegroom cometh in the middle of the night,
   And blest is he whose loins are girt, whose lamp is burning bright;
   But woe to that dull servant, whom the Master shall surprise
   With lamp untrimmed, unburning, and with slumber in his eyes.

2 Do thou, my soul, beware, beware lest thou in sleep sink down,
   Lest thou be given o'er to death, and lose the golden crown;
   But see that thou be sober, with watchful eye, and thus
   Cry, "Holy, holy, holy God, have mercy upon us."

3 That day, the day of fear, shall come; my soul slack not thy toil,
   But light thy lamp, and feed it well, and make it bright with oil;
   Who knowest not how soon may sound the cry at eventide,
   "Behold the Bridegroom comes. Arise! Go forth to meet the Bride."

4 Beware, my soul, take thou good heed, lest thou in slumber lie,
   And, like the five, remain without, and knock, and vainly cry;
   But watch, and bear thy lamp undimmed, and Christ shall gird thee on
   His own bright wedding-robe of light, the glory of the Son.
      Rev. Gerard Moultrie. 1867.

JUDGMENT AND ETERNITY.

1344   *"Hora novissima."*   7, 6.

1 THE world is very evil,
    The times are waxing late:
Be sober and keep vigil,
    The Judge is at the gate;
The Judge that comes in mercy,
    The Judge that comes with might,
To terminate the evil,
    To diadem the right.

2 Arise, arise, good Christian,
    Let right to wrong succeed;
Let penitential sorrow
    To heavenly gladness lead;
To light that hath no evening,
    That knows no moon nor sun,
The light so new and golden,
    The light that is but one.

3 O Home of fadeless splendor,
    Of flowers that fear no thorn,
Where they shall dwell as children
    Who here as exiles mourn.
'Midst power that knows no limit,
    Where wisdom has no bound,
The beatific vision
    Shall glad the saints around.

4 O happy, holy portion,
    Refection for the blest,
True vision of true beauty,
    Sweet cure of all distrest;
Strive, man, to win that glory;
    Toil, man, to gain that light;
Send hope before to grasp it,
    Till hope be lost in sight.

5 O sweet and blesséd country,
    The home of God's elect,
O sweet and blesséd country
    That eager hearts expect:
Jesus, in mercy bring us
    To that dear land of rest;
Who art, with God the Father,
    And Spirit, ever blest.

        Bernard of Cluny, c. 1145.
Tr. by Rev. John Mason Neale. (1818—1866.) 1858. sl. alt.

1345   *Death and Judgment anticipated.*   C. P. M.

1 Lo, on a narrow neck of land,
  'Twixt two unbounded seas, I stand,
    Secure, insensible;
A point of time, a moment's space,
Removes me to that heavenly place,
    Or shuts me up in hell.

2 O God, mine inmost soul convert,
And deeply on my thoughtful heart
    Eternal things impress;
Give me to feel their solemn weight,
And tremble on the brink of fate,
    And wake to righteousness.

3 Before me place, in dread array,
The pomp of that tremendous day,
    When Thou with clouds shalt come
To judge the nations at Thy bar;
And tell me, Lord, shall I be there
    To meet a joyful doom?

4 Be this my one great business here,
With holy trembling, holy fear,
    To make my calling sure,
Thine utmost counsel to fulfil,
And suffer all Thy righteous will,
    And to the end endure.

5 Then, Saviour, then my soul receive,
Transported from this vale to live,
    And reign with Thee above,
Where faith is sweetly lost in sight,
And hope in full, supreme delight,
    And everlasting love.

        Rev. Charles Wesley. 1749. ab. and alt.

1346   *Prayer for Grace.*   C. P. M.

1 WHEN Thou, my righteous Judge, shalt come
To fetch Thy ransomed people home,
    Shall I among them stand?
Shall such a worthless worm as I,
Who sometimes am afraid to die,
    Be found at Thy right hand?

2 I love to meet among them now,
Before Thy gracious feet to bow,
    Though vilest of them all;
But can I bear the piercing thought,
What if my name should be left out,
    When Thou for them shalt call?

3 Prevent, prevent it by Thy grace;
Be Thou, dear Lord, my hiding-place,
    In this th' accepted day;
Thy pardoning voice, O let me hear,
To still my unbelieving fear,
    Nor let me fall, I pray.

4 Among Thy saints let me be found,
  Whene'er th' archangel's trump shall sound,
  To see Thy smiling face;
  Then loudest of the crowd I'll sing,
  While heaven's resounding mansions ring
  With shouts of sovereign grace.
Selina, Countess of Huntingdon. (1707—1791.) 1772. alt.

347 *"Es ist gewisslich an der Zeit."*   8, 7.

1 GREAT God, what do I see and hear?
  The end of things created;
  The Judge of man I see appear,
  On clouds of glory seated;
  The trumpet sounds, the graves restore
  The dead which they contained before;
  Prepare, my soul, to meet Him.

2 The dead in Christ shall first arise,
  At the last trumpet's sounding;
  Caught up to meet Him in the skies,
  With joy their Lord surrounding;
  No gloomy fears their souls dismay,
  His presence sheds eternal day
  On those prepared to meet Him.

3 But sinners, filled with guilty fears,
  Behold His wrath prevailing:
  For they shall rise, and find their tears
  And sighs are unavailing;
  The day of grace is past and gone;
  Trembling they stand before the throne,
  All unprepared to meet Him.

4 Great God, what do I see and hear?
  The end of things created;
  The Judge of man I see appear,
  On clouds of glory seated;
  Beneath His cross I view the day,
  When heaven and earth shall pass away,
  And thus prepare to meet Him.
Rev. Bartholomew Ringwaldt. (1530—1598.) 1585 ab.
Tr. by Rev. William Bengo Collyer. (1782—1854.) 1812. alt.

348   *Earth and Heaven shaken.*   8, 7.
      Heb. xii. 26.

1 THE Lord of Might from Sinai's brow
  Gave forth His voice of thunder;
  And Israel lay on earth below,
  Outstretched in fear and wonder:
  Beneath His feet was pitchy night,
  And at His left hand and His right
  The rocks were rent asunder.

2 The Lord of Love, on Calvary,
  A meek and suffering stranger,
  Upraised to heaven His languid eye
  In nature's hour of danger:
  For us He bore the weight of woe,
  For us He gave His blood to flow,
  And met His Father's anger.

3 The Lord of Love, the Lord of Might,
  The King of all created,
  Shall back return to claim His right,
  On clouds of glory seated;
  With trumpet-sound, and angel-song,
  And hallelujahs loud and long,
  O'er death and hell defeated.
Bp. Reginald Heber. (1783—1826.) 1827.

349   *"Dies iræ, dies illa."*   L. M.

1 DAY of wrath, O day of mourning!
  See fulfilled the prophets' warning,
  Heaven and earth in ashes burning!
  O what fear man's bosom rendeth,
  When from heaven the Judge descendeth,
  On whose sentence all dependeth!

2 Wondrous sound the trumpet flingeth;
  Through earth's sepulchres it ringeth;
  All before the throne it bringeth.
  Death is struck, and nature quaking;
  All creation is awaking,
  To its Judge an answer making.

3 Lo, the book exactly worded,
  Wherein all hath been recorded:
  Thence shall judgment be awarded.
  When the Judge His seat attaineth,
  And each hidden deed arraigneth,
  Nothing unavenged remaineth.

4 What shall I, frail man, be pleading?
  Who for me be interceding,
  When the just are mercy needing?
  King of Majesty tremendous,
  Who dost free salvation send us,
  Fount of pity, then befriend us.

5 Think, good Jesus, my salvation
  Cost Thy wondrous incarnation;
  Leave me not to reprobation.
  Faint and weary Thou hast sought me,
  On the cross of suffering bought me.
  Shall such grace be vainly brought me?

6 Righteous Judge, for sin's pollution,
Grant Thy gift of absolution,
Ere that day of retribution.
Guilty, now I pour my moaning,
All my shame with anguish owning;
Spare, O God, Thy suppliant groaning.

7 Thou the sinful woman saved'st;
Thou the dying thief forgavest;
And to me a hope vouchsafest.
Worthless are my prayers and signing,
Yet, good Lord, in grace complying,
Rescue me from fires undying.

8 With Thy favored sheep O place me;
Nor among the goats abase me;
But to Thy right hand upraise me.
While the wicked are confounded,
Doomed to flames of woe unbounded,
Call me, with Thy saints surrounded.

9 Low I kneel with heart submission,
See, like ashes, my contrition;
Help me in my last condition.
Ah, that day of tears and mourning!
From the dust of earth returning,
Man for judgment must prepare him.

Thomas of Celano, c. 1280.
Rev. William Josiah Irons. (1812—) 1848. alt. and abr.

1350   "*Dies iræ, dies illa.*"   L. M.

1 THAT day of wrath, that dreadful day,
When heaven and earth shall pass away,
What power shall be the sinners stay?
How shall he meet that dreadful day?

2 When, shrivelling like a parched scroll,
The flaming heavens together roll;
When louder yet, and yet more dread,
Swells the high trump that wakes the dead.

3 O on that day, that wrathful day,
When man to judgment wakes from clay,
Be Thou the trembling sinner's stay,
Though heaven and earth shall pass away.

Thomas of Celano, c. 1280.
Sir Walter Scott. (1771—1832.) 1805.

1351   "*He cometh to judge the Earth.*"   L. M.
Ps. xcvi. 13.

1 THE Lord will come, the earth shall quake,
The hills their fixed seat forsake,
And, withering from the vault of night,
The stars withdraw their feeble light.

2 The Lord will come, but not the same
As once in lowly form He came,
A silent Lamb to slaughter led,
The bruised, the suffering, and the dead.

3 The Lord will come, a dreadful form,
With wreath of flame and robe of storm,
On cherub wings, and wings of wind,
Anointed Judge of human kind.

4 Can this be He who wont to stray
A pilgrim on the world's highway,
By power oppressed, and mocked by pride,
O God, is this the Crucified?

5 Go, tyrants, to the rocks complain,
Go, seek the mountain's cleft in vain;
But faith, victorious o'er the tomb,
Shall sing for joy, "The Lord is come."

Bp. Reginald Heber. 1811.

1352   Τῆν ἡμέραν τῆν φρικτήν.   L. M.

1 THAT fearful day, that day of dread,
When Thou shalt judge the quick and dead;
O God, I shudder to foresee
The awful things which then shall be.

2 When Thou shalt come, Thine angels round
With legions, and with trumpet sound;
O Saviour, grant me in the air
With all Thy saints, to meet Thee there.

3 Weep, O my soul, ere that great day,
When God shall shine in plain array;
O weep thy sin, that thou may'st be
In that severest judgment free.

4 O Christ, forgive, remit, protect,
And set Thy servant with the elect;
That I may hear the voice, that calls
The righteous to Thy heavenly halls.

Theodore of the Studium. (759—826.)
Tr. by Rev. John Mason Neale. (1818—1866.) 1853. alt.

1353   *Looking forward to the Judgment.*   S. M.

1 THOU Judge of quick and dead,
Before whose bar severe,
With holy joy, or guilty dread,
We all shall soon appear.

2 Our cautioned souls prepare
For that tremendous day;
And fill us now with watchful care,
And stir us up to pray;

3 To pray, and wait the hour,
   That awful hour unknown,
  When robed in majesty and power,
   Thou shalt from heaven come down,—

4 The immortal Son of Man,
   To judge the human race,
  With all Thy Father's dazzling train,
   With all Thy glorious grace.

5 O may we thus be found
   Obedient to His word,
  Attentive to the trumpet's sound,
   And looking for our Lord.

6 O may we thus insure
   Our lot among the blest;
  And watch a moment to secure
   An everlasting rest.
      Rev. Charles Wesley. (1702—1788.) 1749. ab.

1354   *The Day of Doom.*   S. M.
              Matt. xxv. 41.

1 AND will the Judge descend,
   And must the dead arise,
  And not a single soul escape
   His all-discerning eyes?

2 How will my heart endure
   The terrors of that day,
  When earth and heaven before His face
   Astonished shrink away?

3 But ere that trumpet shakes
   The mansions of the dead,
  Hark, from the gospel's cheering sound
   What joyful tidings spread.

4 Ye sinners, seek His grace
   Whose wrath ye cannot bear;
  Fly to the shelter of His cross,
   And find salvation there.

5 So shall that curse remove,
   By which the Saviour bled;
  And the last awful day shall pour
   His blessings on your head.
      Rev. Philip Doddridge. (1702–1751.) 1755. ab.

1355   *Fear and Joy at Christ's Coming.*   S. M.

1 BEHOLD, the day is come,
   The righteous Judge is near,
  And sinners, trembling at their doom,
   Shall soon their sentence hear.

2 Angels in bright attire
   Conduct Him through the skies;
  Darkness and tempests, smoke and fire,
   Attend Him as He flies.

3 How awful is the sight,
   How loud the thunders roar;
  The sun forbears to give his light,
   And stars are seen no more.

4 The whole creation groans,
   But saints arise and sing;
  They are the ransomed of the Lord,
   And He their God and King.
      Rev. Benjamin Beddome. (1717–1795.) 1818.

1356   *Advent.*   S. M.

1 THE Church has waited long
   Her absent Lord to see;
  And still in loneliness she waits,
   A friendless stranger she.

2 Age after age has gone,
   Sun after sun has set,
  And still, in weeds of widowhood,
   She weeps a mourner yet.

3 Saint after saint on earth
   Has lived, and loved, and died;
  And as they left us one by one,
   We laid them side by side;

4 We laid them down to sleep,
   But not in hope forlorn;
  We laid them but to ripen there
   Till the last glorious morn.

5 The whole creation groans,
   And waits to hear that voice
  That shall restore her comeliness,
   And make her wastes rejoice.

6 Come, Lord, and wipe away
   The curse, the sin, the stain,
  And make this blighted world of ours
   Thine own fair world again.
      Rev. Horatius Bonar. (1808–) 1857. ab.

1357   *Waiting for Christ.*   S. M.

1 IN expectation sweet
   We wait, and sing, and pray,
  Till Christ's triumphal car we meet,
   And see an endless day.

JUDGMENT AND ETERNITY.   353

2 He comes, the Conqueror comes;
　　Death falls beneath His sword;
　　The joyful prisoners burst their tombs,
　　And rise to meet their Lord.
3 Thrice happy mourn for those
　　Who love the ways of peace;
　　No night of sorrow e'er shall close
　　Or shade their perfect bliss.
　　　　Rev. Joseph Swain. (1761—1796.) 1791. ab.

1358　　"Come, Lord."　　S. M.
1 COME, Lord, and tarry not:
　　Bring the long-looked-for day,
　　O why these years of waiting here,
　　These ages of delay?
2 Come, for creation groans,
　　Impatient of Thy stay,
　　Worn out with these long years of ill,
　　These ages of delay.
3 Come, for the corn is ripe,
　　Put in Thy sickle now;
　　Reap the great harvest of the earth,
　　Sower and Reaper, Thou.
4 Come in Thy glorious might,
　　Come with the iron rod,
　　Scattering Thy foes before Thy face,
　　Most mighty Son of God.
5 Come, and make all things new;
　　Build up this ruined earth;
　　Restore our faded Paradise,
　　Creation's second birth.
6 Come, and begin Thy reign
　　Of everlasting peace;
　　Come, take the kingdom to Thyself,
　　Great King of righteousness.
　　　　Rev. Horatius Bonar. 1857. ab.

1359　"A new Heaven and a new Earth." C. M.
　　　　Rev. xxi. 1—4.
1 Lo, what a glorious sight appears
　　To our believing eyes:
　　The earth and seas are passed away,
　　And the old rolling skies.
2 From the third heaven where God resides,
　　That holy, happy place,
　　The New Jerusalem comes down,
　　Adorned with shining grace.
3 Attending angels shout for joy,
　　And the bright armies sing,
　　"Mortals, behold the sacred seat
　　Of your descending King.

4 "The God of glory down to men
　　Removes His blest abode;
　　Men, the dear objects of His grace,
　　And He the loving God.
5 "His own soft hand shall wipe the tears
　　From every weeping eye;
　　And pains,and groans,and griefs,and fears,
　　And death itself shall die."
6 How long, dear Saviour, O how long
　　Shall this bright hour delay?
　　Fly swifter round, ye wheels of time,
　　And bring the welcome day.
　　　　Rev. Isaac Watts. (1674—1748.) 1709.

1360　　The Resurrection.　　C. M.
　　　　1 Thess. iv. 14—17.
1 Lo, I behold the scattering shades,
　　The dawn of heaven appears;
　　The sweet immortal morning spreads
　　Its blushes round the spheres.
2 I see the Lord of glory come,
　　And flaming guards around;
　　The skies divide to make Him room,
　　The trumpet shakes the ground.
3 I hear the voice, "Ye dead, arise,"
　　And lo, the graves obey;
　　And waking saints, with joyful eyes,
　　Salute the expected day.
4 They leave the dust, and on the wing
　　Rise to the middle air,
　　In shining garments meet their King,
　　And low adore Him there.
5 O may my humble spirit stand
　　Amongst them clothed in white:
　　The meanest place at His right hand
　　Is infinite delight.
　　　　Rev. Isaac Watts. 1706. ab.

1361　　Breathing after Heaven.　　C. M.
　　　　Ps. xc. 13.
1 RETURN, O God of love, return;
　　Earth is a tiresome place:
　　How long shall we, Thy children, mourn
　　Our absence from Thy face?
2 Let heaven succeed our painful years,
　　Let sin and sorrow cease;
　　And, in porportion to our tears,
　　So make our joys increase.
3 Thy wonders to Thy servants show,
　　Make Thine own work complete;
　　Then shall our souls Thy glory know,
　　And own Thy love was great.

HEAVEN.

4 Then shall we shine before Thy throne
   In all Thy beauty, Lord;
And the poor service we have done
   Meet a divine reward.
               Rev. Isaac Watts. (1674–1748.) 1719.

1362   *"Come, Lord Jesus."*
           Rev. xxii. 20.

1 HOPE of our hearts, O Lord, appear:
   Thou glorious Star of day,
Shine forth, and chase the dreary night,
   With all our tears, away.

2 Strangers on earth, we wait for Thee;
   O leave the Father's throne,
Come with a shout of victory, Lord,
   And claim us as Thine own.

3 O bid the bright archangel, now,
   The trump of God prepare,
To call Thy saints—the quick, the dead,
   To meet Thee in the air.

4 No resting place we seek on earth,
   No loveliness we see;
Our eye is on the royal crown,
   Prepared for us and Thee.

5 There, near Thy heart, upon the throne,
   Thy ransomed Bride shall see
What grace was in the bleeding Lamb,
   Who died to make her free.
             Sir Edward Denny. (1796–) 1839. ab.

1363   *"Sanctorum meritis inclyta gaudia."*

1 THE triumphs of the martyred Saints
   The joyous lay demand,
The heart delights in song to dwell
   On that victorious band.

2 For Thee they braved the tyrant's rage,
   The scourge's cruel smart:
The wild beast's claw their bodies tore,
   But vanquished not the heart.

3 Like lambs before the sword they fell,
   Nor cry nor plaint expressed:
For patience kept the concious mind,
   And armed the fearless breast.

4 What tongue can tell Thy crown prepared
   To wreathe the martyr's head?
What voice Thy robe of white to clothe
   His limbs with torture red?

5 Vouchsafe us, Lord, if such Thy will,
   Clear skies and seasons calm:
If not, the martyr's cross to bear,
   And win the martyr's palm.
        Unknown Author of the 8th century.
     Tr. by Bp. Richard Mant. (1776–1848.) 1837. ab.

1364   *"Te læta, mundi Conditor."*

1 MAKER of earth, to Thee alone
   Perpetual rest belongs;
To Thee bright choirs around Thy throne
   Pour forth their endless songs.

2 But we, as sinless now no more,
   Are doomed to toil and pain;
Yet exiles on a foreign shore
   May sing the heavenly strain.

3 Father, whose promise binds Thee still
   To make the captive free,
Grant us to mourn the deeds of ill
   That banish us from Thee.

4 And, mourning, grant us faith to rest
   Upon Thy love and care;
Till Thou restore us with the blest,
   The joys of heaven to share.

5 O God the Father, God the Son,
   And God the Holy Ghost,
To Thee we praise, Great Three in One,
   From Thy created host.
        Prof. Charles Coffin. (1676–1749.) 1736.
   Tr. by Rev. John Mason Neale. (1818–1866.) 1863.

1365   *Heaven in Prospect.*   7. D.
           Rev. vii. 9.

1 PALMS of glory, raiment bright,
   Crowns that never fade away,
Gird and deck the saints in light,
   Priests, and kings, and conquerors they.
Yet the conquerors bring their palms
   To the Lamb amidst the throne,
And proclaim, in joyful psalms,
   Victory through His cross alone.

2 Kings for harps their crowns resign,
   Crying, as they strike the chords,
"Take the kingdom, it is Thine,
   King of kings, and Lord of lords."
Round the altar priests confess,
   If their robes are white as snow,
'Twas the Saviour's righteousness,
   And His blood, that made them so.

3 Who were these?—On earth they dwell
   Sinners once of Adam's race,
Guilt, and fear, and suffering felt,
   But were saved by sovereign grace.
They were mortal, too, like us:
   Ah, when we, like them, shall die,
May our souls, translated thus,
   Triumph, reign, and shine on high.
        James Montgomery. (1771–1854.) 1825.

HEAVEN.

1366 *The Song of the Sealed.* 7. D.
Rev. vii. 9—16.

1 WHAT are these in bright array,
    This innumerable throng,
Round the altar night and day,
    Hymning one triumphant song:
"Worthy is the Lamb, once slain,
    Blessing, honor, glory, power,
Wisdom, riches, to obtain,
    New dominion every hour."

2 These through fiery trials trod;
    These from great afflictions came;
Now, before the throne of God,
    Sealed with His Almighty Name;
Clad in raiment pure and white,
    Victor-palms in every hand,
Through their dear Redeemer's might,
    More than conquerors they stand.

3 Hunger, thirst, disease unknown,
    On immortal fruits they feed;
Them the Lamb amidst the throne,
    Shall to living fountains lead;
Joy and gladness banish sighs,
    Perfect love dispels all fear,
And forever from their eyes
    God shall wipe away the tear.
                James Montgomery. 1819, 1853.

1367 *The happy Saints.* 7. D.

1 HIGH in yonder realms of light,
    Dwell the raptured saints above,
Far beyond our feeble sight,
    Happy in Immanuel's love;
Pilgrims in this vale of tears,
    Once they knew, like us below,
Gloomy doubts, distressing fears,
    Torturing pain, and heavy woe.

2 Mid the chorus of the skies,
    Mid th' angelic lyres above,
Hark, their songs melodious rise,
    Songs of praise to Jesus' love:
Happy spirits, ye are fled,
    Where no grief can entrance find;
Lulled to rest the aching head,
    Soothed the anguish of the mind.

3 All is tranquil and serene,
    Calm and undisturbed repose,
There no cloud can intervene,
    There no angry tempest blows:

Every tear is wiped away,
    Sighs no more shall heave the breast,
Night is lost in endless day,
    Sorrow, in eternal rest.
            Rev. Thomas Raffles. (1788—1863.) 1812. ab. and alt.

1368 *The Sons of Light.* 7. D.

1 WHAT are these arrayed in white,
    Brighter than the noon-day sun,
Foremost of the sons of light,
    Nearest the eternal throne?
These are they that bore the cross,
    Nobly for their Master stood,
Sufferers in His righteous cause,
    Followers of the dying God.

2 Out of great distress they came;
    Washed their robes by faith below
In the blood of Christ, the Lamb,
    Blood that washes white as snow.
Therefore are they next the throne,
    Serve their Maker day and night;
God resides among His own,
    God doth in His saints delight.

3 More than conquerors at last,
    Here they find their trials o'er;
They have all their sufferings passed,
    Hunger now and thirst no more;
No excessive heat they feel
    From the sun's directer ray;
In a milder clime they dwell,
    Region of eternal day.

4 He that on the throne doth reign,
    Them the Lamb shall always feed,
With the tree of life sustain,
    To the living fountains lead;
He shall all their sorrows chase,
    All their wants at once remove;
Wipe the tears from every face;
    Fill up every soul with love.
                Rev. Charles Wesley. (1708—1788.) 1745.

1369 *Saints and Angels before the Throne.* 7. D.

1 LIFT your eyes of faith, and see
    Saints and angels joined in one;
What a countless company
    Stand before yon dazzling throne.
Each before his Saviour stands,
    All in milk-white robes arrayed;
Palms they carry in their hands,
    Crowns of glory on their head.

2 Saints, begin the endless song,
   Cry aloud, in heavenly lays,
 Glory doth to God belong,
   God the glorious Saviour praise;
 All salvation from Him came,
   Him who reigns enthroned on high;
 Glory to the bleeding Lamb,
   Let the morning stars reply.

3 Angel powers the throne surround;
   Next the saints in glory they;
 Lulled with the transporting sound,
   They their silent homage pay;
 Prostrate on their face, before
   God and His Messiah fall;
 Then in hymns of praise adore,
   Shout the Lamb that died for all.
      Rev. Charles Wesley. (1708—1788.) 1745. ab.

1370   *"O Mother dear, Jerusalem."*   C. M. D.

1 O MOTHER dear, Jerusalem,
   When shall I come to thee?
 When shall my sorrows have an end?
   Thy joys when shall I see?
 O happy harbor of God's saints,
   O sweet and pleasant soil;
 In thee no sorrow can be found,
   Nor grief, nor care, nor toil.

2 No dimming cloud o'ershadows thee,
   Nor gloom, nor darksome night;
 But every soul shines as the sun,
   For God Himself gives light.
 Thy walls are made of precious stone,
   Thy bulwarks diamond-square,
 Thy gates are all of orient pearl;
   O God, if I were there!

3 Right thro' thy streets with pleasing sound
   The flood of life doth flow,
 And on the banks, on either side,
   The trees of life do grow.
 Those trees each month yield ripened fruit;
   For evermore they spring,
 And all the nations of the earth
   To thee their honors bring.

4 There the blest souls that hardly 'scaped
   The snare of death and hell,
 Triumph in joy eternally,
   Whereof no tongue can tell.

 O mother dear, Jerusalem,
   When shall I come to thee?
 When shall my sorrows have an end?
   Thy joys when shall I see?
      Rev. Francis Baker? 1616. alt.
      Rev. David Dickson. (1583—1663.) 1649. ab.

1371   *Resigned to Death.*   C. M. D

1 AND let this feeble body fail,
   And let it faint or die,
 My soul shall quit the mournful vale,
   And soar to worlds on high;
 Shall join the disembodied saints,
   And find its long-sought rest,
 That only bliss for which it pants,
   In my Redeemer's breast.

2 O what hath Jesus bought for me!
   Before my ravished eyes
 Rivers of life divine I see,
   And trees of Paradise:
 I see a world of spirits bright,
   Who reap the pleasures there;
 They all are robed in spotless white,
   And conquering palms they bear.

3 O what are all my sufferings here,
   If, Lord, Thou count me meet
 With that enraptured host to appear,
   And worship at Thy feet!
 Give joy or grief, give ease or pain,
   Take life or friends away,
 I come, to find them all again
   In that eternal day.
      Rev. Charles Wesley. 1759. ab.

1372   *"Jerusalem, my happy Home."*   C. M.

1 JERUSALEM, my happy home,
   Name ever dear to me,
 When shall my labors have an end
   In joy, and peace, and thee?

2 When shall these eyes thy heaven-built walls
   And pearly gates behold;
 Thy bulwarks with salvation strong,
   And streets of shining gold?

3 O when, thou City of my God,
   Shall I thy courts ascend,
 Where congregations ne'er break up,
   And Sabbaths have no end?

HEAVEN.

4 There happier bowers than Eden's bloom,
   Nor sin nor sorrow know;
   Blest seats, through rude and stormy scenes
   I onward press to you.

5 Apostles, martyrs, prophets, there
   Around my Saviour stand;
   And soon my friends in Christ below
   Will join the glorious band.

6 Jerusalem, my happy home,
   My soul still pants for thee:
   Then shall my labors have an end
   When I thy joys shall see.
     Unknown. Williams and Boden's Collection, 1801. ab.

1373   *The heavenly Fold.*   C. M.

1 THERE is a fold, whence none can stray,
   And pastures ever green,
   Where sultry sun, or stormy day,
   Or night is never seen.

2 Far up the everlasting hills,
   In God's own light it lies;
   His smile its vast dimension fills
   With joy that never dies.

3 One narrow vale, one darksome wave,
   Divides that land from this:
   I have a Shepherd pledged to save
   And bear me home to bliss.

4 Soon at His feet my soul will lie
   In life's last struggling breath;
   But I shall only seem to die,
   I shall not taste of death.

5 Far from this guilty world to be
   Exempt from toil and strife,
   To spend eternity with Thee,
   My Saviour, this is life.
     Bp. John East. 1836. ab.

1374   *Heaven invisible and holy.*   C. M.
     1 Cor. ii. 9, 10. Rev. xxi. 27.

1 NOR eye hath seen, nor ear hath heard,
   Nor sense, nor reason known,
   What joys the Father has prepared,
   For those that love the Son.

2 But the good Spirit of the Lord
   Reveals a heaven to come;
   The beams of glory in His word
   Allure and guide us home.

3 Pure are the joys above the sky,
   And all the region peace;
   No wanton lips, nor envious eye,
   Can see or taste the bliss.

4 Those holy gates for ever bar
   Pollution, sin, and shame;
   None shall obtain admittance there
   But followers of the Lamb.
     Rev. Isaac Watts. (1674—1748.) 1709. ab.

1375   *"Hic breve vivitur."*   7, 6. D.

1 BRIEF life is here our portion;
   Brief sorrow, short-lived care;
   The life that knows no ending,
   The tearless life, is there.
   O happy retribution:
   Short toil, eternal rest;
   For mortals and for sinners
   A mansion with the blest.

2 And now we fight the battle,
   But then shall wear the crown
   Of full and everlasting
   And passionless renown.
   But He whom now we trust in
   Shall then be seen and known;
   And they that know and see Him
   Shall have Him for their own.

3 The morning shall awaken,
   The shadows shall decay,
   And each true-hearted servant
   Shall shine as doth the day.
   There God our King and Portion,
   In fulness of His grace,
   Shall we behold forever,
   And worship face to face.
     Bernard of Cluny. c. 1145.
     Tr. by Rev. John Mason Neale. (1818—1866.) 1851. ab.

1376   *"O bona Patria."*   7, 6. D.

1 FOR thee, O dear, dear Country,
   Mine eyes their vigils keep;
   For very love, beholding
   Thy happy name, they weep.
   The mention of thy glory
   Is unction to the breast,
   And medicine in sickness,
   And love, and life, and rest.

2 O one, O only Mansion,
   O Paradise of joy,

HEAVEN.

Where tears are ever banished,
And smiles have no alloy;
The Lamb is all thy splendor,
The Crucified thy praise;
His laud and benediction
Thy ransomed people raise.

3 With jasper glow thy bulwarks,
Thy streets with emerald blaze;
The sardius and the topaz
Unite in thee their rays;
Thine ageless walls are bonded
With amethyst unpriced;
The saints build up its fabric,
And the Corner-stone is Christ.

4 Thou hast no shore, fair ocean;
Thou hast no time, bright day:
Dear fountain of refreshment
To pilgrims far away.
Upon the Rock of Ages
They raise thy holy tower;
Thine is the victor's laurel,
And thine the golden dower.
Bernard of Cluny. c. 1145.
Tr. by Rev. John Mason Neale. 1851. alt.

1377 *"Urbs Syon aurea."* 7, 6. D.

1 JERUSALEM the golden,
With milk and honey blest,
Beneath thy contemplation
Sink heart and voice opprest:
I know not, O I know not
What social joys are there;
What radiancy of glory,
What light beyond compare.

2 They stand, those halls of Zion,
All jubilant with song,
And bright with many an angel,
And all the martyr throng:
The Prince is ever in them,
The daylight is serene;
The pastures of the blessèd
Are decked in glorious sheen.

3 There is the throne of David;
And there, from care released,
The shout of them that triumph,
The song of them that feast;
And they who, with their leader,
Have conquered in the fight,

For ever and for ever
Are clad in robes of white.
Bernard of Cluny. c. 1145.
Tr. by Rev. John Mason Neale. 1851. alt.

1378 *"Urbs Syon inclyta, Gloria."* 7, 6. D.

1 JERUSALEM the glorious,
The home of the elect,
O dear and future vision
That eager hearts expect:
E'en now by faith I see thee,
E'en here thy walls discern;
To thee my thoughts are kindled,
And strive and pant and yearn.

2 New mansion of new people,
Whom God's own love and light
Promote, increase, make holy,
Identify, unite.
And there the band of prophets
United praise ascribes,
And there the twelve-fold chorus
Of Israel's ransomed tribes.

3 And there the Sole-Begotten
Is Lord in regal state;
He, Judah's mystic Lion,
He, Lamb immaculate.
O fields that know no sorrow,
O state that fears no strife,
O princely bowers, O land of flowers,
O realm and home of life.
Bernard of Cluny. c. 1145.
Tr. by Rev. John Mason Neale. 1851. alt.

1379 *General Ending of the four preceding Hymns.* 7, 6.

1 O SWEET and blessèd country,
The home of God's elect,
O sweet and blessèd country
That eager hearts expect:
Jesus, in mercy bring us
To that dear land of rest;
Who art with God the Father,
And Spirit, ever blest.
Bernard of Cluny. c. 1145.
Tr. by Rev. John Mason Neale. 1851.

1380 *The Country beyond the Stars.* 7, 6.

1 MY soul, there is a country
Afar beyond the stars,
Where stands a wingèd sentry,
All skilful in the wars.

There, above noise and danger,
  Sweet Peace sits crowned with smiles,
And One born in a manger
  Commands the beauteous files.
2 If thou canst get but thither,
  There grows the flower of peace,
The rose that cannot wither,
  Thy fortress and thine ease.
Leave then thy foolish ranges,
  For none can thee secure,
But One, who never changes,
  Thy God, thy Life, thy Cure.
          Henry Vaughan. (1621—1695.) 1650.

1381   *The Saints marching up.*   7, 6, 8, 6.
1 TEN thousand times ten thousand,
    In sparkling raiment bright,
  The armies of the ransomed saints
    Throng up the steeps of light:
  'T is finished, all is finished,
    Their fight with death and sin:
  Fling open wide the golden gates,
    And let the victors in.

2 What rush of Hallelujahs
    Fills all the earth and sky;
  What ringing of a thousand harps
    Bespeaks the triumph nigh.
  O day, for which Creation
    And all its tribes were made;
  O joy, for all its former woes
    A thousand fold repaid.

3 O then what raptured greetings
    On Canaan's happy shore;
  What knitting severed friendships up,
    Where partings are no more.
  Then eyes with joy shall sparkle,
    That brimmed with tears of late:
  Orphans no longer fatherless,
    Nor widows desolate.
          Rev. Henry Alford. (1810—1871.) 1866.

1382   *The Heavenly Rest.*   C. M.
1 THERE is an hour of peaceful rest,
    To mourning wanderers given;
  There is a joy for souls distrest,
  A balm for every wounded breast,
    'T is found above, in heaven.

2 There is a home for weary souls
    By sin and sorrow driven;

When tossed on life's tempestuous shoals,
Where storms arise, and ocean rolls,
  And all is drear but heaven.

3 There, faith lifts up her cheerful eye,
    To brighter prospects given;
  And views the tempest passing by,
  The evening shadows quickly fly,
    And all serene in heaven.

4 There, fragrant flowers, immortal, bloom,
    And joys supreme are given;
  There, rays divine disperse the gloom:
  Beyond the confines of the tomb
    Appears the dawn of heaven.
     Rev. William Bingham Tappan. (1794—1849.) 1822, 1846. ab.

1383   *Sowing in Tears, Reaping in Joy.*   C. M.
1 THERE is an hour of hallowed peace
    For those with cares distrest,
  When sighs and sorr'wing tears shall cease
    And all be hushed to rest.

2 'T is then the soul is freed from fears
    And doubts, which here annoy;
  And they, that oft have sown in tears,
    Shall reap again in joy.

3 There is a home of sweet repose,
    Where storms assail no more;
  The stream of endless pleasure flows,
    On that celestial shore.

4 There smiling peace with love appears,
    And bliss without alloy;
  There, they, who once have sown in tears,
    Now reap eternal joy.
          Rev. William Bingham Tappan. 1822. ab.

1384   *The Beatific Vision of Christ.*   C. M.
1 FROM Thee, my God, my joys shall rise,
    And run eternal rounds,
  Beyond the limits of the skies,
    And all created bounds.

2 The holy triumphs of my soul
    Shall death itself outbrave,
  Leave dull mortality behind,
    And fly beyond the grave.

3 There, where my blessèd Jesus reigns,
    In heaven's unmeasured space,
  I'll spend a long eternity
    In pleasure and in praise.

HEAVEN.

4 Millions of years my wondering eyes
   Shall o'er Thy beauties rove,
And endless ages I'll adore
   The glories of Thy love.

5 Sweet Jesus, every smile of Thine
   Shall fresh endearments bring,
And thousand tastes of new delight
   From all Thy graces spring.

6 Haste, my Belovéd, fetch my soul
   Up to Thy blest abode;
Fly, for my spirit longs to see
   My Saviour and my God.
       Rev. Isaac Watts. (1674—1748.) 1709.

1385   "The goodly Land."   6, 8, 4.

1 THE goodly land I see,
   With peace and plenty blest;
A land of sacred liberty,
   And endless rest:
There milk and honey flow,
   And oil and wine abound,
And trees of life forever grow
   With mercy crowned.

2 There dwells the Lord, our King,
   The Lord, our righteousness:
Triumphant o'er the world and sin,
   The Prince of Peace,
On Zion's sacred height,
   His kingdom still maintains,
And glorious, with His saints in light,
   For ever reigns.

3 Before the Saviour's face
   The ransomed nations bow,
O'erwhelmed at His almighty grace,
   For ever new:
He shows His prints of love;
   They kindle to a flame,
And sound, through all the worlds above,
   "The slaughtered Lamb!"

4 The whole triumphant host
   Give thanks to God on high;
"Hail, Father, Son, and Holy Ghost,"
   They ever cry.
Hail, Abrah'm's God and mine!
   (I join the heavenly lays)
All might and majesty are Thine,
   And endless praise.
       Rev. Thomas Olivers. (1725—1799.) 1770. ab.

1386   *The God of Abraham praised.*   6, 8, 4
       Ex. iii. 6. Ps. cxlvi. 2.

1 THE God of Abrah'm praise,
   Who reigns enthroned above;
Ancient of everlasting days,
   And God of love:
Jehovah, Great I Am!
   By earth and heaven confest:
I bow and bless the sacred Name,
   For ever blest.

2 The God of Abrah'm praise,
   At whose supreme command
From earth I rise, and seek the joys
   At His right hand:
I all on earth forsake,
   Its wisdom, fame, and power;
And Him my only portion make,
   My shield and tower.

3 He by Himself hath sworn,
   I on His oath depend;
I shall on eagles' wings upborne
   To heaven ascend;
I shall behold His face,
   I shall His power adore,
And sing the wonders of His grace
   For evermore.
       Rev. Thomas Olivers. 1770. ab.

1387   *Moving onward.*   10.

1 JOYFULLY, joyfully onward I move,
Bound for the land of bright spirits above;
Angelic choristers sing as I come,
Joyfully, joyfully haste to thy home.
Soon with my pilgrimage ended below,
Home to that land of delight will I go;
Pilgrim and stranger, no more shall I roam,
Joyfully, joyfully resting at home.

2 Friends, fondly cherished, have passed on before.   [shore;
Waiting, they watch me approaching the
Singing to cheer me through death's chilling gloom,
Joyfully, joyfully haste to Thy home.
Sounds of sweet melody fall on my ear;
Harps of the blesséd, your voices I hear;
Rings with the harmony heaven's high dome,
Joyfully, joyfully haste to thy home.

3 Death, with thy weapons of war, lay me low,
Strike, king of terrors, I fear not the blow
Jesus hath broken the bars of the tomb;
Joyfully, joyfully will I go home.

Bright will the morn of eternity dawn,
Death shall be banished, his sceptre be gone;
Joyfully, then, shall I witness his doom,
Joyfully, joyfully, safely at home.
Rev. William Hunter. (1811—) 1843.

1388 *The happy Release.* 10.

1 HAPPY the spirit released from its clay;
Happy the soul that goes bounding away;
Singing, as upward it hastes to the skies,
Victory, victory! homeward I rise.
Many the toils it has passed through below,
Many the seasons of trial and woe;
Many the doubtings it never should sing,
Victory, victory! thus on the wing.

2 How can we wish them recalled from their home,
Longer in sorrowing exile to roam?
Safely they passed from their troubles beneath,
Victory, victory! shouting in death.
Thus let them slumber, till Christ from the skies
Bids them in glorified body arise;
Singing, as upward they spring from the tomb,
Victory, victory! Jesus hath come.
Rev. William Hunter. 1843.

1389 *The River of Life.* 8, 7.
Rev. xxii. 1.

1 SHALL we gather at the river
Where bright angel feet have trod;
With its crystal tide forever
Flowing by the throne of God?
Cho. Yes, we'll gather at the river,
The beautiful, the beautiful river;
Gather with the saints at the river,
That flows by the throne of God.

2 On the margin of the river,
Washing up its silver spray,
We will walk and worship ever,
All the happy golden day. *Cho.*

3 On the bosom of the river,
Where the Saviour-King we own,
We shall meet, and sorrow never
'Neath the glory of the throne. *Cho.*

4 Ere we reach the shining river,
Lay we every burden down;
Grace our spirits will deliver,
And provide a robe and crown. *Cho.*

5 At the smiling of the river,
Mirror of the Saviour's face,
Saints whom death will never sever,
Lift their songs of saving grace. *Cho.*

6 Soon we'll reach the silver river,
Soon our pilgrimage will cease;
Soon our happy hearts will quiver
With the melody of peace. *Cho.*
Rev. Robert Lowry. (1826—) 1864.

1390 *"The City God hath made."* 8, 7.

1 DAILY, daily sing the praises
Of the City God hath made;
In the beauteous fields of Eden
Its foundation-stones are laid.
Cho. O the beauty of that city,
The wonderful, the wonderful city,
With its gates of pearl ever open,
That who will may enter in.

2 In the midst of that dear City
Christ is reigning on His seat,
And the angels swing their censers
In a ring about His feet. *Cho.*

3 From the throne a river issues,
Clear as crystal, passing bright,
And it traverses the City
Like a sudden beam of light. *Cho.*

4 There the wind is sweetly fragrant,
And is laden with the song
Of the seraphs, and the elders,
And the great redeemed throng. *Cho.*

5 O I would my ears were open
Here to catch that happy strain;
O I would my eyes some vision
Of that Eden could attain. *Cho.*
Rev. Sabine Baring Gould. (1834—) 1867. ab

1391 *The Multitude before the Throne.* 8, 7.
Rev. iv. 6; vii. 9.

1 HARK the sound of holy voices,
Chanting at the crystal sea,
Hallelujah, Hallelujah,
Hallelujah! Lord to Thee.

2 Multitude, which none can number,
Like the stars in glory stand,
Clothed in white apparel, holding
Palms of victory in their hand.

3 They have come from tribulation,
And have washed their robes in blood,
Washed them in the blood of Jesus;
Tried they were, and firm they stood.

4 Gladly, Lord, with Thee they suffered,
Gladly, Lord, with Thee they died;
And by death to life immortal
They were born, and glorified.

5 Now they reign in heavenly glory,
    Now they walk in golden light,
  Now they drink, as from a river,
    Holy bliss and infinite.

6 Love and peace they taste forever,
    And all truth and knowledge see
  In the beatific vision
    Of the Blessèd Trinity.
    Bp. Christopher Wordsworth. (1807—) 1863. ab.

1392 *"Welt, lebewohl, ich bin dein müde."* 8, 7.

1 TIME, thou speedest on but slowly,
    Hours, how tardy is your pace,
  Ere with Him, the High and Holy,
    I hold converse face to face.

2 Here is nought but care and mourning,
    Comes a joy, it will not stay;
  Fairly shines the sun at dawning,
    Night will soon o'ercloud the day.

3 Onward then: not long I wander
    Ere my Saviour comes for me,
  And with Him abiding yonder,
    All His glory I shall see.

4 O the music and the singing
    Of the host redeemed by love;
  O the hallelujahs ringing
    Through the halls of light above.
    Rev. Johann Georg Albinus. (1624—1679.) 1652.
    Tr. by Miss Catherine Winkworth. (1829—) 1858. ab.

1393 *"Alleluia! dulce carmen."* 8, 7.

1 HALLELUJAH! best and sweetest
    Of the hymns of praise above;
  Hallelujah! thou repeatest,
    Angel-host, these notes of love:
      This ye utter,
    While your golden harps ye move.

2 Hallelujah! church victorious,
    Join the concert of the sky;
  Hallelujah! bright and glorious,
    Lift, ye saints, this strain on high:
      We, poor exiles,
    Join not yet your melody.

3 Hallelujah! strains of gladness
    Suit not souls with anguish torn;
  Hallelujah! sounds of sadness
    Best become our state forlorn:
      Our offences
    We with bitter tears must mourn.

4 But our earnest supplication,
    Holy God, we raise to Thee:
  Visit us with Thy salvation,
    Make us all Thy joys to see.
      Hallelujah!
    Ours at length this strain shall be.
    Unknown Author of the 14th or 15th century.
    Tr. by Rev. John Chandler. (1806—) 1837.

1394 *The Lamb in the Midst of the Throne.* 8, 7.
Rev. vii. 17.

1 JESUS, blessèd Mediator,
    Thou the airy path hast trod;
  Thou the Judge, the Consummator,
    Shepherd of the fold of God.
  Can I trust a fellow-being?
    Can I trust an angel's care?
  O Thou merciful All-seeing,
    Beam around my spirit there.

2 Blessèd fold, no foe can enter,
    And no friend departeth thence;
  Jesus is their sun, their centre,
    And their shield Omnipotence.
  Blessèd, for the Lamb shall feed them,
    All their tears shall wipe away,
  To the living fountains lead them,
    Till fruition's perfect day.

3 Lo, it comes, that day of wonder;
    Louder chorals shake the skies,
  Hades' gates are burst asunder;
    See, the new-clothed myriads rise:
  Thought, repress thy weak endeavor;
    Here must reason prostrate fall;
  O the ineffable For Ever,
    And the eternal All in all.
    Josiah Conder. (1789—1855.) 1837. ab.

1395 *"Wer sind die vor Gottes Throne?"* 8, 7.

1 WHO are these like stars appearing,
    These, before God's throne who stand?
  Each a golden crown is wearing,
    Who are all this glorious band?
  Alleluia! hark, they sing,
    Praising loud their heavenly King.

2 These are they who have contended
    For their Saviour's honor long,
  Wrestling on till life was ended,
    Following not the sinful throng;
  These, who well the fight sustained,
    Triumph through the Lamb have gained.

3 These are they whose hearts were riven,
  Sore with woe and anguish tried,
Who in prayer full oft have striven
  With the God they glorified:
Now, their painful conflict o'er,
God has bid them weep no more.

4 These, like priests have watched and waited,
  Offering up to Christ their will,
Soul and body consecrated,
  Day and night they serve Him still:
Now, in God's most holy place,
Blest they stand before His face.

5 Lo, the Lamb Himself now feeds them,
  On Mount Zion's pastures fair;
From His central throne He leads them
  By the living fountain there:
Lamb and Shepherd, Good Supreme,
Free He gives the cooling stream.
  Rev. Heinrich Theodor Schenk. (—1727.)
  Tr. by Miss Frances Elizabeth Cox. 1841. ab.

1396 *"Clothed with white Robes."* L. M.
  Rev. vii. 9.

1 O HAPPY saints, who dwell in light,
  And walk with Jesus, clothed in white;
Safe landed on that peaceful shore,
Where pilgrims meet to part no more.

2 Released from sin, and toil, and grief,
  Death was their gate to endless life;
An opened cage, to let them fly
And build their happy nest on high.

3 And now they range the heavenly plains,
  And sing their hymns in melting strains;
And now their souls begin to prove
The heights and depths of Jesus' love.

4 He cheers them with eternal smile;
  They sing hosannas all the while;
Or, overwhelmed with rapture sweet,
Sink down adoring at His feet.

5 Ah, Lord, with tardy steps I creep,
  And sometimes sing, and sometimes weep;
Yet strip me of this house of clay,
And I will sing as loud as they.
  Rev. John Berridge. (1716—1793.) 1785.

1397 *The Sight of God and Christ in Heaven.* L. M.

1 DESCEND from heaven, Immortal Dove,
  Stoop down and take us on Thy wings,
And mount and bear us far above
  The reach of these inferior things.

2 O for a sight, a pleasing sight,
  Of our Almighty Father's throne:
There sits our Saviour crowned with light,
  Clothed in a body like our own.

3 Adoring saints around Him stand,
  And thrones and powers before Him fall;
The God shines gracious through the Man,
  And sheds sweet glories on them all.

4 When shall the day, dear Lord, appear,
  That I shall mount to dwell above,
And stand and bow amongst them there,
  And view Thy face, and sing, and love?
  Rev. Isaac Watts. (1674—1748.) 1709. ab.

1398 *With Christ in Glory.* L. M.
  John xvii. 24.

1 O FOR a sweet, inspiring ray,
  To animate our feeble strains,
From the bright realms of endless day,
  The blissful realms, where Jesus reigns.

2 There, low before His glorious throne,
  Adoring saints and angels fall;
And with delightful worship own
  His smile their bliss, their heaven, their all.

3 Immortal glories crown His head,
  While tuneful hallelujahs rise,
And love, and joy, and triumph spread
  Through all th' assemblies of the skies.

4 He smiles, and seraphs tune their songs
  To boundless rapture while they gaze;
Ten thousand thousand joyful tongues
  Resound His everlasting praise.

5 There, all the favorites of the Lamb
  Shall join at last the heavenly choir:
O may the joy-inspiring theme
  Awake our faith and warm desire.

6 Dear Saviour, let Thy Spirit seal
  Our interest in that blissful place;
Till death remove this mortal veil,
  And we behold Thy lovely face.
  Miss Anne Steele. (1717—1778.) 1760.

1399 *The Return of the Soul to God.* L. M.
  Eccl. xii. 7.

1 Now let our souls, on wings sublime,
  Rise from the vanities of time,
Draw back the parting vail, and see
  The glories of eternity.

2 Born by a new, celestial birth,
  Why should we grovel here on earth?
  Why grasp at vain and fleeting toys,
  So near to heaven's eternal joys?

3 Shall aught beguile us on the road,
  While we are walking back to God?
  For strangers into life we come,
  And dying is but going home.

4 Welcome, sweet hour of full discharge,
  That sets our longing souls at large,
  Unbinds our chains, breaks up our cell,
  And gives us with our God to dwell.

5 To dwell with God, to feel His love,
  Is the full heaven enjoyed above;
  And the sweet expectation now
  Is the young dawn of heaven below.
  Rev. Thomas Gibbons. (1720—1785.) 1762. alt.

1400 *Satisfied with God's Likeness.* L. M.
    Ps. xvii. 15.

1 WHAT sinners value I resign;
  Lord, 'tis enough that Thou art mine:
  I shall behold Thy blissful face,
  And stand complete in righteousness.

2 This life's a dream, an empty show;
  But the bright world to which I go
  Hath joys substantial and sincere:
  When shall I wake and find me there!

3 O glorious hour, O blest abode,
  I shall be near and like my God;
  And flesh and sin no more control
  The sacred pleasures of the soul.

4 My flesh shall slumber in the ground
  Till the last trumpet's joyful sound;
  Then burst the chains with sweet surprise,
  And in my Saviour's image rise.
  Rev. Isaac Watts. (1674—1748.) 1719. ab.

1401 *The Rest that remaineth.* L. M.

1 LORD, Thou wilt bring the joyful day;
  Beyond earth's weariness and pains,
  Thou hast a mansion far away,
  Where, for Thine own, a rest remains.

2 No sun there climbs the morning sky,
  There never falls the shade of night,
  God and the Lamb, for ever nigh,
  O'er all shed everlasting light.

3 The bow of mercy spans the throne,
  Emblem of love and goodness there;
  While notes, to mortals all unknown,
  Float on the calm celestial air.

4 Around the throne bright legions stand,
  Redeemed by blood from sin and hell;
  And shining forms, an angel band,
  The mighty chorus join to swell.

5 There, Lord, Thy way-worn saints shall find
  The bliss for which they longed before;
  And holiest sympathies shall bind
  Thine own to Thee for evermore.

6 O Jesus, bring us to that rest,
  Where all the ransomed shall be found,
  In Thine eternal fulness blest,
  While ages roll their cycles round.
  Rev. Ray Palmer. (1808—) 1865.

1402 *The Promised Land.* C. M.

1 ON Jordan's rugged banks I stand,
  And cast a wishful eye
  To Canaan's fair and happy land,
  Where my possessions lie.

2 O the transporting, rapturous scene
  That rises to my sight:
  Sweet fields arrayed in living green,
  And rivers of delight.

3 All o'er those wide-extended plains
  Shines one eternal day;
  There God, the Son, for ever reigns,
  And scatters night away.

4 No chilling winds, or poisonous breath,
  Can reach that healthful shore;
  Sickness and sorrow, pain and death,
  Are felt and feared no more.

5 When shall I reach that happy place,
  And be for ever blest?
  When shall I see my Father's face,
  And in His bosom rest?

6 Filled with delight, my raptured soul,
  Can here no longer stay:
  Though Jordan's waves around me roll,
  Fearless I'd launch away.
  Rev. Samuel Stennett. (1727—1795.) 1787. ab.

HEAVEN.

1403 *Heavenly Hope.* C. M.

1 WHEN I can read my title clear
   To mansions in the skies,
I bid farewell to every fear,
   And wipe my weeping eyes.

2 Should earth against my soul engage,
   And hellish darts be hurled,
Then I can smile at Satan's rage,
   And face a frowning world.

3 Let cares like a wild deluge come,
   And storms of sorrow fall;
May I but safely reach my home,
   My God, my heaven, my all:

4 There shall I bathe my weary soul
   In seas of heavenly rest,
And not a wave of trouble roll
   Across my peaceful breast.
              Rev. Isaac Watts. 1709.

1404 *The Martyrs glorified.* C. M.
        Rev. vii. 13—17.

1 HOW bright these glorious spirits shine,
   Whence all their white array?
How came they to the blissful seats
   Of everlasting day?

2 Lo, these are they from sufferings great
   Who came to realms of light,
And in the blood of Christ have washed
   Those robes which shine so bright.

3 Now, with triumphal palms, they stand
   Before the throne on high,
And serve the God they love, amidst
   The glories of the sky.

4 The Lamb which dwells amidst the throne
   Shall o'er them still preside,
Feed them with nourishment divine,
   And all their footsteps guide.

5 'Mong pastures green He'll lead His flock,
   Where living streams appear;
And God, the Lord, from every eye
   Shall wipe off every tear.
              Rev. Isaac Watts. 1709. alt.
   Rev. William Cameron. (1751—1811.) 1770. ab.

1405 *The sweet Fields.* C. M.

1 THERE is a land of pure delight,
   Where saints immortal reign;
Infinite day excludes the night,
   And pleasures banish pain,
There, everlasting springs abide,
   And never-withering flowers:
Death, like a narrow sea, divides
   This heavenly land from ours.

2 Sweet fields beyond the swelling flood,
   Stand dressed in living green:
So to the Jews old Canaan stood,
   While Jordan rolled between.
But timorous mortals start and shrink
   To cross this narrow sea,
And linger shivering on the brink,
   And fear to launch away.

3 O could we make our doubts remove,
   Those gloomy doubts that rise,
And see the Canaan that we love
   With unbeclouded eyes;
Could we but climb where Moses stood,
   And view the landscape o'er,
Not Jordan's stream, nor death's cold flood,
   Should fright us from the shore.
              Rev. Isaac Watts. 1709.

1406 *The Blessed Hope.* C. M.

1 O, WHAT a blessèd hope is ours:
   While here on earth we stay,
We more than taste the heavenly powers,
   And ante-date that day.
We feel the resurrection near,
   Our life in Christ concealed,
And with His glorious presence here
   Our earthen vessels filled.

2 O would He more of heaven bestow,
   And let the vessel break,
And let our ransomed spirits go
   To grasp the God we seek:
In rapturous awe on Him to gaze
   Who bought the sight for me;
And shout and wonder at His grace
   Through all eternity.
        Rev. Charles Wesley. (1708—1788.) 1759. ab.

1407 *The Song of Angels above.* C. M.

1 EARTH has engrossed my love too long;
   'Tis time I lift mine eyes
Upward, dear Father, to Thy throne,
   And to my native skies.

HEAVEN.

2 There the blest Man, my Saviour, sits;
The God, how bright He shines!
And scatters infinite delights
On all the happy minds.

3 Seraphs with elevated strains
Circle the throne around;
And move, and charm the starry plains
With an immortal sound.

4 Jesus, the Lord, their harps employs;
Jesus, my love, they sing;
Jesus, the life of both our joys,
Sounds sweet from every string.

5 Now let me dwell on earth no more,
But mount in haste above,
To bless the God that I adore,
And sing the Man I love.
Rev. Isaac Watts. (1674—1748.) 1706. ab. and alt.

1408   Rest for the Weary.   8, 7.

1 IN the Christian's home in glory,
There remains a land of rest;
There my Saviour's gone before me,
To fulfil my soul's request.
Cho. There is rest for the weary,
There is rest for the weary,
There is rest for the weary,
There is rest for you,
On the other side of Jordan,
In the sweet fields of Eden,
Where the tree of life is blooming,
There is rest for you.

2 He is fitting up my mansion,
Which eternally shall stand,
For my stay shall not be transient
In that holy, happy land. *Cho.*

3 Pain and sickness ne'er shall enter,
Grief nor woe my lot shall share;
But in that celestial centre
I a crown of life shall wear. *Cho.*

4 And the grave shall then be conquered,
And the sting of death be lost;
And our bark, all safely anchored,
Never more be tempest-tost. *Cho.*

5 Sing, O sing, ye heirs of glory;
Shout your triumph as you go;
Zion's gate will ope before ye,
You shall find an entrance through. *Cho.*
Rev. Samuel Young Harmer. (1809—) 1855.

1409   "This is not your Rest."   8, 7.
Micah ii. 10.

1 THIS is not my place of resting,
Mine's a city yet to come;
Onward to it I am hasting,
On to my eternal home. *Cho.*

2 In it all is light and glory;
O'er it shines a nightless day;
Every trace of sin's sad story,
All the curse, hath passed away. *Cho.*

3 There the Lamb, our Shepherd, leads us,
By the streams of life along,
On the freshest pastures feeds us,
Turns our sighing into song. *Cho.*

4 Soon we pass this desert dreary,
Soon we bid farewell to pain;
Never more are sad or weary,
Never, never sin again. *Cho.*
Rev. Horatius Bonar. (1808—) 1845.

1410   "New Jerusalem."   7, 6, 7, 7, 7.

1 WE are on our journey home,
Where Christ our Lord is gone;
We shall meet around His throne,
When He makes His people one
‖: In the new :‖ Jerusalem.

2 We can see that distant home,
Though clouds rise dark between;
Faith views the radiant dome,
And a lustre flashes keen
‖: From the new :‖ Jerusalem.

3 O glory shining far
From the never-setting Sun,
O trembling morning-star,
Our journey's almost done
‖: To the new :‖ Jerusalem.

4 O holy, heavenly Home,
O rest eternal there:
When shall the exiles come,
Where they cease from earthly care
‖: In the new :‖ Jerusalem.

5 Our hearts are breaking now
Those mansions fair to see;
O Lord, Thy heavens bow,
And raise us up with Thee
‖: To the new :‖ Jerusalem.
Rev. Charles Beecher. (1819—) 1857.

1411   *"Safe Home."*

1 SAFE Home, safe Home in port!
    Rent cordage, shattered deck,
Torn sails, provisions short,
    And only not a wreck:
But O the joy upon the shore,
To tell our voyage perils o'er!

2 No more the foe can harm:
    No more of leaguered camp,
And cry of night-alarm,
    And need of ready lamp;
And yet how nearly had he failed,
How nearly had that foe prevailed!

3 The lamb is in the fold
    In perfect safety penned:
The lion once had hold,
    And thought to make an end;
But One came by with wounded side,
And for the sheep the Shepherd died.
      Joseph of the Studium. (—883).
    Rev. John Mason Neale (1818—1866.) 1862. ab

1412   *Nearing Home.*   S. M.

1 ONE sweetly solemn thought
    Comes to me o'er and o'er,
Nearer my parting hour am I
    Than e'er I was before.

2 Nearer my Father's house,
    Where many mansions be;
Nearer the throne where Jesus reigns,
    Nearer the crystal sea;

3 Nearer my going home,
    Laying my burden down,
Leaving my cross of heavy grief,
    Wearing my starry crown.

4 Nearer that hidden stream,
    Winding through shades of night,
Rolling its cold, dark waves between
    Me and the world of light.

5 Jesus, to Thee I cling:
    Strengthen my arm of faith;
Stay near me while my way-worn feet
    Press through the stream of death.
      Miss Phœbe Cary. (1825—1871.) 1852. ab. and alt.

7. 1413   *Our Home above.*   S. M.

1 OUR glorious home above,
    The City of our God,
The resting-place of peace and love,
    The pilgrim's sweet abode:

2 O for an angel's wing
    To soar above the skies,
And join the angelic choir who sing
    Their hallowed symphonies.

3 Pure mansions of the blest,
    Prepared by Jesus' hand,
That all His own may sweetly rest
    Safe in Emmanuel's Land.

4 May each we love be there,
    From death and darkness free;
Our joy unspeakable to share
    Throughout eternity.
      Rev. D. T. K. Drummond. 1850.

1414   *Rest after Toil.*   S. M.

1 AND is there, Lord, a rest,
    For weary souls designed,
Where not a care shall stir the breast,
    Or sorrow entrance find?

2 Is there a blissful home,
    Where kindred minds shall meet,
And live, and love, nor ever roam
    From that serene retreat?

3 Are there bright, happy fields,
    Where naught that blooms shall die;
Where each new scene fresh pleasure yields,
    And healthful breezes sigh?

4 Are there celestial streams,
    Where living waters glide,
With murmurs sweet as angel-dreams,
    And flowery banks beside?

5 For ever blessed they,
    Whose joyful feet shall stand,
While endless ages waste away,
    Amid that glorious land!

6 My soul would thither tend,
    While toilsome years are given;
Then let me, gracious God, ascend
    To sweet repose in heaven.
      Rev. Ray Palmer. (1808—) 1843.

HEAVEN.

1415 *Paradise* P. M.

1 O PARADISE, O Paradise,
Who doth not care for rest,
Who would not seek the happy land
Where they that loved are blest?
Cho. Where loyal hearts and true
Stand ever in the light,
All rapture through and through,
In God's most holy sight.

2 O Paradise, O Paradise,
The world is growing old;
Who would not be at rest and free
Where love is never cold? *Cho.*

3 O Paradise, O Paradise,
'T is weary waiting here;
I long to be where Jesus is,
To feel, to see Him near; *Cho.*

4 O Paradise, O Paradise,
I want to sin no more,
I want to be as pure on earth
As on Thy spotless shore; *Cho.*

5 O Paradise, O Paradise,
I greatly long to see
The special place my dearest Lord
In love prepares for me; *Cho.*

6 Lord, Jesus, King of Paradise,
O keep me in Thy love,
And guide me to that happy land
Of perfect rest above; *Cho.*

Rev. Frederick William Faber. (1814—1863.) 1854. ab. and alt.

1416 *"Which was, and is, and is to come."* 11, 12, 12, 10.
Rev. iv. 8.

HOLY, holy, holy, Lord God Almighty!
Early in the morning our song shall rise to Thee;
Holy, holy, holy! Merciful and Mighty!
God in Three Persons, Blessed Trinity!

2 Holy, holy, holy! all the saints adore Thee,
Casting down their golden crowns around the glassy sea;
Cherubim and seraphim falling down before Thee,
Which wert, and art, and evermore shalt be.

3 Holy, holy, holy! though the darkness hide Thee,
Though the eye of sinful man Thy glory may not see,
Only Thou art holy, there is none beside Thee,
Perfect in power, in love, and purity.

4 Holy, holy, holy! Lord God Almighty!
All Thy works shall praise Thy Name, in earth, and sky, and sea;
Holy, holy, holy! Lord God Almighty!
God in Three Persons, Blesséd Trinity!

Bp. Reginald Heber. (1783—1826.) 1827.

DOXOLOGIES.

1   C. M.

To Father, Son, and Holy Ghost,
   The God whom we adore,
Be glory, as it was, is now,
   And shall be ever more.
Tate and Brady. 1696.

2   S. M.

To God the Father, Son,
   And Spirit, One and Three,
Be glory, as it was, is now,
   And shall for ever be.
Rev. John Wesley. (1703—1791.) 1741.

3   L. M.

PRAISE God, from whom all blessings flow;
Praise Him, all creatures here below;
Praise Him above, ye heavenly host;
Praise Father, Son, and Holy Ghost.
Bp. Thomas Ken. (1637—1711.) 1697.

4   L. M.

To God the Father, God the Son,
And God the Spirit, Three in One,
Be honor, praise, and glory given,
By all on earth, and all in heaven.
Rev. Isaac Watts. (1674—1748.) 1709.

5   L. M. 6l.

To God the Father, God the Son,
And God the Spirit, Three in One,
Be honor, praise, and glory given,
By all on earth, and all in heaven;
As was through ages heretofore,
Is now, and shall be evermore.
Rev. Isaac Watts. 1709. First 4 lines.

6   C. P. M.

To Father, Son, and Holy Ghost,
The God whom heaven's triumphant host
   And saints on earth adore;
Be glory as in ages past,
As now it is, and so shall last,
   When time shall be no more.
Tate and Brady. 1696. alt.

7   L. P. M.

Now to the great and sacred Three,
The Father, Son, and Spirit, be
Eternal praise and glory given,
Through all the worlds where God is known,
By all the angels near the throne,
And all the saints in earth and heaven.
Rev. Isaac Watts. 1719.

8   H. M.

O GOD, for ever blest,
   To Thee all praise be given;
Thy Name Triune confest
   By all in earth and heaven;
As heretofore it was, is now,
And shall be so for evermore.
Rev. Edward Henry Bickersteth. [1825—] 1870.

9   8, 7.

PRAISE the Father, earth and heaven,
   Praise the Son, the Spirit praise,
As it was, and is, be given
   Glory through eternal days.
Unknown Author. 1827.

10   8, 7. D.

PRAISE the God of all creation;
   Praise the Father's boundless love;
Praise the Lamb, our Expiation,
   Priest and King enthroned above;
Praise the Fountain of Salvation,
   Him by whom our spirits live:
Undivided adoration
   To the One Jehovah give.
Josiah Conder. (1789—1855.) 1836.

11   8, 7, 4.

GLORY be to God the Father,
   Glory be to God the Son,
Glory be to God the Spirit,
   Great Jehovah, Three in One:
      Glory, glory,
   While eternal ages run.
Rev. Horatius Bonar. (1808—) 1866.

12   7, 6. D.

FATHER, Son, and Holy Ghost,
  One God whom we adore,
Join we with the heavenly host,
  To praise Thee evermore:
Live, by heaven and earth adored,
  Three in One, and One in Three,
Holy, holy, holy Lord,
  All glory be to Thee.
Rev. Charles Wesley. (1708—1788.) 1746. alt.

13   7.

SING we to our God above
Praise eternal as His love:
Praise Him, all ye heavenly host,
Father, Son, and Holy Ghost.
Rev. Charles Wesley. 1740.

14   7. 6l.

PRAISE the Name of God most high,
Praise Him, all below the sky,
Praise Him, all ye heavenly host,
Father, Son, and Holy Ghost;
As through countless ages past,
Evermore His praise shall last.
Unknown Author. 1827.

15   7. 6l.

GOD the Father, God of grace,
Saviour, born of mortal race,
Comforter, our Life and Light,
One in essence, love and might;
Thee whom all in heaven adore,
We would worship evermore.
Rev. Ray Palmer. (1808—) 1873.

16   7. D.

PRAISE our glorious King and Lord,
Angels waiting on His word,
Saints that walk with Him in white,
Pilgrims walking in His light:
Glory to the Eternal One,
Glory to His Only Son,
Glory to the Spirit be
Now, and through eternity.
Rev. Alexander Ramsay Thompson. (1822—) 1869.

17   6, 4.

To the great One in Three
  The highest praises be,
    Hence evermore;
His sovereign majesty
May we in glory see,
And to eternity
    Love and adore.
Rev. Charles Wesley. 1757.

18   6, 4.

To God, the Father, Son,
And Spirit, Three in One,
  All praise be given:
Crown Him in every song;
To Him your hearts belong,
Let all His praise prolong
  On earth, in heaven.
Rev. Edwin Francis Hatfield. (1807—) 1843.

19   10.

To Father, Son, and Spirit, ever blest,
Eternal praise and worship be addrest;
From age to age, ye saints, His name adore,
And spread His fame, till time shall be no more.
Rev. Simon Browne. (1680—1732.) 1720. alt.

20   10, 11.

ALL glory to God, the Father and Son,
And Spirit of grace, the great Three in One;
Let highest ascriptions forever be given
By all the creation on earth and in heaven.
Rippon's Collection. 1778.

21   11.

O FATHER Almighty, to Thee be addrest,
With Christ and the Spirit, One God ever blest,
All glory and worship, from earth and from heaven,
As was, and is now, and shall ever be given.
Unknown Author.

Chants.

1
Ps. xcv.

1 O COME, let us sing un- | to the | Lord; ‖ Let us heartily rejoice in the | strength of | our sal- | vation.
2 Let us come before His presence | with thanks- | giving; ‖ And show ourselves | glad in | Him with | psalms.
3 For the Lord is a | great— | God; ‖ And a great | King a- | bove all | gods.
4 In His hands are all the corners | of the | earth; ‖ And the strength of the | hills is | His— | also.
5 The sea is His | and He | made it; ‖ And His hands pre- | pared | the dry | land.
6 O come, let us worship and fall | down; ‖ And kneel be- | fore the | Lord our | Maker.
7 For He is the | Lord our | God; ‖ And we are the people of His pasture, and the | sheep of | His— | hand.
8 O worship the Lord in the | beauty of | holiness; ‖ Let the whole | earth stand in | awe of | Him.
*9 For He cometh, for He cometh to judge the | earth; ‖ And with righteousness to judge the world, and the | people | with His | truth.
10 Glory be to the Father, and | to the | Son, ‖ And | to the | Holy | Ghost;
11 As it was in the beginning, is now, and | ever shall | be, ‖ World without | end. A- | men, A- | men.

2
Lætatus Sum.
Ps. cxxii.

1 I WAS glad when they said | unto | me, ‖ Let us go into the | house- | of the | Lord.
2 Our feet shall stand with- | in thy | gates, ‖ O— | —Je- | rusa- | lem!
3 Jerusalem is builded | as a | city ‖ That | is com- | pact to- | gether:
4 Whither the tribes go up, the | tribes of the | Lord, ‖ Unto the testimony of Israel, to give thanks unto the | name— | of the | Lord.
5 For there are set | thrones of | judgment, ‖ The thrones of the | house of | Da- | vid.
6 Pray for the peace of Je- | rusa- | lem: ‖ They shall | prosper that | love— | thee.
7 Peace be with- | in thy | walls, ‖ And prosperity with- | in thy | pala- | ces.
8 For my brethren and com- | panions' | sakes, ‖ I will now say, | Peace— | be with- | in thee.
*9 Because of the house of the | Lord our | God ‖ I will | seek— | thy— | good.
Glory be to the Father, &c.

(371)

CHANTS.

TE DEUM LAUDAMUS.

3
1. WE praise Thee, | O— | God; || we acknowledge | Thee to | be the | Lord. || All the earth doth | worship | Thee, || the Father | ever- | last- — | ing.
2. To Thee all Angels | cry a- | loud; || the Heavens, and | all the | powers·· there- | in. || To Thee Cherubim, and | Sera- | phim || con- | tin-ual- | ly do | cry,
3. Holy, | Holy, | Holy, || Lord | God of | Saba- | oth; || Heaven and earth are full of the | Majes- | ty || of | Thy— | glo- — | ry.
4. The glorious company | of the | Apostles || praise | — — | — — | Thee; || The goodly fellowship | of the | Prophets || praise | — — | — — | Thee.
5. The noble army | of — | Martyrs || praise | — — | — — | Thee. || The holy Church throughout | all the | world || doth | — ac- | knowledge | Thee,
6. The | Fa- — | ther || of an | infinite | Majes- | ty; || Thine ad- | ora-ble, | true, || and on- — | ly — | Son;
7. Also the | Holy | Ghost, || the | Com — | — fort- | er. || Thou art the | King of | Glo-ry, || O | — — | — — | Christ.
8. Thou art the ever- | lasting | Son || of | — the | Fa- — | ther. || When Thou tookest upon Thee to de- | liver | man, || Thou didst humble Thyself to be | born — | of a | Virgin.
9. When Thou hadst overcome the | sharpness·· of | death, || Thou didst open the Kingdom of Heaven to | all be- | liev- — | ers. || Thou sittest at the right hand | of — God || in the glory | of the | Fa- — | ther.
10. We believe that | Thou shalt | come || to | be — | our — | Judge. || We therefore pray Thee, | help Thy | servants, || whom Thou hast redeemed | with Thy | pre-cious | blood.
11. Make them to be numbered | with Thy | saints || in glory | ever- | last- — | ing. || O Lord, | save Thy | people, || and | bless Thine | heri- | tage.
12. Gov- | — ern | them || and | lift them | up for- | ever. || Day | by — | day || we | mag-ni- | fy — | Thee.
13. And we worship | Thy — | Name, || ever, | world with- | out — | end. || Vouchsafe, | O — | Lord, || to keep us | this day | without | sin.
14. O Lord, have mercy up- | on — | us, || have | mercy·· up- | on — | us. || O Lord, let Thy mercy be up- | on — | us, || as our | trust — | is in | Thee.
*15. O Lord, in Thee | have I | trusted, || let me never | be con- | found- — | ed.

GLORIA PATRI.

GLORY be to the Father, and | to the | Son, || and | to the | Ho · ly | Ghost. || As it was in the beginning, | ever shall | be, || world without | end, A - | men, A · | men. || is now, and............. |

5
Ps. c.
1. O BE joyful in the Lord, | all ye | lands; || Serve the Lord with gladness, And come before His | presence | with a | song.
2. Be sure that the Lord | He is | God; || It is He that hath made us, and not we our-selves: We are His | people; and the | sheep of·· His | pasture.
3. O go your way into His gates with thanksgiving, And into His | courts with | praise; || Be thankful unto Him, and speak good | of His | name.

CHANTS.

4 For the Lord is gracious, His mercy is | ever- | lasting ; || And His truth endureth from gene- | ration · · to | gene- | ration.
5 Glory be to the Father, and | to the | Son, || And | to the | Holy | Ghost;
6 As it was in the beginning, is now, and | ever · · shall | be, || World|without | end. A- | men.

6   Luke i. 68—71.

1 BLESSED be the Lord | God of | Israel, || For He hath visited | and re- | deemed His | people;
2 And hath raised up a horn of sal- | vation | for us, || In the house | of His | servant | David;
3 As He spake by the mouth of His | holy | prophets, || Which have been | since the | world be- | gan ;
4 That we should be saved | from our | enemies, || And from the | hand of | all that | hate us.
5 Glory be to the Father, and | to the | Son, || And | to the | Holy | Ghost ; ||
6 As it was in the beginning, is now, and | ever | shall be, || World | without | end. A- | men.

GLORIA IN EXCELSIS.

7
1 GLORY be to | God on | high, || and on earth | peace, good- | will · · towards | men.
2 We praise Thee, we bless Thee, we | worship | Thee, || we glorify Thee, we give thanks to | Thee for | Thy great | glory.
3 O Lord God, | heavenly | King, || God the | Father | Al- — | mighty.
4 O Lord, the only begotten Son, | Jesus | Christ; || O Lord God, Lamb of ' God, Son | of the | Father,
5 That takest away the | sins · · of the | world, || have mercy | upon | us.
6 Thou that takest away the | sins · · of the | world, || have mercy | upon | us.
7 Thou that takest away the | sins · · of the | world, re- | ceive our | prayer.
8 Thou that sittest at the right hand of | God the | Father, || have mercy | upon | us.
9 For Thou | only · · art | holy : || Thou | only | art the | Lord:
10 Thou only, O Christ, with the | Holy | Ghost, || art most high in the | glory · · of | God the | Father. || A- | men

GLORIA PATRI.

GLORY be to the Father, and | to   the | Son: || And | to   the | Ho - ly | Ghost; ||
As it was in the beginning, is now, and | ev - er | shall be, || World | with-out | end. A - | men. ||

9   Ps. xcviii.

1 O sing unto the Lord | a new | song ; || For | He hath · done | marvel · · lous | things. ||
2 With His own right hand and with His | holy | arm, || Hath He gotten Him- | self the | victo- | ry.
3 The Lord declared | His | sal- | vation ; || His righteousness hath He openly | showed · · in the | sight · · of the | heathen. ||
4 He hath remembered His mercy and truth toward the | house of | Israel, || And all the ends of the world have seen the sal- | vation | of our | God.
5 Show yourselves joyful unto the Lord, | all ye | lands : || Sing, re- | joice, and | give — | thanks. ||

CHANTS.

6 Praise the Lord up- | on the | harp; || Sing to the Lord with a | psalm of | thanks— | giv-ing.
7 With trumpets | also · ·and | (cornet, or shawms,) || O show yourselves joyful be- | fore the | Lord the | King. ||
8 Let the sea make a noise, and all that | therein | is; || The round world, and | they that | dwell there- | in.
*9 Let the floods clap their hands, and let the hills be joyful together be- | fore the | Lord; || For He | cometh · ·to | judge the | earth.
10 With righteousness shall He | judge the | world; || And the | people | with— | equity. Glory be to the Father, &c.

10   *Magnificat.*
                        Luke i. 46—55.

1 MY soul doth magni- | fy the | Lord, || And my spirit hath re- | joiced in | God my | Saviour. ||
2 For He hath regarded the low estate of | His hand- | maiden: || For behold, from hence-forth all gener- | ations · ·shall | call me | blessed.
3 For He that is mighty hath done to me | great— | things, || And | holy | is His | Name.
4 And His mercy is on | them that | fear Him, || From gener- | ation to | gener- | ation.
5 He hath showed strength | with His | arm, || He hath scattered the proud in the imagi- | nation | of their | hearts. ||
6 He hath put down the mighty | from their | seats, || And exalted | them of | low de- | gree.
7 He hath filled the hungry with | good— | things, || And the rich He | hath sent | empty · · a- | way.
8 He hath holpen His | servant | Israel, || In re- | membrance | of His | mercy.
*9 As He spake to our fathers, to | Abra- | ham, || And | to his | seed for- | ever.

11   Ps. lxvii.

1 GOD be merciful unto | us, and | bless us; || And show us the light of His countenance, and be | merci · ·ful | unto | us.
2 That Thy way may be known | up · ·on | earth; || Thy saving | health a- | mong all | nations.
3 Let the people praise Thee, | O — | God. || Yea, let | all the · ·people | praise — | Thee.
4 O let the nations rejoice | and be | glad; || For Thou shalt judge the people righteous-ly, and govern the | na · ·tions | upon | earth.
5 Let the people praise Thee, | O — | God; || Yea, let | all the · ·people | praise — | Thee.
6 Then shall the earth bring | forth her | increase; || And God, even our own | God shall | give us · ·His | blessing.
7 God shall | bless — | us; || And all the ends of the | world shall | fear — | Him.
8 Glory be to the Father, and | to the | Son, || And | to the | Holy | Ghost; ||
9 As it was in the beginning, is now, and | ever | shall be, || World | without | end. A- | men.

12   Ps. xcii.

1 It is a good thing to give thanks un- | to the | Lord; || And to sing praises unto Thy | name — | O most | Highest.

CHANTS.

2 To tell of Thy loving kindness | early··in the | morning; || A: d of Thy | truth··in the | night — | season.
3 Upon an instrument of ten strings, | and, up- | on the | lute; || Upon a loud instrument, | and up- | on the | harp.
4 For Thou, Lord, hast made me glad | through Thy | works; || And I will rejoice in giving praise for the ope- | ration | of Thy | hands.
5 Glory be to the Father, and | to the | Son, || And | to the | Holy | Ghost;
6 As it was in the beginning, is now, and | ever··shall | be, || World without | end. A- | men, A- | men.

13
Ps. ciii.

1 PRAISE the Lord, | O my | soul; || And all that is within me, | praise His | holy | name. ||
2 Praise the Lord, | O my | soul; || And for- | get not | all His | benefits.
3 Who forgiveth | all Thy | sin, || And | healeth··all | Thine in- | firmities. ||
4 Who saveth thy | life··from de- | struction; || And crowneth thee with | mercy··and | loving-kindness.
5 O praise the Lord, ye angels of His, ye that ex- | cel in | strength; || Ye that fulfil His commandment, and hearken unto the | voice of | His — | word. ||
6 O praise the Lord, | all··ye His | hosts; || Ye servants of | His that | do His | pleasure.
*7 O speak good of the Lord, all ye works of His, in all places of | His do- | minion. || Praise thou the | Lord, O | — my | soul.
8 Glory be to the Father and | to the | Son, And | to the | Holy | Ghost;
9 As it was in the beginning, is now, and | ever··shall | be, || World without | end. A- | — — | men.

GLORIA PATRI.

GLORY be to the Father, and | to the | Son: || And | to the | Ho - ly | Ghost; || As it was in the beginning, is now, and | ev - er | shall be, || World | with-out | end. A - | men. ||

15
Ps. viii.

1 O LORD, our Lord, how excellent is Thy name in | all the | earth! || Who hast set thy | glory a- | bove the | heavens. || Out of the mouth of babes and sucklings hast Thou ordained strength be- | cause··of Thine | enemies, || That Thou mightest still the | enemy | and the a- | venger.
2 When I consider Thy heavens, the | work of··Thy | fingers, || The moon and the stars | which Thou | hast or- | dained; || What is man, that Thou art | mindful··of | him? || And the son of man | that Thou | visitest | him?
3 For Thou hast made him a little lower | than the | angels, || And hast crowned him with | glory | and — | honor. || Thou madest Him to have dominion over the | works··of Thy | hands; || Thou hast put | all things | under··His | feet:
4 All | sheep and | oxen, || Yea, and the | beasts— | of the | field; || The fowl of the air, and the ; fish··of the | sea, || And whatsoever passeth through the | paths— | of the | seas.
*5 O | Lord our | Lord, || How excellent is Thy | name in | all the | earth!

CHANTS.

16
Ps. xix.

1 THE heavens declare the | glory·· of | God; || And the firmament | showeth··His | handy | work. || Day unto day uttereth speech, and night unto | night showeth | knowledge. || There is no speech nor language, where their | voice— | is not | heard.

2 Their line is gone out through | all the | earth, || And their words to the | end — | of the world. || In them hath He set a tabernacle | for the | sun, || Which is as a bridegroom coming out of his chamber, and rejoiceth as a strong | man to | run a | race.

3 His going forth is from the end of the heaven, and his circuit unto the | ends— | of it : || And there is nothing | hid··from the | heat there- | of. || The law of the Lord is perfect, con- | verting··the | soul: || The testimony of the Lord is sure, | making | wise the | simple.

4 The statutes of the Lord are right, re- | joicing··the | heart: || The commandment of the Lord is | pure, en- | lightening··the | eyes. || The fear of the Lord is clean, en- | during for | ever. || The judgments of the Lord are true and | righteous | altogether.

5 More to be desired are they than gold, yea, than | much fine | gold: || Sweeter also than honey | and the | honey- | comb, || Moreover by them is Thy | servant | warned: || || And in keeping of them | there is | great re- | ward.

6 Who can under- | stand his errors? || Cleanse Thou | me from | secret | faults. || Keep back Thy servant also from presumptuous sins; let them not have do- | minion | over me: || Then shall I be upright, and I shall be innocent | from the | great trans- | gression.

*7 Let the words of my mouth, and the meditation of my heart, be acceptable | in Thy | sight, || O Lord, my | Strength, and | my Re- | deemer.

17
Ps. xxiii.

1 THE Lord is my Shepherd; I | shall not | want. || He maketh me to lie down in green pastures; He leadeth me beside the | still — | waters.

2 He restoreth my soul; He leadeth me in the paths of righteousness for His | name's — | sake. || Yea, though I walk through the valley of the shadow of death, I will fear no evil: for Thou art with me; Thy rod and Thy staff | they — | comfort me.

3 Thou preparest a table before me in the presence of mine enemies, Thou anointest my head with oil: my | cup··runneth | over. || Surely goodness and mercy shall follow me all the days of my life; and I will dwell in the house of the | Lord, for | ever. || A- | men.

18
Ps. xxiv.

1 THE earth is the Lord's, and the | fulness | thereof; || The world and | they that | dwell there- | in. || For He hath founded it up- | on the | seas, || And established it up- | on the | floods.

2 Who shall ascend into the | hill··of the | Lord? || Or who shall | stand··in His | holy | place? || He that hath clean hands, and a | pure — | heart; || Who hath not lifted up his soul unto — | vanity, nor | sworn de- | ceitfully.

3 He shall receive the blessing | from the | Lord, || And righteousness from the | God of | his sal- | vation. || This is the generation of them that | seek — | Him, || That | seek | Thy | face, | O Jacob. ||

CHANTS.

4 Lift up your heads, O ye gates; and be ye lift up, ye ever- | lasting | doors; || And the King of | glory | shall come | in. || Who is this | King of | glory? || The Lord, strong and mighty, | the Lord | mighty ·· in | battle.

5 Lift up your heads, O ye gates; even lift them up, ye ever- | lasting | doors; || And the King of | glory | shall come | in. | Who is this | King of | glory? || The Lord of hosts, He | is the | King of | glory.

19
Ps. xlii.

1 As the hart panteth after the | water | brooks, || So panteth my soul after | Thee · O — | God.
2 My soul thirsteth for God, for the | living | God! || When shall I come and ap- | pear be- | fore — · | God?
3 My tears have been my meat | day and | night, || While they continually say unto me, | where is | thy — | God?
4 When I re- | member ·· these | things, || I pour | out my | soul — | in me;
5 For I had gone with the multitude, I went with them to the | house of | God, || With the voice of joy and praise, with a multitude that | kept — | holy- | day.
6 Why art thou cast down, | O my | soul? || And why are thou dis- | quiet- | ed in | me?
7 Hope | thou in | God: || For I shall yet praise Him for the | help of | His — | countenance.
8 O send out Thy light and Thy truth: | let them | lead me; || Let them bring me unto Thy holy hill, and | to Thy | taber - na - | cles.
9 Then will I go unto the altar of God, unto God my ex- | ceeding | joy: || Yea, upon the harp will I praise | Thee, O | God, my | God.
10 Why art thou cast down, | O my | soul? || And why art Thou dis- | quiet- | ed with- | in me?
11 Hope | in — | God: || For I shall yet praise Him, who is the health of my | countenance, | and my | God.

20
Ps. xlvi.

1 GOD is our | refuge ·· and | strength, || A very | present | help in | trouble.
2 Therefore will not we fear, though the | earth be | removed, || And though the mountains be carried | into ·· the | midst ·· of the | sea.
3 Though the waters thereof | roar ·· and be | troubled, || Though the mountains | shake ·· with the | swelling ·· there- | of.
4 There is a river, the streams whereof shall make glad the | city of | God, || The holy place of the | tabernacles of | the Most | High.
5 God is in the midst of her; she | shall ·· not be | moved: || God shall help her, | and — | that right | early.
6 The heathen raged, the | kingdoms ·· were | moved: || He uttered His | voice, the | earth — | melted.
7 The Lord of | Hosts is | with us; || The God of | Jacob | is our | refuge.
Glory be to the Father, &c.

21
Ps. 51.

1 HAVE mercy upon me, O God, according to Thy | loving- | kindness: || According unto the multitude of Thy tender mercies | blot out | my trans- | gressions.
2 Wash me thoroughly from | mine in- | iquity, || And | cleanse me | from my | sin.

CHANTS.

3 For I acknowledge | my trans- | gressions: || And my | sin is | ever··be- | fore me.
4 Hide Thy face | from my | sins, || And blot out | all — | mine in- | iquities.
5 Create in me a clean | heart, O | God; || And renew a right | spirit··with- | in — | me.
6 Cast me not away | from Thy | presence; || And take not Thy | Holy | Spirit | from me.
7 Restore unto me the joy of | Thy sal- | vation; || And uphold me | with Thy | free — | Spirit.
8 Then will I teach trans- | gressors··Thy | ways; || And sinners shall be con- | verted | unto | Thee.
9 Deliver me from blood-guiltiness, O God, thou God of | my sal- | vation: || And my tongue shall sing aloud | of Thy | righteous- | ness.
10 O Lord, open | Thou my | lips: || And my mouth shall | shew forth | Thy — | praise.
11 For Thou desirest not sacrifice; | else··would I | give it: || Thou delightest | not in | burnt — | offering.
12 The sacrifices of God are a | broken | spirit: || A broken and contrite heart, O God, | Thou wilt | not de- | spise.

22
Ps. lvii.

1 BE Thou exalted, O God, a- | bove the | heavens; || Let Thy glory be a- | bove — | all the | earth.
2 My heart is fixed, O God, my | heart is | fixed; || I will | sing and | give — | praise.
3 Awake up, my glory; awake, | psaltery··and | harp: || I my- | self··will a- | wake — | early.
4 I will praise Thee, O Lord, a- | mong the | people: || I will sing unto | Thee a- | mong the | nations.
5 For Thy mercy is great | unto··the | heavens, || And Thy | truth — | unto··the | clouds.
6 Be Thou exalted, O God, a- | bove the | heavens; || Let Thy glory be a- | bove — | all the | earth.

23
Ps. lxiii.

1 O GOD, Thou | art my | God; || Early | will I | seek — | Thee:
2 My soul thirsteth for Thee, my flesh | longeth··for | Thee || In a dry and thirsty land, | where no | water | is;
3 To see Thy power | and Thy | glory, || So as I have seen Thee | in the | sanctu- | ary.
4 Because Thy loving-kindness is | better··than | life, || My | lips shall | praise — | Thee.
5 Thus will I bless Thee | while I | live; || I will lift up my | hands in | Thy— | name.
6 My soul shall be satisfied as with | marrow··and | fatness; || And my mouth shall praise | Thee with | joyful | lips:
7 When I remember Thee up- | on my | bed, || And meditate on Thee | in the | night — | watches.
8 Because Thou hast | been my | help, || Therefore in the shadow of Thy | wings will | I re- | joice.

CHANTS.

24
Ps. lxxxiv.

1 How amiable are Thy | taber- | nacles, || O | Lord — | of — | hosts!
2 My soul longeth, yea, even fainteth for the | courts·· of the | Lord: || My heart and flesh crieth out | for the | living | God.
3 Yea, the sparrow hath found a house, and the swallow a nest for herself, where she may | lay her | young, || Even Thine altars, O Lord of hosts, my | King — | and my | God.
4 Blessed are they that | dwell·· in Thy | house: || They will be | still — | praising | Thee.
5 Behold, O | God our | Shield, || And look upon the | face of | Thine A- | nointed.
6 For a day in Thy courts is better | than a | thousand. || I had rather be a doorkeeper in the house of my God, than to dwell in the | tents of | wicked- | ness.
7 For the Lord God is a | Sun and | Shield: || The Lord will give grace and glory: no good thing will He withhold from | them that | walk up- | rightly.
8 O | Lord of | hosts, || Blessed is the | man that | trusteth·· in | **Thee.**

25
Ps. xc.

1 LORD, Thou hast been our | dwelling | place || In | all — | gener- | ations. || Before the mountains were brought forth, or ever Thou hadst formed the | earth·· and the | world, || Even from everlasting to ever- | lasting, | Thou art | God.
2 Thou turnest | man·· to de- | struction; || And sayest, Re- | turn, ye | children·· of | men. || For a thousand years in Thy sight are but as yesterday | when·· it is | past, || And as a | watch — | in the | night.
3 Thou carriest them away as with a flood; they | are·· as a | sleep: || In the morning they are like | grass which | groweth | up; || In the morning it flourisheth, and | groweth | up; || In the evening it is cut | down and | wither- | eth.
4 For we are consumed | by Thine | anger, || And by Thy | wrath — | are we | troubled. || Thou hast set our iniquities be- | fore — | Thee, || Our secret sins in the | light of | Thy — | countenance.
5 For all our days are passed away | in Thy | wrath: || We spend our years as a | tale — | that is | told. || The days of our years are threescore | years and | ten; || And if by reason of | strength·· they be | fourscore | years,
6 Yet is their strength | labor·· and | sorrow; || For it is soon cut off, | and we | fly a- | way. || Who knoweth the power | of Thine | anger? || Even according to Thy | fear, so | is Thy | wrath.
7 So teach us to | number·· our | days, || That we may apply our | hearts — | unto | wisdom. || Return, O | Lord, how | long? || And let it repent Thee con- | cerning | Thy — | servants.
8 O satisfy us early | with thy | mercy; || That we may rejoice and be | glad — | all our | days. || Make us glad according to the days wherein Thou | hast af- | flicted us, || And the years where- | in we | have seen | evil

CHANTS.

9 Let Thy work appear | unto · · Thy | servants, || And Thy | glory | unto · · their | children ||
And let the beauty of the Lord our God | be up- | on us: || And establish Thou the
work of our hands upon us; yea, the work of our | hands es- | tablish · · Thou | it.

10 Glory be to the Father, and | to the | Son, || And | to the | Holy | Ghost; || As it
was in the beginning, is now, and | ever · · shall | be, || World | without | end. A- |
men.

26
Ps. xcviii.

1 O SING unto the Lord a new song; for He hath done | marvel - ous | things: || His
right hand, and His holy arm, hath | gotten | Him the | victory. || The Lord hath
made known | His sal- | vation: || His righteousness hath He openly shewed in the |
sight — | of the | heathen.
2 He hath remembered His mercy and His truth toward the | house of | Israel: || All the
ends of the earth have seen the sal- | vation | of our | God. || Make a joyful noise unto
the Lord, | all the | earth; || Make a loud noise, and re- | joice, and | sing — | praise.
3 Sing unto the Lord | with the | harp; || With the harp, and the | voice — | of a | psalm. ||
With trumpets and | sound of | cornet || Make a joyful noise be- | fore the | Lord,
the | King.
4 Let the sea roar, and the | fulness · · there- | of; || The world, and | they that | dwell
there- | in. || Let the floods | clap their | hands: || Let the hills be joyful to- |
gether · · be- | fore the | Lord;
*5 For He cometh to | judge the | earth; || With righteousness shall He judge the world,
and the | people | with — | equity.

27
Trisagion.

1 HOLY, holy, holy, | Lord · · God of | Sabbaoth; || Heaven and | earth are | full · · of Thy |
glory
2 Hosanna in the highest! Blessed is He that cometh in the | name of the | Lord. || Ho-
sanna | in the | highest!
3 Therefore with Angels, | and Arch- | angels, || and with | all the | company of | Heaven, ||
we laud and magnify Thy | glorious | Name, || evermore praising | Thee, and | say-
— | ing, ||
4 Holy, holy, holy, | Lord · · God of | hosts; Heaven and | earth are | full · · of Thy | glory; ||
5 Glory | be to | Thee, || O | Lord Most | High. A- | men.

"THY WILL BE DONE."
28
1 "THY will be | done!" || In devious way The hurrying stream of | life may | run; ||
Yet still our grateful hearts shall say, | "Thy will be | done."
2 "Thy will be | done!" || If o'er us shine a gladdening and a | prosperous | sun, ||
This prayer will make it more divine — | "Thy will be | done!"
3 "Thy will be | done!" || Though shrouded o'er Our path with | gloom, || one com-
fort — one || is ours: — to breathe, while we adore, | "Thy will be | done."

Sir John Bowring. (1792—1872.) 1825. ab.

CHANTS.

BAPTISMAL CHANT.

29 *Before the Administration.*

1 AND Jesus said, Suffer little children, and forbid them not to | come·· unto | Me ; ||
For of | such·· is the | kingdom·· of | heaven.

2 He shall feed His | flock·· like a | shepherd : || He shall gather the lambs with His arm
and | carry·· them | in His | bosom.

3 I will pour My Spirit upon thy seed, and My blessing up- | on thine | offspring ; ||
And they shall spring up as among the grass, as | willows·· by the | water— | courses.

After the Administration.

1 THEN will I sprinkle clean | water·· up- | on you, || And | ye shall | be — | clean :

2 A new heart also | will I | give you, || And a new spirit | will I | put with- | in you,

3 And I will take away the stony heart | out of·· your | flesh, || And I will | give·· you a |
heart of | flesh.

EUCHARISTIC.

NETTLETON. 8, 7. D.

1 SWEET the moments, rich in blessing,
　Which before the cross I spend ;
Life, and health, and peace possessing,
　From the sinner's dying Friend.
While I see divine compassion
　Beaming in His gracious eye,
Truly blessèd is this station,
　Low before His cross to lie.

2 Love and grief my heart dividing,
　With my tears His feet I'll bathe ;
Constant still, in faith abiding,
　Life deriving from His death.
May I still enjoy this feeling,
　Still to my Redeemer go,
Prove His wounds each day more
　healing,
And Himself more truly know.

Rev. James Allen. (1734—1804.) 1757. much alt.
Hon. and Rev. Walter Shirley. (1725--1786.) 1774. ab.
and alt.

Index of Scripture Texts.

	HYMN.
GENESIS.	
1: 3	3
5: 24	684
8:	476
12: 7	1171
17: 7	862
24: 31	876
24: 56	636
27: 34	4-7
28: 10—13	734
28: 20—22	1173
31: 26	1227
EXODUS.	
3: 6	1386
13: 21	119
14: 15	639
33: 20	19
LEVITICUS.	
8: 35	631
NUMBERS.	
10: 2	993
10: 33	18
23: 10	1293
DEUTERONOMY.	
4: 31	91
RUTH.	
1: 16, 17	875
1st SAMUEL.	
1: 28	865
3: 10	962
15: 32	1274
2d SAMUEL.	
23: 5	787
1st KINGS.	
3: 5	823, 979
2d CHRONICLES.	
6: 18	1032
15: 15	872
EZRA.	
8: 21	846
NEHEMIAH.	
9: 5	57
13: 31	762
JOB.	
11: 7	21
23: 10	1233
29: 2	678, 686
PSALMS.	
1	1229, 1234
4: 4	478
5	979
5: 3	957
8	60, 153
9	654

	HYMN.
21	44
14	1095
15	693
17: 15	140
18	122, 128, 156
19	63, 67, 386, 403, 404
19: 5, 8	1198
23	82, 84, 85, 9s, 132, 664, 710, 759, 1154
24	154 2-0
24: 7—10	300
26: 2	552
27	766, 954
29	138, 1227
31	777
31: 15	797, 806
32	511
33	114
34	142
35	130
36: 5—9	104, 141
39	1380
40: 5—7	146
41	1654
42	6-7
44	1155
45	313, 1088
46	121
48	299, 836, 837, 840
51	428, 465, 466, 467, 480
51: 10	741
55	1286
55: 6	211
55: 17	821
55: 22	794
56	3-7
57	52, 134
58: 1	1175
63	86, 977, 1003, 1010
65	69, 998, 1154, 1252
65: 2	1256
66: 2	3-8
67	956, 959, 1159
68	49, 241, 1325
68: 18	267
70	6-8
71	750, 782
71: 5—9	1226
71: 17—21	1295
72	1115, 1139
72: 15	1122
73: 24—26	892
74: 23—28	714
73: 25	584, 740, 754, 1198
74: 16, 17	66
77	641
78	1158
78: 53	663
80	1046
81	936
84	950, 951, 984, 987, 1003, 1017
87	9-5
90: 11, 12	120
90: 7	94
90	71
90: 2	27
90: 3—5	1087
90: 13	1361
90: 17	1171
91	765, 1247

	HYMN.
92	935, 944, 1004
93	41, 45, 101, 103
93: 3—5	109
95	58, 946
95: 1—6	103, 982
96	145
96: 2	714
96: 13	1354
97	41, 110
99	61
100	46, 47, 48, 107, 841, 955
100: 3	2
102	7
13—21	1109
104	97, 135, 537, 1154
103: 1—7	87
104: 1—12	88
104: 13—18	82
104	56, 136
106	100
107: 23—30	1144
107: 24	694
107: 35	139
109: 20	775
110: 4	562
111: 9	144
113	78, 137
115	96
116: 12	755
117	1, 35, 30, 72, 1023
118	939, 968
118: 24	941
119	394, 395, 396, 397, 399, 400, 715
119: 3	393
119: 71, 75	774
119: 136, 158	1061
121: 5	1243
122	960, 970, 973, 976, 984, 1011, 1112, 1113
125: 2	814
126	602, 857
127	1234
130	463, 695
132	1036
133	924, 1169
135: 2	409
136	81, 105, 1153
137	725, 655, 1059
138	699
139: 5	603
139	94, 95, 130
143	102, 131
146	4, 111
146: 2	1386
147	1254
147: 3	1282
148	39, 40, 51, 53, 58, 79
150	23, 80, 83
PROVERBS.	
3: 9	1075
8: 22—31	149
12: 24	544
ECCLESIASTES.	
9: 10	421
11: 1	1054
12: 7	1390

	HYMN.
CANTICLES.	
5: 2	428
ISAIAH.	
2: 1—4	1107
6: 1—3	152
6: 3	12
9: 1—7	157
9: 6	1103
9: 6	172, 176
12: 1	579
21: 11	174
25: 3	521
25: 13	508
27: 8	143
32: 2	555
32: 20	833
33: 17, 21	733, 1313
33: 20, 21	831
35: 8—10	627
40: 28—31	655
42: 10—12	1106
45	1072
45: 2	308
45: 7	1200
51: 9	1049
52: 1, 2	1116
52: 7	1128
52: 10	1079
52: 15	1078
53	199, 791
53: 4, 5, 12	218
53: 5	516
53: 6—12	235
53: 7—9	851
53: 1—2	416
55: 4, 5	1299
58: 1	1083, 1084
60: 20	1312
61	155
62: 6, 7	1053
63: 1	1116
64: 7	535
66: 19, 20	1073
JEREMIAH.	
3: 22	690
29: 13	981
31: 18—20	431
LAMENTATIONS.	
3: 22, 23	1199
3: 23	150
3: 24	1633
EZEKIEL.	
18: 31	416
36: 37	849
37: 3	1032
37: 27	830
HOSEA.	
6: 1—4	685
14: 4	410
MICAH.	
2: 10	1409
4: 1, 2	1107
6: 9	709

INDEX OF SCRIPTURE TEXTS.

HABAKKUK.
2: 20 961

HAGGAI.
2: 7 303

ZECHARIAH.
1: 5 1270
13: 1 .... 301, 545, 556, 1129

MATTHEW.
2: 10 190
4: 16 1051
5: 4 70
5: 8 736
6: 25 ....
8: 25 1145
11: 24 .... 433, 468
11: 2—30 .... 415, 420
12: 20 330
13: 16, 17 851
14: 27 705
14: 35, 36 211
17: 4 212
18: 20 .... 735, 968, 969
18: 34 661
21: 1—11 217
21: 15, 16 1195
22: 4 441
25: 7 614
25: 40 1045
25: 41 1354
26: 11 1040
26: 29 902
28: 6 336

MARK.
1: 32 1214
4: 35 1147
5: 1—21 200
10: 14—16 861
10: 25 610
10: 45 .... 492, 517
10: 51, 52 51
13: 10 1056
16: 6 209
16: 15 .... 845, 1160

LUKE.
1: 47 716
2: 7—15 160
2: 10 181
2: 11 163
2: 32 1050
2: 40 1150
4: 22 205
6: 12 620
7: 13 1253
9: 58 1229
10: 42 422
12: 33 1015
12: 35—48 854
14: 16—24 426
14: 17 .... 427, 433
14: 22 448
18: 1 751
18: 1—7 825
19: 13 .... 481, 492
24: 19 691

HYMN.
24: 1—10 962
24: 29 .... 1029, 1029
24: 32 743
24: 34 .... 206, 277

JOHN.
1: 1, 3, 14 150
1: 16 509
2: 2 1165
3: 16, 17 449
4: 21—23 986
6: 37 483
7: 37 .... 408, 447
10: 16 930
12: 41 ....
14: 1 347
14: 6 ...... 304, 752, 1006
14: 16, 17 367
14: 19 698
15: 13 .... 595, 624
16: 7 .... 333, 340
17: 24 139
19: 30 246
21: 11—16 270
21: 29 ....
21: 15 503
21: 17 730

ACTS.
1: 4 382
2: 1—4 .... 341, 342
9: 6 522
9: 11 803
9: 36 322
10: 38 .... 192, 1013
10: 44 355
16: 9 1070
17: 24—28 63
20: 35 1033
26: 22 157

ROMANS.
1: 14 622
1: 16 616
1: 20 39
4: 4 460
8: 14, 16 353
8: 33 701
11: 23 1060
12: 1 319
13: 2 1251
14: 8 .... 99, 721
15: 11 1

1ST CORINTHIANS.
1: 22—29 731
1: 23, 24 ....
1: 30 .... 485, 605
3: 9—10 ....
5: 7 1374
6: 17 963
6: 17 726
7: 23 884
11: 26 .... 697, 904
12: 9 117
12: 13 1040
15: 20—23 311

HYMN.
15: 47, 49 325
16: 13 642

2D CORINTHIANS.
4: 4 395
4: 6 3
5: 1 1171
5: 17 529
6: 2 439

GALATIANS.
3: 22 469
6: 2 1056
6: 6 781
6: 14 .... 612, 618

EPHESIANS.
1: 13, 14 355
2: 5 604
2: 13—18 809
2: 20 929
3: 16 360
4: 8 822
4: 32 987
5: 14 632
6: 11—18 628

PHILIPPIANS.
1: 21 .... 549, 1276
2: 22 619
2: 21 .... 1260, 1290
3: 7—9 860
3: 8 466
3: 12—14 643
4: 6, 7 1279
4: 13 751

COLOSSIANS.
1: 27 1242
2: 2 913
3: 11 574
4: 2 846

1ST THESSALONIANS.
4: 13 1327
4: 14—17 1360
4: 13 1298
5: 17 622

1ST TIMOTHY.
1: 15 584
1: 17 16
2: 5 333
3: 16 ....
4: 6, 7, 18 1277
6: 12 .... 652, 671

2D TIMOTHY.
1: 12 623
3: 16 .... 397, 404

TITUS.
2: 10—13 621
2: 12 814

HEBREWS.
1: 6 307
2: 10 302

HYMN.
2: 11 616
2: 18 801
3: 4 133
4: 9 1312
4: 16 320
5: 1 1318
5: 6 562
6: 19 692
7: 25 245
10: 23 42
10: 24 395
10: 29 471
11: 14 658
11: 13 .... 720, 1218
12: 26 1348
13: 14 657

JAMES.
4: 13—15 1267
4: 14 1228

1ST PETER.
1: 8 .... 530, 545
2: 4, 5 827
2: 7 .... 563, 757
2: 21 290
5: 7 .... 635, 713, 775
5: 10 732

2D PETER.
1: 4 709

1ST JOHN.
1: 3 722
2: 6 684
3: 1 723
3: 2 705
4: 8 51
4: 11 1043

JUDE.
24, 25 62

REVELATION.
3: 17 439
3: 20 428
3: 21 900
4: 6 1391
4: 8 1416
4: 11 .... 55, 301
5: 6—12 326
5: 9 28
5: 11—13 .... 330, 551
5: 12 315
7: 9 .... 1365, 1391, 1396
7: 9—16 1366
7: 13 1194
7: 13—17 1404
7: 17 1394
11: 15 305
13: 8 1322
15: 3 .... 301, 606
19: 12 396
19: 16 318
21: 1—4 1330
21: 3, 4, 23, 25 1305
21: 27 1374
22: 1 1359
22: 17—20 443
22: 20 .... 1357, 1362

Index of Subjects.

THE FIGURES REFER TO THE NUMBERS OF THE HYMNS.

ABBA, FATHER, 610, 723.
Abiding with Believers—See *Christ*.
Abrahamic Covenant, 862, 867.
Accepted Time, 425, 439—See *Day of Grace*.
Access to God, 322, 513, 722, 823.
Activity, Calls to, 894, 1039, 1051, 1092, 1343, 1344.
Adoption, 125, 723, 1010.
Adoration, 5, 26, 48, 986—See *Christ*, and *Trinity*.
Advent—See *Christ*.
Advocate, Christ our—See *Christ*.
Afflictions:
 Blessings of, 116, 622, 647, 774, 798, 799.
 Comfort Under, 1298–1336.
 Courage in, 337, 586, 625, 709, 710, 728, 927, 1264, 1266.
 Prayer in, 665, 706, 761–763, 791, 792, 1269.
 Refuge in, 121, 122, 317, 434, 437, 635, 666, 667, 671–680, 692–713, 764, 765, 766, 773, 775, 794, 805, 1237, 1279–1283.
 Submission in, 88–91, 123–127, 636, 767–772, 776, 777, 788, 1221.
All in all—See *Christ*, and *God*.
All is Well, 672.
Alms—See *Charity*.
Angels:
 At Advent of Christ, 147, 150—See *Song of*.
 At Coronation of Christ, 296, 305, 329, 330.
 At Resurrection of Christ, 262, 263, 265, 266, 273.
 Joy of, 730.
 Ministry of, 30, 1210, 1241, 1287, 1290.
 Song of, 158–164, 166, 170, 176, 185, 194, 195.

Ark of God, 444.
Ascension of Christ — See *Christ*.
Ashamed of Jesus, 616, 623.
Asleep in Jesus, 1292, 1294, 1333.
Aspirations, 681–683, 726, 727.
For Divine Grace, 18, 36, 86, 99, 125, 624, 631, 704, 706, 741, 745, 746, 749, 751, 753, 761–763, 817, 823, 826, 979, 990, 1170, 1172.
For Heaven—See *Longing for Heaven*.
For Nearness to Christ, 660–670, 687, 689, 720, 728, 729, 734–737, 752, 753, 757, 758, 1029, 1173, 1191.
Of Faith—See *Faith*.
Of Hope—See *Hope*.
Assurance, 355, 513, 651, 698, 728, 759.
Atonement:
 Completed, 146, 147, 222–338, 408–450, 499, 501, 534, 587, 588, 1129.
 Necessary, 223, 234, 235, 245, 321, 453, 460, 464, 465, 467, 499, 502, 605.
 Sufficient, 230, 234, 238, 310, 408, 411, 419, 420, 429, 432, 446, 503, 515, 534, 605, 608, 618.
Attributes of God—See *God*.
Autumn—See *Seasons*.

BACKSLIDING, 471, 678, 684–688, 690.
Baptism, 861–871.
 Adult, 863, 864.
 Infant, 861, 862, 865–871.
 Of Holy Spirit, 912, 1067.
Beatitudes, 756, 1169.
Being of God—See *God*.
Believers—See *Saints*.

Believing—See *Faith*.
Benediction, 943, 1005—See *Close of Service*.
Benevolence:
 Of Christ—See *Christ*.
 Human—See *Charity*.
Bereavement—See *Afflictions*, and *Funeral Hymns*.
Bible, 386–407.
Blessedness of the Pardoned, 511.
Blessing Sought, 487, 488, 489, 517, 519, 1174.
Blindness, 517–519.
Blind Bartimeus, 517.
Blood of Christ—See *Christ*. See also *Atonement*.
Book of Life, 115.
Bread of Heaven—See *Christ*.
Bread of Life—See *Christ*.
Brevity of Life—See *Life*.
Bridegroom, Coming of, 894, 1343.
Brotherly Love, 913–915, 918, 924, 925, 1049—See also *Communion of Saints*.
Burdens, 512, 794—See *Afflictions*.
Burial—See *Death*, and *Funeral Hymns*.

CALL, GOD'S, 477.
Calmness, 761, 763, 810, 814.
Calvary, 229, 247, 249, 253—See *Christ, Crucified*.
Captain of Salvation — See *Christ*.
Carnal Joys, 558.
Change of Heart—See *Conversion*.
Charity, 1038, 1041–1046, 1052, 1053, 1055, 1056—See also *Brotherly Love*.
Chastenings—See *Afflictions*.
Children, 1176, 1177, 1181, 1184–1195.
Hosannas of, 218, 219, 1177, 1186, 1195.

385

Childlike Spirit, 796.
Choosing Christ, 494, 495, 878.
Christ, 145-338.
  Abiding with Believers, 802, 883, 1020,1024,1029.
  Adoration of, 151, 239, 307, 310, 326, 330, 568.
  Advent, First, 145-197.
  Advent, Second, 180, 182, 1337-1364.
  Advocate, 284, 322, 324.
  Agony of, 220-233, 247.
  All in All, 527, 531, 532, 569, 574, 592.
  Ascension of, 278-282, 285-290, 298, 299, 309, 312, 333.
  Atonement of, 485, 516, 1179.
  Beauty of, 313, 580, 582.
  Benevolence of, 204, 390, 1038.
  Best Friend, 544, 909.
  Birth of, 161-166, 169-179, 183-188, 190, 191, 194, 195.
  Blood of, 242, 253-256, 267, 268, 324.
  Bread of Heaven, 898.
  Bread of Life, 893, 895, 896.
  Burial of, 257-259.
  Captain of Salvation, 586, 634, 651, 724.
  Character of, 198, 199, 200, 206, 207, 208, 215, 313.
  Childhood of, 197, 216.
  Choice of—See *Choosing Christ*.
  Compassion of, 153, 199, 209, 320, 780.
  Condescension of, 180.
  Conqueror, 266, 267, 271, 275, 279, 280, 290, 294-301, 312, 314, 318, 331, 336, 971, 1196.
  Consoler, 801, 802, 805.
  Corner-Stone, 827, 828, 830, 833, 929, 939.
  Coronation of, 296, 305, 329.
  Cross of—See *Cross*.
  Crucified, 578, 583.
  Crucifixion of, 227-256, 283.
  Day Star, 185, 192, 193, 406, 958, 1225.
  Death of—See *Atonement of*, and *Crucifixion of*.

Christ:
  Delight in, 149, 212, 213, 214, 316, 527—529, 572.
  Deliverer, 673, 674, 679, 708, 709, 801.
  Desire of Nations, 165, 170, 181, 303.
  Divinity of, 150, 151, 167, 170, 171, 177, 210, 236, 313, 315, 330.
  Eternity of, 150, 315, 318.
  Exaltation of, 235, 302, 315, 329.
  Example, 198, 200, 333, 624, 1038, 1176, 1177, 1188.
  Excellency of, 330, 568, 588.
  Faith in, 234—See *Faith*.
  First Fruits, 311.
  Fountain, 242, 253, 254, 501, 515, 550, 599.
  Friend of Sinners, 214, 323, 457, 469.
  Fullness of, 430, 728, 729.
  Gift of God, 700.
  Glorying in, 612-618, 623.
  Glory of, 212, 213, 273, 302, 306, 310, 313.
  Grace of, 208, 313, 450, 479, 572, 804.
  Gratitude to, 180, 238, 325, 536-556.
  Hiding Place, 453, 555, 642, 676.
  High Priest, 268, 269, 317, 328.
  Hope of His People, 310, 319-328, 336-338, 549, 691, 693, 694, 698, 772.
  Hosanna to, 218, 219, 331.
  Humanity of, 150, 198-208, 214-216, 317, 321, 323-325, 333.
  Humility of, 198, 206.
  Humiliation of, 197, 216, 235, 315.
  Immanuel, 189, 318, 321, 325.
  Incarnate, 196, 201, 203, 321, 332, 333.
  Incomparable, 189, 505, 546, 561, 670.
  Indwelling, 494, 666.
  In Gethsemane, 220, 223-226, 366.
  Intercession of, 240, 284, 286, 317, 666.
  Invitation of, 205, 209, 408,

Christ:
  415, 416, 429, 447, 599, 707.
  Judge, 338, 1338-1341,1345-1355.
  King of Glory, 152, 181, 260-265, 271, 280, 281, 300, 301, 307, 318, 323.
  King of Saints, 291, 314, 334, 335.
  King, Sovereign, 151, 285, 297, 313, 338, 514, 532.
  Knocking at the Door, 241, 428.
  Lamb of God, 236, 310, 315, 326, 330, 573, 899.
  Leader, 641, 651-654, 660-670.
  Life, 556, 599.
  Light 464, 556, 571, 599, 738, 1202.
  Love of, 146, 215, 216, 328, 347, 471, 544, 571, 587, 589, 881, 882, 886, 909, 1190.
  Loveliness of, 531, 561, 562, 598.
  Majesty of, 62, 151, 214, 217, 307.
  Man of Sorrows, 248, 791.
  Mediator, 236, 237, 324, 534.
  Meekness of, 198, 200, 206, 208.
  Ministry of, 198, 202,205, 210, 211.
  Miracles of, 202, 204, 209, 210.
  Mission of, 153, 198, 202, 449.
  Names of, 157, 171, 504, 514.
  Nativity of—See *Birth of*.
  Offices of, 171, 504, 514, 533.
  Only Plea, 451, 453, 455, 469, 475, 496, 497, 583, 584, 590.
  Our Passover, 265, 310, 899.
  Passion, 221, 222, 227-256.
  Patience of, 198, 208, 222, 244.
  Pattern—See *Example*.
  Pearl of Great Price, 527, 700.
  Physician, 204, 517, 518.
  Power of—See *Divinity of*.

Christ:
 Praise to—See *Praise*.
 Prayer to—See *Prayer*.
 Preciousness of, 503-508, 563-566.
 Presence of, 203, 581, 637, 667, 755, 1173.
 Priest, 164, 196, 324, 514, 527, 562.
 Prince of Grace, 303.
 Prince of Peace, 315, 335.
 Prince of Salvation, 1124.
 Prophet, 164, 196, 514, 527.
 Ransom, 250, 264, 267, 308, 327, 502, 526, 534.
 Redeemer, 147, 167, 168, 282, 306, 308, 319, 326, 327.
 Refuge, 642, 676, 679.
 Reigning, 145, 156, 274, 275, 279, 283, 294-302, 305, 307, 334, 335, 338, 1121, 1122, 1139-1141.
 Resurrection of, 180, 260-267, 270, 272-283, 311, 336, 933, 948, 969, 971, 973.
 Resurrection, Pledge of, 311, 312, 316.
 Righteousness of, 485, 605, 889.
 Rock of Ages, 499, 831.
 Sacrifice, 198, 227-256, 513, 579—See . *Atonement*.
 Saviour, the, 209, 210, 211, 237, 289, 316, 318.
 Second Coming of — See *Advent, Second*.
 Sepulchre of, 257, 258, 259, 270, 272.
 Shepherd, 82, 84, 85, 98, 333, 539, 565, 661, 710, 759, 906, 1175, 1178, 1191, 1193.
 Son of God, 145, 150, 151, 162, 171, 195, 197, 213, 216, 240, 247, 248, 261, 284, 313, 315, 318.
 Substitute, 228, 250, 516, 584.
 Sufferings of, 198, 199, 220-256.
 Sufficient, 677, 702.
 Sun of Righteousness, 99, 479, 957, 958, 1029, 1236.
 Surety, 277, 513.
 Sympathy of, 214, 215, 317, 320, 328, 453, 561, 615, 701, 791-794.

Christ :
 Teacher, 205.
 Temptations of, 201.
 Transfiguration of, 212, 213.
 Triumphal Entry of, 152, 217-219.
 Trust in—See *Trust*.
 Victorious—See *Conqueror*.
 Way, Truth, and Life, 304, 752.
 Weeping over Sinners, 459.
 Wisdom of, 148.
 Wonderful, 532.
 Word of God, 150, 177, 407.
 Work Finished, 260, 269.
Christ's Grace Extolled, 599-609.
Christians :
 At the Cross, 230, 243, 245, 703.
 Christ the Life of, 549, 698, 735.
 Comfort of—See *Comfort*.
 Confidence in God, 1328—See *Faith*, and *Trust*.
 Conflicts of, 111, 471, 671-697, 797, 809—See also *Warfare*.
 Conquerors through Christ, 586, 605, 648-650.
 Courage of—See *Courage*.
 Death of—See *Death of Saints*.
 Debt of, to Christ, 681, 682, 881.
 Dependence on Christ, 99, 321, 666, 670, 728, 777, 877, 1295, 1296.
 Duties of, 99, 621, 631, 853, 1038, 1039, 1197-1201, 1268.
 Encouragements of, 585, 634, 645, 651, 655, 671, 672, 691, 708-710, 759, 1051.
 Example of, 621, 648, 919, 920.
 Fellowship of—See *Brotherly Love*.
 Graces of, 603, 621, 656, 741, 746, 751, 756, 761, 763, 1040, 1041, 1182.
 Love of, for Christ, 504, 530-535, 545, 547, 548, 559-568, 577, 593-598, 721, 736.
 Perseverance of, 543, 642-656, 701, 759, 787.

Christians :
 Safety of, in God, 43, 44, 49, 52, 56, 74, 82-85, 118, 121, 142, 777.
 Race of, 648-657.
 Warfare of, 586, 625-654.
Christian Ministry—See *Ministry*.
Christian Work, 1038-1057, 1192.
Christmas Song—See *Song of the Angels*.
Church, 827-842.
 Afflicted, 1058, 1059, 1066, 1356, 1358.
 Beloved of God, 831, 834, 835, 837.
 Beloved of Saints, 830, 832, 835, 836, 841, 878, 974-978.
 Birth Place of the Saints, 985.
 Glory of, 831, 836, 985, 1102, 1108, 1111, 1116, 1359.
 God the Strength of, 830, 837, 840, 842, 984.
 In the Desert, 1066.
 Joining the, 876, 878, 879.
 Ministry of—See *Ministry*.
 Missions of—See *Missions*.
 Ordinances of—See *Baptism*, and *Lord's Supper*.
 Revival of—See *Revival*.
 The Safety of the Nation, 837.
 Triumph of, 174, 1068, 1116, 1125-1141, 1393.
 Unity of, 829.
City of God, 1390—See *Zion*.
Close of Service, 918, 925, 943, 963, 1005, 1014, 1015, 1022, 1023, 1025.
Come and Welcome, 408, 419, 876, 879.
Comfort, 270, 434, 435, 437, 450, 1282, 1283, 1298.
Comforter—See *Holy Spirit*.
Coming of Christ-See *Christ, Advent*.
 Anticipated, 1337, 1338, 1342, 1356-1364.
Commemoration, 884, 887, 891, 897, 900-908, 926.
Communion :
 Of Saints, 911-930.
 With God, 738-740.
 With Christ, 559, 722.
 At the Lord's Table—See *Lord's Supper*.

Compassion:
  Of Christ—See *Christ*.
  Of God—See *God*.
Condescension — See *Christ*, and *God*.
Confession:
  Of Faith—See *Faith*.
  Of Sin—See *Sin*.
Confidence—See *Faith*, and *Trust*.
Conflict with Sin—See *Christians, Conflicts of*.
Conformity to Christ, 741—See *Christ, Example*.
Conqueror—See *Christ*.
Conscience, 234, 744, 745.
Consecration, of Possessions, 245, 486, 1052, 1053, 1055.
  Of Self, 36, 873, 874, 880.
  Renewed, 684–690.
  To Christ, 619–621.
Consolation, in God, 773–776.
  In the Sympathy of Christ, 791–794.
  Sought, 764–766.
  Under Bereavement, 1298–1306, 1311, 1321, 1323, 1327–1330.
Constancy, 643–645, 648, 650–657.
Contributions—See *Charity*.
Contrition, 227, 230–232, 524.
Conversion, 152, 256, 472–477, 479, 486, 492–498, 509–511, 518, 522–524, 529, 533, 535, 538, 539, 554, 557, 558, 599–603, 610, 892.
Conviction — See *Pardon Sought*.
Corner-Stone—See *Christ*.
Coronation—See *Christ*.
Country, our, 1152, 1157–1166.
Courage, 625, 628, 633, 643–655, 1092, 1094, 1096.
Covenant, entering into, 864, 872–880.
  Of Grace, 695, 701, 787, 862, 867.
Creation—See *God, Creator*.
Cross:
  And Crown, 927.
  Bearing, 610, 611, 617, 621–624.
  Glorying in, 612, 613, 616–618, 647.
  Lessons of, 251, 502.

Cross:
  Salvation by, 227–256, 302, 314.
  Soldier of, 625, 643, 644, 1096.
  Crowns of Glory, 609, 622, 627, 648, 651, 730, 885, 920.
Crucifixion of Christ — See *Christ*.
Crucifixion to the World, 245 — See *Renouncing all for Christ*.

DARKNESS, SPIRITUAL, 359, 678, 684–690, 695, 809, 1361.
Day of Grace, 413, 414, 421, 425, 428, 439, 450, 497, 946.
Day Spring, 406, 958.
Day Star, 185, 406, 958, 1225.
Death:
  Confidence in, 1274–1278, 1289–1292, 1294, 1318, 1371.
  Conquered, 1271, 1302, 1321–1326.
  Fear of, Overcome, 1317.
  Of Children, 1299, 1300.
  Of Friends, 1311, 1316.
  Of Infants, 1301, 1303.
  Of a Minister, 1329, 1331.
  Of Saints, 1284, 1292, 1293, 1298, 1304, 1305, 1307–1310, 1317–1336.
  Prevalence of, 1272, 1273, 1306.
  Second, 462.
Declension Deplored, 471, 678, 684–688.
Decrees of God—See *God*.
Dedicating Places of Worship, 1032–1037.
Delay, Danger of, 413, 414, 416, 421, 424, 425, 428, 450.
Dependence on God, 73, 74, 77, 92, 98, 99, 794, 1200, 1213, 1223, 1226, 1237, 1238, 1245.
  On Grace, 387, 584, 600, 601, 603, 604.
Deliverance Sought and Gained, 695–697.
Depravity:
  Native, 467, 496, 1061, 1062.
  Universal, 147, 235, 605, 1061, 1062.

Despondency — See *Christians, Conflicts of*.
Devotions—See *Prayer*, and *Worship*.
Dismissions — See *Close of Service*.
Distress, Spiritual—See *Christians, Conflicts of*.
Doubt—See *Christians, Conflicts of*.
Doxologies; Hymns 15, 18, 38, 55, 72, 97, 551, 1025; Pages 529, 530.
Duties, Daily — See *Christians, Duties of*.

EARLY PIETY — See *Children*.
Earnest of the Spirit — See *Holy Spirit, Earnest of*.
Earnestness—See *Zeal*.
Earthly Pleasures—See *Renunciation*.
Easter Hymns—See *Christ, Resurrection of*.
Ebenezer, 536, 1211.
Effectual Calling—See *Election*.
Effort, Christian, 625, 628–633, 643, 652, 853, 1038, 1057, 1091.
Election—See *God, Decrees of*.
Encouragements—See *Christians, Encouragements of*.
Energy—See *Effort, Zeal*.
Erection of Churches — See *Dedicating Places of Worship*.
Espousals to Christ — See *Faith, Confession of*.
Eternal Life—See *Life*.
Eternal Punishment — See *Future Punishment*.
Eternity, 76, 462, 1318, 1323, 1334, 1337–1364.
Evening, 1026, 1187, 1200, 1210, 1211, 1214, 1216, 1217, 1222–1224, 1228–1244, 1246, 1248, 1249.
  Of Lord's Day—See *Lord's Day*.
  Of Life, 1024.
Exaltation of Christ — See *Christ*.
Example:
  Of Christ—See *Christ*.
  Of Christians—See *Christians*.

INDEX OF SUBJECTS. 389

Expostulation, 410, 413, 416, 420, 422-425, 428, 431, 439, 448, 497, 946.

FAINT HEARTEDNESS, 645, 651, 655.
Faith, 496-526.
　Aspiration of, 500, 728, 729, 919, 920.
　Assurance of, 501-508.
　Blessedness of, 521.
　Confession of, 872-880.
　Gift of God, 601, 603, 604.
　Justification by, 234, 496-499, 526.
　Prayer for, 784, 1016.
　Prayer of, 525.
　Triumph of, 701.
　Walking by, 656, 919, 920.
Faithfulness of God — See *God*.
Fall of Man — See *Depravity*.
Family, 1169, 1171.
Family Worship, 1168-1249.
Fast Days, 1156, 1160-1164.
Father, God our — See *God*.
Fearfulness — See *Faint Heartedness*.
Feast:
　Gospel — See *Gospel Feast*.
　Sacramental — See *Lord's Supper*.
Festivals and Fasts, 1149-1168.
Filial Yearning, 723-725, 749.
Forbearance, Divine — See *God, Forbearance of*.
Forefathers' Day, 1157, 1158, 1162.
For Those at Sea, 1142-1148.
Following Christ, 626, 627, 629, 649, 651-654, 659-670, 1047.
Following hard after God, 734-737.
Forgiveness of Sin — See *Pardon Found*.
Foreign Missions — See *Missions*.
Formality, 359.
Forsaking all for Christ — See *Renouncing all for Christ*.
Fountain:
　Of Blood, 242, 253, 254, 501.
　Of Living Water, 446, 447, 831, 895, 896, 1129.

Foundation of Hope — See *Christ, Hope of His People*.
Frailty of Man — See *Life, Brevity of*.
Free Salvation, 237, 253, 408-450, 472, 497, 520, 536, 587, 600.
Friend of Sinners — See *Christ*.
Friends, Burial of — See *Funeral Hymns*.
　Glorified, 916, 917, 1240, 1311, 1327.
Fruits of Grace, 621, 749.
Fulness of Grace, 408-450.
Funeral Hymns, 1272, 1307, 1316, 1319-1321, 1324, 1327.
Future Punishment, 423, 462 — See *Judgment Day*.

GENTLENESS, 1382.
Gethsemane, 220, 223-226.
Gloria in Excelsis, 25, 71.
Glorified Saints — See *Saints, Glorified*.
Glory:
　Of Christ — See *Christ*.
　Of God — See *God*.
Glorying in the Cross — See *Cross*.
God, 1-144.
　Abode of, 19.
　All in all, 92, 754.
　All-Seeing, 95.
　All Things present to, 33.
　Almighty — See *Omnipotent*.
　Attributes of, 27, 77, 93, 102, 106, 140.
　Being of, 63, 115, 403.
　Calling yet, 477.
　Communion with, 722, 738-740, 748, 749, 754, 810, 813, 815, 1213.
　Compassion of, 87, 88, 89, 131, 135, 141, 142.
　Condescension of, 78, 106, 137.
　Covenant Keeping, 787.
　Creator, 4, 39, 40, 55, 56, 58, 63, 79, 103, 105, 129, 133, 827.
　Decrees of, 115, 116, 123.
　Eternal, 27, 74, 76, 77, 108.
　Faithfulness of, 42, 96, 120, 794.
　Father, 41, 77, 91, 543, 547, 723, 787, 826.

God:
　Forbearance of, 87, 471, 690.
　Glory of, 13, 15, 16, 17, 63, 64, 67, 75, 112, 136, 403.
　Goodness of, 4, 60, 107, 131, 143, 153, 460.
　Grace of, 36, 52, 81, 104, 105.
　Greatness of, 102, 134, 137.
　Guardian, 82, 118, 119.
　Guide, 18, 43, 82, 119, 139, 660.
　Helper, 74, 634, 635, 748.
　Holiness of, 6, 12, 14, 15, 61, 70, 144, 1416.
　Immutable — See *Unchangeable*.
　Incarnate, 30.
　Incomprehensible, 102, 116, 117, 123.
　Indwelling of, 7, 26.
　Infinite, 76.
　In Nature, 39, 40, 51, 53, 63, 66, 67, 112, 129, 133, 398, 403, 406, 1252.
　Jehovah, 8, 41, 45.
　Judge, 1275 — See *Christ, Judge*.
　Justice of, 123, 140, 141.
　King — See *Sovereign*.
　Kingdom of, 101.
　Light of his Saints, 1312.
　Love of, 38, 54, 55, 135, 347, 723, 832, 1199, 1200.
　Majesty of, 45, 49, 56, 93, 113, 128, 134, 136.
　Mercy of, 49, 56, 81, 91, 120, 135, 140, 141, 143.
　Mercies of, Recounted, 90, 778.
　Mysterious, 19, 27, 116, 117, 123.
　Omnipotent, 109, 113, 138.
　Omnipresent, 92, 94, 130, 753, 1213.
　Omniscient, 33, 127, 130.
　Patience of — See *Forbearance of*.
　Perfections of, 106.
　Pity of — See *Compassion of*.
　Praise to — See *Praise*.
　Prayer Hearing, 456, 466, 525, 826, 986.
　Preserver, 43, 786.
　Presence of, 94, 139, 984, 987, 992, 997, 1226.

God :
  Promises of, 42.
  Providence of, 63, 64, 81, 104, 133.
  Purposes of—See *Decrees of*.
  Reconciled, 513.
  Refuge, 1, 43, 121, 764-766.
  Ruler, 39, 40, 41.
  Saviour, 555, 714, 716.
  Safety in, 44, 96, 111, 121, 142, 777, 789.
  Shepherd, 82, 84, 85, 98, 710.
  Source of Blessing, 87, 114, 124, 140.
  Sovereign, 41, 58, 59, 60, 101, 108, 110, 128, 138, 797.
  Stronghold, 1, 45, 121.
  Supreme, 2, 48, 76, 115, 797.
  Triune—See *Trinity*.
  Trust in—See *Trust*.
  Truth of, 4, 42, 48, 50, 52, 104, 135, 709, 1023, 1227, 1386.
  Unchangeable, 48, 53, 73, 74, 76, 100, 101.
  Unsearchable, 21, 116, 117, 123.
  Watchful Care of, 44, 65, 86, 87, 99, 100, 118, 132, 773, 803.
  Wisdom of, 41, 54, 62, 112, 123, 127, 129.
  Works of, 40, 41, 56, 60, 63, 73, 81, 105, 106, 108, 112, 129, 133, 398.
  Worshipped, 46-48, 61, 93, 97, 107, 144.
Good Works, 400, 621, 889.
Good Tidings, 1128, 1134.
Gospel :
  Banner, 1101, 1123.
  Excellency of, 403, 405, 851, 1227.
  Feast, 408, 426, 427, 433, 441, 446, 448.
  Freeness of, 408—450.
  Fulness of, 408, 411, 432, 433, 434, 446.
  Invitations, 408-420, 426-429, 431-450.
  Message, 420, 436, 1093, 1094.
  Power of, 465, 1088.
  Reception of, 476, 477, 486, 494-496, 509-512, 520-524, 527-609.

Gospel :
  Rejection of, 416, 423, 425, 428.
  Spread of, 1102, 1103, 1106, 1138 — See also *Missions*, and *Kingdom of Christ, Progress of*.
  Success of, 858.
  Triumph of, 1113, 1115, 1116, 1121, 1122, 1132 — See also *Missions*, and *Kingdom of Christ, Progress of*.
  Trumpet, 438.
Grace :
  Aspiration for Divine — See *Aspirations*.
  Converting, 344, 350, 352, 359, 363, 364, 366, 369, 370, 378, 381, 528, 600, 603, 604.
  Free, 408-450, 520, 536, 584, 600.
  Justifying, 498, 499, 523, 535, 604, 889, 892.
  Miracle of, 533.
  Quickening, 343, 344, 350, 359, 361, 365, 379-381.
  Renewing, 344, 381, 561, 602, 1075.
  Restoring, 359, 381, 699.
  Reviving, 343, 349, 352, 359, 362, 381, 849.
  Sanctifying, 344, 352, 361, 365, 366, 369, 370, 384, 605.
  Saving, 584, 588, 600, 604.
  Sovereign, 540, 600, 603-605.
Graces, Christian, 1040—See *Faith, Hope*, and *Love*.
Gratitude, 536-556.
Grave, 421, 665, 1310, 1321-1327, 1329, 1333.
Grieving the Spirit — See *Holy Spirit*.
Growth in Grace, 198, 200, 621, 624, 704, 726, 751, 811, 822, 823, 979.
Guest, Divine, 241, 428.
Guidance, Divine, 18, 82, 84, 85, 98, 353, 366, 405, 407, 662, 709, 710, 759, 1172, 1191.
Guiding Star, 190, 192, 193.
Guilt—See *Sin*.

HALLELUJAHS, 51, 78, 182, 311, 332, 537, 1121, 1241, 1192, 1318, 1393.
Happiness, 521, 527-535, 603, 759, 872, 982, 1387.
Hardness of Heart, 483.
Harvest, Spiritual, 853, 857, 1091, 1155.
Temporal, 1155, 1167 — See *Thanksgiving*.
Hearing the Word, 946, 953, 962-965, 974, 978, 1015, 1022.
Heart :
  Change of—See *Regeneration*.
  Clean, 352, 741.
  Contrite, 480-482, 511, 741.
  New—See *Regeneration*.
  Searching of, 94, 95, 478, 678, 704, 1309.
  Stony, 483.
  Surrender of, 152, 477, 480, 496, 509, 510, 512, 522, 538, 610, 910.
  Vile, 524, 690.
Heathen, 1082, 1103.
Heaven, 1365-1416.
  Anticipated, 657, 658, 717-719, 769, 1265, 1285-1288, 1344, 1371, 1399, 1403, 1406-1415.
  Blessedness of, 730, 731, 1312, 1313, 1383, 1389, 1404, 1405.
  Christ There, 1384, 1385, 1394-1398, 1407, 1415.
  Friends There, 1311, 1381.
  Home, 1314, 1334, 1336, 1344, 1372, 1373, 1375-1379, 1387, 1388, 1403, 1410-1413.
  Holiness of, 1374.
  Longed for—See *Longing for Heaven*.
  Nearness to, 1375, 1412.
  Praise of, 1385, 1386, 1392-1398.
  Prospect of, 611, 1365, 1367, 1370, 1380.
  Rest of, 769, 1382, 1401, 1408, 1409, 1414.
  Society of, 1365-1369, 1381.
  Security of, 1373.
  Songs of, 730, 1366, 1367, 1391, 1407.
  Treasure in, 1048.
  Worship of, 1390, 1391, 1398, 1416.

INDEX OF SUBJECTS.   391

Heavens, Starry, 406.
Heavenly Race, 648, 655.
Heirship of Saints, 723, 1403.
Hell — See *Future Punishment*.
Heralds of the Gospel, 851, 1100, 1128, 1134.
Hiding Place—See *Christ*.
High Priest—See *Christ*.
Holiness—See *God, Heaven,* and *Saints*.
Holy Scriptures—See *Bible*.
Holy Spirit, 339-385.
 Absence of, 351, 359 —See *Declensions*.
 Baptism of, 912, 1057.
 Comforter, 358, 362, 370, 375, 382, 383.
 Descent of, 339-342, 344, 348, 349, 372.
 Divine, 343, 349, 362, 363, 369, 370, 372, 376, 381, 384.
 Earnest of, 355, 356, 364, 367, 369.
 Enlightener, 353, 360, 370, 375, 376, 382.
 Fruits of, 352, 353, 362, 377.
 Grieved, 414, 425, 450, 470.
 Indwelling, 348, 355, 360, 367, 373, 379, 385.
 Influences of, 340, 356, 361-363, 368-370, 372, 374.
 Inspirer, 379-381, 385.
 Invoked, 343-347, 349-352, 354, 355-357, 359-385, 470, 475, 849, 1057, 1130.
 Leadings of, 353, 365, 383.
 Refining, 350, 361-363, 365, 384.
 Rejoicing in, 339, 344, 358, 371.
 Regenerating, 340, 360-363, 365, 381, 1075.
 Sought, 826.
 Striving, 354, 425, 442, 470.
 Teachings of, 344, 364, 377, 380.
 Witnessing, 355, 356, 360, 361, 367, 369, 385.
Home — See *Family,* and *Heaven*.
Home Missions, 1064, 1110.
Hope, Aspiration of, 414, 507, 609, 622, 627, 648, 651, 655, 691, 723, 726, 730-733, 919, 920, 1276, 1314, 1315, 1344, 1403, 1406.

Hope:
 In Affliction, 434-437, 692, 694, 695, 697, 769, 774, 1279, 1282, 1298-1301.
 In darkness—See *Spiritual Trouble*.
 In Death, 1284-1294, 1304, 1310, 1311, 1317-1333.
 In God, 691-697, 782.
 Of Heaven — See *Heaven Anticipated*.
Hosannas, 28, 38, 196, 331, 939, 969, 973, 996.
House of God — See *Sanctuary*.
Household—See *Family*.
Humanity of Christ — See *Christ*.
Humble Service, 1183.
Humiliation:
 Days of—See *Fast Days*.
 Of Christ—See *Christ*.
Humility, 1185 — See also *Calmness*.

IMMANUEL—See *Christ*.
Immortality, 336, 462, 1273, 1302, 1318, 1325, 1329-1336—See also *Heaven*.
Importunity, 525, 822, 825, 981.
Imputation, 230, 234, 235, 238, 310, 485, 516, 601, 791, 889.
In the Depths, 671-680.
Incarnation—See *Christ*.
Inconstancy, 688, 690.
Infant Baptism — See *Baptism*.
Infant Salvation, 1180, 1194, 1299-1301.
Ingratitude, 460, 483, 690.
Infinity of God—See *God*.
Inspiration, 388, 395, 397, 404.
Installation—See *Pastor, Installation of*.
Intercession—See *Christ*.
Invitations of the Gospel—See *Gospel*.
Invocation, 2, 3, 26, 343-347, 938-943, 947, 948, 953, 954, 956-959, 962, 964, 965, 972, 981, 988-993, 996-999, 1001, 1002, 1009, 1010, 1016, 1027, 1028.
Israel, in Captivity, 1059.
 Outcast, 1060.
 Restoration of, 1108, 1109.
 Salvation of, 1095.

JACOB'S VOW, 1172.
Jehovah—See *God*.
Jerusalem, 1370, 1372, 1377, 1378, 1410.
Jesus is Mine, 735-737.
Jesus Watching over Children, 1181.
Joining the Church — See *Lord's Supper*.
Joy, in Christ, 527-529.
 In the Lord, 114, 585, 739, 740.
 Of the Believer, 557, 564, 607, 712-716, 872.
Joyous Trust in Christ, 747-750, 888, 880, 890.
Jubilee, 417, 418, 1113, 1134, 1140, 1141.
Judgment and Eternity, 1337-1364.
Judgment Day, 1337-1355.
Justice of God—See *God*.
Justification — See *Faith, Justification by*.

KINDNESS — See *Brotherly Love*.
Kingdom of Christ, 1058-1141.
 Prayer for, 838, 1058, 1060, 1064, 1067-1078, 1112, 1118.
 Progress of, 1079-1081, 1085-1088, 1098, 1099, 1113, 1115, 1121, 1131-1134.

LABOR—See *Activity,* and *Christian Work*.
Lamb of God —See *Christ*.
Land of Peace, 443.
Latter Day, 1107, 1111, 1117, 1126, 1133.
Law of God, 386, 393-400.
 And Gospel, 234, 249, 342.
 Conviction under — See *Penitence*.
Liberality—See *Charity*.
Life and Death, 462, 1264-1336.
Life:
 Brevity of, 727, 1250, 1251, 1261, 1268, 1269, 1270, 1288, 1306, 1375.
 Object of, 411, 462, 631, 633, 1306, 1353.
 Solemnity of, 631, 1268, 1275, 1345, 1353.

INDEX OF SUBJECTS.

Life:
　Uncertainty of, 1242, 1267, 1268, 1272, 1345, 1412.
　Vanity of, 1265, 1269, 1272.
Light of the World — See *Christ*.
Likeness to Christ—See *Conformity*.
Litany, 500, 675, 791.
Little Things, 1041, 1183, 1192, 1199.
Little Travelers, 1184.
Longing:
　For Christ, 468, 490, 559, 589, 689, 732, 733, 736, 755, 757, 758, 771.
　For God, 493, 703, 704-706, 734, 749, 811, 817.
　For Heaven, 658, 659, 717-719, 725-727, 730-733, 1019, 1285-1288, 1314, 1315, 1361.
　For Holiness, 741-743, 745, 746.
Long Suffering — See *God, Forbearance of*.
Looking to Jesus, 337, 615, 728, 729.
Lord's Day, and Worship, 931-1031.
　Delight in, 932, 935-937, 939, 942, 949-952, 960, 961, 966-969, 974-978, 983, 987,1003,1004,1011, 1012, 1017.
　Evening, 1007, 1008, 1013, 1018, 1020, 1021, 1024, 1026, 1029-1031.
　Morning, 272, 940, 941, 944-948, 953-959, 971, 972-978, 994, 1227.
　Welcomed, 931-934, 938, 970, 995—See also *Invocation*, and *Close of Service*.
Lord's Prayer, 1170.
Lord's Supper, 881-910.
Lord our Righteousness, 711.
Loss, of all Things—See *Renouncing all for Christ*.
　Of the Soul—See *Future Punishment*.
Lost State of Man—See *Depravity*.
Love of Christ—See *Christ*.
　Of God—See *God*.
　Of Holy Spirit, 347, 348, 354, 355, 357, 360, 367, 368.

Love to Christ, 545, 547, 548, 560, 563, 570, 577, 593-598.
　To God, 358, 543, 547, 566, 738-740, 754.
　To Saints—See *Brotherly Love*.
　To the Church, 829, 835, 878, 882.
Love, Joy, Trust, 530-535.
Loving-kindness, 575, 576.
Lukewarmness, 359.

MAJESTY of Christ — See *Christ*.
　Of God—See *God*.
Man, Fallen—See *Depravity*.
Mariners—See *Sailors*.
Martyrs, 613, 649, 920, 1365-1368, 1404.
Mediator—See *Christ*.
Mediatorial Reign — See *Kingdom of Christ*.
Meditation, 399, 478, 580, 810, 814, 942, 1231, 1232, 1279.
Meekness, 198, 200, 206, 208, 624, 1185.
Mercifulness, 1041, 1044, 1056.
Mercy:
　Free, 520.
　Of God—See *God*.
　Seat, 268, 269, 455, 576, 764, 937, 1000, 1002.
　Sought, 452, 454-458, 461, 463, 465, 470, 471, 481, 482, 487, 488, 491, 492.
Message of the Gospel—See *Gospel*.
Messiah, 154, 1139.
Millenium—See *Latter Day*.
Ministry, 843-860.
　Commission of, 843, 851-854, 857.
　Christ's Call to, 860.
　Convocation of, 845, 851, 854, 1114.
　Installation of—See *Pastor*.
　Ordination of, 847, 856, 859.
　Prayer for, 844, 845, 855.
Ministry of Christ—See *Christ*.
Miracles—See *Christ, Miracles of*.
Miracle of Grace, 533.
Mission of Christ—See *Christ*.
Missions, 1114, 1119, 1121, 1138.
Missionaries, 856, 1073, 1083, 1097, 1100, 1104, 1105, 1120.

Missionary Hymn, 1119.
　Meeting, 1114.
　Work, Calls to, 1084, 1089-1092.
Morning, 1197-1209, 1215, 1245, 1247.
　Of Lord's Day--See *Lord's Day*.
Mortality — See *Death* and *Life*.
Mountains, Three, 249.
Mystery of God's Abode, 19.
　Of Providence — See *God, Mysterious*.

NATIONAL, 1150, 1152, 1157-1160, 1163-1166.
Nativity of Christ — See *Christ, Birth of*.
Nature:
　Beauties of, 39, 40, 63, 66, 67, 112, 129, 406.
　God seen in, 39, 40, 51, 53, 63, 66, 67, 112, 129, 133, 398, 403, 406, 1252.
Nearness to God, 64, 684, 734, 1029.
　To Heaven, 719, 727, 1264, 1288, 1334, 1378, 1412.
Need of God, 1238.
　Of Salvation—See *Atonement, Necessary*.
Needful, one Thing, 422.
New Birth — See *Regeneration*.
New Jerusalem, 1359, 1370, 1372, 1377, 1378, 1410.
New Song—See *Song, New*.
New Year, 1256-1259.
New Year's Eve, 1263.
Now, 425, 439—See *Day of Grace*.

OBEDIENCE:
　Of Christ—See *Christ*.
　Of the Christian, 58, 521, 619, 749, 889, 946, 1057, 1201.
Offers of Grace—See *Pardon, Offered*.
Offices of Christ—See *Christ*.
Old Age, 1295, 1296.
Omnipotence—See *God*.
Omnipresence—See *God*.
Omniscience—See *God*.
Oneness with Christ, 597, 760.
Onward, 611, 638, 639, 640, 644, 648, 659, 671, 1387.

INDEX OF SUBJECTS.

Opening of Service—See *Invocation*.
Ordinances — See *Baptism*, and *Lord's Supper*.
Ordination—See *Ministry*.
Original Sin—See *Depravity*.
Out of the Depths, 695.

PANOPLY, 628.
Paradise, 1415.
Pardon Found, 256, 510, 511, 516, 517-524, 527, 529, 531, 533-539, 554-558, 575, 578, 579, 599-610, 711, 737.
  Offered, 237, 253, 408-450, 472, 497, 587, 879, 946.
  Sought, 369, 451-493, 522, 525, 675, 690, 707, 979, 1345, 1346.
Parting—See *Close of Service*.
Passover, 265, 310, 899.
Pastor, Death of, 1329, 1331.
  Installation of, 844, 847, 849-851, 857-859, 1067.
  Prayed for, 844.
  Sought, 846.
  Welcomed, 848, 851.
Patience, 116, 123.
Peace, Christian, 124, 284, 520, 635, 744, 781, 1035, 1036.
  For the Troubled, 409, 435, 437, 443.
  Of God, 781, 943.
  National, 1150, 1152, 1160, 1163, 1164, 1166.
Peace-Makers, 914, 924.
Pearl of Great Price, 527, 700.
Penitence, 451-493 → See *Pardon Sought*.
Pentecost, 341, 342, 371.
Peril, 1142.
Perseverance, 543, 641-656, 731, 759, 787.
Pestilence, 1237, 1241.
Pilgrim Band, 911.
Pilgrim Church, 839.
Pilgrim Fathers, 1162, 1165.
Pilgrim's Prayer, 662, 663, 668, 669, 670.
Pilgrim's Song, 585, 726, 1218, 1264, 1266.
Pilgrim-Spirit, 585, 691, 719, 725, 728, 729, 1218, 1264, 1299.
Pilgrimage, 658-670, 713, 921, 1218, 1260, 1264, 1266, 1330.

Pity of God—See *God, Compassion of*.
Sought, 783.
To the Poor, 1043-1046.
Pleading with Jesus, 452, 457, 517, 518, 598.
Pleasures, Worldly—See *Renouncing all for Christ*.
Poor, Care for, 1043, 1046, 1056.
Praise, 23, 30, 35, 50, 51, 52, 68, 69, 70, 97, 111, 952, 980, 1023.
Calls to, 1, 53, 57-59, 72, 79, 80, 83, 103, 607, 1251.
For Creation, 28.
  " Deliverance, 142, 537.
  " Divine Goodness, and Truth, 4, 52, 537.
  " Pardoning Grace, 535, 540, 982.
  " Redemption, 28, 167.
  " Salvation, 9.
To Christ, 151, 152, 156, 168, 169, 207, 214, 218, 219, 252, 271, 292, 293, 306-338, 528, 552, 553, 557-592, 608, 609, 899, 1186.
  " God, 1, 4, 5, 11, 13, 15, 24, 25, 26, 33, 39-43, 71, 97, 387, 818, 1256, 1386.
  " the Creator, 112, 133.
  " " Father, 24, 55, 77, 125.
  " " Son, 149, 196.
  " " Spirit, 344, 362-364, 368, 383.
  " " nity—See *Trinity*.
Prayer, 807-825 — See also *Family Worship*.
Encouragements to, 823, 825, 879.
Hour of, 813, 821, 1212, 1219, 1231.
Importunity in, 525, 822, 825, 981.
Lord's, 1170.
Nature of, 807, 808.
Power of, 812, 816, 979.
For Baptized Children, 865-871.
  " Comfort, 792, 1282.
  " Deliverance, 683, 790, 800.

Prayer
For Extension of Christ's Kingdom—See *Kingdom of Christ*.
  " Guidance, 18, 662-665, 668, 669, 770, 795, 806, 1191.
  " Perfect Peace, 696, 761-764, 789, 824, 892.
  " Revival—See *Revival*.
  " Union, 912.
To Christ, 201, 203, 211, 238, 240, 243, 494, 500, 567, 568, 620, 793, 850, 956-959, 979, 1029, 1171, 1173, 1175, 1181, 1187, 1191, 1193, 1202, 1208, 1220, 1241, 1242.
  " the Holy Spirit, 343, 345-347, 352, 365, 366, 369, 370, 374, 378, 849.
  " " Trinity, 2, 3, 18, 29, 31, 954, 1249.
Preaching—See *Ministry*.
Preciousness of Christ—See *Christ*.
Predestination—See *God, Decrees of*.
Pride—See *Humility*.
Priesthood of Christ — See *Christ*.
Prince of Peace—See *Christ*.
Probation—See *Day of Grace*.
Procrastination—See *Decay*.
Prodigal's Welcome, 498.
Profession, 785, 863, 864, 872-880.
Progress, Christian — See *Growth in Grace*.
Of Christ's Kingdom—See *Kingdom of Christ*.
Promised Land, 1264, 1313, 1376, 1402, 1405, 1415.
Promises, 42, 709.
Prophecy, 332, 404.
Providence—See *God, Providence of*.
Punishment, Future — See *Future Punishment*.
Pure in Heart, 741, 756.
Purposes of God—See *God, Decrees of*.

RACE, CHRISTIAN, 648-657.
Ransom — See *Christ, Ransom*.

25

INDEX OF SUBJECTS.

Reconciliation—See *Pardon Found.*
Redeeming Love—See *Christ, Love of.*
Redemption — See *Atonement.*
Refuge—See *Christ,* and *God.*
Regeneration:
  Necessary, 353, 359, 363, 376, 378, 467, 523.
  Prayed for, 343, 346, 347, 349, 350, 354, 356, 357, 359, 363, 364, 366, 369, 370, 374, 376, 378, 741, 849.
  Wrought by God, 344, 348, 352, 355, 358, 360, 363, 380, 385.
Rejoicing in God—See *Joy of the Believer.*
Remembrance of Christ — See *Commemoration.*
Renewed Consecration, 684–690.
Renouncing all for Christ, 199, 422, 486, 510, 529, 538, 558, 610, 614, 878, 889, 1409.
Repentance—See *Penitence.*
Resignation, 124, 125, 126, 761–763, 767–772, 776, 798, 799, 1221.
Resolves — See *Renouncing all for Christ.*
Rest for the Weary — See *Weary, Rest for.*
Rest of Heaven—See *Heaven.*
Resurrection:
  Of Christ—See *Christ.*
  Of Believers, 1285, 1308, 1310, 1318, 1319, 1321, 1324–1327, 1333, 1335, 1338, 1360, 1400.
Retirement, 478, 810, 814, 815, 1231, 1232.
Return to God, 431, 471, 473, 498, 530—See also *Pardon Sought.*
Revelation, 3, 192, 386–407, 1085, 1227.
Revival:
  Hoping for, 351, 1063, 1098.
  Prayer for, 346, 351, 912, 1062, 1066, 1135.
  Thanksgiving for, 1136.
Riches, 245, 486, 726.
Righteousness of Christ — See *Christ.*

Rock of Ages—See *Christ.*
Royal Priesthood—See *Christ, Priest.*
SABBATH—See *Lord's Day.*
Sacraments — See *Baptism,* and *Lord's Supper.*
Sacrifice, Vicarious — See *Atonement.*
Safety in God, 1237.
Safety of Believers, 765.
Sailors, 1142–1148.
Saints:
  Blessedness of, 832, 1365–1369.
  Communion of—See *Communion.*
  Death of—See *Death.*
  Glorified, 730, 731, 733, 919, 920, 921, 928—See also *Heaven.*
  Holiness of, 621, 744.
  Security of, 765.
  Union of, with Christ, 720–722, 760, 928–930.
  Union of, with Each Other, 912–918, 922, 923, 924, 925, 928.
Salvation — See *Atonement,* and *Free Salvation.*
Sanctification — See *Growth in Grace.*
Sanctuary:
  Corner-Stone Laid, 1032.
  Dedication of, 1002, 1033–1037.
  Love for, 931–1004, 1011, 1012, 1017.
Saviour—See *Christ.*
Scriptures, Holy—See *Bible.*
Seamen—See *Sailors.*
Seasons, 66, 1153–1156, 1167, 1250–1263.
Second Birth—See *Regeneration.*
Second Death—See *Future Punishment.*
Security of Saints—See *Saints.*
Seeking God, 86.
Seed Time and Harvest, 1255—See *Seasons.*
Self-Deception, 678, 688, 690.
Dedication—See *Consecration.*
Denial, 245, 486, 622, 624, 625, 885, 889.
Renunciation — See *Renouncing all for Christ.*

Shepherd — See *Christ,* and *God.*
Showers of Grace, 487.
Sickness, 1214, 1279–1281.
Sin:
  Confession of, 451–493 — See *Pardon Sought.*
  Hatred of, 744–746.
  Original, 467, 496, 661, 1062.
Sinai, 249, 523.
Sinners Invited and Warned — See *Pardon Offered.*
  Penitent — See *Pardon Sought.*
Slavery, 1094, 1097, 1105, 1122.
Sleep, 1197, 1199, 1200, 1204, 1205, 1210, 1211, 1222–1230, 1234, 1237–1239, 1241, 1244, 1249.
Soldiers, Christian, 586, 625, 628, 640, 643, 644, 875, 1096.
Soul of Man—See *Immortality.*
Son of God—See *Christ.*
Song of Moses and the Lamb, 606.
Song, New, 330, 573, 1366.
Song of the Angels, 158–164, 166, 170, 176, 185, 194, 195.
Sorrow—See *Afflictions.*
  For Sin—See *Penitence.*
Sorrowing Comforted — See *Comfort.*
Sovereignty of God—See *God, Sovereign.*
Sowing and Reaping, 602, 853, 857, 1048, 1054, 1091, 1383.
Speak Gently, 1182.
Spirit—See *Holy Spirit.*
Spring—See *Seasons.*
Star of Bethlehem, 169, 186, 187.
Star of the East, 174, 175, 183, 190, 192, 193.
Starry Heavens, 406.
Steadfastness—See *Perseverance.*
Still with Thee, 1213, 1226.
Storms, 56, 109, 113, 128, 138, 143.
Strength as our Days, 680, 762.
Submission—See *Afflictions,* and *Resignation.*

Index of Subjects.

Substitution — See *Atonement*.
Sufficiency of Christ — See *Christ*.
Sufferings of Christ — See *Christ*.
Suffering with Christ — See *Martyrs*.
Summer—See *Seasons*.
Sun of Righteousness — See *Christ*.
Supper, Lord's, 881-910.
Supremacy of God—See *God*.
Surety—See *Christ*.
Surrender, 241, 509, 510, 522, 538, 541.
"Sweet Will of God," 126.
Sweet Subjection, 512.
Sympathy of Christ — See *Christ*.
 Christian — See *Brotherly Love*.

TABLE, LORD'S—See *Lord's Supper*.
Tabor, 249.
Teacher, the Great — See *Christ*.
Te Deum Laudamus, 5, 11, 24.
Temptation, 800—See *Christians, Conflicts of*.
Thankfulness, 100, 1205, 1256.
Thanksgiving, 57, 1149-1159, 1162, 1167.
Throne of Grace, 761, 809, 823.
Thy Kingdom Come, 1058-1141.
Thy Will be Done, 1221.
Time — See *Death, Life, Year*.
Times and Seasons, 1250-1263.
Titles of Christ—See *Christ, Names of*.
To-Day, 414, 425, 439, 450, 946.
To-Morrow, 450, 1267.
Transfiguration, 213.
Trials—See *Afflictions*.
Tribulation—See *Afflictions*.
Trinity :
 Adoration of, 6, 7, 10, 12, 32, 1416.
 Invocation of, 2, 3.
 Praise to, 2, 9, 10, 14, 16, 17, 20, 22, 28, 30, 34, 36, 37, 38.

Trinity :
 Worship of, 8, 16, 27, 29, 954.
 Prayer to—See *Prayer*.
Triumphal Entry, 217-219.
Trust in Christ, 276, 288, 289, 319, 530, 591, 697-712, 747, 750, 759, 760, 794.
 In God, 44, 122, 124, 125, 127, 634, 635, 674, 779, 797, 803-806.
 In Providence, 775, 779-790, 1297.
Truth of God—See *God*.
Trumpet, Gospel, 417, 418, 438, 446.
Judgment, 1338-1341, 1346-1350, 1352-1354, 1360, 1362.

UNSEEN BUT LOVED, 530.
Unchangeableness of God—See *God*.
Union of Saints—See *Saints*.
Unsearchableness of God—See *God*.

VANITY OF LIFE—See *Life*.
Victory of Believers, 1388—See *Warfare*.
 Of Christ — See *Christ, Conqueror*.
Vows to God, 626, 785, 864, 872-874, 880.

WAITING ON GOD, 751, 1050.
Walking with God, 684.
Wanderer—See *Backsliding*.
Wanderer Invited, 431, 472.
 Restored, 456, 539, 690.
Warfare, Christian, 586, 625-654.
Warnings, 411, 413, 414, 416, 421-426, 428.
Watchfulness, 614, 630, 631, 632, 653, 751, 854, 894, 1343, 1345, 1353.
Watching and Praying, 751, 819, 894.
Watchmen, 174, 851, 852, 854, 859.
Waters of Life—See *Fountain*.
Way of Salvation—See *Free Salvation*, and *Atonement*.
Way to God, 554, 585.
Way to Zion, 627.
Way, Truth, and Life—See *Christ*.

Wealth—See *Riches*.
Use of—See *Charity*.
Weary, Rest for the, 432, 436, 437, 472, 476, 599, 1408, 1409, 1414.
Welcome to the, 415, 419, 429.
Wedding Hymn, 1168.
Weeping, 459, 602, 857, 1091, 1383.
Winter—See *Seasons*.
Wisdom — See *God*, and *Christ*.
Witness—See *Holy Spirit*.
Witnesses, Cloud of, 644, 648.
Word of God—See *Bible*.
Works of God—See *God*.
Working in the Vineyard, 1192.
Working and Giving, 1038-1057.
World Renounced—See *Renouncing all for Christ*.
Worship, 8.
 Call to, 46, 58, 181.
 Cheerful, 47.
 Delight in, 107, 149, 942—See also *Lord's Day*.
 Family—See *Family Worship*.
 Public—See *Lord's Day*.
 Universal, 986.
"Worthy the Lamb," 292, 293.
Wrath of God—See *Future Punishment*.

YEAR :
 Beginning—See *New Year*.
 Close, 1262, 1263.
 Of Jubilee, 417, 418, 1113, 1134, 1140, 1141.
Yielding to Christ, 451-512, 522, 538, 539, 541, 767, 768, 770, 771, 874, 880.
Yoke of Christ, 429, 512.

ZEAL, 590, 592, 593, 611, 625, 626, 631, 648, 651, 655, 920.
Zion—See also *Church*.
 City of God, 831, 836.
 Enlarged, 1099, 1102, 1103, 1137.
 Favored Hour of, 1068.
 Highway to, 627.
 Prayer for, 1058.
 Rejoicing, 1065, 1126-1129.
 Restored, 1109, 1116.
 Secure, 834.

Index of First Lines.

	HYMN		HYMN
A BROKEN heart, my God, my King.	480	Arm these Thy soldiers, mighty Lord	875
A charge to keep I have	631	Around the throne of God in heaven.	1194
A few more years shall roll	1266	Art thou weary, art thou languid	436
A little child the Saviour came	866	As Jesus died, and rose again	1323
A pilgrim through this lonely world..	199	As pants the hart for cooling streams.	687
A safe stronghold our God is still	842	As thy day, thy strength shall be	680
Abide with me: fast falls the eventide	1024	As when the weary traveller gains	719
According to Thy gracious word	905	As with gladness men of old	190
Again the Lord of life and light	971	Ascend Thy throne, almighty King..	1118
Ah, what avails my strife	509	Ask ye what great thing I know	578
Alas, and did my Saviour bleed	230	Asleep in Jesus: blessed sleep	1292
All hail, incarnate God	1087	Assembled at Thy great command...	1114
All hail the power of Jesus' name	329	At even, ere the sun was set	1214
All is dying; hearts are breaking	1306	At the door of mercy sighing	519
All is o'er, the pain, the sorrow	259	At the Lamb's high feast we sing	899
All my heart this night rejoices	163	At Thy command, our dearest Lord..	885
All people that on earth do dwell	46	Awake, and sing the song	606
All praise to Thee, eternal Lord	184	Awake, awake, O Zion	1133
All praise to Thee, my God, this night	1222	Awake, my soul, and with the sun...	1197
All that I was, my sin and guilt	601	Awake, my soul, in joyful lays	575
All things are ready, Come	441	Awake, my soul, lift up thine eyes....	653
All ye Gentiles, praise the Lord	72	Awake, my soul, stretch every nerve..	648
Almighty Father of mankind	1297	Awake, our drowsy souls	948
Almighty God of love	1073	Awake, our souls, away our fears	655
Almighty God, to-night	1229	Awake, ye saints, and raise your eyes.	1251
Always with us, always with us	667	Awaked by Sinai's awful sound	523
Am I a soldier of the cross	625	Awhile in spirit, Lord, to Thee	201
Amazing grace, how sweet the sound.	600		
Amplest grace in Thee I find	191	BE joyful in God, all ye lands of the..	841
And can I yet delay	510	Be Thou, O God, exalted high	134
And is the time approaching	930	Before Jehovah's awful throne	48
And is there, Lord, a rest	1414	Behold, a stranger's at the door	428
And let this feeble body fail	1371	Behold, the blind their sight receive..	202
And must I part with all I have	486	Behold, the Bridegroom cometh	1343
And must this body die	1271	Behold, the day is come	1355
And will the Judge descend	1354	Behold the glories of the Lamb	326
Angels, from the realms of glory	181	Behold the man! How glorious He...	221
Angels rejoiced and sweetly sung	195	Behold, the morning sun	1227
Angels, roll the rock away	263	Behold, the Mountain of the Lord	1107
Another six days' work is done	940	Behold the Saviour of mankind	231
Another year, another year	1258	Behold, the shade of night	1215
Approach, my soul, the mercy-seat...	455	Behold, the throne of grace	823
Arise, my soul, arise	513	Behold, the western evening light!....	1284
Arise, my tenderest thoughts, arise...	1061	Behold, what wondrous grace	723
Arise, O King of grace, arise	1036	Behold, where, in the Friend of man.	198
Arm of the Lord, awake	1069	Beneath our feet and o'er our head...	1272

INDEX OF FIRST LINES.

First Line	Hymn
Bethlehem, of noblest cities	169
Beyond the glittering starry skies	295
Bless God, my soul; Thou, Lord, alone	136
Bless, O my soul, the living God	97
Blessed Fountain, full of grace	550
Blessed Jesus, ere we part	551
Blessed Saviour, Thee I love	590
Blest are the pure in heart	756
Blest are the sons of peace	1169
Blest be the dear, uniting love	918
Blest be the Father, and His love	20
Blest be the tie that binds	925
Blest be Thy love, dear Lord	507
Blest Comforter Divine	354
Blest day of God, most calm	966
Blest hour, when mortal man retires	813
Blest inhabitants of Zion	832
Blest is the man, whose spirit shares	1043
Blest morning, whose young dawning	973
Blest Trinity, from mortal sight	10
Blow ye the trumpet, blow	417
Bread of heaven, on Thee I feed	898
Bread of the world, in mercy broken	893
Breast the wave, Christian	671
Brethren, while we sojourn here	646
Brief life is here our portion	1375
Bright and joyful is the morn	171
Bright King of glory, dreadful God	151
Bright was the guiding star that led	192
Brightest and best of the sons of the	183
Brightness of the Father's glory	168
Brother, now thy toils are o'er	1308
Brother, though from yonder sky	1307
By cool Siloam's shady rill	1176
By faith I view my Saviour dying	520
Call Jehovah thy salvation	1237
Calm me, my God, and keep me calm	763
Calm on the listening ear of night	159
Calmer of the troubled heart	1006
Cast thy bread upon the waters	1054
Cast thy burden on the Lord	794
Cheer up, desponding soul	772
Child of sin and sorrow	450
Children of light, arise and shine	337
Children of the Heavenly King	585
Chosen not for good in me	682
Christ and His cross are all our theme	858
Christ, by heavenly hosts adored	1156
Christ for the world we sing	1086
Christ is made the sure foundation	833
Christ is our Corner-stone	828
Christ, of all my hopes the ground	549
Christ, the Lord, is risen again	265
Christ, the Lord, is risen to-day, Our	264
Christ, the Lord, is risen to-day, Sons	260
Christ to heaven is gone before	333
Christ, whose glory fills the skies	958
Cling to the mighty One	674
Come, all ye saints of God	293
Come at the morning hour	821
Come, blessed Spirit, Source of light	364
Come, dearest Lord, descend and dwell	990
Come, divine Emmanuel, come	1135
Come, every pious heart	180
Come, happy souls, approach your	449
Come hither, all ye weary souls	429
Come, Holy Ghost, all-quickening fire	379
Come, Holy Ghost, in love	374
Come, Holy Ghost, our souls inspire	380
Come, Holy Spirit, calm my mind	365
Come, Holy Spirit, come, Let Thy	352
Come, Holy Spirit, come, With energy	350
Come, Holy Spirit, heavenly Dove	366
Come, Holy Spirit, heavenly Dove, With	359
Come, humble sinner, in whose breast	484
Come in, thou blessed of the Lord	876
Come, kingdom of our God	838
Come, let our voices join to raise	946
Come, let us anew	1259
Come, let us anew	1260
Come, let us join in songs of praise	324
Come, let us join our cheerful songs	330
Come, let us join our friends above	916
Come, let us lift our joyful eyes	322
Come, let us sing the song of songs	573
Come, let us to the Lord, our God	685
Come, Lord, and tarry not	1358
Come, my Redeemer, come	494
Come, my soul, thy suit prepare	979
Come, O Creator Spirit blest	362
Come, O my soul, in sacred lays	112
Come, O promised Comforter	375
Come on, my partners in distress	638
Come, sacred Spirit, from above	849
Come, said Jesus' sacred voice	415
Come see the place where Jesus lay	336
Come, see the place where Jesus lies	257
Come, sinners, to the gospel feast	426
Come, sound His praise abroad	58

INDEX OF FIRST LINES.

	HYMN.		HYMN.
Come, take His offers now............	529	Dread Sovereign, let my evening song.	1255
Come, Thou almighty King..........	2		
Come, Thou everlasting Spirit.......	345	EARLY, my God, without delay......	977
Come, thou Fount of every blessing..	536	Earth has engrossed my love too long.	1407
Come, Thou long-expected Jesus.....	165	Earth has nothing sweet or fair.......	580
Come, Thou soul-transforming Spirit.	965	Earth, with its dark and dreadful ills..	1278
Come to Calvary's holy mountain....	253	Earthly joys no longer please us......	614
Come to the land of peace...........	443	Enthroned on high, Almighty Lord..	360
Come unto me, when shadows darkly.	437	Ere another Sabbath's close..........	1007
Come, we that love the Lord.........	607	Ere earth's foundations yet were laid..	705
Come, weary souls, with sin distrest..	432	Ere God had built the mountains.....	148
Come, ye disconsolate, where'er ye...	434	Ere the blue heavens were stretched..	150
Come, ye faithful, raise the anthem..	308	Ere the waning light decay..........	1244
Come, ye sinners, poor and wretched.	419	Eternal Father, strong to save.......	1142
Come, ye sinners, to your Lord......	433	Eternal Father, Thou hast said......	1113
Come, ye thankful people, come.....	1155	Eternal Father, when to Thee.......	7
Come, ye weary sinners, come.......	472	Eternal Source of every joy.........	1256
Commit thou all thy griefs..........	775	Eternal Spirit, Source of light.......	381
Compared with Christ, in all beside..	566	Eternal Spirit, Source of truth.......	361
Creator Spirit, by whose aid.........	384	Eternal Spirit, we confess...........	363
Cross, reproach, and tribulation.....	613	Eternal Wisdom, Thee we praise.....	129
Crown Him with many crowns......	296	Ever would I fain be reading........	390
		Every morning mercies new..........	1245
DAILY, daily sing the praises........	1390	Exalt the Lord our God.............	61
Daughter of Zion, awake from thy...	1127		
Daughter of Zion, from the dust.....	1108	FADE, fade, each earthly joy........	735
Day divine, when sudden streaming...	348	Fading, still fading, the last beam is..	1026
Day of judgment, day of wonders....	1341	Faint not, Christian, though the road.	645
Day of wrath, O day of mourning...	1349	Fair shines the morning star.........	418
Days and moments quickly flying....	1243	Fairest Lord Jesus..................	582
Dayspring of eternity................	1027	Faith, hope, and charity, these three.	1040
Dear as Thou wert, and justly dear...	1283	Far as Thy name is known..........	836
Dear Friend, whose presence in the..	1173	Far down the ages now..............	839
Dear is the hallowed morn to me.....	945	Far from my heavenly home........	725
Dear Jesus, ever at my side..........	1181	Far from my thoughts, vain world...	942
Dear Lord and Master mine.........	512	Far from the world, O Lord, I flee...	810
Dear Refuge of my weary soul.......	763	Far from these narrow scenes of night	1313
Dear Saviour, I am Thine...........	720	Fastened within the veil.............	692
Dear Saviour, if these lambs should..	867	Father, at Thy footstool see.........	31
Dearest of all the names above......	321	Father, by Thy love and power......	1249
Death may dissolve my body now....	1277	Father, I know that all my life......	806
Deathless spirit, now arise...........	1317	Father, in these reveal Thy Son.....	868
Depth of mercy, can there be........	471	Father of heaven, whose love profound	8
Descend from heaven, Immortal Dove	1397	Father of love, our Guide and Friend.	779
Did Christ o'er sinners weep.........	459	Father of mercies, bow Thine ear....	844
Dismiss us with Thy blessing, Lord...	1015	Father of mercies, God of love.......	91
Do not I love Thee, O my Lord......	593	Father of mercies, in Thy house.....	847
Does the Gospel word proclaim......	476	Father of mercies, in Thy word......	396
Done is the work that saves.........	269	Father, Son, and Holy Ghost........	36
Draw near, O Holy Dove, draw near..	891	Father, Thine Elect who lovest......	17

INDEX OF FIRST LINES.

	HYMN.		HYMN.
Father, Thy will, not mine be done..	636	Go to dark Gethsemane............	226
Father, whate'er of earthly bliss.....	761	Go to the grave in all thy glorious....	1329
Father, who didst fashion me........	29	Go, worship at Immanuel's feet......	189
Fear not, O little flock..............	634	Go, ye messengers of God..........	1097
Fear not, poor, weary one...........	805	God bless our native land..........	1166
Fierce was the wild billow...........	673	God calling yet! shall I not hear.....	477
Fight the good fight with all Thy....	652	God eternal, Lord of all............	11
Fling our the banner; let it float.....	1101	God in His earthly temple lays......	985
For all the saints, who from their.....	928	God, in the Gospel of His Son.......	405
For all Thy saints, O Lord..........	926	God is in His holy temple...........	964
For ever with the Lord..............	1334	God is love; His mercy brightens....	54
For me vouchsafed the unspotted.....	228	God is the name my soul adores......	21
For thee, O dear, dear Country......	1376	God is the refuge of His saints.......	121
For Thy mercy and Thy grace.......	1263	God moves in a mysterious way......	116
Forth from the dark and stormy sky..	991	God, my supporter and my hope.....	748
Forth in Thy Name, O Lord, I go...	1201	God of mercy, God of grace.........	956
Forth to the Land of promise bound.	921	God of my childhood, and my youth.	1295
Forward! be our watchword.........	639	God of my life, through all its days...	111
Fount of everlasting love............	1136	God of my life, to Thee I call........	706
Fountain of grace, rich, full, and free.	702	God of that glorious gift of grace....	865
Fountain of mercy, God of love.....	1255	God of the morning, at whose voice..	1198
Frequent the day of God returns.....	1016	God of the sun-light hours, how sad..	1018
Friend after friend departs...........	1311	God, that madest earth and heaven..	1217
From all that dwell below the skies...	50	God, the All-Terrible, Thou who.....	1163
From Calvary a cry was heard.......	247	Good news from heaven the angels...	188
From Egypt lately come............	658	Grace, like an uncorrupted seed......	749
From every stormy wind that blows..	1000	Grace, 'tis a charming sound........	604
From foes that would the land devour.	1164	Gracious Redeemer, shake..........	632
From Greenland's icy mountains.....	1119	Gracious Spirit, Dove Divine........	369
From the cross the blood is falling...	251	Gracious Spirit, dwell with me.......	373
From the cross uplifted high.........	408	Gracious Spirit, Holy Ghost.........	377
From the vast and veiled throng.....	13	Granted is the Saviour's prayer......	372
From Thee, my God, my joys shall...	1384	Great Creator, who this day.........	954
GENTLY, Lord, O gently lead us.....	665	Great Father of each perfect gift.....	356
Gently, my Saviour, let me down....	1294	Great God, attend while Zion sings...	984
Gird on Thy conquering sword.......	1088	Great God, how infinite art Thou....	76
Give me the wings of faith, to rise...	919	Great God, indulge my humble claim.	1010
Give thanks to God; He reigns above	139	Great God, the nations of the earth..	1076
Give to our God immortal praise.....	105	Great God, to Thee my evening song.	1224
Give to the Lord, ye sons of fame....	138	Great God, we sing that mighty hand	1257
Give to the winds thy fears..........	803	Great God, what do I see and hear...	1347
Give us room, that we may dwell.....	1099	Great God, who hid from mortal sight	999
Glorious things of Thee are spoken..	831	Great God, whose universal sway.....	1112
Glory be to God on high............	71	Great is the Lord our God..........	837
Glory be to God the Father.........	16	Great Ruler of all nature's frame.....	143
Glory, glory everlasting.............	306	Great Shepherd of Thine Israel......	1066
Glory to God on high, Let praises....	292	Guide me, O Thou great Jehovah....	662
Go forward, Christian soldier........	644		
Go, labor on; spend and be spent....	1039	HAIL, all hail, the joyful morn.......	172
Go, preach My gospel, saith the Lord.	843	Hail, everlasting Spring.............	515

INDEX OF FIRST LINES.

First line	Hymn
Hail, morning known among the blest	941
Hail, my ever blessed Jesus	533
Hail, sacred truth, whose piercing rays	402
Hail, sovereign Love, that first began	555
Hail the day that sees Him rise	286
Hail the joyful day's return	371
Hail the night, all hail the morn	173
Hail, thou bright and sacred morn	955
Hail, Thou God of grace and glory	912
Hail, Thou once despiséd Jesus	310
Hail to the brightness of Zion's glad	1126
Hail to the Lord's Anointed	1122
Hail to the Sabbath day	938
Hail to Thee, our risen King	262
Hail, tranquil hour of closing day	1232
Hallelujah! best and sweetest	1393
Hallelujah! hallelujah!	311
Hallelujah! praise to God	332
Hallelujah, raise, O raise	78
Happy soul, thy days are ended	1304
Happy the man, who knows	1057
Happy the souls to Jesus joined	915
Happy the spirit released from its clay	1388
Hark, a voice divides the sky	1319
Hark, hark, my soul: Angelic songs	1330
Hark, hark, the notes of joy	179
Hark, how the watchmen cry	852
Hark, my soul, it is the Lord	881
Hark, ten thousand harps and voices	307
Hark, the distant isles proclaim	1138
Hark, the glad sound, the Saviour	155
Hark, the herald angels sing	170
Hark, the hosts of heaven are singing	166
Hark, the judgment-trumpet sounding	1339
Hark, the song of jubilee	1141
Hark, the sound of holy voices	1391
Hark, the voice of Jesus calling	1089
Hark, the voice of love and mercy	252
Hark, what celestial sounds	176
Hark, what mean those holy voices	164
Hark, what mean those lamentations	1090
Haste, traveller, haste! the night comes	424
Hasten, Lord, the glorious time	1139
Hasten, Lord, to my release	683
Have mercy, Lord, on me	458
Have mercy on us, God most High	27
He comes in blood-stained garments	1196
He dies, the Friend of sinners dies	283
He is gone! and we remain	287
He leadeth me: O blessed thought	660

First line	Hymn
He lives, the Great Redeemer lives	284
He that goeth forth with weeping	1091
He who on earth as man was known	323
He, who once in righteous vengeance	255
Hear, gracious God, a sinner's cry	482
Hear my prayer, O heavenly Father	1239
Hear what the voice from heaven	1322
Heart-broken, friendless, poor, cast	479
Heart of stone, relent, relent	410
Heavenly Father, to whose eye	795
Heralds of creation, cry	79
Here at Thy table, Lord, we meet	903
Here I can firmly rest	543
High in the heavens, eternal God	
High in yonder realms of light	1367
High let us swell our tuneful notes	194
Holy and reverend is the name	144
Holy Bible, book divine	389
Holy Ghost that, promised, came	383
Holy Ghost, the Infinite	376
Holy Ghost, with light divine	370
Holy, holy, holy Lord, be Thy	70
Holy, holy, holy, Lord God Almighty	1416
Holy, holy, holy, Lord God of Hosts	12
Holy, holy, holy, Lord God of Hosts	14
Holy, holy, holy Lord, God the Father	32
Holy Spirit, from on high	475
Holy Spirit, Lord of light	382
Hope of our hearts, O Lord, appear	1362
Hosanna, raise the pealing hymn	196
Hosanna to our conquering King	331
Hosanna to the living Lord	996
How beauteous are their feet	851
How beauteous on the mountains	1134
How beauteous were the marks divine	206
How blest the righteous, when he dies	1293
How bright these glorious spirits shine	1404
How can I sink with such a prop	747
How calm and beautiful the morn	272
How charming is the place	937
How did my heart rejoice to hear	975
How firm a foundation, ye saints of	709
How gentle God's commands	773
How heavy is the night	605
How large the promise, how divine	862
How lovely are Thy dwellings fair	1017
How oft, alas, this wretched heart	690
How pleasant, how divinely fair	987
How pleased and blest was I	960
How precious is the book divine	397

INDEX OF FIRST LINES.

401

First Line	Hymn
How shall we show our love to Thee..	1049
How shall the young secure their.....	394
How sweet and awful is the place.....	901
How sweet, how heavenly is the sight.	914
How sweet the melting lay...........	820
How sweet the Name of Jesus sounds.	504
How sweet to leave the world awhile..	988
How sweetly flowed the gospel's sound	205
How swift the torrent rolls...........	1270
How tedious and tasteless the hours..	581
How tender is Thy hand.............	774
How vain is all beneath the skies.....	1265
How welcome was the call...........	1168
I BLESS the Christ of God...........	506
I did thee wrong, my God...........	768
I give immortal praise...............	37
I heard the voice of Jesus say........	599
I know no life divided..............	760
I know that my Redeemer lives, And.	319
I know that my Redeemer lives, What	282
I'll praise my Maker with my breath..	4
I long to behold Him arrayed........	733
I love the volumes of Thy word......	386
I love Thy kingdom, Lord...........	835
I love to steal awhile away...........	1231
I love to tell the story..............	1093
I'm a pilgrim, and I'm a stranger....	1218
I'm not ashamed to own my Lord....	623
I need Thee, precious Jesus.........	757
I once was a stranger to grace and to.	711
I say to all men far and near........	274
I see the crowd in Pilate's hall.......	227
I send the joys of earth away........	558
I sing the almighty power of God....	133
I thirst, but not as once I did........	703
I've found the pearl of greatest price.	527
I want a principle within............	746
I was a wandering sheep............	539
I will love Thee, all my treasure......	545
I will praise Thee every day.........	579
I worship Thee, sweet will of God....	126
I would love Thee, God and Father..	547
I would not live alway; I ask not to...	1285
If human kindness meets return.....	904
In all my Lord's appointed ways.....	626
In all my vast concerns with Thee....	94
In Christ I've all my soul's desire.....	574
In evil long I took delight...........	256
In expectation sweet................	1357
In heavenly love abiding............	759
In love, the Father's sinless Child....	216
In prayer together let us fall.........	1161
In sleep's serene oblivion laid........	1204
In stature grows the Heavenly Child..	197
In the Christian's home in glory......	1408
In the cross of Christ I glory.........	612
In the dark and cloudy day..........	792
In the vineyard of our Father........	1192
In Thee I put my steadfast trust.....	782
In this calm, impressive hour........	1247
In Thy name, O Lord, assembling...	962
In time of tribulation...............	641
In us the hope of glory.............	1342
Indulgent Sovereign of the skies.....	1058
Infinite excellence is Thine..........	303
Inspirer and hearer of prayer........	1210
Is this the kind return..............	460
Is this the Son of God..............	541
It came upon the midnight clear.....	158
It is not death to die................	1332
It is Thy hand, my God.............	776
JEHOVAH, God, Thy gracious power..	130
Jehovah reigns; He dwells in light....	108
Jehovah reigns; His throne is high...	106
Jerusalem, my happy home.........	1372
Jerusalem the glorious..............	1378
Jerusalem the golden...............	1377
Jesus, and shall it ever be...........	616
Jesus, be near us when we wake......	1208
Jesus, blessed Mediator.............	1394
Jesus came, the heavens adoring.....	182
Jesus, cast a look on me............	796
Jesus Christ is risen to-day..........	261
Jesus Christ, my Lord and Saviour...	1188
Jesus, full of all compassion.........	492
Jesus, grant me this, I pray.........	883
Jesus, how sweet Thy memory is.....	572
Jesus, I live to Thee................	721
Jesus, I love Thee evermore.........	577
Jesus, I love Thy charming name....	563
Jesus, I my cross have taken........	610
Jesus is the Name we treasure.......	546
Jesus, Lord of Life eternal..........	309
Jesus, Lover of my soul.............	676
Jesus, Master, whose I am..........	592
Jesus, my All, to Heaven is gone.....	554
Jesus, my heart within me burns.....	560
Jesus, my Lord, attend.............	696

INDEX OF FIRST LINES.

First line	Hymn	First line	Hymn
Jesus, my Lord, how rich Thy grace	1045	Let children hear the mighty deeds	1158
Jesus, my Lord, my chief Delight	700	Let every creature join	59
Jesus, my Lord, my God	804	Let every heart exulting beat	214
Jesus, my Lord, my God, my all	568	Let every mortal ear attend	446
Jesus, my Saviour, look on me	1220	Let me go, the day is breaking	1287
Jesus, my Strength, my Hope	751	Let songs of praises fill the sky	344
Jesus, my Truth, my Way	752	Let the world their virtue boast	584
Jesus, Name all names above	491	Let them neglect Thy glory, Lord	28
Jesus, once for sinners slain	900	Let us awake our joys	291
Jesus, one word from Thee	697	Let us sing, with one accord	1186
Jesus, our best beloved Friend	620	Let us, with a gladsome mind	81
Jesus shall reign where'er the sun	1115	Let worldly minds the world pursue	529
Jesus spreads His banner o'er us	907	Let Zion and her sons rejoice	1109
Jesus, still lead on	669	Let Zion's watchmen all awake	859
Jesus, Sun of righteousness	957	Life is a span, a fleeting hour	1300
Jesus, tender Shepherd, hear me	1187	Life is the time to serve the Lord	421
Jesus, the Christ of God	236	Lift up your heads, eternal gates	300
Jesus, the Name high over all	505	Lift up your heads, ye mighty gates	152
Jesus, the sinner's Friend, to Thee	469	Lift your eyes of faith, and see	1369
Jesus, the very thought of Thee	564	Lift your heads, ye friends of Jesus	1131
Jesus, these eyes have never seen	530	Light of the lonely pilgrim's heart	1077
Jesus, Thou art my Righteousness	485	Light of those whose dreary dwelling	346
Jesus, Thou art the sinner's Friend	457	Like Noah's weary dove	444
Jesus, Thou joy of loving hearts	888	Like sheep we went astray	235
Jesus, Thy boundless love to me	571	Little travellers Zion-ward	1184
Jesus, transporting sound	495	Lo, God is here; let us adore	997
Jesus, the Conqueror, reigns	279	Lo, God, our God, has come	177
Jesus, we bow before Thy throne	1117	Lo, He comes, with clouds descending	1340
Jesus, we look to Thee	755	Lo, He cometh: countless trumpets	1338
Jesus, where'er Thy people meet	1002	Lo, I behold the scattering shades	1360
Jesus, who can be	670	Lo, on a narrow neck of land	1345
Join all the glorious names	514	Lo, the prisoner is released	1320
Join, all ye servants of the Lord	387	Lo, what a glorious sight appears	1359
Joy to the world, the Lord is come	156	Look down, O Lord, with pitying eye	1062
Joyful be the hours to-day	982	Look from Thy sphere of endless day	1064
Joyfully, joyfully onward I move	1387	Look, ye saints, the sight is glorious	305
Just as I am, without one plea	496	Lord, as to Thy dear cross we flee	624
Just as Thou art, without one trace	497	Lord, at Thy feet a sinner lies	452
		Lord, dismiss us with Thy blessing	963
KEEP silence, all created things	115	Lord, forever at Thy side	1185
Kingdoms and thrones to God belong	49	Lord God of morning and of night	1205
		Lord God, the Holy Ghost	349
LADEN with guilt, and full of fears	392	Lord God, we worship Thee	1150
Lamb of God, whose bleeding love	892	Lord, I am Thine, entirely Thine	874
Lamp of our feet, whereby we trace	401	Lord, I am vile, conceived in sin	467
Lead, kindly Light, amid th' encircling	668	Lord, I have made Thy word my	393
Lead on, almighty Lord	629	Lord, I hear of showers of blessings	487
Lead us, heavenly Father, lead us	18	Lord, I know Thy grace is nigh me	518
Let all the heathen writers join	400	Lord, I was blind! I could not see	556
Let all the just, to God with joy	114	Lord, in the morning Thou shalt hear	972

INDEX OF FIRST LINES.

	HYMN.		HYMN.
Lord, in this Thy mercy's day	224	My country, 'tis of thee	1165
Lord, in Thy Name Thy servants	1253	My days are gliding swiftly by	1264
Lord, it belongs not to my care	1276	My dear Redeemer, and my Lord	200
Lord Jesus, are we one with Thee	597	My faith looks up to Thee	728
Lord Jesus, by Thy passion	758	My former hopes are fled	464
Lord Jesus, when we stand afar	243	My God and Father, while I stray	1221
Lord, lead the way the Saviour went	1046	My God, how endless is Thy love	1200
Lord, let me know mine end	1269	My God, how wonderful Thou art	77
Lord, now we part in Thy blest name	1014	My God, I love Thee; not because	596
Lord of all being; throned afar	64	My God, in whom are all the springs	52
Lord of all power and might	1085	My God, is any hour so sweet	1219
Lord of glory, who hast bought us	1052	My God, my everlasting hope	1296
Lord of hosts, how bright, how fair	983	My God, my Father, blissful name	125
Lord of hosts, to Thee we raise	1035	My God, my King, Thy various praise	102
Lord of mercy and of might	793	My God, my Life, my Love	754
Lord of the harvest, hear	855	My God, my Portion, and my Love	740
Lord of the Sabbath, hear our vows	1012	My God, my reconciled God	358
Lord of the worlds above	950	My God, permit me not to be	814
Lord, Thou art my Rock of strength	679	My God, permit my tongue	86
Lord, Thou hast searched and seen me	95	My God, the covenant of Thy love	787
Lord, Thou hast taught our hearts to	860	My God, the Spring of all my joys	738
Lord, Thou hast won, at length I yield	522	My God, what monuments I see	120
Lord, Thou wilt bring the joyful day	1401	My gracious Lord, I own Thy right	619
Lord, Thou wilt hear me when I pray	1234	My heavenly home is bright and fair	718
Lord, Thy Church hath seen Thee rise	281	My Jesus, as Thou wilt	767
Lord, we come before Thee now	981	My Lord, how full of sweet content	1213
Lord, with glowing heart I'd praise Thee	535	My Lord, my Love, was crucified	968
Loud hallelujahs to the Lord	51	My precious Lord, for Thy dear Name	617
Love Divine, all love excelling	347	My Saviour and my King	1072
Lowly and solemn be	1316	My Saviour, my Almighty Friend	750
		My soul, amid this stormy world	1314
MAJESTIC sweetness sits enthroned	561	My soul, be on thy guard	630
Make haste, O man, to live	1268	My soul, repeat His praise	88
Maker of earth, to Thee alone	1364	My soul, there is a country	1380
Many woes had Christ endured	223	My soul, weigh not thy life	633
Mary to her Saviour's tomb	270	My spirit longs for Thee	771
Meet and right it is to sing	22	My spirit, on Thy care	777
Men of God, go take your stations	1083	My trust is in the Lord	44
Mercy, O Thou Son of David	517		
Messiah, at Thy glad approach	154	NEAR the cross was Mary weeping	250
'Mid evening shadows let us all be	1216	Nearer, my God, to Thee	734
'Mid scenes of confusion and creature	717	New every morning is the love	1199
Mighty God, the First, the Last	33	No change of times shall ever shock	122
Mighty God, while angels bless Thee	167	No more, my God, I boast no more	889
Millions within Thy courts have met	1031	No, no, it is not dying	1302
More love to Thee, O Christ	736	No track is on the sunny sky	341
Mortals, awake, with angels join	161	Nor eye hath seen, nor ear hath heard	1374
Much in sorrow, oft in woe	586	Not all the blood of beasts	234
Must Jesus bear the cross alone	622	Not unto us, Almighty Lord	96
My blessèd Saviour, is Thy love	595	Nothing, either great or small	776

INDEX OF FIRST LINES.

	HYMN		HYMN
Now be my heart inspired to sing	313	O God of sovereign grace	1074
Now be the Gospel banner	1123	O God, Thy power is wonderful	75
Now begin the heavenly theme	587	O God, we praise Thee, and confess	24
Now from labor and from care	1248	O God, who metest in Thy hand	1144
Now I have found a Friend	737	O great is Jehovah, and great be His	840
Now I have found the ground wherein	289	O had I, my Saviour, the wings of	1286
Now is the accepted time	439	O happy band of pilgrims	713
Now let our cheerful eyes survey	328	O happy day, that fixed my choice	872
Now let our souls, on wings sublime	1399	O happy saints, who dwell in light	1396
Now let our voices join	609	O happy soul, that lives on high	744
Now, my soul, thy voice upraising	254	O help us, Lord, each hour of need	790
Now thank we all our God	1149	O Holy, holy, holy Lord	6
Now that the sun is gleaming bright	1209	O Holy Spirit, Fount of love	357
Now with angels round the throne	34, 351	O how happy are they	521
		O how I love Thy holy law	399
O BLESS the Lord, my soul	87	O how shall I receive Thee	149
O blessèd feet of Jesus	240	O Jesus, bruised and wounded sore	887
O blessèd God, to Thee I raise	818	O Jesus Christ, grow Thou in me	567
O blessèd souls are they	511	O Jesus, Jesus, dearest Lord	531
O Bread of Life from heaven	896	O Jesus, King most wonderful	532
O Bread to pilgrims given	895	O Jesus, Lord of light and grace	1202
O Christ, our hope, our hearts' desire	327	O Jesus, sweet the tears I shed	232
O Christ, our King, Creator, Lord	314	O Jesus, Thou art standing	241
O Christ, the Lord of heaven, to Thee	318	O Jesus, Thou the beauty art	598
O city of the Lord, begin	1106	O Jesus, we adore Thee	239
O come, all ye faithful, triumphantly	162	O Jesus, when I think of Thee	276
O come, and mourn with me awhile	244	O Lamb of God, still keep me	642
O come, loud anthems let us sing	103	O Lord, another day is flown	1236
O come to the merciful Saviour that	412	O Lord, encouraged by Thy grace	869
O come, ye sinners, to your God	433	O Lord, how good, how great art Thou	153
O could I find, from day to day	689	O Lord, how happy should we be	635
O could I speak the matchless worth	588	O Lord, how infinite Thy love	146
O day of rest and gladness	931	O Lord, how joyful 'tis to see	1001
O deem not they are blest alone	798	O Lord, I would delight in Thee	739
O'er the distant mountains breaking	1337	O Lord, impart Thyself to me	742
O'er the gloomy hills of darkness	1081	O Lord most High, Eternal King	285
O'er the realms of pagan darkness	1080	O Lord, my best desire fulfil	788
O'erwhelmed in depths of woe	233	O Lord of heaven, and earth, and sea	1042
O for a closer walk with God	684	O Lord, our fathers oft have told	1157
O for a faith that will not shrink	784	O Lord our God, arise	1071
O for a glance of heavenly day	483	O Lord, our heavenly King	60
O for a heart to praise my God	741	O Lord, Thou art my Lord	508
O for a shout of sacred joy	299	O Lord, Thy mercy, my sure hope	141
O for a sweet inspiring ray	1398	O Lord, turn not Thy face from me	454
O for a thousand tongues to sing	528	O Lord, when we the path retrace	207
O for the death of those	1333	O Lord, within Thy sacred gate	1009
O for the happy hour	351	O Love divine, how sweet Thou art	589
O gift of gifts! O grace of faith	603	O Love, who formedst me to wear	886
O God, beneath Thy guiding hand	1162	O Master, it is good to be	212
O God of Bethel, by whose hand	1172	O mean may seem this house of clay	325

INDEX OF FIRST LINES.

First Line	Hymn
O mighty joy to all our race	316
O Mother dear, Jerusalem	1370
O Paradise, O Paradise	1415
O praise our God to-day	1056
O render thanks to God above	100
O sacred Head, now wounded	238
O Saviour, is Thy promise fled	850
O Source divine and Life of all	65
O Spirit of the living God	1067
O sweet and blesséd country	1379
O, sweetly breathe the lyres above	873
O that I could forever dwell	559
O that I knew the secret place	809
O that my load of sin were gone	468
O that the Lord's salvation	1095
O that the Lord would guide my ways	745
O the sweet wonders of that cross	890
O Thou from whom all goodness flows	762
O Thou great Ruler of the sky	1206
O Thou, great Teacher from the skies	1047
O Thou, my soul, forget no more	877
O Thou that hearest prayer	826
O Thou that hear'st the prayer of faith	525
O Thou that hear'st when sinners cry	466
O Thou to whom, in ancient time	986
O Thou, to whose all-searching sight	704
O Thou, who by a star didst guide	193
O Thou, who driest the mourner's tear	1282
O Thou, who lov'st to send relief	1280
O Thou, who in the olive shade	1281
O Thou, whose filméd and failing eye	780
O Thou, whose own vast temple stands	1037
O Thou, whose tender mercy hears	456
O turn ye, O turn ye, for why will ye	413
O 'twas a joyful sound to hear	976
O Unity of Threefold Light	26
O very God of very God	1050
O what a blessed hope is ours	1406
O what, if we are Christ's	927
O what stupendous mercy shines	1044
O when shall I see Jesus	715
O, where is He that trod the sea	210
O where shall rest be found	462
O why should Israel's sons, once blest	1060
O wondrous type, O vision fair	213
O word of God incarnate	407
O worship the King all glorious above	56
Of Him who did salvation bring	430
Oft when the waves of passion rise	637
On Jordan's bank the Baptist's cry	203
On Jordan's rugged banks I stand	1402
On the mountain's top appearing	1128
On Thy Church, O Power divine	959
On Zion and on Lebanon	1116
Once blind with sin and self	542
Once I thought my mountain strong	678
Once more, before we part	1022
Once more, my soul, the rising day	1207
One cup of healing oil and wine	1041
One sole baptismal sign	829
One sweetly solemn thought	1412
One there is above all others	544, 909
Onward, Christian soldiers	640
Open, Lord, my inward ear	490
Our blest Redeemer, ere he breathed	340
Our Captain leads us on	724
Our day of praise is done	1021
Our glorious home above	1413
Our God, our God, Thou shinest here	1111
Our God, our help in ages past	74
Our heavenly Father calls	722
Our heavenly Father, hear	1170
Our journey is a thorny maze	650
Our Lord is risen from the dead	280
Our Lord, who knows full well	825
Our Saviour alone, the Lord let us bless	335
Our souls, by love together knit	913
Our yet unfinished story	127
Out of the deep I call	463
Out of the depths of woe	695
PALMS of glory, raiment bright	1365
Part in peace, Christ's life was peace	1005
Pass me not, O gentle Saviour	488
Peace, troubled soul, whose plaintive	435
People of the living God	878
Pilgrim burdened with thy sin	879
Pleasant are Thy courts above	1003
Plunged in a gulf of dark despair	147
Pour out Thy Spirit from on high	845
Praise, Lord, for Thee in Zion waits	998
Praise, my soul, the King of Heaven	537
Praise, O praise our God and King	1153
Praise on Thee in Zion's gates	69
Praise the Lord, His glories show	80
Praise the Lord, His power confess	83
Praise the Lord, who reigns above	23
Praise the Lord, ye heavens, adore	53
Praise the Rock of our salvation	830
Praise the Saviour, all ye nations	1053

INDEX OF FIRST LINES.

First Line	Hymn
Praise to God, immortal praise	1154
Praise to God, who reigns above	30
Praise to Thee, Thou great Creator	55
Praises to Him, whose love has given	9
Pray, without ceasing, pray	822
Prayer is the breath of God in man	807
Prayer is the soul's sincere desire	808
Prostrate, dear Jesus, at Thy feet	451
Raise your triumphant songs	237
Rejoice, rejoice, believers	894
Rejoice, the Lord is King	338
Rejoice to-day with one accord	1
Rest for the toiling hand	1335
Resting from His work to-day	258
Return, my roving heart, return	478
Return, O God of love, return	1361
Return, O wanderer, return	431
Ride on, ride on in majesty!	217
Rise, crowned with light, imperial	1125
Rise, glorious Conqueror, rise	290
Rise, O my soul, pursue the path	920
Rise, my soul, and stretch thy wings	726
Rock of ages, cleft for me	499
Roll on, thou mighty ocean	1120
Round the Lord in glory seated	15
Safe Home, safe Home in port	1411
Safely thro' another week	953
Saints in glory, we together	553
Salvation! O the joyful sound	445
Saviour, again to Thy dear name we	1025
Saviour, breathe an evening blessing	1241
Saviour, happy would I be	591
Saviour, I look to Thee	729
Saviour, like a Shepherd lead us	1191
Saviour, sprinkle many nations	1078
Saviour, through the desert lead us	663
Saviour, when in dust to Thee	675
Saviour, who Thy flock art feeding	871
Say, sinner, hath a voice within	425
Scorn not the slightest word or deed	1183
See, from Zion's sacred mountain	1129
See how great a flame aspires	1098
See how He loved! exclaimed the	215
See, Israel's gentle Shepherd stands	861
See the Conqueror mounts in triumph	312
See what a living stone	939
Servant of God, well done	1351
Servants of God, in joyful lays	137

First Line	Hymn
Shall hymns of grateful love	949
Shall man, O God of light and life	1325
Shall we gather at the river	1389
Shepherd of Israel, bend Thine ear	846
Shepherd of Israel, from above	1175
Shepherd of souls, refresh and bless	906
Shepherd of tender youth	1193
Shepherd of Thine Israel, lead us	664
Shine on our land, Jehovah, shine	1159
Shine on our souls, eternal God	1174
Show pity, Lord, O Lord forgive	465
Silently the shades of evening	1240
Sing of Jesus, sing forever	552
Sing to the Lord most high	952
Sing to the Lord, our Might	936
Sing to the Lord with heart and voice	1033
Sing to the Lord, ye distant lands	145
Sing we the song of those who stand	917
Sing, ye redeemed of the Lord	627
Sinners, lift up your hearts	339
Sinners, obey the gospel word	427
Sinners, turn, why will ye die?	416
Sinners, will you scorn the message	420
So let our lips and lives express	621
Softly fades the twilight ray	1008
Softly now the light of day	1246
Soldiers of Christ, arise	628
Soldiers of the cross, arise	1096
Something every heart is loving	548
Sometimes a light surprises	712
Songs of praise the angels sang	68
Son of God, to Thee I cry	500
Sons of men, behold from far	175
Sons of Zion, raise your songs	271
Soon as I heard my Father say	766
Soon may the last glad song arise	1070
Sovereign Ruler, Lord of all	473
Sovereign of worlds, display Thy	1068
Sovereign Ruler of the skies	797
Sound, sound the truth abroad	1084
Souls in heathen darkness lying	1082
Sow in the morn thy seed	853
Speak gently: it is better far	1182
Speed Thy servants, Saviour, speed	1105
Spirit Divine, attend our prayers	343
Spirit, leave thy house of clay	1518
Spirit of mercy, truth, and love	368
Spirit of power and might, behold	1073
Spirit of Truth, essential God	388
Spread, O spread, Thou mighty word	391

INDEX OF FIRST LINES.

	HYMN.		HYMN.
Stand up, and bless the Lord	57	The God of Abrah'm praise	1376
Stand up, my soul, shake off thy fears	651	The God of harvest praise	1107
Stand up, stand up for Jesus	643	The goodly land I see	1385
Star of peace, to wanderers weary	1146	The happy morn is come	267
Stay, Thou insulted Spirit, stay	470	The harvest dawn is near	857
Still, still with Thee, my God	1226	The head that once was crowned with	302
Strangers and pilgrims here below	1171	The heavens declare Thy glory, Lord	403
Sun of my soul, Thou Saviour dear	1029	The hour is come; the feast is spread	902
Sure the blest Comforter is nigh	367	The hour of my departure's come	1291
Surely Christ thy griefs hath borne	248	The long-expected morn	178
Sweet hour of prayer	1212	The Lord descended from above	128
Sweet is the light of Sabbath eve	1013	The Lord Himself doth condescend	661
Sweet is the memory of Thy grace	131	The Lord Himself, the mighty Lord	132
Sweet is the solemn voice that calls	1011	The Lord, how wondrous are His ways	135
Sweet is the work, my God, my King	944	The Lord is King: lift up thy voice	110
Sweet is the work, O Lord	935	The Lord is my Shepherd, no want	710
Sweet is Thy mercy, Lord	778	The Lord is risen indeed	277
Sweet Saviour, bless us ere we go	1030	The Lord Jehovah reigns, And royal	45
Sweet the time, exceeding sweet	882	The Lord Jehovah reigns, His throne	41
Sweet was the time when first I felt	686	The Lord my pasture shall prepare	98
Swell the anthem, raise the song	1152	The Lord my Shepherd is	84
Sweet the moments... *See Chants, page*	381	The Lord of glory is my light	974
TAKE me, O my Father, take me	493	The Lord of Might from Sinai's brow	1348
Take my heart, O Father, take it	910	The Lord on high ascends	298
Take, my soul, thy full salvation	611	The Lord our God is full of might	113
Talk with me, Lord: Thyself reveal	743	The Lord our God is Lord of all	92
Tarry with me, O my Saviour	1242	The Lord will come, the earth shall	1351
Teach me, my God and King	753	The morning dawns upon the place	222
Ten thousand times ten thousand	1381	The morning light is breaking	1132
Tender Shepherd, Thou hast stilled	1303	The morning purples all the sky	273
Thank and praise Jehovah's name	35	The peace which God alone reveals	943
That day of wrath, that dreadful day	1350	The people of His choice	693
That fearful day, that day of dread	1352	The perfect world, by Adam trod	1034
That we might walk with God	353	The pity of the Lord	89
Th' atoning work is done	268	The praying spirit breathe	824
The billows swell, the winds are high	800	The Prince of salvation in triumph is	1124
The bird let loose in Eastern skies	811	The promises I sing	42
The Church has waited long	1356	The race that long in darkness pined	157
The Church's one foundation	929	The roseate hues of early dawn	1315
The dawn is sprinkling in the east	1203	The royal banner is unfurled	502
The day is past and gone, Great God	1230	The Saviour calls, let every ear	447
The day is past and gone, The evening	1228	The Saviour! O what endless charms	503
The day, O Lord, is spent	1020	The seeds, which piety and love	1048
The day of rest once more comes round	993	The Son of God goes forth to war	649
The day of resurrection	933	The spacious firmament on high	63
The eternal gates lift up their heads	301	The Spirit breathes upon the word	395
The festal morn, my God, is come	994	The Spirit in our hearts	442
The floods, O Lord, lift up their voice	109	The starry firmament on high	406
The gentle Saviour calls	870	The triumphs of the martyred saints	1363

INDEX OF FIRST LINES.

	HYMN.		HYMN.
The twilight falls, the night is near...	1233	Though now the nations sits beneath.	1103
The voice of free grace cries, Escape.	411	Three in One, and One in Three.....	1028
The wanderer no more will roam.....	498	Throned high is Jesus now..........	297
The winds were howling o'er the deeps	209	Through all the changing scenes of life	142
The world can neither give nor take..	781	Through endless years, Thou art the.	73
The world is very evil..............	1344	Through sorrow's night and danger's.	1273
Thee to laud in songs divine........	980	Through the love of God our Saviour.	672
Thee we adore, eternal Lord........	5	Through the night of doubt and.....	911
Thee we adore, Eternal Name.......	1250	Thus far the Lord has led me on.....	1223
Thee will I love, my Strength, and...	570	Thy glory, Lord, the heavens declare.	67
There is a blessed home............	769	Thy holy day's returning...........	932
There is a book, who runs may read..	398	Thy loving-kindness, Lord, I sing....	576
There is a fold whence none can stray	1373	Thy name, Almighty Lord..........	1023
There is a fountain filled with blood..	501	Thy way is in the deep, O Lord......	789
There is a glorious world of light.....	1180	Thy way, not mine, O Lord.........	770
There is a green hill far away........	1179	Thy way, O God, is in the sea.......	117
There is a land of pure delight......	1405	Thy works, not mine, O Christ......	516
There is a little lonely fold..........	1178	Till He come, O let the words........	897
There is a safe and secret place......	765	Time is winging us away...........	727
There is an eye that never sleeps.....	812	Time, thou speedest on but slowly....	1392
There is an hour of hallowed peace...	1383	'Tis a pleasant thing to see..........	924
There is an hour of peaceful rest.....	1382	'Tis by the faith of joys to come.....	656
They pray the best who pray and watch	819	'Tis by Thy strength the mountains..	1252
They whose course on earth is o'er...	922	"'Tis finished!" so the Saviour cried.	246
Thine forever!—God of Love........	880	'Tis heaven begun below...........	961
Thine, Lord, is wisdom, Thine alone.	140	'Tis midnight; and on Olive's brow..	220
Thine arm, O Lord, in days of old...	211	'Tis my happiness below............	647
Think, O ye, who fondly languish....	1305	'Tis thus in solitude I roam.........	815
Think well how Jesus trusts Himself..	594	To Calvary, Lord, in spirit now......	229
This is not my place of resting.......	1409	To Christ, the Prince of peace.......	608
This is the day of toil..............	659	To-day the Saviour calls...........	414
This is the day the Lord hath made...	960	To God be glory, peace on earth.....	25
This place is holy ground..........	1310	To God I cried when troubles rose....	699
This stone to Thee in faith we lay....	1032	To God the only wise...............	62
Those whom many a land divides....	923	To heaven I lift my waiting eyes.....	786
Thou art gone to the grave..........	1327	To Him that chose us first..........	38
Thou art gone up on high...........	278	To Jesus, the Crown of my hope....	732
Thou art, O God, the life and light...	66	To-morrow, Lord, is Thine..........	1267
Thou art the Way: to Thee alone...	304	To spend one sacred day...........	951
Thou dear Redeemer, dying Lamb...	562	To Thee be glory, honor, praise.....	218
Thou hidden Source of calm repose..	569	To Thee, my God and Saviour.......	714
Thou Judge of quick and dead.......	1353	To Thee, my God, whose presence fills	783
Thou Lord of all above.............	461	To Thee, my Shepherd and my Lord.	565
Thou, O Christ, art all I want.......	677	To Thee, O dear, dear Saviour......	716
Thou who art enthroned above.......	1004	To Thee, O God, we raise..........	1151
Thou who didst on Calvary bleed....	474	To Thy pastures fair and large......	82
Thou who like the wind dost come...	378	To Thy temple I repair.............	978
Thou who roll'st the year around....	1262	Tossed upon life's raging billow.....	1147
Thou, whose almighty Word........	3	Tossed with rough winds, and faint...	708

INDEX OF FIRST LINES.

	HYMN		HYMN
Trembling before Thine awful Throne	557	When all Thy mercies, O my God....	90
Triumphant Zion, lift Thy head.....	1116	When bending o'er the brink of life..	1274
'Twas by an order from the Lord.....	404	When gathering clouds around I view	801
'Twas on that dark, that doleful night	884	When God of old came down from...	342
		When God revealed His gracious name	602
Unveil thy bosom, faithful tomb....	1324	When His salvation bringing........	1195
Up to the hills I lift mine eyes.......	118	When I can read my title clear.......	1403
Uphold me, Lord, too prone to stray.	654	When I survey the wondrous cross...	245
Uplift the blood-red banner..........	1094	When I view my Saviour bleeding...	534
Upward I lift mine eyes.............	43	When in the hour of lonely woe.....	802
		When Israel of the Lord beloved.....	119
Vain, delusive world, adieu..........	583	When Jesus dwelt in mortal clay.....	1038
Vainly through night's weary hours..	1238	When Jesus left His Father's throne..	1177
		When Jordan hushed his waters still..	185
Wait, O my soul, thy Maker's will..	123	When languor and disease invade....	1279
Wake the song of jubilee............	1140	When like a stranger on our sphere..	204
Watchman, tell us of the night......	174	When marshalled on the nightly plain	187
We are little Christian children......	1189	When, O dear Jesus, when shall I....	1019
We are living, we are dwelling.......	1092	When on Sinai's top I see...........	249
We are on our journey home........	1410	When our heads are bowed with woe.	791
We bid thee welcome, in the name...	848	When rising from the bed of death...	1275
We did not see Thee lifted high.....	288	When shall I hear the inward voice..	385
We give Thee but Thine own........	1055	When shall the voice of singing.....	1121
We have a house above.............	1336	When sins and fears prevailing rise...	698
We lift our hearts to Thee...........	1225	When, streaming from the eastern skies	99
We long to move and breathe in Thee	863	When the worn spirit wants repose...	967
We're bound for yonder land........	694	When this passing world is done.....	681
We sing His love who once was slain.	1526	When Thou, my righteous Judge,...	1346
We sing the praise of Him who died.	618	When thro' the torn sail the wild.....	1145
We speak of the realms of the blest..	731	When we, our wearied limbs to rest..	1059
We've no abiding city here..........	657	When with a mind devoutly pressed..	524
Welcome, delightful morn...........	947	When wounded sore the stricken soul.	453
Welcome, sweet day, of days the best,	995	Where high the heavenly temple stands	317
Welcome, sweet day of rest.........	934	Where is my God? does He retire....	817
Welcome, Thou victor in the strife...	294	Where two or three, with sweet accord	989
Welcome, welcome, dear Redeemer..	538	While I to grief my soul gave way...	1063
What a strange and wondrous story..	1190	While in sweet communion feeding...	908
What are these arrayed in white.....	1368	While Life prolongs its precious light..	423
What are these in bright array.......	1366	While my Redeemer's near..........	85
What are those soul-reviving strains..	219	While o'er our guilty land, O Lord...	1160
What equal honors shall we bring....	315	While o'er the deep Thy servants sail.	1143
What grace, O Lord, and beauty shone	208	While on the verge of life I stand...	1290
What is life? 'T is but a vapor.......	1288	While shepherds watched their flocks.	160
What secret place, what distant star..	19	While Thee I seek, protecting Power.	124
What shall I render to my God......	785	While Thou, O my God, art my Helper	1328
What sinners value, I resign.........	1400	While with ceaseless course the sun..	1261
What star is this, with beams so bright	186	Who are these like stars appearing...	1395
What, though my frail eye-lids refuse.	1211	Who are these that come from far....	1137
What various hindrances we meet....	816	Who but Thou, almighty Spirit......	1130

26

INDEX OF FIRST LINES.

	HYMN.		HYMN.
Who can forbear to sing	540	Ye angels, who stand round the throne	730
Who, O Lord, when life is o'er	1309	Ye boundless realms of joy	39
Who shall the Lord's elect condemn?	701	Ye choirs of new Jerusalem	275
Why do we mourn departing friends	1321	Ye Christian heralds, go, proclaim	1100
Why is my heart so far from Thee	688	Ye golden lamps of heaven, farewell	1312
Why, on the bending willows hung	1065	Ye messengers of Christ	856
Why should I murmur or repine	799	Ye mourning saints, whose streaming	1299
Why should our tears in sorrow flow	1298	Ye nations round the earth, rejoice	107
Why should the children of a King	355	Ye servants of God, your Master	334
Why should we start and fear to die?	1289	Ye servants of the Lord	854
Why will ye waste on trifling cares	422	Ye that in His courts are found	409
With broken heart and contrite sigh	481	Ye that pass by, behold the Man	242
With ecstacy of joy	827	Ye trembling captives, hear	438
With glory clad, with strength arrayed	101	Ye tribes of Adam, join	40
With joy I see a thousand charms	1301	Ye wretched, hungry, starving poor	448
With joy we hail the sacred day	970	Yes, for me, for me He careth	666
With joy we meditate the grace	320	Yes, He knows the way is dreary	615
With one consent, let all the earth	47	Yes, my native land, I love thee	1104
With rev'rence let the saints appear	93	Yes, the Redeemer rose	266
With songs and honors sounding loud	1254	Yes, we trust the day is breaking	1079
With tearful eyes I look around	707	Your harps, ye trembling saints	691
Witness, ye men and angels, now	864		
Workman of God, O lose not heart	1051	Zion, awake, thy strength renew	1132
Wrecked and struggling in mid-ocean	1148	Zion's Daughter, weep no more	225
Wretched, helpless, and distrest	489	Zion stands by hills surrounded	834

Index to Chants.

	PAGE.		PAGE.
As the hart panteth after the water	377	Lord, Thou hast been our dwelling	379
Baptismal Chant	381	My soul doth magnify the Lord	374
Be Thou exalted, O God, above the	378	O be joyful in the Lord, all ye lands	372
Blessed be the Lord God of Israel	373	O come, let us sing unto the Lord	371
Glory be to God on high	373	O God, Thou art my God	378
Glory be to the Father, and to the Son,	372	O Lord, our Lord, how excellent is Thy	375
Glory be to the Father, and to the Son,	373	O sing unto the Lord a new song	373
Glory be to the Father, and to the Son,	375	O sing unto the Lord a new song	380
God be merciful unto us, and bless us	374	Praise the Lord, O my soul	375
God is our refuge and strength	377	The earth is the Lord's, and the fulness	376
Have mercy upon me, O God	377	The heavens declare the glory of God	376
Holy, holy, holy, Lord God of Sabbaoth,	380	The Lord is my Shepherd; I shall not	376
How amiable are Thy tabernacles	379	"Thy will be done!"	380
It is a good thing to give thanks unto	374	We praise Thee, O God	372
I was glad when they said unto me	371	Then will I sprinkle clean water	381

Index of Authors of Hymns.

Adams, Rev. Nehemiah, 440.
Adams, Mrs. Sarah Flower, 734, 1205.
Addison, Joseph, 63, 90, 98, 1275.
Adolphus, Gustavus, 634.
Alderson, Mrs., 1032.
Alexander, Mrs. Cecil Frances, 301, 453, 887, 1092, 1179, 1180, 1313.
Alexander, Rev. James Waddell, 238, 250, 572.
Albinus, Rev. Johann Georg, 1392.
Alford, Rev. Henry, 639, 921, 1155, 1381.
Allen, G. N., 622.
Allen, Rev. James, 292.
Allen, Rev. Jonathan, 420.
Ambrose of Milan, 273, 285, 298, 316, 1202, 1244.
Ambrosian, 327, 1203, 1208.
Anatolius of Constantinople, 673.
Anstice, Prof. Joseph, 635, 1249.
Auber, Miss Harriet, 146, 172, 192, 340, 387, 935, 959, 970, 1139, 1238.
Austin, John, 507.
Aveling, Rev. Thomas William, 912.
A., S., 262.

Bache, Mrs. Sarah, 215.
Bacon, Rev. Leonard, 1103, 1140, 1162, 1232.
Bahnmaier, Rev. Jonathan Frederic, 391.
Baker, Rev. Francis, 1370.
Baker, Rev. Sir Henry Williams, 1, 10, 29, 225, 254, 463, 537, 769, 833, 927, 999, 1036, 1153, 1161, 1168.
Bakewell, Rev. John, 310.
Ball, William, 332.
Bancroft, Mrs. Charitie Lees, 1196.
Bancroft, Rev. James Henry, 1307.
Barbauld, Mrs. Anna Laetitia, 415, 653, 971, 1154, 1293.
Barton, Bernard, 401.
Bateman, Rev. Christian Henry, 551.
Bathurst, Rev. Wm. Hiley, 475, 784, 1138, 1175, 1298.
Baxter, Rev. Richard, 1276.
Beddome, Rev. Benjamin, 123, 350, 353, 364, 405, 459, 461, 486, 508, 700, 807, 844, 864, 1118, 1355.
Beecher, Rev. Charles, 1410.
Beman, Rev. Nathan Sidney Smith, 1117, 1339.
Benedict, Erastus Cornelius, 577.
Bennett, Henry, 674.
Benson, Rev. Richard Meux, 30.
Bernard of Clairvaux, 238, 430, 532, 564, 572, 598, 888.
Bernard of Cluny, 1344, 1375, 1376, 1377, 1378, 1379.
Berridge, Rev. John, 796, 1306.
Bethune, Rev. Geo. Washington, 276, 351, 1147, 1332.
Bickersteth, Rev. Edward Henry, 897, 902.
Blacklock, Rev. Thomas, 112.
Blew, Rev. William John, 1230.
Boden, Rev. James, 293.
Boehm, Rev. Anthony Wilhelm, 430.
Bonar, Rev. Horatius, 9, 16, 177, 216, 227, 236, 251, 269, 506, 516, 539, 599, 601, 659, 666, 763, 768, 770, 839, 1039, 1245, 1260, 1268, 1335, 1356, 1358, 1409.
Bonar, Mrs. Horatius, 735.
Borthwick, Miss Jane, 477, 545, 669, 767, 894, 930, 957.
Bowring, Sir John, 54, 174, 205, 612.
Boyce, Samuel, 438.
Breviary, Le Mans, 29.
Breviary, Paris, 1209.
Breviary, Roman, 225, 233, 255, 608, 899.
Breviary, Sarum, 213.
Brewer, Rev. Jehoida, 555.
Bridges, Mathew, 290, 296.

Briggs' Collection, 443.
Browne, Rev. Moses, 524.
Brown, Mrs. Phœbe Hinsdale, 820, 1231.
Browne, Rev. Simon, 366, 452, 995, 1016.
Bruce, Michael, 154, 317, 1106, 1107, 1172, 1291, 1297, 1323.
Bryant, William Cullen, 798, 1037, 1064.
Bulfinch, Rev. Stephen Greenleaf, 938.
Burder, Rev. George, 882.
Burder's Collection, 365.
Burdsall, Rev. Richard, 411.
Burgess, Bp. George, 109, 857, 1143.
Burnham, Rev. Richard, 457.
Burns, Rev. James Drummond, 474, 1226.
Burton, John, 826.
Burton, John, 389, 727.
Buttress, John, 402.
Byrom, John, 771, 772.

C., 218.
Cameron, Rev. William, 1404.
Campbell, Robert, 275, 371, 899.
Campbell, Thomas, 185.
Carlyle, Thomas, 842.
Cary, Miss Alice, 1278.
Cary, Miss Phœbe, 1412.
Caswall, Rev. Edward, 162, 169, 233, 255, 362, 382, 532, 564, 596, 598, 608, 1203, 1208, 1243.
Cawood, Rev. John, 164, 1090.
Cennick, Rev. John, 335, 554, 562, 585, 1019, 1338.
Chambers, Rev. John David, 214.
Chandler, Rev. John, 186, 197, 203, 307, 502, 828, 1001, 1202, 1393.
Chapman, Robert Cleaver, 1314.
Charles, Mrs. Elizabeth, 316, 708.
Cheever, Rev. George Barrell, 576.
Chorley, Henry Fothergill, 1163.
Christian Magazine, 574.
Clarke, Rev. James Freeman, 1173.
Clement of Alexandria, 1193.
Cleveland, Benjamin, 689.
Codner, Mrs. Elizabeth, 487.
Coffin, Prof. Charles, 186, 203, 357, 999, 1364.
Collins, Rev. Henry, 568.
Collyer, Rev. Wm. Bengo, 424, 431, 1114, 1274, 1305, 1347.
Conder, Josiah, 34, 69, 78, 110, 664, 795, 802, 898, 1394.
Cook, Rev. Russell Sturgis, 497.
Cooper, John, 8.
Cosin, Bp. John, 380.
Cotterill, Rev. Thomas, 5, 344, 361, 405, 1080.
Cowper, William, 116, 148, 395, 464, 501, 579, 647, 684, 703, 706, 712, 732, 783, 800, 810, 816, 831, 1002, 1213.
Cox, C. C., 1240.
Cox, Miss Frances Elizabeth, 580, 1395.
Coxe, Bp. Arthur Cleveland, 206, 1078, 1092.
Crabbe, Rev. George, 879.
Croswell, Rev. William, 1046.
Cummins, Rev. James J., 949.
Cunningham, Rev. John William, 247, 945.

Dale, Rev. Thomas, 1283.
Dana, Mrs. Mary S. B., 1218.
Davies, Rev. Samuel, 381, 874, 1160.
Deck, James George, 207, 597, 642, 776.
De Fleury, Miss Maria, 730.
Denham, Rev. David, 717.
Denny, Sir Edward, 199, 208, 229, 337, 90?, 1077, 1362.
Dexter, Rev. Henry Martyn, 1193.

(411)

Index of Authors of Hymns.

Dickson, Rev. David, 1370.
Dix, William Chatterton, 190.
Doane, Bp. George Washington, 304, 1101, 1246.
Dobell, John, 439.
Dobell's Collection, 574, 947, 948.
Doddridge, Rev. Philip, 42, 111, 143, 155, 194, 266, 328, 355, 422, 478, 515, 561, 592, 604, 609, 612, 627, 618, 720, 722, 752, 787, 825, 846, 847, 849, 854, 859, 861, 872, 1012, 1015, 1036, 1058, 1061, 1262, 1088, 1116, 1152, **1174, 1251,** 1256, 1263, 1267, 1270, 1290, 1299, 1301, 1312, 1354.
Downton, Rev. Henry, 1263.
Doane, Rev. John, 1014.
Drummond, Rev. D. T. K., 1413.
Drummond, Rev. William Hamilton, 1041.
Dryden, John, 383.
Duffield, Rev. George, Jr., 590, 643.
Duncan, Mrs. Mary Lundie, 1187.
Dunn, Prof. Robinson Potter, 1302.
Dwight, Rev. John Sullivan, 1166.
Dwight, Rev. Timothy, 443, 835, 952, **1325.**

East, Bp. John, 1373.
Eastburn, Rev. James Wallis, 6.
Edmeston, James, 18, 702, 967, 1013, 1120, 1121, 1184, 1241.
Ellerton, Rev. John, 1021, 1025.
Elliott, Miss Charlotte, 496, 707, 1219, 1221.
Elliott, Mrs. Julia Anne, 954, 955.
Elven, Rev. Cornelius, 481.
Enfield, Prof. William, 198.
"Eriphas," Evangelical Magazine, 1130.
Evans, Rev. James Harrington, 645.
Evans, Rev. Jonathan, 252, 965.

Faber, Frederick William, 27, 75, 77, 126, **244, 341,** 412, 531, 594, 603, 1030, 1051, 1181, 1330, 1415.
Fabricius, Rev. Jacob, 634.
Fanch, Rev. James, 235.
Fawcett, Rev. John, 55, 117, 303, 397, **925.**
Fitzgerald's Collection, 1127.
Flowerdew, Mrs. Alice, 1253.
Ford, Charles Lawrence, 614.
Ford, Rev. David Everard, 1265.
Fortunatus, Venantius, 502.
Francis, Rev. Benjamin, 616, 1053.
Franke, Rev. August Hermann, 679.
Frank, Johann, 1150.
Freylinghausen, Rev. Johann Anastasius, 670.
Fulbert of Chartres, 275.

Gambold, Bp. John, 670.
Ganse, Rev. Hervey Doddridge, 7, 13, 378, 518, 541, 697.
Gaskell, Mrs. Elizabeth Cleghorn, 33.
Gerhardt, Rev. Paul, 149, 163, 238, 543, 571, 775, 803.
German, from the, 173.
Gibbons, Rev. Thomas, 783, 1038, 1044, 1076, 1399.
Gill, Thomas Hornblower, 17, 19, 325, 348, 512, 1111.
Gilmore, Rev. J. H., 660.
Goode, Rev. William, 281.
Gotter, Ludwig Andreas, 613.
Gough, Benjamin, 1005, 1133, 1134.
Gould, Rev. Sabine Baring, 640, 911, 1390.
Grant, Sir Robert, 36, 406, 675, 301.
Greek, Sabbath Hymn-Book, 818.
Gregory the Great, 314, 1215, 1216.
Grigg, Rev. Joseph, 428, 616.
Gurney, Rev. John Hampden, 288, 624.
Guyon, Madame Jeanne M. B. de la M., 547, 1213.
G., W., 574.

Hammond, Rev. William, 606, 981.
Hanaford, Mrs. J. H., 1054.
Hangford, George Washington, 1182.
Hankey, Miss Kate, 1093.
Hankinson, Rev. Thomas Edwards, 257.
Hardenburg, Friedrich von, 274.
Harbaugh, Rev. Henry, 721, 1156.
Harmer, Rev. Samuel Young, 1408.
Hart, Rev. Joseph, 223, 352, 361, 419, **483** 900, 1015, 1022.
Hastings, Thomas, 272, 414, 434, 450, 665, 729, 774, 1091, 1123, 1126, 1247, 1248.
Havergal, Miss Frances Ridley, 127, 592, 615, 680.

Havergal, Rev. William, 196.
Haweis, Rev. Thomas, 252, 300, 408, 714, 762.
Hawkesworth, John, 1204.
Hayward, 947.
Heath, George, 630.
Heber, Bp. Reginald, 183, 209, 649, 703, 810, 892, 921, 996, 1110, 1145, 1164, 1176, 1217, 1272, 1327, 1348, 1351, 1416.
Hegindbothom, Rev. Ottiwell, 91, 568.
Hensel, Miss Luise, 350.
Herbert, Rev. George, 752.
Hermans, Mrs. Felicia Dorothea, **1281, 1316.**
Hermann, Rev. Johann Gottfried, 705.
Herrick, Rev. Robert, 792.
Hill, Rev. Rowland, 465, 704, **1294, 1326.**
Hillhouse, Abraham Lucas, 557.
Holmes, Oliver Wendell, 64.
Hope, Henry Joy McCracken, 737.
Hopkins, Rev. Josiah, 413.
Hopper, Rev. Edward, 819, 1145.
How, Rev. Wm. Walsham, 241, 243, 407, 928, **1055, 1096**
Hunter, Rev. William, 718, 1387, 1388.
Hupton, Rev. Job, 308.
Hurn, Rev. William, 192.
Hyde, Mrs. Ann Bradley, **425, 867.**

Ingemann, Bernhardt Severin, 911.
Irons, Rev. William Josiah, 779, 1349.

John of Damascus, 933.
Johns, Rev. Henry D., 838.
Jones, Rev. Edmund, 484.
Joseph of the Studium, 309, 713, 1411.
Joyce, Rev. James, 1060, 1065.
Judkin, Rev. Thomas James, 297.
Jukes, R., 520.

Keble, Rev. John, 342, 398, 756, 1029, 1199, 1253.
Keith, George, 709.
Kelly, Rev. Thomas, 178, 221, 268, 255, 277, 302, 305, 306, 307, 336, 550, 592, 618, 629, 657, 658, 765, 693, 834, 856, 962, 982, 985, 993, 1079, 1083, 1084, 1099, 1108, 1125, 1129, 1137, 1288.
Kempthorne, Rev. John, 53.
Ken, Bp. Thomas, 1197, 1222.
Kethe, Rev. William, 46.
Key, Francis Scott, 535.
King, Rev. Joshua, 1195.
Kingsbury, Rev. William, 291.
Kyle, Rev. R. W., 368.

Lange, Ernest, 140.
Laurenti, Laurentius, 894.
Lavater, Rev. Johann Caspar, 567.
Lee, Richard, 534.
Lesson, Miss Jane E., 357.
Leland, Rev. John, 715, 1228.
Littledale, Rev. Richard Frederick, 1144, 1258.
Lowry, Rev. Robert, 1389.
Luther, Martin, 184, 188, 842.
Lynch, Rev. Thomas Toke, 210, 373.
Lyte, Rev. Henry Francis, 44, 80, 96, 120, 153, 537, 610, 611, 654, 687, 725, 763, 777, 924, 936, 956, 998, 1003, 1011, 1024, 1043, 1093, 1286.

Macduff, Rev. John Robert, 1220.
Mackay, Mrs. Margaret, 1222.
Madan, Rev. Martin, 587, 606, 1340.
Maclehose's Santolius, 10, 254.
Mahmed, S. F., 333.
Maitland, Miss Fanny Fuller, 486.
Malan, Rev. Cesar Henri Abraham, 1102, 1332.
Mant, Bp. Richard, 15, 500, 926, 1244, 1363.
March, Rev. Daniel 1089.
Mardley, John, 484.
Marriott, Rev. John, 3.
Marsden, Rev. Joshua, 1007.
Marshman, Rev. Joshua, 877.
Mason, Rev. John, 318, 427, 781, 966, 968.
Mason, Rev. William, 128.
Massie, Richard, 869, 1276.
Matson, Rev. William Tidd, 536.

Index of Authors of Hymns. 413

Maude, Mrs. Mary Fawler, 880.
McCheyne, Rev. Robert Murray, 681, 682, 711.
MacKellar, Thomas, 519, 1192.
Medley, Rev. Samuel, 161, 282, 482, 575, 588.
Meinhold, Rev. Wilhelm, 1303.
Melrose, 1074.
Merrick, Rev. James, 82, 994, 1309.
Metrophanes of Smyrna, 26.
Midlane, Albert, 441.
Millard, Rev. James Elwin, 11.
Miller, Rev. William Edward, 913.
Mills, Mrs. Elizabeth, 731.
Milman, Rev. Henry Hart, 217, 790, 791.
Milton, John, 81, 1017.
Monsell, Rev. John Samuel Bewley, 578, 652, 716, 778, 865, 1337.
Montgomery, James, 12, 35, 57, 67, 68, 72, 79, 137, 171, 181, 204, 219, 222, 226, 249, 253, 349, 418, 462, 479, 573, 620, 636, 641, 683, 695, 710, 803, 821, 840, 841, 845, 848, 853, 878, 905, 906, 917, 964, 978, 1031, 1032, 1035, 1040, 1067, 1075, 1108, 1122, 1141, 1167, 1170, 1177, 1185, 1237, 1269, 1287, 1310, 1311, 1318, 1329, 1331, 1334, 1365, 1366.
Moore, Thomas, 66, 434, 811, 1282.
Moravian Collection, 5, 613, 617.
Morrison, Rev. John, 157, 685.
Moultrie, Rev. Gerard, 1308, 1343.
Moultrie, Rev. John, 259.
Muhlenberg, Rev. William Augustus, 444, 871, 1285.

Neale, Rev. John Mason, 26, 193, 213, 285, 308, 309, 436, 491, 546, 673, 713, 833, 922, 923, 933, 1020, 1050, 1161, 1171, 1229, 1280, 1344, 1352, 1364, 1375, 1376, 1377, 1378, 1379, 1411.
Needham, Rev. John, 144, 920.
Nelson, Rev. David, 1264.
Nettleton, Rev. Asahel, 523.
Nettleton's Village Hymns, 1074.
Nevin, Rev. Edwin H., 591, 667.
Newman, Rev. John Henry, 663, 1209.
Newton, Rev. John, 256, 270, 323, 455, 476, 504, 517, 522, 523, 544, 581, 600, 678, 686, 719, 823, 825, 831, 832, 909, 913, 953, 979, 1063, 1261, 1341.
New York Dutch Reformed Collection of Psalms, 661.
Noel, Hon. and Rev. Gerard Thomas, 904.
Noel's Selection, 1007.

Occum, Rev. Sampson, 523.
Olivers, Rev. Thomas, 1285, 1386.
Onderdonk, Bp. Henry Ustick, 442, 870, 1110.

Pal, Krishnoo, 877.
Palgrave, Francis Turner, 1205.
Palmer, Rev. Ray, 232, 314, 318, 374, 383, 493, 530, 560, 728, 860, 873, 883, 895, 932, 1113, 1136, 1215, 1216, 1262, 1401, 1414.
Park, Rev. Roswell, 907.
Parr, Miss Harriet, 1239.
Peabody, Rev. William Bourn Oliver, 1284.
Perronet, Rev. Edward, 329.
Peters, Mrs. Mary Bowly, 672.
Pierpont, Rev. John, 986.
Pierson, Rev. Arthur Tappan, 1151.
Pirie, Rev. Alexander, 324.
Plumptre, Rev. Edward Hayes, 166, 211.
Pope, Alexander, 1125.
Pratt's Collection, 264.
Prentiss, Mrs. Elizabeth Payson, 736.
Procter, Rev. James, 526.
Prudentius, Aurelius Clemens, 169.

Raffles, Rev. Thomas, 473, 513, 1367.
Rawson, George, 333, 376, 794.
Reed, Rev. Andrew, 179, 343, 370, 494, 559.
Ringwaldt, Rev. Bartholomew, 1347.
Rinkart, Rev. Martin, 1149.
Robert II., King of France, 374, 382.
Robertson, Rev. William, 366.
Robinson, George, 829.
Robinson, Rev. Robert, 167, 168, 536.
Robinson, Rev. Gilbert, 1023.

Rosenroth, Christian Knorr von, 957, 1027.
Rothe, Rev. John Andrew, 289.
Russell, Rev. Arthur Tozer, 149, 188, 239, 375.
Ryland, Rev. John, 626, 733, 797.

Sabbath Hymn-Book, 173, 818, 910.
Saffery, Mrs. Maria Grace, 1018, 1178.
Salisbury Collection, 176.
Sandys, George, 1004.
Schaff, Rev. Philip, 896.
Schenk, Rev. Heinrich, Theodor, 1395.
Schmolke, Rev. Benjamin, 294, 767.
Scott, Miss Elizabeth, 948, 1087.
Scott, Rev. Thomas, 263.
Scott, Sir Walter, 119, 1350.
Seagrave, Rev. Robert, 726.
Sears, Rev. Edmund Hamilton, 158, 159.
Selina, Countess of Huntington, 781, 1346.
Shepherd, Mrs. Anne Houlditch, 1194.
Shirley, Hon. and Rev. Walter, 435, 963.
Shrubsole, William, Jr., 99, 1069, 1102.
Sigourney, Mrs. Lydia Howard Huntley, 354.
Silesius, Johann Angelus, 545, 570, 580, 886.
Simpson, Mrs. Jane Cross Bell, 1146.
Singleton, Robert Cordet, 298.
Smith, Mrs. Caroline Sprague, 1242.
Smith, Mrs. Elizabeth Lee, 567.
Smith, Rev. Samuel Francis, 414, 1008, 1104, 1124, 1132, 1165, 1333.
Spitta, Rev. Carl Johann Philipp, 760, 1306.
Stammers, Joseph, 671.
Stanley, Rev. Arthur Penrhyn, 212, 287.
Steele, Miss Anne, 85, 125, 284, 367, 396, 432, 447, 448, 456, 503, 690, 698, 761, 764, 817, 869, 1224, 1300, 1313, 1398.
Stennett, Rev. Joseph, 595, 940.
Stennett, Rev. Samuel, 180, 246, 451, 561, 903, 917, 981, 1402.
Stephen of St. Sabas, 436.
Sterling, Rev. John, 65.
Sternhold, Thomas, 128.
Stocker, John, 369.
Stone, Rev. Samuel John, 929.
Stowell, Rev. Hugh, 1000, 1085.
Strong, Rev. Nathan, 1152.
Swain, Rev. Joseph, 540, 646, 914, 961, 1357.

Tappan, Rev. William Bingham, 220, 1382, 1383.
Tate and Brady, 39, 47, 73, 100, 101, 103, 114, 122, 134, 136, 141, 142, 300, 458, 687, 782, 976, 1059, 1157.
Tate and Brady's Supplement, 24, 25, 160, 261.
Taylor, Miss Jane, 1180, 1188.
Tersteegen, Gerhard, 477, 542, 543, 704, 992, 977.
Theoctistus of the Studium, 491.
Theodore of the Studium, 1352.
Theodulph, Bp. of Orleans, 218.
Thomas of Celano, 1349, 1350.
Thompson, Rev. Alexander Ramsay, 273, 780.
Thomson, Rev. John, 130.
Thring, Rev. Godfrey, 182.
Thrupp, Miss Dorothy Ann, 1186, 1190, 1191.
Thrupp, Rev. Joseph Francis, 201.
Todi, Jacoponi da, 250.
Toke, Mrs. Emma, 278.
Toplady, Rev. Augustus Montague, 191, 228, 243, 310, 499, 525, 566, 691, 692, 693, 1210, 1211, 1279, 1317.
Tritton, Joseph, 1033.
Turner, Rev. Daniel, 295, 492, 983.
Tuttiett, Rev. Laurence, 644.
Twells, Rev. Henry, 1214.

Unknown Author, 162, 214, 261, 362, 380, 334, 437, 546, 577, 582, 633, 758, 783, 799, 804, 828, 833, 863, 883, 895, 896, 1007, 1026, 1183, 1233, 1342, 1363, 1372, 1393.
Unknown Spanish Author, 1009.
Upham, Rev. Thomas Cogswell, 805, 815, 1047, 1057, 1206.

Van Alstyne, Mrs. Fanny Jane Crosby, 433.
Vaughan, Henry, 180.
Victorinus, Santolius, 197, 1001.
Voke, Mrs., 856, 1068, 1070, 1100.

Index of Authors of Hymns.

WALKER, MRS. MARY JANE, 498.
WALLACE, REV. JOHN AIKMAN, 812.
WARDLAW, REV. RALPH, 549, 941, 1071.
WARING, MISS ANNA LAETITIA, 759, 806.
WATTS, REV. ISAAC, 1, 20, 21, 28, 37, 38, 40, 41, 43, 45, 48, 49, 50, 51, 52, 58, 59, 60, 61, 62, 74, 76, 84, 86, 87, 88, 89, 93, 94, 95, 97, 102, 104, 105, 106, 107, 108, 115, 118, 121, 129, 131, 133, 135, 138, 139, 145, 147, 150, 151, 156, 139, 200, 202, 230, 234, 235, 237, 245, 283, 299, 313, 315, 320, 321, 322, 326, 330, 331, 355, 359, 363, 386, 392, 393, 394, 399, 400, 403, 404, 421, 429, 445, 446, 449, 460, 465, 466, 467, 480, 511, 514, 558, 602, 605, 607, 621, 623, 625, 650, 651, 655, 656, 688, 699, 701, 723, 738, 740, 744, 745, 747, 748, 749, 750, 754, 766, 785, 796, 809, 814, 836, 837, 843, 851, 858, 862, 884, 885, 889, 890, 901, 919, 934, 939, 942, 944, 946, 950, 951, 960, 969, 972, 973, 974, 975, 977, 984, 985, 987, 970, 1010, 1023, 1036, 1056, 1072, 1102, 1112, 1115, 1158, 1159, 1169, 1198, 1200, 1207, 1223, 1227, 1234, 1235, 1250, 1252, 1254, 1271, 1277, 1289, 1295, 1296, 1321, 1322, 1324, 1359, 1360, 1361, 1374, 1384, 1397, 1400, 1403, 1404, 1405, 1407.
WEBB, REV. BENJAMIN, 830.
WEISSE, REV. MICHAEL, 265.
WEISSEL, REV. GEORGE, 152.
WESLEY, REV. CHARLES, 2, 22, 23, 31, 32, 36, 71, 165, 170, 175, 242, 260, 279, 282, 286, 319, 334, 338, 345, 346, 347, 372, 379, 385, 388, 410, 416, 417, 426, 427, 432, 440, 468, 469, 470, 471, 472, 485, 489, 490, 495, 505, 509, 510, 513, 521, 528, 569, 583, 584, 589, 628, 631, 632, 637, 638, 676, 677, 696, 724, 733, 741, 742, 743, 746, 751, 752, 755, 796, 822, 824, 852, 855, 868, 832, 915, 916, 918, 958, 980, 1006, 1073, 1098, 1131, 1135, 1201, 1239, 1260, 1304, 1319, 1320, 1336, 1340, 1345, 1353, 1368, 1369, 1371, 1406.

WESLEY, REV. JOHN, 48, 140, 283, 289, 339, 472, 570, 571, 704, 775, 803, 992, 997, 1005, 1225.
WESLEY, REV. SAMUEL, 231.
WHATELY, ABP. RICHARD, 1217.
WHITE, HENRY KIRKE, 92, 113, 187, 586, 1236, 1273.
WHITFIELD, REV. FREDERICK, 757.
WHITING, WILLIAM, 1142.
WHYTEHEAD, REV. THOMAS, 258.
WILLIAMS, REV. BENJAMIN, 70.
WILLIAMS AND BODEN'S COLLECTION, 1372.
WILLIAMS, MISS HELEN MARIA, 124.
WILLIAMS, REV. ISAAC, 224, 1049.
WILLIAMS, REV. PETER, 662.
WILLIAMS, REV. WILLIAM, 662, 1081.
WILLIS, NATHANIEL PARKER, 1034.
WINGROVE, JOHN, 533.
WINKWORTH, MISS CATHERINE, 152, 163, 265, 274, 294, 390, 391, 542, 543, 634, 679, 705, 836, 1027, 1149, 1150, 1303, 1392.
WINSLOW, MISS MARGARET ELIZABETH, 246.
WOLCOTT, REV. SAMUEL, 1086.
WOLFE, REV. AARON ROBARTS, 891.
WORDSWORTH, BP. CHRISTOPHER, 14, 311, 312, 377, 875, 931, 1042, 1371.
WRANGHAM, WILLIAM, 83.

XAVIER, FRANCIS, 596.

YOUNG, REV. WILLIAM, 1328.

ZINZENDORF, NICOLAUS LUDWIG, 669.

By the Same Editors.

HYMNS AND SONGS,

FOR

SOCIAL AND SABBATH WORSHIP,

EDITED BY

ROSWELL D. HITCHCOCK, ZACHARY EDDY,
PHILIP SCHAFF.

Musical Editors: J. K. PAINE, U. C. BURNAP,
JAMES FLINT.

CONTAINING

360 Pages, over 650 Hymns, nearly 300 Tunes and Chants, 4to. Price, ... $1.25
Without Music. . . *In Preparation.* . .

ANSON D. F. RANDOLPH & CO.,
900 Broadway, New York.

www.ingramcontent.com/pod-product-compliance
Lightning Source LLC
Chambersburg PA
CBHW032143010526
44111CB00035B/986